READINGS IN SOCIAL THEORY
The Classic Tradition to Post-Modernism

READINGS IN SOCIAL THEORY
The Classic Tradition to Post-Modernism

FOURTH EDITION

Edited with Introductions by

James Farganis
Vassar College
New School University

Boston   Burr Ridge, IL   Dubuque, IA   Madison, WI   New York   San Francisco   St. Louis
Bangkok   Bogotá   Caracas   Kuala Lumpur   Lisbon   London   Madrid   Mexico City
Milan   Montreal   New Delhi   Santiago   Seoul   Singapore   Sydney   Taipei   Toronto

The McGraw·Hill Companies

Higher Education

READINGS IN SOCIAL THEORY: THE CLASSIC TRADITION TO POST-MODERNISM
Published by McGraw-Hill, a business unit of The McGraw-Hill Companies, Inc., 1221 Avenue of
the Americas, New York, NY, 10020. Copyright © 2004, 2000, 1996, 1993, by The McGraw-Hill
Companies, Inc. All rights reserved. No part of this publication may be reproduced or distributed
in any form or by any means, or stored in a data base or retrieval system, without the prior written
consent of The McGraw-Hill Companies, Inc., including, but not limited to, in any network or other
electronic storage or transmission, or broadcast for distance learning. Some ancillaries, including
electronic and print components, may not be available to customers outside the United States.

This book is printed on acid-free paper.

1 2 3 4 5 6 7 8 9 0 FGR/FGR 0 9 8 7 6 5 4 3

ISBN 0-07-282577-4

Publisher: *Phillip A. Butcher*
Sponsoring editor: *Sherith H. Pankratz*
Developmental editor: *Jill Gordon*
Senior marketing manager: *Daniel M. Loch*
Project manager: *Jill Moline*
Production supervisor: *Janean A. Utley*
Associate designer: *George Kokkonas*
Lead supplement producer: *Marc Mattson*
Typeface: *10/12 Palatino*
Compositor: *Electronic Publishing Services Inc., TN*
Printer: *Quebecor World Fairfield Inc.*

Library of Congress Cataloging-in-Publication Data

Readings in social theory : the classic tradition to post-modernism / edited with
    introductions by James Farganis. — 4th ed.
        p.   cm.
    Includes bibliographical references.
    ISBN 0-07-282577-4 (softcover : alk. paper)
    1. Sociology—Philosophy. I. Farganis, James.
HM585.R43 2004
301'.01—dc21   2003046354

www.mhhe.com

About the Author

JAMES FARGANIS was born and raised in New York City, attended its public schools, and received his B.A. from Brooklyn College and his Ph.D. in government from Cornell University. He has taught at several colleges and universities, including Harpur College at SUNY Binghamton, Brooklyn College, Queens College, and The Graduate Faculty of the New School for Social Research. He is currently Professor Emeritus of Sociology at Vassar College, where he taught social theory and political sociology, chaired the Sociology Department and helped establish, and later chaired, the college's first program in multidisciplinary studies, the Program in Science, Technology, and Society. He has been the recipient of an NEH Summer Fellowship, an NEH Program Development Grant, and a Fulbright Senior Scholar Grant to Australia. His published articles on social theory have appeared in *The British Journal of Sociology, Sociological Focus, Journal of Psychiatry and Law,* and *Theory and Society,* and he has reviewed for *Contemporary Sociology, Social Forces, Polity,* and *The American Political Science Review.* He has served on the editorial board of *Polity* and as a corresponding editor to *Theory and Society.* He currently teaches social theory at the New School University.

Contents

Preface   xi

Introduction. The Classic Tradition to Post-Modernism: An Overview   1

PART 1: THE CLASSIC TRADITION   21

1. KARL MARX: ALIENATION, CLASS STRUGGLE, AND CLASS CONSCIOUSNESS   23

Introduction   23

From Karl Marx and Frederick Engels: *The Manifesto of the Communist Party*   26

From Karl Marx: *Economic and Philosophic Manuscripts of 1844*   37

From Karl Marx and Frederick Engels: *The German Ideology*   43

From Karl Marx: "The Fetishism of Commodities and the Secret Thereof"   47

2. ÉMILE DURKHEIM: ANOMIE AND SOCIAL INTEGRATION   55

Introduction   55

From Émile Durkheim: *The Rules of Sociological Method*   59

From Émile Durkheim: "Egoistic Suicide and Anomic Suicide"   64

From Émile Durkheim: *The Elementary Forms of Religious Life*   73

From Émile Durkheim: "Individualism and the Intellectuals"   81

3. MAX WEBER: THE IRON CAGE   91

Introduction   91

From Max Weber: *The Protestant Ethic and the Spirit of Capitalism*   95

From Max Weber: "Bureaucracy"   99

From Max Weber: "'Objectivity' in Social Science and Social Policy"   109

From Max Weber: "Class, Status, Party"   116

4. GEORG SIMMEL: DIALECTIC OF INDIVIDUAL AND SOCIETY   127

Introduction   127

From Georg Simmel: "The Metropolis and Mental Life"   129

From Georg Simmel: "The Stranger"   138

5. GEORGE HERBERT MEAD: THE EMERGENT SELF   143

Introduction   143

From George Herbert Mead: *Mind, Self and Society*   145

6. W. E. B. Du BOIS: DOUBLE-CONSCIOUSNESS AND THE PUBLIC INTELLECTUAL   165

Introduction   165

From W. E. B. Du Bois: *The Philadelphia Negro: A Social Study*   167

From W. E. B. Du Bois: *The Souls of Black Folk*   171

PART 2: CONTEMPORARY SOCIOLOGICAL THEORY   179

7. FUNCTIONALISM   181

Introduction   181

From Kingsley Davis and Wilbert E. Moore: "Some Principles of Stratification"   183

From Talcott Parsons: "Age and Sex in the Social Structure of the United States"   191

From Robert K. Merton: "Manifest and Latent Functions"   201

8. CONFLICT THEORY   219

Introduction   219

From Ralf Dahrendorf: "Social Structure, Group Interests, and Conflict Groups"   222

From C. Wright Mills: "The Structure of Power in America"   241

From Richard L. Zweigenhaft and G. William Domhoff: "The Ironies of Diversity"   250

9. EXCHANGE THEORY AND RATIONAL CHOICE   263

Introduction   263

From Peter Blau: "The Structure of Social Associations"   265

From George C. Homans: "Social Behavior as Exchange"   279

From James S. Coleman: "Social Capital in the Creation of Human Capital"   289

10. PHENOMENOLOGICAL SOCIOLOGY AND ETHNOMETHODOLOGY   303

Introduction   303

From Alfred Schutz: "Common-Sense and Scientific Interpretation of Human Action"   305

From Peter Berger and Thomas Luckmann: "Foundations of Knowledge in Everyday Life"   331

From Harold Garfinkel: "Studies of the Routine Grounds of Everyday Activities"   340

11. SYMBOLIC INTERACTION   349

Introduction   349

From Herbert Blumer: "Society as Symbolic Interaction"   351

From Erving Goffman: *The Presentation of Self in Everyday Life*   259

12. **FEMINIST THEORY**   369

Introduction   369

From Dorothy Smith: "Women's Experience as a Radical Critique of Sociology"   372

From Michèle Barrett: "Words and Things: Materialism and Method in Contemporary Feminist Analysis"   381

PART 3: MODERNITY AND POST-MODERNISM   395

13. **CRITICAL THEORY**   397

Introduction   397

From Herbert Marcuse: *One-Dimensional Man*   400

From Jürgen Habermas: "Three Normative Models of Democracy"   413

14. **POST-MODERNISM**   423

Introduction   423

From Michel Foucault: "The Carceral"   425

From Jean-François Lyotard: *The Post-Modern Condition: A Report on Knowledge*   435

Preface

The fourth edition of this selection of readings in social theory contains a number of significant changes that reflect the growth and development in the field. These changes are also designed to present the reader with a broader and richer range of selections, adding to the core readings and remaining current with others.

In Part 1, dealing with the Classic Tradition, the Marx chapter now includes "The Fetishism of Commodities," the Durkheim chapter incorporates "Individualism and Intellectuals," and the chapter on Simmel has been expanded to include "The Stranger." Part 2 on Contemporary Theory has likewise been enlarged and now contains a chapter from Zweigenhaft and Domhoff's *Diversity in the Power Elite*, an extended chapter on "Exchange Theory and Rational Choice" that contains selections by George Homans and James S. Coleman, and an expanded "Phenomenology and Ethnomethodology" chapter that incorporates Harold Garfinkel's work on "breach experiments." Michele Barrett's essay, "Words and Things: Materialism and Method in Contemporary Feminist Analysis," provides an important counterpoint to Dorothy Smith in the chapter on "Feminist Theory." In Part 3, a recent essay by Jürgen Habermas brings the student into contact with Habermas's reflections on the possibility of deliberative democracy in a multicultural society and sets him apart from Marcuse's critique of technological rationality and domination.

A website has been developed to accompany the fourth edition. It includes non-text-specific features such as: chapter objectives, web links, Internet exercises, glossary terms, and flashcards. Visit the Social Theory Supersite by going to www.mhhe.com/socialtheory.

I am very appreciative and thankful for the insightful and encouraging reviews submitted for this edition by Richard Garnett, Marshall University; Carol Ray, San Jose State University; Glenna Colclough, University of Alabama, Huntsville, Scott Applerouth, California State University, Northridge; Steve Buechler, Minnesota State University; Terri LeMoyne, University of Tennessee, Chattanooga; Emilia McGulken, Case Western Reserve; and Basil Kardaras, Capital University. The careful reading of the text and the considered suggestions made by these reviewers are reflected in the changes that I have undertaken for this revision; changes, for which, I of course, assume full responsibility as editor.

Working closely with the supportive staff at McGraw-Hill has made it possible to bring the process of revision and rewriting to successful conclusion with ease. Phil Butcher (Publisher), Sherith Pankratz (Sociology Editor), Jill Gordon

(Assistant Editor), Amy Shaffer (Editorial Coordinator), and Jill Moline (Project Manager) all deserve my special thanks for their conscientious and thoughtful oversight of this project. Finally, I want to thank George Ritzer for endorsing the original idea for this reader, for his continuing support of the project as a consulting editor, and for his sustained friendship.

James Farganis
Poughkeepsie, New York
New York City, New York
2003

READINGS IN SOCIAL THEORY
The Classic Tradition to Post-Modernism

Introduction

The Classic Tradition to Post-Modernism: An Overview

James Farganis

I The Classic Tradition

Although theories about society date back to the Greeks, sociology as a disciplined, scientific inquiry is of more recent origin. Auguste Comte (1798–1857) coined the term "sociology" in 1822 to connote the systematic study of society. The influences upon him date back to Charles de Montesquieu (1689–1755) and to the reflections of the *philosophes* during the Enlightenment. Of equal importance to Comte were those conservative thinkers who surfaced after the French Revolution to condemn the Enlightenment and its doctrines. Francois Marie Arouet de Voltaire (1694–1778), Jean Jacques Rousseau (1712–1778), Denis Diderot (1713–1784), and Jean Antoine de Condorcet (1742–1794) were the eighteenth-century Enlightenment thinkers whose optimistic views about individual rights, human perfectibility, and social progress were absorbed into sociological theory, as were the conservative views of Louis de Bonald (1754–1840) and Joseph de Maistre (1754–1821) regarding the primacy of the social, the role of custom and tradition in social life, and the centrality of the family, the community, groups, and institutions in ordering, regulating, and shaping the lives of individuals. In the next few pages we will review briefly the key ideas of the Enlightenment *philosophes* and their conservative critics.

Montesquieu's *Persian Letters,* published in 1721 when he was thirty-two years old, illustrate the idea of sociological perspective. Montesquieu wrote these letters as if they were an exchange between Persian visitors to France. He published them anonymously, claiming that the Persians who wrote them had stayed with him during their visit. In the letters Montesquieu comments, often satirically, on the customs and habits of French society of his time. The ability to step outside of one's society, to distance oneself from what seems to be natural, and to develop a different perspective from the one taken for granted, are sociological attitudes exhibited in this early work.

The Spirit of the Laws, Montesquieu's most famous work, appeared in 1748. In it he develops systematically his views on how the culture of a people is affected by their geography and climate and temperament. Laws, customs, and forms of government are not natural phenomena, but are shaped by the surrounding conditions under which a particular people have to live. Montesquieu's method combines observation with reflection, and his conclusions reflect a careful study of the relationship between the behavior and beliefs of people and their environmental context. In addition, Montesquieu explored population densities and property distribution in order to arrive at his social and political typologies.

Enlightenment *philosophes* like Montesquieu were the eighteenth-century precursors of the classical sociological theorists. The *philosophes* were impressed with the revolutionary advances wrought in the natural sciences, particularly by Newtonian physics, and sought to discover the scientific truths about society:

What is new and original about Enlightenment thought, therefore, is the whole-hearted adoption of the methodological pattern of Newton's physics; and what is even more important for our consideration of the philosophical foundations of sociological theory is the fact that immediately with its adoption it was generalized and employed in realms other than the mathematical and physical. (Zeitlin 1968, 7).

Social order, the inequalities of class, the domination by an aristocracy were no longer to be accepted as divinely ordained and unchangeable truths. Science was to be a critical instrument in the pursuit of truth, a truth that would liberate people from the dark myths of the divine right of kings and religious dogma and lead them toward a progressively democratic order based on the newly discovered truths about the "rights of man." Rousseau wrote of the inequalities between people caused by social institutions and practices, and noted that in the "natural" state the differences between people were far less acute than in society. It is society, he argued, that distorts the basic goodness, decency, and equality that are the natural condition of mankind:

> I conceive that there are two kinds of inequality among the human species; one, which I call natural or physical, because it is established by nature, and consists in difference of age, health, bodily strength, and the qualities of mind or of the soul: and another, which may be called moral or political inequality, because it depends on a kind of convention, and is established, or at least authorized, by the consent of men. This latter consists of the different privileges which some men enjoy to the prejudice of others; such as that of being more rich, more honored, more powerful, or even in a position to extract obedience. (Rousseau 1947, 160).

Condorcet, a mathematician who endorsed the idea that the social sciences would progress faster if they followed the methods of the natural sciences, firmly believed in the notion of human perfectibility and progress in the achievement of a just society. Condorcet supported equal rights for women, strongly opposed slavery, called for universal suffrage, and endorsed the separation of church and state, freedom of opinion, and a wide range of social welfare measures to help the less fortunate members of society.

The ideas of the *philosophes* took hold in the climate of prerevolutionary France, and the French Revolution is arguably the political culmination of those ideas in action. The Revolution challenged the legitimacy of the aristocratic state and those religious, social, and political institutions that supported it.

In place of the *ancien régime*, a new social order was legislated into being based on rational principles, consciously constructed by politicized and informed individuals. Laws were passed which transformed the political, economic, social, and cultural life of France. The aristocracy was abolished, the church was abolished, the industrial guilds were abolished. Divorce became legalized, the educational system was reformed and centralized, and a new governing structure was created. What informed these revolutionary changes were the ideas developed by the *philosophes* concerning the rights of individuals to establish collectively their own government and to remake their social institutions according to their notions of progress and justice.

Out of the revolutionary upheaval in France there emerged a long period of instability, of counterrevolution, of attempts at monarchical restoration, and Napoleonic imperial domination. Rather than the steady progress toward a free and democratic society in which human reason would order the affairs of politics and society, there followed a period of bloodshed, division, domination, and reaction. The Enlightenment *philosophes* were seen by their critics as naive mythmakers who had substituted their own *a priori* ideals of progress, reason, and freedom for the earlier mythologies. Far from undertaking a scientific examination of society and the human condition, the *philosophes* had actually engaged in a form of moral philosophising. Carl Becker (1959, 101) asks the question:

> Is it, then, possible that the Philosophers were not really interested in establishing the rights suitable to man's nature on the facts of experience? Is it possible that they were engaged in that nefarious medieval enterprise of reconciling the facts of human experience with the truths already, in some fashion, revealed to them?

To these questions Becker answers with an emphatic "yes" as he likens the science of the *philosophes* to a religious faith in progress, reason, and human goodness.

In the aftermath of the French Revolution, a group of social theorists led by Louis de Bonald and Joseph de Maistre emerged as a conservative, counter-Enlightenment, intellectual force. They were distressed at the condition of France following the Revolution, its social dislocation, political turmoil, and general disintegration, and they held the *philosophes* directly accountable. Not only had the *philosophes* and their followers badly misjudged the social needs of people to belong to groups and communities greater than themselves, to abide by collective ideals, and to partake in collective rituals, but they had falsely assumed that humans are rational and progressive creatures, and that they are constituted as individuals by their natural rights rather than shaped by their social environment.

The primacy of the social over the individual is a fundamental point of difference between the Enlightenment *philosophes* and their conservative critics. Whereas the *philosophes* saw the individual as endowed with natural and inalienable rights and society as a contract entered into by individuals, the counter-Enlightenment conservatives viewed society as primary and the individual as shaped by social institutions to meet the needs of the larger social order. The ideology of individualism was a distortion of the truly social nature of human life. Family, community, church, town, and guild are functionally interrelated and provide for the material and spiritual needs of ordinary people. Tradition, custom, and institutions that have stood the test of time should inform us about the social nature of humankind, they claimed. The Church was to be seen as a necessary binding and integrative force, and the family, not the individual, was viewed as the basic unit of society.

The past and the present form a seamless web, and it is only the arrogance of individualism, or more particularly the presumption of the power of human reason, that has allowed some people to believe that they can legislate a new social order. The result of this arrogance, the conservatives seemed to be saying, was the social chaos and instability that confronted France following the Revolution, and by extension, would be the fate of all social change inspired by abstract deductive reason.

The classic tradition begins with Karl Marx (1818–1883) and ends with Karl Mannheim's (1893–1947) writings on the sociology of knowledge. The classical social theorists wished to distinguish their work from speculative moral philosophy and to contribute to a scientific study of society. This is the objective that unites them, but their success in achieving it is debatable. Despite their best intentions the social theorists of the classic tradition were, for the most part, unable to leave behind the moral presuppositions that impelled their inquiries. Their greatness for us lies as much in their cogent analyses of the forces of modernization and its impact on the human condition as in their noble efforts at a science of society.

The classical texts do not speak with one voice about any matter, and so it is difficult to ascribe common characteristics to them. Even on the critical question of their commitment to science as against philosophy, it should be noted that these theorists held differing views of what they meant by science. They were divided over the question of whether the methods of science as they had been developed in the physical sciences were appropriate to the subject matter of the social sciences. Some saw the quest for social laws as no different from the discovery of the laws of nature, whereas others found compelling the claim that human beings are unique in their rational and linguistic abilities. Distinctions were made between the natural and the cultural, or social, sciences, and arguments were advanced that each requires a different methodology.

Although the classical theorists agree that claims must be substantiated by appeal to evidence, there is little unity on what constitutes evidence. If history is the dense and rich source of sociological evidence, some approached history as if it were governed by laws of social development that must be uncovered, while others viewed history as contingent and unknowable in its totality. To some, history connotes progressive evolution toward emancipation, or social justice, or democracy; to others, history is nothing but a factual chaos until order is imposed on it temporarily by the researcher and his or her theory.

Nor was there any unity with respect to what constitutes society. On the one hand, some maintained that society can be studied as a totality, whereas others saw individuals as the component parts of society and the source of all observable action. If the latter were the case, then some feared that sociology would be reduced to psychology and could make no contribution of its own. On the other hand, if society could be studied as an entity unto itself, there was the danger of inventing a metaphysical group mind and thereby defeating the purpose of scientific investigation.

The classic tradition is not a single tradition speaking with a uniform voice. It is mired in conflicting views and often irreconcilable perspectives that reflect deeply held moral assumptions. Science is powerless to resolve these moral differences, and as a result many of these divergences continue to surface in contemporary social theory. Today the controversy takes the form of an intense dispute between adherents who claim that sociological truths can be established by a strict observance of the rules of positivism and those who think that sociology is a discursive discipline whose truths can be established through rational, generalized, speculative, and persuasive argument (Alexander 1987).

In what follows we will discuss the intellectual conflicts and tensions within the classic tradition. These differences stem from the varied attitudes of the classical theorists to the legacy of the Enlightenment. Did they believe in progress? Did they view science as an unalloyed blessing? Would human reason lead to a more just and humane society, or would new forms of domination emerge in the age of science? The different responses to these questions stake out the relationship of these theorists to the Enlightenment traditions. They also demonstrate how their unarticulated moral presuppositions led the classical theorists to define their science, their methods, and their sociology in radically diverse ways.

The principal contributors to the classic tradition are both scientists and discursive theorists, and their work is both a continuation of the Enlightenment tradition and a departure from it. The classical theorists were more attentive systematically than their Enlightenment predecessors to empirical evidence and to historical analysis. Their avoidance of unfounded and broadly speculative generalizations marks them as social theorists who relied on evidence and rational argument.

It has been suggested (Salomon 1945, 596) that much of the development of sociological theory can be understood as a debate with the ghost of Karl Marx. On this view Marx emerges as the child of the Enlightenment, and the conflicts and contradictions within the classic tradition are explained by reference to Marx and his adversaries. However, the development of sociological theory may also be said to owe much to the philosophy of Friedrich Nietzsche (1844–1900), especially in light of his influence on Max Weber and Georg Simmel and the growing recognition of his significance for post-modernist social thought (Chapter 14).

The Marxist tradition represents a continuation of many of the Enlightenment's rationalist and progressive convictions. This humanistic project of a just and democratic rational social order has been carried forward in the works of Jürgen Habermas (Chapter 13). By contrast, Nietzsche's critique of scientific objectivity, his view of reason as a form of domination, his disdain for democratic culture and politics, and his romantic vision of the heroic triumph of the *Übermensch* over the "last men" who seek happiness find resonance in the works of Max Weber, Georg Simmel, and the post-modernists.

It is against this backdrop of continuities and discontinuities with the Enlightenment and the internal tensions that mark the classic tradition that some of the key social theorists will be discussed. Our aim is to present the different perspectives, the different ideas concerning the relationship of the individual to society, and the different methodologies that constitute the classic tradition, and to dispel the notion that it is a singular tradition that represents a unified perspective.

The classic tradition represents those works that have come to be considered the foundational texts of the discipline of sociology. They are generally regarded to be excellent examples of the kind of work that people who claim to be sociologists ought to engage in, and, because they are exemplary, they continue to serve as a source of ideas and hypotheses about, and orientations to, social reality.

For the most part, these works tend to address a broad range of problems emerging from the transition from an agrarian to an industrial society. While reading from the works of Marx, Durkheim, and Weber, the student should constantly question the relevance and importance of what is being said. For example, how significant for our time are Marx's ideas of class and class conflict? Does it matter at all that America and other Western industrial societies are moving into a post-industrial age, into a service economy in which industrial labor is on the decline and in which the service sector is expanding? Does the emergence of the information age with its emphasis on knowledge create new class relationships, or is this an age in which class categories are no longer relevant? What are the sources of conflict in our contemporary society and are they traceable to economic discrepancies between rich and poor, or do the lines of conflict fall among different status groups, that is, racial, ethnic, religious, and sexual? Similar questions can and should be formulated about other readings in this anthology.

Even when these classical texts seem to be dated, they nevertheless provide us with the important questions that must be upppermost in the mind of a sociologist. Do they alert us to observe those around us, to listen closely to their expressions of belief and to ponder where these views come from? Are the values that people hold a reflection of their class background, or is it their status groups that most closely influence their beliefs? How people speak, what clothes they wear, what habits they exhibit should lead us to inquire as to the social antecedents of these behaviors and to ask what kind of image is being projected and for what purpose.

More broadly, the classical texts compel us to ask what we mean by the term "society." We all take it for granted that we know what society is, yet a moment's reflection will cause the reader to pause and think. Is society nothing more than a collection of individuals? How are these different individuals brought together so that they can cooperate and understand one another? Does society have an existence outside of us, or is society in us, in our consciousness, and, if so, how did it get there? If, as some would maintain, society is a collective system of commonly shared beliefs and agreed-on rules of behavior, who makes up the beliefs and the rules and are they in the interest of all or the dominant few? Marx and Durkheim wrestle with these questions and come up with very different answers. But despite their differences, they are concerned with fundamental questions that define the sociological enterprise, and the student is invited to think through these questions with the skilled guidance of some of the great minds in social theory.

Auguste Comte (1798–1857), often cited as the first to use the word sociology to refer to the new discipline, sought to use historical evidence to establish laws of social development. He was less rigorous and systematic in his research than those who followed him, and for this reason he may be viewed as a proto-sociologist. The contradictory influences which shaped his work are evident in his commitment to science and progress on the one hand and his view that individualism was "the disease of the Western world" on the other. It will be recalled that the Enlightenment thinkers endorsed the view that scientific progress and individual rights were part of an emerging democratic social order. It was the counter-Enlightenment that condemned the idea of individualism and offered the notion that society and its institutions are primary and shape the behavior of individuals. Comte taps into the Enlightenment for his views on science and progress and draws on the counter-Enlightenment for his views on the relationship of the individual to society.

Comte's theory of society was based on his conviction that the scientific approach, or positivism, was the most appropriate method for understanding social order and social change. By positivism Comte meant a study of society based on sensory observation, historical comparison, and experimentation in the quest for universal laws, rather than reliance on abstract moral principles about human nature and social justice. Comte represents a viewpoint that disdains the untidiness of democratic politics and leads to an endorsement of rule by a knowledge elite. Unlike Plato's philosopher-kings, however, the rulers of modern society would be sociologist-kings, people with technical knowledge of the operations of society and their consequences. Today we refer to this kind of thinking as technocratic, and hence for us Comte is the first technocrat.

Karl Marx (1818–1883), Émile Durkheim (1858–1917), and Max Weber (1864–1920) are generally considered the "holy trinity" of the classic tradition. Although there are important conceptual similarities between them, there are considerable methodological and substantive differences, some of which have already been alluded to; yet the significant points of contrast for what follows will be in their often irreconcilable moral assumptions, which provide them with critical perspectives on modernity, and in the different ways in which they carry on the sociological enterprise.

Marx and Comte were only superficially similar in their approach. Both are interested in a science of society, both view history as the source of empirical data, and both tend to think in terms of stages of historical development and the predictive value of their social theories. But Marx is a dialectical thinker in contrast to Comte's positivism, so that Marx sees social development as a consequence of conflicting classes acting to shape a future society. Dialectical reasoning attempts to capture the dynamic character of social reality by viewing change as a consequence of historically evolving oppositional forces. In this case it refers to the capacity of one class to negate, to challenge, and to overthrow the domination of another and bring about revolutionary change.

In place of Comtean technocrats, whose prevision allows them privileged access to the future course of social development, Marx evokes an active and politically conscious proletariat whose collective oppression compels them to act in behalf of their own liberation and thus profoundly alter the social, economic, and political circumstances of their existence.

At the heart of Marx's theory of industrial society is the moral view of human beings as essentially free and of capitalism as a mode of production that enslaves people through institutional arrangements which define the relationship between wage labor and capital. Marx observed the development of capitalism and saw in it a system that legitimated the exploitation of one class by another. He sought to expose the true nature of that relationship by challenging the accepted notions of private property and individual freedom. Marx projected a revolutionary destruction of capitalism as a necessary stage in the emancipatory development of mankind.

No less sincere and profoundly troubled by the advent of modern industrial society, Durkheim analyzed the central problem of modernity as the breakdown of those shared moral beliefs that develop as a result of a common commitment to common ideals and values by the members of a community. For Durkheim the condition of modernity is characterized by the breakdown of communal ties and bonds as individuals are compelled to live in a social environment that is characterized as *anomic*, i.e, normless and lawless. The similarities to the views of the conservative counter-Enlightenment should be noted, although Durkheim did not seek to return to the old order. The term *anomie* literally means without law, and it is Durkheim's view that this pervasive condition of modernity quite literally destroys individuals who must exist within it, for such conditions are responsible for increases in the suicide rate. Whereas Marx sees the rules and regulations of capitalist society as so many manifestations of class interest and domination, and argues for their destruction in order to liberate the proletariat from domination, Durkheim argues that legitimate rules and regulations are a necessary and essential feature of social life. People need ideals to believe in, and they need rules to guide their social life. Moral regulation and social integration are positive features of a healthy society in which individuals may thrive as members of a community.

Durkheim wrestled with the destructive features of anomie and the growth of individualism in modern society. The "cult of the individual" was Durkheim's attempt to reconcile the central tendency of modernity toward individualism

with the view that moral consensus is threatened by fragmentation, extreme differentiation, and individualization. In "Individualism and the Intellectuals" (Durkheim 1973), he distinguished between egoistic individualism and a moral individualism, arguing that the latter was the "cult of the individual" and had become the basis of the new consensus of modernity. According to this view, the individual is a subject with rights and with the moral responsibility to act in accordance with principles of justice and the common good. Moral individualism is a social creation supported and encouraged by social institutions and moral practices. Durkheim argued that the idea of the egoistic individual intent on self-interest is a metaphysical construct that depicts a natural and atomistic creation whose primacy is justified philosophically, not sociologically.

Much of the disagreement between Marx and Durkheim turns on the moral assumptions they make regarding the relationship of the individual to society. Marx's emancipatory view precedes his empirical analyses and provides the foundation for his theory. Marx questions the legitimacy of any community, ideals, or institutions that tolerate, support, or justify inequality, i.e., the domination of one class over another. It is Marx's claim that with the destruction of private property the equality of all can be secured under communism as all the members become equal participants in the social, political, and economic life of the community.

By contrast, Durkheim rejects this egalitarian conception as utopian and impossible to realize. As a result, he argues that certain inequalities are natural and cannot be eradicated. It is possible to reform institutions so as to make them conform more faithfully to the established egalitarian ideals of society. Thus Durkheim would favor policies that foster equality of opportunity because they allow the natural talents and abilities of individuals to be judged irrespective of race, gender, and ethnicity. If the institutions of society keep faith with that principle of justice, then individuals will identify with the community, sharing its ideals and its moral consensus, and will judge its outcomes as just and legitimate. If, by contrast, economic institutions favor the privileged and risk the formation of classes and class conflict, then the binding ideals of the community will be shattered. Alternatively, if economic policies favor the least privileged by attempting to equalize outcomes, society runs the risk of losing support from the vast majority of its members who believe that rewards are due to those who demonstrate ability. Consequently, Durkheim recommends social and economic reforms that will equalize conditions and make the social ideals of equality of opportunity credible because these reforms would foster integration and the acceptance of regulative norms as legitimate.

For Durkheim, in sharp contrast to Marx, it is possible to have community with inequality, provided the inequality is a consequence of merit and achievement. Marx's theory seeks to liberate people from the very system that Durkheim wishes to reform and legitimate. Although both theorists are analyzing and interpreting industrial capitalism, they do so from the different perspectives that are formed from the moral presuppositions they hold about the individual and society.

Durkheim's views on sociological method are clearly patterned after the natural sciences, and some of his work reflects a commitment to statistical analysis and systematic data gathering that make it exemplary for scientific sociology. Durkheim is meticulous in the way he constructs his argument, impeccable in his use of logical analysis, and precise in the way he marshals evidence leading to his generalizations. Durkheim's study, *Suicide,* is taken as a model of how a sociological analysis should be conducted, and his *Rules of Sociological Method* is widely recognized as a major contribution to the methodology of the social sciences.

Max Weber's theory of action focuses attention on the individual as a social actor, and his *verstehende* methodology invites us to explore the subjective meaning of action from the actor's point of view. In this respect, Weber's work seems to be in conflict with the more systematic and positivistic inclinations of Durkheim's methodology and the dialectical approach taken by Karl Marx.

Weber's *Protestant Ethic and the Spirit of Capitalism* argues that religious beliefs may have profound and even revolutionary economic consequences; for ideas are not simply epiphenomenal consequences of economic modes of production. In this study Weber reveals how belief in the tenets of Calvinism led to changes in the believers' attitudes toward work that became an important factor in the emergence of capitalism. In opposition to Marx's rational view of history as an ordered development leading to a logically determined endpoint, or *telos,* Weber views history as contingent and accidental, and human action as often entailing unforeseen and unanticipated results. Weber seems to be saying, however tentatively, that capitalism was the unanticipated consequence of Protestant beliefs and not the programmatic and rational transition from feudalism as depicted by Marx.

"Class, Status, Party" focuses on Weber's views on power in modern society in contrast to Marx's notion of the ruling class. Weber seems to share Marx's definition of class but denies the singular importance that Marx ascribes to it. Rather than viewing classes and class consciousness as a necessary development under capitalism, Weber sees status groups as natural communities that impact more directly and immediately on the consciousness and actions of individuals. Furthermore, the Marxist view that there is a single avenue to power in society and that the dominant economic class is the ruling class is challenged by Weber's analysis. Economic class position, status honor, and persuasive leadership of a party are distinctive means to power. They may overlap, but they are not identical and are not always found together in the same individual.

Excerpts from Weber's essay on methodology provide an excellent discussion of problems surrounding the idea of objectivity and detail Weber's contributions to a distinctively socio- logical method. Weber employs an interpretive methodology, using rational models or ideal types to develop themes or generalizations from a painstaking examination of the historical data. He approaches historical information from the perspective of a sociologist; from this rich empirical data he draws observations about class, status, party, religion, and modernity.

The differences between Weber's approach and Marx's dialectical method signal an endur- ing and irresolvable conflict over the relation- ship between thought and action, and between reason and reality. For Marx the object of social analysis is to change the world; for Weber it is enough to try to understand it. And whereas Marx believes that his dialectical methodology uncovers the forces of revolutionary change, Weber maintains that rational thought is limited and prescriptions for change are the province of politicians and not of social scientists.

Weber argues that objectivity in the social sciences is possible, although only under care- fully defined conditions. He recognizes the influ- ence of moral values in social research but claims that these values enter at specific junctures and should not influence the outcomes of the research. Social analysts holding radically dif- ferent values should be able to agree on the facts even if their interpretations of their meaning and significance might differ. As a result, Weber believes that it is impossible to conduct social research without recognizing the role that values play. He does not argue for the elimination of values from research, a clear impossibility for Weber. On the other hand, such a recognition need not lead to the view that all research is tainted by subjectivity and is therefore unscien- tific. Weber's position is more subtle and more complex. Although acknowledging the role of values Weber circumscribes their impact and refuses to surrender rational discourse to the arbitrary claims of power.

The relationship between knowledge and power is developed by Michel Foucault (Chapter 14), whose post-modernist theory is greatly influenced by Nietzsche. However, although Foucault follows Friedrich Nietzsche more closely, Weber's reluctance to undermine scien- tific rationality attests to his critical relationship to Nietzsche. In other respects as well, there are affinities between these two thinkers. Weber's belief that charismatic politics can overcome the ossified bureaucratic system resonates with the idea of the *Übermensch*, and Weber's worst fears that instrumental rationality would create technical and passionless men extends Niet- zsche's intuitive insights into the realm of so- ciological analysis.

Following Nietzsche it was Weber who saw the darker side of scientific rationality and who pointed to the enduring resistances to politically directed change. Weber wrote of the disen- chantment of the world under the pressure of scientific reason and recounted the emergence of a new form of domination with the spread of a rational bureaucratic order. In a variation of Nietzsche's theme that God is dead, Weber saw conflicts over moral values as a ceaseless strug- gle between "Gods" and "Demons." Contrary to the Enlightenment, this was not a world in which politics would necessarily usher in a new order of harmony and justice. Politics is an enduring conflict of interests, a struggle for power. As Weber puts it, politics is the "strong and slow boring of hard boards" (Weber 1958, 128), and only those who endure the struggle and maintain their vision can hope to bring about change.

Georg Simmel, George Herbert Mead, and Karl Mannheim occupy a place just slightly behind that of Marx, Durkheim, and Weber. Simmel viewed modernity as a mixture of pos- itive and negative outcomes rather than unal- loyed blessing or an unrelieved failure. His social analysis reveals a new form of cultural alienation in the presence of unprecedented individual freedom. For Simmel, modernity connotes the breakdown of small, rural com- munities and their personal styles of interaction. In their place, urban centers of production and culture have emerged that tend toward anonymity and impersonality in social interactions. Although it is true that modern society provides manifold opportunities for individuals to express themselves freely and to adopt different roles and to interact in different social arenas, Simmel's dialectical view reveals the urban condition that supports this new-found freedom as well as the way in which the modern urban culture comes to dominate the individual. Simmel, like Weber, understands the complexity and contingency of modernity and ascribes to it outcomes that are more tempered than the confident optimism of the Enlightenment *philosophes.*

In contrast to the structural and deterministic theories of several Europeans, the social psychology developed by George Herbert Mead (1863–1931), the first American in this group of classical theorists, views the self as a consequence of complex social interactive processes. In this sense, Mead's views are consistent with the progressive ideals and the democratic faith of the Enlightenment. The self emerges in action that results from an internal dialogue between the "I" and the "me." Rather than considering the self as an object determined by external forces or as a fixed entity that somehow "resides" inside the person, Mead emphasized self-reflection and adaptability. In placing emphasis on gestures, symbols, and reflective interaction, Mead's theory evolves a democratic character type, i.e., an individual who can make the actions of the self the objects of thought, and can adjust, adapt, and control behavior based on that reflection. The more individuals are capable of controlling their own actions, the more capable they are at self-government, the less need there is for an external authority to control them. Mead's theories are at odds with the Durkheimian conception of the individual as socially determined by external forces, or Marx's view that the class position of an individual is a vital factor in understanding consciousness and collective action. Perhaps Mead's perception of the fluidity of American life and the ideology of American individualism led him to develop a theory that minimizes external or objective structures. In any event, we see in Mead's work a continuation of the Enlightenment ideals of democratic progress, but without the dialectical methodology or the structural characteristics of Marxist thought.

W. E. B. Du Bois (1868–1963) began his career as a sociologist with a strong commitment to objectivity and truth in scientific inquiry. His classic study, *The Philadelphia Negro: A Social Study* (1899), represents a careful and systematic study of the conditions of African-Americans in Philadelphia, one of the earliest urban sociological studies that has become a paradigm for later generations. It was Du Bois's belief that sociology should combine theory and empirical study; that abstract theorizing without empirical grounding was as empty as factual study without some guiding generalizations. Du Bois's reflective essays in *The Souls of Black Folk* and elsewhere draw on his personal experiences and situate these in a historical and cultural context. They give expression to the unique vision of a black man in white America, captured in the idea of "double consciousness." Apart from his singular efforts in establishing the legitimacy of an empirical sociology of the African-American, Du Bois embraced the role of activist and public intellectual, thereby uniting his intellectual gifts in the service of the cause for equal justice. In bringing together theory and action, Du Bois abandoned the teachings of Max Weber and came closer to the *praxis* of Karl Marx. His life as an empirical sociologist and public intellectual captures the dilemma of being a black academic, at once committed to objectivity and social justice.

Karl Mannheim (1893–1947) represents a fusion of certain aspects of Marx's thought with a Weberian orientation. Mannheim turns to a Marxian insight on the relationship of ideas to interests and their location in the social structure and develops it into a full study, the sociology of knowledge. Marx had claimed that the ruling ideas were the ideas of the ruling class and that the dominant interests in society used ideas to legitimate their position. As Marx looked toward the proletariat as the agent of change, he argued that as a class, the proletariat was acting on behalf of a universal principle and not just for its narrow class interest. Socialism was a truly just system for all members of society, not only for the working classes. In this sense then, Marx believed that all classes developed ideologies to justify their domination, but the proletariat possessed a truth that was universal in scope and aimed at the liberation of mankind.

Although impressed with Marx's analysis of ideology, Mannheim was unprepared to follow him in his depiction of the proletariat as a universal class. Instead Mannheim viewed socialism as that complex of ideas which represented the interests of the workers and sought to change the *status quo*. His analysis led him to conclude that sociology can establish the relationship between ideas and their historical and social context; it can tell us who holds particular ideas, which groups benefit from the belief in certain ideas, what interests are advanced, and which are deterred. However, sociology cannot establish the substantive truth about any complex of ideas or declare them to be universally true. In establishing the relativity of perspectives, and applying it to the proletariat as well as to the bourgeoisie, Mannheim's sociology of knowledge departs from Marx and embraces a Weberian position. Thus, Mannheim's *Ideology and Utopia* represents both a continuation of Marxist thought and a critical departure from it.

Mannheim's analysis of the role of intellectuals in society exhibits a similar critical tension. In his earlier work, Mannheim had described the intellectuals as "free-floating" and unattached to any class interest. Hence, unlike others, intellectuals were able to establish distance and assess arguments dispassionately, seeing different perspectives and the interests they advance. During World War II, in exile from his native Germany, Mannheim wrote that the crisis of Western society required the active engagement of intellectuals in the politics of the

time, and he attributed to them a powerful role in extending democratic ideas. Mannheim came to see that progress and other Enlightenment ideals were to be advanced by a politically engaged intellectual elite and not by a detached intelligentsia. Why intellectuals should be so significant to the preservation of a democratic order, and indeed whether their role as described by Mannheim in his later work is compatible with democratic processes, are continuing questions that stem from his analysis.

The different perspectives held by the classical theorists illustrate how basic assumptions about the relationship of the individual to society provide the framework within which the facts are interpreted, questions formulated, and answers provided. Models of society and alternative perspectives on social reality are the legacy of the classics. As C. Wright Mills (1960, 4) summarizes:

> The classic tradition, then, may not be defined by one specific method, certainly not by any one theory of society, history, or human nature. . . . The classic tradition is most readily defined by the character of the questions that have guided and do now guide those who are part of it. These questions are generally of wide scope: they concern total societies, their transformations, and the varieties of individual men and women that inhabit them. The answers given by classic sociologists provide conceptions about society, about history and about biography, and in their work these three are usually linked closely together.

II Contemporary Sociological Theory

Part Two of this collection attempts to capture the development of sociological theory in the post-World War II period. During the 1950s, the field of sociology was dominated by Talcott Parsons and his integrative theoretical efforts in the form of structural functionalism. At the same time, the discipline seemed to be committed to a positivistic model of scientific knowledge, so that for the duration of the decade, sociology appeared to be well on the road to establishing its scientific legitimacy. By the end of the decade, functionalism and the positivistic model were under attack. C. Wright Mills (1959) launched a powerful critique against "grand theory," by which he meant Parsonian functionalism, and against "abstracted empiricism," in which he ridiculed the scientific pretensions of sociology. Alvin Gouldner (1970) ended the decade with an enormously influential critical analysis of functionalism and positivism.

The debate within sociology was supported by developments outside the field as well. Thomas Kuhn's *The Structure of Scientific Revolutions* (1962) challenged the old orthodoxies with respect to the evolutionary character of scientific disciplines. In discussing the ambiguous and controversial concept of "paradigm," Kuhn demonstrated how an exemplary model tends to dominate a field and narrow the focus of practitioners' vision to problem solving, or what he called "normal science." What was significant, however, for the social sciences, and for sociology in particular, was the way in which Kuhn described changes in the dominant paradigm, or theory. Kuhn's thesis departed from the conventional interpretations when he claimed that changes are not the consequence of the rational assessment of the evidence to see which of two competing theories ought to prevail. Rather, Kuhn used the language of politics and characterized the change as "revolutionary." Practitioners confronted with anomalies and unable to find a resolution often experience a change in the way they see the world that is closer to a religious conversion than to the process of methodical calculations described in the conventional theories of scientific progress. Because changes in the dominant theory were now seen as matters of conversion, unrelated to disconfirmation by "neutral" or "objective" facts, political strategies for paradigmatic dominance began to take hold in the social sciences.

These intellectual developments in the history and philosophy of science were taking place simultaneously with the tumultuous political and cultural events of the 1960s. Whereas functionalism stressed harmony, integration, consensus, and order, the civil rights movement, the anti-war movement, and the acid-rock countercultural movement generated conflict, critique, disorder, and confrontation. Functional theory was out of step with reality, and Kuhn had made it possible for social scientists to see how arbitrary the prevailing paradigms were, and how much their continued dominance depended on the unquestioning acceptance by practitioners. There followed a period of two decades of theoretical diversification and proliferation in sociology, leading George Ritzer (1975) to label sociology a "multiple paradigm science."

Part Two begins with an essay by Kingsley Davis and Wilbert E. Moore, which presents the functionalist analysis of social stratification. It is followed by an essay by Talcott Parsons on age and sex in America, and an extract from Robert K. Merton's essay on manifest and latent functions. The student will recognize similarities with Durkheim's theory of society and his approach to it. Central to the functionalist perspective is the notion that a society is a system of interrelated and differentiated parts, all of which work together to maintain a stable order in a changing environment. Functionalism avows the objective reality of the social system, whose needs exist and must be fulfilled irrespective of the wishes of the particular individuals who live within it. Functionalism views social facts as *sui generis* and does not engage in reductionist explanations. The functionalist perspective is preoccupied with the problem of social order and finds an explanation in the ways in which shared norms and values serve to bring forth an integrated and consensual order. Functionalists emphasize social integration and consensus, and they tend to minimize the phenomenon of conflict in their quest for integrative mechanisms.

Our presentation of contemporary theory continues with a reading in "conflict theory" which attempts to highlight the limitations of functionalism. Ralf Dahrendorf demonstrates how a conflict model restructures our perception of the social world by recognizing that conflict is a necessary feature of social life. Conflict theory draws on Marxist and Weberian formulations about the basis of social order, positing that order is ultimately based on force rather than consent, as the functionalists would have it, and that the dominant interests are the beneficiaries of social order. The essay by C. Wright Mills, which follows the Dahrendorf selection, illustrates the structure of power in American society and raises questions about the feasibility of democratic control. Conflict theorists place considerable emphasis on the dynamics of social change, the sources of conflict and dissent in society, and the differences in the power resources of those at the top of the social order as against those at the bottom. These emphases clearly distinguish conflict theory from functionalism and its consensual approach to social order.

Exchange theory and rational choice theory are further examples of proliferation and diversity following the demise of functionalism. In an attempt to move away from abstract conceptualization and to refocus sociology onto the behavior of real people in their everyday life, George Homans, a Harvard sociologist, turned to the psychological theories of B. F. Skinner, a colleague at Harvard, to ground exchange theory in the behavior of individuals. Arguing that individuals are engaged in exchange relations in which rewards and punishments are elicited by particular behaviors, Homans went on to describe how behavior is reinforced by negative or positive responses. What emerged from Homans' formulations was an elaborate scheme that depicted individuals as actors able to calculate costs and risks attendant on particular behaviors.

Peter Blau, another exchange theorist, shares some of the antipathy expressed by Homans toward Parsonian functionalism. However, Blau is also aware of the limitations of Homans' approach, and as we shall see below, he extends exchange theory beyond the narrow scope of face-to-face interactions to speak of larger social structures and what makes them possible.

Exchange theory and rational choice theory, represented here by James S. Coleman, have much in common. They focus on the behavior of individuals as their starting point and evince less concern for large-scale structures and institutions, although as we have noted, Blau's work, as well as other recent developments, point in the direction of efforts to integrate micro and macro approaches.

Phenomenological sociology and Ethnomethodology develop out of a commitment to a *verstehende* approach to social reality. The focus is on the subjective meaning of action as opposed to the objective meaning attributed to action by the observer. It is imperative to capture the shared meaning structures of the participants in a social act by empathic understanding or rational reconstruction and to guard against the imposition of meanings as they are deduced from abstract scientific theories or models of the real world. The shared life-world of commonsense meanings is the everyday reality of ordinary people, and it is the purpose of sociological inquiry to understand that social reality. This is the burden of the work of Alfred Schutz (1967) and of Peter Berger and Thomas Luckmann (1967) and Harold Garfinkel (1967), (Chapter 10).

These theorists maintain that sociology must inquire into how ordinary people see the social world, how they organize their daily activities, why they act as they do, and what explanations they give to their behavior. Sociologists must first learn the language of everyday life in order to understand the experience of ordinary people, and they must eschew the scientific obligation to construct abstract theories and explain the data of everyday life in terms of those intellectual constructions. Failure to do so may lead to erroneous explanations that may make logical sense as derivatives from theory, but may have no connection to what meaning ordinary people impart to their actions.

In a somewhat related fashion, ethnomethodology proceeds to uncover the shared meaning structures and to demonstrate their reality and their fragility. Only as a result of shared meanings is social interaction possible, and when these meanings are disavowed and behavioral expectations denied interaction becomes difficult if not impossible. Ethnomethodologists, such as Harold Garfinkel (1967), demonstrate these claims with concrete experimental evidence.

The work of George Herbert Mead inspired a number of students to continue working with the theoretical concepts that he developed. Symbolic Interactionism is the name of the orientation taken by those who have followed in Mead's wake. The approach places considerable emphasis on the self as a social construction, on the interactive processes as central to understanding human behavior, and on the use of symbols as a distinctively human form of communication. Through language human beings can make themselves the objects of their reflection, i.e., they are able to think about their actions and change their future behavior based on their understanding. Mead pioneered this view of the reflexive self with the internal dialogue between the "I" and the "me" (Chapter 5). Herbert Blumer, a graduate student of sociology during Mead's time at the University of Chicago, coined the term *symbolic interaction* as he extended Mead's work beyond small groups to broader social processes. For Blumer social reality is defined by interactive processes and less importantly by objective structures external to the individual. What we observe in everyday life are people acting jointly, fitting their behaviors to one another, and adjusting their actions so as to fit together with the actions of others in order to achieve collective goals.

Erving Goffman may also be counted among Mead's followers. Having studied with Blumer, Goffman went on to write a number of works that celebrated the capacity of the self to play many roles and to survive under duress through creative invention in varied contexts. Goffman's *dramaturgy* is intended to capture the idea that social life is very much like a stage play, and that only if people play their roles and understand the limits of the interactive process can social life proceed. If expectations are denied, if individuals allow irrelevant emotions to intrude, or if they fail to read the cues of others properly, the interaction between people suffers a breakdown. It should be noted that the interactionists shift the focus of their attention away from social structures such as class, and place far greater significance on the experienced reality of everyday life and the self as the agent of reflective action.

Feminist social theory as it has emerged over the past twenty-five years draws from different perspectives of the sociological tradition. Liberal feminism, Marxian feminism, radical feminism, and socialist feminism are among the varieties of feminist theory that provide critical perspectives on mainstream theorizing in sociology. Dorothy Smith's work, (Chapter 12) extends the phenomenological insights as it makes the claim that not only does the objective science to which many mainstream sociologists subscribe impose an abstract meaning structure onto the activities of everyday life, but that the imposition is linked to larger socioeconomic structures of male domination. The danger in the scientific approach to truth is that it ignores the subjective or experiential meaning that actors bring to interaction situations. In particular, Smith claims, this process leads to "bifurcation of consciousness" in women, who must at once suppress their experiential understanding of their life-world in order to participate in the abstract, yet socially constructed, world of male domination. To the degree that mainstream sociology adheres to an objective view of knowledge and eschews the phenomenological approach, it simply appends women's issues to its male-oriented research program and excludes the experiential mode of knowing the meaning of the lives of women. Michele Barrett's essay, "Words and Things . . . " (chapter 12) raises an important cautionary note in respect to the paradigm shift in feminist theory, particularly the embrace of "post-structuralism" and its implications for universal ideals of equality and human rights.

III Modernity and Post-Modernism

Part Three points to the most recent developments in continental social theory. The debates among the modernists and post-modernists have had significant impact among American scholars, especially in the humanities and in the field of literary criticism. Within sociology the influence of these debates has been confined to social theory, and even there it has been marginal to mainstream concerns about micro- and macro-integration, and metatheory as opposed to empirical research, as a programmatic paradigm (Ritzer 1990; Giddens and Turner 1987).

C. Wright Mills (1959, 1960) criticized sociology for its hyperfactualism, its narrowness, and its lack of support for theory, most particularly the kind of theory produced by the social theorists of the classical tradition. What Mills meant was that social theory should be broadly based, morally involved, and actively engaged with the vital issues of the day. He saw the retreat to neutral facts as indicative of a "crisis of social reflection," as if social problems could be resolved by resort to facts alone. Thus the crisis Mills feared was not only a crisis among sociologists, but among intellectuals who were seduced by the siren song of a science of society, and who retreated from value judgments in their quest for technical solutions to moral questions. This would not augur well for our political future because it would support the superiority of narrow expertise in decision making and tend to legitimate technocratic as against democratic tendencies in the society.

The readings in Part Three, most particularly the contributions of Herbert Marcuse, Jürgen Habermas, and Michel Foucault, address some of these issues directly. Marcuse and Habermas represent critical social theory, which addresses the central issue of the future viability of democratic initiative and control under conditions that favor narrow expertise and instrumental rationality in problem solving. In a one-dimensional society (Marcuse 1966), where the traditional sources of negativity have been absorbed, political initiatives reflecting community needs give way to the formulations of experts in the policy process. Habermas, (1970) speaks of a process of disenfranchisement that develops as ordinary citizens are overwhelmed by social problems, politicians become media celebrities, and the public sphere of discourse is gradually eroded. In reflecting on the tasks of a critical theory of society, Habermas brings into focus the questions that contemporary social theory must address, how it should be grounded to avoid the charge of relativism, and how it may help to revitalize democratic politics by reviving questions about moral purpose and supporting the efforts of the new social movements as progressive forces (Habermas 1985). If Habermas represents the continuation of the Enlightenment project of rational knowledge as a source of control over political and social destiny, he also affirms the distinction between reason and power and projects the capacity of an autonomous reason to hold power to account.

Approaching the problematic of modern society from an entirely different vantage point, Michel Foucault challenges the idea that reason is autonomous, and he substitutes the notion of knowledge/power. What Foucault means to do is to expose the false claims of objectivity and neutrality with respect to knowledge and to argue that knowledge is a form of power. In *Discipline and Punish,* Foucault (1977) demonstrates how the human sciences evolved from ameliatory and humanely motivated inquiries about prison conditions and prisoners into intrusive forms of psychological investigation into the inner recesses of a prisoner's mind. Under the aegis of a rational scientific approach, causal inquiries are undertaken to provide explanations for criminal or deviant behavior. In order to pursue the more enlightened purpose of rehabilitation rather than punishment, intimate knowledge of prisoners was necessary to understand the causes of crime. Furthermore, in order to work with inmates and restore them to mainstream society, psychological counselors needed detailed personal information, not only about the inmate but also about his family and friends, his childhood, his secret longings, and so forth. Foucault sees in this development the formation of scientifically grounded codes of behavior that distinguish the normal from the abnormal or deviant. The human sciences produce moral norms of right behavior and become agents in the achievement of social control. Social scientific knowledge becomes a means of producing and legitimating the normal personality.

Foucault's work is very much in line with Weber's view of the "iron cage" and the "totally administered society" as formulated by Max Horkheimer and T. W. Adorno (1975) in an early work on critical theory. It demonstrates "the end of the subject" in the sense that the individual becomes the object of knowledge and those with access to that knowledge have the power to produce standards of normality and create new types of individuals. Contrary to the Enlightenment promise, rational knowledge is not a source of liberation from dogma and myth, but creates new forms of control based on the human sciences of normality. Foucault sees this phenomenon throughout modern society. He describes it as the "carceral society" (Foucault 1977, 304).

> The judges of normality are present everywhere. We are in the society of the teacher-judge, the doctor-judge, the educator-judge, the social-worker judge. It is on them that the universal reign of the normative is based; and each individual, wherever he may find himself, subjects to it his body, his gestures, his behaviour, his aptitudes, his achievements. The carceral network, in its compact or disseminated forms, with its systems of insertion, distribution, surveillance, observation, has been the greatest support, in modern society, of the normalizing of power.

Jean-Francois Lyotard's work (1984) carries this analysis further to an inquiry about the condition of knowledge in the post-modern age. Foucault and Lyotard provide a powerful challenge to social theory as well as to the claims of an objective and value-neutral science of society. The impact of Lyotard's work has been to challenge all truth claims and to expose them as a function of power. Scientific knowledge develops unevenly, often accidentally and contingently. The myth of evolutionary development through tests and experimentation is challenged in the way in which Thomas Kuhn (1962) earlier wrote about revolutionary science.

Lyotard's argument centers on his view of metanarratives and their role in the legitimation of science. By metanarratives, Lyotard means broadly based social themes such as progressive and emancipatory theories which tend to order history according to some teleological notion that places past and current events in a context and provides an abstract interpretation of these events, guided by a deductive logic rather than by empirical demonstration. Reason, Progress, Knowledge, and Enlightenment are part of the myth, the great story, the grand metanarratives that provide totalizing explanations of human history and justify current scientific and political practices in light of the promised *telos*. These metanarratives aim to achieve a true and just social order, one that is not subject to the contingencies of power and interest. A pure reason is able to identify the good, the true, and the just beyond the distortions of everyday political and cultural practice.

Post-modernism signifies the end of these claims as the post-modern society witnesses emerging pluralities, diversities, and the collapse of philosophy and social theory. What Lyotard describes is a post-modern world in which all metanarratives are discredited and in which no claim to a privileged position can be granted to philosophy or social theory. All such previous claims are today met with oppositional responses in which the hegemonic positions of the rationalist philosophies are viewed as repressive. In Lyotard's view there is no intellectual tribunal which has privileged access to truth and justice. Rather, in a pluralistic, contingent, and decentralized world, knowledge must become plural, contingent, and decentered. What this means in the realm of knowledge is a proliferation of discourses in which scholars pursue intellectual interests and form groups with those of like mind. As a group, they work out the rules and principles by which they conduct their inquiries rather than seek approval or legitimation for their work from some philosophically privileged court that holds an answer to the question, "What is true knowledge?" As Fraser and Nicholson (1988, 377) state:

> In *The Postmodern Condition*, Lyotard argues that metanarratives, whether philosophies of history or non-narrative foundational philosophies, are merely modern and dépassé. We can no longer believe, he claims, in the availability of a privileged metadiscourse capable of capturing once and for all the truth of every first order discourse. The claim to meta status does not stand up. A so-called metadiscourse is in fact simply one more discourse among others. It follows for Lyotard that legitimation, both epistemic and political, can no longer reside in philosophical metanarratives.

Between Habermas the modernist and rationalist, and Foucault and Lyotard the postmodernists, there exists an enormous chasm. Habermas refuses to surrender the idea that human reason is capable of grounding a critique of society that avoids relativism and he identifies the new social movements as political forces that will enhance the formation of a just society through democratic and consensual means. His analysis presupposes the capacity of human reason to identify the good, the true, and the just and to act in order to bring it about. Post-

modernists, by contrast, not only deny Habermas' basic assumptions about reason, communication, and action; they fear that his programmatic critical theory may become yet another legitimating ideology, another metanarrative.

Foucault's response to the new forms of power/knowledge domination and the potential for the creation of new standards of political and social "normality" is a radical affirmation of the Nietzschean individual whose creative and unique capabilities are sources of truth and freedom. The social nature of existence is no longer viewed as an opportunity to become a truly human being; rather social existence is increasingly seen as a politically manipulated and controlled existence in Foucault's analysis. It is the "poetic" or "aesthetic" self that Foucault (1988) finds as the source of negativity in the all-pervasive system of knowledge/power and technocratic domination.

Within the classic tradition, Weber's challenge to Marxist thought and to the metanarratives that have historically preceded it anticipates much of the post-modernist critique. In "Science as a Vocation," Weber (1958, 143) reviews the justifications for science as so many illusions:

> Under these internal presuppositions, what is the meaning of science as a vocation, now after all these former illusions, the "way to true being," the "way to true art," the "way to true nature," the "way to true God," the "way to true happiness" have been dispelled? Tolstoi has given the simplest answer, with the words: "Science is meaningless because it gives no answer to our question, the only question important for us: 'What shall we do and how shall we live?'"

In this passage as well as in his other writings, Weber reveals himself to be a skeptic of metanarratives and most especially of the Enlightenment myth of reason and progress. It was Weber (1958, 181–2) who characterized modern rational society as "the iron cage" and referred to our future as a "polar night of icy darkness" (1958a, 128). Weber's science sought no justification in the mythologies of an emancipatory future. Weber challenged all of this and more. Can Weber then be said to be the first post-modernist? Is the modernist/post-modernist debate a replay of the debate between Marx and Weber?

What I wish to argue in the concluding sections of this essay is that the condition of post-modernity presents sociological theory with a unique and unprecedented range of social problems. Most particularly, I want to argue that if sociology is to maintain its vitality in the future it must recouple with philosophy in order to chart new directions and develop the critical constructs necessary to a new age or risk the fate of becoming a source of ideological legitimation for a liberal technocracy.

Recent debates over the meaning and purpose of sociological theory point to a pervasive disagreement over the current state of the field. In *Frontiers of Social Theory* (Ritzer 1990), a collection of essays on the current state of sociological theory, George Ritzer, Jonathan Turner, and Norbert Wiley, in their concluding essays, fail to arrive at any agreement as to the meaning and significance of contemporary developments. Ritzer discovers syntheses within each of the major schools or subfields of social theory and supports the idea that the integration of concepts and micro, macro perspectives is better than further diversification. Turner reads the proliferation of theory subfields as symptomatic of the collapse of sociology. His unreconstructed positivism leads him to claim that sociology loses credibility and legitimacy the more it departs from the models of scientific investigation. On the other hand, Norbert Wiley uses the metaphors of politics to describe the struggles for theoretical dominance in the post-modern age. When knowledge is neither disinterested nor objective the claim to truth collapses into a struggle for power. Other critics (Seidman 1990) find contemporary theory empty because it makes no linkage to an emerging social reality and is beset by the professionals' agenda.

Anthony Giddens in his recent *Modernity and Self-Identity* (1991) argues that modernity entails a constant challenge to traditional beliefs, customs, and institutions. This is nothing new, but what is novel here is the way in which Giddens ties these developments to the self and the formation of identity. We might term this the central problematic for a post-modern sociology. Giddens describes the process of identity breakdown and the need of individuals to create new identities as they are caught in a maelstrom of social change and old institutions are rendered irrelevant or obsolete. The present age encourages an experimental attitude toward life that increasingly begs for answers to the most fundamental questions of meaning and purpose. These are precisely the questions that Weber admonished sociologists as sociologists to avoid because they cannot be answered scientifically. However, were social theory to turn toward philosophy, then its future might be secured and its relevance for a post-modern age made palpable.

Both Habermas and the later Foucault are responding to these new needs for a philosophically oriented sociology. Habermas' critical theory attempts to ground a critical sociology in the universal emancipatory ideals of Marxism. A value-free sociology is, for Habermas, an instrumentalist sociology that functions to support the liberal ideology of modern society but develops no fundamental critique of it. Rather, it functions as a reformist and ameliatory sociology. Habermas' project is to link sociology to an emancipatory and democratic political philosophy so as to ensure its relevance to an emerging social order. To this end Habermas endorses the new social movements as social forces that are expressive of moral concerns about the public good and questions of identity formation that point to a new style of politics for the future.

Foucault's earlier work, as we have seen, is an extension of Weber's views of modernity and the administered society. His later work, *The Care of the Self* (1988), in particular, is an attempt to link sociology to questions of self and identity at which Giddens only hints. Foucault returns to ancient Greece in his quest for answers to the question of what constitutes the self when "the social" becomes transparently manipulative and all-controlling. By exploring the Greek ethic of the self, Foucault points us in the direction of an aesthetic concept of the self, the self as a work of art.

What is significant is that both Habermas and Foucault, from radically different perspectives, are attempting to focus their social analyses on the deeply disturbing contemporary issues that seem to require philosophical reflection in order to provide a critical awareness of the historical moment that we occupy. In this sense, their writings seem closer to the concerns of the classical tradition than they are to the contemporary American theorists, and for that reason they provide us with an alternative to the professionals' definition of the tasks of theory.

REFERENCES

ALEXANDER, JEFFREY, 1987: "The Centrality of the Classics." In *Social Theory Today*. Edited by Anthony Giddens, and Jonathan Turner. Stanford: Stanford University Press.

BECKER, CARL L., 1959: *The Heavenly City of the Eighteenth Century Philosophers*. New Haven: Yale University Press.

BERGER, PETER L., AND THOMAS LUCKMANN, 1967: *The Social Construction of Reality: A Treatise in the Sociology of Knowledge*. Garden City: Anchor.

DURKHEIM, ÉMILE, 1973: "Individualism and the Intellectuals." In *Émile Durkheim on Morality and Society*. Edited by Robert N. Bellah. Chicago: The University of Chicago Press.

FOUCAULT, MICHEL, 1977: *Discipline and Punish: The Birth of the Prison*. Trans. by Alan Sheridan. New York: Pantheon Books.; 1988: *The Care of the Self: The History of Sexuality*. Vol. 3. Trans. by Robert Hurley. New York: Random House.

FRASER, NANCY, AND LINDA NICHOLSON, 1988: "Social Criticism Without Philosophy: An Encounter Between Feminism and Post-Modernism." *Theory, Culture and Society* 5(2–3):373–394.

GARFINKEL, HAROLD, 1967: *Studies in Ethnomethodology*. Englewood Cliffs: Prentice Hall.

GIDDENS, ANTHONY, 1991: *Modernity and Self-Identity: Self and Society in the Late Modern Age*. Stanford: Stanford University Press.

GIDDENS, ANTHONY, AND JONATHAN TURNER, EDS., 1987: *Social Theory Today*. Stanford: Stanford University Press.

GOULDNER, ALVIN, 1970: *The Coming Crisis of Western Sociology*. New York: Basic Books.

HABERMAS, JÜRGEN, 1970: *Towards Rational Society: Student Protest, Science and Politics*. Trans. by Jeremy Shapiro. Boston: Beacon Press; 1985: *The Theory of Communicative Action*. Vol. 1, *Reason and the Rationalization of Society*. Trans. by Thomas McCarthy. Boston: Beacon Press.

HORKHEIMER, MAX, AND THEODOR W. ADORNO, 1975: *The Dialectic of Enlightenment*. Trans. by John Cumming. New York: Continuum.

KUHN, THOMAS, 1962: *The Structure of Scientific Revolutions*. Chicago: University of Chicago Press.

LYOTARD, JEAN-FRANCOIS, 1984: *The Post-Modern Condition: A Report of Knowledge*. Trans. by Geoff Bennington and Brian Mossumi. Minneapolis: University of Minnesota Press.

MARCUSE, HERBERT, 1966: *One-Dimensional Man*. Boston: Beacon Press.

MILLS, C. WRIGHT, 1959: *The Sociological Imagination*. New York: Oxford University Press; 1960: *Images of Man*. New York: George Braziller.

RITZER, GEORGE, 1975: *Sociology: A Multiple Paradigm Science*. Boston: Allyn and Bacon.

RITZER, GEORGE, ED., 1990: *Frontiers of Social Theory: The New Syntheses*. New York: Columbia University Press.

ROUSSEAU, JEAN JACQUES, 1947: "What Is the Origin of Inequality among Men?" In *The Social Contract and Discourse*. London: Everyman's Library, J. M.Dent.

SALOMON, ALBERT, 1945: "German Sociology." In *Twentieth Century Sociology*. Edited by George Gurvitch and Wilbert E. Moore, New York: The Philosophical Library; 1967: *Collected Papers*. Vol. 1, *The Problem of Social Reality*. Edited and introduced by Maurice Natanson. The Hague: Martinus Nijhoff.

SEIDMAN, STEVEN, 1990: "Against Theory as a Foundationalist Discourse." *Perspectives: Theory Section Newsletter* (American Sociological Association) 13(2):1–3.

WEBER, MAX, 1958: *The Protestant Ethic and the Spirit of Capitalism*. New York: Scribner's; 1958a: Hans H. Gerth, and C. Wright Mills, eds. *From Max Weber: Essays in Sociology*. New York: Oxford University Press.

ZEITLIN, IRVING, 1968: *Ideology and the Development of Sociological Theory*. Englewood Cliffs: Prentice Hall.

The Classic Tradition

21

Chapter 1

Karl Marx: Alienation, Class Struggle, and Class Consciousness

Introduction

Why should one bother to read Marx, one might ask, particularly after the collapse of Communism in Eastern Europe and the Soviet Union? These historic events, it has been argued, have brought the Cold War to an end, and with this a victorious West is able to establish a liberal, capitalist, and democratic world order. Yet Marx continues to be of interest, less so because of his failed predictions than for his analysis of the structure of power in capitalist societies and his comprehensive view of the close interrelationship of economic class dominance, political power, and ideology. These structural relationships have much to recommend them to the student of society for they point to significant questions of economic, social, and political power and provide us with a view of history that explains how, and under what conditions, these relationships change. Although Marx claimed to be committed to a scientific study of society, his unique dialectical approach allowed him to fuse his philosophical views about human emancipation with his sociological and historical analyses of social change and revolution.

Marx was born in Trier in 1818 to a middle-class German-Jewish family. He attended the University of Bonn and later the University of Berlin, where he became associated with a group of intellectuals, the Young Hegelians, who applied Hegel's philosophical approach to a radical critique of German politics. Hegel's dialectical approach attempted to capture the reality of dynamic change in the world by urging that we examine things as they are and as

they have the potential to become in the future. Just as the seedling gives rise to the tree so too do individuals and societies have the potential to develop and realize themselves under appropriate conditions. It was Marx's objectives to recount the conditions of human development under capitalism and logically to project the dynamic changes that would ensue, bringing people to a fuller realization of their free and creative potentialities.

In 1843 Marx left Germany for Paris, where he worked as a journalist and wrote the essays that were eventually published as the *Economic and Philosophical Manuscripts of 1844*. It was in Paris that Marx met up with Frederick Engels, who was to become his greatest friend and colleague. In 1845 Marx visited London, where he and Engels worked together on *The German Ideology*. Later, in 1847, a socialist group called "The League of the Just" commissioned Marx and Engels to write the *Communist Manifesto*.

Revolutionary upheavals against the old monarchical order were sweeping across Europe in 1848, the year the *Manifesto* was published. Marx returned to London following these failed revolutions and spent the greater part of his remaining life in exile there. He was supported primarily by his rich friend Engels and earned a small income from his work for the *New York Daily Tribune* as their European correspondent.

The period between 1848 and 1863 was a particularly difficult one for Marx. The revolutions of 1848 having failed, Marx was left without an audience for his work. Yet he continued to write his masterpiece, *Capital*, encouraged by

Engels and driven by his vision of historical progress and revolutionary transformation. In 1863 Marx discovered an audience for his work once again with the founding of The International, an organization of representatives from various European worker parties dedicated to ending the prevailing system of economic domination. Marx became heavily involved with the organization, writing speeches and pamphlets and eventually becoming its head, as he worked tirelessly to forge a united front out of the various ideological viewpoints that were represented. When the first volume of *Capital* was published in 1867, it was well received among Russian and German socialists and by the membership of The International, who celebrated Marx and his work as scientific socialism and accorded it canonical status.

Internal conflicts brought about the dissolution of the The International in 1876, and Marx completed very little serious intellectual work in his later life. He died in 1883 and is buried in Highgate Cemetery.

Marx believed that, through labor, humankind would be able to realize its "species-being," i.e., its potential for creative and purposeful activity through work. Human labor was not simply energy expended for subsistence, although it was clearly that under capitalism. What Marx envisioned was the use of labor for enhancement of human life beyond material necessity, for the creation of a society in which aesthetic as well as material needs could be fulfilled. Labor could potentially provide such an opportunity, for it allowed persons to display creative and purposeful activity through their work under the appropriate conditions.

Under capitalism, however, the owners of the means of production, the bourgeoisie, are in control of the productive process. Whereas Marx assumed that the determination of what labor produces, how labor produces, and how the products of labor are distributed should be made by the working class, under capitalism the bourgeoisie pays workers a wage and then appropriates and disposes of what they produce. In other words, the conditions under which labor produces are alienating conditions insofar as workers are no longer in control of the object of their labor, i.e., its product. All the important determinations are made by others. Not being permitted to perform the inherent functions of a species-being, or even to view one's labor-power as one's own, the worker feels demoralized and dehumanized.

As a mode of production, capitalism entails structured relationships between labor and capital which result in the alienation of workers from the most important aspects of their labor. They are alienated first from their productive activity. The industrial labor force is organized on the assembly line, in which specific, repetitive, and tedious tasks must be performed. Work becomes a mechanical means to an end, requiring neither intelligence nor imagination, and the worker reverts to a subhuman condition instead of being elevated to realize "species-being." Workers are also alienated from the products they produce. Their energy is congealed in those products, but workers do not own what they produce. Finally, workers are alienated from their fellow workers as capitalists promote competition among them for the available jobs at subsistence wages. Instead of the solidarity and comradeship that comes from working together on a collective project, the work force is deliberately kept at subsistence wages, engendering great fear in workers that they will not be able to survive if their jobs are taken from them. The reserve army of labor, as Marx called the mass of the unemployed, acts as a constant threat to workers who may try to organize themselves and demand higher wages. Thus alienated and mechanized, the worker feels inhuman in the activity which should most naturally express humanity.

Marx viewed history as a record of oppression and domination in which members of the upper classes were able to exploit those in the lower classes. However, history is also progressive and points in the direction of improved conditions and greater freedom. Capitalism is but a stage in that historical development. Just as feudalism gave way to capitalism when the economic conditions were ripe, so too will capitalism give way to socialism and later communism, as the ultimate form of an emancipated existence. How this would come about is recounted on the following pages in the *Communist Manifesto.*

Marx's categories for social analysis still have considerable validity. In attempting to analyze a society, Marx questions how the social order has come to be what it is, what the structures of power are that maintain it, and what the relationship is between wealth and power. These are the questions that should be uppermost in the reader's mind in reading the materials in this chapter.

Central to Marx's theory of society was his view that the way in which production is organized is a key to understanding the important relationships in any social order. The mode of production, be it a slave economy, a feudal system, a capitalist order, or a socialist system must be analyzed in terms of the basic relationships that define that system. Moreover, the economic base of society, its substructure, was seen to influence, if not determine the superstructure, i.e., the ideas, values, laws, and social and political institutions. The content of our consciousness and our ideological orientation to the world are a function of the material, or productive, base of society. Changes in the economic substructure produce changes in the political and ideological superstructure. In *The German Ideology,* Marx recounts his materialist conception of history and fully develops his ideas concerning the interrelationship of the economy to politics and society.

In his view of capitalist society Marx reveals a theory of class structure. The class that controls the means of production is also the dominant political and ideological force in society. The ruling ideas are the ideas of the ruling class, Marx tells us. The content of consciousness under capitalism centers on the liberal ideas of individual rights, principally property rights. Power is maintained by the ruling class, at least in part, because the proletariat does not, in the early stages of capitalism, possess "true consciousness." Only after prolonged and unrelieved suffering and wretchedness does the proletariat begin to see itself as a class, gradually mobilize, and develop an alternative ideology that posits the objective relations of labor and capital.

Marx believed that history was driven by class struggle and that important social changes were the outcomes of inevitable conflicts between irreconcilable interests. Capitalism would give way as the struggle between the bourgeoisie and the proletariat could no longer be contained by the framework of law and social institutions. The *Communist Manifesto* offers a brief historical analysis of how the bourgeois class came into being, demonstrates how the bourgeoisie no longer has control over its dominions, and delineates the basic doctrines of the usurping class: the proletariat. Marx believed that socialism would replace capitalism and that the triumph of the proletariat would usher in a new and progressive order that would fulfill mankind's highest aspiration for a free and creative social order.

KARL MARX AND FREDERICK ENGELS:
THE MANIFESTO OF THE COMMUNIST PARTY

A specter is haunting Europe—the specter of Communism. All the powers of old Europe have entered into a holy alliance to exorcise this specter: Pope and Czar, Metternich and Guizot, French Radicals and German police-spies.

Where is the party in opposition that has not been decried as communistic by its opponents in power? Where the Opposition that has not hurled back the branding reproach of Communism, against the more advanced opposition parties, as well as against its reactionary adversaries?

Two things result from this fact:

I. Communism is already acknowledged by all European powers to be itself a power.

II. It is high time that Communists should openly, in the face of the whole world, publish their views, their aims, their tendencies, and meet this nursery tale of the specter of Communism with a manifesto of the party itself.

To this end, Communists of various nationalities have assembled in London, and sketched the following manifesto, to be published in the English, French, German, Italian, Flemish, and Danish languages.

I Bourgeois and Proletarians

The history of all hitherto existing society is the history of class struggles.

Freeman and slave, patrician and plebeian, lord and serf, guild-master and journeyman, in a word, oppressor and oppressed, stood in constant opposition to one another, carried on an uninterrupted, now hidden, now open fight, a fight that each time ended, either in a revolutionary reconstitution of society at large, or in the common ruin of the contending classes.

In the earlier epochs of history, we find almost everywhere a complicated arrangement of society into various orders, a manifold gradation of social rank. In ancient Rome we have patricians, knights, plebeians, slaves; in the Middle Ages, feudal lords, vassals, guild-masters, journeymen, apprentices, serfs; in almost all of these classes, again, subordinate gradations.

The modern bourgeois society that has sprouted from the ruins of feudal society, has not done away with class antagonisms. It has but established new classes, new conditions of oppression, new forms of struggle in place of the old ones.

Our epoch, the epoch of the bourgeoisie, possesses, however, this distinctive feature: It has simplified the class antagonisms. Society as a whole is more and more splitting up into two great hostile camps, into two great classes directly facing each other—bourgeoisie and proletariat.

From the serfs of the Middle Ages sprang the chartered burghers of the earliest towns. From these burgesses the first elements of the bourgeoisie were developed.

The discovery of America, the rounding of the Cape, opened up fresh ground for the rising bourgeoisie. The East Indian and Chinese markets, the colonization of America, trade with the colonies, the increase in the means of exchange and in commodities generally, gave to commerce, to navigation, to industry, an impulse never before known, and thereby, to the revolutionary element in the tottering feudal society, a rapid development.

The feudal system of industry, in which industrial production was monopolized by closed guilds, now no longer sufficed for the growing wants of the new markets. The manufacturing system took its place. The guild-masters were pushed aside by the manufacturing middle class; division of labor between the different corporate guilds vanished in the face of division of labor in each single workshop.

Meantime the markets kept ever growing, the demand ever rising. Even manufacture no longer sufficed. Thereupon, steam and machinery revolutionized industrial production. The place of manufacture was taken by the giant, modern industry, the place of the industrial middle class, by industrial millionaires—the leaders of whole industrial armies, the modern bourgeois.

Modern industry has established the world market, for which the discovery of America paved the way. This market has given an immense development to commerce, to navigation, to communication by land. This development has, in its turn, reacted on the extension of industry; and in proportion as industry, commerce, navigation, railways extended, in the same proportion the bourgeoisie developed, increased its capital, and pushed into the background every class handed down from the Middle Ages.

We see, therefore, how the modern bourgeoisie is itself the product of a long course of development, of a series of revolutions in the modes of production and of exchange.

Each step in the development of the bourgeoisie was accompanied by a corresponding political advance of that class. An oppressed class under the sway of the feudal nobility, it became an armed and self-governing association in the medieval commune; here independent urban republic (as in Italy and Germany), there taxable "third estate" of the monarchy (as in France); afterwards, in the period of manufacture proper, serving either the semi-feudal or the absolute monarchy as a counterpoise against the nobility, and, in fact, cornerstone of the great

monarchies in general—the bourgeoisie has at last, since the establishment of modern industry and of the world market, conquered for itself, in the modern representative state, exclusive political sway. The executive of the modern state is but a committee for managing the common affairs of the whole bourgeoisie.

The bourgeoisie has played a most revolutionary role in history.

The bourgeoisie, wherever it has got the upper hand, has put an end to all feudal, patriarchal, idyllic relations. It has pitilessly torn asunder the motley feudal ties that bound man to his "natural superiors," and has left no other bond between man and man than naked self-interest, than callous "cash payment." It has drowned the most heavenly ecstasies of religious fervor, of chivalrous enthusiasm, of philistine sentimentalism, in the icy water of egotistical calculation. It has resolved personal worth into exchange value and in place of the numberless indefeasible chartered freedoms, has set up that single, unconscionable freedom—Free Trade. In one word, for exploitation, veiled by religious and political illusions, it has substituted naked, shameless, direct, brutal exploitation.

The bourgeoisie has stripped of its halo every occupation hitherto honored, and looked up to with reverent awe. It has converted the physician, the lawyer, the priest, the poet, the man of science, into its paid wage-laborers.

The bourgeoisie has torn away from the family its sentimental *veil*, and has reduced the family relation to a mere money relation.

The bourgeoisie has disclosed how it came to pass that the brutal display of vigor in the Middle Ages, which reactionaries so much admire, found its fitting complement in the most slothful indolence. It has been the first to show what man's activity can bring about. It has accomplished wonders far surpassing Egyptian pyramids, Roman aqueducts, and Gothic cathedrals; it has conducted expeditions that put in the shade all former migrations of nations and crusades.

The bourgeoisie cannot exist without constantly revolutionizing the instruments of production, and thereby the relations of production, and with them the whole relations of society. Conservation of the old modes of production in unaltered form, was, on the contrary, the first condition of existence for all earlier industrial classes. Constant revolutionizing of production, uninterrupted disturbance of all social conditions, everlasting uncertainty and agitation distinguish the bourgeois epoch from all earlier ones. All fixed, fast-frozen relations, with their train of ancient and venerable prejudices and opinions, are swept away, all new-formed ones become antiquated before they can ossify. All that is solid melts into air, all that is holy is profaned, and man is at last compelled to face with sober senses his real conditions of life and his relations with his kind.

The need of a constantly expanding market for its products chases the bourgeoisie over the whole surface of the globe. It must nestle everywhere, settle everywhere, establish connections everywhere.

The bourgeoisie has through its exploitation of the world market given a cosmopolitan character to production and consumption in every country. To the great chagrin of reactionaries, it has drawn from under the feet of industry the national ground on which it stood. All old-established national industries have been destroyed or are daily being destroyed. They are dislodged by new industries, whose introduction becomes a life and death question for all civilized nations, by industries that no longer work up indigenous raw material, but raw material drawn from the remotest zones; industries whose products are consumed, not only at home, but in every corner of the globe. In place of the old wants, satisfied by the production of the country, we find new wants, requiring for their satisfaction the products of distant lands and climes. In place of the old local and national seclusion and self-sufficiency, we have intercourse in every direction, universal inter-dependence of nations.

And as in material, so also in intellectual production. The intellectual creations of individual nations become common property. National one-sidedness and narrow-mindedness become more and more impossible, and from the numerous national and local literatures there arises a world literature.

The bourgeoisie, by the rapid improvement of all instruments of production, by the immensely facilitated means of communication, draws all nations, even the most barbarian, into civilization. The cheap prices of its commodities are the heavy artillery with which it batters down all Chinese walls, with which it forces the barbarians' intensely obstinate hatred of foreigners to capitulate. It compels all nations, on pain of extinction, to adopt the bourgeois mode of production; it compels them to introduce what it calls civilization into their midst, i.e., to become bourgeois themselves. In a word, it creates a world after its own image.

The bourgeoisie has subjected the country to the rule of the towns. It has created enormous cities, has greatly increased the urban population as compared with the rural, and has thus rescued a considerable part of the population from the idiocy of rural life. Just as it has made the country dependent on the towns, so it has made barbarian and semi-barbarian countries dependent on the civilized ones, nations of peasants on nations of bourgeois, the East on the West.

More and more the bourgeoisie keeps doing away with the scattered state of the population, of the means of production, and of property. It has agglomerated population, centralized means of production, and has concentrated property in a few hands. The necessary consequence of this was political centralization. Independent, or but loosely connected provinces, with separate interests, laws, governments, and systems of taxation, became lumped together into one nation, with one government, one code of laws, one national class interest, one frontier, and one customs tariff.

The bourgeoisie, during its rule of scarce one hundred years, has created more massive and more colossal productive forces than have all preceding generations together. Subjection of nature's forces to man, machinery, application of chemistry to industry and agriculture, steam-navigation, railways, electric telegraphs, clearing of whole continents for cultivation, canalization of rivers, whole populations conjured out of the ground—what earlier century had even a pre-sentiment that such productive forces slumbered in the lap of social labor?

We see then that the means of production and of exchange, which served as the foundation for the growth of the bourgeoisie, were generated in feudal society. At a certain stage in the development of these means of production and of exchange, the conditions under which feudal society produced and exchanged, the feudal organization of agriculture and manu-facturing industry, in a word, the feudal rela-tions of property became no longer compatible with the already developed productive forces; they became so many fetters. They had to be burst asunder; they were burst asunder.

Into their place stepped free competition, accompanied by a social and political constitu-tion adapted to it, and by the economic and political sway of the bourgeois class.

A similar movement is going on before our own eyes. Modern bourgeois society with its relations of production, of exchange and of prop-erty, a society that has conjured up such gigan-tic means of production and of exchange, is like the sorcerer who is no longer able to control the powers of the nether world whom he has called up by his spells. For many a decade past the his-tory of industry and commerce is but the history of the revolt of modern productive forces against modern conditions of production, against the property relations that are the conditions for the existence of the bourgeoisie and of its rule. It is enough to mention the commercial crises that by their periodical return put the existence of the entire bourgeois society on trial, each time more threateningly. In these crises a great part not only of the existing products, but also of the previ-ously created productive forces, are periodically destroyed. In these crises there breaks out an epi-demic that, in all earlier epochs, would have seemed an absurdity—the epidemic of over-production. Society suddenly finds itself put back into a state of momentary barbarism; it appears as if a famine, a universal war of dev-astation had cut off the supply of every means of subsistence; industry and commerce seem to be destroyed. And why? Because there is too much civilization, too much means of subsistence, too much industry, too much commerce. The pro-ductive forces at the disposal of society no longer tend to further the development of the conditions of bourgeois property; on the con-trary, they have become too powerful for these conditions, by which they are fettered, and no sooner do they overcome these fetters than they bring disorder into the whole of bourgeois soci-ety, endanger the existence of bourgeois prop-erty. The conditions of bourgeois society are too narrow to comprise the wealth created by them. And how does the bourgeoisie get over these crises? On the one hand, by enforced destruction of a mass of productive forces; on the other, by the conquest of new markets, and by the more thorough exploitation of the old ones. That is to say, by paving the way for more extensive and more destructive crises, and by diminishing the means whereby crises are prevented.

The weapons with which the bourgeoisie felled feudalism to the ground are now turned against the bourgeoisie itself.

But not only has the bourgeoisie forged the weapons that bring death to itself; it has also called into existence the men who are to wield those weapons—the modern working class—the proletarians.

In proportion as the bourgeoisie, i.e., capital, is developed, in the same proportion is the pro-letariat, the modern working class, developed—a class of laborers, who live only so long as they find work, and who find work only so long as their labor increases capital. These laborers, who must sell themselves piecemeal, are a commodity, like every other article of commerce, and are consequently exposed to all the vicissitudes of competition, to all the fluctuations of the market.

Owing to the extensive use of machinery and to division of labor, the work of the proletarians has lost all individual character, and, consequently, all charm for the workman. He becomes an appendage of the machine, and it is only the most simple, most monotonous, and most easily acquired knack, that is required of him. Hence, the cost of production of a workman is restricted, almost entirely, to the means of subsistence that he requires for his maintenance, and for the propagation of his race. But the price of a commodity, and therefore also of labor, is equal to its cost of production. In proportion, therefore, as the repulsiveness of the work increases, the wage decreases. Nay more, in proportion as the use of machinery and division of labor increases, in the same proportion the burden of toil also increases, whether by prolongation of the working hours, by increase of the work exacted in a given time, or by increased speed of the machinery, etc.

Modern industry has converted the little workshop of the patriarchal master into the great factory of the industrial capitalist. Masses of laborers, crowded into the factory, are organized like soldiers. As privates of the industrial army they are placed under the command of a perfect hierarchy of officers and sergeants. Not only are they slaves of the bourgeois class, and of the bourgeois state; they are daily and hourly enslaved by the machine, by the over-looker, and, above all, by the individual bourgeois manufacturer himself. The more openly this despotism proclaims gain to be its end and aim, the more petty, the more hateful and the more embittering it is.

The less the skill and exertion of strength implied in manual labor, in other words, the more modern industry develops, the more is the labor of men superseded by that of women. Differences of age and sex have no longer any distinctive social validity for the working class. All are instruments of labor, more or less expensive to use, according to their age and sex.

No sooner has the laborer received his wages in cash, for the moment escaping exploitation by the manufacturer, than he is set upon by the other portions of the bourgeoisie, the landlord, the shopkeeper, the pawnbroker, etc.

The lower strata of the middle class—the small tradespeople, shopkeepers, and retired tradesmen generally, the handicraftsmen and peasants—all these sink gradually into the proletariat, partly because their diminutive capital does not suffice for the scale on which modern industry is carried on, and is swamped in the competition with the large capitalists, partly because their specialized skill is rendered worthless by new methods of production. Thus the proletariat is recruited from all classes of the population.

The proletariat goes through various stages of development. With its birth begins its struggle with the bourgeoisie. At first the contest is carried on by individual laborers, then by the work people of a factory, then by the operatives of one trade, in one locality, against the individual bourgeois who directly exploits them. They direct their attacks not against the bourgeois conditions of production, but against the instruments of production themselves; they destroy imported wares that compete with their labor, they smash machinery to pieces, they set factories ablaze, they seek to restore by force the vanished status of the workman of the Middle Ages.

At this stage the laborers still form an incoherent mass scattered over the whole country, and broken up by their mutual competition. If anywhere they unite to form more compact bodies, this is not yet the consequence of their own active union, but of the union of the bourgeoisie, which class, in order to attain its own political ends, is compelled to set the whole proletariat in motion, and is moreover still able to do so for a time. At this stage, therefore, the proletarians do not fight their enemies, but the enemies of their enemies, the remnants of absolute monarchy, the landowners, the non-industrial bourgeois, the petty bourgeoisie. Thus the whole historical movement is concentrated in the hands of the bourgeoisie; every victory so obtained is a victory for the bourgeoisie.

But with the development of industry the proletariat not only increases in number; it becomes concentrated in greater masses, its strength grows, and it feels that strength more. The various interests and conditions of life within the ranks of the proletariat are more and more equalized, in proportion as machinery obliterates all distinctions of labor and nearly everywhere reduces wages to the same low level. The growing competition among the bourgeois, and the resulting commercial crises, make the wages of the workers ever more fluctuating. The unceasing improvement of machinery, ever more rapidly developing, makes their livelihood more and more precarious; the collisions between individual workmen and individual bourgeois take more and more the character of collisions between two classes. Thereupon the workers begin to form combinations (trade unions) against the bourgeoisie; they club together in order to keep up the rate of wages; they found permanent associations in order to make provision beforehand for these occasional revolts. Here and there the contest breaks out into riots.

Now and then the workers are victorious, but only for a time. The real fruit of their battles lies, not in the immediate result, but in the ever expanding union of the workers. This union is furthered by the improved means of communication which are created by modern industry, and which place the workers of different localities in contact with one another. It was just this contact that was needed to centralize the numerous local struggles, all of the same character, into one national struggle between classes. But every class struggle is a political struggle. And that union, to attain which the burghers of

the Middle Ages, with their miserable highways, required centuries, the modern proletarians, thanks to railways, achieve in a few years.

This organization of the proletarians into a class, and consequently into a political party, is continually being upset again by the competition between the workers themselves. But it ever rises up again, stronger, firmer, mightier. It compels legislative recognition of particular interests of the workers, by taking advantage of the divisions among the bourgeoisie itself. Thus the ten-hour bill in England was carried.

Altogether, collisions between the classes of the old society further the course of development of the proletariat in many ways. The bourgeoisie finds itself involved in a constant battle. At first with the aristocracy; later on, with those portions of the bourgeoisie itself whose interests have become antagonistic to the progress of industry; at all times with the bourgeoisie of foreign countries. In all these battles it sees itself compelled to appeal to the proletariat, to ask for its help, and thus, to drag it into the political arena. The bourgeoisie itself, therefore, supplies the proletariat with its own elements of political and general education, in other words, it furnishes the proletariat with weapons for fighting the bourgeoisie.

Further, as we have already seen, entire sections of the ruling classes are, by the advance of industry, precipitated into the proletariat, or are at least threatened in their conditions of existence. These also supply the proletariat with fresh elements of enlightenment and progress.

Finally, in times when the class struggle nears the decisive hour, the process of dissolution going on within the ruling class, in fact within the whole range of old society, assumes such a violent, glaring character, that a small section of the ruling class cuts itself adrift, and joins the revolutionary class, the class that holds the future in its hands. Just as, therefore, at an earlier period, a section of the nobility went over to the bourgeoisie, so now a portion of the bourgeoisie goes over to the proletariat, and in particular, a portion of the bourgeois ideologists, who have raised themselves to the level of comprehending theoretically the historical movement as a whole.

Of all the classes that stand face to face with the bourgeoisie today, the proletariat alone is a really revolutionary class. The other classes decay and finally disappear in the face of modern industry; the proletariat is its special and essential product.

The lower middle class, the small manufacturer, the shopkeeper, the artisan, the peasant, all these fight against the bourgeoisie, to save from extinction their existence as fractions of the middle class. They are therefore not revolutionary, but conservative. Nay more, they are reactionary, for they try to roll back the wheel of history. If by chance they are revolutionary, they are so only in view of their impending transfer into the proletariat; they thus defend not their present, but their future interests; they desert their own standpoint to adopt that of the proletariat.

The "dangerous class," the social scum (*Lumpenproletariat),* that passively rotting mass thrown off by the lowest layers of old society, may, here and there, be swept into the movement by a proletarian revolution; its conditions of life, however, prepare it far more for the part of a bribed tool of reactionary intrigue.

The social conditions of the old society no longer exist for the proletariat. The proletarian is without property; his relation to his wife and children has no longer anything in common with bourgeois family relations; modern industrial labor, modern subjection to capital, the same in England as in France, in America as in Germany, has stripped him of every trace of national character. Law, morality, religion, are to him so many bourgeois prejudices, behind which lurk in ambush just as many bourgeois interests.

All the preceding classes that got the upper hand, sought to fortify their already acquired status by subjecting society at large to their conditions of appropriation. The proletarians cannot become masters of the productive forces of society, except by abolishing their own previous mode of appropriation, and thereby also every other previous mode of appropriation. They have nothing of their own to secure and to fortify; their mission is to destroy all previous securities for, and insurances of, individual property.

All previous historical movements were movements of minorities, or in the interest of minorities. The proletarian movement is in the self-conscious, independent movement of the immense majority, in the interest of the immense majority. The proletariat, the lowest stratum of our present society, cannot stir, cannot raise itself up, without the whole superincumbent strata of official society being sprung into the air.

Though not in substance, yet in form, the struggle of the proletariat with the bourgeoisie is at first a national struggle. The proletariat of each country must, of course, first of all settle matters with its own bourgeoisie.

In depicting the most general phases of the development of the proletariat, we traced the more or less veiled civil war, raging within existing society, up to the point where that war breaks out into open revolution, and where the violent overthrow of the bourgeoisie lays the foundation for the sway of the proletariat.

Hitherto, every form of society has been based, as we have already seen, on the antagonism of oppressing and oppressed classes. But in order to oppress a class, certain conditions must be assured to it under which it can, at least, continue its lavish existence. The serf, in the period of serfdom, raised himself to membership in the commune, just as the petty bourgeois, under the yoke of feudal absolutism, managed to develop into a bourgeois. The modern laborer, on the contrary, instead of rising with the progress of industry, sinks deeper and deeper below the conditions of existence of his own class. He becomes a pauper, and pauperism develops more rapidly than population and wealth. And here it becomes evident, that the bourgeoisie is unfit any longer to be the ruling class in society, and to impose its conditions of existence upon society as an overriding law. It is unfit to rule because it is incompetent to assure an existence to its slave within his slavery, because it cannot help letting him sink into such a state, that it has to feed him, instead of being fed by him. Society can no longer live under this bourgeoisie, in other words, its existence is no longer compatible with society.

The essential condition for the existence and sway of the bourgeois class, is the formation and augmentation of capital; the condition for capital is wage-labor. Wage-labor rests exclusively on competition between the laborers. The advance of industry, whose involuntary promoter is the bourgeoisie, replaces the isolation of the laborers, due to competition, by their revolutionary combination, due to association. The development of modern industry, therefore, cuts from under its feet the very foundation on which the bourgeoisie produces and appropriates products. What the bourgeoisie therefore produces, above all, are its own grave-diggers. Its fall and the victory of the proletariat are equally inevitable.

II Proletarians and Communists

In what relation do the Communists stand to the proletarians as a whole?

The Communists do not form a separate party opposed to other working-class parties.

They have no interests separate and apart from those of the proletariat as a whole.

They do not set up any sectarian principles of their own, by which to shape and mould the proletarian movement.

The Communists are distinguished from the other working-class parties by this only: 1. In the national struggles of the proletarians of the different countries, they point out and bring to the front the common interests of the entire proletariat, independently of all nationality. 2. In the various stages of development which the struggle of the working class against the bourgeoisie has to pass through, they always and

everywhere represent the interests of the movement as a whole.

The Communists, therefore, are on the one hand, practically, the most advanced and resolute section of the working-class parties of every country, that section which pushes forward all others; on the other hand, theoretically, they have over the great mass of the proletariat the advantage of clearly understanding the line of march, the conditions, and the ultimate general results of the proletarian movement.

The immediate aim of the Communists is the same as that of all the other proletarian parties: Formation of the proletariat into a class, overthrow of bourgeois supremacy, conquest of political power by the proletariat.

The theoretical conclusions of the Communists are in no way based on ideas or principles that have been invented, or discovered, by this or that would-be universal reformer.

They merely express, in general terms, actual relations springing from an existing class struggle, from a historical movement going on under our very eyes. The abolition of existing property relations is not at all a distinctive feature of Communism.

All property relations in the past have continually been subject to historical change consequent upon the change in historical conditions.

The French Revolution, for example, abolished feudal property in favor of bourgeois property.

The distinguishing feature of Communism is not the abolition of property generally, but the abolition of bourgeois property. But modern bourgeois private property is the final and most complete expression of the system of producing and appropriating products that is based on class antagonisms, on the exploitation of the many by the few.

In this sense, the theory of the Communists may be summed up in the single sentence: Abolition of private property.

We Communists have been reproached with the desire of abolishing the right of personally acquiring property as the fruit of a man's own labor, which property is alleged to be the groundwork of all personal freedom, activity, and independence.

Hard-won, self-acquired, self-earned property! Do you mean the property of the petty artisan and of the small peasant, a form of property that preceded the bourgeois form? There is no need to abolish that; the development of industry has to a great extent already destroyed it, and is still destroying it daily.

Or do you mean modern bourgeois private property?

But does wage-labor create any property for the laborer? Not a bit. It creates capital, i.e., that kind of property which exploits wage-labor, and which cannot increase except upon condition of begetting a new supply of wage-labor for fresh exploitation. Property, in its present form, is based on the antagonism of capital and wage-labor. Let us examine both sides of this antagonism.

To be a capitalist, is to have not only a purely personal, but a social *status* in production. Capital is a collective product, and only by the united action of many members, nay, in the last resort, only by the united action of all members of society, can it be set in motion.

Capital is therefore not a personal, it is a social power.

When, therefore, capital is converted into common property, into the property of all members of society, personal property is not thereby transformed into social property. It is only the social character of the property that is changed. It loses its class character.

Let us now take wage-labor.

The average price of wage-labor, is the minimum wage, i.e., that quantum of the means of subsistence which is absolutely requisite to keep the laborer in bare existence as a laborer. What, therefore, the wage-laborer appropriates by means of his labor, merely suffices to prolong and reproduce a bare existence. We by no means intend to abolish this personal appropriation of the products of labor, an appropriation that is made for the maintenance and reproduction of human life, and that leaves no surplus wherewith to command the labor of others. All that we want to do away with is the miserable character of this appropriation, under which the laborer lives merely to increase capital, and is allowed to live only insofar as the interest of the ruling class requires it.

In bourgeois society, living labor is but a means to increase accumulated labor. In Communist society, accumulated labor is but a means to widen, to enrich, to promote the existence of the laborer.

In bourgeois society, therefore, the past dominates the present; in Communist society, the present dominates the past. In bourgeois society capital is independent and has individuality, while the living person is dependent and has no individuality.

And the abolition of this state of things is called by the bourgeois, abolition of individuality and freedom! And rightly so. The abolition of bourgeois individuality, bourgeois independence, and bourgeois freedom is undoubtedly aimed at.

By freedom is meant, under the present bourgeois conditions of production, free trade, free selling and buying.

But if selling and buying disappears, free selling and buying disappears also. This talk about free selling and buying, and all the other "brave words" of our bourgeoisie about freedom in general, have a meaning, if any, only in contrast with restricted selling and buying, with the fettered traders of the Middle Ages, but have no meaning when opposed to the Communist abolition of buying and selling, of the bourgeois conditions of production, and of the bourgeoisie itself.

You are horrified at our intending to do away with private property. But in your existing society, private property is already done away with for nine-tenths of the population; its existence for the few is solely due to its nonexistence in the hands of those nine-tenths. You reproach us, therefore, with intending to do away with a form of property, the necessary condition for whose existence is the non-existence of any property for the immense majority of society.

In a word, you reproach us with intending to do away with your property. Precisely so; that is just what we intend.

From the moment when labor can no longer be converted into capital, money, or rent, into a social power capable of being monopolized, i.e., from the moment when individual property can no longer be transformed into bourgeois property, into capital, from that moment, you say, individuality vanishes.

You must, therefore, confess that by "individual" you mean no other person than the bourgeois, than the middle-class owner of property. This person must, indeed, be swept out of the way, and made impossible.

Communism deprives no man of the power to appropriate the products of society; all that it does is to deprive him of the power to subjugate the labor of others by means of such appropriation.

It has been objected, that upon the abolition of private property all work will cease, and universal laziness will overtake us.

According to this, bourgeois society ought long ago to have gone to the dogs through sheer idleness; for those of its members who work, acquire nothing, and those who acquire anything, do not work. The whole of this objection is but another expression of the tautology: There can no longer be any wage-labor when there is no longer any capital.

All objections urged against the Communist mode of producing and appropriating material products, have, in the same way, been urged against the Communist modes of producing and appropriating intellectual products. Just as, to the bourgeois, the disappearance of class property is the disappearance of production itself, so the disappearance of class culture is to him identical with the disappearance of all culture.

That culture, the loss of which he laments, is, for the enormous majority, a mere training to act as a machine.

But don't wrangle with us so long as you apply, to our intended abolition of bourgeois property, the standard of your bourgeois notions of freedom, culture, law, etc. Your very ideas are but the outgrowth of the conditions of your bourgeois production and bourgeois property, just as your jurisprudence is but the will of your class made into a law for all, a will whose essential character and direction are determined by the economic conditions of existence of your class.

The selfish misconception that induces you to transform into eternal laws of nature and of reason, the social forms springing from your present mode of production and form of property—historical relations that rise and disappear in the progress of production—this misconception you share with every ruling class that has preceded you. What you see clearly in the case of ancient property, what you admit in the case of feudal property, you are of course forbidden to admit in the case of your own bourgeois form of property. . . .

The Communists are further reproached with desiring to abolish countries and nationality.

The workingmen have no country. We cannot take from them what they have not got. Since the proletariat must first of all acquire political supremacy, must rise to be the leading class of the nation, must constitute itself *the* nation, it is, so far, itself national, though not in the bourgeois sense of the word.

National differences and antagonisms between peoples are vanishing gradually from day to day, owing to the development of the bourgeoisie, to freedom of commerce, to the world market, to uniformity in the mode of production and in the conditions of life corresponding thereto.

The supremacy of the proletariat will cause them to vanish still faster. United action, of the leading civilized countries at least, is one of the first conditions for the emancipation of the proletariat.

In proportion as the exploitation of one individual by another is put an end to, the exploitation of one nation by another will also be put an end to. In proportion as the antagonism between classes within the nation vanishes, the hostility of one nation to another will come to an end.

The charges against Communism made from a religious, a philosophical, and, generally, from an ideological standpoint, are not deserving of serious examination.

Does it require deep intuition to comprehend that man's ideas, views, and conceptions, in one word, man's consciousness, changes with every change in the conditions of his material existence, in his social relations and in his social life?

What else does the history of ideas prove, than that intellectual production changes its character in proportion as material production is changed? The ruling ideas of each age have ever been the ideas of its ruling class.

When people speak of ideas that revolutionize society, they do but express the fact that within the old society the elements of a new one have been created, and that the dissolution of the old ideas keeps even pace with the dissolution of the old conditions of existence.

When the ancient world was in its last throes, the ancient religions were overcome by Christianity. When Christian ideas succumbed in the 18th century to rationalist ideas, feudal society fought its death-battle with the then revolutionary bourgeoisie. The ideas of religious liberty and freedom of conscience, merely gave expression to the sway of free competition within the domain of knowledge.

"Undoubtedly," it will be said, "religion, moral, philosophical, and juridical ideas have been modified in the course of historical development. But religion, morality, philosophy, political science, and law, constantly survived this change.

"There are, besides, eternal truths, such as Freedom, Justice, etc., that are common to all states of society. But Communism abolishes eternal truths, it abolishes all religion, and all morality, instead of constituting them on a new basis; it therefore acts in contradiction to all past historical experience."

What does this accusation reduce itself to? The history of all past society has consisted in the development of class antagonisms, antagonisms that assumed different forms at different epochs.

But whatever form they may have taken, one fact is common to all past ages, viz., the exploitation of one part of society by the other. No wonder, then, that the social consciousness of past ages, despite all the multiplicity and variety it displays, moves within certain common forms, or general ideas, which cannot completely vanish except with the total disappearance of class antagonisms.

The Communist revolution is the most radical rupture with traditional property relations; no wonder that its development involves the most radical rupture with traditional ideas.

But let us have done with the bourgeois objections to Communism.

We have seen above, that the first step in the revolution by the working class, is to raise the proletariat to the position of ruling class, to establish democracy.

The proletariat will use its political supremacy to wrest, by degrees, all capital from the bourgeoisie, to centralize all instruments of production in the hands of the state, i.e., of the proletariat organized as the ruling class; and to increase the total of productive forces as rapidly as possible.

Of course, in the beginning, this cannot be effected except by means of despotic inroads on the rights of property, and on the conditions of bourgeois production; by means of measures, therefore, which appear economically insufficient and untenable, but which, in the course of the movement, outstrip themselves, necessitate further inroads upon the old social order, and are unavoidable as a means of entirely revolutionizing the mode of production.

These measures will of course be different in different countries.

Nevertheless in the most advanced countries, the following will be pretty generally applicable.

1. Abolition of property in land and application of all rents of land to public purposes.

2. A heavy progressive or graduated income tax.

3. Abolition of all right of inheritance.

4. Confiscation of the property of all emigrants and rebels.

5. Centralization of credit in the hands of the state, by means of a national bank with state capital and an exclusive monopoly.

6. Centralization of the means of communication and transport in the hands of the state.

7. Extension of factories and instruments of production owned by the state; the bringing into cultivation of waste lands, and the improvement of the soil generally in accordance with a common plan.

8. Equal obligation of all to work. Establishment of industrial armies, especially for agriculture.

9. Combination of agriculture with manufacturing industries; gradual abolition of the distinction between town and country, by a more equable distribution of the population over the country.

10. Free education for all children in public schools. Abolition of child factory labor in its present form. Combination of education with industrial production, etc.

When, in the course of development, class distinctions have disappeared, and all production has been concentrated in the hands of a vast association of the whole nation, the public power will lose its political character. Political power, properly so called, is merely the organized power of one class for oppressing another. If the proletariat during its contest with the bourgeoisie is compelled, by the force of circumstances, to organize itself as a class; if, by means of a revolution, it makes itself the ruling class, and, as such sweeps away by force the old conditions of production, then it will, along with these conditions, have swept away the conditions for the existence of class antagonisms, and of classes generally, and will thereby have abolished its own supremacy as a class.

In place of the old bourgeois society, with its classes and class antagonisms, we shall have an association, in which the free development of each is the condition for the free development of all.

KARL MARX: ECONOMIC AND PHILOSOPHIC MANUSCRIPTS OF 1844

Estranged Labour

We have proceeded from the premises of political economy. We have accepted its language

From Karl Marx, *Economic and Philosophic Manuscripts of 1844* (New York: International Publishers). Copyright 1964. Reprinted with permission.

and its laws. We presupposed private property, the separation of labour, capital and land, and of wages, profit of capital and rent of land—likewise division of labour, competition, the concept of exchange-value, etc. On the basis of political economy itself, in its own words, we have shown that the worker sinks to the level of a commodity and becomes indeed the most wretched of commodities; that the wretchedness of the worker is in inverse proportion to the power and magnitude of his production; that the necessary result of competition is the accumulation of capital in a few hands, and thus the restoration of monopoly in a more terrible form; that finally the distinction between capitalist and land-rentier, like that between the tiller of the soil and the factory-worker, disappears and that the whole of society must fall apart into the two classes—the property-*owners* and the propertyless *workers*.

Political economy proceeds from the fact of private property, but it does not explain it to us. It expresses in general, abstract formulae the *material* process through which private property actually passes, and these formulae it then takes for *laws*. It does not *comprehend* these laws—i.e., it does not demonstrate how they arise from the very nature of private property. Political economy does not disclose the source of the division between labour and capital, and between capital and land. When, for example, it defines the relationship of wages to profit, it takes the interest of the capitalists to be the ultimate cause; i.e., it takes for granted what it is supposed to evolve. Similarly, competition comes in everywhere. It is explained from external circumstances. As to how far these external and apparently fortuitous circumstances are but the expression of a necessary course of development, political economy teaches us nothing. We have seen how, to it, exchange itself appears to be a fortuitous fact. The only wheels which political economy sets in motion are *avarice* and the *war amongst the avaricious—competition.*

Precisely because political economy does not grasp the connections within the movement, it was possible to counterpose, for instance, the doctrine of competition to the doctrine of monopoly, the doctrine of craft-liberty to the doctrine of the corporation, the doctrine of the division of landed property to the doctrine of the big estate—for competition, craft-liberty and the division of landed property were

explained and comprehended only as fortuitous, premediated and violent consequences of monopoly, the corporation, and feudal property, not as their necessary, inevitable and natural consequences.

Now, therefore, we have to grasp the essential connection between private property, avarice, and the separation of labour, capital and landed property; between exchange and competition, value and the devaluation of men, monopoly and competition, etc.; the connection between this whole estrangement and the *money*-system.

Do not let us go back to a fictitious primordial condition as the political economist does, when he tries to explain. Such a primordial condition explains nothing. He merely pushes the question away into a grey nebulous distance. He assumes in the form of fact, of an event, what he is supposed to deduce—namely, the necessary relationship between two things—between, for example, division of labour and exchange. Theology in the same way explains the origin of evil by the fall of man: that is, it assumes as a fact, in historical form, what has to be explained.

We proceed from an *actual* economic fact.

The worker becomes all the poorer the more wealth he produces, the more his production increases in power and range. The worker becomes an ever cheaper commodity the more commodities he creates. With the *increasing value* of the world of things proceeds in direct proportion the *devaluation* of the world of men. Labour produces not only commodities: it produces itself and the worker as a *commodity*—and does so in the proportion in which it produces commodities generally.

This fact expresses merely that the object which labour produces—labour's product—confronts it as *something alien*, as a *power independent* of the producer. The product of labour is labour which has been congealed in an object, which has become material: it is the *objectification* of labour. Labour's realization is its objectification.

In the conditions dealt with by political economy this realization of labour appears as *loss of reality* for the workers: objectification as *loss of the object* and *object-bondage:* appropriation as *estrangement,* as *alienation.*

So much does labour's realization appear as loss of reality that the worker loses reality to the point of starving to death. So much does objectification appear as loss of the object that the worker is robbed of the objects most necessary not only for his life but for his work. Indeed, labour itself becomes an object which he can get hold of only with the greatest effort and with the most irregular interruptions. So much does the appropriation of the object appear as estrangement that the more objects the worker produces the fewer can he possess and the more he falls under the dominion of his product, capital.

All these consequences are contained in the definition that the worker is related to the *product of his labour* as to an *alien* object. For on this premise it is clear that the more the worker spends himself, the more powerful the alien objective world becomes which he creates over-against himself, the poorer he himself—his inner world—becomes, the less belongs to him as his own. It is the same in religion. The more man puts into God, the less he retains in himself. The worker puts his life into the object; but now his life no longer belongs to him but to the object. Hence, the greater this activity, the greater is the worker's lack of objects. Whatever the product of his labour is, he is not. Therefore the greater this product, the less is he himself. The *alienation* of the worker in his product means not only that his labour becomes an object, an *external* existence, but that it exists *outside* him, independently, as something alien to him, and that it becomes a power on its own confronting him; it means that the life which he has conferred on the object confronts him as something hostile and alien.

Let us now look more closely at the *objectification,* at the production of the worker; and therein at the *estrangement,* the *loss* of the object, his product.

The worker can create nothing without *nature,* without the *sensuous external world.* It is the material on which his labour is manifested, in which it is active, from which and by means of which it produces.

But just as nature provides labour with the *means of life* in the sense that labour cannot *live* without objects on which to operate, on the other hand, it also provides the *means of life* in the more restricted sense—i.e., the means for the physical subsistence of the *worker* himself.

Thus the more the worker by his labour *appropriates* the external world, sensuous nature, the more he deprives himself of *means of life* in the double respect: first, that the sensuous external world more and more ceases to be an object belonging to his labour—to be his labour's *means of life:* and secondly, that it more and more ceases to be *means of life* in the immediate sense, means for the physical subsistence of the worker.

Thus in this double respect the worker becomes a slave of his object, first, in that he receives an *object of labour,* i.e., in that he receives *work;* and secondly, in that he receives *means of subsistence.* Therefore, it enables him to exist, first, as a *worker;* and, second, as a *physical subject.* The extremity of this bondage is that it is only as a *worker* that he continues to maintain himself as a *physical subject,* and that it is only as a *physical subject* that he is a *worker.*

(The laws of political economy express the estrangement of the worker in his object thus: the more the worker produces, the less he has to consume; the more values he creates, the more valueless, the more unworthy he becomes; the better formed his product, the more deformed becomes the worker; the more civilized his object, the more barbarous becomes the worker; the mightier labour becomes, the more powerless becomes the worker; the more ingenious labour becomes, the duller becomes the worker and the more he becomes nature's bondsman.)

Political economy conceals the estrangement inherent in the nature of labour by not considering the direct relationship between the worker (labour) *and production.* It is true that labour produces for the rich wonderful things—but for the worker it produces privation. It produces palaces—but for the worker, hovels. It produces beauty—but for the worker, deformity. It replaces labour by machines—but some of the workers it throws back to a barbarous type of labour, and the other workers it turns into machines. It produces intelligence—but for the worker idiocy, cretinism.

The direct relationship of labour to its produce is the relationship of the worker to the objects of his production. The relationship of the man of means to the objects of production and to production itself is only a *consequence* of this first relationship— and confirms it. We shall consider this other aspect later.

When we ask, then, what is the essential relationship of labour we are asking about the relationship of the *worker* to production.

Till now we have been considering the estrangement, the alienation of the worker only in one of its aspects, i.e., the worker's *relationship to the products of his labour.* But the estrangement is manifested not only in the result but in the *act of production*—within the *producing activity* itself. How would the worker come to face the product of his activity as a stranger, were it not that in the very act of production he was estranging himself from himself? The product is after all but the summary of the activity, of production. If then the product of labour is alienation, production itself must be active alienation, the alienation of activity, the activity of alienation. In the estrangement of the object of labour is merely summarized the estrangement, the alienation, in the activity of labour itself.

What, then, constitutes the alienation of labour?

First, the fact that labour is *external* to the worker, i.e., it does not belong to his essential being; that in his work, therefore, he does not affirm himself but denies himself, does not feel content but unhappy, does not develop freely his physical and mental energy but mortifies his body and ruins his mind. The worker therefore only feels himself outside his work, and in his work feels outside himself. He is at home when he is not working, and when he is not working he is not at home. His labour is therefore not voluntary, but coerced; it is *forced labour.* It is therefore not the satisfaction of a need; it is merely a *means* to satisfy needs external to it. Its alien character emerges clearly in the fact that as soon as no physical or other compulsion exists, labour is shunned like the plague. External labour, labour in which man alienates himself, is a labour of self-sacrifice, of mortification. Lastly, the external character of labour for the worker appears in the fact that it is not his own, but someone else's, that it does not belong to him, that in it he belongs, not to himself, but to another. Just as in religion the spontaneous activity of the human imagination, of the human brain and the human heart, operates independently of the individual—that is, operates on him as an alien, divine or diabolical activity—in the same way the worker's activity is not his spontaneous activity. It belongs to another; it is the loss of his self.

As a result, therefore, man (the worker) no longer feels himself to be freely active in any but his animal functions—eating, drinking, procreating, or at most in his dwelling and in dressing-up, etc.; and in his human functions he no longer feels himself to be anything but an animal. What is animal becomes human and what is human becomes animal.

Certainly eating, drinking, procreating, etc., are also genuinely human functions. But in the abstraction which separates them from the sphere of all other human activities and turns them into sole and ultimate ends, they are animal. . . .

Man is a species being, not only because in practice and in theory he adopts the species as his object (his own as well as those of other things), but—and this is only another way of expressing it—but also because he treats himself as the actual, living species; because he treats himself as a *universal* and therefore a free being.

The life of the species, both in man and in animals, consists physically in the fact that man (like the animal) lives on inorganic nature; and the more universal man is compared with an animal, the more universal is the sphere of inorganic nature on which he lives. Just as plants, animals, stones, the air, light, etc., constitute a part of human consciousness in the realm of theory, partly as objects of natural science, partly as objects of art—his spiritual inorganic nature, spiritual nourishment which he must first prepare to make it palatable and digestable—so too in the realm of practice they constitute a part of human life and human activity. Physically man lives only on these products of nature, whether they appear in the form of food, heating, clothes, a dwelling, or whatever it may be. The universality of man is in practice manifested precisely in the universality which makes all nature his *inorganic* body—both inasmuch as nature is (1) his direct means of life, and (2) the material, the object, and the instrument of his life-activity. Nature is man's *inorganic body*— nature, that is, in so far as it is not itself the human body. Man *lives* on nature—means that nature is his *body*, with which he must remain in continuous intercourse if he is not to die. That man's physical and spiritual life is linked to nature means simply that nature is linked to itself, for man is a part of nature.

In estranging from man (1) nature, and (2) himself, his own active functions, his life-activity, estranged labour estranges the *species* from man. It turns for him the *life of the species* into a means of individual life. First it estranges the life of the species and individual life, and secondly it makes individual life in its abstract form the purpose of the life of the species, likewise in its abstract and estranged form.

For in the first place labour, *life-activity, productive life* itself, appears to man merely as a *means* of satisfying a need—the need to maintain the physical existence. Yet the productive life is the life of the species. It is life-engendering life. The whole character of a species—its species character—is contained in the character of its life-activity; and free, conscious activity is man's species character. Life itself appears only as a *means to life*.

The animal is immediately identical with its life-activity. It does not distinguish itself from it. It is *its life-activity*. Man makes his life-activity itself the object of his will and of his consciousness. He has conscious life-activity. It is not a determination with which he directly merges. Conscious life-activity directly distinguishes man from animal life-activity. It is just because of this that he is a species being. Or it is only because he is a species being that he is a Conscious Being, i.e., that his own life is an object for him. Only because of that is his activity free activity. Estranged labour reverses this relationship, so that it is just because man is a conscious being that he makes his life-activity, his *essential* being, a mere means to his *existence*.

In creating an *objective world* by his practical activity, in *working-up* inorganic nature, man proves himself a conscious species being, i.e., as a being that treats the species as its own essential being, or that treats itself as a species being. Admittedly animals also produce. They build themselves nests, dwellings, like the bees, beavers, ants, etc. But an animal only produces what it immediately needs for itself or its young. It produces one-sidedly, whilst man produces universally. It produces only under the dominion of immediate physical need, whilst man produces even when he is free from physical need and only truly produces in freedom therefrom. An animal produces only itself, whilst man reproduces the whole of nature. An animal's product belongs immediately to its physical body, whilst man freely confronts his product. An animal forms things in accordance with the standard and the need of the species to which it belongs, whilst man knows how to produce in accordance with the standard of every species, and knows how to apply everywhere the inherent standard to the object. Man therefore also forms things in accordance with the laws of beauty.

It is just in the working-up of the objective world, therefore, that man first really proves himself to be a *species-being.* This production is his active species life. Through and because of this production, nature appears as *his* work and his reality. The object of labour is, therefore, the *objectification of man's species life:* for he duplicates himself not only, as in consciousness, intellectually, but also actively, in reality, and therefore he contemplates himself in a world that he has created. In tearing away from man the object of his production, therefore, estranged labour tears from him his *species life,* his real species objectivity, and transforms his advantage over animals into the disadvantage that his inorganic body, nature, is taken from him.

Similarly, in degrading spontaneous activity, free activity, to a means, estranged labour makes man's species life a means to his physical existence.

The consciousness which man has of his species is thus transformed by estrangement in such a way that the species life becomes for him a means.

Estranged labour turns thus (3) *Man's species-being,* both nature and his spiritual species property, into a being *alien* to him, into a *means* to his *individual existence.* It estranges man's own body from him, as it does external nature and his spiritual essence, his *human* being. (4) An immediate consequence of the fact that man is estranged from the product of his labour, from his life-activity, from his species being is the *estrangement of man* from *man.* If a man is confronted by himself, he is confronted by the *other* man. What applies to a man's relation to his work, to the product of his labour and to himself, also holds of a man's relation to the other man, and to the other man's labour and object of labour.

In fact, the proposition that man's species nature is estranged from him means that one man is estranged from the other, as each of them is from man's essential nature.

The estrangement of man, and in fact every relationship in which man stands to himself, is first realized and expressed in the relationship in which a man stands to other men.

Hence within the relationship of estranged labour each man views the other in accordance with the standard and the position in which he finds himself as a worker.

We took our departure from a fact of political economy—the estrangement of the worker and his production. We have formulated the concept of this fact—*estranged, alienated* labour. We have analysed this concept—hence analysing merely a fact of political economy.

Let us now see, further, how in real life the concept of estranged, alienated labour must express and present itself.

If the product of labour is alien to me, if it confronts me as an alien power, to whom, then, does it belong?

If my own activity does not belong to me, if it is an alien, a coerced activity, to whom, then, does it belong?

To a being *other* than me.

Who is this being? . . .

The *alien* being, to whom labour and the produce of labour belongs, in whose service labour is done and for whose benefit the produce of labour is provided, can only be *man* himself.

If the product of labour does not belong to the worker, if it confronts him as an alien power, this can only be because it belongs to some *other man than the worker.* If the worker's activity is a torment to him, to another it must be *delight* and his life's joy. Not the gods, not nature, but only man himself can be this alien power over man.

We must bear in mind the above-stated proposition that man's relation to himself only becomes *objective* and *real* for him through his relation to the other man. Thus, if the product of his labour, his labour *objectified,* is for him an *alien,* hostile, powerful object independent of him, then his position towards it is such that someone else is master of this object, someone who is alien, hostile, powerful, and independent of him. If his own activity is to him an unfree activity, then he is treating it as activity performed in the service, under the dominion, the coercion and the yoke of another man.

Every self-estrangement of man from himself and from nature appears in the relation in which he places himself and nature to men other than and differentiated from himself. For this reason religious self-estrangement necessarily appears in the relationship of the layman to the priest, or again to a mediator, etc., since we are here dealing with the intellectual world. In the real practical world self-estrangement can only become manifest through the real practical relationship to other men. The medium through which estrangement takes place is itself *practical*. Thus through estranged labour man not only engenders his relationship to the object and to the act of production as to powers that are alien and hostile to him; he also engenders the relationship in which other men stand to his production and to his product, and the relationship in which he stands to these other men. Just as he begets his own production as the loss of his reality, as his punishment; just as he begets his own product as a loss, as a product not belonging to him; so he begets the dominion of the one who does not produce over production and over the product. Just as he estranges from himself his own activity, so he confers to the stranger activity which is not his own.

Till now we have only considered this relationship from the standpoint of the worker and later we shall be considering it also from the standpoint of the non-worker.

Through *estranged, alienated labour,* then, the worker produces the relationship to this labour of a man alien to labour and standing outside it. The relationship of the worker to labour engenders the relation to it of the capitalist, or whatever one chooses to call the master of labour. *Private property* is thus the product, the result, the necessary consequence, of *alienated labour,* of the external relation of the worker to nature and to himself.

Private property thus results by analysis from the concept of *alienated labour*—i.e., of *alienated man,* of estranged labour, of estranged life, of *estranged* man.

True, it is as a result of the *movement of private property* that we have obtained the concept of *alienated labour* (of *alienated life*) from political economy. But on analysis of this concept it becomes clear that though private property appears to be the source, the cause of alienated labour, it is really its consequence, just as the gods *in the beginning* are not the cause but the effect of man's intellectual confusion. Later this relationship becomes reciprocal.

Only at the very culmination of the development of private property does this, its secret, reemerge, namely, that on the one hand it is the *product* of alienated labour, and that secondly it is the *means* by which labour alienates itself, the *realization of this alienation.*

KARL MARX AND FREDERICK ENGELS: THE GERMAN IDEOLOGY

The production of life, both of one's own in labour and of fresh life in procreation, now appears as a double relationship: on the one hand as a natural, on the other as a social relationship.

From Karl Marx and Frederick Engels, *The German Ideology* (New York: International Publishers). Copyright 1974. Reprinted with permission.

By social we understand the co-operation of several individuals, no matter under what conditions, in what manner and to what end. It follows from this that a certain mode of production, or industrial stage, is always combined with a certain mode of co-operation, or social stage, and this mode of co-operation is itself a "productive force." Further, that the multitude of productive forces accessible to men determines the nature of society, hence, that the "history of humanity" must always be studied and treated in relation to the history of industry and exchange. . . .

Consciousness is. . . . therefore, from the very beginning a social product, and remains so as long as men exist at all. Consciousness is at first, of course, merely consciousness concerning the *immediate* sensuous environment and consciousness of the limited connection with other persons and things outside the individual who is growing self-conscious. At the same time it is consciousness of nature, which first appears to men as a completely alien, all-powerful and unassailable force, with which men's relations are purely animal and by which they are over-awed like beasts; it is thus a purely animal consciousness of nature (natural religion) just because nature is as yet hardly modified historically. . . . On the other hand, man's consciousness of the necessity of associating with the individuals around him is the beginning of the consciousness that he is living in society at all. This beginning is as animal as social life itself at this stage. It is mere herd-consciousness, and at this point man is only distinguished from sheep by the fact that with him consciousness takes the place of instinct or that his instinct is a conscious one. This sheep-like or tribal consciousness receives its further development and extension through increased productivity, the increase of needs, and, what is fundamental to both of these, the increase of population. With these there develops the division of labour, which was originally nothing but the division of labour in the sexual act, then that division of labour which develops spontaneously or "naturally" by virtue of natural predisposition (e.g., physical strength), needs, accidents, etc., etc. Division of labour only becomes truly such from the moment when a division of material and mental labour appears. (The first form of ideologists, *priests*, is concurrent.) From this moment onwards consciousness *can* really flatter itself that it is something other than consciousness of existing practice, that it *really* represents something without representing something real; from now on consciousness is in a position to emancipate itself from the world and to proceed to the formation of "pure" theory, theology, philosophy, ethics, etc. But even if this theory, theology, philosophy, ethics, etc. comes into contradiction with the existing relations, this can only occur because existing social relations have come into contradiction with existing forces of production; this, moreover, can also occur in a particular national sphere of relations through the appearance of the contradiction, not within the national orbit, but between this national consciousness and the practice of other nations, i.e. between the national and the general consciousness of a nation (as we see it now in Germany).

Moreover, it is quite immaterial what consciousness starts to do on its own: out of all such muck we get only the one inference that these three moments, the forces of production, the state of society, and consciousness, can and must come into contradiction with one another, because the *division of labour* implies the possibility, nay the fact that intellectual and material activity—enjoyment and labour, production and consumption—devolve on different individuals, and that the only possibility of their not coming into contradiction lies in the negation in its turn of the division of labour. It is self-evident, moreover, that "spectres," "bonds," "the higher being," "concept," "scruple," are merely the idealistic, spiritual expression, the conception apparently of the isolated individual, the image of very empirical fetters and limitations, within which the mode of production of life and the form of intercourse coupled with it move.

Private Property and Communism

With the division of labour, in which all these contradictions are implicit, and which in its turn is based on the natural division of labour in the family and the separation of society into individual families opposed to one another, is given simultaneously the *distribution,* and indeed the *unequal* distribution, both quantitative and qualitative, of labour and its products, hence property: the nucleus, the first form, of which lies in the family, where wife and children are the slaves of the husband. This latent slavery in the family, though still very crude, is the first property, but even at this early stage it corresponds perfectly to the definition of modern economists who call it the power of disposing of the labour-power of others. Division of labour and private property are, moreover, identical expressions: in the one the same thing is affirmed with reference to activity as is affirmed in the other with reference to the product of the activity.

Further, the division of labour implies the contradiction between the interest of the separate individual or the individual family and the communal interest of all individuals who have intercourse with one another. And indeed, this communal interest does not exist merely in the imagination, as the "general interest," but first of all in reality, as the mutual interdependence of the individuals among whom the labour is divided. And finally, the division of labour offers us the first example of how, as long as man remains in natural society, that is, as long as a cleavage exists between the particular and the common interest, as long, therefore, as activity is not voluntarily, but naturally, divided, man's own deed becomes an alien power opposed to him, which enslaves him instead of being controlled by him. For as soon as the distribution of labour comes into being, each man has a particular, exclusive sphere of activity, which is forced upon him and from which he cannot escape. He is a hunter, a fisherman, a shepherd, or a critical critic, and must remain so if he does not want to lose his means of livelihood; while in communist society, where nobody has one exclusive sphere of activity but each can become accomplished in any branch he

wishes, society regulates the general production and thus makes it possible for me to do one thing today and another tomorrow, to hunt in the morning, fish in the afternoon, rear cattle in the evening, criticise after dinner, just as I have a mind, without ever becoming hunter, fisherman, shepherd or critic. This fixation of social activity, this consolidation of what we ourselves produce into an objective power above us, growing out of our control, thwarting our expectations, bringing to naught our calculations, is one of the chief factors in historical development up till now. . . .

Ruling Class and Ruling Ideas

The ideas of the ruling class are in every epoch the ruling ideas, i.e. the class which is the ruling *material* force of society, is at the same time its ruling *intellectual* force. The class which has the means of material production at its disposal, has control at the same time over the means of mental production, so that thereby, generally speaking, the ideas of those who lack the means of mental production are subject to it. The ruling ideas are nothing more than the ideal expression of the dominant material relationships, the dominant material relationships grasped as ideas; hence of the relationships which make the one class the ruling one, therefore, the ideas of its dominance. The individuals composing the ruling class possess among other things consciousness, and therefore think. Insofar, therefore, as they rule as a class and determine the extent and compass of an epoch, it is self-evident that they do this in its whole range, hence among other things rule also as thinkers, as producers of ideas, and regulate the production and distribution of the ideas of their age: thus their ideas are the ruling ideas of the epoch. . . .

The division of labour, which we already saw above as one of the chief forces of history up till now, manifests itself also in the ruling class as the division of mental and material labour, so that inside this class one part appears as the thinkers of the class (its active, conceptive ideologists, who make the perfecting of the illusion of the class about itself their chief source of livelihood), while the others' attitude to these ideas and illusions is more passive and receptive, because they are in reality the active members of this class and have less time to make up illusions and ideas about themselves. Within this class this cleavage can even develop into a certain opposition and hostility between the two parts, which, however, in the case of a practical collision, in which the class itself is endangered, automatically comes to nothing, in which case there also vanishes the semblance that the ruling ideas were not the ideas of the ruling class and had a power distinct from the power of this class. The existence of revolutionary ideas in a particular period presupposes the existence of a revolutionary class; about the premises for the latter sufficient has already been said above.

If now in considering the course of history we detach the ideas of the ruling class from the ruling class itself and attribute to them an independent existence, if we confine ourselves to saying that these or those ideas were dominant at a given time, without bothering ourselves about the conditions of production and the producers of these ideas, if we thus ignore the individuals and world conditions which are the source of the ideas, we can say, for instance, that during the time that the aristocracy was dominant, the concepts honour, loyalty, etc. were dominant, during the dominance of the bourgeoisie the concepts freedom, equality, etc. The ruling class itself on the whole imagines this to be so. This conception of history, which is common to all historians, particularly since the eighteenth century, will necessarily come up against the phenomenon that increasingly abstract ideas hold sway, i.e., ideas which increasingly take on the form of universality. For each new class which puts itself in the place of one ruling before it, is compelled, merely in order to carry through its aim, to represent its interest as the common interest of all the members of society, that is, expressed in ideal form: it has to give its ideas the form of universality, and represent them as the only rational, universally valid ones. The class making a revolution appears from the very start, if only because it is opposed to a *class*, not as a class but as the representative of the whole of society; it appears as the whole mass of society confronting the one ruling class. It can do this because, to start with, its interest really is more connected with the common interest of all other non-ruling classes, because under the pressure of hitherto existing conditions its interest has not yet been able to develop as the particular interest of a particular class. Its victory, therefore, benefits also many individuals of the other classes which are not winning a dominant position, but only insofar as it now puts these individuals in a position to raise themselves into the ruling class. When the French bourgeoisie overthrew the power of the aristocracy, it thereby made it possible for many proletarians to raise themselves above the proletariat, but only insofar as they become bourgeois. Every new class, therefore, achieves its hegemony only on a broader basis than that of the class ruling previously, whereas the opposition of the non-ruling class against the new ruling class later develops all the more sharply and profoundly. Both these things determine the fact that the struggle to be waged against this new ruling class, in its turn, aims at a more decided and radical negation of the previous conditions of society than could all previous classes which sought to rule.

This whole semblance, that the rule of a certain class is only the rule of certain ideas, comes to a natural end, of course, as soon as class rule in general ceases to be the form in which society is organised, that is to say, as soon as it is no longer necessary to represent a particular interest as general or the "general interest" as ruling.

Once the ruling ideas have been separated from the ruling individuals and, above all, from the relationships which result from a given stage of the mode of production, and in this way the conclusion has been reached that history is always under the sway of ideas, it is very easy to abstract from these various ideas *"the* idea," the notion, etc., as the dominant force in history, and thus to understand all these separate ideas and concepts as "forms of self-determination" on the part of *the* concept developing in history. It follows then naturally, too, that all the relationships of men can be derived from the concept of man, man as conceived, the essence of man, *Man.* This has been done by the speculative philosophers. . . .

No. 1. One must separate the ideas of those ruling for empirical reasons, under empirical conditions and as empirical individuals, from these actual rulers, and thus recognise the rule of ideas or illusions in history.

No. 2. One must bring an order into this rule of ideas, prove a mystical connection among the successive ruling ideas, which is managed by understanding them as "acts of self-determination on the part of the concept" (this is possible because by virtue of their empirical basis these ideas are really connected with one another and because, conceived as *mere* ideas, they become self-distinctions, distinctions made by thought).

No. 3. To remove the mystical appearance of this "self-determining concept" it is changed into a person—"Self-Consciousness"—or, to appear thoroughly materialistic, into a series of persons, who represent the "concept" in history, into the "thinkers," the "philosophers," the ideologists, who again are understood as the manufacturers of history, as the "council of guardians," as the rulers. Thus the whole body of materialistic elements has been removed from history and now full rein can be given to the speculative steed.

Whilst in ordinary life every shopkeeper is very well able to distinguish between what somebody professes to be and what he really is, our historians have not yet won even this trivial insight. They take every epoch at its word and believe that everything it says and imagines about itself is true.

KARL MARX: THE FETISHISM OF COMMODITIES AND THE SECRET THEREOF

A commodity appears, at first sight, a very trivial thing, and easily understood. Its analysis shows that it is, in reality, a very queer thing, abounding in metaphysical subtleties and theological niceties. So far as it is a value in use, there is nothing mysterious about it, whether we consider it from the point of view that by its properties it is capable of satisfying human wants, or from the point that those properties are the product of

human labour. It is as clear as noon-day, that man, by his industry, changes the forms of the materials furnished by Nature, in such a way as to make them useful to him. The form of wood, for instance, is altered, by making a table out of it. Yet, for all that, the table continues to be that common, every-day thing, wood. But, so soon as it steps forth as a commodity, it is changed into something transcendent. It not only stands with its feet on the ground, but, in relation to all other commodities, it stands on its head, and evolves out of its wooden brain grotesque ideas, far more wonderful than "table-turning" ever was.

The mystical character of commodities does not originate, therefore, in their use-value. Just as little does it proceed from the nature of the determining factors of value. For, in the first place, however varied the useful kinds of labour, or productive activities, may be, it is a physiological fact, that they are functions of the human organism, and that each such function, whatever may be its nature or form, is essentially the expenditure of human brain, nerves, muscles, &c. Secondly, with regard to that which forms the ground-work for the quantitative determination of value, namely, the duration of that expenditure, or the quantity of labour, it is quite clear that there is a palpable difference between its quantity and quality. In all states of society, the labour-time that it costs to produce the means of subsistence, must necessarily be an object of interest to mankind, though not of equal interest in different stages of development. And lastly, from the moment that men in any way work for one another, their labour assumes a social form.

Whence, then, arises the enigmatical character of the product of labour, so soon as it assumes the form of commodities? Clearly from this form itself. The equality of all sorts of human labour is expressed objectively by their products all being equally values; the measure of the expenditure of labour-power by the duration of that expenditure, takes the form of the quantity of value of the products of labour; and finally, the mutual relations of the producers, within which the social character of their labour affirms itself, take the form of a social relation between the products.

A commodity is therefore a mysterious thing, simply because in it the social character of men's labour appears to them as an objective character stamped upon the product of that labour; because the relation of the producers to the sum total of their own labour is presented to them as a social relation, existing not between themselves, but between the products of their labour. This is the reason why the products of

labour become commodities, social things whose qualities are at the same time perceptible and imperceptible by the senses. In the same way the light from an object is perceived by us not as the subjective excitation of our optic nerve, but as the objective form of something outside the eye itself. But, in the act of seeing, there is at all events, an actual passage of light from one thing to another, from the external object to the eye. There is a physical relation between physical things. But it is different with commodities. There, the existence of the things *quâ* commodities, and the value-relation between the products of labour which stamps them as commodities, have absolutely no connexion with their physical properties and with the material relations arising therefrom. There it is a definite social relation between men, that assumes, in their eyes, the fantastic form of a relation between things. In order, therefore, to find an analogy, we must have recourse to the mist-enveloped regions of the religious world. In that world the productions of the human brain appear as independent beings endowed with life, and entering into relation both with one another and the human race. So it is in the world of commodities with the products of men's hands. This I call the Fetishism which attaches itself to the products of labour, so soon as they are produced as commodities, and which is therefore inseparable from the production of commodities.

This Fetishism of commodities has its origin, as the foregoing analysis has already shown, in the peculiar social character of the labour that produces them.

As a general rule, articles of utility become commodities, only because they are products of the labour of private individuals or groups of individuals who carry on their work independently of each other. The sum total of the labour of all these private individuals forms the aggregate labour of society. Since the producers do not come into social contact with each other until they exchange their products, the specific social character of each producer's labour does not show itself except in the act of exchange. In other words, the labour of the individual asserts itself as a part of the labour of society, only be means of the relations which the act of exchange establishes directly between the products, and indirectly, through them, between the producers. To the latter, therefore, the relations connecting the labour of one individual with that of the rest appear, not as direct social relations between individuals at work, but as what they really are, material relations between persons and social relations between things. It is only by being exchanged that the products of labour acquire, as values, one uniform social status, distinct from their varied forms of existence as objects of utility. This division of a product into a useful thing and a value becomes practically important, only when exchange has acquired such an extension that useful articles are produced for the purpose of being exchanged, and their character as values has therefore to be taken into account, beforehand, during production. From this moment the labour of the individual producer acquires socially a two-fold character. On the one hand, it must, as a definite useful kind of labour, satisfy a definite social want, and thus hold its place as part and parcel of the collective labour of all, as a branch of a social division of labour that has sprung up spontaneously. On the other hand, it can satisfy the manifold wants of the individual producer himself, only in so far as the mutual exchangeability of all kinds of useful private labour is an established social fact, and therefore the private useful labour of each producer ranks on an equality with that of all others. The equalisation of the most different kinds of labour can be the result only of an abstraction from their inequalities, or of reducing them to their common denominator, viz., expenditure of human labour-power or human labour in the abstract. The two-fold social character of the labour of the individual appears to him, when reflected in his brain, only under those forms which are impressed upon that labour in

every-day practice by the exchange of products. In this way, the character that his own labour possesses of being socially useful takes the form of the condition, that the product must be not only useful, but useful for others, and the social character that his particular labour has of being the equal of all other particular kinds of labour, takes the form that all the physically different articles that are the products of labour, have one common quality, viz., that of having value.

Hence, when we bring the products of our labour into relation with each other as values, it is not because we see in these articles the material receptacles of homogeneous human labour. Quite the contrary: whenever, by an exchange, we equate as values our different products, by that very act, we also equate, as human labour, the different kinds of labour expended upon them. We are not aware of this, nevertheless we do it.[1] Value, therefore, does not stalk about with a label describing what it is. It is value, rather, that converts every product into a social hieroglyphic. Later on, we try to decipher the hieroglyphic, to get behind the secret of our own social products; for to stamp an object of utility as a value, is just as much a social product as language. The recent scientific discovery, that the products of labour, so far as they are values, are but material expressions of the human labour spent in their production, marks, indeed, an epoch in the history of the development of the human race, but, by no means, dissipates the mist through which the social character of labour appears to us to be an objective character of the products themselves. The fact, that in the particular form of production with which we are dealing, viz., the production of commodities, the specific social character of private

---

[1] When, therefore, Galiani says: Value is a relation between persons—"La Ricchezza è una ragione tra due persone,"—he ought to have added: a relation between persons expressed as relation between things. (Galiani: Della Moneta, p. 221, V. III. of Custodi's collection of "Scrittori Classici Italiani di Economia Poltica." Parte Moderna, Milano, 1803.)

labour carried on independently, consists in the equality of every kind of that labour, by virtue of its being human labour, which character, therefore, assumes in the product the form of value—this fact appears to the producers, notwithstanding the discovery above referred to, to be just as real and final, as the fact, that, after the discovery by science of the component gases of air, the atmosphere itself remained unaltered.

What, first of all, practically concerns producers when they make an exchange, is the question, how much of some other product they get for their own? in what proportions the products are exchangeable? When these proportions have, by custom, attained a certain stability, they appear to result from the nature of the products, so that, for instance, one ton of iron and two ounces of gold appear as naturally to be of equal value as a pound of gold and a pound of iron in spite of their different physical and chemical qualities appear to be of equal weight. The character of having value, when once impressed upon products, obtains fixity only by reason of their acting and re-acting upon each other as quantities of value. These quantities vary continually, independently of the will, foresight and action of the producers. To them, their own social action takes the form of the action of objects, which rule the production of commodities before, from accumulated experience alone, the scientific conviction springs up, that all the different kinds of private labour, which are carried on independently of each other, and yet as spontaneously developed branches of the social division of labour, are continually being reduced to the quantitative proportions in which society requires them. And why? Because, in the midst of all the accidental and ever fluctuating exchange-relations between the products, the labour-time socially necessary for their production forcibly asserts itself like an over-riding law of Nature. The law of gravity thus asserts itself when a house falls about our ears.[2] The determination of the magnitude of value by labour-time is therefore a secret, hidden under the apparent fluctuations in the relative values of commodities. Its discovery, while removing all appearance of mere accidentality from the determination of the magnitude of the values of products, yet in no way alters the mode in which that determination takes place.

Man's reflections on the forms of social life, and consequently, also, his scientific analysis of those forms, take a course directly opposite to that of their actual historical development. He begins, post festum, with the results of the process of development ready to hand before him. The characters that stamp products as commodities, and whose establishment is a necessary preliminary to the circulation of commodities, have already acquired the stability of natural, self-understood forms of social life, before man seeks to decipher, not their historical character, for in his eyes they are immutable, but their meaning. Consequently it was the analysis of the prices of commodities that alone led to the determination of the magnitude of value, and it was the common expression of all commodities in money that alone led to the establishment of their characters as values. It is, however, just this ultimate money-form of the world of commodities that actually conceals, instead of disclosing, the social character of private labour, and the social relations between the individual producers. When I state that coats or boots stand in a relation to linen, because it is the universal incarnation of abstract human labour, the absurdity of the statement is self-evident. Nevertheless, when the producers of coats and boots compare those articles with linen, or, what is the same thing, with gold or silver, as the universal equivalent, they express

---

[2] "What are we to think of a law that asserts itself only by periodic revolutions? It is just nothing but a law of Nature, founded on the want of knowledge of those whose action is the subject of it." (Friedrich Engels: "Umrisse zu einer Kritik der National-ökonomie," in the "Deutsch-Französische Jahrbücher," edited by Arnold Ruge and Karl Marx. Paris, 1844.)

the relation between their own private labour and the collective labour of society in the same absurd form.

The categories of bourgeois economy consist of such like forms. They are forms of thought expressing with social validity the conditions and relations of a definite, historically determined mode of production, viz., the production of commodities. The whole mystery of commodities, all the magic and necromancy that surrounds the products of labour as long as they take the form of commodities, vanishes therefore, so soon as we come to other forms of production.

Since Robinson Crusoe's experiences are a favourite theme with political economists,[3] let us take a look at him on his island. Moderate though he be, yet some few wants he has to satisfy, and must therefore do a little useful work of various sorts, such as making tools and furniture, taming goats, fishing and hunting. Of his prayers and the like we take no account, since they are a source of pleasure to him, and he looks upon them as so much recreation. In spite of the variety of his work, he knows that his labour, whatever its form, is but the activity of one and the same Robinson, and consequently, that it consists of nothing but different modes of human labour. Necessity itself compels him to apportion his time accurately between his different kinds of work. Whether one kind occupies a greater space in his general activity than another, depends on the difficulties, greater or less as the case may be, to be overcome in attaining the useful effect aimed at. This our friend Robinson soon learns by

experience, and having rescued a watch, ledger, and pen and ink from the wreck, commences, like a true-born Briton, to keep a set of books. His stock-book contains a list of the objects of utility that belong to him, of the operations necessary for their production; and lastly, of the labour-time that definite quantities of those objects have, on an average, cost him. All the relations between Robinson and the objects that form this wealth of his own creation, are here so simple and clear as to be intelligible without exertion, even to Mr. Sedley Taylor. And yet those relations contain all that is essential to the determination of value.

Let us now transport ourselves from Robinson's island bathed in light to the European middle ages shrouded in darkness. Here, instead of the independent man, we find everyone dependent, serfs and lords, vassals and suzerains, laymen and clergy Personal dependence here characterises the social relations of production just as much as it does the other spheres of life organised on the basis of that production. But for the very reason that personal dependence forms the ground-work of society, there is no necessity for labour and its products to assume a fantastic form different from their reality. They take the shape, in the transactions of society, of services in kind and payments in kind. Here the particular and natural form of labour, and not, as in a society based on production of commodities, its general abstract form is the immediate social form of labour. Compulsory labour is just as properly measured by time, as commodity-producing labour; but every serf knows that what he expends in the service of his lord, is a definite quantity of his own personal labour-power. The tithe to be rendered to the priest is more matter of fact than his blessing. No matter, then, what we may think of the parts played by the different classes of people themselves in this society, the social relations between individuals in the performance of their labour, appear at all events as their own mutual personal relations, and are not disguised under the shape of social relations between the products of labour.

---

[3] Even Ricardo has his stories a la Robinson. "He makes the primitive hunter and the primitive fisher straightway, as owners of commodities, exchange fish and game in the proportion in which labour-time is incorporated in these exchange-values. On this occasion he commits the anachronism of making these men apply to the calculation, so far as their implements have to be taken into account, the annuity tables in current use on the London Exchange in the year 1817. The parallelograms of Mr. Owen' appear to be the only form of society, besides the bourgeois form, with which he was acquainted." (Karl Marx: "Zur Kritik, &c.," pp. 38, 39).

For an example of labour in common or directly associated labour, we have no occasion to go back to that spontaneously developed form which we find on the threshold of the history of all civilised races.[4] We have one close at hand in the patriarchal industries of a peasant family, that produces corn, cattle, yarn, linen, and clothing for home use. These different articles are, as regards the family, so many products of its labour, but as between themselves, they are not commodities. The different kinds of labour, such as tillage, cattle tending, spinning, weaving and making clothes, which result in the various products, are in themselves, and such as they are, direct social functions, because functions of the family, which, just as much as a society based on the production of commodities, possesses a spontaneously developed system of division of labour. The distribution of the work within the family, and the regulation of the labour-time of the several members, depend as well upon differences of age and sex as upon natural conditions varying with the seasons. The labour-power of each individual, by its very nature, operates in this case merely as a definite portion of the whole labour-power of the family, and therefore, the measure of the expenditure of individual labour-power by its duration, appears here by its very nature as a social character of their labour.

Let us now picture to ourselves, by way of change, a community of free individuals, carrying on their work with the means of production in common, in which the labour-power of all the different individuals is consciously applied as the combined labour-power of the community. All the characteristics of Robinson's labour are here repeated, but with this difference, that they are social, instead of individual. Everything produced by him was exclusively the result of his own personal labour, and therefore simply an object of use for himself. The total product of our community is a social product. One portion serves as fresh means of production and remains social. But another portion is consumed by the members as means of subsistence. A distribution of this portion amongst them is consequently necessary. The mode of this distribution will vary with the productive organisation of the community, and the degree of historical development attained by the producers. We will assume, but merely for the sake of a parallel with the production of commodities, that the share of each individual producer in the means of subsistence is determined by his labour-time. Labour-time would, in that case, play a double part. Its apportionment in accordance with a definite social plan maintains the proper proportion between the different kinds of work to be done and the various wants of the community. On the other hand, it also serves as a measure of the portion of the common labour borne by each individual, and of his share in the part of the total product destined for individual consumption. The social relations of the individual producers, with regard both to their labour and to its products, are in this case perfectly simple and intelligible, and that with regard not only to production but also to distribution.

The religious world is but the reflex of the real world. And for a society based upon the production of commodities, in which the producers in general enter into social relations with one another by treating their products as commodities and values, whereby they reduce their individual private labour to the standard of homogeneous human labour—for such a society, Christianity with its *cultus* of abstract man,

---

[4] "A ridiculous presumption has latterly got abroad that common property in its primitive form is specifically a Slavonian, or even exclusively Russian form. It is the primitive form that we can prove to have existed amongst Romans, Teutons, and Celts, and even to this day we find numerous examples, ruins though they be, in India. A more exhaustive study of Asiatic, and especially of Indian forms of common property, would show how from the different forms of primitive common property, different forms of its dissolution have been developed. Thus, for instance, the various original types of Roman and Teutonic private property are deducible from different forms of Indian common property." (Karl Marx, "Zur Kritik, &c.," p. 10.)

more especially in its bourgeois developments, Protestantism, Deism, &c., is the most fitting form of religion. In the ancient Asiatic and other ancient modes of production, we find that the conversion of products into commodities, and therefore the conversion of men into producers of commodities, holds a subordinate place, which, however, increases in importance as the primitive communities approach nearer and nearer to their dissolution. Trading nations, properly so called, exist in the ancient world only in its interstices, like the gods of Epicurus in the Intermundia, or like Jews in the pores of Polish society. Those ancient social organisms of production are, as compared with bourgeois society, extremely simple and transparent. But they are founded either on the immature development of man individually, who has not yet severed the umbilical cord that unites him with his fellowmen in a primitive tribal community, or upon direct relations of subjection. They can arise and exist only when the development of the productive power of labour has not risen beyond a low stage, and when, therefore, the social relations within the sphere of material life, between man and man, and between man and Nature, are correspondingly narrow. This narrowness is reflected in the ancient worship of Nature, and in the other elements of the popular religions. The religious reflex of the real world can, in any case, only then finally vanish, when the practical relations of every-day life offer to man none but perfectly intelligible and reasonable relations with regard to his fellowmen and to Nature.

The life-process of society, which is based on the process of material production, does not strip off its mystical veil until it is treated as production by freely associated men, and is consciously regulated by them in accordance with a settled plan. This, however, demands for society a certain material ground-work or set of conditions of existence which in their turn are the spontaneous product of a long and painful process of development.

Political Economy has indeed analysed, however incompletely, value and its magnitude, and has discovered what lies beneath these forms. But it has never once asked the question why labour is represented by the value of its product and labour-time by the magnitude of that value. These formulae, which bear it stamped upon them in unmistakable letters that they belong to a state of society, in which the process of production has the mastery over man, instead of being controlled by him, such formulae appear to the bourgeois intellect to be as much a self-evident necessity imposed by Nature as productive labour itself. Hence forms of social production that preceded the bourgeois form, are treated by the bourgeoisie in much the same way as the Fathers of the Church treated pre-Christian religions.

To what extent some economists are misled by the Fetishism inherent in commodities, or by the objective appearance of the social characteristics of labour, is shown, amongst other ways, by the dull and tedious quarrel over the part played by Nature in the formation of exchange-value. Since exchange-value is a definite social manner of expressing the amount of labour bestowed upon an object, Nature has no more to do with it, than it has in fixing the course of exchange.

The mode of production in which the product takes the form of a commodity, or is produced directly for exchange, is the most general and most embryonic form of bourgeois production. It therefore makes its appearance at an early date in history, though not in the same predominating and characteristic manner as now-a-days. Hence its Fetish character is comparatively easy to be seen through. But when we come to more concrete forms, even this appearance of simplicity vanishes. Whence arose the illusions of the monetary system? To it gold and silver, when serving as money, did to represent a social relation between producers, but were natural objects with strange social properties. And modern economy, which looks down with such disdain on the monetary system, does not its superstition come out as clear as noon-day, whenever it treats of capital? How long is it since economy discarded the physiocratic illusion, that rents grow out of the soil and not out of society?

But not to anticipate, we will content ourselves with yet another example relating to the commodity-form. Could commodities themselves speak, they would say: Our use-value may be a thing that interests men. It is no part of us as objects. What, however, does belong to us as objects, is our value. Our natural intercourse as commodities proves it. In the eyes of each other we are nothing but exchange-values. Now listen how those commodities speak through the mouth of the economist. "Value"— (*i.e.,* exchange-value) "is a property of things, riches"—(*i.e.,* use-value) "of man. Value, in this sense, necessarily implies exchanges, riches do not." "Riches" (use-value) "are the attribute of men, value is the attribute of commodities. A man or a community is rich, a pearl or a diamond is valuable. . . A pearl or a diamond is valuable" as a pearl or a diamond. So far no chemist has ever discovered exchange-value either in a pearl or a diamond. The economic discoverers of this chemical element, who by-the-by lay special claim to critical acumen, find however that the use-value of objects belongs to them independently of their material properties, while their value, on the other hand, forms a part of them as objects. What confirms them in this view, is the peculiar circumstance that the use-value of objects is realised without exchange, by means of a direct relation between the objects and man, while, on the other hand, their value is realised only by exchange, that is; by means of a social process. Who fails here to call to mind our good friend, Dogberry, who informs neighbour Seacoal, that, "To be a well-favoured man is the gift of fortune; but reading and writing comes by Nature."

Chapter 2

Emile Durkheim: Anomie and Social Integration

Introduction

Émile Durkheim's scholarly writings were dedicated to the proposition that society was an entity *sui generis,* i.e., one that could be studied in itself without reducing it to individuals and their motivations. Although individuals clearly are the component parts of a society, nevertheless society is more than the individuals who constitute it. According to Durkheim, we know of its existence because society exercises control over our behavior, as rules of conduct, as laws, as customs, and as norms and values that we believe in and that shape our conscience and make us part of a collectively. Society is external to us in that we feel its pressures to conform, but it is also internal to us in that it forms the collective moral conscience. Durkheim published several major works that have become classics in the field, among them *The Division of Labor* (1893), *Suicide* (1897), *The Elementary Forms of Religious Life* (1912), and he established *L'Année Sociologique,* the first French journal of sociology. French sociology became closely identified with Durkheim's work in the early years of its development. Although Comte may have been the first to use the term "sociology," it was Durkheim who founded the field by defining its subject matter and its methodology.

Émile Durkheim was born in eastern France at Épinal in 1858 to Jewish parents. The descendant of a long line of rabbis, Durkheim originally planned to become a rabbi himself, but in his early teens he turned away from religious beliefs and became an agnostic. A brilliant and dedicated student, he eventually worked his way into the École Normale Supérieure, the school for France's intellectual elite, by passing the difficult entrance examination on his third attempt. After graduating he spent five years teaching philosophy at high schools before becoming a professor of philosophy at the University of Bordeaux in 1887, where he specialized in the fields of education and social science.

After a lifetime of effort to establish the field of sociology by demonstrating how social phenomena could be studied empirically and not simply discussed speculatively, Durkheim was granted recognition and acclaim with a chair at the Sorbonne, France's most prestigious academic institution. In 1913 the title of his chair was officially changed from Professor of the Science of Education to Professor of the Science of Education and Sociology, and Durkheim thus became the first official sociologist in France, a major victory for a discipline that had been formerly considered illegitimate by most academics.

In the excerpt reprinted on the following pages from *The Rules of Sociological Method,* Durkheim presents his case for sociology as an independent field of inquiry with its own subject matter that is not reducible to individual psychology. There are "social facts," he claims that exist outside of us and that compel us to behave in conformity with norms that are not of our making. In short, Durkheim is pointing to the existence of constraints on individual behavior and claiming that these external forces are the substance of the "social" and warrant a systematic examination on their own terms by sociologists. What are these constraints? How do they emerge? How do we know of their existence? Can they be changed and under what conditions?

Durkheim's classic study, *Suicide,* demonstrates his view that larger social forces exist which can account for a phenomenon that on the surface appears to be strictly a case of individual action. In other words, Durkheim believed that if he could demonstrate that there are social causes of suicide, which many understood to be the ultimate individual act, he would go to the heart of the psychological and reductionist argument and prove its inadequacy. In addition, *Suicide* is a model of sociological method. It demonstrates how a sociologist can proceed to establish significant correlations with statistical data, how inferences can be drawn from the data, and, finally, how broader generalizations are formulated from the empirical data and lead to a general theory.

In the extracts from *Suicide* reprinted below, Durkheim describes the variations in the rates of suicide among different groups in society. At the very outset we are invited to ask about social rates of suicide rather than individual incidents. In other words, Durkheim shifts our attention away from psychological questions about the motivations of particular individuals who commit suicide, a focus that he viewed as reductionist, to sociological questions concerning the larger social conditions associated with the suicide rates. In the process Durkheim develops the notion that suicide rates increase as the degree of integration and regulation of the individual by the group decreases. Put differently and somewhat more simply, the more free the individual is from external restraints, and the more isolated from group life, the more prone the individual is to suicide. Durkheim's quest, then, is to determine the social conditions that lead to the breakdown of moral regulation and group integration. Beyond that, Durkheim is aware that social conditions will have different effects on different individuals, and in a later chapter he deals with the question of the role of psychology.

Durkheim saw society as an elaborate organism in which each separate part performs its specific task in the functioning of the whole. This is analogous to the human body, in which each separate organ performs a bodily function in order to enable the person to survive. Though each organ performs a different function, each is vitally important, and none of them can survive or be understood except in the context of every other organ. The phrase "the body social" refers to this typically Durkheimian way of viewing society.

In *The Division of Labor in Society,* Durkheim demonstrates the dramatic increase in the differentiation and specialization of functions in modern society. He distinguishes two basic forms of social organization, *mechanical solidarity* and *organic solidarity,* corresponding roughly to traditional and modern society. In societies characterized by mechanical solidarity people are basically similar in their social roles; there is little specialization or division of labor. As a result, people tend to share many things, having a common culture and a common morality. The members of such societies are thus very closely knit together, and their unity is based on their similarity. Modern societies, on the other hand, are characterized by organic solidarity, which replaces mechanical solidarity as the differentiation in the division of labor in society increases. As the name suggests, the cohesion of such societies depends less on the common culture and morality of its members than on their mutual interdependence.

Durkheim's discussion of law extends this analysis further and sharpens the distinction between traditional and modern societies. Simpler societies sharing a common culture and moral code are also governed by *repressive law,* in which severe punishments are meted out as expressions of the collective outrage at the violation of the morality of the community. *Restitutive law* is characteristic of modern societies, in which the common moral ground may be weak because of differentiation and specialization and the diverse groups and moral codes that define contemporary society. Here the meaning of law changes, and in place of strong, commonly held moral codes is a bureaucratic legal system in which violations are not perceived as moral transgressions against the community but as infractions that can be paid for through adjudicated fines and terms of imprisonment. In contrast to repressive law, where the function is to extract retribution, restitutive law aims to restore the situation to its condition prior to the violation.

The idea of organic solidarity, or unity based on the interdependence that characterizes modern society, was Durkheim's functional response to the fear that with the passing of traditional society and the breakdown of a common moral value system society itself was threatened. Durkheim saw in the modern division of labor the possibility of reducing social conflict and war. In contrast to mechanical solidarity, where different groups performed the same functions, could exist independently of one another, and thus were liable to fight among themselves for scarce resources, the increasing interdependence of social groups under organic solidarity would, according to Durkheim, make it harder for any group to be done away with or oppressed.

Nevertheless, Durkheim was deeply troubled by the development of modern society and particularly by the breakup of traditional ways of life and morality. In sharp contrast to those who saw society as the result of a contract entered into by self-interested individuals, Durkheim saw people as very much socially constructed and society as preceding and forming the individual. Humans are always found in groups and their lives as individuals are always shaped by social conditions. The notion that individuals exist as atomized entities in a state of nature prior to the formation of society is a convenient myth used to justify liberal utilitarian ideology rather than an accurate and empirical description. People's personalities and morality are not created *a priori* but are a result of social

conditioning and regulating, and if society fails to regulate its members well or consistently, they are liable to suffer. Modern society, with its rapid changes, has often failed to provide a stable set of norms for individuals to absorb and live by; on the contrary, it has tended to destroy such systems of belief. As a result, many people are afflicted by a debilitating sense of purposelessness and normlessness in their lives, a social condition to which Durkheim gave the now famous term *anomie*, and which he considered to be one of the leading causes of suicide and unhappiness in his time.

The Elementary Forms of Religious Life, arguably Durkheim's most creative work and considered by some to be his best, explores the nature of religious belief by studying the religions of very simple societies. Durkheim thought that the essential qualities of religious belief could be best understood under conditions less complex than those of the highly differentiated modern society. From his study of the religions of Australian aboriginal tribes he concluded that the one thing all religions have in common is a division between the *sacred*—the realm of the extraordinary, and/or the divine—and the *profane*—the realm of the everyday, the commonplace, the ordinary. Durkheim claimed that the distinction between the sacred and profane is one that is socially constructed and not one that inheres in the object so designated. Thus tribal people attribute sacred meaning to a bird or an animal, designate it as their totem, and build up rituals surrounding it, and the symbol in turn becomes a source of unity through a shared belief. Every society and every religion designates certain objects—in Christianity the cross, holy water, icons, etc.—as sacred. These sacred objects act as focal points for the attitudes of awe, reverence, mystery, and respect that are associated with religious belief.

But Durkheim's most original formulation was his view that these symbols and beliefs are all actually representations of society; in other words, he claims that all religious symbols and ideas are actually symbols for society, i.e., symbols of moral unity. These symbols represent the collective ideals and morality that are the basis of social order. "God" and such phenomena as totems are society personified, and when we worship in a religious ceremony, we are really worshipping the collective ideals that unite us with one another. The feelings of awe or reverence that are associated with the realm of the sacred are feelings of awe or reverence for society.

Durkheim's analysis points to the functions that are served by religious symbols and beliefs. Having established this, Durkheim believes that he has found possibilities for replacing religion in modern society, so that one need not fear that social collapse is inevitable with the disintegration of traditional religious beliefs. For, if we ask about the function of these symbols and beliefs, rather than about the truth of their content, we may be able better to understand the modern condition and the passing of traditional religious beliefs.

A contemporary sociologist, Robert Bellah, has pointed to the "civil religion" in America as the functional equivalent of traditional religious beliefs. On this view, the Constitution, the Bill of Rights, and our democratic institutions affirming human rights represent the fundamental moral consensus of society. The national anthem, the flag, and the national holidays are contemporary symbols and common rituals of unity in the presence of diversity and differentiation. Contemporary debates over multiculturalism and diversity underscore the continuing relevance of Durkheim's formulations and his attempt to provide a moral foundation for the modern, differentiated, and individualistic society.

Durkheim was deeply troubled by the condition of modernity: the rationalism of science, the complex division of labor brought on by industrialization, and the emphasis on individualism. However, he found in modern individualism, "the cult of the individual," the moral basis of modern society. In "Individualism and the Intellectuals," Durkheim distinguished between the egoistic or self-interested individualism of Herbert Spencer and the moral individualism of Immanuel Kant. The latter stressed the dignity and the rights of the individual as a member of the human community. Such membership entailed a recognition and respect for the rights of others in the pursuit of a just social order. It did not mean, as Spencer and others had claimed, that social life was a constant struggle of egos in the survival of the fittest.

Durkheim's influence has been enormous, and he is without question to be counted with Marx and Weber as one of the main founders of modern sociology. His empirical method and functional style of analysis have been adopted by many schools of anthropology, sociology, and other social sciences, and although certain qualities of his methodology are controversial, such as his claim that values need not enter social research and analysis, the style of statistical analysis he pioneered in such books as *Suicide* has been widely utilized ever since. His legacy remains particularly strong in the functional school of American sociology, and figures such as Talcott Parsons and Robert K. Merton have acknowledged Durkheim as one of their primary influences.

ÉMILE DURKHEIM: THE RULES OF SOCIOLOGICAL METHOD

What is a Social Fact?

Before inquiring into the method suited to the study of social facts, it is important to know which facts are commonly called "social." This information is all the more necessary since the designation "social" is used with little precision. It is currently employed for practically all phenomena generally diffused within society, however small their social interest. But on that basis, there are, as it were, no human events that may not be called social. Each individual drinks, sleeps, eats, reasons; and it is to society's interest that these functions be exercised in an orderly manner. If, then, all these facts are counted as "social" facts, sociology would have no subject matter exclusively its own, and its domain would be confused with that of biology and psychology.

But in reality there is in every society a certain group of phenomena which may be differentiated from those studied by the other natural sciences. When I fulfill my obligations as brother, husband, or citizen, when I execute my contracts, I perform duties which are defined, externally to myself and my acts, in law and in custom. Even if they conform to my own sentiments and I feel their reality subjectively, such reality is still objective, for I did not create them; I merely inherited them through my education. How many times it happens, moreover, that we are ignorant of the details of the obligations incumbent upon us, and that in order to acquaint ourselves with them

we must consult the law and its authorized interpreters! Similarly, the church-member finds the beliefs and practices of his religious life ready-made at birth; their existence prior to his own implies their existence outside of himself. The system of signs I use to express my thought, the system of currency I employ to pay my debts, the instruments of credit I utilize in my commercial relations, the practices followed in my profession, etc., function independently of my own use of them. And these statements can be repeated for each member of society. Here, then, are ways of acting, thinking, and feeling that present the noteworthy property of existing outside the individual consciousness.

These types of conduct or thought are not only external to the individual but are, moreover, endowed with coercive power, by virtue of which they impose themselves upon him, independent of his individual will. Of course, when I fully consent and conform to them, this constraint is felt only slightly, if at all, and is therefore unnecessary. But it is, nonetheless, an intrinsic characteristic of these facts, the proof thereof being that it asserts itself as soon as I attempt to resist it. If I attempt to violate the law, it reacts against me so as to prevent my act before its accomplishment, or to nullify my violation by restoring the damage, if it is accomplished and reparable, or to make me expiate it if it cannot be compensated for otherwise.

In the case of purely moral maxims; the public conscience exercised a check on every act which offends it by means of the surveillance it exercises over the conduct of citizens, and the appropriate penalties at its disposal. In many cases the constraint is less violent, but nevertheless it always exists. If I do not submit to the conventions of society, if in my dress I do not conform to the customs observed in my country and in my class, the ridicule I provoke, the social isolation in which I am kept, produce, although in an attenuated form, the same effects as a punishment in the strict sense of the word. The constraint is nonetheless efficacious for being indirect. I am not obliged to speak French with my fellow-countrymen nor to use the legal currency, but I cannot possibly do otherwise. If I tried to escape this necessity, my attempt would fail miserably. As an industrialist, I am free to apply the technical methods of former centuries; but by doing so, I should invite certain ruin. Even when I free myself from these rules and violate them successfully, I am always compelled to struggle with them. When finally overcome, they make their constraining power sufficiently felt by the resistance they offer. The enterprises of all innovators, including successful ones, come up against resistance of this kind.

Here, then, is a category of facts with very distinctive characteristics: it consists of ways of acting, thinking, and feeling, external to the individual, and endowed with a power of coercion, by reason of which they control him. These ways of thinking could not be confused with biological phenomena, since they consist of representations and of actions; nor with psychological phenomena, which exist only in the individual consciousness and through it. They constitute, thus, a new variety of phenomena; and it is to them exclusively that the term "social" ought to be applied. And this term fits them quite well, for it is clear that, since their source is not in the individual, their substratum can be no other than society, either the political society as a whole or some one of the partial groups it includes, such as religious denominations, political, literary, and occupational associations, etc. On the other hand, this term "social" applies to them exclusively, for it has a distinct meaning only if it designates exclusively the phenomena which are not included in any of the categories of facts that have already been established and classified. These ways of thinking and acting therefore constitute the proper domain of soci-

ology. It is true that, when we define them with this word "constraint," we risk shocking the zealous partisans of absolute individualism. For those who profess the complete autonomy of the individual, man's dignity is diminished whenever he is made to feel that he is not completely self-determinant. It is generally accepted today, however, that most of our ideas and our tendencies are not developed by ourselves but come to us from without. How can they become a part of us except by imposing themselves upon us? This is the whole meaning of our definition. And it is generally accepted, moreover, that social constraint is not necessarily incompatible with the individual personality.[1]

Since the examples that we have just cited (legal and moral regulations, religious faiths, financial systems, etc.) all consist of established beliefs and practices, one might be led to believe that social facts exist only where there is some social organization. But there are other facts without such crystallized form which have the same objectivity and the same ascendancy over the individual. These are called "social currents." Thus the great movements of enthusiasm, indignation, and pity in a crowd do not originate in any one of the particular individual consciousness. They come to each one of us from without and can carry us away in spite of ourselves. Of course, it may happen that, in abandoning myself to them unreservedly, I do not feel the pressure they exert upon me. But it is revealed as soon as I try to resist them. Let an individual attempt to oppose one of these collective manifestations, and the emotions that he denies will turn against him. Now, if this power of external coercion asserts itself so clearly in cases of resistance, it must exist also in the first-mentioned cases, although we are unconscious of it. We are then victims of the illusion of having ourselves created that which actually forces itself from without. . . .

---

[1] We do not intend to imply, however, that all constraint is normal. We shall return to this point later.

To confirm this definition of the social fact by a characteristic illustration from common experience, one need only observe the manner in which children are brought up. Considering the facts as they are and as they have always been, it becomes immediately evident that all education is a continuous effort to impose on the child ways of seeing, feeling, and acting which he could not have arrived at spontaneously. From the very first hours of his life, we compel him to eat, drink, and sleep at regular hours; we constrain him to cleanliness, calmness, and obedience; later we exert pressure upon him in order that he may learn proper consideration for others, respect for customs and conventions, the need for work, etc. If, in time, this constraint ceases to be felt, it is because it gradually gives rise to habits and to internal tendencies that render constraint unnecessary; but nevertheless it is not abolished, for it is still the source from which these habits were derived. It is true that, according to Spencer, a rational education ought to reject such methods, allowing the child to act in complete liberty; but as this pedagogic theory has never been applied by any known people, it must be accepted only as an expression of personal opinion, not as a fact which can contradict the aforementioned observations. What makes these facts particularly instructive is that the aim of education is, precisely, the socialization of the human being; the process of education, therefore, gives us in a nutshell the historical fashion in which the social being is constituted. This unremitting pressure to which the child is subjected in the very pressure of the social milieu which tends to fashion him in its own image, and of which parents and teachers are merely the representatives and intermediaries.

It follows that sociological phenomena cannot be defined by their universality. A thought which we find in every individual consciousness, a movement repeated be all individuals, is not thereby a social fact. If sociologists have been satisfied with defining them by this characteristic, it is because they confused them with what one might call their reincarnation in the individual. It is, however, the collective aspects of the beliefs, tendencies, and practices of a group that characterize truly social phenomena. As for the forms that the collective states assume when refracted in the individual, these are things of another sort. This duality is clearly demonstrated by the fact that these two orders of phenomena are frequently found dissociated from one another. Indeed, certain of these social manners of acting and thinking acquire, by reason of their repetition, a certain rigidity which on its own account crystallizes them, so to speak, and isolates them from the particular events which reflect them. They thus acquire a body, a tangible form, and constitute a reality in their own right, quite distinct from the individual facts which produce it. Collective habits are inherent not only in the successive acts which they determine but, by a privilege of which we find no example in the biological realm, they are given permanent expression in a formula which is repeated from mouth to mouth, transmitted by education, and fixed even in writing. Such is the origin and nature of legal and moral rules, popular aphorisms and proverbs, articles of faith wherein religious or political groups condense their beliefs, standards of taste established by literary schools, etc. None of these can be found entirely reproduced in the applications made of them by individuals, since they can exist even without being actually applied.

No doubt, this dissociation does not always manifest itself with equal distinctness, but its obvious existence in the important and numerous cases just cited is sufficient to prove that the social fact is a thing distinct from its individual manifestations. Moreover, even when this dissociation is not immediately apparent, it may often be disclosed by certain devices of method. Such dissociation is indispensable if one wishes to separate social facts from their alloys in order to observe them in a state of purity. Currents of opinion, with an intensity varying according to the time and place, impel certain groups either to more marriages, for example, or to more suicides, or to a higher or lower birthrate, etc. These currents are plainly social facts. At first sight they seem inseparable from the forms they take in individual cases. But statistics furnish us with means of isolating them. They are, in fact, represented with considerable exactness by the rates of births, marriages, and suicides, that is, by the number obtained by dividing the average annual total of marriages, births, suicides, by the number of persons whose ages lie within the range in which marriages, births, and suicides occur.[2] Since each of these figures contains all the individual cases indiscriminately, the individual circumstances which may have had a share in the production of the phenomenon are neutralized and, consequently, do not contribute to its determination. The average, then, expresses a certain state of the group mind (*l'âme collective*).

Such are social phenomena, when disentangled from all foreign matter. As for their individual manifestations, these are indeed, to a certain extent, social, since they partly reproduce a social model. Each of them also depends, and to a large extent, on the organopsychological constitution of the individual and on the particular circumstances in which he is placed. Thus they are not sociological phenomena in the strict sense of the word. They belong to two realms at once; one could call them sociopsychological. They interest the sociologist without constituting the immediate subject matter of sociology. There exist in the interior of organisms similar phenomena, compound in their nature, which form in their turn the subject matter of the "hybrid sciences," such as physiological chemistry, for example.

The objection may be raised that a phenomenon is collective only if it is common to all members of society, or at least to most of them—in other words, if it is truly general. This may be true; but it is general because it is collective (that is, more or less obligatory), and certainly not collective because general. It is a group condition repeated in the individual because imposed on him. It is to be found in each part because it exists in the whole, rather than in the whole because it exists in the parts. This becomes conspicuously evident in those beliefs and practices which are transmitted to us ready-made by previous generations; we receive and adopt them because, being both collective and ancient, they are invested with a particular authority that education has taught us to recognize and respect. It is, of course, true that a vast portion of our social culture is transmitted to us in this way; but even when the social fact is due in part to our direct collaboration, its nature is not different. A collective emotion which bursts forth suddenly and violently in a crowd does not express merely what all the individual sentiments had in common; it is something entirely different, as we have shown. It results form their being together, a product of the actions and reactions which take place between individual consciousnesses; and if each individual consciousness echoes the collective sentiment, it is by virtue of the special energy resident in its collective origin. If all hearts beat in unison, this is not the result of a spontaneous and pre-established harmony but rather because an identical force propels them in the same direction. Each is carried along by all.

We thus arrive at the point where we can formulate and delimit in a precise way the domain of sociology. It comprises only a limited group of phenomena. A social fact is to be recognized by the power of external coercion which it exercises or is capable of exercising over individuals, and the presence of this power may be recognized in its turn either by the existence of some specific sanction or by the resistance offered against every individual effort that tends to violate it. One can, however, define it also by

---

[2] Suicides do not occur at every age, and they take place with varying intensity at the different ages in which they occur.

its diffusion within the group, provided that, in conformity with our previous remarks, one takes care to add as a second and essential characteristic that its own existence is independent of the individual forms it assumes in its diffusion. This last criterion is perhaps, in certain cases, easier to apply then the preceding one. In fact, the constraint is easy to ascertain when it expresses itself externally by some direct reaction of society, as is the case in law, morals, beliefs, customs, and even fashions. But when it is only indirect, like the constraint which an economic organization exercises, it cannot always be so easily detected. Generality combined with externality may, then, be easier to establish. Moreover, this second definition is but another form of the first; for if a mode of behavior whose existence is external to individual consciousnesses become general, this can only be brought about by its being imposed upon them.[3]

But these several phenomena present the same characteristic by which we defined the others. These "ways of existing" are imposed on the individual precisely in the same fashion as the "ways of acting" of which we have spoken. Indeed, when we wish to know how a society is

divided politically, of what themselves are composed, and the fusion existing between th achieve our purpose by physical inspecuu̶̶ᴜ̶ᴜ̶̶ by geographical observations; for these phenomena are social, even when they have some basis in physical nature. It is only by a study of public law that a comprehension of this organization is possible, for it is this law that determines the organization, as it equally determines our domestic and civil relations. This political organization is, then, no less obligatory than the social facts mentioned above. If the population crowds into our cities instead of scattering into the country, this is due to a trend of public opinion, a collective drive that imposes this concentration upon the individuals. We can no more choose the style of our houses than of our clothing—at least, both are equally obligatory. The channels of communication prescribe the direction of internal migrations and commerce, etc., and even their extent. Consequently, at the very most, it should be necessary to add to the list of phenomena which we have enumerated as presenting the distinctive criterion of a social fact only one additional category, "ways of existing"; and, as this enumeration was not meant to be rigorously exhaustive, the addition would not be absolutely necessary.

Such an addition is perhaps not necessary, for these "ways of existing" are only crystallized "ways of acting." The political structure of a society is merely the way in which its component segments have become accustomed to live with one another. If their relations are traditionally intimate, the segments tend to fuse with one another, or, in the contrary case, to retain their identity. The type of habitation imposed upon us is merely the way in which our contemporaries and our ancestors have been accustomed to construct their houses. The methods of communication are merely the channels which the regular currents of commerce and migrations have dug, by flowing in the same direction. To be sure, if the phenomena of a structural

[3] It will be seen how this definition of the social fact diverges from that which forms the basis of the ingenious system of M. Tarde. First of all, we wish to state that our researches have nowhere led us to observe that preponderant influence in the genesis of collective facts which M. Tarde attributes to imitation. Moreover, from the preceding definition, which is not a theory but simply a résumé of the immediate data of observation, it seems indeed to follow, not only that imitation does not always express the essential and characteristic features of the social fact, but even that it never expresses them. No doubt, every social fact is imitated; it has as we have just shown, a tendency to become general, but that is because it is social, i.e., obligatory. Its power of expansion is not the cause but the consequence of its sociological character. If, further, only social facts produced this consequence, imitation could perhaps serve, if not to explain them, at least to define them. But an individual condition which produces a whole series of effects remains individual nevertheless. Moreover, one may ask whether the word "imitation" is indeed fitted to designate an effect due to a coercive influence. Thus, by this single expression, very different phenomena, which ought to be distinguished, are confused.

 naracter alone presented this permanence, one might believe that they constituted a distinct species. A legal regulation is an arrangement no less permanent than a type of architecture, and yet the regulation is a "physiological" fact. A simple moral maxim is assuredly somewhat more malleable, but it is much more rigid than a simple professional custom or a fashion. There is thus a whole series of degrees without a break in continuity between the facts of the most articulated structure and those free currents of social life which are not yet definitely molded. The differences between them are, therefore, only differences in the degree of consolidation they present. Both are simply life, more or less crystallized. No doubt, it may be of some advantage to reserve the term "morphological" for those social facts which concern the social substratum, but

only on condition of not overlooking the fact that they are of the same nature as the others. Our definition will then include the whole relevant range of facts if we say: *A social fact is every way of acting, fixed or not, capable of exercising on the individual an external constraint; or again, every way of acting which is general throughout a given society, while at the same time existing in its own right independent of its individual manifestations.*[4]

---

[4] This close connection between life and structure, organ and function, may be easily proved in sociology because between these two extreme terms there exists a whole series of immediately observable intermediate stages which show the bond between them. Biology is not in the same favorable position. But we may well believe that the inductions on this subject made by sociology are applicable to biology and that, in organisms as well as in societies, only differences in degree exist between these two orders of facts.

ÉMILE DURKHEIM: EGOISTIC SUICIDE AND ANOMIC SUICIDE

Egoistic Suicide

We have thus successively set up the three following propositions:

> *Suicide varies inversely with the degree of integration of religious society.*
> *Suicide varies inversely with the degree of integration of domestic society.*
> *Suicide varies inversely with the degree of integration of political society.*

This grouping shows that whereas these different societies have a moderating influence upon

suicide, this is due not to special characteristics of each but to a characteristic common to all. Religion does not owe its efficacy to the special nature of religious sentiments, since domestic and political societies both produce the same effects when strongly integrated. This, moreover, we have already proved when studying directly the manner of action of different religions upon suicide. Inversely, it is not the specific nature of the domestic or political tie which can explain the immunity they confer, since religious society has the same advantage. The cause can only be found in a single quality possessed by all these social groups, though perhaps to varying degrees. The only quality satisfying this condition is that they are all strongly integrated social groups. So we reach the general conclusion: suicide varies inversely with the degree of integration of the social groups of which the individual forms a part.

But society cannot disintegrate without the individual simultaneously detaching himself from social life, without his own goals becoming preponderant over those of the community, in a word without his personality tending to surmount the collective personality. The more weakened the groups to which he belongs, the less he depends on them, the more he consequently depends only on himself and recognizes no other rules of conduct than what are founded on his private interests. If we agree to call this state egoism, in which the individual ego asserts itself to excess in the face of the social ego and at its expense, we may call egoistic the special type of suicide springing from excessive individualism.

But how can suicide have such an origin?

First of all, it can be said that, as collective force is one of the obstacles best calculated to restrain suicide, its weakening involves a development of suicide. When society is strongly integrated, it holds individuals under its control, considers them at its service and thus forbids them to dispose wilfully of themselves. Accordingly it opposes their evading their duties to it through death. But how could society impose its supremacy upon them when they refuse to accept this subordination as legitimate? It no longer then possesses the requisite authority to retain them in their duty if they wish to desert; and conscious of its own weakness, it even recognizes their right to do freely what it can no longer prevent. So far as they are the admitted masters of their destinies, it is their privilege to end their lives. They, on their part, have no reason to endure life's sufferings patiently. For they cling to life more resolutely when belonging to a group they love, so as not to betray interests they put before their own. The bond that unites them with the common cause attaches them to life and the lofty goal they envisage prevents their feeling personal troubles so deeply. There is, in short, in a cohesive and animated society a constant interchange of ideas and feelings from all to each and each to all, something like a mutual moral support, which instead of throwing the individual on his own resources, leads him to share in the collective energy and supports his own when exhausted.

But these reasons are purely secondary. Excessive individualism not only results in favoring the action of suicidogenic causes, but it is itself such a cause. It not only frees man's inclination to do away with himself from a protective obstacle, but creates this inclination out of whole cloth and thus gives birth to a special suicide which bears its mark. This must be clearly understood for this is what constitutes the special character of the type of suicide just distinguished and justifies the name we have given it. What is there then in individualism that explains this result? . . .

Indeed, a whole range of functions concern only the individual; these are the ones indispensable for physical life. Since they are made for this purpose only, they are perfected by its attainment. In everything concerning them, therefore, man can act reasonably without thought of transcendental purposes. These functions serve by merely serving him. In so far as he has no other needs, he is therefore self-sufficient and can live happily with no other objective than living. This is not the case, however, with the civilized adult. He has many ideas, feelings and practices unrelated to organic needs. The roles of art, morality, religion, political faith, science itself are not to repair organic exhaustion nor to provide sound functioning of the organs. All this supra-physical life is built and expanded not because of the demands of the cosmic environment but because of the demands of the social environment. The influence of society is what has aroused in us the sentiments of sympathy and solidarity drawing us toward others; it is society which, fashioning us in its image, fills us with religious, political and moral beliefs that control our actions. To play our social role we have striven to extend our intelligence and it is still society that has supplied us with tools for this development by transmitting to us its trust fund of knowledge.

Through the very fact that these superior forms of human activity have a collective origin, they have a collective purpose. As they derive from society they have reference to it; rather they are society itself incarnated and individualized in each one of us. But for them to have a raison d'être in our eyes, the purpose they envisage must be one not indifferent to us. We can cling to these forms of human activity only to the degree that we cling to society itself. Contrariwise, in the same measure as we feel detached from society we become detached from that life whose source and aim is society. For what purpose do these rules of morality, these precepts of law binding us to all sorts of sacrifices, these restrictive dogmas exist, if there is no being outside us whom they serve and in whom we participate? . . .

If, in other words, as has often been said, man is double, that is because social man superimposes himself upon physical man. Social man necessarily presupposes a society which he expresses and serves. If this dissolves, if we no longer feel it in existence and action about and above us, whatever is social in us is deprived of all objective foundation. All that remains is an artificial combination of illusory images, a phantasmagoria vanishing at the least reflection; that is, nothing which can be a goal for our action. Yet this social man is the essence of civilized man; he is the masterpiece of existence. Thus we are bereft of reasons for existence; for the only life to which we could cling no longer corresponds to anything actual; the only existence still based upon reality no longer meets our needs. Because we have been initiated into a higher existence, the one which satisfies an animal or a child can satisfy us no more and the other itself fades and leaves us helpless. So there is nothing more for our efforts to lay hold of, and we feel them lose themselves in emptiness. In this sense it is true to say that our activity needs an object transcending it. We do not

need it to maintain ourselves in the illusion of an impossible immortality; it is implicit in our moral constitution and cannot be even partially lost without this losing its raison d'être in the same degree. No proof is needed that in such a state of confusion the least cause of discouragement may easily give birth to desperate resolutions. If life is not worth the trouble of being lived, everything becomes a pretext to rid ourselves of it. . . .

For individuals share too deeply in the life of society for it to be diseased without their suffering infection. What it suffers they necessarily suffer. Because it is the whole, its ills are communicated to its parts. Hence it cannot disintegrate without awareness that the regular conditions of general existence are equally disturbed. Because society is the end on which our better selves depend, it cannot feel us escaping it without a simultaneous realization that our activity is purposeless. Since we are its handiwork, society cannot be conscious of its own decadence without the feeling that henceforth this work is of no value. Thence are formed currents of depression and disillusionment emanating from no particular individual but expressing society's state of disintegration. They reflect the relaxation of social bonds, a sort of collective asthenia, or social malaise, just as individual sadness, when chronic, in its way reflects the poor organic state of the individual. Then metaphysical and religious systems spring up which, by reducing these obscure sentiments to formulae, attempt to prove to men the senselessness of life and that it is self-deception to believe that it has purpose. Then new moralities originate which, by elevating facts to ethics, commend suicide or at least tend in that direction by suggesting a minimal existence. On their appearance they seem to have been created out of whole cloth by their makers who are sometimes blamed for the pessimism of their doctrines. In reality they are an effect rather than a cause; they merely symbolize in abstract language and systematic form the physiological distress of the body social. As these currents are collective, they have, by virtue of their origin, an authority which they impose upon the individual and they drive him more vigorously on the way to which he is already inclined by the state of moral distress directly aroused in him by the disintegration of society. Thus, at the very moment that, with excessive zeal, he frees himself from the social environment, he still submits to its influence. However individualized a man may be, there is always something collective remaining—the very depression and melancholy resulting from this same exaggerated individualism. He effects communion through sadness when he no longer has anything else with which to achieve it.

Hence this type of suicide well deserves the name we have given it. Egoism is not merely a contributing factor in it; it is its generating cause. In this case the bond attaching man to life relaxes because that attaching him to society is itself slack. The incidents of private life which seem the direct inspiration of suicide and are considered its determining causes are in reality only incidental causes. The individual yields to the slightest shock of circumstance because the state of society has made him a ready prey to suicide. . . .

Anomic Suicide

No living being can be happy or even exist unless his needs are sufficiently proportioned to his means. In other words, if his needs require more than can be granted, or even merely something of a different sort, they will be under continual friction and can only function painfully. Movements incapable of production without pain tend not to be reproduced. Unsatisfied tendencies atrophy, and as the impulse to live is merely the result of all the rest, it is bound to weaken as the others relax.

In the animal, at least in a normal condition, this equilibrium is established with automatic spontaneity because the animal depends on purely material conditions. All the organism needs is that the supplies of substance and energy constantly employed in the vital process should be periodically renewed by equivalent quantities; that replacement be equivalent to use. When the void created by existence in its own resources is filled, the animal, satisfied, asks nothing further. Its power of reflection is not sufficiently developed to imagine other ends than those implicit in its physical nature. On the other hand, as the work demanded of each organ itself depends on the general state of vital energy and the needs of organic equilibrium, use is regulated in turn by replacement and the balance is automatic. The limits of one are those of the other; both are fundamental to the constitution of the existence in question, which cannot exceed them.

This is not the case with man, because most of his needs are not dependent on his body or not to the same degree. Strictly speaking, we may consider that the quantity of material supplies necessary to the physical maintenance of a human life is subject to computation, though this be less exact than in the preceding case and a wider margin left for the free combinations of the will; for beyond the indispensable minimum which satisfies nature when instinctive, a more awakened reflection suggests better conditions, seemingly desirable ends craving fulfillment. Such appetites, however, admittedly sooner or later reach a limit which they cannot pass. But how determine the quantity of well-being, comfort or luxury legitimately to be craved by a human being? Nothing appears in man's organic nor in his psychological constitution which sets a limit to such tendencies. The functioning of individual life does not require them to cease at one point rather than at another; the proof being that they have constantly increased since the beginnings of history, receiving more and more complete satisfaction, yet with no weakening of average health. Above all, how establish their proper variation with different conditions of life, occupations, relative importance of services, etc.?

In no society are they equally satisfied in the different stages of the social hierarchy. Yet human nature is substantially the same among all men, in its essential qualities. It is not human nature which can assign the variable limits necessary to our needs. They are thus unlimited so far as they depend on the individual alone. Irrespective of any external regulatory force, our capacity for feeling is in itself an insatiable and bottomless abyss.

But if nothing external can restrain this capacity, it can only be a source of torment to itself. Unlimited desires are insatiable by definition and insatiability is rightly considered a sign of morbidity. Being unlimited, they constantly and infinitely surpass the means at their command; they cannot be quenched. Inextinguishable thirst is constantly renewed torture. It has been claimed, indeed, that human activity naturally aspires beyond assignable limits and sets itself unattainable goals. But how can such an undetermined state be any more reconciled with the conditions of mental life than with the demands of physical life? All man's pleasure in acting, moving and exerting himself implies the sense that his efforts are not in vain and that by walking he has advanced. However, one does not advance when one walks toward no goal, or—which is the same thing—when his goal is infinity. Since the distance between us and it is always the same, whatever road we take, we might as well have made the motions without progress from the spot. Even our glances behind and our feeling of pride at the distance covered can cause only deceptive satisfaction, since the remaining distance is not proportionately reduced. To pursue a goal which is by definition unattainable is to condemn oneself to a state of perpetual unhappiness. . . .

To achieve any other result, the passions first must be limited. Only then can they be harmonized with the faculties and satisfied. But since the individual has no way of limiting them, this must be done by some force exterior to him. A regulative force must play the same role for moral needs which the organism plays for physical needs. This means that the force can only be moral. The awakening of conscience interrupted the state of equilibrium of the animal's dormant existence; only conscience, therefore, can furnish the means to re-establish it. Physical restraint would be ineffective; hearts cannot be touched by physio-chemical forces. So far as the appetites are not automatically restrained by physiological mechanisms, they can be halted only by a limit that they recognize as just. Men would never consent to restrict their desires if they felt justified in passing the assigned limit. But, for reasons given above, they cannot assign themselves this law of justice. So they must receive it from an authority which they respect, to which they yield spontaneously. Either directly and as a whole, or through the agency of one of its organs, society alone can play this moderating role; for it is the only moral power superior to the individual, the authority of which he accepts. It alone has the power necessary to stipulate law and to set the point beyond which the passions must not go. Finally, it alone can estimate the reward to be prospectively offered to every class of human functionary, in the name of the common interest.

As a matter of fact, at every moment of history there is a dim perception, in the moral consciousness of societies, of the respective value of different social services, the relative reward due to each, and the consequent degree of comfort appropriate on the average to workers in each occupation. The different functions are graded in public opinion and a certain coefficient of well-being assigned to each, according to its place in the hierarchy. According to accepted ideas, for example, a certain way of living is considered the upper limit to which a workman may aspire in his efforts to improve his existence, and there is another limit below which he is not willingly permitted to fall unless he has seriously demeaned himself. Both differ for city and country workers, for the domestic servant and the day-laborer, for the business clerk and the official, etc. Likewise the man of wealth is reproved if he lives the life of a poor man, but also if he seeks the refinements of luxury overmuch. Economists may protest in vain; public feeling will always be scandalized if an individual spends too much wealth for wholly superfluous use, and it even seems that this severity relaxes only in times of moral disturbance. A genuine regimen exists, therefore, although not always legally formulated, which fixes with relative precision the maximum degree of ease of living to which each social class may legitimately aspire. However, there is nothing immutable about such a scale. It changes with the increase or decrease of collective revenue and the changes occurring in the moral ideas of society. Thus what appears luxury to one period no longer does so to another; and the well-being which for long periods was granted to a class only by exception and supererogation, finally appears strictly necessary and equitable.

Under this pressure, each in his sphere vaguely realizes the extreme limit set to his ambitions and aspires to nothing beyond. At least if he respects regulations and is docile to collective authority, that is, has a wholesome moral constitution, he feels that it is not well to ask more. Thus, an end and goal are set to the passions. Truly, there is nothing rigid nor absolute about such determination. The economic ideal assigned each class of citizens is itself confined to certain limits, within which the desires have free range. But it is not infinite. This relative limitation and the moderation it involves, make men contented with their lot while stimulating them moderately to improve it; and this average contentment causes the feeling of calm, active happiness, the pleasure in existing and living which characterizes health for societies as well as for individuals. Each person is then at least, generally speaking, in harmony with his condition, and desires only what he may legitimately hope for as the normal reward of his activity. Besides, this does not

condemn man to a sort of immobility. He may seek to give beauty to his life; but his attempts in this direction may fail without causing him to despair. For, loving what he has and not fixing his desire solely on what he lacks, his wishes and hopes may fail of what he has happened to aspire to, without his being wholly destitute. He has the essentials. The equilibrium of his happiness is secure because it is defined, and a few mishaps cannot disconcert him.

But it would be of little use for everyone to recognize the justice of the hierarchy of functions established by public opinion, if he did not also consider the distribution of these functions just. The workman is not in harmony with his social position if he is not convinced that he has his deserts. If he feels justified in occupying another, what he has would not satisfy him. So it is not enough for the average level of needs for each social condition to be regulated by public opinion, but another, more precise rule, must fix the way in which these conditions are open to individuals. There is no society in which such regulation does not exist. It varies with times and places. Once it regarded birth as the almost exclusive principle of social classification; today it recognizes no other inherent inequality than hereditary fortune and merit. But in all these various forms its object is unchanged. It is also only possible, everywhere, as a restriction upon individuals imposed by superior authority, that is, by collective authority. For it can be established only by requiring of one or another group of men, usually of all, sacrifices and concessions in the name of the public interest.

Some, to be sure, have thought that this moral pressure would become unnecessary if men's economic circumstances were only no longer determined by heredity. If inheritance were abolished, the argument runs, if everyone began life with equal resources and if the competitive struggle were fought out on a basis of perfect equality, no one could think its results unjust. Each would instinctively feel that things are as they should be.

Truly, the nearer this ideal equality were approached, the less social restraint will be necessary. But it is only a matter of degree. One sort of heredity will always exist, that of natural talent. Intelligence, taste, scientific, artistic, literary or industrial ability, courage and manual dexterity are gifts received by each of us at birth, as the heir to wealth receives his capital or as the nobleman formerly received his title and function. A moral discipline will therefore still be required to make those less favored by nature accept the lesser advantages which they owe to the chance of birth. Shall it be demanded that all have an equal share and that no advantage be given those more useful and deserving? But then there would have to be a discipline far stronger to make these accept a treatment merely equal to that of the mediocre and incapable.

But like the one first mentioned, this discipline can be useful only if considered just by the peoples subject to it. When it is maintained only by custom and force, peace and harmony are illusory; the spirit of unrest and discontent are latent; appetites superficially restrained are ready to revolt. This happened in Rome and Greece when the faiths underlying the old organization of the patricians and plebeians were shaken, and in our modern societies when aristocratic prejudices began to lose their old ascendancy. But this state of upheaval is exceptional; it occurs only when society is passing through some abnormal crisis. In normal conditions the collective order is regarded as just by the great majority of persons. Therefore, when we say that an authority is necessary to impose this order on individuals, we certainly do not mean that violence is the only means of establishing it. Since this regulation is meant to restrain individual passions, it must come from a power which dominates individuals; but this power must also be obeyed through respect, not fear.

It is not true, then, that human activity can be released from all restraint. Nothing in the world can enjoy such a privilege. All existence being a part of the universe is relative to the remainder; its nature and method of manifestation accordingly depend not only on itself but on other beings, who consequently restrain and regulate it. Here there are only differences of degree and form between the mineral realm and the thinking person. Man's characteristic privilege is that the bond he accepts is not physical but moral; that is, social. He is governed not by a material environment brutally imposed on him, but by a conscience superior to his own, the superiority of which he feels. Because the greater, better part of his existence transcends the body, he escapes the body's yoke, but is subject to that of society.

But when society is disturbed by some painful crisis or by beneficent but abrupt transitions, it is momentarily incapable of exercising this influence; thence come the sudden rises in the curve of suicides which we have pointed out above. . . .

Then, truly, as the conditions of life are changed, the standard according to which needs were regulated can no longer remain the same; for it varies with social resources, since it largely determines the share of each class of producers. The scale is upset; but a new scale cannot be immediately improvised. Time is required for the public conscience to reclassify men and things. So long as the social forces thus freed have not regained equilibrium, their respective values are unknown and so all regulation is lacking for a time. The limits are unknown between the possible and the impossible, what is just and what is unjust, legitimate claims and hopes and those which are immoderate. Consequently, there is no restraint upon aspirations. If the disturbance is profound, it affects even the principles controlling the distribution of men among various occupations. Since the relations between various parts of society are necessarily modified, the ideas expressing these relations must change. Some particular class especially favored by the crisis is no longer resigned to its former lot, and, on the other hand, the example of its greater good fortune arouses all sorts of jealousy below and about it. Appetites, not being controlled by a public opinion become disoriented, no longer recognize the limits proper to them. Besides, they are at the same time seized by a sort of natural erethism simply by the greater intensity of public life. With increased prosperity desires increase. At the very moment when traditional rules have lost their authority, the richer prize offered these appetites stimulates them and makes them more exigent and impatient of control. The state of de-regulation or anomie is thus further heightened by passions being less disciplined, precisely when they need more disciplining.

But then their very demands make fulfillment impossible. Overweening ambition always exceeds the results obtained, great as they may be, since there is no warning to pause here. Nothing gives satisfaction and all this agitation is uninterruptedly maintained without appeasement. Above all, since this race for an unattainable goal can give no other pleasure but that of the race itself, if it is one, once it is interrupted the participants are left empty-handed. At the same time the struggle grows more violent and painful, both from being less controlled and because competition is greater. All classes contend among themselves because no established classification any longer exists. Effort grows, just when it becomes less productive. How could the desire to live not be weakened under such conditions?

This explanation is confirmed by the remarkable immunity of poor countries. Poverty protects against suicide because it is a restraint in itself. No matter how one acts, desires have to depend upon resources to some extent; actual possessions are partly the criterion of those aspired to. So the less one has the less he is tempted to extend the range of his needs indefinitely. Lack of power, compelling moderation, accustoms men to it, while nothing excites envy if no one has superfluity. Wealth, on the other hand, by the power it bestows, deceives us into believing that we depend on ourselves only.

Reducing the resistance we encounter from objects, it suggests the possibility of unlimited success against them. The less limited one feels, the more intolerable all limitation appears. . . .

If anomy never appeared except, as in the above instances, in intermittent spurts and acute crisis, it might cause the social suicide-rate to vary from time to time, but it would not be a regular, constant factor. In one sphere of social life, however—the sphere of trade and industry—it is actually in a chronic state.

For a whole century, economic progress has mainly consisted in freeing industrial relations from all regulation. . . .

Ultimately, this liberation of desires has been made worse by the very development of industry and the almost infinite extension of the market. So long as the producer could gain his profits only in his immediate neighborhood, the restricted amount of possible gain could not much overexcite ambition. Now that he may assume to have almost the entire world as his customer, how could passions accept their former confinement in the face of such limitless prospects?

Such is the source of the excitement predominating in this part of society, and which has thence extended to the other parts. There, the state of crisis and anomy is constant and, so to speak, normal. From top to bottom of the ladder, greed is aroused without knowing where to find ultimate foothold. Nothing can calm it, since its goal is far beyond all it can attain. Reality seems valueless by comparison with the dreams of fevered imaginations; reality is therefore abandoned, but so too is possibility abandoned when it in turn becomes reality. A thirst arises for novelties, unfamiliar pleasures, nameless sensations, all of which lose their savor once known. Henceforth one has no strength to endure the least reverse. The whole fever subsides and the sterility of all the tumult is apparent, and it is seen that all these new sensations in their infinite quantity cannot form a solid foundation of happiness to support one during days of trial. The wise man, knowing how to enjoy achieved results without having constantly to replace them with others, finds in them an attachment to life in the hour of difficulty. But the man who has always pinned all his hopes on the future and lived with his eyes fixed upon it, has nothing in the past as a comfort against the present's afflictions, for the past was nothing to him but a series of hastily experienced stages. What blinded him to himself was his expectation always to find further on the happiness he had so far missed. Now he is stopped in his tracks; from now on nothing remains behind or ahead of him to fix his gaze upon. Weariness alone, moreover, is enough to bring disillusionment, for he cannot in the end escape the futility of an endless pursuit.

We may even wonder if this moral state is not principally what makes economic catastrophes of our day so fertile in suicides. In societies where a man is subjected to a healthy discipline, he submits more readily to the blows of chance. The necessary effort for sustaining a little more discomfort costs him relatively little, since he is used to discomfort and constraint. But when every constraint is hateful in itself, how can closer constraint not seem intolerable? There is no tendency to resignation in the feverish impatience of men's lives. When there is no other aim but to outstrip constantly the point arrived at, how painful to be thrown back! Now this very lack of organization characterizing our economic condition throws the door wide to every sort of adventure. Since imagination is hungry for novelty, and ungoverned, it gropes at random. Setbacks necessarily increase with risks and thus crises multiply, just when they are becoming more destructive.

Yet these dispositions are so inbred that society has grown to accept them and is accustomed to think them normal. It is everlastingly repeated that it is man's nature to be eternally dissatisfied, constantly to advance, without relief or rest, toward an indefinite goal. The longing for infinity is daily represented as a mark of moral distinction, whereas it can only appear within unregulated consciences which elevate to a rule the lack of rule from which they suffer. The doctrine of the most ruthless and swift progress has become an article of faith. But other theories appear parallel with those praising the advantages of instability, which, generalizing the situation that gives them birth, declare life evil, claim that it is richer in grief than in pleasure and that it attracts men only by false claims. Since this disorder is greatest in the economic world, it has most victims there. . . .

Anomy, therefore, is a regular and specific factor in suicide in our modern societies; one of the springs from which the annual contingent feeds. So we have here a new type to distinguish from the others. It differs from them in its dependence, not on the way in which individuals are attached to society, but on how it regulates them. Egoistic suicide results from man's no longer finding a basis for existence in life; altruistic suicide, because this basis for existence appears to man situated beyond life itself. The third sort of suicide, the existence of which has just been shown, results from man's activity's lacking regulation and his consequent sufferings. By virtue of its origin we shall assign this last variety the name of *anomic suicide.*

Certainly, this and egoistic suicide have kindred ties. Both spring from society's insufficient presence in individuals. But the sphere of its absence is not the same in both cases. In egoistic suicide it is deficient in truly collective activity, thus depriving the latter of object and meaning. In anomic suicide, society's influence is lacking in the basically individual passions, thus leaving them without a check-rein. In spite of their relationship, therefore, the two types are independent of each other. We may offer society everything social in us, and still be unable to control our desires; one may live in an anomic state without being egoistic, and vice versa. These two sorts of suicide therefore do not draw their chief recruits from the same social environments; one has its principal field among intellectual careers, the world of thought—the other, the industrial or commercial world.

ÉMILE DURKHEIM: THE ELEMENTARY FORMS OF RELIGIOUS LIFE

The study which we are undertaking is therefore a way of taking up again, *but under new conditions,* the old problem of the origin of religion. To be sure, if by origin we are to understand the very first beginning, the question has nothing scientific about it, and should be resolutely discarded. There was no given moment when religion began to exist, and there is consequently no need of finding a means of transporting ourselves thither in thought. Like every human institution, religion did not commence anywhere. Therefore, all speculations of this sort are justly discredited; they can only consist in subjective and arbitrary constructions which are subject to no sort of control. But the problem which we raise is quite another one. What we want to do is to find a means of discerning the ever-present causes upon which the most essential forms of religious thought and practice depend.

* * *

For a long time it has been known that the first systems of representations with which men have pictured to themselves the world and themselves were of religious origin. There is no religion that is not a cosmology at the same time that it is a speculation upon divine things. If philosophy and the sciences were born of religion, it is because religion began by taking the place of the sciences and philosophy. But it has been less frequently noticed that religion has not confined itself to enriching the human intellect, formed beforehand, with a certain number of ideas; it has contributed to forming the intellect itself. Men owe to it not only a good part of the substance of their knowledge, but also the form in which this knowledge has been elaborated.

At the roots of all our judgments there are a certain number of essential ideas which dominate all our intellectual life; they are what philosophers since Aristotle have called the categories of the understanding: ideas of time, space, class, number, cause, substance, personality, etc. They correspond to the most universal properties of things. They are like the solid frame which encloses all thought; this does not seem to be able to liberate itself from them without destroying itself, for it seems that we cannot think of objects that are not in time and space, which have no number, etc. Other ideas are contingent and unsteady; we can conceive of their being unknown to a man, a society or an epoch; but these others appear to be nearly inseparable from the normal working of the intellect. They are like the framework of the intelligence. Now when primitive religious beliefs are systematically analyzed, the principal categories are naturally found. They are born in religion and of religion; they are a product of religious thought. This is a statement that we are going to have occasion to make many times in the course of this work.

This remark has some interest of itself already; but here is what gives it its real importance.

The general conclusion of the book which the reader has before him is that religion is something eminently social. Religious representations are collective representations which express collective realities; the rites are a manner of acting which take rise in the midst of the assembled groups and which are destined to excite, maintain or recreate certain mental states in these groups. So if the categories are of religious origin, they ought to participate in this nature common to all religious facts; they too should be social affairs and the product of collective thought. At least—for in the actual condition of our knowledge of these matters, one

Reprinted from Émile Durkheim, *The Elementary Forms of Religious Life* (New York: The Free Press).

should be careful to avoid all radical and exclusive statements—it is allowable to suppose that they are rich in social elements.

* * *

All known religious beliefs, whether simple or complex, present one common characteristic: they presuppose a classification of all the things, real and ideal, of which men think, into two classes or opposed groups, generally designated by two distinct terms which are translated well enough by the words *profane* and *sacred (profane, sacré)*. This division of the world into two domains, the one containing all that is sacred, the other all that is profane, is the distinctive trait of religious thought; the beliefs, myths, dogmas and legends are either representations or systems of representations which express the nature of sacred things, the virtues and powers which are attributed to them, or their relations with each other and with profane things.

* * *

The opposition of these two classes manifests itself outwardly with a visible sign by which we can easily recognize this very special classification, wherever it exists. Since the idea of the sacred is always and everywhere separated from the idea of the profane in the thought of men, and since we picture a sort of logical chasm between the two, the mind irresistibly refuses to allow the two corresponding things to be confounded, or even to be merely put in contact with each other; for such a promiscuity, or even too direct a contiguity, would contradict too violently the dissociation of these ideas in the mind. The sacred thing is *par excellence* that which the profane should not touch, and cannot touch with impunity. To be sure, this interdiction cannot go so far as to make all communication between the two worlds impossible; for if the profane could in no way enter into relations with the sacred, this latter could be good for nothing. But, in addition to the fact that this establishment of relations is always a delicate operation in itself, demanding great precautions and a more or less complicated initiation, it is

quite impossible, unless the profane is to lose its specific characteristics and become sacred after a fashion and to a certain degree itself. The two classes cannot even approach each other and keep their own nature at the same time.

Thus we arrive at the first criterium of religious beliefs. Undoubtedly there are secondary species within these two fundamental classes which, in their turn, are more or less incompatible with each other. But the real characteristic of religious phenomena is that they always suppose a bipartite division of the whole universe, known and knowable, into two classes which embrace all that exists, but which radically exclude each other. Sacred things are those which the interdictions protect and isolate; profane things, those to which these interdictions are applied and which must remain at a distance from the first. Religious beliefs are the representations which express the nature of sacred things and the relations which they sustain, either with each other or with profane things. Finally, rites are the rules of conduct which prescribe how a man should comport himself in the presence of these sacred objects.

* * *

The really religious beliefs are always common to a determined group, which makes profession of adhering to them and of practicing the rites connected with them. They are not merely received individually by all the members of this group; they are something belonging to the group, and they make its unity. The individuals which compose it feel themselves united to each other by the simple fact that they have a common faith. A society whose members are united by the fact that they think in the same way in regard to the sacred world and its relations with the profane world, and by the fact that they translate these common ideas into common practices, is what is called a Church. In all history, we do not find a single religion without a Church. Sometimes the Church is strictly national, sometimes it passes the frontiers; sometimes it embraces an entire people (Rome,

Athens, the Hebrews), sometimes it embraces only a part of them (the Christian societies since the advent of Protestantism); sometimes it is directed by a corps of priests, sometimes it is almost completely devoid of any official directing body. But wherever we observe the religious life, we find that it has a definite group as its foundation. Even the so-called private cults, such as the domestic cult or the cult of a corporation, satisfy this condition; for they are always celebrated by a group, the family or the corporation. Moreover, even these particular religions are ordinarily only special forms of a more general religion which embraces all; these restricted Churches are in reality only chapels of a vaster Church which, by reason of this very extent, merits this name still more.

* * *

Thus we arrive at the following definition: *A religion is a unified system of beliefs and practices relative to sacred things, that is to say, things set apart and forbidden—beliefs and practices, which unite into one single moral community called a Church, all those who adhere to them.* The second element which thus finds a place in our definition is no less essential than the first; for by showing that the idea of religion is inseparable from that of the Church, it makes it clear that religion should be an eminently collective thing.

* * *

The proposition established in the preceding chapter determines the terms in which the problem of the origins of totemism should be posed. Since totemism is everywhere dominated by the idea of a quasi-divine principle, imminent in certain categories of men and things and thought of under the form of an animal or vegetable, the explanation of this religion is essentially the explanation of this belief; to arrive at this, we must seek to learn how men have been led to construct this idea and out of what materials they have constructed it.

It is obviously not out of the sensations which the things serving as totems are able to arouse in the mind; we have shown that these things are frequently insignificant. The lizard, the caterpillar, the rat, the ant, the frog, the turkey, the bream-fish, the plum-tree, the cockatoo, etc., to cite only those names which appear frequently in the lists of Australian totems, are not of a nature to produce upon men these great and strong impressions which in a way resemble religious emotions and which impress a sacred character upon the objects they create. It is true that this is not the case with the stars and the great atmospheric phenomena, which have, on the contrary, all that is necessary to strike the imagination forcibly; but as a matter of fact, these serve only very exceptionally as totems. It is even probable that they were very slow in taking this office. So it is not the intrinsic nature of the thing whose name the clan bears that marked it out to become the object of a cult. Also, if the sentiments which it inspired were really the determining cause of the totemic rites and beliefs, it would be the pre-eminently sacred thing; the animals or plants employed as totems would play an eminent part in the religious life. But we know that the centre of the cult is actually elsewhere. It is the figurative representations of this plant or animal and the totemic emblems and symbols of every sort, which have the greatest sanctity; so it is in them that is found the source of that religious nature, of which the real objects represented by these emblems receive only a reflection.

Thus the totem is before all a symbol, a material expression of something else. But of what?

From the analysis to which we have been giving our attention, it is evident that it expresses and symbolizes two different sorts of things. In the first place, it is the outward and visible form of what we have called the totemic principle or god. But it is also the symbol of the determined society called the clan. It is its flag; it is the sign by which each clan distinguishes itself from the others, the visible mark of its personality, a mark borne by everything which is a part of the clan under any title whatsoever, men, beasts or things. So if it is at once the symbol of the god and of the society, is that not because the god and the society are only one? How could the emblem of the group have been able to become the figure of this quasi-divinity, if the group and the divinity were two distinct realities? The god of the clan, the totemic principle, can therefore be nothing else than the clan itself, personified and represented to the imagination under the visible form of the animal or vegetable which serves as totem.

But how has this apotheosis been possible, and how did it happen to take place in this fashion?

In a general way, it is unquestionable that a society has all that is necessary to arouse the sensation of the divine in minds, merely by the power that it has over them; for to its members it is what a god is to his worshippers. In fact, a god is, first of all, a being whom men think of as superior to themselves, and upon whom they feel that they depend. Whether it be a conscious personality, such as Zeus or Jahveh, or merely abstract forces such as those in play in totemism, the worshipper, in the one case as in the other, believes himself held to certain manners of acting which are imposed upon him by the nature of the sacred principle with which he feels that he is in communion. Now society also gives us the sensation of a perpetual dependence. Since it has a nature which is peculiar to itself and different from our individual nature, it pursues ends which are likewise special to it; but, as it cannot attain them except through our intermediacy, it imperiously demands our aid. It requires that, forgetful of our own interest, we make ourselves its servitors, and it submits us to every sort of inconvenience, privation and sacrifice, without which social life would be impossible. It is because of this that at every instant we are obliged to submit ourselves to rules of conduct and of thought which we have neither made nor desired, and which are sometimes even contrary to our most fundamental inclinations and instincts.

Even if society were unable to obtain these concessions and sacrifices from us except by a material constraint, it might awaken in us only the idea of a physical force to which we must give way of necessity, instead of that of a moral power such as religions adore. But as a matter of fact, the empire which it holds over consciences is due much less to the physical supremacy of which it has the privilege than to the moral authority with which it is invested. If we yield to its orders, it is not merely because it is strong enough to triumph over our resistance; it is primarily because it is the object of a venerable respect. . . .

Since it is in spiritual ways that social pressure exercises itself, it could not fail to give men the idea that outside themselves there exist one or several powers, both moral and, at the same time, efficacious, upon which they depend. They must think of these powers, at least in part, as outside themselves, for these address them in a tone of command and sometimes even order them to do violence to their most natural inclinations. It is undoubtedly true that if they were able to see that these influences which they feel emanate from society, then the mythological system of interpretations would never be born. But social action follows ways that are too circuitous and obscure, and employs physical mechanisms that are too complex to allow the ordinary observer to see when it comes. As long as scientific analysis does not come to teach it to them, men know well that they are acted upon, but they do not know by whom. So they must invent by themselves the idea of these powers with which they feel themselves in connection, and from that, we are able to catch a glimpse of the way by which they were led to represent them under forms that are really foreign to their nature and to transfigure them by thought.

But a god is not merely an authority upon whom we depend; it is a force upon which our strength relies. The man who has obeyed his god and who for this reason, believes the god is with him, approaches the world with confidence and with the feeling of an increased energy. Likewise, social action does not confine itself to demanding sacrifices, privations and efforts from us. For the collective force is not entirely outside of us; it does not act upon us wholly from without; but rather, since society cannot exist except in and through individual consciousness, this force must also penetrate us and organize itself within us; it thus becomes an integral part of our being and by that very fact this is elevated and magnified.

There are occasions when this strengthening and vivifying action of society is especially apparent. In the midst of an assembly animated by a common passion, we become susceptible of acts and sentiments of which we are incapable when reduced to our own forces; and when the assembly is dissolved and when, finding ourselves alone again, we fall back to our ordinary level, we are then able to measure the height to which we have been raised above ourselves. History abounds in examples of this sort. It is enough to think of the night of the Fourth of August, 1789, when an assembly was suddenly led to an act of sacrifice and abnegation which each of its members had refused the day before, and at which they were all surprised the day after. This is why all parties political, economic or confessional, are careful to have periodical reunions where their members may revivify their common faith by manifesting it in common. To strengthen those sentiments which, if left to themselves, would soon weaken, it is sufficient to bring those who hold them together and to put them into closer and more active relations with one another. . . .

Besides these passing and intermittent states, there are other more durable ones, where this strengthening influence of society makes itself felt with greater consequences and frequently even with greater brilliancy. There are periods in history when, under the influence of some great collective shock, social interactions have become much more frequent and active. Men look for each other and assemble together more than ever. That general effervescence results which is characteristic of revolutionary or creative epochs. Now this greater activity results in a general stimulation of individual forces. Men see more and differently now than in normal times. Changes are not merely of shades and degrees; men become different. The passions moving them are of such an intensity that they cannot be satisfied except by violent and unrestrained actions, actions of superhuman heroism or of bloody barbarism.

* * *

In addition to men, society also consecrates things, especially ideas. If a belief is unanimously shared by a people, then, for the reason which we pointed out above, it is forbidden to touch it, that is to say, to deny it or to contest it. Now the prohibition of criticism is an interdiction like the others and proves the presence of something sacred. Even today, howsoever great may be the liberty which we accord to others, a man who should totally deny progress or ridicule the human ideal to which modern societies are attached, would produce the effect of a sacrilege. There is at least one principle which those the most devoted to the free examination of everything tend to place above discussion and to regard as untouchable, that is to say, as sacred: this is the very principle of free examination.

* * *

This aptitude of society for setting itself up as a god or for creating gods was never more apparent than during the first years of the French Revolution. At this time, in fact, under the influence of the general enthusiasm, things purely laical by nature were transformed by public opinion into sacred things: these were the Fatherland, Liberty, Reason.

* * *

We are now able to understand how the totemic principle, and in general, every religious force, comes to be outside of the object in which it resides. It is because the idea of it is in no way made up of the impressions directly produced by this thing upon our senses or minds. Religious force is only the sentiment inspired by the group in its members, but projected outside of the consciousnesses that experience them, and objectified. To be objectified, they are fixed upon some object which thus becomes sacred; but any object might fulfill this function. In principle, there are none whose nature predestines them to it to the exclusion of all others; but also there are none that are necessarily impossible. Everything depends upon the circumstances which lead the sentiment creating religious ideas to establish itself here or there, upon this point or upon that one. Therefore, the sacred character assumed by an object is not implied in the intrinsic properties of this latter: *it is added to them*. The world of religious things is not one particular aspect of empirical nature; *it is superimposed upon it*.

* * *

In addition to all the reasons which have been given to justify this conception, a final one may be added here, which is the result of our whole work. As we have progressed, we have established the fact that the fundamental categories of thought, and consequently of science, are of religious origin. We have seen that the same is true for magic and consequently for the different processes which have issued from it. On the other hand, it has long been known that up until a relatively advanced moment of evolution, moral and legal rules have been indistinguishable from ritual prescriptions. In summing up, then, it may be said that nearly all the great social institutions have been born in religion. Now in order that these principal aspects of the collective life may have commenced by being only varied aspects of the religious life, it is obviously necessary that the religious life be the eminent form and, as it were, the concentrated expression of the whole collective life. If religion had given birth to all that is essential in society, it is because the idea of society is the soul of religion.

Religious forces are therefore human forces, moral forces.

* * *

But, it is said, what society is it that has thus made the basis of religion? Is it the real society,

such as it is and acts before our very eyes, with the legal and moral organization which it has laboriously fashioned during the course of history? This is full of defects and imperfections. In it, evil goes beside the good, injustice often reigns supreme, and the truth is often obscured by error. How could anything so crudely organized inspire the sentiments of love, the ardent enthusiasm and the spirit of abnegation which all religions claim of their followers? These perfect beings which are gods could not have taken their traits from so mediocre, and sometimes even so base a reality.

But, on the other hand, does someone think of a perfect society, where justice and truth would be sovereign, and from which evil in all its forms would be banished for ever? No one would deny that this is in close relations with the religious sentiment; for, they would say, it is towards the realization of this that all religions strive. But that society is not an empirical fact, definite and observable; it is a fancy, a dream with which men have lightened their sufferings, but in which they have never really lived. It is merely an idea which comes to express our more or less obscure aspirations towards the good, the beautiful and the ideal. Now these aspirations have their roots in us; they come from the very depths of our being; then there is nothing outside of us which can account for them. Moreover, they are already religious in themselves; thus it would seem that the ideal society presupposes religion, far from being able to explain it.

But, in the first place, things are arbitrarily simplified when religion is seen only on its idealistic side: in its way, it is realistic. There is no physical or moral ugliness, there are no vices or evils which do not have a special divinity. There are gods of theft and trickery, of lust and war, of sickness and of death. Christianity itself, howsoever high the idea which it has made of the divinity may be, has been obliged to give the spirit of evil a place in its mythology. Satan is an essential piece of the Christian system; even if he is an impure being, he is not a profane one. The anti-god is a god, inferior and subordinated, it is true, but nevertheless endowed with extended powers; he is even the object of rites, at least of negative ones. Thus religion, far from ignoring the real society and making abstraction of it, is in its image; it reflects all its aspects, even the most vulgar and the most repulsive. All is to be found there, and if in the majority of cases we see the good victorious over evil, life over death, the powers of light over the powers of darkness, it is because reality is not otherwise. If the relation between these two contrary forces were reversed, life would be impossible; but, as a matter of fact, it maintains itself and even tends to develop. . . .

The explanation of religion which we have proposed has precisely this advantage, that it gives an answer to this question. For our definition of the sacred is that it is something added to and above the real: now the ideal answers to this same definition; we cannot explain one without explaining the other. In fact, we have seen that if collective life awakens religious thought on reaching a certain degree of intensity, it is because it brings about a state of effervescence which changes the conditions of psychic activity. Vital energies are over-excited, passions more active, sensations stronger; there are even some which are produced only at this moment. A man does not recognize himself; he feels himself transformed and consequently he transforms the environment which surrounds him. In order to account for the very particular impressions which he receives, he attributes to the things with which he is in most direct contact properties which they have not, exceptional powers and virtues which the objects of everyday experience do not possess. In a word, above the real world where his profane life passes he has placed another which, in one sense, does not exist except in thought, but to which he attributes a higher sort of dignity than to the first. Thus, from a double point of view it is an ideal world. . . .

A society can neither create itself or recreate itself without at the same time creating an ideal. This creation is not a sort of work of supererogation for it, by which it would complete itself, being already formed; it is the act by which it is periodically made and remade. Therefore when some oppose the ideal society to the real society, like two antagonists which would lead us in opposite directions, they materialize and oppose abstractions. The ideal society is not outside of the real society; it is a part of it. Far from being divided between them as between two poles which mutually repel each other, we cannot hold to one without holding to the other. For a society is not made up merely of the mass of individuals who compose it, the ground which they occupy, the things which they use and the movements which they perform, but above all is the idea which it forms of itself. It is undoubtedly true that it hesitates over the manner in which it ought to conceive itself; it feels itself drawn in divergent directions. But these conflicts which break forth are not between the ideal and reality, but between two different ideals, that of yesterday and that of today, that which has the authority of tradition and that which has the hope of the future. There is surely a place for investigating whence these ideals evolve; but whatever solution may be given to this problem, it still remains that all passes in the world of the ideal.

Thus the collective ideal which religion expresses is far from being due to a vague innate power of the individual, but it is rather at the school of collective life that the individual has learned to idealize. It is in assimilating the ideals elaborated by society that he has become capable of conceiving the ideal. It is society which, by leading him within its sphere of action, has made him acquire the need of raising himself above the world of experience and has at the same time furnished him with the means of conceiving another. For society has constructed this new world in constructing itself, since it is society which this expresses.

Thus both with the individual and in the group, the faculty of idealizing has nothing mysterious about it. It is not a sort of luxury which a man could get along without, but a condition of his very existence. He could not be a social being, that is to say, he could not be a man, if he had not acquired it.

* * *

Thus there is something eternal in religion which is destined to survive all the particular symbols in which religious thought has successively enveloped itself. There can be no society which does not feel the need of upholding and reaffirming at regular intervals the collective sentiments and the collective ideas which make its unity and its personality. Now this moral remaking cannot be achieved except by the means of reunions, assemblies and meetings where the individuals, being closely united to one another, reaffirm in common their common sentiments; hence come ceremonies which do not differ from regular religious ceremonies, either in their object, the results which they produce, or the processes employed to attain these results. What essential difference is there between an assembly of Christians celebrating the principal dates of the life of Christ, or of Jews remembering the exodus from Egypt or the promulgation of the decalogue, and a reunion of citizens commemorating the promulgation of a new moral or legal system or some great event in the national life?

If we find a little difficulty today in imagining what these feasts and ceremonies of the future could consist in, it is because we are going through a stage of transition and moral mediocrity. The great things of the past which filled our fathers with enthusiasm do not excite the same ardour in us, either because they have come into common usage to such an extent that we are unconscious of them, or else because they no longer answer to our actual aspirations; but as yet there is nothing to replace them. We can no longer impassionate ourselves for the principles in the name of which Christianity recommended to masters that they treat their slaves humanely, and, on the other hand, the idea which it has formed of human equality and fraternity seems to us today to leave too large a place for unjust inequalities. Its pity for the outcast seems to us too Platonic; we desire another which would be more practicable; but as yet we cannot clearly see what it should be nor how it could be realized in facts. In a word, the old gods are growing old or already dead, and others are not yet born. . . . But this state of incertitude and confused agitation cannot last for ever. A day will come when our societies will know again those hours of creative effervescence, in the course of which new ideas arise and new formulae are found which serve for a while as a guide to humanity; and when these hours shall have been passed through once, men will spontaneously feel the need of reliving them from time to time in thought, that is to say, of keeping alive their memory by means of celebrations which regularly reproduce their fruits. . . .

* * *

Thus sociology appears destined to open a new way to the science of man. Up to the present, thinkers were placed before this double alternative: either explain the superior and specific faculties of men by connecting them to the inferior forms of his being, the reason to the senses, or the mind to matter, which is equivalent to denying their uniqueness; or else attach them to some super-experimental reality which was postulated, but whose existence could be established by no observation. What put them in this difficulty was the fact that the individual passed as being the *finis naturæ*—the ultimate creation of nature; it seemed that there was nothing beyond him, or at least nothing that science could touch. But from the moment when it is recognized that above the individual there is society, and that this is not a nominal being created by reason, but a system of active forces, a new manner of explaining men becomes possible. To conserve his distinctive traits it is no longer necessary to put them outside experience. At least, before going to this last extremity, it would be well to see if that which surpasses the individual, though it is within him, does not come from this super-individual reality which we experience in society. To be sure, it cannot be said at present to what point these explanations may be able to reach, and whether or not they are of a nature to resolve all the problems. But it is equally impossible to mark in advance a limit beyond which they cannot go. What must be done is to try the hypothesis and submit it as methodically as possible to the control of facts. This is what we have tried to do.

ÉMILE DURKHEIM: INDIVIDUALISM AND THE INTELLECTUALS

The question that has so painfully divided our country for the past six months is in the process of being transformed: originally a simple factual question, it has been generalized little by little. The recent intervention of a well-known man of letters has greatly contributed to this result. It seems that the moment has arrived to renew in a brilliant move a polemic which was bogged down in repetitiveness. This is why, instead of resuming once again the discussion of facts, we have passed on, in a single bound, to the level of principles: it is the mental state of the "intellectuals," the basic ideas they profess, and no longer the details of their reasoning which are being attacked. If they obstinately refuse "to bend their logic before the word of an army general," it is evidently because they presume the right to decide the question for themselves; it is because they place their reason above authority, because the rights of the individual seem to them inalienable. It is therefore their individualism which has determined their schism. But then, it is said, if we wish to restore peace in our minds and to prevent the return of similar discord, this individualism must be fought tooth and nail. This inexhaustible source of internal division must be dried up once and for all. And so a veritable crusade has begun against this public scourge, against "this great sickness of the present age."

We gladly accept the debate in these terms. We also believe that the controversies of yesterday only gave superficial expression to a more profound disagreement, and that opinion was divided far more over a question of principle than over a question of fact. Let us therefore leave aside the arguments over circumstances which have been exchanged on both sides. Let us forget the matter itself and the sad spectacles we have witnessed. The problem before us goes infinitely beyond the present incidents and must be distinguished from them.

There is one ambiguity that must be cleared up before all else.

In order to prosecute individualism more easily, they confuse it with the strict utilitarianism and the utilitarian egoism of Spencer and the economists. But that is to make the contest too easy. It is indeed an easy game to denounce as an ideal without grandeur this crass commercialism which reduces society to nothing more than a vast apparatus of production and exchange. For it is exceedingly clear that all communal life is impossible without the existence of interests

Reprinted from Émile Durkheim, "Individualism and the Intellectuals," in *Émile Durkheim on Morality and Society,* edited by Robert N. Bellah. Copyright © 1973 by The University of Chicago Press.
Originally published as "L'individualisme et les intellectuels," *Revue bleue,* 4e série, 10 (1898): 7–13. Translated by Mark Traugott.

superior to those of the individual. We quite agree that nothing is more deserved than that such doctrines be considered anarchical. But what is inadmissable is that they should reason as though this form of individualism were the only one which existed or was even possible. Quite the contrary—it is more and more becoming a rarity and an exception. The practical philosophy of Spencer is morally so impoverished that it can hardly claim any adherents anymore. As for the economists, though they formerly allowed themselves to be seduced by the simplicity of this theory, for some time they have sensed the necessity of tempering the rigor of their primitive orthodoxy and of opening themselves to more generous sentiments. Molinari is just about alone in France in remaining intractable, and I do not believe he has exercised a great influence on the ideas of our epoch. In truth, if individualism had no other representatives, it would be quite useless thus to move heaven and earth to combat an enemy who is in the process of quietly dying a natural death.

But there exists another sort of individualism which is less easily overcome. It has been professed, for the past century, by the vast majority of thinkers: this is the individualism of Kant and Rousseau, of the idealists—the one which the Declaration of the Rights of Man attempted, more or less happily, to formulate and which is currently taught in our schools and has become the basis of our moral catechism. They hope to deal a blow to this form of individualism by striking instead at the former type; but this one is profoundly different, and the criticisms which apply to the one could hardly suit the other. For from making personal interest the objective of conduct, this one sees in all personal motives the very source of evil. According to Kant, I am sure of acting properly only if the motives which determine my behavior depend not on the particular circumstances in which I find myself, but on my humanity in the abstract. Inversely, my actions are bad when they can be logically justified only by my favored position or by my social

condition, by my class or caste interests, by my strong passions, and so on. This is why immoral conduct can be recognized by the fact that it is closely tied to the actor's individuality and cannot be generalized without manifest absurdity. In the same way, if, according to Rousseau, the general will, which is the basis of the social contract, is infallible, if it is the authentic expression of perfect justice, it is because it is the sum of all individual wills; it follows that it constitutes a sort off impersonal average from which all individual considerations are eliminated, because, being divergent and even antagonistic, they neutralize each other and cancel each other out. Thus, for both these men, the only moral ways of acting are those which can be applied to all men indiscriminately; that is, which are implied in the general notion of "man."

Here we have come a long way from that apotheosis of well-being and private interest, from that egoistic cult of the self for which utilitarian individualism has been rightly criticized. Quite the contrary, according to these moralists, duty consists in disregarding all that concerns us personally, all that derives from our empirical individuality, in order to seek out only that which our humanity requires and which we share with all our fellowmen. This ideal so far surpasses the level of utilitarian goals that it seems to those minds who aspire to it to be completely stamped with religiosity. This human person (*personne humaine*), the definition of which is like the touchstone which distinguishes good from evil, is considered sacred in the ritual sense of the word. It partakes of the transcendent majesty that churches of all time lend to their gods; it is conceived of as being invested with that mysterious property which creates a void about sacred things, which removes them from vulgar contacts and withdraws them from common circulation. And the respect which is given it comes precisely from this source. Whoever makes an attempt on a man's life, on a man's liberty, on a man's honor, inspires in us a feeling of horror analogous in every way to that which the believer experiences when he sees his idol profaned. Such an ethic is therefore not simply a hygienic discipline or a prudent economy of existence; it is a religion in which man is at once the worshiper and the god.

But this religion is individualistic, since it takes man as its object and since man is an individual by definition. What is more, there is no system whose individualism is more intransigent. Nowhere are the rights of the individual affirmed with greater energy, since the individual is placed in the ranks of sacrosanct objects; nowhere is the individual more jealously protected from encroachments from the outside, whatever their source. The doctrine of utility can easily accept all sorts of compromises without belying its fundamental axiom; it can admit of individual liberties' being suspended whenever the interest of the greater number requires that sacrifice. But no compromise is possible with a principle which is thus placed outside and above all temporal interests. There is no political reason which can excuse an attack upon the individual when the rights of the individual are above those of the state. If then, individualism is, in and of itself, the catalyst of moral dissolution, we should see it here manifest its antisocial essence. Now we understand the gravity of the question. For this eighteenth-century liberalism which is at bottom the whole object of the dispute is not simply a drawing-room theory, a philosophical construct; it has become a fact, it has penetrated our institutions and our mores, it has blended with our whole life, and if, truly, we had to give it up, we would have to recast our whole moral organization at the same stroke.

Now it is already a remarkable fact that all those theoreticians of individualism are no less sensitive to the rights of the collectivity than to those of the individual. No one has insisted more strongly than Kant upon the supraindividual character of ethics and of law; he makes of them a sort of commandment that man must obey without any discussion simply because it is a commandment. And if he has sometimes been reproached for having exaggerated the autonomy of reason, one could equally well say, and not without foundation, that he placed at the base of his ethics an irrational act of faith and submission. Moreover, doctrines are judged above all by what they produce—that is, by the spirit of the doctrines to which they give birth. Now Kantianism gave rise to the ethics of Fichte, which are already quite impregnated with socialism, and the philosophy of Hegel, of whom Marx was the disciple. As for Rousseau, we know how his individualism is complemented by his authoritarian conception of society. Following him, the men of the Revolution, even while promulgating the famous Declaration of Rights, made of France an indivisible and centralized entity. Perhaps we should see in the work of the Revolution above all a great movement of national concentration. Finally, the principal reason the idealists have fought against the utilitarian ethic is that it appeared to them incompatible with social necessities.

This eclecticism, it is said, is not without contradictions. To be sure, we do not dream of defending the way these different thinkers went about fusing these two aspects of their systems of thought. If, with Rousseau, we begin by making of the individual a sort of absolute which can and must suffice unto itself, it is evidently difficult then to explain how it was possible for the civil state to be established. But the pesent question is to know not whether this or that moralist succeeded in showing how these two tendencies are reconciled, but whether or not they are, in and of themselves, reconcilable. The reasons given for establishing their unity may be worthless, and yet this unity may be real; and already the fact that they generally coincide in the same minds leads us to believe that they go together; from all this, it follows that they must depend on a single social state of which they are probably only different aspects.

And, in fact, once we have stopped confusing individualism with its opposite—that is, with utilitarianism—all these supposed contradictions disappear like magic. This religion of humanity has everything it needs to speak to its faithful in a no less imperative tone than the religions it replaces. Far from limiting itself to flattering our instincts, it fixes before us an ideal which infinitely surpasses nature. For ours is not naturally a wise and pure reason which, purged of all personal motives, would legislate in the abstract its own conduct. Doubtless, if the dignity of the individual came from his personal characteristics, from the peculiarities which distinguish him from others, we might fear that it would shut him off in a sort of moral egoism which would make any solidarity impossible. But in reality he receives dignity from a higher source, one which he shares with all men. If he has a right to this religious respect, it is because he partakes of humanity. It is humanity which is worthy of respect and sacred. Now it is not all in him. It is diffused among all his fellowmen and consequently he cannot adopt it as the aim of his conduct without being obliged to come out of himself and relate to others. The cult, of which he is at once both object and agent, does not address itself to the particular being with he is and which bears his name, but to the human person *(la personne humaine)* wherever it is to be found, and in whatever form it is embodied. Impersonal and anonymous, such an aim, then, soars far above all individual minds *(consciences particulières)* and can thus serve them as a rallying point. The fact that it is not alien to us (by the simple fact that it is human) does not prevent it from dominating us. Now, the only thing necessary for a society to be coherent is that its members have their eyes fixed on the same goal, concur in the same faith. But it is in no way necessary that the object of this common faith be unrelated to individual natures. After all, individualism thus extended is the glorification not of the self but of the individual in general. It springs not from egoism but from sympathy for all that is human, a broader pity for all sufferings, for all human miseries, a more ardent need to combat them and mitigate them, a greater thirst for justice. Is there not herein what is needed to place all men of good will in communion? Without doubt, it can happen that individualism is practiced in a completely different spirit. Some use it for their personal ends, as a means of disguising their egoism and of more easily escaping their duties to society. But this abusive exploitation of individualism proves nothing against it, just as the utilitarian falsehoods about religious hypocrisy prove nothing against religion.

But I am anxious to come to the great objection. This cult of man has as its primary dogma the autonomy of reason and as its primary rite the doctrine of free inquiry. But, we are told, if all opinions are free, by what miracle will they be in harmony? If they are formed without mutual awareness and without having to take one another into account, how can they not be incoherent? Intellectual and moral anarchy would thus be the inevitable result of liberalism. Such is the argument, always refuted and always renewed, to which the eternal adversaries of reason periodically return with a perseverance which nothing discourages, every time a momentary lassitude of the human spirit places it more at their mercy. Yes, it is quite true that individualism implies a certain intellectualism; for freedom of thought is the first of the freedoms. But where has it been seen to have as a consequence this absurd infatuation with oneself which shuts everyone up in his own feelings and creates a vacuum between intellects? What it requires is the right for each individual to know the things he legitimately can know. But it in no way consecrates some sort of right to incompetence. On a question on which I can form no knowledgeable opinion, it costs my intellectual independence nothing to follow more competent opinions. The collaboration of learned men is possible only thanks to this mutual deference; every science constantly borrows from its neighboring disciplines propositions that it accepts without further verification. However, my reason requires reasons before it bows before someone else's. Respect for authority is in no way incompatible with rationalism as long as the authority is rationally grounded.

This is why, when it comes to calling upon certain men to rally themselves to an opinion which is not their own, it is not enough, in order to convince them, to recall to them that commonplace of banal rhetoric that society is not possible without mutual sacrifices and without a certain spirit of subordination. The docility which is asked of them must still be justified for the particular case by demonstrating their incompetence. For if, on the contrary, it were one of those questions which, be definition, come under the jurisdiction of common judgment, a similar abdication would be contrary to all reason and, consequently, to their duty. To know whether a tribunal can be permitted to condemn an accused man without having heard his defense requires no special intelligence. It is a problem of practical ethics for which every man of good sense is competent and to which no one should be indifferent. If, therefore, in recent times, a certain number of artists, and especially scholars, believed they had to refuse to concur in a judgment whose legality appeared to them suspect, it was not because, in their capacity as chemists or philologists, as philosophers or historians, they attributed to themselves some sort of special privilege and a sort of eminent right of control over the thing being judged. It is because, being men, they intend to exercise all their human rights and retain before them a matter which is amenable to reason alone. It is true that they have shown themselves to be more jealous of that right than has the rest of the society; but it is simply because in consequence of their professional practices they take it more to heart. Since they are accustomed by the practice of the scientific method to reserve their judgment as long as they do not feel themselves enlightened,

it is natural that they should yield less easily to the sway of the masses and the prestige of authority.

Not only is individualism not anarchical, but it henceforth is the only system of beliefs which can ensure the moral unity of the country.

We often hear it said today that religion alone can produce this harmony. This proposition, which modern prophets believe they must develop in mystic tones, is essentially a simple truism about which everyone can agree. For we know today that a religion does not necessarily imply symbols and rites, properly speaking, or temples and priests. This whole exterior apparatus is only the superficial part. Essentially, it is nothing other than a body of collective beliefs and practices endowed with a certain authority. As soon as a goal is pursued by an entire people, it acquires, in consequence of this unanimous adherence, a sort of moral supremacy which raises it far above private aims and thus gives it a religious character. From another viewpoint, it is apparent that a society cannot be coherent if there does not exist among its members a certain intellectual and moral community. However, after recalling once again this sociological truism, we have not gotten very far. For if it is true that religion is, in a sense, indispensable, it is no less certain that religions change—that the religion of yesterday could not be the religion of tomorrow. What is important therefore is to say what the religion of today should be.

Now everything converges in the belief that this religion of humanity, of which the individualistic ethic is the rational expression, is the only one possible. Hereafter, to what can the collective sensitivity cling? To the extent that societies become more voluminous and expand over vaster territories, traditions and practices, in order to accommodate themselves to the diversity of situations and to the mobility of circumstances, are obliged to maintain themselves in a state of plasticity and inconstancy which no longer offers enough resistance to individual variations. These variations, being less well restrained, are produced more freely and multiply; that is to say, everyone tends to go off in his own direction. At the same time, as a result of a more developed division of labor, each mind finds itself oriented to a different point on the horizon, reflecting a different aspect of the world, and consequently the contents of consciousness (*conscience*) differ from one person to another. Thus, we make our way, little by little, toward a state, nearly achieved as of now, where the members of a single social group will have nothing in common among themselves except their humanity, except the constitutive attributes of the human person (*personne humaine*) in general. This idea of the human person, given different nuances according to the diversity of national temperaments, is therefore the only idea which would be retained, unalterable and impersonal, above the changing torrent of individual opinions. And the feelings it awakens would be the only ones which could be found in almost every heart. The communion of spirits can no longer be based on definite rites and prejudices, since rites and prejudices are overcome by the course of events. Consequently, nothing remains which men can love and honor in common if not man himself. That is how man has become a god for man and why he can no longer create other gods without lying to himself. And since each of us incarnates something of humanity, each individual consciousness contains something divine and thus finds itself marked with a character which renders it sacred and inviolable to others. Therein lies all individualism; and that is what makes it a necessary doctrine. For in order to halt its advance it would be necessary to prevent men from differentiating themselves more and more from each other, to equalize their personalities, to lead them back to the old conformism of former times, to contain, as a result, the tendency for societies to become always more extended and more centralized, and to place an obstacle in the way of the unceasing progress of the division of

labor. Such an enterprise, whether desirable or not, infinitely exceeds all human capability.

Moreover, what are we offered in place of this despised individualism? The merits of Christian morality are praised and we are discreetly invited to embrace them. But are we to ignore the fact that the originality of Christianity consisted precisely in a remarkable development of the individualistic spirit? Whereas the religion of the ancient city-state was quite entirely made of external practices, from which the spiritual was absent, Christianity demonstrated in its inner faith, in the personal conviction of the individual, the essential condition of piety. First, it taught that the moral value of acts had to be measured according to the intention, a preeminently inward thing which by its very nature escapes all external judgments and which only the agent could competently appraise. The very center of moral life was thus transported from the external to the internal, and the individual was thus elevated to be sovereign judge of his own conduct, accountable only to himself and to his God. Finally, in consummating the definitive separation of the spiritual and the temporal, in abandoning the world to the disputes of men, Christ delivered it at once to science and to free inquiry. This explains the rapid progress made by the scientific spirit from the day when Christian societies were established. Individualism should not, then, be denounced as the enemy which must be combated at any cost! We combat it only to return to it, so impossible is it to escape it. We can oppose to it only itself; but the whole question is to know its proper bounds and whether there is some advantage in disguising it beneath symbols. Now if it is as dangerous as we are told, how can it become inoffensive or beneficial by simply having its true nature dissimulated with the help of metaphors? And looking at it from another point of view, if this restrained individualism which is Christianity was necessary eighteen centuries ago, there is a good chance that a more fully developed individualism is indispensable today. For things have changed. It is therefore a singular error to present the individualistic ethic as the antagonist of Christian morality. Quite the contrary—the former derived from the latter. By attaching ourselves to the first, we do not deny our past; we only continue it.

We are now in a better position to understand why certain minds believe they must oppose an opinionated resistance against everything that seems to threaten the individualistic creed. If every enterprise directed against the rights of an individual revolts them, it is not only out of sympathy for the victim; nor is it from fear of having to suffer similar injustices. Rather, it is because such attempts cannot remain unpunished without compromising the national existence. Indeed, it is impossible for them to occur freely without weakening the feelings they transgress against. And since these feelings are the only ones we hold in common, they cannot be weakened without disturbing the cohesion of society. A religion which tolerates sacrilege abdicates all dominion over men's minds (*consciences*). The religion of the individual therefore cannot let itself be scoffed at without resistance, under penalty of undermining its authority. And since it is the only tie which binds us all to each other, such a weakness cannot exist without a beginning of social dissolution. Thus the individualist who defends the rights of the individual defends at the same time the vital interests of society, for he prevents the criminal impoverishment of that last reserve of collective ideas and feelings which is the very soul of the nation. He renders to his country the same service the aged Roman once rendered to his city in defending the traditional rites against foolhardy innovators. And if there is a country among all others where the cause of individualism is truly national, it is our own; for there is no other which has created such rigorous solidarity between its fate and the fate of these ideas. We have given them their most recent formulation, and it is from us that other peoples have received them. And this is why even now we are considered their most

authoritative representatives. Therefore we cannot disavow them today without disavowing ourselves, without diminishing ourselves in the eyes of the world, without committing a veritable moral suicide. Not long ago, people wondered whether it would not perhaps be convenient to consent to a temporary eclipse of these principles, in order not to disturb the functioning of a public administration which everyone recognized to be indispensable to the security of the state. We do not know if the antinomy really poses itself in this acute form; but, in any case, if a choice truly is necessary between these two evils, to thus sacrifice what has been to this day our historical raison d´être would be to choose the worst. An organ of public life, however important, is only an instrument, a means to an end. What purpose does it serve to maintain the means with such care if the end is dispensed with? And what a sad way of figuring to renounce everything that makes life worthwhile and lends it dignity in order to live,

Et propter vitam vivendi perdere causas!

In truth, I fear there may have been some frivolity in the way this campaign was undertaken. A verbal similarity has permitted the belief that "individualism" necessarily derived from "individual" and therefore egoistic feelings. In reality, the religion of the individual was socially instituted, as were all known religions. It is society which fixes for us this ideal as the sole common goal which can rally our wills. To take it away from us when we have nothing else to put in its place is, then, to precipitate us into that moral anarchy which is precisely what we wish to combat.

Yet we have almost considered the eighteenth-century formulation of individualism perfect and definitive and have made the mistake of preserving it almost without modification. Although it was sufficient a century ago, it now needs to be enlarged and made complete. It presents individualism only in its most negative light. Our fathers undertook exclusively the task of freeing the individual from the political shackles which impeded his development. The freedom to think, the freedom to write, the freedom to vote were therefore placed by them in the ranks of the primary benefits to be obtained, and this emancipation was certainly the necessary precondition of all subsequent progress. However, quite completely carried away by the fervor of the struggle toward the objective they pursued, they ended by no longer seeing beyond it and by erecting as a sort of final goal this proximate term of their efforts. Now political freedom is a means, not an end; its worth lies in the manner in which it is used. If it does not serve some end which goes beyond itself, it is not simply useless; it becomes dangerous. It is a battle weapon; if those who wield it do not know how to use it in fruitful struggles, they soon end by turning it against themselves.

And this is precisely the reason why today it has fallen into a certain disrepute. Men of my generation recall how great our enthusiasm was when, twenty years ago, we finally saw the fall of the last barriers which restrained our restlessness. But alas! Disenchantment quickly followed. For we soon had to admit that we did not know what to do with this hard-won freedom. Those to whom we owed this freedom used it only to tear each other to pieces. And from that moment on, we felt that wind of sadness and discouragement rise over the land which daily grew stronger and eventually finished by disheartening the least resistant spirits.

Thus, we cannot limit ourselves to this negative ideal. We must go beyond the results achieved, if only to preserve them. If we do not finally learn to put to work the means of action we have in our hands, they will inevitably lose their worth. Let us therefore make use of our liberties to seek out what we must do and to do it, to smooth the functioning of the social machine, still so harsh on individuals, to place within their reach all possible means of developing their abilities without hindrance, to work finally to make a reality of the famous precept: to each

according to his labor! Let us even recognize that in a general way liberty is a delicate instrument which one must learn to handle; and let us train our children accordingly. All moral education should be oriented to this end. Clearly, we have no lack of matters on which to take action. However, though it is certain that we will hereafter have to set up new goals beyond those already attained, it would be senseless to renounce the latter in order to better pursue the former. For the necessary progress is possible only thanks to progress already achieved. It is a matter of completing, extending, and organizing individualism, not of restraining and combating it. It is a matter of using reflection, not of imposing silence upon it. Reflection alone can help us emerge from our present difficulties. We do not see what could replace it. It is not, however, by meditating upon *Politics in the Holy Scriptures* that we will ever find the means of organizing economic life and of introducing greater justice in contractual relations!

In these circumstances, is our duty not clear? All those who believe in the utility or simply in the necessity of the moral transformations accomplished in the past century have the same interest: they must forget the differences which separate them and unite in their efforts to preserve the already acquired position. Once the crisis has passed, there will certainly be cause to recall the teachings of experience, so that we do not again fall into that sterile inaction for which we are now paying the penalty. But that is tomorrow's task. Today, the urgent task which must come before all others is to save our moral patrimony; once it is secure, we will see that it prospers. Let the common danger at least shake us from our torpor and give us back a taste for action! And already, indeed, we see across the country initiative wakening and men of good will seeking each other out. If someone would come to group them together and lead them into battle, then victory might not be far off. For what should reassure us to a certain extent is that our adversaries are strong only because of our own weakness. They have neither the profound faith nor the generous impulses which irresistibly lead peoples to great reactions, as to great revolutions. We certainly would not dream of questioning their sincerity! But how could we fail to sense to what extent their conviction is improvised? They are neither apostles who let their anger or their enthusiasm overflow nor scholars who bring us the product of their research and reflections; they are men of letters seduced by an interesting theme. It would therefore seem impossible that these dilettantes' games could long succeed in holding back the masses if we know how to act. But also, what a humiliation it would be if reason, dealing with so weak an opponent, should end by being worsted, even if only for a time!

Chapter 3

Max Weber: The Iron Cage

Introduction

Writing in the mid-1950s, Leo Strauss, a renowned political philosopher and severe critic of Max Weber wrote: "Whatever may have been his errors, he is the greatest social scientist of our century." Weber's contribution is truly immense in both breadth and complexity. His methodological work provides a framework for research and instruction, and his substantive explorations in religion, economics, history, and politics give a unique insight into the origins of the modern world and its evolution. Central to Weber's sociology is the idea of rationalization and its consequences for modern life. Unlike Marx and Durkheim, both of whom projected optimistic outcomes in the transition to modernity, Weber rejects the Enlightenment's view of evolutionary progress and happiness. Instead he projects a "polar night of icy darkness," a highly rational and bureaucratically organized social order, an "iron cage" in which people are trapped. Modernity also produces a new character type, a technical as opposed to a cultured individual, a passionless, coldly calculating, and instrumentally rational actor.

Max Weber was born into a middle-class family on April 21, 1864, in Erfurt, Germany. His father was an active politician serving at various levels of local and national government, and his mother was a devout Protestant who raised a family and tended to the household. The Webers moved to Berlin in 1869 and settled in a fashionable suburb favored by academics and politicians. The Weber household hosted many notables from Berlin society. Weber studied law

at the universities in Berlin and Göttingen and went on to take a Ph.D. in economic and legal history in 1889. He married Marianne Schnitger in 1893, and her devotion to him is evidenced throughout her famous biography, *Max Weber: A Life*. The death of Weber's father in 1897 and the circumstances surrounding it had a profound impact on Weber's life. Since he had had a fearsome quarrel with his father shortly before his death, Weber felt guilt and overwhelming remorse to the point of depression. His life fluctuated between manic periods of extraordinary productivity and severe, almost catatonic depression. After a brief stay in a mental hospital Weber returned to his research and scholarly writing. In 1904 the Webers came to visit the United States, a trip which aided his recovery and left him with an enduring fascination with America. Upon his return to Heidelberg, Weber assumed a full schedule of writing and was active in the intellectual life of the community. Following a brief period of service during World War I as a captain in charge of running several Heidelberg hospitals, Weber resumed work on his major project, *Economy and Society*. During the last few years of his life, Weber began lecturing again, in Vienna in 1918, and in Munich in 1919. He died in June 1920, leaving behind a monumental scholarly corpus.

In *The Protestant Ethic and the Spirit of Capitalism*, a study of the relationship of religious ideas to economic activity, Weber offers an insight into the process of transformation and rationalization. Weber argued that seventeenth-century beliefs in predestination and asceticism flowing from Calvinism shaped the actions of the faithful and contributed to the rise of capitalism. Specifically, Calvinists adopted attitudes toward work and money that revolutionized their daily lives. To ease the pain of living with the doctrine of predestination, i.e., the uncertainty of one's eternal fate as a member of the elect or the damned, true believers sought a sign that they were favored. Hard work and economic success were taken as signs of salvation. Asceticism led to a frugal way of life and the resulting accumulation of capital. The preconditions for capitalism, namely available capital for investment in nascent industries, were set into motion by the belief in Calvinism. Good Calvinists who wished to save their souls inadvertently engaged in those actions of industriousness and frugality that contributed to capitalism's rise.

Weber concludes his essay with some reflections on the future course of capitalist development. The Protestant beliefs that initiated this activity have long since ceased to function as a justification for economic action. As Weber writes, capitalism is now perpetuated by the desire to make money for its own sake; its religious inspiration is gone. Like other modern institutions, capitalism has become a rational system, an "iron cage," in which people have become money-making instruments who no longer believe passionately in salvation and damnation. Weber does not long romantically for the return of an earlier era of Protestant belief. There is no turning back from modernity and the scientific and industrial revolutions that made it possible. However, Weber wants us to recognize what we have become and to face up to the realities of a disenchanted world.

Whereas Marx predicted a proletarian revolution that would shatter the capitalist order and usher in the new age of socialism, Weber saw no such progressive future. Were socialism to arise, Weber claimed, it would not escape the bureaucratic fate of modern institutions but would succumb to the rationalization process. He regarded the creation of a centralized state administration to oversee the economy under socialism as an even greater threat to individual freedom than the separate and oppositional spheres of state and economy under capitalism.

What was this rationalization process and why was it significant for Weber's social theory? Weber's reflections on bureaucracy, excerpted in the following pages, provide us with an important point of departure. Weber argued that the characteristic form of modern institutional organizations, including the state, the corporation, the military, the university, the church, is bureaucratic. Highly specialized tasks are coordinated in a hierarchical order, with each level of organization reporting to the one above in a pyramidal fashion until one reaches the head of the organization. Depersonalization, routinization, and mechanical predictability are the characteristics of bureaucracies, and they survive and expand because they are the most efficient method for coordinating a large number of different tasks. Decision making within bureaucracies is based on a particular mode of thinking, instrumental reasoning, or *Zweckrational*, as Weber called it. This form of reasoning breaks down all problems into a means-ends chain and entails rational calculation of costs incurred and benefits to be secured if a particular line of action is pursued.

Apart from his careful depiction of the role and function of the official, Weber characterizes bureaucratic organizations as operating with "calculable rules" and "without regard for persons." What does he mean by these terms? Does "dehumanization," as Weber describes it, have any positive consequences?

Bureaucracy and democracy exist in an uneasy relationship. Is the expertise that is fostered by bureaucratic organization compatible with democratic processes? What are the potential sources of abuse by experts and how can these be overcome? What does Weber have to say about the possibility of revolution in the age of bureaucracy? Finally, how does bureaucracy impact on the educational system and with what kinds of results?

The reader should keep in mind that the rationalization process in modern society as Weber describes it anticipates Michel Foucault's "carceral society" (Chapter 14) and his description of instrumental rationality, as the prevalent mode of thought in modern society, gives concrete empirical expression to Nietzsche's Apollonian type.

Max Weber's essays on the methodology of the social sciences likewise demonstrate a Nietzschean influence and anticipate the postmodernist critique of truth and objectivity (Chapter 14). Reprinted on the following pages are excerpts from one of those essays, in which Weber probes deeply into the question of the relationship of values to science and the possibility of objective research in sociology. Weber's position is complex and not easily summarized. He characterizes the social reality in which we move as infinite; yet out of this infinity of facts a particular focus is necessary before one can even begin to think about a social question. What problem one chooses to study is a consequence of the values one holds and the relevance of particular events or phenomena to those value assumptions.

Sociology falls somewhere between the methodology of the natural sciences and of literary interpretation. It is not a hard science, although it respects the need for systematic study and empirical analysis in order to arrive at generalizations. On the other hand, because sociology deals with human behavior, it is obliged to inquire into the subjective meaning of action. Weber's *verstehende* sociology meets this need by supplementing the more objective methodologies with an interpretive one in which the sociologist attempts a deeper understanding by probing subjective meaning structures.

Weber warned against the conflation of reason and reality. The Hegelian-Marxist claim to grasp the totality of history was rejected by Weber, who saw the mind as a limited instrument capable of dealing empirically with a particular slice of reality. Weber suspected totalistic views leading to prophecies because they misconstrued the relation between the reasoning mind and social reality. Social theorists construct models or ideal types that explain the interrelationships of relevant key elements of the social

world. Weber's essay on bureaucracy, presented on the following pages, provides an example of a rational model or ideal type. The ideal type is a rational construct that helps orient us to the confusing infinity of social facts. The model is not the reality; it provides a framework with which to observe and determine how social processes deviate from the ways in which the rational model organizes them. In other words, social reality is more complex, more contingent, and more subject to unanticipated consequences than our rational models are able to predict. If we mistake reason, i.e., the models or ideal types, for the reality, we do violence to the complexities of everyday life, and rather than respect the integrity of our subject, we may compel it to fit the rational demands of our model.

If these models emanate from academic establishments, think tanks, or governmental agencies and they are implemented, they may become blueprints for social engineering, thus empowering a technocratic elite to shape the future, a development decried by Habermas (Chapter 13) and Foucault (Chapter 14).

For Weber, scientific analysis was a tool for understanding social reality and not an appropriate instrument for social change. Directed social change presupposes the achievement of a valued objective; it deals with moral conceptions of justice and right. Science is an enterprise limited to factual analysis and interpretation, and therefore it cannot make valid judgments about moral claims. Weber argued that the appropriate arena for the struggle over different policies and the moral claims that they support is the political arena and not the scientific one. In so doing, Weber placed science and politics in different spheres, each with very different functions to perform. Analysis of society was not the equivalent of changing it, and the obligation of the sociologist was to understand social reality and not to transform it. If social change was needed, then political parties and their leaders were the effective vehicle to accomplish these ends in a representative system.

The essay "Class, Status, Party," reprinted on the following pages, reveals yet another aspect of

Weber's sociology. Weber deals with the question of the relationship of political power to economic class and offers an alternative to Marx's ruling class. Marx claims that the ruling class controls economic and political power in capitalist society. The owners of the means of production are the dominant class because they control the wealth of society and therefore also political power. Although they may not run for office, they either directly or indirectly control those who do. The dominant ideas—the ruling ideas—are the ideas of the ruling class.

For Weber, this is an oversimplification. He distinguishes three avenues to power in modern society; class, status, and party. Weber and Marx share similar views on the meaning and significance of economic class. Ownership of property and its disposition on the open market are signs of considerable power. However, the political significance of economic power is more problematic for Weber, as he questions whether economic class identity is the basis for collective action. When does a class act for itself? Weber makes collective class action more problematic than does Marx.

Social status may be yet another dimension of power. Those with high status in society may also be wealthy; but they need not be. Moreover, those who are rich do not necessarily enjoy high status. For example, wealthy criminals do not have social status, and the *nouveaux riches* are not admitted to high society. But status groups are also ethnic and religious groups, and for Weber, these emerge as more significant in shaping values and behavior than the objective categories of class. Contemporary events in the former Soviet Union seem to bear out these Weberian observations, as witness the reemergence of powerful religious and nationalistic emotions despite a seventy-year regime of proletarian class consciousness.

Weber turns to the third dimension of power in contemporary society, namely, the political party. The fact that people are rich or that they enjoy high social status does not guarantee their success in politics. Politicians must also win elections and gain support for their positions. The abilities required of a political leader in order to rise to prominence within a political party and to win elections reside in his persuasive personal characteristics and social skills. Those talents constitute yet another avenue to power beyond class and status. Despite the powerful linkages that connect class, status, and party, Weber's analytic distinctions recognize ethnic, racial, and charismatic claims to political leadership.

When he turned to politics, Weber saw the possibility that "the iron cage" might be shattered. Political leaders with a new vision of the future, a charismatic leadership, might project a moral vision of the just society and gather the support needed to bring about social change. But politics also entailed rational calculation. Weber wrote that the "ethic of ultimate ends," the moral vision, had to be accompanied by the "ethic of responsibility," the cool calculation as to how to overcome obstacles and achieve the desired goals. In any event, academics trained in social analysis were neither intellectually equipped nor temperamentally suited to engage in the politics of social change. Weber urged their participation as citizens, of course, and as writers, their work was bound to express their value preferences, but because as teachers they enjoyed their legitimacy through the special claims of science, Weber saw their politicization of the classroom as dishonest.

At the end of *The Protestant Ethic and the Spirit of Capitalism,* Weber allows us to glimpse at what modernity has in store when he writes:

> No one knows who will live in this cage in the future, or whether at the end of this tremendous development entirely new prophets will arise, or, if neither, mechanized petrification, embellished with a sort of convulsive self-importance. For of the last stage of this cultural development, it might well be truly said: "Specialists without spirit, sensualists without heart; this nullity imagines that it has attained a level of civilization never before achieved."

MAX WEBER: THE PROTESTANT ETHIC AND THE SPIRIT OF CAPITALISM

Let us now try to clarify the points in which the Puritan idea of the calling and the premium it placed upon ascetic conduct was bound directly to influence the development of a capitalistic way of life. As we have seen, this asceticism turned with all its force against one thing: the spontaneous enjoyment of life and all it had to offer. This is perhaps most characteristically brought out in the struggle over the *Book of Sports* which James I and Charles I made into law expressly as a means of counteracting Puritanism, and which the latter ordered to be read from all the pulpits. The fanatical opposition of the Puritans to the ordinances of the King, permitting certain popular amusements on Sunday outside of Church hours by law, was not only explained by the disturbance of the Sabbath rest, but also by resentment against the intentional diversion from the ordered life of the saint, which it caused. And, on his side, the King's threats of severe punishment for every attack on the legality of those sports were motivated by his purpose of breaking the anti-authoritarian ascetic tendency of Puritanism, which was so dangerous to the State. The feudal and monarchical forces protected the pleasure seekers against the rising middle-class morality and the anti-authoritarian ascetic conventicles, just as to-day capitalistic society tends to protect those willing to work against the class morality of the proletariat and the anti-authoritarian trade union.

As against this the Puritans upheld their decisive characteristic, the principle of ascetic conduct. For otherwise the Puritan aversion to sport, even for the Quakers, was by no means simply one of principle. Sport was accepted if it served a rational purpose, that of recreation necessary for physical efficiency. But as a means

for the spontaneous expression of undisciplined impulses, it was under suspicion; and in so far as it became purely a means of enjoyment, or awakened pride, raw instincts or the irrational gambling instinct, it was of course strictly condemned. Impulsive enjoyment of life, which leads away both from work in a calling and from religion, was as such the enemy of rational asceticism, whether in the form of seigneurial sports, or the enjoyment of the dance-hall or the publichouse of the common man.

Its attitude was thus suspicious and often hostile to the aspects of culture without any immediate religious value. It is not, however, true that the ideals of Puritanism implied a solemn, narrow-minded contempt of culture. Quite the contrary is the case at least for science, with the exception of the hatred of Scholasticism. Moreover, the great men of the Puritan movement were thoroughly steeped in the culture of the Renaissance. The sermons of the Presbyterian divines abound with classical allusions, and even the Radicals, although they objected to it, were not ashamed to display that kind of learning in theological polemics. Perhaps no country was ever so full of graduates as New England in the first generation of its existence. The satire of their opponents, such as, for instance, Butler's *Hudibras,* also attacks primarily the pedantry and highly trained dialectics of the Puritans. This is partially due to the religious valuation of knowledge which followed from their attitude to the Catholic *fides implicita.*

But the situation is quite different when one looks at non-scientific literature, and especially the fine arts. Here asceticism descended like a frost on the life of "Merrie old England." And not only worldly merriment felt its effect. The Puritan's ferocious hatred of everything which smacked of superstition, of all survivals of magical or sacramental salvation, applied to the Christmas festivities and the May Pole and all spontaneous religious art. That there was room in Holland for a great, often uncouthly realistic art proves only how far from completely the authoritarian moral discipline of that country was able to counteract the influence of the court and the regents (a class of *rentiers*), and also the joy of life of the parvenu bourgeoisie, after the short supremacy of the Calvinistic theocracy had been transformed into a moderate national Church, and with it Calvinism had perceptibly lost in its power of ascetic influence.

The theatre was obnoxious to the Puritans, and with the strict exclusion of the erotic and of nudity from the realm of toleration, a radical view of either literature or art could not exist. The conceptions of idle talk, of superfluities, and of vain ostentation, all designations of an irrational attitude without objective purpose, thus not ascetic, and especially not serving the glory of God, but of man, were always at hand to serve in deciding in favour of sober utility as against any artistic tendencies. This was especially true in the case of decoration of the person, for instance clothing. That powerful tendency toward uniformity of life, which to-day so immensely aids the capitalistic interest in the standardization of production, had its ideal foundations in the repudiation of all idolatry of the flesh.

Of course we must not forget that Puritanism included a world of contradictions, and that the instinctive sense of eternal greatness in art was certainly stronger among its leaders than in the atmosphere of the Cavaliers. Moreover, a unique genius like Rembrandt, however, little his conduct may have been acceptable to God in the eyes of the Puritans, was very strongly influenced in the character of his work by his religious environment. But that does not alter the picture as a whole. In so far as the development of the Puritan tradition could, and in part did, lead to a powerful spiritualization of personality, it was a decided benefit to literature. But for the most part that benefit only accrued to later generations.

Although we cannot here enter upon a discussion of the influence of Puritanism in all these directions, we should call attention to the fact that the toleration of pleasure in cultural goods, which contributed to purely aesthetic or athletic enjoyment, certainly always ran up against one characteristic limitation: they must not cost anything. Man is only a trustee of the goods which have come to him through God's grace. He must, like the servant in the parable, give an account of every penny entrusted to him, and it is at least hazardous to spend any of it for a purpose which does not serve the glory of God but only one's own enjoyment. What person, who keeps his eyes open, has not met representatives of this viewpoint even in the present? The idea of a man's duty to his possessions, to which he subordinates himself as an obedient steward, or even as an acquisitive machine, bears with chilling weight on his life. The greater the possessions the heavier, if the ascetic attitude toward life stands the test, the feeling of responsibility for them, for holding them undiminished for the glory of God and increasing them by restless effort. The origin of this type of life also extends in certain roots, like so many aspects of the spirit of capitalism, back into the Middle Ages. But it was in the ethic of ascetic Protestantism that it first found a consistent ethical foundation. Its significance for the development of capitalism is obvious.

This worldly Protestant asceticism, as we may recapitulate up to this point, acted powerfully against the spontaneous enjoyment of possessions; it restricted consumption, especially of luxuries. On the other hand, it had the psychological effect of freeing the acquisition of goods from the inhibitions of traditionalistic ethics. It broke the bonds of the impulse of acquisition in that it not only legalized it, but (in the sense discussed) looked upon it as directly willed by God. The campaign against the temptations of the flesh, and the dependence on external things was, as besides the Puritans the great Quaker apologist Barclay expressly says, not a struggle against the rational acquisition, but against the irrational use of wealth.

But this irrational use was exemplified in the outward forms of luxury which their code condemned as idolatry of the flesh, however natural they had appeared to the feudal mind. On the other hand, they approved the rational and utilitarian uses of wealth which were willed by God for the needs of the individual and the community. They did not wish to impose mortification on the man of wealth, but the use of his means for necessary and practical things. The idea of comfort characteristically limits the extent of ethically permissible expenditures. It is naturally no accident that the development of a manner of living consistent with that idea may be observed earliest and most clearly among the most consistent representatives of this whole attitude toward life. Over against the glitter and ostentation of feudal magnificence which, resting on an unsound economic basis, prefers a sordid elegance to a sober simplicity, they set the clean and solid comfort of the middle-class home as an ideal.

On the side of the production of private wealth, asceticism condemned both dishonesty and impulsive avarice. What was condemned as covetousness, Mammonism, etc., was the pursuit of riches for their own sake. For wealth in itself was a temptation. But here asceticism was the power "which ever seeks the good but ever creates evil"; what was evil in its sense was possession and its temptation. For, in conformity with the Old Testament and in analogy to the ethical valuation of good works, asceticism looked upon the pursuit of wealth as an end in itself as highly reprehensible; but the attainment of it as a fruit of labour in a calling was a sign of God's blessing. And even more important: the religious valuation of restless, continuous, systematic work in a worldly calling, as the highest means to asceticism, and at the same time the surest and most evident proof of rebirth and genuine faith, must have been the most powerful conceivable lever for the expansion of the attitude toward life which we have here called the spirit of capitalism.

When the limitation of consumption is combined with this release of acquisitive activity, the inevitable practical result is obvious: accumulation of capital through ascetic compulsion to save. The restraints which were imposed upon the consumption of wealth naturally served to increase it by making possible the productive investment of capital. . . .

As far as the influence of the Puritan outlook extended, under all circumstances—and this is, or course, much more important than the mere encouragement of capital accumulation—it favoured the development of a rational bourgeois economic life; it was the most important, and above all the only consistent influence in the development of that life. It stood at the cradle of the modern economic man. . . .

We may hence quote here a passage from John Wesley himself which might well serve as a motto for everything which has been said above. For it shows that the leaders of these ascetic movements understood the seemingly paradoxical relationships which we have here analysed perfectly well, and in the same sense that we have given them. He wrote:

> I fear, wherever riches have increased, the essence of religion has decreased in the same proportion. Therefore I do not see how it is possible, in the nature of things, for any revival of true religion to continue long. For religion must necessarily produce both industry and frugality, and these cannot but produce riches. But as riches increase, so will price, anger, and love of the world in all its branches. How then is it possible that Methodism, that is, a religion of the heart, though it flourishes now as a green bay tree, should continue in this state? For the Methodists in every place grow diligent and frugal; consequently they increase in goods. Hence they proportionately increase in pride, in anger, in the desire of the flesh, the desire of the eyes, and the pride of life. So, although the form of religion remains, the spirit is swiftly vanishing away. Is there no way to prevent this—this continual decay of pure religion? We ought not to prevent people from being

diligent and frugal; *we must exhort all Christians to gain all they can, and to save all they can; that is, in effect, to grow rich. . . .*

A specifically bourgeois economic ethic had grown up. With the consciousness of standing in the fullness of God's grace and being visibly blessed by Him, the bourgeois business man, as long as he remained within the bounds of formal correctness, as long as his moral conduct was spotless and the use to which he put his wealth was not objectionable, could follow his pecuniary interest as he would and feel that he was fulfilling a duty in doing so. The power of religious asceticism provided him in addition with sober, conscientious, and unusually industrious workmen, who clung to their work as to a life purpose willed by God.

Finally, it gave him the comforting assurance that the unequal distribution of the goods of this world was a special dispensation of Divine Providence, which in these differences, as in particular grace, pursued secret ends unknown to men. . . .

One of the fundamental elements of the spirit of modern capitalism, and not only of that but of all modern culture: rational conduct on the basis of the idea of the calling, was born— that is what this discussion has sought to demonstrate—from the spirit of Christian asceticism. One has only to re-read the passage from Franklin, quoted at the beginning of this essay, in order to see that the essential elements of the attitude which was there called the spirit of capitalism are the same as what we have just shown to be the content of the Puritan worldly asceticism, only without the religious basis, which by Franklin's time had died away. . . .

The Puritan wanted to work in a calling; we are forced to do so. For when asceticism was carried out of monastic cells into everyday life, and began to dominate worldly morality, it did its part in building the tremendous cosmos of the modern economic order. This order is now bound to the technical and economic conditions of machine production which to-day determine the lives of all the individuals who are born into this mechanism, not only those directly concerned with economic acquisition, with irresistible force. Perhaps it will so determine them until the last ton of fossilized coal is burnt. In Baxter's view the care for external goods should only lie on the shoulders of the "saint like a light cloak, which can be thrown aside at any moment." But fate decreed that the cloak should become an iron cage.

Since asceticism undertook to remodel the world and to work out its ideals in the world, material goods have gained an increasing and finally an inexorable power over the lives of men as at no previous period in history. To-day the spirit of religious asceticism—whether finally, who knows?—has escaped from the cage. But victorious capitalism, since it rests on mechanical foundations, needs its support no longer. The rosy blush of its laughing heir, the Enlightenment, seems also to be irretrievably fading, and the idea of duty in one's calling prowls about in our lives like the ghost of dead religious beliefs. Where the fulfilment of the calling cannot directly be related to the highest spiritual and cultural values, or when, on the other hand, it need not be felt simply as economic compulsion, the individual generally abandons the attempt to justify it at all. In the field of its highest development, in the United States, the pursuit of wealth, stripped of its religious and ethical meaning, tends to become associated with purely mundane passions, which often actually give it the character of sport.

No one knows who will live in this cage in the future, or whether at the end of this tremendous development entirely new prophets will arise, or there will be a great rebirth of old ideas and ideals, or, if neither, mechanized petrification, embellished with a sort of convulsive self-importance. For of the last stage of this cultural development, it might well be truly said: "Specialists without spirit, sensualists without heart; this nullity imagines that it has attained a level of civilization never before achieved."

MAX WEBER: BUREAUCRACY

Characteristics of Modern Bureaucracy

Modern officialdom functions in the following manner:

I. There is the principle of official *jurisdictional areas*, which are generally ordered by rules, that is, by laws or administrative regulations. This means:

(1) The regular activities required for the purposes of the bureaucratically governed structure are assigned as official duties.

(2) The authority to give the commands required for the discharge of these duties is distributed in a stable way and is strictly delimited by rules concerning the coercive means, physical, sacerdotal, or otherwise, which may be placed at the disposal of officials.

(3) Methodical provision is made for the regular and continuous fulfillment of these duties and for the exercise of the corresponding rights; only persons who qualify under general rules are employed.

In the sphere of the state these three elements constitute a bureaucratic *agency*, in the sphere of the private economy they constitute a bureaucratic *enterprise*. Bureaucracy, thus understood, is fully developed in political and ecclesiastical communities only in the modern state, and in the private economy only in the most advanced institutions of capitalism. Permanent agencies, with fixed jurisdiction, are not the historical rule but rather the exception. This is even true of large political structures such as those of

the ancient Orient, the Germanic and Mongolian empires of conquest, and of many feudal states. In all these cases, the ruler executes the most important measures through personal trustees, table-companions, or court-servants. Their commissions and powers are not precisely delimited and are temporarily called into being for each case.

II. The principles of *office hierarchy* and of channels of appeal (*Instanzenzug*) stipulate a clearly established system of super- and subordination in which there is a supervision of the lower offices by the higher ones. Such a system offers the governed the possibility of appealing, in a precisely regulated manner, the decision of a lower office to the corresponding superior authority. With the full development of the bureaucratic type, the office hierarchy is *monocratically* organized. The principle of hierarchical office authority is found in all bureaucratic structures: in state and ecclesiastical structures as well as in large party organizations and private enterprises. It does not matter for the character of bureaucracy whether its authority is called "private" or "public."

When the principle of jurisdictional "competency" is fully carried through, hierarchical subordination—at least in public office—does not mean that the "higher" authority is authorized simply to take over the business of the "lower." Indeed, the opposite is the rule; once an office has been set up, a new incumbent will always be appointed if a vacancy occurs.

III. The management of the modern office is based upon written documents (the "files"), which are preserved in their original or draft form, and upon a staff of subaltern officials and scribes of all sorts. The body of officials working in an agency along with the respective apparatus of material implements and the files makes up a *bureau* (in private enterprises often called the "counting house," *Kontor*).

In principle, the modern organization of the civil service separates the bureau from the private domicile of the official and, in general, segregates official activity from the sphere of private life. Public monies and equipment are divorced from the private property of the official. This condition is everywhere the product of a long development. Nowadays, it is found in public as well as in private enterprises; in the latter, the principle extends even to the entrepreneur at the top. In principle, the *Kontor* (office) is separated from the household, business from private correspondence, and business assets from private wealth. The more consistently the modern type of business management has been carried through, the more are these separations the case. The beginnings of this process are to be found as early as the Middle Ages.

It is the peculiarity of the modern entrepreneur that he conducts himself as the "first official" of his enterprise, in the very same way in which the ruler of a specifically modern bureaucratic state [Frederick II of Prussia] spoke of himself as "the first servant" of the state. The idea that the bureau activities of the state are intrinsically different in character from the management of private offices is a continental European notion and, by way of contrast, is totally foreign to the American way.

IV. Office management, at least all specialized office management—and such management is distinctly modern—usually presupposes thorough training in a field of specialization. This, too, holds increasingly for the modern executive and employee of a private enterprise, just as it does for the state officials.

V. When the office is fully developed, official activity demands the *full working capacity* of the official, irrespective of the fact that the length of his obligatory working hours in the bureau may be limited. In the normal case, this too is only the product of a long development, in the public as well as in the private office. Formerly the normal state of affairs was the reverse: Official business was discharged as a secondary activity.

VI. The management of the office follows *general rules*, which are more or less stable, more or less exhaustive, and which can be learned. Knowledge of these rules represents a special technical expertise which the officials possess. It involves jurisprudence, administrative or business management.

The reduction of modern office management to rules is deeply embedded in its very nature. The theory of modern public administration, for instance, assumes that the authority to order certain matters by decree—which has been legally granted to an agency—does not entitle the agency to regulate the matter by individual commands given for each case, but only to regulate the matter abstractly. This stands in extreme contrast to the regulation of all relationships through individual privileges and bestowals of favor, which, as we shall see, is absolutely dominant in patrimonialism, at least in so far as such relationships are not fixed by sacred tradition.

The Position of the Official Within and Outside of Bureaucracy

All this results in the following for the internal and external position of the official:

I. Office Holding as a Vocation

That the office is a "vocation" *(Beruf)* finds expression, first, in the requirement of a prescribed course of training, which demands the entire working capacity for a long period of time, and in generally prescribed special examinations as prerequisites of employment. Furthermore, it finds expression in that the position of the official is in the nature of a "duty" *(Pflicht)*. This determines the character of his relations in the following manner: Legally and actually, office holding is not considered ownership of a source of income, to be exploited for rents or emoluments in exchange for the rendering of certain services, as was normally the case during the

Middle Ages and frequently up to the threshold of recent times, nor is office holding considered a common exchange of services, as in the case of free employment contracts. Rather, entrance into an office, including one in the private economy, is considered an acceptance of a specific duty of fealty to the purpose of the office *(Amtstreue)* in return for the grant of a secure existence. It is decisive for the modern loyalty to an office that, in the pure type, it does not establish a relationship to a *person*, like the vassal's or disciple's faith under feudal or patrimonial authority, but rather is devoted to *impersonal* and *functional* purposes. These purposes, of course, frequently gain an ideological halo from cultural values, such as state, church, community, party or enterprise, which appear as surrogates for a this-worldly or other-worldly personal master and which are embodied by a given group.

The political official—at least in the fully developed modern state—is not considered the personal servant of a ruler. Likewise, the bishop, the priest and the preacher are in fact no longer, as in early Christian times, carriers of a purely personal charisma, which offers other-worldly sacred values under the personal mandate of a master, and in principle responsible only to him, to everybody who appears worthy of them and asks for them. In spite of the partial survival of the old theory, they have become officials in the service of a functional purpose, a purpose which in the present-day "church" appears at once impersonalized and ideologically sanctified.

II. The Social Position of the Official

Social Esteem and Status Convention. Whether he is in a private office or a public bureau, the modern official, too, always strives for and usually attains a distinctly elevated *social esteem* vis-à-vis the governed. His social position is protected by prescription about rank order and, for the political official, by special prohibitions of the criminal code against "insults to the office" and "contempt" of state and church authorities.

The social position of the official is normally highest where, as in old civilized countries, the following conditions prevail: a strong demand for administration by trained experts; a strong and stable social differentiation, where the official predominantly comes from socially and economically privileged strata because of the social distribution of power or the costliness of the required training and of status conventions. The possession of educational certificates or patents—discussed below—is usually linked with qualification for office; naturally, this enhances the "status element" in the social position of the official. Sometimes the status factor is explicitly acknowledged; for example, in the prescription that the acceptance of an aspirant to an office career depends upon the consent ("election") by the members of the official body. This is the case in the officer corps of the German army. Similar phenomena, which promote a guild-like closure of officialdom, are typically found in the patrimonial and, particularly, in prebendal officialdom of the past. The desire to resurrect such policies in changed forms is by no means infrequent among modern bureaucrats; it played a role, for instance, in the demands of the largely proletarianized [zemstvo-] officials (the *tretii element*) during the Russian revolution [of 1905].

Usually the social esteem of the officials is especially low where the demand for expert administration and the hold of status conventions are weak. This is often the case in new settlements by virtue of the great economic opportunities and the great instability of their social stratification: witness the United States.

* * *

Rank as the Basis of Regular Salary. The official as a rule receives a *monetary* compensation in the form of a *salary*, normally fixed, and the old age security provided by a pension. The salary is not measured like a wage in terms of work done, but according to "status," that is, according to the kind of function (the "rank") and, possibly, according to the length of service. The relatively great security of the official's income, as well as the rewards of social esteem, make the office a sought-after position, especially in countries which no longer provide opportunities for colonial profits. In such countries, this situation permits relatively low salaries for officials.

Fixed Career Lines and Status Rigidity. The official is set for a "career" within the hierarchical order of the public service. He expects to move from the lower, less important and less well paid, to the higher positions. The average official naturally desires a mechanical fixing of the conditions of promotion: if not of the offices, at least of the salary levels. He wants these conditions fixed in terms of "seniority," or possibly according to grades achieved in a system of examinations. Here and there, such grades actually form a *character indelebilis* of the official and have lifelong effects on his career. To this is joined the desire to reinforce the right to office and to increase status group closure and economic security. All of this makes for a tendency to consider the offices as "prebends" of those qualified by educational certificates. The necessity of weighing general personal and intellectual qualifications without concern for the often subaltern character of such patents of specialized education, has brought it about that the highest political offices, especially the "ministerial" positions, are as a rule filled without reference to such certificates.

The Technical Superiority of Bureaucratic Organization over Administration by Notables

The decisive reason for the advance of bureaucratic organization has always been its purely *technical* superiority over any other form of organization. The fully developed bureaucratic apparatus compares with other organizations exactly as does the machine with the nonmechanical modes of production. Precision, speed, unambiguity, knowledge of the files, continuity, discretion, unity, strict subordination, reduction of friction and of material and personal costs— these are raised to the optimum point in the strictly bureaucratic administration, and especially in its monocratic form. As compared with all collegiate, honorific, and avocational forms of administration, trained bureaucracy is superior on all these points. And as far as complicated tasks are concerned, paid bureaucratic work is not only more precise but, in the last analysis, it is often cheaper than even formally unremunerated honorific service.

* * *

Today, it is primarily the capitalist market economy which demands that the official business of public administration be discharged precisely, unambiguously, continuously, and with as much speed as possible. Normally, the very large modern capitalist enterprises are themselves unequaled models of strict bureaucratic organization. Business management throughout rests on increasing precision, steadiness, and, above all, speed of operations. This, in turn, is determined by the peculiar nature of the modern means of communication, including, among other things, the news service of the press. The extraordinary increase in the speed by which public announcements, as well as economic and political facts, are transmitted exerts a steady and sharp pressure in the direction of speeding up the tempo of administrative reaction towards various situations. The optimum of such reaction time is normally attained only by a strictly bureaucratic organization. (The fact that the bureaucratic apparatus also can, and indeed does, create certain definite impediments for the discharge of business in a manner best adapted to the individuality of each case does not belong into the present context.)

Bureaucratization offers above all the optimum possibility for carrying through the principle of specializing administrative functions according to purely objective considerations.

Individual performances are allocated to functionaries who have specialized training and who by constant practice increase their expertise. "Objective" discharge of business primarily means a discharge of business according to *calculable rules* and "without regard for persons."

"Without regard for persons," however, is also the watchword of the market and, in general, of all pursuits of naked economic interests. Consistent bureaucratic domination means the leveling of "status honor." Hence, if the principle of the free market is not at the same time restricted, it means the universal domination of the "class situation." That this consequence of bureaucratic domination has not set in everywhere proportional to the extent of bureaucratization is due to the differences between possible principles by which polities may supply their requirements. However, the second element mentioned, calculable rules, is the most important one for modern bureaucracy. The peculiarity of modern culture, and specifically of its technical and economic basis, demands this very "calculability" of results. When fully developed, bureaucracy also stands, in a specific sense, under the principle of *sine ira ac studio*. Bureaucracy develops the more perfectly, the more it is "dehumanized," the more completely it succeeds in eliminating from official business love, hatred, and all purely personal, irrational, and emotional elements which escape calculation. This is appraised as its special virtue by capitalism.

The more complicated and specialized modern culture becomes, the more its external supporting apparatus demands the personally detached and strictly objective *expert*, in lieu of the lord of older social structures who was moved by personal sympathy and favor, by grace and gratitude. Bureaucracy offers the attitudes demanded by the external apparatus of modern culture in the most favorable combination. In particular, only bureaucracy has established the foundation for the administration of a rational law conceptually systematized on the basis of "statutes," such as the later Roman Empire first created with a high degree of technical perfection. During the Middle Ages, the reception of this [Roman] law coincided with the bureaucratization of legal administration: The advance of the rationally trained expert displaced the old trial procedure which was bound to tradition or to irrational presuppositions.

The Leveling of Social Differences

In spite of its indubitable technical superiority, bureaucracy has everywhere been a relatively late development. A number of obstacles have contributed to this, and only under certain social and political conditions have they definitely receded into the background.

A. Administrative Democratization   Bureaucratic organization has usually come into power on the basis of a leveling of economic and social differences. This leveling has been at least relative, and has concerned the significance of social and economic differences for the assumption of administrative functions.

Bureaucracy inevitably accompanies modern *mass democracy*, in contrast to the democratic self-government of small homogeneous units. This results from its characteristic principle: the abstract regularity of the exercise of authority, which is a result of the demand for "equality before the law" in the personal and functional sense—hence, of the horror of "privilege," and the principled rejection of doing business "from case to case." Such regularity also follows from the social preconditions of its origin. Any nonbureaucratic administration of a large social structure rests in some way upon the fact that existing social, material, or honorific preferences and ranks are connected with administrative functions and duties. This usually means that an economic or a social exploitation of position, which every sort of administrative activity provides to its bearers, is the compensation for the assumption of administrative functions.

Bureaucratization and democratization within the administration of the state therefore signify an increase of the cash expenditures of the public treasury, in spite of the fact that bureaucratic administration is usually more "economical" in character than other forms. Until recent times—at least from the point of view of the treasury—the cheapest way of satisfying the need for administration was to leave almost the entire local administration and lower judicature to the landlords of Eastern Prussia. The same is true of the administration by justices of the peace in England. Mass democracy which makes a clean sweep of the feudal, patrimonial, and—at least in intent—the plutocratic privileges in administration unavoidably has to put paid professional labor in place of the historically inherited "avocational" administration by notables.

B. Mass Parties and the Bureaucratic Consequences of Democratization   This applies not only to the state. For it is no accident that in their own organizations the democratic mass parties have completely broken with traditional rule by notables based upon personal relationships and personal esteem. Such personal structures still persist among many old conservative as well as old liberal parties, but democratic mass parties are bureaucratically organized under the leadership of party officials, professional party and trade union secretaries, etc. In Germany, for instance, this has happened in the Social Democratic party and in the agrarian mass-movement; in England earliest in the caucus democracy of Gladstone and Chamberlain which spread from Birmingham in the 1870's. In the United States, both parties since Jackson's administration have developed bureaucratically. In France, however, attempts to organize disciplined political parties on the basis of an election system that would compel bureaucratic organization have repeatedly failed. The resistance of local circles of notables against the otherwise unavoidable bureaucratization of the parties, which would encompass the entire country and break their influence, could not be overcome. Every advance

of simple election techniques based on numbers alone as, for instance, the system of proportional representation, means a strict and inter-local bureaucratic organization of the parties and therewith an increasing domination of party bureaucracy and discipline, as well as the elimination of the local circles of notables—at least this holds for large states.

The progress of bureaucratization within the state administration itself is a phenomenon paralleling the development of democracy, as is quite obvious in France, North America, and now in England. Of course, one must always remember that the term "democratization" can be misleading. The *demos* itself, in the sense of a shapeless mass, never "governs" larger associations, but rather is governed. What changes is only the way in which the executive leaders are selected and the measure of influence which the *demos*, or better, which social circles from its midst are able to exert upon the content and the direction of administrative activities by means of "public opinion." "Democratization," in the sense here intended, does not necessarily mean an increasingly active share of the subjects in government. This may be a result of democratization, but it is not necessarily the case.

We must expressly recall at this point that the political concept of democracy, deduced from the "equal rights" of the governed, includes these further postulates: (1) prevention of the development of a closed status group of officials in the interest of a universal accessibility of office, and (2) minimization of the authority of officialdom in the interest of expanding the sphere of influence of "public opinion" as far as practicable. Hence, wherever possible, political democracy strives to shorten the term of office through election and recall, and to be relieved from a limitation to candidates with special expert qualifications. Thereby democracy inevitably comes into conflict with the bureaucratic tendencies which have been produced by its very fight against the notables. The loose term "democratization" can not be used here, in so far as it is understood to mean the minimization of the civil servants' power in favor of the greatest possible "direct" rule of the *demos,* which in practice means the respective party leaders of the *demos.* The decisive aspect here—indeed it is rather exclusively so—is the *leveling of the governed* in face of the governing and bureaucratically articulated group, which in its turn may occupy a quite autocratic position, both in fact and in form.

The Objective and Subjective Bases of Bureaucratic Perpetuity

Once fully established, bureaucracy is among those social structures which are the hardest to destroy. Bureaucracy is *the* means of transforming social action into rationally organized action. Therefore, as an instrument of rationally organizing authority relations, bureaucracy was and is a power instrument of the first order for one who controls the bureaucratic apparatus. Under otherwise equal conditions, rationally organized and directed action (*Gesellschaftshandeln*) is superior to every kind of collective behavior (*Massenhandeln*) and also social action (*Gemeinschaftshandeln*) opposing it. Where administration has been completely bureaucratized, the resulting system of domination is practically indestructible.

The individual bureaucrat cannot squirm out of the apparatus into which he has been harnessed. In contrast to the "notable" performing administrative tasks as a honorific duty or as a subsidiary occupation (avocation), the professional bureaucrat is chained to his activity in his entire economic and ideological existence. In the great majority of cases he is only a small cog in a ceaselessly moving mechanism which prescribes to him an essentially fixed route of march. The officialis entrusted with specialized tasks, and normally the mechanism cannot be put into motion or arrested by him, but only from the very top. The individual bureaucrat is, above all, forged to the common interest of all the functionaries in the perpetuation of the

apparatus and the persistence of its rationally organized domination.

The ruled, for their part, cannot dispense with or replace the bureaucratic apparatus once it exists, for it rests upon expert training, a functional specialization of work, and an attitude set on habitual virtuosity in the mastery of single yet methodically integrated functions. If the apparatus stops working, or if its work is interrupted by force, chaos results, which it is difficult to master by improvised replacements from among the governed. This holds for public administration as well as for private economic management. Increasingly the material fate of the masses depends upon the continuous and correct functioning of the ever more bureaucratic organizations of private capitalism, and the idea of eliminating them becomes more and more utopian.

Increasingly, all order in public and private organizations is dependent on the system of files and the discipline of officialdom, that means, its habit of painstaking obedience within its wonted sphere of action. The latter is the more decisive element, however important in practice the files are. The naive idea of Bakuninism of destroying the basis of "acquired rights" together with "domination" by destroying the public documents overlooks that the settled orientation of *man* for observing the accustomed rules and regulations will survive independently of the documents. Every reorganization of defeated or scattered army units, as well as every restoration of an administrative order destroyed by revolts, panics, or other catastrophes, is effected by an appeal to this conditioned orientation, bred both in the officials and in the subjects, of obedient adjustment to such [social and political] orders. If the appeal is successful it brings, as it were, the disturbed mechanism to "snap into gear" again.

The objective indispensability of the once-existing apparatus, in connection with its peculiarly "impersonal" character, means that the mechanism—in contrast to the feudal order based upon personal loyalty—is easily made to work for anybody who knows how to gain control over it. A rationally ordered officialdom continues to function smoothly after the enemy has occupied the territory; he merely needs to change the top officials. It continues to operate because it is to the vital interest of everyone concerned, including above all the enemy.

After Bismarck had, during the long course of his years in power, brought his ministerial colleagues into unconditional bureaucratic dependence by eliminating all independent statesmen, he saw to his surprise that upon his resignation they continued to administer their offices unconcernedly and undismayedly, as if it had not been the ingenious lord and very creator of these tools who had left, but merely some individual figure in the bureaucratic machine which had been exchanged for some other figure. In spite of all the changes of masters in France since the time of the First Empire, the power apparatus remained essentially the same.

Such an apparatus makes "revolution," in the sense of the forceful creation of entirely new formations of authority, more and more impossible—technically, because of its control over the modern means of communication (telegraph etc.), and also because of its increasingly rationalized inner structure. The place of "revolutions" is under this process taken by *coups d'état*, as again France demonstrates in the classical manner since all successful transformations there have been of this nature.

Bureaucracy and Education

A. Educational Specialization, Degree Hunting and Status Seeking

We cannot here analyze the far-reaching and general cultural effects that the advance of the rational bureaucratic structure of domination develops quite independently of the areas in which it takes hold. Naturally, bureaucracy promotes a "rationalist" way of life, but the concept of rationalism allows for widely differing contents. Quite generally, one can only say that the bureaucratization of all domination very strongly furthers the development of "rational matter-of-factness" and the personality type of the professional expert. This has far-reaching ramifications, but only one important element of the process can be briefly indicated here: its effect upon the nature of education and personal culture *(Erziehung und Bildung)*.

Educational institutions on the European continent, especially the institutions of higher learning—the universities, as well as technical academies, business colleges, gymnasia, and other secondary schools—are dominated and influenced by the need for the kind of "education" which is bred by the system of specialized examinations or tests of expertise *(Fachprüfungswesen)* increasingly indispensable for modern bureaucracies.

The "examination for expertise" in the modern sense was and is found also outside the strictly bureaucratic structures: today, for instance, in the so-called "free" professions of medicine and law, and in the guild-organized trades. Nor is it an indispensable accompaniment of bureaucratization: the French, English and American bureaucracies have for a long time done without such examinations either entirely or to a large extent, using in-service training and performance in the party organizations as a substitute.

"Democracy" takes an ambivalent attitude also towards the system of examinations for expertise, as it does towards all the phenomena of the bureaucratization which, nevertheless, it promotes. On the one hand, the system of examinations means, or at least appears to mean, selection of the qualified from all social strata in place of the rule by notables. But on the other, democracy fears that examinations and patents of education will create a privileged "caste," and for that reason opposes such a system.

Finally, the examination for expertise is found already in prebureaucratic or semibureaucratic epochs. Indeed, its earliest regular historical locus is in *prebendally* organized structures of domination. The expectation of prebends, first of church prebends—as in the Islamic Orient and in the Occidental Middle Ages—and then, as was especially the case in China, also of secular prebends, is the typical prize for which people study and are examined. These examinations, however, have only in part the character of tests for specialized "expertise."

Only the modern development of full bureaucratization brings the system of rational examinations for expertise irresistibly to the fore. The American Civil-Service Reform movement gradually imports expert training and specialized examinations into the United States; the examination system also advances into all other countries from its main (European) breeding ground, Germany. The increasing bureaucratization of administration enhances the importance of the specialized examination in England. In China, the attempt to replace the old semipatrimonial bureaucracy by a modern bureaucracy brought the expert examination; it took the place of the former and quite differently structured system of examinations. The bureaucratization of capitalism, with its demand for expertly trained technicians, clerks, etc., carries such examinations all over the world.

This development is, above all, greatly furthered by the social prestige of the "patent of education" acquired through such specialized examinations, the more so since this prestige can again be turned to economic advantage. The role played in former days by the "proof of ancestry," as prerequisite for equality of birth, access to noble prebends and endowments and, wherever the nobility retained social power, for the qualification to state offices, is nowadays taken by the patent of education. The elaboration of the diplomas from universities, business and engineering colleges, and the universal clamor for the creation of further educational certificates in all fields serve the formation of a privileged stratum in bureaus and in offices.

Such certificates support their holders' claims for connubium with the notables (in business offices, too, they raise hope for preferment with the boss's daughter), claims to be admitted into the circles that adhere to "codes of honor," claims for a "status-appropriate" salary instead of a wage according to performance, claims for assured advancement and old-age insurance, and, above all, claims to the monopolization of socially and economically advantageous positions. If we hear from all sides demands for the introduction of regulated curricula culminating in specialized examinations, the reason behind this is, of course, not a suddenly awakened "thirst for education," but rather the desire to limit the supply of candidates for these positions and to monopolize them for the holders of educational patents. For such monopolization, the "examination" is today the universal instrument—hence its irresistible advance. As the curriculum required for the acquisition of the patent of education requires considerable expenses and a long period of gestation, this striving implies a repression of talent (of the "charisma") in favor of property, for the intellectual costs of the educational patent are always low and decrease, rather than increase, with increasing volume. The old requirement of a knightly style of life, the prerequisite for capacity to hold a fief, is nowadays in Germany replaced by the necessity of participating in its surviving remnants, the duelling fraternities of the universities which grant the patents of education; in the Anglo-Saxon countries, the athletic and social clubs fulfill the same function.

On the other hand, bureaucracy strives everywhere for the creation of a "right to the office" by the establishment of regular disciplinary procedures and by the elimination of the completely arbitrary disposition of the superior over the subordinate official. The bureaucracy seeks to secure the official's position, his orderly advancement, and his provision for old age. In this, it is supported by the "democratic" sentiment of the governed which demands that domination be minimized; those who hold this attitude believe themselves able to discern a weakening of authority itself in every weakening of the lord's arbitrary disposition over the officials. To this extent bureaucracy, both in business offices and in public service, promotes the rise of a specific status group, just as did the quite different officeholders of the past. We have already pointed out that these status characteristics are usually also exploited for, and by their nature contribute to, the technical usefulness of bureaucracy in fulfilling its specific tasks.

It is precisely against this unavoidable status character of bureaucracy that "democracy" reacts in its striving to put the election of officials for short terms in place of the appointment of officials and to substitute the recall of officials by referendum for a regulated disciplinary procedure, thus seeking to replace the arbitrary disposition of the hierarchically superordinate "master" by the equally arbitrary disposition of the governed or rather, of the party bosses dominating them.

B. Excursus on the "Cultivated Man"

Social prestige based upon the advantage of schooling and education as such is by no means specific to bureaucracy. On the contrary. But educational prestige in other structures of domination rests upon substantially different foundations with respect to content. Expressed in slogans, the "cultivated man," rather than the "specialist," was the end sought by education and the basis of social esteem in the feudal, theocratic, and patrimonial structures of domination, in the English administration by notables, in the old Chinese patrimonial bureaucracy, as well as under the rule of demagogues in the Greek states during the so-called Democracy. The term "cultivated man" is used here in a completely value-neutral sense; it is understood to mean solely that a quality of life conduct which *was held* to be "cultivated" was the goal of education, rather than a specialized training

in some expertise. Such education may have been aimed at a knightly or at an ascetic type, at a literary type (as in China) or at a gymnastic-humanist type (as in Hellas), or at a conventional "gentleman" type of the Anglo-Saxon variety. A personality "cultivated" in this sense formed the educational ideal stamped by the structure of domination and the conditions of membership in the ruling stratum of the society in question. The qualification of this ruling stratum rested upon the possession of a "plus" of such *cultural quality* (in the quite variable and value-neutral sense of the term as used here), rather than upon a "plus" of expert knowledge. Military, theological and legal expertise was, of course, intensely cultivated at the same time. But the point of gravity in the Hellenic, in the medieval, as well as in the Chinese educational curriculum was formed by elements entirely different from those which were "useful" in a technical sense.

Behind all the present discussions about the basic questions of the educational system there lurks decisively the struggle of the "specialist" type of man against the older type of the "cultivated man," a struggle conditioned by the irresistibly expanding bureaucratization of all public and private relations of authority and by the ever-increasing importance of experts and specialised knowledge. This struggle affects the most intimate aspects of personal culture.

Conclusion

During its advance, bureaucratic organization has had to overcome not only those essentially negative obstacles, several times previously mentioned, that stood in the way of the required leveling process. In addition, administrative structures based on different principles did and still do cross paths with bureaucratic organization. Some of these have already been mentioned in passing. Not all of the types existing in the real world can be discussed here—this would lead us much too far afield; we can analyze only some of the most important *structural principles* in much simplified schematic exposition. We shall proceed in the main, although not exclusively, by asking the following questions:

1. How far are these administrative structures in their developmental chances subject to economic, political or any other external determinants, or to an "autonomous" logic inherent in their technical structure? 2. What, if any, are the economic effects which these administrative structures exert? In doing this, one must keep one's eye on the fluidity and the overlapping of all these organizational principles. Their "pure" types, after all, are to be considered merely border cases which are of special and indispensable

analytical value, and bracket historical reality which almost always appears in mixed forms.

The bureaucratic structure is everywhere a late product of historical development. The further back we trace our steps, the more typical is the absence of bureaucracy and of officialdom in general. Since bureaucracy has a "rational" character, with rules, means-ends calculus, and matter-of-factness predominating, its rise and expansion has everywhere had "revolutionary" results, in a special sense still to be discussed, as had the advance of *rationalism* in general. The march of bureaucracy accordingly destroyed structures of domination which were not rational in this sense of the term. Hence we may ask: What were these structures?

MAX WEBER: "OBJECTIVITY" IN SOCIAL SCIENCE AND SOCIAL POLICY[1]

All serious reflection about the ultimate elements of meaningful human conduct is oriented primarily in terms of the categories "end" and "means." We desire something concretely either "for its own sake" or as a means of achieving something else which is more highly desired. The question of the appropriateness of the means for achieving a given end is undoubtedly accessible to scientific analysis. Inasmuch as we are able to determine (within the present limits of our knowledge) which means for the achievement of a proposed end are appropriate or inappropriate, we can in this way estimate the chances of attaining a certain end by certain available means. In this way we can indirectly

criticize the setting of the end itself as practically meaningful (on the basis of the existing historical situation) or as meaningless with reference to existing conditions. Furthermore, when the possibility of attaining a proposed end appears to exist, we can determine (naturally within the limits of our existing knowledge) the consequences which the application of the means to be used will produce in addition to the eventual attainment of the proposed end, as a result of the interdependence of all events. We can then provide the acting person with the ability to weigh and compare the undesirable as over against the desirable consequences of his action. Thus, we can answer the question: what will the

[1] This essay was published when the editorship of the *Archiv fur Sozialwissenschaft und Sozialpolitik* was transferred to Edgar Jaffé, Werner Sombart, and Max Weber. Its form was influenced by the occasion for which it was written and the content should be considered in this light. (Marianne Weber.)

attainment of a desired end "cost" in terms of the predictable loss of other values? Since, in the vast majority of cases, every goal that is striven for does "cost" or can "cost" something in this sense, the weighing of the goal in terms of the incidental consequences of the action which realizes it cannot be omitted from the deliberation of persons who act with a sense of responsibility. One of the most important functions of the *technical criticism* which we have been discussing thus far is to make this sort of analysis possible. To apply the results of this analysis in the making of a decision, however, is not a task which science can undertake; it is rather the task of the acting, willing person: he weighs and chooses from among the values involved according to his own conscience and his personal view of the world. Science can make him realize that all action and naturally, according to the circumstances, inaction imply in their consequences the espousal of certain values—and herewith—what is today so willingly overlooked—the rejection of certain others. The act of choice itself is his own responsibility.

We can also offer the person, who makes a choice, insight into the significance of the desired object. We can teach him to think in terms of the context and the meaning of the ends he desires, and among which he chooses. We do this through making explicit and developing in a logically consistent manner the "ideas" which actually do or which can underlie the concrete end. It is self-evident that one of the most important tasks of every science of cultural life is to arrive at a rational understanding of these "ideas" for which men either really or allegedly struggle. This does not overstep the boundaries of a science which strives for an "analytical ordering of empirical reality," although the methods which are used in this interpretation of cultural *(geistig)* values are not "inductions" in the usual sense. At any rate, this task falls at least partly beyond the limits of economics as defined according to the conventional division of labor. It belongs among the tasks of

social philosophy. However, the historical influence of ideas in the development of social life has been and still is so great that our journal cannot renounce this task. It shall rather regard the investigation of this phenomenon as one of its most important obligations.

But the scientific treatment of value-judgments may not only understand and empathically analyze *(nacherleben)* the desired ends and the ideals which underlie them; it can also "judge" them critically. This criticism can of course have only a dialetical character, i.e., it can be no more than a formal logical judgment of historically given value-judgments and ideas, a testing of the ideals according to the postulate of the internal *consistency* of the desired end. It can, insofar as it sets itself this goal, aid the acting willing person in attaining self-clarification concerning the final axioms from which his desired ends are derived. It can assist him in becoming aware of the ultimate standards of value which he does not make explicit to himself or, which he must presuppose in order to be logical. The elevation of these ultimate standards, which are manifested in concrete value-judgments, to the level of explicitness is the utmost that the scientific treatment of value-judgments can do without entering into the realm of speculation. As to whether the person expressing these value-judgments *should* adhere to these ultimate standards is his personal affair; it involves will and conscience, not empirical knowledge. . . .

Certainly, the dignity of the "personality" lies in the fact that for it there exist values about which it organizes its life;—even if these values are in certain cases concentrated exclusively within the sphere of the person's "individuality," then "self-realization" in *those* interests for which it claims *validity* as *values*, is the idea with respect to which its whole existence is oriented. Only on the assumption of belief in the validity of values is the attempt to espouse value-judgments meaningful. However, to *judge* the *validity* of such values is a matter of *faith*. It may perhaps be a task for the speculative interpretation of life and the universe in quest of their meaning. But it certainly does not fall within the province of an empirical science in the sense in which it is to be practised here. The empirically demonstrable fact that these ultimate ends undergo historical changes and are debatable does not affect this distinction between empirical science and value-judgments, contrary to what is often thought. For even the knowledge of the most certain proposition of our theoretical sciences—e.g., the exact natural sciences or mathematics, is, like the cultivation and refinement of the conscience, a product of culture. . . . Only positive religions—or more precisely expressed: dogmatically bound *sects*—are able to confer on the content of *cultural values* the status of unconditionally valid *ethical* imperatives. Outside these sects, cultural ideals which the individual wishes to realize and ethical obligations which he *should* fulfill do not, in principle, share the same status. The fate of an epoch which has eaten of the tree of knowledge is that it must know that we cannot learn the *meaning* of the world from the results of its analysis, be it ever so perfect; it must rather be in a position to create this meaning itself. It must recognize that general views of life and the universe can never be the products of increasing empirical knowledge, and that the highest ideals, which move us most forcefully, are always formed only in the struggle with other ideals which are just as sacred to others as ours are to us. . . .

* * *

There is no absolutely "objective" scientific analysis of culture—or put perhaps more narrowly but certainly not essentially differently for our purposes—of "social phenomena" independent of special and "one-sided" viewpoints according to which—expressly or tacitly, consciously or unconsciously—they are selected, analyzed and organized for expository purposes. The reasons for this lie in the character of the cognitive goal of all research in social science which seeks to transcend the purely *formal* treatment of the legal or conventional norms regulating social life.

The type of social science in which we are interested is an *empirical science* of concrete *reality* (*Wirklichkeitswissenschaft*). Our aim is the understanding of the characteristic uniqueness of the reality in which we move. We wish to understand on the one hand the relationships and the cultural significance of individual events in their contemporary manifestations and on the other the causes of their being historically *so* and not *otherwise*. Now, as soon as we attempt to reflect about the way in which life confronts us in immediate concrete situations, it presents an infinite multiplicity of successively and coexistently emerging and disappearing events, both "within" and "outside" ourselves. The absolute infinitude of this multiplicity is seen to remain undiminished even when our attention is focused on a single "object," for instance, a concrete act of exchange, as soon as we seriously attempt an exhaustive description of *all* the individual components of this "individual phenomena," to say nothing of explaining it causally. All the analysis of infinite reality which the finite human mind can conduct rests on the tacit assumption that only a finite portion of this reality constitutes the object of scientific investigation, and that only it is "important" in the sense of being "worthy of being known." But what are the criteria by which this segment is selected? It has often been thought that the decisive criterion in the cultural sciences, too, was in the last analysis, the "regular" recurrence of certain causal relationships. The "laws" which we are able to perceive in the infinitely manifold stream of events must—according to this conception—contain the scientifically "essential" aspect of reality. . . .

We seek knowledge of an historical phenomenon, meaning by historical: significant in its individuality (*Eigenart*). And the decisive element in this is that only through the presupposition that a finite part alone of the infinite variety of phenomena is significant, does the knowledge of an individual phenomenon become logically meaningful. Even with the widest imaginable knowledge of "laws," we are helpless in the face of the question: how is the *causal explanation* of an *individual* fact possible—since a *description* of even the smallest slice of reality can never be exhaustive? The number and type of causes which have influenced any given event are always infinite and there is nothing in the things themselves to set some of them apart as alone meriting attention. A chaos of "existential judgments" about countless individual events would be the only result of a serious attempt to analyze reality "without presuppositions." And even this result is only seemingly possible, since every single perception discloses on closer examination an infinite number of constituent perceptions which can never be exhaustively expressed in a judgment. Order is brought into this chaos only on the condition that in every case only a *part* of concrete reality is interesting and *significant* to us, because only it is related to the *cultural values* with which we approach reality. Only certain sides of the infinitely complex concrete phenomenon, namely those to which we attribute a general *cultural significance*—are therefore worthwhile knowing. They alone are objects of causal explanation. And even this causal explanation evinces the same character; an *exhaustive* causal investigation of any concrete phenomena in its full reality is not only practically impossible—it is simply nonsense. We select only those causes to which are to be imputed in the individual case, the "essential" feature of an event. Where the *individuality* of a phenomenon is concerned, the question of causality is not a question of *laws* but of concrete causal *relationships;* it is not a question of the subsumption of the event under some general rubric as a representative case but of its imputation as a consequence of some constellation. It is in brief a *question of imputation.* Wherever the causal explanation of a "cultural phenomenon—an "historical individual" is under consideration, the knowledge of causal *laws* is not the *end* of the investigation but only a means. It facilitates and renders possible the

causal imputation to their concrete causes of those components of a phenomenon the individuality of which is culturally significant. So far and only so far as it achieves this, is it valuable for our knowledge of concrete relationships. And the more "general," i.e., the more abstract the laws, the less they can contribute to the causal imputation of *individual* phenomena and, more indirectly, to the understanding of the significance of cultural events.

* * *

The conclusion which follows from the above is that an "objective" analysis of cultural events, which proceeds according to the thesis that the ideal of science is the reduction of empirical reality of "laws," is meaningless. It is not meaningless, as is often maintained, because cultural or psychic events for instance are "objectively" less governed by laws. It is meaningless for a number of other reasons. Firstly, because the knowledge of social laws is not knowledge of social reality but is rather one of the various aids used by our minds for attaining this end; secondly, because knowledge of *cultural* events is inconceivable except on a basis of the *significance* which the concrete constellations of reality have for us in certain *individual* concrete situations. In *which* sense and in *which* situations this is the case is not revealed to us by any law; it is decided according to the *value-ideas* in the light of which we view "culture" in each individual case. "Culture" is a finite segment of the meaningless infinity of the world process, a segment on which *human beings* confer meaning and significance. This is true even for the human being who views a *particular* culture as a mortal enemy and who seeks to "return to nature." He can attain this point of view only after viewing the culture in which he lives from the standpoint of his values, and finding it "too soft." This is the purely logical-formal fact which is involved when we speak of the logically necessary rootedness of all historical entities *(historische Individuen)* in "evaluative ideas." The transcendental presupposition of every *cultural science* lies not in our finding a certain culture or any "culture" in general to be *valuable* but rather in the fact that we are *cultural beings,* endowed with the capacity and the will to take a deliberate attitude towards the world and to lend it *significance.* Whatever this significance may be, it will lead us to judge certain phenomena of human existence in its light and to respond to them as being (positively or negatively) meaningful. Whatever may be the content of this attitude—these phenomena have cultural significance for us and on this significance alone rests its scientific interest. Thus when we speak here of the conditioning of cultural knowledge through *evaluative* ideas *(Wertideen)* (following the terminology of modern logic), it is done in the hope that we will not be subject to crude misunderstandings such as the opinion that cultural significance should be attributed only to *valuable* phenomena. Prostitution is a *cultural* phenomenon just as much as religion or money. All three are cultural phenomena *only* because and *only* insofar as their existence and the form which they historically assume touch directly or indirectly on our cultural *interests* and arouse our striving for knowledge concerning problems brought into focus by the evaluative ideas which give *significance* to the fragment of reality analyzed by those concepts.

All knowledge of cultural reality, as may be seen, is always knowledge from *particular points of view.* When we require from the historian and social research worker as an elementary presupposition that they distinguish the important from the trivial and that they should have the necessary "point of view" for this distinction, we mean that they must understand how to relate the events of the real world consciously or unconsciously to universal "cultural values" and to select out those relationships which are significant for us. If the notion that those standpoints can be derived from the "facts themselves" continually recurs, it is due to the naive self-deception of the specialist who is unaware that it is due to the evaluative ideas with which

he unconsciously approaches his subject matter, that he has selected from an absolute infinity a tiny portion with the study of which he *concerns* himself. In connection with this selection of individual special "aspects" of the event which always and everywhere occurs, consciously or unconsciously, there also occurs that element of cultural-scientific work which is referred to by the often-heard assertion that the "personal" element of a scientific work is what is really valuable in it, and that personality must be expressed in every work if its existence is to be justified. To be sure, without the investigator's evaluative ideas, there would be no principle of selection of subject-matter and no meaningful knowledge of the concrete reality. Just as without the investigator's conviction regarding the significance of particular cultural facts, every attempt to analyze concrete reality is absolutely meaningless, so the direction of his personal belief, the refraction of values in the prism of his mind, gives direction to his work. And the values to which the scientific genius relates the object of his inquiry may determine, i.e., decide the "conception" of a whole epoch, not only concerning what is regarded as "valuable" but also concerning what is significant or insignificant, "important" or "unimportant" in the phenomena.

Accordingly, cultural science in our sense involves "subjective" presuppositions insofar as it concerns itself only with those components of reality which have some relationship, however indirect, to events to which we attach cultural significance. . . .

Accordingly the synthetic concepts used by historians are either imperfectly defined or, as soon as the elimination of ambiguity is sought for, the concept becomes an abstract ideal type and reveals itself therewith as a theoretical and hence "one-sided" viewpoint which illuminates the aspect of reality with which it can be related. But these concepts are shown to be obviously inappropriate as schema into which reality could be completely *integrated.* For none of those systems of ideas, which are absolutely indispensable in the understanding of those segments of reality which are meaningful at a particular moment, can exhaust its infinite richness. They are all attempts, on the basis of the present state of our knowledge and the available conceptual patterns, to bring order into the chaos of those facts which we have drawn into the field circumscribed by our *interest*. The intellectual apparatus which the past has developed through the analysis, or more truthfully, the analytical rearrangement of the immediately given reality, and through the latter's integration by concepts which correspond to the state of its knowledge and the focus of its interest, is in constant tension with the new knowledge which we can and *desire* to wrest from reality. The progress of cultural science occurs through this conflict. Its result is the perpetual reconstruction of those concepts through which we seek to comprehend reality. The history of the social sciences is and remains a continuous process passing from the attempt to order reality analytically through the construction of concepts—the dissolution of the analytical constructs so constructed through the expansion and shift of the scientific horizon—and the reformulation anew of concepts on the foundations thus transformed. It is not the error of the attempt to construct conceptual systems *in general* which is shown by this process—every science, even simple descriptive history, operates with the conceptual stock-in-trade of its time. Rather, this process shows that in the cultural sciences concept-construction depends on the setting of the problem, and the latter varies with the content of culture itself. The relationship between concept and reality in the cultural sciences involves the transitoriness of all such syntheses. The great attempts at theory-construction in our science were always useful for revealing the limits of the significance of those points of view which provided their foundations. The greatest advances in the sphere of the social sciences are substantively tied up with the shift in practical cultural problems and take the guise of a critique of concept-construction. Adherence to the purpose of this critique and therewith the investigation of the *principles of syntheses* in the social sciences shall be among the primary tasks of our journal.

In the conclusions which are to be drawn from what has been said, we come to a point where perhaps our views diverge here and there from those of many, and even the most outstanding, representatives of the Historical School, among whose offspring we too are to be numbered. The latter still hold in many ways, expressly or tacitly, to the opinion that it is the end and the goal of every science to order its data into a system of concepts, the content of which is to be acquired and slowly perfected through the observation of empirical regularities, the construction of hypotheses, and their verification, until finally a "completed" and *hence* deductive science emerges. For this goal, the historical-inductive work of the present-day is a preliminary task necessitated by the imperfections of our discipline. Nothing can be more suspect, from this point of view, than the construction and application of clear-cut concepts since this seems to be an overhasty anticipation of the remote future.

This conception was, in principle, impregnable within the framework of the classical-scholastic epistemology which was still fundamentally assumed by the majority of the research-workers identified with the Historical School. The function of concepts was assumed to be the *reproduction* of "objective" reality in the analyst's imagination. Hence the recurrent references to the *unreality* of all clear-cut concepts. If one perceives the implications of the fundamental ideas of modern epistemology which ultimately derives from Kant; namely, that concepts are primarily analytical instruments for the intellectual mastery of empirical data and can be only that, the fact that precise genetic concepts are necessarily ideal types will not cause him to desist from constructing them. The relationship between concept and historical research is reversed for those who appreciate this; the goal of the Historical School then appears as logically impossible, the concepts are not ends but are means to the end of understanding phenomena which are significant from concrete individual viewpoints.

* * *

We are now at the end of this discussion, the only purpose of which was to trace the course of the hair-line which separates science from faith and to make explicit the *meaning* of the quest for social and economic knowledge. The *objective* validity of all empirical knowledge rests exclusively upon the ordering of the given reality according to categories which are *subjective* in a specific sense, namely, in that they present the *presuppositions* of our knowledge and are based on the presupposition of the *value* of those *truths* which empirical knowledge alone is able to give us. The means available to our science offer nothing to those persons to whom this truth is of no value. It should be remembered that the belief in the value of scientific truth is the product of certain cultures and is not a product of man's original nature. Those for whom scientific truth is of no value will seek in vain for some other truth to take the place of science in just those respects in which it is unique, namely, in the provision of concepts and judgments which are neither empirical reality nor reproductions of it but which facilitate its analytical ordering in a valid manner. In the empirical social sciences, as we have seen, the possibility of meaningful knowledge of what is essential for us in the infinite richness of events is bound up with the unremitting application of viewpoints of a specifically particularized character, which, in the last analysis, are oriented on the basis of evaluative ideas. These evaluative ideas are for their part empirically discoverable and analyzable as elements of meaningful human

conduct, but their validity can *not* be deduced from empirical data as such. The "objectivity" of the social sciences depends rather on the fact that the empirical data are always related to those evaluative ideas which alone make them worth knowing and the significance of the empirical data is derived from these evaluative ideas. But these data can never become the foundation for the empirically impossible proof of the validity of the evaluative ideas. . . .

All research in the cultural sciences in an age of specialization, once it is oriented towards a given subject matter through particular settings of problems and has established its methodological principles, will consider the analysis of the data as an end in itself. It will discontinue assessing the value of the individual facts in terms of their relationships to ultimate value-ideas. Indeed, it will lose its awareness of its ultimate rootedness in the value-ideas in general. And it is well that should be so. But there comes a moment when the atmosphere changes. The significance of the unreflectively utilized viewpoints becomes uncertain and the road is lost in the twilight. The light of the great cultural problems moves on. Then science too prepares to change its standpoint and its analytical apparatus and to view the streams of events from the heights of thought. It follows those stars which alone are able to give meaning and direction to its labors:

> "... der neue Trieb erwacht,
> Ich eile fort, ihr ewiges Licht zu trinken,
> Vor mir den Tag und unter mir die Nacht,
> Den Himmel; auuber mir und unter mir die Wellen."[2]

---

[2] *Faust:* Act I, Scene II. (Translated by Bayard-Taylor) "The newborn impulse fires my mind.

I hasten on, his beams eternal drinking,
The Day before me and the Night behind,
Above me Heaven unfurled, the floor of waves beneath me."

MAX WEBER: CLASS, STATUS, PARTY

A. Economically Determined Power and the Status Order. The structure of every legal order directly influences the distribution of power, economic or otherwise, within its respective community. This is true of all legal orders and not only that of the state. In general, we understand by "power" the chance of a man or a number of men to realize their own will in a social action even against the resistance of others who are participating in the action.

"Economically conditioned" power is not, of course, identical with "power" as such. On the contrary, the emergence of economic power may be the consequence of power existing on other grounds. Man does not strive for power only in order to enrich himself economically. Power, including economic power, may be valued for its own sake. Very frequently the striving for power is also conditioned by the social honor it entails. Not all power, however, entails social honor: The typical American Boss, as well as the typical big speculator, deliberately relinquishes social honor. Quite generally, "mere economic" power, and especially "naked" money power, is by no means a recognized basis of social honor. Nor is power the only basis of social honor. Indeed, social honor, or prestige, may even be the basis of economic power, and very frequently has been. Power, as well as honor, may be guaranteed by the legal order, but, at least normally, it is not their primary source. The legal order is rather an additional factor that enhances the chance to hold power or honor; but it can not always secure them.

The way in which social honor is distributed in a community between typical groups participating in this distribution we call the "status order." The social order and the economic order are related in a similar manner to the legal order. However, the economic order merely defines the way in which economic goods and services are distributed and used. Of course, the status order is strongly influenced by it, and in turn reacts upon it.

Now: "classes," "status groups," and "parties" are phenomena of the distribution of power within a community.

B. Determination of Class Situation by Market Situation. In our terminology, "classes" are not communities; they merely represent possible, and frequent, bases for social action. We may speak of a "class" when (1) a number of people have in common a specific causal component of their life chances, insofar as (2) this component is represented exclusively by economic interests in the possession of goods and opportunities for income, and (3) is represented under the conditions of the commodity or labor markets. This is "class situation."

It is the most elemental economic fact that the way in which the disposition over material property is distributed among a plurality of people, meeting competitively in the market for the purpose of exchange, in itself creates specific life chances. The mode of distribution, in accord with the law of marginal utility, excludes the non-wealthy from competing for highly valued goods; it favors the owners and, in fact, gives to them a monopoly to acquire such goods. Other things being equal, the mode of distribution monopolizes the opportunities for profitable deals for all those who, provided with goods, do not necessarily have to exchange them. It increases, at least generally, their power in the price struggle with those who, being propertyless, have nothing to offer but their labor or the resulting products, and who are compelled to get rid of these products in order to subsist at all. The mode of distribution gives to the propertied a monopoly on the possibility of transferring property from the sphere of use as "wealth" to the sphere of "capital," that is, it gives them the entrepreneurial function and all chances to share directly or indirectly in returns on capital. All this holds true within the area in which pure market conditions prevail. "Property" and "lack of property" are, therefore, the basic categories of all class situations. It does not matter whether these two categories become effective in the competitive struggles of the consumers or of the producers.

Within these categories, however, class situations are further differentiated: on the one hand, according to the kind of property that is usable for returns; and, on the other hand, according to the kind of services that can be offered in the market. Ownership of dwellings; workshops; warehouses; stores; agriculturally usable land in large or small holdings—a quantitative difference with possibly qualitative consequences; ownership of mines; cattle; men (slaves); disposition over mobile instruments of production, or capital goods of all sorts, especially money or objects that can easily be exchanged for money; disposition over products of one's own labor or of others' labor differing according to their various distances from consumability; disposition over transferable monopolies of any kind—all these distinctions differentiate the class situations of the propertied just as does the "meaning" which they can give to the use of property, especially to property which has money equivalence. Accordingly, the propertied, for instance, may belong to the class of rentiers or to the class of entrepreneurs.

Those who have no property but who offer services are differentiated just as much according to their kinds of services as according to the way in which they make use of these services,

in a continuous or discontinuous relation to a recipient. But always this is the generic connotation of the concept of class: that the kind of chance in the *market* is the decisive moment which presents a common condition for the individual's fate. Class situation is, in this sense, ultimately market situation. The effect of naked possession *per se,* which among cattle breeders gives the non-owning slave or serf into the power of the cattle owner, is only a fore-runner of real "class" formation. However, in the cattle loan and in the naked severity of the law of debts in such communities for the first time mere "possession" as such emerges as decisive for the fate of the individual; this is much in contrast to crop-raising communities, which are based on labor. The creditor-debtor relation becomes the basis of "class situations" first in the cities, where a "credit market," however primitive, with rates of interest increasing according to the extent of dearth and factual monopolization of lending in the hands of a plutocracy could develop. Therewith "class struggles" begin.

Those men whose fate is not determined by the chance of using goods or services for themselves on the market, e.g., slaves, are not, however, a class in the technical sense of the term. They are, rather, a status group.

C. Social Action Flowing from Class Interest. According to our terminology, the factor that creates "class" is unambiguously economic interest, and indeed, only those interests involved in the existence of the market. Nevertheless, the concept of class-interest is an ambiguous one: even as an empirical concept it is ambiguous as soon as one understands by it something other than the factual direction of interests following with a certain probability from the class situation for a certain average of those people subjected to the class situation. The class situation and other circumstances remaining the same, the direction in which the individual worker, for instance, is likely to pursue his interests may vary widely, according to whether he is constitutionally qualified for the task at hand to a high, to an average, or to a low degree. In the same way, the direction of interests may vary according to whether or not social action of a larger or smaller portion of those commonly affected by the class situation, or even an association among them, e.g., a trade union, has grown out of the class situation, from which the individual may expect promising results for himself. The emergence of an association or even of mere social action from a common class situation is by no means a universal phenomenon.

The class situation may be restricted in its efforts to the generation of essentially *similar* reactions, that is to say, within our terminology, of "mass behavior." However, it may not even have this result. Furthermore, often merely amorphous social action emerges. For example, the "grumbling" of workers known in ancient Oriental ethics: The moral disapproval of the work-master's conduct, which in its practical significance was probably equivalent to an increasingly typical phenomenon of precisely the latest industrial development, namely, the slowdown of laborers by virtue of tacit agreement. The degree in which "social action" and possibly associations emerge from the mass behavior of the members of a class is linked to general cultural conditions, especially to those of an intellectual sort. It is also linked to the extent of the contrasts that have already evolved, and is especially linked to the transparency of the connections between the causes and the consequences of the class situation. For however different life chances may be, this fact in itself, according to all experience, by no means gives birth to "class action" (social action by the members of a class). For that, the real conditions and the results of the class situation must be distinctly recognizable. For only then the contrast of life chances can be felt not as an absolutely given fact to be accepted, but as a resultant from either (1) the given distribution

of property, or (2) the structure of the concrete economic order. It is only then that people may react against the class structure not only through acts of intermittent and irrational protest, but in the form of rational association. There have been "class situations" of the first category (1), of a specifically naked and transparent sort, in the urban centers of Antiquity and during the Middle Ages: especially then when great fortunes were accumulated by factually monopolized trading in local industrial products or in foodstuffs; furthermore, under certain conditions, in the rural economy of the most diverse periods, when agriculture was increasingly exploited in a profit-making manner. The most important historical example of the second category (2) is the class situation of the modern proletariat.

D. Types of Class Struggle. Thus every class may be the carrier of any one of the innumerable possible forms of class action, but this is not necessarily so. In any case, a class does not in itself constitute a group *(Gemeinschaft)*. To treat "class" conceptually as being equivalent to "group" leads to distortion. That men in the same class situation regularly react in mass actions to such tangible situations as economic ones in the direction of those interests that are most adequate to their average number is an important and after all simple fact for the understanding of historical events. However, this fact must not lead to that kind of pseudo-scientific operation with the concepts of class and class interests which is so frequent these days and which has found its most classic expression in the statement of a talented author, that the individual may be in error concerning his interests but that the class is infallible about its interests.

If classes as such are not groups, nevertheless class situations emerge only on the basis of social action. However, social action that brings forth class situations is not basically action among members of the identical class; it is an action among members of different classes. Social actions that directly determine the class situation of the worker and the entrepreneur are: the labor market, the commodities market, and the capitalistic enterprise. But, in its turn, the existence of a capitalistic enterprise presupposes that a very specific kind of social action exists to protect the possession of goods *per se,* and especially the power of individuals to dispose, in principle freely, over the means of production: a certain kind of legal order. Each kind of class situation, and above all when it rests upon the power of property *per se,* will become most clearly efficacious when all other determinants of reciprocal relations are, as far as possible, eliminated in their significance. It is in this way that the use of the power of property in the market obtains its most sovereign importance.

Now status groups hinder the strict carrying through of the sheer market principle. In the present context they are of interest only from this one point of view. Before we briefly consider them, note that not much of a general nature can be said about the more specific kinds of antagonism between classes (in our meaning of the term). The great shift, which has been going on continuously in the past, and up to our times, may be summarized, although at a cost of some precision: the struggle in which class situations are effective has progressively shifted from consumption credit toward, first, competitive struggles in the commodity market and then toward wage disputes on the labor market. The class struggles of Antiquity—to the extent that they were genuine class struggles and not struggles between status groups—were initially carried on by peasants and perhaps also artisans threatened by debt bondage and struggling against urban creditors. For debt bondage is the normal result of the differentiation of wealth in commercial cities, especially in seaport cities. A similar situation has existed among cattle breeders. Debt relationships as such produced class action up to the days of Catilina. Along with this, and with an increase in provision of grain for the city by transporting it from the outside, the struggle over the means of sustenance emerged. It centered in the first place around the provision of bread and determination of the price of bread. It lasted throughout Antiquity and the entire Middle Ages. The propertyless flocked together against those who actually and supposedly were interested in the dearth of bread. This fight spread until it involved all those commodities essential to the way of life and to handicraft production. There were only incipient discussions of wage disputes in Antiquity and in the Middle Ages. But they have been slowly increasing up into modern times. In the earlier periods they were completely secondary to slave rebellions as well as to conflicts in the commodity market.

The propertyless of Antiquity and of the Middle Ages protested against monopolies, pre-emption, forestalling, and the withholding of goods from the market in order to raise prices. Today the central issue is the determination of the price of labor. The transition is represented by the fight for access to the market and for the determination of the price of products. Such fights went on between merchants and workers in the putting-out system of domestic handicraft during the transition to modern times. Since it is quite a general phenomenon we must mention here that the class antagonisms that are conditioned through the market situations are usually most bitter between those who actually and directly participate as opponents in price wars. It is not the rentier, the shareholder, and the banker who suffer the ill will of the worker, but almost exclusively the manufacturer and the business executives who are the direct opponents of workers in wage conflicts. This is so in spite of the fact that it is precisely the cash boxes of the rentier, the shareholder, and the banker into which the more or less unearned gains flow, rather than into the pockets of the manufacturers or of the business executives. This simple state of affairs has very frequently been decisive for the role the class situation has played in the formation of political parties. For example, it has made possible the varieties of patriarchal socialism and the frequent attempts—formerly, at least—of threatened status groups to form alliances with the proletariat against the bourgeoisie.

E. Status Honor.   In contrast to classes, *Stände (status groups)* are normally groups. They are, however, often of an amorphous kind. In contrast to the purely economically determined "class situation," we wish to designate as *status situation* every typical component of the life of men that is determined by a specific, positive or negative, social estimation of *honor.* This honor may be connected with any quality shared by a plurality, and, of course, it can be knit to a class situation: class distinctions are linked in the most varied ways with status distinctions. Property as such is not always recognized as a status qualification, but in the long run it is, and with extraordinary regularity. In the subsistence economy of neighborhood associations, it is often simply the richest who is the "chieftain." However, this often is only an honorific preference. For example, in the so-called pure modern democracy, that is, one devoid of any expressly ordered status privileges for individuals, it may be that only the families coming under approximately the same tax class dance with one another. This example is reported of certain smaller Swiss cities. But status honor need not necessarily be linked with a class situation. On the contrary, it normally stands in sharp opposition to the pretensions of sheer property.

Both propertied and propertyless people can belong to the same status group, and frequently they do with very tangible consequences. This equality of social esteem may, however, in the long run become quite precarious. The equality of status among American gentlemen, for instance, is expressed by the fact that outside the subordination determined by the different functions of business, it would be considered strictly repugnant—wherever the old tradition still prevails—if even the richest

boss, while playing billiards or cards in his club would not treat his clerk as in every sense fully his equal in birthright, but would bestow upon him the condescending status-conscious "benevolence" which the German boss can never dissever from his attitude. This is one of the most important reasons why in America the German clubs have never been able to attain the attraction that the American clubs have.

In content, status honor is normally expressed by the fact that above all else a specific *style of life* is expected from all those who wish to belong to the circle. Linked with this expectation are restrictions on social intercourse (that is, intercourse which is not subservient to economic or any other purposes). These restrictions may confine normal marriages to within the status circle and may lead to complete endogamous closure. Whenever this is not a mere individual and socially irrelevant imitation of another style of life, but consensual action of this closing character, the status development is under way.

In its characteristic form, stratification by status groups on the basis of conventional styles of life evolves at the present time in the United States out of the traditional democracy. For example, only the resident of a certain street ("the Street") is considered as belonging to "society," is qualified for social intercourse, and is visited and invited. Above all, this differentiation evolves in such a way as to make for strict submission to the fashion that is dominant at a given time in society. This submission to fashion also exists among men in America to a degree unknown in Germany; it appears as an indication of the fact that a given man puts forward a *claim* to qualify as a gentleman. This submission decides, at least *prima facie,* that he will be treated as such. And this recognition becomes just as important for his employment chances in swank establishments, and above all, for social intercourse and marriage with "esteemed" families, as the qualification for dueling among Germans. As for the rest, status honor is usurped by certain families resident for a long time, and, of course, correspondingly wealthy (e.g. F.F.V., the First Families of Virginia), or by the actual or alleged descendants of the "Indian Princess" Pocahontas, of the Pilgrim fathers, or of the Knickerbockers, the members of almost inaccessible sects and all sorts of circles setting themselves apart by means of any other characteristics and badges. In this case stratification is purely conventional and rests largely on usurpation (as does almost all status honor in its beginning). But the road to legal privilege, positive or negative, is easily traveled as soon as a certain stratification of the social order has in fact been "lived in" and has achieved stability by virtue of a stable distribution of economic power.

F. Ethnic Segregation and Caste. Where the consequences have been realized to their full extent, the status group evolves into a closed caste. Status distinctions are then guaranteed not merely by conventions and laws, but also by religious sanctions. This occurs in such a way that every physical contact with a member of any caste that is considered to be lower by the members of a higher caste is considered as making for a ritualistic impurity and a stigma which must be expiated by a religious act. In addition, individual castes develop quite distinct cults and gods.

In general, however, the status structure reaches such extreme consequences only where there are underlying differences which are held to be "ethnic." The caste is, indeed, the normal form in which ethnic communities that believe in blood relationship and exclude exogamous marriage and social intercourse usually associate with one another. As mentioned before, such a caste situation is part of the phenomenon of pariah peoples and is found all over the world. These people form communities, acquire specific occupational traditions of handicrafts or of other arts, and cultivate a belief in their ethnic community. They live in a diaspora strictly segregated from all personal intercourse, except that of an unavoidable sort, and their situation is legally precarious. Yet, by virtue of their economic indispensability, they are tolerated, indeed frequently privileged, and they live interspersed in the political communities. The Jews are the most impressive historical example.

A status segregation grown into a caste differs in its structure from a mere ethnic segregation: the caste structure transforms the horizontal and unconnected coexistences of ethnically segregated groups into a vertical social system of super- and subordination. Correctly formulated: a comprehensive association integrates the ethnically divided communities into one political unit. They differ precisely in this way: ethnic coexistence, based on mutual repulsion and disdain, allows each ethnic community to consider its own honor as the highest one; the caste structure brings about a social subordination and an acknowledgment of "more honor" in favor of the privileged caste and status groups. This is due to the fact that in the caste structure ethnic distinctions as such have become "functional" distinctions within the political association (warriors, priests, artisans that are politically important for war and for building, and so on). But even pariah peoples who are most despised (for example, the Jews) are usually apt to continue cultivating the belief in their own specific "honor," a belief that is equally peculiar to ethnic and to status groups.

However, with the negatively privileged status groups the sense of dignity takes a specific deviation. A sense of dignity is the precipitation in individuals of social honor and of conventional demands which a positively privileged status group raises for the deportment of its members. The sense of dignity that characterizes positively privileged status groups is naturally related to their "being" which does not transcend itself, that is, it is related to their "beauty and excellence" (καλοκἀγαθία). Their kingdom is "of this world." They live for the present and by exploiting their great past. The sense of dignity of the negatively privileged strata naturally refers to a future lying beyond the present, whether it is of this life or of another. In other words, it must be nurtured by the belief in a providential mission and by a belief in a specific honor before God. The chosen people's dignity is nurtured by a belief either that in the beyond "the last will be the first," or that in this life a Messiah will appear to bring forth into the light of the world which has cast them out the hidden honor of the pariah people. This simple state of affairs, and not the resentment which is so strongly emphasized in Nietzsche's much-admired construction in the *Genealogy of Morals,* is the source of the religiosity cultivated by pariah status groups moreover, resentment applies only to a limited extent; for one of Nietzsche's main examples, Buddhism, it is not at all applicable.

For the rest, the development of status groups from ethnic segregations is by no means the normal phenomenon. On the contrary. Since objective "racial differences" are by no means behind every subjective sentiment of an ethnic community, the question of an ultimately racial foundation of status structure is rightly a question of the concrete individual case. Very frequently a status group is instrumental in the production of a thoroughbred anthropological type. Certainly status groups are to a high degree effective in producing extreme types, for they select personally qualified individuals (e.g. the knighthood selects those who are fit for warfare, physically and psychically). But individual selection is far from being the only, or the predominant, way in which status groups are formed: political membership or class situation has at all times been at least as frequently decisive. And today the class situation is by far the predominant factor. After all, the possibility of a style of life expected for members of a status group is usually conditioned economically.

G. Status Privileges.   For all practical purposes, stratification by status goes hand in hand with a monopolization of ideal and material goods or opportunities, in a manner we have come to know as typical. Besides the specific status honor,

which always rests upon distance and exclusiveness, honorific preferences may consist of the privilege of wearing special costumes, of eating special dishes taboo to others, of carrying arms—which is most obvious in its consequences—the right to be a dilettante, for example, to play certain musical instruments. However, material monopolies provide the most effective motives for the exclusiveness of a status group; although, in themselves, they are rarely sufficient, almost always they come into play to some extent. Within a status circle there is the question of intermarriage: the interest of the families in the monopolization of potential bridegrooms is at least of equal importance and is parallel to the interest in the monopolization of daughters. The daughters of the members must be provided for. With an increased closure of the status group, the conventional preferential opportunities for special employment grow into a legal monopoly of special offices for the members. Certain goods become objects for monopolization by status groups, typically, entailed estates, and frequently also the possession of serfs or bondsmen and, finally, special trades. This monopolization occurs positively when the status group is exclusively entitled to own and to manage them; and negatively when, in order to maintain its specific way of life, the status group must *not* own and manage them. For the decisive role of a style of life in status honor means that status groups are the specific bearers of all conventions. In whatever way it may be manifest, all stylization of life either originates in status groups or is at least conserved by them. Even if the principles of status conventions differ greatly, they reveal certain typical traits, especially among the most privileged strata. Quite generally, among privileged status groups there is a status disqualification that operates against the performance of common physical labor. This disqualification is now "setting in" in America against the old tradition of esteem for labor. Very frequently every rational economic pursuit, and especially entrepreneurial activity, is looked upon as a disqualification of status. Artistic and literary activity is also considered degrading work as soon as it is exploited for income, or at least when it is connected with hard physical exertion. An example is the sculptor working like a mason in his dusty smock as over against the painter in his salon-like studio and those forms of musical practice that are acceptable to the status group.

H. Economic Conditions and Effects of Status Stratification.

The frequent disqualification of the gainfully employed as such is a direct result of the principle of status stratification, and of course, of this principle's opposition to a distribution of power which is regulated exclusively through the market. These two factors operate along with various individual ones, which will be touched upon below.

We have seen above that the market and its processes knows no personal distinctions: "functional" interests dominate it. It knows nothing of honor. The status order means precisely the reverse: stratification in terms of honor and styles of life peculiar to status groups as such. The status order would be threatened at its very root if mere economic acquisition and naked economic power still bearing the stigma of its extra-status origin could bestow upon anyone who has won them the same or even greater honor as the vested interests claim for themselves. After all, given equality of status honor, property *per se* represents an addition even if it is not overtly acknowledged to be such. Therefore all groups having interest in the status order react with special sharpness precisely against the pretensions of purely economic acquisition. In most cases they react the more vigorously the more they feel themselves threatened. Calderon's respectful treatment of the peasant, for instance, as opposed to Shakespeare's simultaneous ostensible disdain of the *canaille* illustrates the different way in which a firmly structured status order reacts as compared with a status

order that has become economically precarious. This is an example of a state of affairs that recurs everywhere. Precisely because of the rigorous reactions against the claims of property *per se*, the "parvenu" is never accepted, personally and without reservation, by the privileged status groups, no matter how completely his style of life has been adjusted to theirs. They will only accept his descendants who have been educated in the conventions of their status group and who have never besmirched its honor by their own economic labor.

As to the general *effect* of the status order, only one consequence can be stated, but it is a very important one: the hindrance of the free development of the market. This occurs first for those goods that status groups directly withhold from free exchange by monopolization, which may be effected either legally or conventionally. For example, in many Hellenic cities during the "status era" and also originally in Rome, the inherited estate (as shown by the old formula for placing spendthrifts under a guardian) was monopolized, as were the estates of knights, peasants, priests, and especially the clientele of the craft and merchant guilds. The market is restricted, and the power of naked property *per se*, which gives its stamp to class formation, is pushed into the background. The results of this process can be most varied. Of course, they do not necessarily weaken the contrasts in the economic situation. Frequently they strengthen these contrasts, and in any case, where stratification by status permeates a community as strongly as was the case in all political communities of Antiquity and of the Middle Ages, one can never speak of a genuinely free market competition as we understand it today. There are wider effects than this direct exclusion of special goods from the market. From the conflict between the status order and the purely economic order mentioned above, it follows that in most instances the notion of honor peculiar to status absolutely abhors that which is essential to the market: hard bargaining. Honor abhors hard bargaining among peers and occasionally it taboos it for the members of a status group in general. Therefore, everywhere some status groups, and usually the most influential, consider almost any kind of overt participation in economic acquisition as absolutely stigmatizing.

With some over-simplification, one might thus say that classes are stratified according to their relations to the production and acquisition of goods; whereas status groups are stratified according to the principles of their *consumption* of goods as represented by special styles of life.

An "occupational status group," too, is a status group proper. For normally, it successfully claims social honor only by virtue of the special style of life which may be determined by it. The differences between classes and status groups frequently overlap. It is precisely those status communities most strictly segregated in terms of honor (viz. the Indian castes) who today show, although within very rigid limits, a relatively high degree of indifference to pecuniary income. However, the Brahmins seek such income in many different ways.

As to the general economic conditions making for the predominance of stratification by status, only the following can be said. When the bases of the acquisition and distribution of goods are relatively stable, stratification by status is favored. Every technological repercussion and economic transformation threatens stratification by status and pushes the class situation into the foreground. Epochs and countries in which the naked class situation is of predominant significance are regularly the periods of technical and economic transformations. And every slowing down of the change in economic stratification leads, in due course, to the growth of status structures and makes for a resuscitation of the important role of social honor.

I. Parties. Whereas the genuine place of classes is within the economic order, the place of status groups is within the social order, that is, within the sphere of the distribution of honor.

From within these spheres, classes and status groups influence one another and the legal order and are in turn influenced by it. "*Parties*" reside in the sphere of power. Their action is oriented toward the acquisition of social power, that is to say, toward influencing social action no matter what its content may be. In principle, parties may exist in a social club as well as in a state. As over against the actions of classes and status groups, for which this is not necessarily the case, party-oriented social action always involves association. For it is always directed toward a goal which is striven for in a planned manner. This goal may be a cause (the party may aim at realizing a program for ideal or material purposes), or the goal may be personal (sinecures, power, and from these, honor for the leader and the followers of the party). Usually the party aims at all these simultaneously. Parties are, therefore, only possible within groups that have an associational character, that is, some rational order and a staff of persons available who are ready to enforce it. For parties aim precisely at influencing this staff, and if possible, to recruit from it party members.

In any individual case, parties may represent interests determined through class situation or status situation, and they may recruit their following respectively from one or the other. But they need be neither purely class nor purely status parties; in fact, they are more likely to be mixed types, and sometimes they are neither. They may represent ephemeral or enduring structures. Their means of attaining power may be quite varied, ranging from naked violence of any sort to canvassing for votes with coarse or subtle means: money, social influence, the force of speech, suggestion, clumsy hoax, and so on to the rougher or more artful tactics of obstruction in parliamentary bodies.

The sociological structure of parties differs in a basic way according to the kind of social action which they struggle to influence; that means, they differ according to whether or not the community is stratified by status or by classes. Above all else, they vary according to the structure of domination. For their leaders normally deal with its conquest. In our general terminology, parties are not only products of modern forms of domination. We shall also designate as parties the ancient and medieval ones, despite the fact that they differ basically from modern parties. Since a party always struggles for political control *(Herrschaft)*, its organization too is frequently strict and "authoritarian." Because of these variations between the forms of domination, it is impossible to say anything about the structure of parties without discussing them first. Therefore, we shall now turn to this central phenomenon of all social organization.

Before we do this, we should add one more general observation about classes, status groups and parties: The fact that they presuppose a larger association, especially the framework of a polity, does not mean that they are confined to it. On the contrary, at all times it has been the order of the day that such association (even when it aims at the use of military force in common) reaches beyond the state boundaries. This can be seen in the [interlocal] solidarity of interests of oligarchs and democrats in Hellas, of Guelphs and Ghibellines in the Middle Ages, and within the Calvinist party during the age of religious struggles; and all the way up to the solidarity of landlords (International Congresses of Agriculture), princes (Holy Alliance, Karlsbad Decrees [of 1819]), socialist workers, conservatives (the longing of Prussian conservatives for Russian intervention in 1850). But their aim is not necessarily the establishment of a new territorial dominion. In the main they aim to influence the existing polity.

Chapter 4

Georg Simmel: Dialectic of Individual and Society

Introduction

Simmel's approach to sociology differs from those of Comte and Durkheim in that he rejects the notion that one can study society as a whole and attempt to discover its laws of evolution and development. Society is a moral and cultural enterprise involving the association of free individuals, and therefore it must be approached differently from the way in which we study nature and nature's laws in the physical sciences. For Simmel, society is made up of the interactions between and among individuals, and the sociologist should study the patterns and forms of these associations, rather than quest after social laws.

Simmel attempts to capture the complexity and the ambiguity of social life by viewing it dialectically. Although individuals are free and creative spirits and not the mere objects of social determination, they are nevertheless part of the socialization process and play a role in its continuation. It is this dynamic tension that Simmel wishes to capture in his social theory. Simmel's explorations of social forms and social types place the reader in a vortex of interactions. Thus, for example, Simmel's typology of the stranger not only addresses the marginality of the person who exists on the fringes of a group, but also describes how the stranger becomes an element of the life of the group when its members seek to confide in the stranger. The marginality of the stranger connotes a role that is in but not of the group. Thus the stranger can have detachment and objectivity and be sought after by group members as an intermediary or

as someone who can keep secrets. It is this interactive relationship, from the perspective of the individual and the group, that Simmel so effectively captures in his writings.

Simmel began his inquiries from the bottom up, observing the smallest of social interactions and attempting to see how larger-scale institutions emerged from them. In doing so he often noticed phenomena that other theorists missed. For example, Simmel observed that the number of parties to an interaction can effect its nature. The interaction between two people, a *dyad*, will be very different from that which is possible in a three-party relationship, or *triad*. Within a *dyadic* relationship, each individual can maintain his or her identity. When one party to the interaction is no longer interested in maintaining it, the relationship is over. As soon as another person is added, however, the situation and its possibilities change markedly, and group structures which are separate from and influence the individuals involved begin to emerge. Two of the people can form a group against the third, one person can become the mediator or the object of competition between the remaining two, and so on. Simmel saw the forms of these interactions as entailing similar options and strategies whether one was dealing with roommates, nation-states, or corporate groups.

Simmel was very interested in and troubled by this relation between the individual and society, and he was particularly acute at relating the most intimate details of individual psychology to larger social structures. Modern civilization in his view was both an aid and a hindrance to the free development of the individual.

Simmel's reflections on culture and alienation as well as his writings on the philosophy of money point to his willingness to write about weighty themes that have moral implications. But Simmel does not moralize: He approaches his subject dialectically and analyzes the tensions that define the modern experience.

Modern society has moved to liberate individuals from the stifling constraints of earlier forms of association. Urban life today allows individuals to play a variety of roles in different social spaces thereby enhancing freedom from the constraints of a fixed, static, and communal life of an earlier era. Yet the price of this freedom is to be found in the increasing sense of alienation that people experience in respect to the culture of urban life.

This latter theme forms the focus of the essay, "The Metropolis and Mental Life," which appears on the following pages. On the one hand, Simmel sees the modern emergence of cities and cosmopolitan living as having freed individuals to an unprecedented degree from the narrow constraints of small town life, a promising development; on the other, the impersonal nature of city life, especially its tendency to cause people to treat others merely as means toward ends, and in purely monetary terms, threatens to become an alienating structure that would dominate and distort this newfound individualism. The essay is a good example of Simmel's eclecticism: He borrows heavily from Durkheim in his analysis of the relation between personality type and the division of labor, and from Marx in his discussion of alienation and objectification. In the end, however, he comes closest in his overall vision to Weber's pessimistic view of the "iron cage," seeing the new metropolitan way of life as threatening to personal freedom and the quality of mental life.

Georg Simmel was born in 1858 in Berlin, the youngest of the seven children of his prosperous and cultured Jewish parents. After graduating from the German equivalent of high school, the *Gymnasium*, he studied at the University of Berlin, then a locus of intellectual activity in central Europe. Although he was officially a philosophy student, Simmel quickly acquired what was to be a lifelong taste for intellectual eclecticism, studying a broad array of disciplines including history, social psychology, art, anthropology, and sociology, and cultivating a mild contempt for academic procedures such as extensive footnoting and the establishment of strict disciplinary boundaries.

This rebelliousness and the refusal to limit himself to a single academic subject, combined with the considerable anti-Semitism of German university administrations, caused Simmel significant setbacks in his academic career. After receiving his doctorate he became a *Privatdozent* at the University of Berlin in 1885, and despite the many books and articles he was to write, the international fame he was to acquire during his years there, and the efforts of many of his fellow professors, including Max Weber, to obtain him a professorship, he was repeatedly to be denied a regular academic appointment. It was not until 1914, four years before his death, that Simmel received a normal professorship, at the University of Strasbourg, and even this achievement was marred by the fact that the university shut down almost immediately with the outbreak of World War I.

Despite his ostracism from mainstream academic life, Simmel became a noted figure in the intellectual circles of Berlin and even worldwide. Because he was one of the most brilliant lecturers of his day, his classes were not only favored by students but became intellectual events, with many of the cultural elite of the city in attendance. He was friends with many of the leading intellectual figures of the day, including Max Weber and Edmund Husserl, and a he was a frequent guest at dinner parties and social events. Many of his six books and over seventy articles were translated into English, French, Italian, Polish, and Russian.

Simmel has had an enormous effect on sociology and is considered perhaps the major founding figure of microsociology. His influence has been particularly strong in America. Albion Small, a translator of several Simmel articles, Robert Park, who studied with Simmel in Berlin in 1899 and 1900, and George Herbert Mead (Chapter 5), who reviewed Simmel's *Philosophy of Money*, all played a major role in the founding of the Chicago School and its main theoretical bent, symbolic interactionism (Chapter 11).

GEORG SIMMEL: THE METROPOLIS AND MENTAL LIFE

The deepest problems of modern life derive from the claim of the individual to preserve the autonomy and individuality of his existence in the face of overwhelming social forces, of historical heritage, of external culture, and of the technique of life. The fight with nature which primitive man has to wage for his *bodily* existence attains in this modern form its latest transformation. The eighteenth century called upon man to free himself of all the historical bonds in the state and in religion, in morals and in economics. Man's nature, originally good and common to all, should develop unhampered. In addition to more liberty, the nineteenth century demanded the functional specialization of man and his work; this specialization makes one individual incomparable to another, and each of them indispensable to the highest possible extent. However, this specialization makes each man the more directly dependent upon the supplementary activities of all others. Nietzsche sees the full development of the individual conditioned by the most ruthless struggle of individuals; socialism believes in the suppression of all competition for the same reason. Be that as it may, in all these positions the same basic motive is at work: the person resists to being leveled down and worn out by a social-technological mechanism. An inquiry into the inner meaning of specifically modern life and its products, into the soul of the cultural body, so to speak, must seek to solve the equation which structures like the metropolis set up between the individual and the super-individual contents of life. Such an inquiry must answer the question of how the personality accommodates itself in the adjustments to external forces. This will be my task today.

The psychological basis of the metropolitan type of individuality consists in the *intensification of nervous stimulation* which results from the swift and uninterrupted change of outer and inner stimuli. Man is a differentiating creature. His mind is stimulated by the difference between a momentary impression and the one which preceded it. Lasting impressions, impressions which differ only slightly from one another, impressions which take a regular and habitual course and show regular and habitual contrasts—all these use up, so to speak, less consciousness than does the rapid crowding of changing images, the sharp discontinuity in the grasp of a single glance, and the unexpectedness of onrushing impressions. These are the psychological conditions which the metropolis creates. With each crossing of the street, with the tempo and multiplicity of economic, occupational and social life, the city sets up a deep contrast with small town and rural life with reference to the sensory foundations of psychic life. The metropolis exacts from man as a discriminating creature a different amount of consciousness than does rural life. Here the rhythm of life and sensory mental imagery flows more slowly, more habitually, and more evenly. Precisely in this connection the sophisticated character of metropolitan psychic life becomes understandable—as over against small town life which rests more upon deeply felt and emotional relationships. These latter are rooted in the more unconscious layers of the psyche and grow most readily in the steady rhythm of uninterrupted habituations. The intellect, however, has its locus in the transparent, conscious, higher layers of the psyche; it is the most adaptable of our inner forces. In order to accommodate to change and to the contrast of phenomena, the intellect does not require any shocks and inner upheavals; it is only through such upheavals that the more conservative mind could accommodate to the metropolitan rhythm of events. Thus the metropolitan type of man—which, of course, exists in a thousand individual variants—develops an organ protecting him against the threatening currents and discrepancies of his external environment which would uproot him. He reacts with his head instead of his heart. In this an increased awareness assumes the psychic prerogative. Metropolitan life, thus, underlies a heightened awareness and a predominance of intelligence in metropolitan man. The reaction to metropolitan phenomena is shifted to that organ which is least sensitive and quite remote from the depth of the personality. Intellectuality is thus seen to preserve subjective life against the overwhelming power of metropolitan life, and intellectuality branches out in many directions and is integrated with numerous discrete phenomena.

The metropolis has always been the seat of the money economy. Here the multiplicity and concentration of economic exchange gives an importance to the means of exchange which the scantiness of rural commerce would not have allowed. Money economy and the dominance of the intellect are intrinsically connected. They share a matter-of-fact attitude in dealing with men and with things; and, in this attitude, a formal justice is often coupled with an inconsiderate hardness. The intellectually sophisticated person is indifferent to all genuine individuality, because relationships and reactions result from it which cannot be exhausted with logical operations. In the same manner, the individuality of phenomena is not commensurate with the pecuniary principle. Money is concerned only with what is common to all: it asks for the exchange value, it reduces all quality and individuality to the question: How much? All intimate emotional relations between persons are founded in their individuality, whereas in rational relations man is reckoned with like a number, like an element which is in itself indifferent. Only the objective measurable achievement is of interest. Thus metropolitan man reckons with his merchants and customers, his domestic servants and often even with persons with whom he is obliged to have social intercourse. These features of intellectuality contrast with the nature of the small circle in which the inevitable knowledge of individuality as inevitably produces a warmer tone of behavior, a behavior which is beyond a mere objective balancing of service and return. In the sphere of the economic psychology of the small group it is of importance that under primitive conditions production serves the customer who orders the good, so that the producer and the consumer are acquainted. The modern metropolis, however, is supplied almost entirely by production for the market, that is, for entirely unknown purchasers who never personally enter the producer's actual field of vision. Through this anonymity the interests of each party acquire an unmerciful matter-of-factness; and the intellectually calculating economic egoisms of both parties need not fear any deflection because of the imponderables of personal relationships. The money economy dominates the metropolis; it has displaced the last survivals of domestic production and the direct barter of goods; it minimizes, from day to day, the amount of work ordered by customers. The matter-of-fact attitude is obviously so intimately interrelated with the money economy, which is dominant in the metropolis, that nobody can say whether the intellectualistic mentality first promoted the money economy or whether the latter determined the former. The metropolitan way of life is certainly the most fertile soil for this reciprocity, a point which I shall document merely by citing the dictum of the most eminent English constitutional historian: throughout the whole course of English history, London has never acted as England's heart but often as England's intellect and always as her moneybag!

In certain seemingly insignificant traits, which lie upon the surface of life, the same psychic currents characteristically unite. Modern mind has become more and more calculating. The calculative exactness of practical life which the money economy has brought about corresponds to the ideal of natural science: to transform the world into an arithmetic problem, to fix every part of the world by mathematical formulas. Only money economy has filled the days of so many people with weighing, calculating, with numerical determinations, with a reduction of qualitative values to quantitative ones. Through the calculative nature of money a new precision, a certainty in the definition of identities and differences, an unambiguousness in agreements and arrangements has been brought about in the relations of life-elements—just as externally this precision has been effected by the universal diffusion of pocket watches. However, the conditions of metropolitan life are at once cause and effect of this trait. The relationships and affairs of the typical metropolitan usually are so varied and complex that without the strictest punctuality in promises and services the whole structure would break down into an inextricable chaos. Above all, this necessity is brought about by the aggregation of so many people with such differentiated interests, who must integrate their relations and activities into a highly complex organism. If all clocks and watches in Berlin would suddenly go wrong in different ways, even if only by one hour, all economic life and

communication of the city would be disrupted for a long time. In addition an apparently mere external factor: long distances, would make all waiting and broken appointments result in an ill-afforded waste of time. Thus, the technique of metropolitan life is unimaginable without the most punctual integration of all activities and mutual relations into a stable and impersonal time schedule. Here again the general conclusions of this entire task of reflection become obvious, namely, that from each point on the surface of existence—however closely attached to the surface alone—one may drop a sounding into the depth of the psyche so that all the most banal externalities of life finally are connected with the ultimate decisions concerning the meaning and style of life. Punctuality, calculability, exactness are forced upon life by the complexity and extension of metropolitan existence and are not only most intimately connected with its money economy and intellectualistic character. These traits must also color the contents of life and favor the exclusion of those irrational, instinctive, sovereign traits and impulses which aim at determining the mode of life from within, instead of receiving the general and precisely schematized form of life from without. Even though sovereign types of personality, characterized by irrational impulses, are by no means impossible in the city, they are, nevertheless, opposed to typical city life. The passionate hatred of men like Ruskin and Nietzsche for the metropolis is understandable in these terms. Their natures discovered the value of life alone in the unschematized existence which cannot be defined with precision for all alike. From the same source of this hatred of the metropolis surged their hatred of money economy and of the intellectualism of modern existence.

The same factors which have thus coalesced into the exactness and minute precision of the form of life have coalesced into a structure of the highest impersonality; on the other hand, they have promoted a highly personal subjectivity. There is perhaps no psychic phenomenon which has been so unconditionally reserved to the metropolis as has the blasé attitude. The blasé attitude results first from the rapidly changing and closely compressed contrasting stimulations of the nerves. From this, the enhancement of metropolitan intellectuality, also, seems originally to stem. Therefore, stupid people who are not intellectually alive in the first place usually are not exactly blasé. A life in boundless pursuit of pleasure makes one blasé because it agitates the nerves to their strongest reactivity for such a long time that they finally cease to react at all. In the same way, through the rapidity and contradictoriness of their changes, more harmless impressions force such violent responses, tearing the nerves so brutally hither and thither that their last reserves of strength are spent; and if one remains in the same milieu they have no time to gather new strength. An incapacity thus emerges to react to new sensations with the appropriate energy. This constitutes that blasé attitude which, in fact, every metropolitan child shows when compared with children of quieter and less changeable milieus.

This physiological source of the metropolitan blasé attitude is joined by another source which flows from the money economy. The essence of the blasé attitude consists in the blunting of discrimination. This does not mean that the objects are not perceived, as is the case with the half-wit, but rather that the meaning and differing values of things, and thereby the things themselves, are experienced as insubstantial. They appear to the blasé person in an evenly flat and gray tone; no one object deserves preference over any other. This mood is the faithful subjective reflection of the completely internalized money economy. By being the equivalent to all the manifold things in one and the same way, money becomes the most frightful leveler. For money expresses all qualitative differences of things in terms of "how much?" Money, with all its colorlessness and indifference, becomes the common denominator of all

values; irreparably it hollows out the core of things, their individuality, their specific value, and their incomparability. All things float with equal specific gravity in the constantly moving stream of money. All things lie on the same level and differ from one another only in the size of the area which they cover. In the individual case this coloration, or rather discoloration, of things through their money equivalence may be unnoticeably minute. However, through the relations of the rich to the objects to be had for money, perhaps even through the total character which the mentality of the contemporary public everywhere imparts to these objects, the exclusively pecuniary evaluation of objects has become quite considerable. The large cities, the main seats of the money exchange, bring the purchasability of things to the fore much more impressively than do smaller localities. That is why cities are also the genuine locale of the blasé attitude. In the blasé attitude the concentration of men and things stimulate the nervous system of the individual to its highest achievement so that it attains its peak. Through the mere quantitative intensification of the same conditioning factors this achievement is transformed into its opposite and appears in the peculiar adjustment of the blasé attitude. In this phenomenon the nerves find in the refusal to react to their stimulation the last possibility of accommodating to the contents and forms of metropolitan life. The self-preservation of certain personalities is brought at the price of devaluating the whole objective world, a devaluation which in the end unavoidably drags one's own personality down into a feeling of the same worthlessness.

Whereas the subject of this form of existence has to come to terms with it entirely for himself, his self-preservation in the face of the large city demands from him a no less negative behavior of a social nature. This mental attitude of metropolitans toward one another we may designate, from a formal point of view, as reserve. If so many inner reactions were responses to the continuous external contacts with innumerable people as are those in the small town, where one knows almost everybody one meets and where one has a positive relation to almost everyone, one would be completely atomized internally and come to an unimaginable psychic state. Partly this psychological fact, partly the right to distrust which men have in the face of the touch-and-go elements of metropolitan life, necessitates our reserve. As a result of this reserve we frequently do not even know by sight those who have been our neighbors for years. And it is this reserve which in the eyes of the small-town people makes us appear to be cold and heartless. Indeed, if I do not deceive myself, the inner aspect of this outer reserve is not only indifference but, more often than we are aware, it is a slight aversion, a mutual strangeness and repulsion, which will break into hatred and fight at the moment of a closer contact, however caused. The whole inner organization of such an extensive communicative life rests upon an extremely varied hierarchy of sympathies, indifferences, and aversions of the briefest as well as of the most permanent nature. The sphere of indifference in this hierarchy is not as large as might appear on the surface. Our psychic activity still responds to almost every impression of somebody else with a somewhat distinct feeling. The unconscious, fluid and changing character of this impression seems to result in a state of indifference. Actually this indifference would be just as unnatural as the diffusion of indiscriminate mutual suggestion would be unbearable. From both these typical dangers of the metropolis, indifference and indiscriminate suggestibility, antipathy protects us. A latent antipathy and the preparatory stage of practical antagonism effect the distances and aversions without which this mode of life could not at all be led. The extent and the mixture of this style of life, the rhythm of its emergence and disappearance, the forms in which it is satisfied—all these, with the unifying motives in the narrower sense, form the inseparable whole of the metropolitan style of life. What appears in the metropolitan style of life directly as dissociation is in reality only one of its elemental forms of socialization.

This reserve with its overtone of hidden aversion appears in turn as the form or the cloak of a more general mental phenomenon of the metropolis: it grants to the individual a kind and an amount of personal freedom which has no analogy whatsoever under other conditions. The metropolis goes back to one of the large developmental tendencies of social life as such, to one of the few tendencies for which an approximately universal formula can be discovered. The earliest phase of social formations found in historical as well as in contemporary social structures is this: a relatively small circle firmly closed against neighboring, strange, or in some way antagonistic circles. However, this circle is closely coherent and allows its individual members only a narrow field for the development of unique qualities and free, self-responsible movements. Political and kinship groups, parties and religious associations begin in this way. The self-preservation of very young associations requires the establishment of strict boundaries and a centripetal unity. Therefore they cannot allow the individual freedom and unique inner and outer development. From this stage social development proceeds at once in two different, yet corresponding, directions. To the extent to which the group grows—numerically, spatially, in significance and in content of life—to the same degree the group's direct, inner unity loosens, and the rigidity of the original demarcation against others is softened through mutual relations and connections. At the same time, the individual gains freedom of movement, far beyond the first jealous delimitation. The individual also gains a specific individuality to which the division of labor in the enlarged group gives both occasion and necessity. The state and Christianity, guilds and political parties, and innumerable other groups have developed according to this formula, however much, of course, the special conditions and forces of the respective groups have modified the general scheme. This scheme seems to me distinctly recognizable also in the evolution of individuality within urban life. The small-town life in Antiquity and in the Middle Ages set barriers against movement and relations of the individual toward the outside, and it set up barriers against individual independence and differentiation within the individual self. These barriers were such that under them modern man could not have breathed. Even today a metropolitan man who is placed in a small town feels a restriction similar, at least, in kind. The smaller the circle which forms our milieu is, and the more restricted those relations to others are which dissolve the boundaries of the individual, the more anxiously the circle guards the achievements, the conduct of life, and the outlook of the individual, and the more readily a quantitative and qualitative specialization would break up the framework of the whole little circle.

The ancient *polis* in this respect seems to have had the very character of a small town. The constant threat to its existence at the hands of enemies from near and afar effected strict coherence in political and military respects, a supervision of the citizen by the citizen, a jealousy of the whole against the individual whose particular life was suppressed to such a degree that he could compensate only by acting as a despot in his own household. The tremendous agitation and excitement, the unique colorfulness of Athenian life, can perhaps be understood in terms of the fact that a people of incomparably individualized personalities struggled against the constant inner and outer pressure of a de-individualizing small town. This produced a tense atmosphere in which the weaker individuals were suppressed and those of stronger natures were incited to prove themselves in the most passionate manner. This is precisely why it was that there blossomed in Athens what must be called, without defining it exactly, "the general human character" in the intellectual development of our species. For we maintain factual as well as historical validity for the following connection: the most extensive and the most general contents and forms of life are most intimately connected with the most individual ones. They have a preparatory stage in common, that is, they find their enemy in narrow formations and groupings the maintenance of which places both of them into a state of defense against expanse and generality lying without and the freely moving individuality within. Just as in the feudal age, the "free" man was the one who stood under the law of the land, that is, under the law of the largest social orbit, and the unfree man was the one who derived his right merely from the narrow circle of a feudal association and was excluded from the larger social orbit—so today metropolitan man is "free" in a spiritualized and refined sense, in contrast to the pettiness and prejudices which hem in the small-town man. For the reciprocal reserve and indifference and the intellectual life conditions of large circles are never felt more strongly by the individual in their impact upon his independence than in the thickest crowd of the big city. This is because the bodily proximity and narrowness of space makes the mental distance only the more visible. It is obviously only the obverse of this freedom if, under certain circumstances, one nowhere feels as lonely and lost as in the metropolitan crowd. For here as elsewhere it is by no means necessary that the freedom of man be reflected in his emotional life as comfort.

It is not only the immediate size of the area and the number of persons which, because of the universal historical correlation between the enlargement of the circle and the personal inner and outer freedom, has made the metropolis the locale of freedom. It is rather in transcending this visible expanse that any given city becomes the seat of cosmopolitanism. The horizon of the city expands in a manner comparable to the way in which wealth develops; a certain amount of property increases in a quasi-automatical way in ever more rapid progression. As soon as a certain limit has been passed, the economic, personal, and intellectual relations of the citizenry, the sphere of intellectual predominance of the city over its hinterland, grow as in geometrical progression. Every gain in dynamic extension becomes a step, not for an equal, but for a new and larger extension. From every thread spinning out of the city, ever new threads grow as if by themselves, just as within the city the unearned increment of ground rent, through the mere increase in communication, brings the owner automatically increasing profits. At this point, the quantitative aspect of life is transformed directly into qualitative traits of character. The sphere of life of the small town is, in the main, self-contained and autarchic. For it is the decisive nature of the metropolis that its inner life overflows by waves into a far-flung national or international area. Weimar is not an example to the contrary, since its significance was hinged upon individual personalities and died with them; whereas the metropolis is indeed characterized by its essential independence even from the most eminent individual personalities. This is the counterpart to the independence, and it is the price the individual pays for the independence, which he enjoys in the metropolis. The most significant characteristic of the metropolis is this functional extension beyond its physical boundaries. And this efficacy reacts in turn and gives weight, importance, and responsibility to metropolitan life. Man does not end with the limits of his body or the area comprising his immediate activity. Rather is the range of the person constituted by the sum of effects emanating from him temporally and spatially. In the same way, a city consists of its total effects which extend beyond its immediate confines. Only this range is the city's actual extent in which its existence is expressed. This fact makes it obvious that individual freedom, the logical and historical complement of such extension, is not to be understood only in the negative sense of mere freedom of mobility and elimination of prejudices and petty philistinism. The essential point is that the particularly and incomparability, which ultimately every human being possesses, be somehow expressed in the working-out of a way of life. That we follow the laws of our own nature—and this after all is freedom—becomes obvious and convincing to ourselves and to others only if the expressions of this nature differ from the expressions of others. Only our unmistakability proves that our way of life has not been superimposed by others.

Cities are, first of all, seats of the highest economic division of labor. They produce thereby such extreme phenomena as in Paris the renumerative occupation of the *quatorzième*. They are persons who identify themselves by signs on their residences and who are ready at the dinner hour in correct attire, so that they can be quickly called upon if a dinner party should consist of thirteen persons. In the measure of its expansion, the city offers more and more the decisive conditions of the division of labor. It offers a circle which through its size can absorb a highly diverse variety of services. At the same time, the concentration of individuals and their struggle for customers compel the individual to specialize in a function from which he cannot be readily displaced by another. It is decisive that city life has transformed the struggle with nature for livelihood into an inter-human struggle for gain, which here is not granted by nature but by other men. For specialization does not flow only from the competition for gain but also from the underlying fact that the seller must always seek to call forth new and differentiated needs of the lured customer. In order to find a source of income which is not yet exhausted, and to find a function which cannot readily be displaced, it is necessary to specialize in one's services. This process promotes differentiation, refinement, and the enrichment of the public's needs, which obviously must lead to growing personal differences within this public.

All this forms the transition to the individualization of mental and psychic traits which the city occasions in proportion to its size. There is a whole series of obvious causes underlying this process. First, one must meet the difficulty of asserting his own personality within the dimensions of metropolitan life. Where the quantitative increase in importance and the expense of energy reach their limits, one seizes upon qualitative differentiation in order somehow to attract the attention of the social circle by playing upon its sensitivity for differences. Finally, man is tempted to adopt the most tendentious peculiarities, that is, the specifically metropolitan extravagances of mannerism, caprice, and preciousness. Now, the meaning of these extravagances does not at all lie in the contents of such behavior, but rather in its form of "being different," of standing out in a striking manner and thereby attracting attention. For many character types, ultimately the only means of saving for themselves some modicum of self-esteem and the sense of filling a position is indirect, through the awareness of others. In the same sense a seemingly insignificant factor is operating, the cumulative effects of which are, however, still noticeable. I refer to the brevity and scarcity of the inter-human contacts granted to the metropolitan man, as compared with social intercourse in the small town. The temptation to appear "to the point," to appear concentrated and strikingly characteristic, lies much closer to the individual in brief metropolitan contacts than in an atmosphere in which frequent and prolonged association assures the personality of an unambiguous image of himself in the eyes of the other.

The most profound reason, however, why the metropolis conduces to the urge for the most individual personal existence—no matter whether justified and successful—appears to me to be the following: the development of modern culture is characterized by the preponderance of what one may call the "objective spirit" over the "subjective spirit." This is to say, in language as well as in law, in the technique of production as well as in art, in science as well as in the objects of the domestic environment,

there is embodied a sum of spirit. The individual in his intellectual development follows the growth of this spirit very imperfectly and at an ever increasing distance. If, for instance, we view the immense culture which for the last hundred years has been embodied in things and in knowledge, in institutions and in comforts, and if we compare all this with the cultural progress of the individual during the same period—at least in high status groups—a frightful disproportion in growth between the two becomes evident. Indeed, at some points we notice a retrogression in the culture of the individual with reference to spirituality, delicacy, and idealism. This discrepancy results essentially from the growing division of labor. For the division of labor demands from the individual an ever more one-sided accomplishment, and the greatest advance in a one-sided pursuit only too frequently means dearth to the personality of the individual. In any case, he can cope less and less with the overgrowth of objective culture. The individual is reduced to a negligible quantity, perhaps less in his consciousness than in his practice and in the totality of his obscure emotional states that are derived from this practice. The individual has become a mere cog in an enormous organization of things and powers which tear from his hands all progress, spirituality, and value in order to transform them from their subjective form into the form of a purely objective life. It needs merely to be pointed out that the metropolis is the genuine arena of this culture which outgrows all personal life. Here in buildings and educational institutions, in the wonders and comforts of space-conquering technology, in the formations of community life, and in the visible institutions of the state, is offered such an overwhelming fullness of crystallized and impersonalized spirit that the personality, so to speak, cannot maintain itself under its impact. On the one hand, life is made infinitely easy for the personality in that stimulations, interests, uses of time and consciousness are offered to it from all sides. They carry the person as if in a stream, and one needs hardly to swim for oneself. On the other hand, however, life is composed more and more of these impersonal contents and offerings which tend to displace the genuine personal colorations and incomparabilities. This results in the individual's summoning the utmost in uniqueness and particularization, in order to preserve his most personal core. He has to exaggerate this personal element in order to remain audible even to himself. The atrophy of individual culture through the hypertrophy of objective culture is one reason for the bitter hatred which the preachers of the most extreme individualism, above all Nietzsche, harbor against the metropolis. But it is, indeed, also a reason why these preachers are so passionately loved in the metropolis and why they appear to the metropolitan man as the prophets and saviors of his most unsatisfied yearnings.

If one asks for the historical position of these two forms of individualism which are nourished by the quantitative relation of the metropolis, namely, individual independence and the elaboration of individuality itself, then the metropolis assumes an entirely new rank order in the world history of the spirit. The eighteenth century found the individual in oppressive bonds which had become meaningless—bonds of a political, agrarian, guild, and religious character. They were restraints which, so to speak, forced upon man an unnatural form and outmoded, unjust inequalities. In this situation the cry for liberty and equality arose, the belief in the individual's full freedom of movement in all social and intellectual relationships. Freedom would at once permit the noble substance common to all to come to the fore, a substance which nature had deposited in every

man and which society and history had only deformed. Besides this eighteenth-century ideal of liberalism, in the nineteenth century, through Goethe and Romanticism, on the one hand, and through the economic division of labor, on the other hand, another ideal arose: individuals liberated from historical bones now wished to distinguish themselves from one another. The carrier of man's values is no longer the "general human being" in every individual, but rather man's qualitative uniqueness and irreplaceability. The external and internal history of our time takes its course within the struggle and in the changing entanglements of these two ways of defining the individual's role in the whole of society. It is the function of the metropolis to provide the arena for this struggle and its reconciliation. For the metropolis presents the peculiar conditions which are revealed to us as the opportunities and the stimuli for the development of both these ways of allocating roles to men. Therewith these conditions gain a unique place, pregnant with inestimable meanings for the development of psychic existence. The metropolis reveals itself as one of those great historical formations in which opposing streams which enclose life unfold, as well as join one another with equal right. However, in this process the currents of life, whether their individual phenomena touch us sympathetically or antipathetically, entirely transcend the sphere for which the judge's attitude is appropriate. Since such forces of life have grown into the roots and into the crown of the whole of historical life in which we, in our fleeting existence, as a cell, belong only as a part, it is not our task either to accuse or to pardon, but only to understand.[1]

---

[1] The content of this lecture by its very nature does not derive from a citable literature. Argument and elaboration of its major cultural-historical ideas are contained in my *Philosophie des Geldes* [*The Philosophy of Money;* München und Leipzig: Duncker und Humblot, 1900].

GEORG SIMMEL: THE STRANGER

If wandering is the liberation from every given point in space, and thus the conceptional opposite to fixation at such a point, the sociological form of the "stranger" presents the unity, as it were, of these two characteristics. This phenomenon too, however, reveals that spatial relations are only the condition, on the one hand, and the symbol, on the other, of human relations. The stranger is thus being discussed here, not in the sense often touched upon in the past, as the wanderer who comes today and goes tomorrow, but rather as the person who comes today and stays tomorrow. He is, so to speak, the *potential* wanderer: although he has not moved on, he has not quite overcome the freedom of coming and going. He is fixed within a particular spatial group, or within a group whose boundaries are similar to spatial boundaries. But his position in this group is determined, essentially, by the fact that he has not belonged to it from the beginning, that he imports qualities into it, which do not and cannot stem from the group itself.

The unity of nearness and remoteness involved in every human relation is organized, in the phenomenon of the stranger, in a way which may be most briefly formulated by saying that in the relationship to him, distance means that he, who is close by, is far, and strangeness means that he, who also is far, is actually near. For, to be a stranger is naturally a very positive relation; it is a specific form of interaction. The inhabitants of Sirius are not really strangers to us, at least not in any sociologically relevant sense: they do not exist for us

at all; they are beyond far and near. The stranger, like the poor and like sundry "inner enemies," is an element of the group itself. His position as a full-fledged member involves both being outside it and confronting it. The following statements, which are by no means intended as exhaustive, indicate how elements which increase distance and repel, in the relations of and with the stranger produce a pattern of coordination and consistent interaction.

Throughout the history of economics the stranger everywhere appears as the trader, or the trader as stranger. As long as economy is essentially self-sufficient, or products are exchanged within a spatially narrow group, it needs no middleman: a trader is only required for products that originate outside the group. Insofar as members do not leave the circle in order to buy these necessities—in which case *they* are the "strange" merchants in that outside territory—the trader *must* be a stranger, since nobody else has a chance to make a living.

This position of the stranger stands out more sharply if he settles down in the place of his activity, instead of leaving it again: in innumerable cases even this is possible only if he can live by intermediate trade. Once an economy is somehow closed, the land is divided up, and handicrafts are established that satisfy the demand for them, the trader, too, can find his existence. For in trade, which alone makes possible unlimited combinations, intelligence always finds expansions and new territories, an achievement which is very difficult to attain for the original producer with his lesser mobility and his dependence upon a circle of customers that can be increased only slowly. Trade can always absorb more people than primary production; it is, therefore, the sphere indicated for the stranger, who intrudes as a supernumerary, so to speak, into a group in which the economic positions are actually occupied—the classical example is the history of

European Jews. The stranger is by nature no "owner of soil"—soil not only in the physical, but also in the figurative sense of a life-substance which is fixed, it not in a point in space, at least in an ideal point of the social environment. Although in more intimate relations, he may develop all kinds of charm and significance, as long as he is considered a stranger in the eyes of the other, he is not an "owner of soil." Restriction to intermediary trade, and often (as though sublimated from it) to pure finance, gives him the specific character of *mobility*. If mobility takes place within a closed group, it embodies that synthesis of nearness and distance which constitutes the formal position of the stranger. For, the fundamentally mobile person comes in contact, at one time or another, with every individual, but is not organically connected, through established ties of kinship, locality, and occupation, with any single one.

Another expression of this constellation lies in the objectivity of the stranger. He is not radically committed to the unique ingredients and peculiar tendencies of the group, and therefore approaches them with the specific attitude of "objectivity." But objectivity does not simply involve passivity and detachment; it is a particular structure composed of distance and nearness, indifference and involvement. I refer to the discussion (in the chapter on "Superordination and Subordination"[1]) of the dominating positions of the person who is a stranger in the group; its most typical instance was the practice of those Italian cities to call their judges from the outside, because no native was free from entanglement in family and party interests.

With the objectivity of the stranger is connected, also, the phenomenon touched upon above,[2] although it is chiefly (but not exclusively) true of the stranger who moves on. This is the fact that he often receives the most surprising openness—confidences which sometimes have the character of confessional and which would be carefully withheld from a more closely related person. Objectivity is by no means non-participation (which is altogether outside both subjective and objective interaction), but a positive and specific kind of participation—just as the objectivity of a theoretical observation does not refer to the mind as a passive *tabula rasa* on which things inscribe their qualities, but on the contrary, to its full activity that operates according to its own laws, and to the elimination, thereby, of accidental dislocations and emphases, whose individual and subjective differences would produce different pictures of the same object.

Objectivity may also be defined as freedom: the objective individual is bound by no commitments which could prejudice his perception, understanding, and evaluation of the given. The freedom, however, which allows the stranger to experience and treat even his close relationships as though from a bird's-eye view, contains many dangerous possibilities. In uprisings of all sorts, the party attacked has claimed, from the beginning of things, that provocation has come from the outside, through emissaries and instigators. Insofar as this is true, it is an exaggeration of the specific role of the stranger: he is freer, practically and theoretically; he surveys conditions with less prejudice; his criteria for them are more general and more objective ideals; he is not tied down in his action by habit, piety, and precendent.[3]

Finally, the proportion of nearness and remoteness which gives the stranger the character of objectivity, also finds practical expression in the more *abstract nature* of the relation to him. That is, with the stranger one has only certain

---

[1] Pp. 216–221 above.—Tr.
[2] On pp. 500–502 of the same chapter from which the present *"Exkurs"* is taken (IX, *"Der Raum und die räumlichen Ordnungen der Gesellschaft,"* Space and the Spatial Organization of Society). The chapter itself is not included in this volume.—Tr.

[3] But where the attacked make the assertion falsely, they do so from the tendency of those in higher position to exculpate inferiors, who, up to the rebellion, have been in a consistently close relation with them. For, by creating the fiction that the rebels were not really guilty, but only instigated, and that the rebellion did not really start with *them,* they exonerate themselves, inasmuch as they altogether deny all real grounds for the uprising.

more general qualities in common, whereas the relation to more organically connected persons is based on the commonness of specific differences from merely general features. In fact, all somehow personal relations follow this scheme in various patterns. They are determined not only by the circumstance that certain common features exist among the individuals, along with individual differences, which either influence the relationship or remain outside of it. For, the common features themselves are basically determined in their effect upon the relation by the question whether they exist only between the participants in this particular relationship, and thus are quite general in regard to this relation, but are specific and incomparable in regard to everything outside of it—or whether the participants feel that these features are common to them because they are common to a group, a type, or mankind in general. In the case of the second alternative, the effectiveness of the common features becomes diluted in proportion to the size of the group composed of members who are similar in this sense. Although the commonness functions as their unifying basis, it does not make *these* particular persons interdependent on one another, because it could as easily connect everyone of them with all kinds of individuals other than the members of his group. This too, evidently, is a way in which a relationship includes both nearness and distance at the same time: to the extent to which the common features are general, they add, to the warmth of the relation founded on them, an element of coolness, a feeling of the contingency of precisely *this* relation—the connecting forces have lost their specific and centripetal character.

In the relation to the stranger, it seems to me, this constellation has an extraordinary and basic preponderance over the individual elements that are exclusive with the particular relationship. The stranger is close to us, insofar as we feel between him and ourselves common features of a national, social, occupational, or generally human, nature. He is far from us, insofar as these common features extend beyond him or us, and connect us only because they connect a great many people.

A trace of strangeness in this sense easily enters even the most intimate relationships. In the stage of first passion, erotic relations strongly reject any thought of generalization: the lovers think that there has never been a love like theirs; that nothing can be compared either to the person loved or to the feelings for that person. An estrangement—whether as cause or as consequence it is difficult to decide—usually comes at the moment when this feeling of uniqueness vanishes from the relationship. A certain skepticism in regard to its value, in itself and for them, attaches to the very thought that in their relation, after all, they carry out only a generally human destiny; that they experience an experience that has occurred a thousand times before; that, had they not accidentally met their particular partner, they would have found the same significance in another person.

Something of this feeling is probably not absent in any relation, however close, because what is common to two is never common to them alone, but is subsumed under a general idea which includes much else besides, many *possibilities* of commonness. No matter how little these possibilities become real and how often we forget them, here and there, nevertheless, they thrust themselves between us like shadows, like a mist which escapes every word noted, but which must coagulate into a solid bodily form before it can be called jealousy. In some cases, perhaps the more general, at least the more unsurmountable, strangeness is not due to different and ununderstandable matters. It is rather caused by the fact that similarity, harmony, and nearness are accompanied by the feeling that they are not really the unique property of this particular relationship: they are something more general, something which potentially prevails between the partners and an indeterminate number of others, and therefore gives the relation, which alone was realized, no inner and exclusive necessity.

On the other hand, there is a kind of "strangeness" that rejects the very commonness based on something more general which embraces the parties. The relation of the Greeks to the Barbarians is perhaps typical here, as are all cases in which it is precisely general attributes, felt to be specifically and purely human, that are disallowed to the other. But "stranger," here, has no positive meaning; the relation to him is a non-relation; he is not what is relevant here, a member of the group itself.

As a group member, rather, he is near and far *at the same time,* as is characteristic of relations founded only on generally human commonness. But between nearness and distance, there arises a specific tension when the consciousness that only the quite general is common, stresses that which is not common. In the case of the person who is a stranger to the country, the city, the race, etc., however, this non-common element is once more nothing individual, but merely the strangeness of origin, which is or could be common to many strangers. For this reason, strangers are not really conceived as individuals, but as strangers of a particular type: the element of distance is no less general in regard to them than the element of nearness.

This form is the basis of such a special case, for instance, as the tax levied in Frankfort and elsewhere upon medieval Jews. Whereas the *Beede* [tax] paid by the Christian citizen changed with the changes of his fortune, it was fixed once for all for every single Jew. This fixity rested on the fact that the Jew had his social position as a *Jew,* not as the individual bearer of certain objective contents. Every other citizen was the owner of a particular amount of property, and his tax followed its fluctuations. But the Jew as a taxpayer was, in the first place, a Jew, and thus his tax situation had an invariable element. This same position appears most strongly, of course, once even these individual characterizations (limited though they were by rigid invariance) are omitted, and all strangers pay an altogether equal head-tax.

In spite of being inorganically appended to it, the stranger is yet an organic member of the group. Its uniform life includes the specific conditions of this element. Only we do not know how to designate the peculiar unity of this position other than by saying that it is composed to certain measures of nearness and distance. Although some quantities of them characterize all relationships, a *special* proportion and reciprocal tension produce the particular, formal relation to the "stranger."

Chapter 5

George Herbert Mead: The Emergent Self

Introduction

George Herbert Mead was born on February 27, 1863, in South Hadley, Massachusetts. His father a clergyman, and his mother well educated, Mead's family encouraged his intellectual development. He spent most of his childhood at Oberlin College in Ohio, where his father held an appointment at the theological seminary, and benefited from the progressive education for which Oberlin is known. He later went to Harvard for his post-graduate degree and studied under William James. After a year, he went to Germany to study philosophy and met Stanley Hall, the psychologist who sparked Mead's interest in that discipline. His work in social psychology, much of which was done at the University of Chicago, is what most consider to be his greatest contribution to sociology. Mead is considered to be a leader of the so-called Chicago School, a group of intellectuals which includes John Dewey, W. I. Thomas and Robert Park. Generally, this group was marked by its pragmatic philosophy, its commitment to social reform, and its democratic ideas. The city of Chicago became a practical laboratory for sociology. Mead and his contemporaries were committed to the idea that sociology can be used to help others; they had an optimistic view of the society and its future and believed that knowledge should guide social action.

Mead's work can best be assessed in comparison to the prevailing behavioristic psychology of his time. Behaviorism tends to view humans as reactive creatures who respond to stimuli. Under the aegis of J. B. Watson, behaviorists adopted a scrupulously scientific methodology and claimed that only observable behavior could be the subject of scientific study. The mental life of an individual was relegated to a "black box" beyond our perceptual grasp, and as a result, behaviorists declared that explanations that relied on the unobservable were unscientific.

Mead's contribution to our understanding of the self and how it is constituted emphasizes the idea that we are thoughtful and reflective creatures whose identities and actions arise as a result of our interaction with others. We are not simply vessels of behaviors waiting to be released by the appropriate stimuli in our environment. That explanation might suffice for pigeons, but Mead was convinced that human behavior was more complex. His most significant insight was his view of human behavior as reflexive, by which he meant that you and I think before we act in many of our important activities. Although it is true that people do engage in behaviors that are not reflexive, it was thoughtful behavior and how it emerges that most concerned Mead.

Reflexivity entails the capacity to use and respond to language, symbols, and thoughts, which Mead called the significant gestures. Our behavior is seen as reflexive because we are able to understand and react to what others think and say about our behavior. Our actions are always engaged with the actions of others, whose responses to what we do send us signals as to their approval or disapproval. We in turn are able to step out of ourselves and make our actions objects to ourselves so that we can analyze and assess the reactions of others. On the basis of this assessment we are able to transform our actions and behavior differently in future situations.

It was Mead's contention that this internal mental dialogue, the dialogue between the "I" and the "me," is what caused the social self to emerge. *Mind, Self and Society*, published after his death on April 26, 1931, best explicates Mead's perspective. What is interesting about this formulation is Mead's insistence that the "self," as it is commonly understood, cannot exist outside its social context. Even consciousness is a social phenomenon, according to Mead. Conversely, the structure of society can be understood as the product of the communication of social acts between individual subjects. The vehicle of this communication is the gesture, which Mead defines as either conscious or unconscious. The unconscious gesture is basically a stimulus-response relationship: a scream of fear or pain, for example. No intentionality is involved. The conscious gestures define human communication. Symbolic interactionism, the school of thought to which Mead's ideas gave rise, claims that the interactive process among humans is generally conducted through the use of conscious gestures, or symbols.

Mead traces the development of these mental abilities in the child. He notes that babies begin to interact on the stimulus-response level and then slowly begin to evolve the skill of "play-acting." Children take on different roles in their play and proceed to more complex games in which the child must conceptualize the roles of many players in order to participate. Learning the game, whether it is baseball or soccer, is learning to be a member of the team. It means learning the positions of one's teammates and the plays that, if executed properly, may bring victory.

The game is a metaphor for democratic life, and Mead is very much the sociologist of democracy. Just as children must learn to cooperate, to restrain their impulsive need to score (the "I") in preference for team play (the "me") so also do individuals reflect on their impulsive behavior and engage in self-analysis and correction. Mead attributes to humans the capacity to reshape their behavior in order to gain approval and acceptance from others. In this way our actions are adjusted to those with whom we interact. It is this constant adjustment, the fitting together of our actions with those of others, that is the substance of social life, and particularly of democratic social life. This process of fitting together entails a respect for the particular other and the "generalized other" or the moral rules. It requires a degree of self-control and adjustment of one's behavior that reduces the need for external authority to compel or coerce behavior. In so far as the self is an emergent property, the result of an internal dialogue, the cooperative dimensions of social interaction are underscored and the willful ego is tempered by the generalized other.

GEORGE HERBERT MEAD: MIND, SELF AND SOCIETY

The self, as that which can be an object to itself, is essentially a social structure, and it arises in social experience. After a self has arisen, it in a certain sense provides for itself its social experiences, and so we can conceive of an absolutely solitary self. But it is impossible to conceive of a self arising outside of social experience. When it has arisen we can think of a person in solitary confinement for the rest of his life, but who still has himself as a companion, and is able to think and to converse with himself as he had communicated with others. That process to which I have just referred, of responding to one's self as another responds to it, taking part in one's own conversation with others, being aware of what one is saying and using that awareness of what one is saying to determine what one is going to say thereafter—that is a process with which we are all familiar. We are continually following up our own address to other persons by an understanding of what we are saying, and using that understanding in the direction of our continued speech. We are finding out what we are going to say, what we are going to do, by saying and doing, and in the process we are continually controlling the process itself. In the conversation of gestures what we say calls out a certain response in another and that in turn changes our own action, so that we shift from what we started to do because of the reply the other makes. The conversation of gestures is the beginning of communication. The individual comes to carry on a conversation of gestures with himself. He says something, and that calls out a certain reply in himself which makes him change what he was going to say. One starts to say something, we will presume an unpleasant something, but when he starts to say it he realizes it is cruel. The effect on himself of what he is saying checks him; there is here a conversation of gestures between the individual and himself. We mean by significant speech that the action is one that affects the individual himself, and that the effect upon the individual himself is part of the intelligent carrying-out of the conversation with others. Now we, so to speak, amputate that social phase and dispense with it for the time being, so that one is talking to one's self as one would talk to another person.

This process of abstraction cannot be carried on indefinitely. One inevitably seeks an audience, has to pour himself out to somebody. In reflective intelligence one thinks to act, and to act solely so that this action remains a part of a social process. Thinking becomes preparatory to social action. The very process of thinking is, of course, simply an inner conversation that goes on, but it is a conversation of gestures which in its completion implies the expression of that which one thinks to an audience. One separates the significance of what he is saying to others from the actual speech and gets it ready before saying it. He thinks it out, and perhaps writes it in the form of a book; but it is still a part of social intercourse in which one is addressing other persons and at the same time addressing one's self, and in which one controls the address to other persons by the response made to one's own gesture. That the person should be responding to himself is necessary to the self, and it is this sort of social conduct which provides behavior within which that self appears. I know of no other form of behavior than the linguistic in which the individual is an object to himself, and, so far as I can see, the individual is not a self in the reflexive sense unless he is an

Reprinted with permission of the University of Chicago Press from George Herbert Mead, *Mind, Self and Society,* Vol. 1, edited by Charles W. Morris. Copyright 1934 by The University of Chicago. Copyright 1962 by Charles W. Morris.

object to himself. It is this fact that gives a critical importance to communication, since this is a type of behavior in which the individual does so respond to himself.

We realize in everyday conduct and experience that an individual does not mean a great deal of what he is doing and saying. We frequently say that such an individual is not himself. We come away from an interview with a realization that we have left out important things, that there are parts of the self that did not get into what was said. What determines the amount of the self that gets into communication is the social experience itself. Of course, a good deal of the self does not need to get expression. We carry on a whole series of different relationships to different people. We are one thing to one man and another thing to another. There are parts of the self which exist only for the self in relationship to itself. We divide ourselves up in all sorts of different selves with reference to our acquaintances. We discuss politics with one and religion with another. There are all sorts of different selves answering to all sorts of different social reactions. It is the social process itself that is responsible for the appearance of the self; it is not there as a self apart from this type of experience.

A multiple personality is in a certain sense normal, as I have just pointed out. There is usually an organization of the whole self with reference to the community to which we belong, and the situation in which we find ourselves. What the society is, whether we are living with people of the present, people of our own imaginations, people of the past, varies, of course, with different individuals. Normally, within the sort of community as a whole to which we belong, there is a unified self, but that may be broken up. To a person who is somewhat unstable nervously and in whom there is a line of cleavage, certain activities become impossible and that set of activities may separate and evolve another self. Two separate "me's" and "I's," two different selves, result, and that is the condition under which there is a tendency to break up the personality. There is an account of a professor of education who disappeared, was lost to the community, and later turned up in a logging camp in the West. He freed himself of his occupation and turned to the woods where he felt, if you like, more at home. The pathological side of it was the forgetting, the leaving out of the rest of the self. This result involved getting rid of certain bodily memories which would identify the individual to himself. We often recognize the lines of cleavage that run through us. We would be glad to forget certain things, get rid of things the self is bound up with in past experiences. What we have here is a situation in which there can be different selves, and it is dependent upon the set of social reactions that is involved as to which self we are going to be. If we can forget everything involved in one set of activities, obviously we relinquish that part of the self. Take a person who is unstable, get him occupied by speech, and at the same time get his eye on something you are writing so that he is carrying on two separate lines of communication, and if you go about it in the right way you can get those two currents going so that they do not run into each other. You can get two entirely different sets of activities going on. You can bring about in that way the dissociation of a person's self. It is a process of setting up two sorts of communication which separate the behavior of the individual. For one individual it is this thing said and heard, and for the other individual there exists only that which he sees written. You must, of course, keep one experience out of the field of the other. Dissociations are apt to take place when an event leads to emotional upheavals. That which is separated goes on in its own way.

The unity and structure of the complete self reflects the unity and structure of the social process as a whole; and each of the elementary selves of which it is composed reflects the unity and structure of one of the various aspects of that process in which the individual is implicated. In other words, the various elementary selves which constitute, or are organized into, a complete self are the various aspects of the structure of that complete self answering to the various aspects of the structure of the social process as a whole; the structure of the complete self is thus a reflection of the complete social process. The organization and unification of a social group is identical with the organization and unification of any one of the selves arising within the social process in which that group is engaged, or which it is carrying on.

The phenomenon of dissociation of personality is caused by a breaking up of the complete, unitary self into the component selves of which it is composed, and which respectively correspond to different aspects of the social process in which the person is involved, and within which his complete or unitary self has arisen; these aspects being the different social groups to which he belongs within that process.

The Background of the Genesis of the Self

The problem now presents itself as to how, in detail, a self arises. We have to note something of the background of its genesis. First of all there is the conversation of gestures between animals involving some sort of co-operative activity. There the beginning of the act of one is a stimulus to the other to respond in a certain way, while the beginning of this response becomes again a stimulus to the first to adjust his action to the oncoming response. Such is the preparation for the completed act, and ultimately it leads up to the conduct which is the outcome of this preparation. The conversation of gestures, however, does not carry with it the reference of the individual, the animal, the organism, to itself. It is not acting in a fashion which calls for a response from the form itself, although it is conduct with reference to the conduct of others. We have seen, however, that there are certain gestures that do affect the organism as they affect other organisms and may, therefore, arouse in the organism responses of the same character as aroused in the other. Here, then, we have a situation in which the individual may at least arouse responses in himself and reply to these responses, the condition being that the social stimuli have an effect on the individual which is like that which they have on the other. That, for example, is what is implied in language; otherwise language as significant symbol would disappear, since the individual would not get the meaning of that which he says.

The peculiar character possessed by our human social environment belongs to it by virtue of the peculiar character of human social activity; and that character, as we have seen, is to be found in the process of communication, and more particularly in the triadic relation on which the existence of meaning is based: the relation of the gesture of one organism to the adjustive response made to it by another organism, in its indicative capacity as pointing to the completion or resultant of the act it initiates (the meaning of the gesture being thus the response of the second organism to it as such, or as a gesture). What, as it were, takes the gesture out of the social act and isolates it as such—what makes it something more than just an early phase of an individual act—is the response of another organism, or of other organisms, to it. Such a response is its meaning, or gives it its meaning. The social situation and process of behavior are here presupposed by the acts of the individual organisms implicated therein. The gesture arises as a separable element in the social act, by virtue of the fact that it is selected out by the sensitivities of other organisms to it; it does not exist as a gesture merely in the experience of the single individual. The meaning of a gesture by one organism, to repeat, is found in the response of another organism to what would be the completion of the act of the first organism which that gesture initiates and indicates.

We sometimes speak as if a person could build up an entire argument in his mind, and then put it into words to convey it to someone else. Actually, our thinking always takes place by means of some sort of symbols. It is possible that one could have the meaning of "chair" in his experience without there being a symbol, but we would not be thinking about it in that case. We may sit down in a chair without thinking about what we are doing, that is, the approach to the chair is presumably already aroused in our experience, so that the meaning is there. But if one is thinking about the chair he must have some sort of a symbol for it. It may be the form of the chair, it may be the attitude that somebody else takes in sitting down, but it is more apt to be some language symbol that arouses this response. In a thought process there has to be some sort of a symbol that can refer to this meaning, that is, tend to call out this response, and also serve this purpose for other persons as well. It would not be a thought process if that were not the case.

Our symbols are all universal. You cannot say anything that is absolutely particular; anything you say that has any meaning at all is universal. You are saying something that calls out a specific response in anybody else provided that the symbol exists for him in his experience as it does for you. There is the language of speech and the language of hands, and there may be the language of the expression of the countenance. One can register grief or joy and call out certain responses. There are primitive people who can carry on elaborate conversations just by expressions of the countenance. Even in these cases the person who communicates is affected by that expression just as he expects somebody else to be affected. Thinking always implies a symbol which will call out the same response in another that it calls out in the thinker. Such a symbol is a universal of discourse; it is universal in its character. We always assume that the symbol we use is one which will call out in the other person the same response, provided it is a part of his mechanism of conduct. A person who is saying something is

saying to himself what he says to others; otherwise he does not know what he is talking about.

There is, of course, a great deal in one's conversation with others that does not arouse in one's self the same response it arouses in others. That is particularly true in the case of emotional attitudes. One tries to bully somebody else; he is not trying to bully himself. There is, further, a whole set of values given in speech which are not of a symbolic character. The actor is conscious of these values; that is, if he assumes a certain attitude he is, as we say, aware that this attitude represents grief. If it does he is able to respond to his own gesture in some sense as his audience does. It is not a natural situation; one is not an actor all of the time. We do at times act and consider just what the effect of our attitude is going to be, and we may deliberately use a certain tone of voice to bring about a certain result. Such a tone arouses the same response in ourselves that we want to arouse in somebody else. But a very large part of what goes on in speech has not this symbolic status.

It is the task not only of the actor but of the artist as well to find the sort of expression that will arouse in others what is going on in himself. The lyric poet has an experience of beauty with an emotional thrill to it, and as an artist using words he is seeking for those words which will answer to his emotional attitude, and which will call out in others the attitude he himself has. He can only test his results in himself by seeing whether these words do call out in him the response he wants to call out in others. He is in somewhat the same position as that of the actor. The first direct and immediate experience is not in the form of communication. We have an interesting light on this from such a poet as Wordsworth, who was very much interested in the technique of the poet's expression; and he has told us in his prefaces and also in his own poetry how his poems, as poems, arose—and uniformly the experience itself was not the immediate stimulus to the poetic expression. A period of ten years might lie between the original experience and the expression of it. This process of finding the expression in language which will call out the emotion once had is more easily accomplished when one is dealing with the memory of it than when one is in the midst of the trance-like experiences through which Wordsworth passed in his contact with nature. One has to experiment and see how the expression that is given does answer to the responses which are now had in the fainter memories of experience. Someone once said that he had very great difficulty in writing poetry; he had plenty of ideas but could not get the language he needed. He was rightly told that poetry was written in words, not in ideas.

A great deal of our speech is not of this genuinely aesthetic character; in most of it we do not deliberately feel the emotions which we arouse. We do not normally use language stimuli to call out in ourselves the emotional response which we are calling out in others. One does, of course, have sympathy in emotional situations; but what one is seeking for there is something which is, after all, that in the other which supports the individual in his own experience. In the case of the poet and actor, the stimulus calls out in the artist that which it calls out in the other, but this is not the natural function of language; we do not assume that the person who is angry is calling out the fear in himself that he is calling out in someone else. The emotional part of our act does not directly call out in us the response it calls out in the other. If a person is hostile the attitude of the other that he is interested in, an attitude which flows naturally from his angered tones, is not one that he definitely recognizes in himself. We are not frightened by a tone which we may use to frighten somebody else. On the emotional side, which is a very large part of the vocal gesture, we do not call out in ourselves in any such degree the response we call out in others as we do in the case of significant speech. Here we should call out in ourselves the type of response we are calling out in others; we must know what we are saying, and the attitude of the other which we arouse in ourselves should control what we do say. Rationality means that the type of the response which we call out in others should be so called out in ourselves, and that this response should in turn take its place in determining what further thing we are going to say and do.

What is essential to communication is that the symbol should arouse in one's self what it arouses in the other individual. It must have that sort of universality to any person who finds himself in the same situation. There is a possibility of language whenever a stimulus can affect the individual as it affects the other. With a blind person such as Helen Keller, it is a contact experience that could be given to another as it is given to herself. It is out of that sort of language that the mind of Helen Keller was built up. As she has recognized, it was not until she could get into communication with other persons through symbols which could arouse in herself the responses they arouse in other people that she could get what we term a mental content, or a self.

Another set of background factors in the genesis of the self is represented in the activities of play and the game.

Among primitive people, as I have said, the necessity of distinguishing the self and the organism was recognized in what we term the "double": the individual has a thing-like self that is affected by the individual as it affects other people and which is distinguished from the immediate organism in that it can leave the body and come back to it. This is the basis for the concept of the soul as a separate entity.

We find in children something that answers to this double, namely, the invisible, imaginary companions which a good many children produce in their own experience. They organize in this way the responses which they call out in other persons and call out also in themselves. Of course, this playing with an imaginary companion is only a peculiarly interesting phase of ordinary play. Play in this sense, especially the stage which precedes the organized games, is a play at something. A child plays at being a mother, at being a teacher, at being a policeman; that is, it is taking different rôles, as we say. We have something that suggests this in what we call the play of animals: a cat will play with her kittens, and dogs play with each other. Two dogs playing with each other will attack and defend, in a process which if carried through would amount to an actual fight. There is a combination of responses which checks the depth of the bite. But we do not have in such a situation the dogs taking a definite rôle in the sense that a child deliberately takes the rôle of another. This tendency on the part of the children is what we are working with in the kindergarten where the rôles which the children assume are made the basis for training. When a child does assume a rôle he has in himself the stimuli which call out that particular response or group of responses. He may, of course, run away when he is chased, as the dog does, or he may turn around and strike back just as the dog does in his play. But that is not the same as playing at something. Children get together to "play Indian." This means that the child has a certain set of stimuli which call out in itself the responses that they would call out in others, and which answer to an Indian. In the play period the child utilizes his own responses to these stimuli which he makes use of in building a self. The response which he has a tendency to make to these stimuli organizes them. He plays that he is, for instance, offering himself something, and he buys it; he gives a letter to himself and takes it away; he addresses himself as a parent, as a teacher; he arrests himself as a policeman. He has a set of stimuli which call out in himself the sort of responses they call out in others. He takes this group of responses and organizes them into a certain whole. Such is the simplest form of being another to one's self. It involves a temporal situation. The child says something in one character and responds in another character, and then his responding in another character is a stimulus to himself in the first character, and so the con-

versation goes on. A certain organized structure arises in him and in his other which replies to it, and these carry on the conversation of gestures between themselves.

If we contrast play with the situation in an organized game, we note the essential difference that the child who plays in a game must be ready to take the attitude of everyone else involved in that game, and that these different rôles must have a definite relationship to each other. Taking a very simple game such as hide-and-seek, everyone with the exception of the one who is hiding is a person who is hunting. A child does not require more than the person who is hunted and the one who is hunting. If a child is playing in the first sense he just goes on playing, but there is no basic organization gained. In that early stage he passes from one rôle to another just as a whim takes him. But in a game where a number of individuals are involved, then the child taking one rôle must be ready to take the rôle of everyone else. If he gets in a ball nine he must have the responses of each position involved in his own position. He must know what everyone else is going to do in order to carry out his own play. He has to take all of these rôles. They do not all have to be present in consciousness at the same time, but at some moments he has to have three or four individuals present in his own attitude, such as the one who is going to throw the ball, the one who is going to catch it, and so on. These responses must be, in some degree, present in his own make-up. In the game, then, there is a set of responses of such others so organized that the attitude of one calls out the appropriate attitudes of the other.

This organization is put in the form of the rules of the game. Children take a great interest in rules. They make rules on the spot in order to help themselves out of difficulties. Part of the enjoyment of the game is to get these rules. Now, the rules are the set of responses which a particular attitude calls out. You can demand a certain response in others if you take a certain attitude. These responses are all in yourself as well. There you get an organized set of such responses as that to which I have referred, which is something more elaborate than the rôles found in play. Here there is just a set of responses that follow on each other indefinitely. At such a stage we speak of a child as not yet having a fully developed self. The child responds in a fairly intelligent fashion to the immediate stimuli that come to him, but they are not organized. He does not organize his life as we would like to have him do, namely, as a whole. There is just a set of responses of the type of play. The child reacts to a certain stimulus, and the reaction is in himself that is called out in others, but he is not a whole self. In his game he has to have an organization of these rôles; otherwise he cannot play the game. The game represents the passage in the life of the child from taking the rôle of others in play to the organized part that is essential to self-consciousness in the full sense of the term.

Play, the Game, and the Generalized Other

We were speaking of the social conditions under which the self arises as an object. In addition to language we found two illustrations, one in play and the other in the game, and I wish to summarize and expand my account on these points. I have spoken of these from the point of view of children. We can, of course, refer also to the attitudes of more primitive people out of which our civilization has arisen. A striking illustration of play as distinct from the game is found in the myths and various of the plays which primitive people carry out, especially in religious pageants. The pure play attitude which we find in the case of little children may not be found here, since the participants are adults, and undoubtedly the relationship of these play processes to that which they interpret is more or less in the minds of even the most primitive people. In the process of interpreta-

tion of such rituals, there is an organization of play which perhaps might be compared to that which is taking place in the kindergarten in dealing with the plays of little children, where these are made into a set that will have a definite structure or relationship. At least something of the same sort is found in the play of primitive people. This type of activity belongs, of course, not to the everyday life of the people in their dealing with the objects about them— there we have a more or less definitely developed self-consciousness—but in their attitudes toward the forces about them, the nature upon which they depend; in their attitude toward this nature which is vague and uncertain, there we have a much more primitive response; and that response finds its expression in taking the rôle of the other, playing at the expression of their gods and their heroes, going through certain rites which are the representation of what these individuals are supposed to be doing. The process is one which develops, to be sure, into a more or less definite technique and is controlled; and yet we can say that it has arisen out of situations similar to those in which little children play at being a parent, at being a teacher— vague personalities that are about them and which affect them and on which they depend. These are personalities which they take, rôles they play, and in so far control the development of their own personality. This outcome is just what the kindergarten works toward. It takes the characters of these various vague beings and gets them into such an organized social relationship to each other that they build up the character of the little child. The very introduction of organization from outside supposes a lack of organization at this period in the child's experience. Over against such a situation of the little child and primitive people, we have the game as such.

The fundamental difference between the game and play is that in the latter the child must have the attitude of all the others involved in that game. The attitudes of the other players which the participant assumes organize into a sort of unit, and it is that organization which controls the response of the individual. The illustration used was of a person playing baseball. Each one of his own acts is determined by his assumption of the action of the others who are playing the game. What he does is controlled by his being everyone else on that team, at least in so far as those attitudes affect his own particular response. We get then an "other" which is an organization of the attitudes of those involved in the same process.

The organized community or social group which gives to the individual his unity of self may be called "the generalized other." The attitude of the generalized other is the attitude of the whole community. Thus, for example, in the case of such a social group as a ball team, the team is the generalized other in so far as it enters—as an organized process or social activity—into the experience of any one of the individual members of it.

If the given human individual is to develop a self in the fullest sense, it is not sufficient for him merely to take the attitudes of other human individuals toward himself and toward one another within the human social process, and to bring that social process as a whole into his individual experience merely in these terms: he must also, in the same way that he takes the attitudes of other individuals toward himself and toward one another, take their attitudes toward the various phases or aspects of the common social activity or set of social undertakings in which, as members of an organized society or social group, they are all engaged; and he must then, by generalizing these individual attitudes of that organized society or social group itself, as a whole, act toward different social projects which at any given time it is carrying out, or toward the various larger phases of the general social process which constitutes its life and of which these projects are specific manifestations. This getting of the broad activities of any given social whole or organized society as such within

the experiential field of any one of the individuals involved or included in that whole is, in other words, the essential basis and prerequisite of the fullest development of that individual's self: only in so far as he takes the attitudes of the organized social group to which he belongs toward the organized, cooperative social activity or set of such activities in which that group as such is engaged, does he develop a complete self or possess the sort of complete self he has developed. And on the other hand, the complex co-operative processes and activities and institutional functionings of organized human society are also possible only in so far as every individual involved in them or belonging to that society can take the general attitudes of all other such individuals with reference to these processes and activities and institutional functionings, and to the organized social whole of experiential relations and interactions thereby constituted—and can direct his own behavior accordingly.

It is in the form of the generalized other that the social process influences the behavior of the individuals involved in it and carrying it on, i.e., that the community exercises control over the conduct of its individual members; for it is in this form that the social process or community enters as a determining factor into the individual's thinking. In abstract thought the individual takes the attitude of the generalized other toward himself, without reference to its expression in any particular other individuals; and in concrete thought he takes that attitude in so far as it is expressed in the attitudes toward his behavior of those other individuals with whom he is involved in the given social situation or act. But only by taking the attitude of the generalized other toward himself, in one or another of these ways, can he think at all; for only thus can thinking—or the internalized conversation of gestures which constitutes thinking—occur. And only through the taking by individuals of the attitude or attitudes of the generalized other toward themselves is the existence of a universe of discourse, as that system of common or social meanings which thinking presupposes at its context, rendered possible.

The self-conscious human individual, then, takes or assumes the organized social attitudes of the given social group or community (or of some one section thereof) to which he belongs, toward the social problems of various kinds which confront that group or community at any given time, and which arise in connection with the correspondingly different social projects or organized cooperative enterprises in which that group or community as such is engaged; and as an individual participant in these social projects or cooperative enterprises, he governs his own conduct accordingly. In politics, for example, the individual identifies himself with an entire political party and takes the organized attitudes of that entire party toward the rest of the given social community and toward the problems which confront the party within the given social situation; and he consequently reacts or responds in terms of the organized attitudes of the party as a whole. He thus enters into a special set of social relations with all the other individuals who belong to that political party; and in the same way he enters into various other special sets of social relations, with various other classes of individuals respectively, the individuals of each of these classes being the other members of some one of the particular organized subgroups (determined in socially functional terms) of which he himself is a member within the entire given society or social community. In the most highly developed, organized, and complicated human social communities—those evolved by civilized man—these various socially functional classes or subgroups of individuals to which any given individual belongs (and with the other individual members of which he thus enters into a special set of social relations) are of two kinds. Some of them are concrete social classes or subgroups, such as political parties, clubs, corporations, which are all actually functional social units, in terms of which their individual members are directly related to one another. The others are abstract social classes or subgroups, such as the class of debtors and the class of creditors, in terms of which their individual members are related to one another only more or less indirectly, and which only more or less indirectly function as social units, but which afford or represent unlimited possibilities for the widening and ramifying and enriching of the social relations among all the individual members of the given society as an organized and unified whole. The given individual's membership in several of these abstract social classes or subgroups makes possible his entrance into definite social relations (however indirect) with an almost infinite number of other individuals who also belong to or are included within one or another of these abstract social classes or subgroups cutting across functional lines of demarcation which divide different human social communities from one another, and including individual members from several (in some cases from all) such communities. Of these abstract social classes or subgroups of human individuals the one which is most inclusive and extensive is, of course, the one defined by the logical universe of discourse (or system of universally significant symbols) determined by the participation and communicative interaction of individuals; for of all such classes or subgroups, it is the one which claims the largest number of individual members, and which enables the largest conceivable number of human individuals to enter into some sort of social relation, however indirect or abstract it may be, with one another—a relation arising from the universal functioning of gestures as significant symbols in the general human social process of communication.

I have pointed out, then, that there are two general stages in the full development of the self. At the first of these stages, the individual's self is constituted simply by an organization of the particular attitudes of other individuals toward himself and toward one another in the specific social acts in which he participates with them. But at the second stage in the full development of the individual's self that self is constituted not only by an organization of these particular individual attitudes, but also by an organization of the social attitudes of the generalized other or the social group as a whole to which he belongs. These social or group attitudes are brought within the individual's field of direct experience, and are included as elements in the structure or constitution of his self, in the same way that the attitudes of particular other individuals are; and the individual arrives at them, or succeeds in taking them, by means of further organizing, and then generalizing, the attitudes of particular other individuals in terms of their organized social bearings and implications. So the self reaches its full development by organizing these individual attitudes of others into the organized social or group attitudes, and by thus becoming an individual reflection of the general systematic pattern of social or group behavior in which it and the others are all involved—a pattern which enters as a whole into the individual's experience in terms of these organized group attitudes which, through the mechanism of his central nervous system, he takes toward himself, just as he takes the individual attitudes of others.

The game has a logic, so that such an organization of the self is rendered possible: there is a definite end to be obtained; the actions of the different individuals are all related to each other with reference to that end so that they do not conflict; one is not in conflict with himself in the attitude of another man on the team. If one has the attitude of the person throwing the ball he can also have the response of catching the ball. The two are related so that they further the purpose of the game itself. They are interrelated in a unitary, organic fashion. There is a definite unity, then, which is introduced into the organization of other selves when we reach such a stage as that of the game, as over against the situation of play where there is a simple succession of one rôle

after another, a situation which is, of course, characteristic of the child's own personality. The child is one thing at one time and another at another, and what he is at one moment does not determine what he is at another. That is both the charm of childhood as well as its inadequacy. You cannot count on the child; you cannot assume that all the things he does are going to determine what he will do at any moment. He is not organized into a whole. The child has no definite character, no definite personality.

The game is then an illustration of the situation out of which an organized personality arises. In so far as the child does take the attitude of the other and allows that attitude of the other to determine the thing he is going to do with reference to a common end, he is becoming an organic member of society. He is taking over the morale of that society and is becoming an essential member of it. He belongs to it in so far as he does allow the attitude of the other that he takes to control his own immediate expression. What is involved here is some sort of an organized process. That which is expressed in terms of the game is, of course, being continually expressed in the social life of the child, but this wider process goes beyond the immediate experience of the child himself. The importance of the game is that it lies entirely inside of the child's own experience, and the importance of our modern type of education is that it is brought as far as possible within this realm. The different attitudes that a child assumes are so organized that they exercise a definite control over his response, as the attitudes in a game control his own immediate response. In the game we get an organized other, a generalized other, which is found in the nature of the child itself, and finds its expression in the immediate experience of the child. And it is that organized activity in the child's own nature controlling the particular response which gives unity, and which builds up his own self.

What goes on in the game goes on in the life of the child all the time. He is continually taking the attitudes of those about him, especially the rôles of those who in some sense control him and on whom he depends. He gets the function of the process in an abstract sort of a way at first. It goes over from the play into the game in a real sense. He has to play the game. The morale of the game takes hold of the child more than the larger morale of the whole community. The child passes into the game and the game expresses a social situation in which he can completely enter; its morale may have a greater hold on him than that of the family to which he belongs or the community in which he lives. There are all sorts of social organizations, some of which are fairly lasting, some temporary, into which the child is entering, and he is playing a sort of social game in them. It is a period in which he likes "to belong," and he gets into organizations which come into existence and pass out of existence. He becomes a something which can function in the organized whole, and thus tends to determine himself in his relationship with the group to which he belongs. That process is one which is a striking stage in the development of the child's morale. It constitutes him a self-conscious member of the community to which he belongs.

Such is the process by which a personality arises. I have spoken of this as a process in which a child takes the rôle of the other, and said that it takes place essentially through the use of language. Language is predominantly based on the vocal gesture by means of which cooperative activities in a community are carried out. Language in its significant sense is that vocal gesture which tends to arouse in the individual the attitude which it arouses in others, and it is this perfecting of the self by the gesture which mediates the social activities that gives rise to the process of taking the rôle of the other. The latter phrase is a little unfortunate because it suggests an actor's attitude which is actually more sophisticated than that which is involved in our own experience. To this degree it does not correctly describe that which I have in mind. We see the

process most definitely in a primitive form in those situations where the child's play takes different rôles. Here the very fact that he is ready to pay out money, for instance, arouses the attitude of the person who receives money; the very process is calling out in him the corresponding activities of the other person involved. The individual stimulates himself to the response which he is calling out in the other person, and then acts in some degree in response to that situation. In play the child does definitely act out the rôle which he himself has aroused in himself. It is that which gives, as I have said, a definite content in the individual which answers to the stimulus that affects him as it affects somebody else. The content of the other that enters into one personality is the response in the individual which his gesture calls out in the other.

We may illustrate our basic concept by a reference to the notion of property. If we say "This is my property, I shall control it," that affirmation calls out a certain set of responses which must be the same in any community in which property exists. It involves an organized attitude with reference to property which is common to all the members of the community. One must have a definite attitude of control of his own property and respect for the property of others. Those attitudes (as organized sets of responses) must be there on the part of all, so that when one says such a thing he calls out in himself the response of the others. He is calling out the response of what I have called a generalized other. That which makes society possible is such common responses, such organized attitudes, with reference to what we term property, the cults of religion, the process of education, and the relations of the family. Of course, the wider the society the more definitely universal these objects must be. In any case there must be a definite set of responses, which we may speak of as abstract, and which can belong to a very large group. Property is in itself a very abstract concept. It is that which the individual himself can control and nobody else can control. The attitude is different from that of a dog toward a bone. A dog will fight any other dog trying to take the bone. The dog is not taking the attitude of the other dog. A man who says "This is my property" is taking an attitude of the other person. The man is appealing to his rights because he is able to take the attitude which everybody else in the group has with reference to property, thus arousing in himself the attitude of others.

What goes to make up the organized self is the organization of the attitudes which are common to the group. A person is a personality because he belongs to a community, because he takes over the institutions of that community into his own conduct. He takes its language as a medium by which he gets his personality, and then through a process of taking the different rôles that all the others furnish he comes to get the attitude of the members of the community. Such, in a certain sense, is the structure of a man's personality. There are certain common responses which each individual has toward certain common things, and in so far as those common responses are awakened in the individual when he is affecting other persons he arouses his own self. The structure, then, on which the self is built is this response which is common to all, for one has to be a member of a community to be a self. Such responses are abstract attitudes, but they constitute just what we term a man's character. They give him what we term his principles, the acknowledged attitudes of all members of the community toward what are the values of that community. He is putting himself in the place of the generalized other, which represents the organized responses of all the members of the group. It is that which guides conduct controlled by principles, and a person who has such an organized group of responses is a man whom we say has character, in the moral sense.

It is a structure of attitudes, then, which goes to make up a self, as distinct from a group of habits. We all of us have, for example, certain groups of habits, such as the particular intona-

tions which a person uses in his speech. This is a set of habits of vocal expression which one has but which one does not know about. The sets of habits which we have of that sort mean nothing to us; we do not hear the intonations of our speech that others hear unless we are paying particular attention to them. The habits of emotional expression which belong to our speech are of the same sort. We may know that we have expressed ourselves in a joyous fashion but the detailed process is one which does not come back to our conscious selves. There are whole bundles of such habits which do not enter into a conscious self, but which help to make up what is termed the unconscious self.

After all, what we mean by self-consciousness is an awakening in ourselves of the group of attitudes which we are arousing in others, especially when it is an important set of responses which go to make up the members of the community. It is unfortunate to fuse or mix up consciousness, as we ordinarily use that term, and self-consciousness. Consciousness, as frequently used, simply has reference to the field of experience, but self-consciousness refers to the ability to call out in ourselves a set of definite responses which belong to the others of the group. Consciousness and self-consciousness are not on the same level. A man alone has, fortunately or unfortunately, access to his own toothache, but that is not what we mean by self-consciousness.

I have so far emphasized what I have called the structures upon which the self is constructed, the framework of the self, as it were. Of course we are not only what is common to all: each one of the selves is different from everyone else; but there has to be such a common structure as I have sketched in order that we may be members of a community at all. We cannot be ourselves unless we are also members in whom there is a community of attitudes which control the attitudes of all. We cannot have rights unless we have common attitudes. That which we have acquired as self-conscious persons makes us such members of society and gives us selves. Selves can only exist in definite relationships to other selves. No hard-and-fast line can be drawn between our own selves and the selves of others, since our own selves exist and enter as such into our experience only in so far as the selves of others exist and enter as such into our experience also. The individual possesses a self only in relation to the selves of the other members of his social group; and the structure of his self expresses or reflects the general behavior pattern of this social group to which he belongs, just as does the structure of the self of every other individual belonging to this social group.

* * *

The "I" and the "Me"

We have discussed at length the social foundations of the self, and hinted that the self does not consist simply in the bare organization of social attitudes. We may now explicitly raise the question as to the nature of the "I" which is aware of the social "me." I do not mean to raise the metaphysical question of how a person can be both "I" and "me," but to ask for the significance of this distinction from the point of view of conduct itself. Where in conduct does the "I" come in as over against the "me"? If one determines what his position is in society and feels himself as having a certain function and privilege, these are all defined with reference to an "I," but the "I" is not a "me" and cannot become a "me." We may have a better self and a worse self, but that again is not the "I" as over against the "me," because they are both selves. We approve of one and disapprove of the other, but when we bring up one or the other they are there for such approval as "me's." The "I" does not get into the limelight; we talk to ourselves, but do not see ourselves. The "I" reacts to the self which arises through the taking of the attitudes of others. Through taking those attitudes we have introduced the "me" and we react to it as an "I."

The simplest way of handling the problem would be in terms of memory. I talk to myself, and I remember what I said and perhaps the emotional content that went with it. The "I" of this moment is present in the "me" of the next moment. There again I cannot turn around quick enough to catch myself. I become a "me" in so far as I remember what I said. The "I" can be given, however, this functional relationship. It is because of the "I" that we say that we are never fully aware of what we are, that we surprise ourselves by our own action. It is as we act that we are aware of ourselves. It is in memory that the "I" is constantly present in experience. We can go back directly a few moments in our experience, and then we are dependent upon memory images for the rest. So that the "I" in memory is there as the spokesman of the self of the second, or minute, or day ago. As given, it is a "me," but it is a "me" which was the "I" at the earlier time. If you ask, then, where directly in your own experience the "I" comes in, the answer is that it comes in as a historical figure. It is what you were a second ago that is the "I" of the "me." It is another "me" that has to take that rôle. You cannot get the immediate response of the "I" in the process. The "I" is in a certain sense that with which we do identify ourselves. The getting of it into experience constitutes one of the problems of most of our conscious experience; it is not directly given in experience.

The "I" is the response of the organism to the attitudes of the others, the "me" is the organized set of attitudes of others which one himself assumes. The attitudes of the others constitute the organized "me," and then one reacts toward that as an "I." I now wish to examine these concepts in greater detail.

There is neither "I" nor "me" in the conversation of gestures; the whole act is not yet carried out, but the preparation takes place in this field of gesture. Now, in so far as the individual arouses in himself the attitudes of the others, there arises an organized group of responses. And it is due to the individual's ability to take the attitudes of these others in so far as they can be organized that he gets self-consciousness. The taking of all of those organized sets of attitudes gives him his "me"; that is the self he is aware of. He can throw the ball to some other member because of the demand made upon him from other members of the team. That is the self that immediately exists for him in his consciousness. He has their attitudes, knows what they want and what the consequence of any act of his will be, and he has assumed responsibility for the situation. Now, it is the presence of those organized sets of attitudes that constitutes that "me" to which he as an "I" is responding. But what that response will be he does not know and nobody else knows. Perhaps he will make a brilliant play or an error. The response to that situation as it appears in his immediate experience is uncertain, and it is that which constitutes the "I."

The "I" is his action over against that social situation within his own conduct, and it gets into his experience only after he has carried out the act. Then he is aware of it. He had to do such a thing and he did it. He fulfills his duty and he may look with pride at the throw which he made. The "me" arises to do that duty—that is the way in which it arises in his experience. He had in him all the attitudes of others, calling for a certain response; that was the "me" of that situation, and his response is the "I."

I want to call attention particularly to the fact that this response of the "I" is something that is more or less uncertain. The attitudes of others which one assumes as affecting his own conduct constitute the "me," and that is something that is there, but the response to it is as yet not given. When one sits down to think anything out, he has certain data that are there. Suppose that it is a social situation which he has to straighten out. He sees himself from the point of view of one individual or another in the group. These individuals, related all together, give him a certain self. Well, what is he going to do? He does not know and nobody else knows. He can

get the situation into his experience because he can assume the attitudes of the various individuals involved in it. He knows how they feel about it by the assumption of their attitudes. He says, in effect, "I have done certain things that seem to commit me to a certain course of conduct." Perhaps if he does so act it will place him in a false position with another group. The "I" as a response to this situation, in contrast to the "me" which is involved in the attitudes which he takes, is uncertain. And when the response takes place, then it appears in the field of experience largely as a memory image.

Our specious present as such is very short. We do, however, experience passing events; part of the process of the passage of events is directly there in our experience, including some of the past and some of the future. We see a ball falling as it passes, and as it does pass part of the ball is covered and part is being uncovered. We remember where the ball was a moment ago and we anticipate where it will be beyond what is given in our experience. So of ourselves; we are doing something, but to look back and see what we are doing involves getting memory images. So the "I" really appears experientially as a part of a "me." But on the basis of this experience we distinguish that individual who is doing something from the "me" who puts the problem up to him. The response enters into his experience only when it takes place. If he says he knows what he is going to do, even there he may be mistaken. He starts out to do something and something happens to interfere. The resulting action is always a little different from anything which he could anticipate. This is true even if he is simply carrying out the process of walking. The very taking of his expected steps puts him in a certain situation which has a slightly different aspect from what is expected, which is in a certain sense novel. That movement into the future is the step, so to speak, of the ego, of the "I." It is something that is not given in the "me."

Take the situation of a scientist solving a problem, where he has certain data which call for certain responses. Some of this set of data call for his applying such and such a law, while others call for another law. Data are there with their implications. He knows what such and such coloration means, and when he has these data before him they stand for certain responses on his part; but now they are in conflict with each other. If he makes one response he cannot make another. What he is going to do he does not know, nor does anybody else. The action of the self is in response to these conflicting sets of data in the form of a problem, with conflicting demands upon him as a scientist. He has to look at it in different ways. That action of the "I" is something the nature of which we cannot tell in advance.

The "I," then, in this relation of the "I" and the "me," is something that is, so to speak, responding to a social situation which is within the experience of the individual. It is the answer which the individual makes to the attitude which others take toward him when he assumes an attitude toward them. Now, the attitudes he is taking toward them are present in his own experience, but his response to them will contain a novel element. The "I" gives the sense of freedom, of initiative. The situation is there for us to act in a self-conscious fashion. We are aware of ourselves, and of what the situation is, but exactly how we will act never gets into experience until after the action takes place.

Such is the basis for the fact that the "I" does not appear in the same sense in experience as does the "me." The "me" represents a definite organization of the community there in our own attitudes, and calling for a response, but the response that takes place is something that just happens. There is no certainty in regard to it. There is a moral necessity but no mechanical necessity for the act. When it does take place then we find what has been done. The above account gives us, I think, the relative position of the "I" and "me" in the situation, and the grounds for the separation of the two in behavior. The two are separated in the process but

they belong together in the sense of being parts of a whole. They are separated and yet they belong together. The separation of the "I" and the "me" is not fictitious. They are not identical, for, as I have said, the "I" is something that is never entirely calculable. The "me" does call for a certain sort of an "I" in so far as we meet the obligations that are given in conduct itself, but the "I" is always something different from what the situation itself calls for. So there is always that distinction, if you like, between the "I" and the "me." The "I" both calls out the "me" and responds to it. Taken together they constitute a personality as it appears in social experience. The self is essentially a social process going on with these two distinguishable phases. If it did not have these two phases there could not be conscious responsibility, and there would be nothing novel in experience.

* * *

The "I" and the "Me" as Phases of the Self

We come now to the position of the self-conscious self or mind in the community. Such a self finds its expression in self-assertion, or in the devotion of itself to the cause of the community. The self appears as a new type of individual in the social whole. There is a new social whole because of the appearance of the type of individual mind I have described, and because of the self with its own assertion of itself of its own identification with the community. The self is the important phase in the development because it is in the possibility of the importation of this social attitude into the responses of the whole community that such a society could arise. The change that takes place through this importation of the conversation of gestures into the conduct of the individual is one that takes place in the experience of all of the component individuals.

These, of course, are not the only changes that take place in the community. In speech definite changes take place that nobody is aware of at all. It requires the investigation of scientists to discover that such processes have taken place. This is also true of other phases of human organization. They change, we say, unconsciously, as is illustrated in such a study of the myth as Wundt has carried out in his *Völkerpsychologie*. The myth carries an account of the way in which organization has taken place while largely without any conscious direction—and that sort of change is going on all the time. Take a person's attitude toward a new fashion. It may at first be one of objection. After a while he gets to the point of thinking of himself in this changed fashion, noticing the clothes in the window and seeing himself in them. The change has taken place in him without his being aware of it. There is, then, a process by means of which the individual in interaction with others inevitably becomes like others in doing the same thing, without that process appearing in what we term consciousness. We become conscious of the process when we do definitely take the attitude of the others, and this situation must be distinguished from the previous one. Perhaps one says that he does not care to dress in a certain fashion, but prefers to be different; then he is taking the attitude of others toward himself into his own conduct. When an ant from another nest is introduced into the nest of other forms, these turn on it and tear it to pieces. The attitude in the human community may be that of the individual himself, refusing to submit himself because he does take that common attitude. The ant case is an entirely external affair, but in the human individual it is a matter of taking the attitudes of the others and adjusting one's self or fighting it out. It is this recognition of the individual as a self in the process of using his self-consciousness which gives him the attitude of self-assertion or the attitude of devotion to the community. He has become, then, a definite self. In such a case of self-assertion there is an entirely different situation from that of the member of the pack who perhaps dominates it, and may turn savagely on different members of

it. There an individual is just acting instinctively, we say, in a certain situation. In the human society we have an individual who not only takes his own attitude but takes the attitude in a certain sense of his subjects; in so far as he is dominating he knows what to expect. When that occurs in the experience of the individual a different response results with different emotional accompaniments, from that in the case of the leader of the pack. In the latter case there is simple anger or hostility, and in the other case there is the experience of the self asserting itself consciously over against other selves, with the sense of power, of domination. In general, when the community reaction has been imported into the individual there is a new value in experience and a new order of response.

We have discussed the self from the point of view of the "I" and the "me," the "me" representing that group of attitudes which stands for others in the community, especially that organized group of responses which we have detailed in discussing the game on the one hand and social institutions on the other. In these situations there is a certain organized group of attitudes which answer to any social act on the part of the individual organism. In any cooperative process, such as the family, the individual calls out a response from the other members of the group. Now, to the extent that those responses can be called out in the individual so that he can answer to them, we have both those contents which go to make up the self, the "other" and the "I." The distinction expresses itself in our experience in what we call the recognition of others and the recognition of ourselves in the others. We cannot realize ourselves except in so far as we can recognize the other in his relationship to us. It is as he takes the attitude of the other that the individual is able to realize himself as a self.

We are referring, of course, to a social situation as distinct from such bare organic responses as reflexes of the organism, some of which we have already discussed, as in the case where a person adjusts himself unconsciously to those about him. In such an experience there is no self-consciousness. One attains self-consciousness only as he takes, or finds himself stimulated to take, the attitude of the other. Then he is in a position of reacting in himself to that attitude of the other. Suppose we find ourselves in an economic situation. It is when we take the attitude of the other in making an offer to us that we can express ourselves in accepting or declining such an offer. That is a different response of the self from a distinctly automatic offering that can take place without self-consciousness. A small boy thrusts an advertising bill into our hand and we take it without any definite consciousness of him or of ourselves. Our thought may be elsewhere but the process still goes on. The same thing is true, of course, in the care of infants. Young children experience that which comes to them, they adjust themselves to it in an immediate fashion, without there being present in their experience a self.

When a self does appear it always involves an experience of another; there could not be an experience of a self simply by itself. The plant or the lower animal reacts to its environment, but there is no experience of a self. When a self does appear in experience it appears over against the other, and we have been delineating the condition under which this other does appear in the experience of the human animal, namely in the presence of that sort of stimulation in the cooperative activity which arouses in the individual himself the same response it arouses in the other. When the response of the other becomes an essential part in the experience or conduct of the individual; when taking the attitude of the other becomes an essential part in his behavior—then the individual appears in his own experience as a self; and until this happens he does not appear as a self.

Rational society, of course, is not limited to any specific set of individuals. Any person who is rational can become a part of it. The attitude of the community toward our own response is

imported into ourselves in terms of the meaning of what we are doing. This occurs in its widest extent in universal discourse, in the reply which the rational world makes to our remark. The meaning is as universal as the community; it is necessarily involved in the rational character of that community; it is the response that the world made up out of rational beings inevitably makes to our own statement. We both get the object and ourselves into experience in terms of such a process; the other appears in our own experience in so far as we do take such an organized and generalized attitude.

If one meets a person on the street whom he fails to recognize, one's reaction toward him is that toward any other who is a member of the same community. He is the other, the organized, generalized other, if you like. One takes his attitude over against one's self. If he turns in one direction one is to go in another direction. One has his response as an attitude within himself. It is having that attitude within himself that makes it possible for one to be a self. That involves something beyond the mere turning to the right, as we say, instinctively, without self-consciousness. To have self-consciousness one must have the attitude of the other in one's own organism as controlling the thing that he is going to do. What appears in the immediate experience of one's self in taking that attitude is what we term the "me." It is that self which is able to maintain itself in the community, that is recognized in the community in so far as it recognizes the others. Such is the phase of the self which I have referred to as that of the "me."

Over against the "me" is the "I." The individual not only has rights, but he has duties; he is not only a citizen, a member of the community, but he is one who reacts to this community and in his reaction to it, as we have seen in the conversation of gestures, changes it. The "I" is the response of the individual to the attitude of the community as this appears in his own experience. His response to that organized attitude in turn changes it. As we have pointed out, this is a change which is not present in his own experience until after it takes place. The "I" appears in our experience in memory. It is only after we have acted that we know what we have done; it is only after we have spoken that we know what we have said. The adjustment to that organized world which is present in our own nature is one that represents the "me" and is constantly there. But if the response to it is a response which is of the nature of the conversation of gestures, if it creates a situation which is in some sense novel, if one puts up his side of the case, asserts himself over against others and insists that they take a different attitude toward himself, then there is something important occurring that is not previously present in experience.

The general conditions under which one is going to act may be present in one's experience, but he is as ignorant of just how he is going to respond as is the scientist of the particular hypothesis he will evolve out of the consideration of a problem. Such and such things are happening that are contrary to the theory that has been held. How are they to be explained? Take the discovery that a gram of radium would keep a pot of water boiling, and seemingly lead to no expenditure of energy. Here something is happening that runs contrary to the theory of physics up to the conception of radium activity. The scientist who has these facts before him has to pick out some explanation. He suggests that the radium atom is breaking down, and is consequently setting free energy. On the previous theory an atom was a permanent affair out of which one could not get energy. But now if it is assumed that the atom itself is a system involving an interrelationship of energies, then the breaking down of such a system sets free what is relatively an enormous amount of energy. The point I am making is that the idea of the scientist comes to him, it is not as yet there in his own mind. His mind, rather, is the process of the appearance of that idea. A person asserting his rights on a certain occasion has rehearsed the situation in his own mind; he has reacted toward

the community and when the situation arises he arouses himself and says something already in his mind. But when he said it to himself in the first place he did not know what he was going to say. He then said something that was novel to himself, just as the scientist's hypothesis is a novelty when it flashes upon him.

Such a novel reply to the social situation involved in the organized set of attitudes constitutes the "I" as over against the "me." The "me" is a conventional, habitual individual. It is always there. It has to have those habits, those responses which everybody has; otherwise the individual could not be a member of the community. But an individual is constantly reacting to such an organized community in the way of expressing himself, not necessarily asserting himself in the offensive sense but expressing himself, being himself in such a co-operative process as belongs to any community. The attitudes involved are gathered from the group, but the individual in whom they are organized has the opportunity of giving them an expression which perhaps has never taken place before.

This brings out the general question as to whether anything novel can appear. Practically, of course, the novel is constantly happening and the recognition of this gets its expression in more general terms in the concept of emergence. Emergence involves a reorganization, but the reorganization brings in something that was not there before. The first time oxygen and hydrogen come together, water appears. Now water is a combination of hydrogen and oxygen, but water was not there before in the separate elements. The conception of emergence is a concept which recent philosophy has made much of. If you look at the world simply from the point of view of a mathematical equation in which there is absolute equality of the different sides, then, of course, there is no novelty. The world is simply a satisfaction of that equation. Put in any values for X and Y and the same equation holds. The equations do hold, it is true, but in their holding something else in fact arises that was not there before. For instance, there is a group of individuals that have to work together. In a society there must be a set of common organized habits of response found in all, but the way in which individuals act under specific circumstances gives rise to all of the individual differences which characterize the different persons. The fact that they have to act in a certain common fashion does not deprive them of originality. The common language is there, but a different use of it is made in every new contact between persons; the element of novelty in the reconstruction takes place through the reaction of the individuals to the group to which they belong. That reconstruction is no more given in advance than is the particular hypothesis which the scientist brings forward given in the statement of the problem. Now, it is that reaction of the individual to the organized "me," the "me" that is in a certain sense simply a member of the community, which represents the "I" in the experience of the self.

The relative values of the "me" and the "I" depend very much on the situation. If one is maintaining his property in the community, it is of primary importance that he is a member of that community, for it is his taking of the attitude of the others that guarantees to him the recognition of his own rights. To be a "me" under those circumstances is the important thing. It gives him his position, gives him the dignity of being a member in the community, it is the source of his emotional response to the values that belong to him as a member of the community. It is the basis for his entering into the experience of others.

At times it is the response of the ego or "I" to a situation, the way in which one expresses himself, that brings to one a feeling of prime importance. One now asserts himself against a certain situation, and the emphasis is on the response. The demand is freedom from conventions, from given laws. Of course, such a situation is only possible where the individual appeals, so to speak, from a narrow and restricted community to a larger one, that is, larger in the logical sense of having rights which are not so restricted. One appeals from fixed conventions which no longer have any meaning to a community in which the rights shall be publicly recognized, and one appeals to others on the assumption that there is a group of organized others that answer to one's own appeal—even if the appeal be made to posterity. In that case there is the attitude of the "I" as over against the "me."

Both aspects of the "I" and "me" are essential to the self in its full expression. One must take the attitude of the others in a group in order to belong to a community; he has to employ that outer social world taken within himself in order to carry on thought. It is through his relationship to others in that community, because of the rational social processes that obtain in that community, that he has being as a citizen. On the other hand, the individual is constantly reacting to the social attitudes, and changing in this cooperative process the very community to which he belongs. Those changes may be humble and trivial ones. One may not have anything to say, although he takes a long time to say it. And yet a certain amount of adjustment and readjustment takes place. We speak of a person as a conventional individual; his ideas are exactly the same as those of his neighbors; he is hardly more than a "me" under the circumstances; his adjustments are only the slight adjustments that take place, as we say, unconsciously. Over against that there is the person who has a definite personality, who replies to the organized attitude in a way which makes a significant difference. With such a person it is the "I" that is the more important phase of the experience. Those two constantly appearing phases are the important phases in the self.

Chapter 6

W. E. B. Du Bois: Double-Consciousness and the Public Intellectual

Introduction

W. E. B. Du Bois was born in Great Barrington, Massachusetts, on February 23, 1868, and died 95 years later in Ghana. His life spans the history of the modern civil rights movement from the end of the Civil War to the March on Washington, and in the course of it Du Bois left his enduring mark as a sociologist, a public intellectual, and a committed activist in the struggle for social justice.

Du Bois was an outstanding young student. While in high school he was trained rigorously in Latin and Greek, and at the age of 16, the youngest in his graduating class, he was ready for college. Although he was regarded as brilliant and had set his sights on Harvard, he lacked the financial resources and, as David Levering Lewis notes in his recent biography, there was a "distinct lack of enthusiasm among so many otherwise kindly, charitable white people for helping even a brilliant 'Negro' attend the nation's leading college." Instead, he attended Fisk University, a Congregational school for blacks, in Nashville, Tennessee. Du Bois received his degree from Fisk in 1888 and then took a second baccalaureate degree at Harvard University. He was by then only the sixth member of his race to have attended the institution since 1870, when the first African-American was admitted.

At Harvard he studied with the leading philosophers of his time, William James, Josiah Royce, and George Santayana, and because Harvard had no sociology department, Du Bois majored in philosophy. He graduated cum laude in 1890 and then enrolled in the Ph.D.

program in history at Harvard. During his graduate studies, Du Bois went to Germany to attend the University of Berlin where he took course work and attended lectures with some of the major figures in German social science, Gustav von Schmoller, Adolph Wagner, and the great sociologist Max Weber. On his return to the United States, Du Bois completed his Ph.D. with a thesis entitled *The Suppression of the African Slave Trade to the United States of America, 1638–1870*, which became the first monograph to be published in the newly created series of Harvard Historical Studies. In 1915, Du Bois became the first African-American to be awarded a Ph.D. from Harvard.

Du Bois held academic appointments at Wilberforce College, at the University of Pennsylvania, and Atlanta University. At the University of Pennsylvania he wrote *The Philadelphia Negro: A Social Study*, a work which recorded his findings from a sociological survey of 4,500 African-Americans living in the Seventh Ward of Philadelphia. It remains a classic work of empirical investigation that stands on a par with contributions from Chicago School sociologists as models of sociological inquiry. Without research assistants, Du Bois conducted a door-to-door survey to get at the facts about the economic, social, religious, and familial life of the inhabitants of the Seventh Ward, in the hope of dispelling the myths and fantasies that circulated in the white community. In keeping with the reformist ethos of the time, Du Bois believed in the utility of scientific research in the solution of outstanding social problems. In this scholarly phase of his career, and indeed throughout his entire life, Du Bois was a prolific writer. For the Atlanta University Studies on the American Negro, he wrote no fewer than nineteen monographs based on studies he conducted into every aspect of black life in America, including questions of health, education, art, religion, crime, family, and economics. Du Bois wanted to build a database that would provide scholars and policymakers with the facts they would need in order to make sound and rational public policy. In this he was a rationalist in the early years, and believed in the power of ideas to shape political and social change.

The strong influence of Du Bois's empirical sociology of African-American life can be seen in Horace Clayton and St. Claire Drake's *Black Metropolis*, E. Franklin Frazier's *The Negro Family in America*, and William Julius Wilson's *The Truly Disadvantaged*. His work remains a guide and inspiration to urban sociologists who have followed in his wake.

In *The Souls of Black Folk*, a famous collection of his early essays, Du Bois develops the prescient concept of "double-consciousness," which captures the enduring enigma of being an African-American. His essays begin with epigraphs from famous European poets and writers followed by the musical notation of a bar or two of a Negro spiritual. This juxtaposition is meant to convey two equal cultures, one black, the other white, each with its contribution to make to the other, and meaningfully anticipates what is called multiculturalism today. In the Forethought to the collection, Du Bois writes: "Herein lie buried many things which if read with patience may show the strange meaning of being black here at the dawning of the Twentieth Century. This meaning is not without interest to you, Gentle Reader; for the problem of the Twentieth Century is the problem of the color line." As you read the essay "Of Our Spiritual Strivings," make careful note of what Du Bois means by "double-consciousness." Does Du Bois seek either assimilation or separatism, and if neither, then what? How do Du Bois's

ideas contribute to our understanding of the contemporary debates over multiculturalism?

It is not only as an academic and scholar that W. E. B. Du Bois is remembered but also as a public intellectual and activist. Throughout his career Du Bois wrote timely political analyses and published novels and biographical essays. These writings gave a clear, passionate and courageous message about the condition of blacks in America. As early as 1905 Du Bois organized the Niagara Movement to give voice to the struggle for civil rights for African-Americans, and four years later on July 4, 1909, the National Association for the Advancement of Colored People held its founding meeting which consisted of the original group of prominent blacks that Du Bois had brought together in the Niagara Movement and a number of white intellectuals and professionals. Du Bois became the editor of *Crisis*, the NAACP journal, which he conceived as an instrument to raise the consciousness of blacks in America. It became his vehicle to mobilize against the evils of racism wherever it existed. Du Bois's uncompromising position on these issues brought him eventually into conflict with the NAACP leadership and forced his resignation from the journal in 1934.

As an early proponent of Pan-Africanism, Du Bois helped found and presided over the first meeting of the Pan-African Congress in 1919 with the express purpose of planning for the future disposition of German colonies in Africa following World War I. The Congress demanded that the African colonies be removed from German control and placed in trusteeship with the League of Nations, in preparation for freedom and nationhood.

In 1926 Du Bois visited the Soviet Union for the first time in order to examine the results of its socialist revolution firsthand. His interest in Marx and Marxism deepened and his career as an activist and public intellectual seemed to have found its theoretical justification in the "Theses on Feuerbach," where Marx writes: "The philosophers have only *interpreted* the world, in various ways; the point is to *change* it." (See "Theses on Feuerbach," Chapter 1, in this text.) Following the Depression and the New Deal, Du Bois's thinking turned to long-range economic planning and he developed increasing sympathy with socialism as an alternative mode of economic organization that would promise and deliver greater equality and social justice.

At the age of 66, in 1934, when others sought retirement, Du Bois embarked on another venture as chair of the sociology department at Atlanta University where for a ten-year period, he taught, carried on his research, and founded the journal *Phylon.*

Du Bois's political difficulties began to mount during the McCarthy period in the 1950s. He had by now left Atlanta University and become increasingly absorbed with the international dimensions of civil rights. Appointed as an NAACP consultant to the United Nations Conference in 1945, Du Bois was also elected international president of the Pan-African Federation. By 1950, Du Bois's politics had swung far to the left and at the age of 82 he became a candidate for the U.S. Senate on the American Labor Party ticket. On February 16, 1951, he was

arrested and arraigned for failure to register as an agent of a foreign government in connection with his membership in the Peace Information Center. Although acquitted of the charges Du Bois was ostracized by former colleagues and friends. In the early 1950s he came to the defense of Julius and Ethel Rosenberg, accepted invitations from the Soviet Union and other Eastern bloc countries, and was lionized wherever he went within the socialist world.

On October 1, 1961, he wrote a long letter to Gus Hall, then head of the Communist Party in the United States, and applied for admission to the party. This letter, rejecting capitalism and the cold war policies of the United States, was to be followed by Du Bois's departure for the Republic of Ghana, whose president, Kwame Nkrumah, a long-time friend and devotee, had extended an invitation to come to Ghana and direct the Encyclopedia Africana project.

In self-exile from the United States, because, as his biographer David Levering Lewis puts it, America, "the promised land, was a cruel, receding mirage for people of color," Du Bois died in Accra, Ghana, on August 27, 1963, on the eve of the massive civil rights March on Washington.

W. E. B. DU BOIS: THE PHILADELPHIA NEGRO: A SOCIAL STUDY

The Scope of This Study

I. General Aim

This study seeks to present the results of an inquiry undertaken by the University of Pennsylvania into the condition of the forty thousand or more people of Negro blood now living in

the city of Philadelphia. This inquiry extended over a period of fifteen months and sought to ascertain something of the geographical distribution of this race, their occupations and daily life, their homes, their organizations, and, above all, their relation to their million white fellow-citizens. The final design of the work is to lay before the public such a body of information as may be a safe guide for all efforts toward the solution of the many Negro problems of a great American city.

W. E. B. Du Bois, *The Philadelphia Negro: A Social Study* (1899).

2. *The Methods of Inquiry*

The investigation began August the first, 1896, and, saving two months, continued until December the thirty-first, 1897. The work commenced with a house-to-house canvass of the Seventh Ward. This long narrow ward, extending from South Seventh street to the Schuylkill River and from Spruce street to South street, is an historic centre of Negro population, and contains today a fifth of all the Negroes in this city.[1] It was therefore thought best to make an intensive study of conditions in this district, and afterward to supplement and correct this information by general observation and inquiry in other parts of the city.

Six schedules were used among the nine thousand Negroes of this ward; a family schedule with the usual questions as to the number of members, their age and sex, their conjugal condition and birthplace, their ability to read and write, their occupation and earnings, etc.; an individual schedule with similar inquiries; a home schedule with questions as to the number of rooms, the rent, the lodgers, the conveniences, etc.; a street schedule to collect data as to the various small streets and alleys, and an institution schedule for organizations and institutions; finally a slight variation of the individual schedule was used for house-servants living at their places of employment.[2]

This study of the central district of Negro settlement furnished a key to the situation in the city; in the other wards therefore a general survey was taken to note any striking differences of condition, to ascertain the general distribution of these people, and to collect information and statistics as to organizations, property, crime and pauperism, political activity, and the like.

This general inquiry, while it lacked precise methods of measurement in most cases, served nevertheless to correct the errors and illustrate the meaning of the statistical material obtained in the house-to-house canvass.

Throughout the study such official statistics and historical matter as seemed reliable were used, and experienced persons, both white and colored, were freely consulted.

3. *The Credibility of the Results*

The best available methods of sociological research are at present so liable to inaccuracies that the careful student discloses the results of individual research with diffidence; he knows that they are liable to error from the seemingly ineradicable faults of the statistical method, to even greater error from the methods of general observation, and, above all, he must ever tremble lest some personal bias, some moral conviction or some unconscious trend of thought due to previous training, has to a degree distorted the picture in his view. Convictions on all great matters of human interest one must have to a greater or less degree, and they will enter to some extent into the most cold-blooded scientific research as a disturbing factor.

Nevertheless here are social problems before us demanding careful study, questions awaiting satisfactory answers. We must study, we must investigate, we must attempt to solve; and the utmost that the world can demand is, not lack of human interest and moral conviction, but rather the heart-quality of fairness, and an earnest desire for the truth despite its possible unpleasantness.

In a house-to-house investigation there are outside the attitude of the investigator, many sources of error: misapprehension, vagueness and forgetfulness, and deliberate deception on the part of the persons questioned, greatly vitiate the value of the answers; on the other hand, conclusions formed by the best trained and most conscientious students on the basis of general

---

[1] I shall throughout this study use the term "Negro," to designate all persons of Negro descent, although the appellation is to some extent illogical. I shall, moreover, capitalize the word, because I believe that eight million Americans are entitled to a capital letter.

[2] See Appendix A for form of schedules used.

observation and inquiry are really inductions from but a few of the multitudinous facts of social life, and these may easily fall far short of being essential or typical.

The use of both of these methods which has been attempted in this study may perhaps have corrected to some extent the errors of each. Again, whatever personal equation is to be allowed for in the whole study is one unvarying quantity, since the work was done by one investigator, and the varying judgments of a score of censustakers was thus avoided.[3]

Despite all drawbacks and difficulties, however, the main results of the inquiry seem credible. They agree, to a large extent, with general public opinion, and in other respects they seem either logically explicable or in accord with historical precedents. They are therefore presented to the public not as complete and without error, but as possessing on the whole enough reliable matter to serve as the scientific basis of further study, and of practical reform.

The Problem

4. *The Negro Problems of Philadelphia*

In Philadelphia, as elsewhere in the United States, the existence of certain peculiar social problems affecting the Negro people are plainly manifest. Here is a large group of people—perhaps forty-five thousand, a city within a city—who do not form an integral part of the larger social group. This in itself is not altogether unusual; there are other unassimilated groups: Jews, Italians, even Americans; and yet in the case of the Negroes the segregation is more conspicuous, more patent to the eye, and so intertwined with a long historic evolution, with

---

[3] The appended study of domestic service was done by Miss Isabel Eaton, Fellow of the College Settlements Association. Outside of this the work was done by the one investigator.

peculiarly pressing social problems of poverty, ignorance, crime and labor, that the Negro problem far surpasses in scientific interest and social gravity most of the other race or class questions.

The student of these questions must first ask, What is the real condition of this group of human beings? Of whom is it composed, what sub-groups and classes exist, what sort of individuals are being considered? Further, the student must clearly recognize that a complete study must not confine itself to the group, but must specially notice the environment; the physical environment of city, sections and houses, the far mightier social environment—the surrounding world of custom, wish, whim, and thought which envelops this group and powerfully influences its social development.

Nor does the clear recognition of the field of investigation simplify the work of actual study; it rather increases it, by revealing lines of inquiry far broader in scope than first thought suggests. To the average Philadelphian the whole Negro question reduces itself to a study of certain slum districts. His mind reverts to Seventh and Lombard streets and to Twelfth and Kater streets of today, or to St. Mary's in the past. Continued and widely known charitable work in these sections makes the problem of poverty familiar to him; bold and daring crime too often traced to these centres has called his attention to a problem of crime, while the scores of loafers, idlers and prostitutes who crowd the sidewalks here night and day remind him of a problem of work.

All this is true—all these problems are there and of threatening intricacy; unfortunately, however, the interest of the ordinary man of affairs is apt to stop here. Crime, poverty and idleness affect his interests unfavorably and he would have them stopped; he looks upon these slums and slum characters as unpleasant things which should in some way be removed for the best interests of all. The social student agrees with him so far, but must point out that the removal of unpleasant features from our complicated modern life is a delicate operation requiring knowledge and skill; that a slum is not a simple fact, it is a symptom and that to know the removable causes of the Negro slums of Philadelphia requires a study that takes one far beyond the slum districts. For few Philadelphians realize how the Negro population has grown and spread. There was a time in the memory of living men when a small district near Sixth and Lombard streets comprehended the great mass of the Negro population of the city. This is no longer so. Very early the stream of the black population started northward, but the increased foreign immigration of 1830 and later turned it back. It started south also but was checked by poor houses and worse police protection. Finally with gathered momentum the emigration from the slums started west, rolling on slowly and surely, taking Lombard street as its main thoroughfare, gaining early foothold in West Philadelphia, and turning at the Schuylkill River north and south to the newer portions of the city.

Thus today the Negroes are scattered in every ward of the city, and the great mass of them live far from the whilom centre of colored settlement. What, then, of this great mass of the population? Manifestly they form a class with social problems of their own—the problems of the Thirtieth Ward differ from the problems of the Fifth, as the black inhabitants differ. In the former ward we have represented the rank and file of Negro working-people; laborers and servants, porters and waiters. This is at present the great middle class of Negroes feeding the slums on the one hand and the upper class on the other. Here are social questions and conditions which must receive the most careful attention and patient interpretation.

Not even here, however, can the social investigator stop. He knows that every group has its upper class; it may be numerically small and socially of little weight, and yet its study is necessary to the comprehension of the whole—it forms the realized ideal of the group, and as

it is true that a nation must to some extent be measured by its slums, it is also true that it can only be understood and finally judged by its upper class.

The best class of Philadelphia Negroes, though sometimes forgotten or ignored in discussing the Negro problems, is nevertheless known to many Philadelphians. Scattered throughout the better parts of the Seventh Ward, and on Twelfth, lower Seventeenth and Nineteenth streets, and here and there in the residence wards of the northern, southern, and western sections of the city is a class of caterers, clerks, teachers, professional men, small merchants, etc., who constitute the aristocracy of the Negroes. Many are well-to-do, some are wealthy, all are fairly educated, and some liberally trained. Here too are social problems—differing from those of the other classes, and differing too from those of the whites of a corresponding grade, because of the peculiar social environment in which the whole race finds itself, which the whole race feels, but which touches this highest class at most points and tells upon them most decisively.

Many are the misapprehensions and misstatements as to the social environment of Negroes in a great Northern city. Sometimes it is said, here they are free; they have the same chance as the Irishman, the Italian, or the Swede; at other times it is said, the environment is such that it is really more oppressive than the situation in Southern cities. The student must ignore both of these extreme statements and seek to extract from a complicated mass of facts the tangible evidence of a social atmosphere surrounding Negroes, which differs from that surrounding most whites; of a different mental attitude, moral standard, and economic judgment shown toward Negroes than toward most other folk. That such a difference exists and can now and then plainly be seen, few deny; but just how far it goes and how large a factor it is in the Negro problems, nothing but careful study and measurement can reveal.

Such then are the phenomena of social condition and environment which this study proposes to describe, analyze, and, so far as possible, interpret.

5. Plan of Presentment

The study as taken up here divides itself roughly into four parts: the history of the Negro people in the city, their present condition considered as individuals, their condition as an organized social group, and their physical and social environment. To the history of the Negro but two chapters are devoted—a brief sketch—although the subject is worthy of more extended study than the character of this essay permitted.

Six chapters consider the general condition of the Negroes: their number, age and sex, conjugal condition, and birthplace; what degree of education they have obtained, and how they earn a living. All these subjects are treated usually for the Seventh Ward somewhat minutely, then more generally for the city, and finally such historical material is adduced as is available for comparison.

Three chapters are devoted to the group life of the Negro; this includes a study of the family, of property, and of organizations of all sorts. It also takes up such phenomena of social maladjustment and individual depravity as crime, pauperism and alcoholism.

One chapter is devoted to the difficult question of environment, both physical and social, one to certain results of the contact of the white and black races, one to Negro suffrage, and a word of general advice in the line of social reform is added.

W. E. B. DU BOIS: THE SOULS OF BLACK FOLK

The Forethought

Herein lie buried many things which if read with patience may show the strange meaning of being black here at the dawning of the Twentieth Century. This meaning is not without interest to you, Gentle Reader; for the problem of the Twentieth Century is the problem of the color line. I pray you, then, receive my little book in all charity, studying my words with me, forgiving mistake and foible for sake of the faith and passion that is in me, and seeking the grain of truth hidden there.

I have sought here to sketch, in vague, uncertain outline, the spiritual world in which ten thousand thousand Americans live and strive. First, in two chapters I have tried to show what Emancipation meant to them, and what was its aftermath. In a third chapter I have pointed out the slow rise of personal leadership, and criticised candidly the leader who bears the chief burden of his race today. Then, in two other chapters I have sketched in swift outline the two worlds within and without the Veil, and thus have come to the central problem of training men for life. Venturing now into deeper detail, I have in two chapters studied the struggles of the massed millions of the black peasantry, and in another have sought to make clear the present relations of the sons of master and man. Leaving, then, the white world, I have stepped within the Veil, raising it that you may view faintly its deeper recesses—the meaning of its religion, the passion of its human sorrow, and the struggle of its greater souls. All this I

From W. E. B. Du Bois, *The Souls of Black Folk* (1903).

have ended with a tale twice told but seldom written, and a chapter of song.

Some of these thoughts of mine have seen the light before in other guise. For kindly consenting to their republication here, in altered and extended form, I must thank the publishers of the *Atlantic Monthly, The World's Work,* the *Dial, The New World,* and the *Annals of the American Academy of Political and Social Science.* Before each chapter, as now printed, stands a bar of the Sorrow Songs—some echo of haunting melody from the only American music which welled up from black souls in the dark past. And, finally, need I add that I who speak here am bone of the bone and flesh of the flesh of them that live within the Veil?

Of Our Spiritual Strivings

O water, voice of my heart, crying in the sand,
　　All night long crying with a mournful cry,
As I lie and listen, and cannot understand
　　　　The voice of my heart in my side or
　　the voice of the sea,
　　O water, crying for rest, is it I, is it I?
　　　　All night long the water is crying to me.
Unresting water, there shall never be rest
　　Till the last moon droop and the last tide fail,
And the fire of the end begin to burn in the west;
　　　　And the heart shall be weary and
　　wonder and cry like the sea,
All life long crying without avail,
　　　　As the water all night long is crying
　　to me.

Arthur Symons

Between me and the other world there is ever an unasked question: unasked by some through feelings of delicacy; by others through the difficulty of rightly framing it. All, nevertheless, flutter round it. They approach me in a half-hesitant sort of way, eye me curiously or compassionately, and then, instead of saying directly, How does it feel to be a problem? they say, I know an excellent colored man in my town; or, I fought at Mechanicsville; or, Do not these Southern outrages make your blood boil? At these I smile, or am interested, or reduce the boiling to a simmer, as the occasion may require. To the real question, How does it feel to be a problem? I answer seldom a word.

And yet, being a problem is a strange experience—peculiar even for one who has never been anything else, save perhaps in babyhood and in Europe. It is in the early days of rollicking boyhood that the revelation first bursts upon one, all in a day, as it were. I remember well when the shadow swept across me. I was a little thing, away up in the hills of New England, where the dark Housatonic winds between Hoosac and Taghkanic to the sea. In a wee wooden schoolhouse, something put it into the boys' and girls' heads to buy gorgeous visiting-cards—ten cents a package—and exchange. The exchange was merry, till one girl, a tall newcomer, refused my card—refused it peremptorily, with a glance. Then it dawned upon me with a certain suddenness that I was different from the others; or like, mayhap, in heart and life and longing, but shut out from their world by a vast veil. I had thereafter no desire to tear down that veil, to creep through; I held all beyond it in common contempt, and lived above it in a region of blue sky and great wandering shadows. That sky was bluest when I could beat my mates at examination-time, or beat them at a foot-race, or even beat their stringy heads. Alas, with the years all this fine contempt began to fade; for the words I longed for, and all their dazzling opportunities, were theirs, not mine. But they should not keep these prizes, I said; some, all, I would wrest from them. Just how I would do it I could never decide: by reading law, by healing the sick, by telling the wonderful tales that swam in my head—some way. With other black boys the strife was not so fiercely sunny: their youth shrunk into tasteless sycophancy, or into silent hatred of the pale world about them and mocking distrust of everything white; or wasted itself in a bitter cry, Why did God make me an outcast and a stranger in mine own house? The shades of the prison-house closed round about us all: walls strait and stubborn to the whitest, but relentlessly narrow, tall, and unscalable to sons of night who must plod darkly on in resignation, or beat unavailing palms against the stone, or steadily, half hopelessly, watch the streak of blue above.

After the Egyptian and Indian, the Greek and Roman, the Teuton and Mongolian, the Negro is a sort of seventh son, born with a veil, and gifted with second-sight in this American world—a world which yields him no true self-consciousness, but only lets him see himself through the revelation of the other world. It is a peculiar sensation, this double-consciousness, this sense of always looking at one's self through the eyes of others, of measuring one's soul by the tape of a world that looks on in amused contempt and pity. One ever feels his twoness—an American, a Negro; two souls, two thoughts, two unreconciled strivings; two warring ideals in one dark body, whose dogged strength alone keeps it from being torn asunder.

The history of the American Negro is the history of this strife—this longing to attain self-conscious manhood, to merge his double self into a better and truer self. In this merging he wishes neither of the older selves to be lost. He would not Africanize America, for America has too much to teach the world and Africa. He would not bleach his Negro soul in a flood of white Americanism, for he knows that Negro blood has a message for the world. He simply wishes to make it possible for a man to be both a Negro and an American, without being cursed and spit upon by his fellows, without having the doors of Opportunity closed roughly in his face.

This, then, is the end of his striving: to be a coworker in the kingdom of culture, to escape both death and isolation, to husband and use his best powers and his latent genius. These powers of body and mind have in the past been strangely wasted, dispersed, or forgotten. The shadow of a mighty Negro past flits through the tale of Ethiopia the Shadowy and of Egypt the Sphinx. Through history, the powers of single black men flash here and there like falling stars, and die sometimes before the world has rightly gauged their brightness. Here in America, in the few days since Emancipation, the black man's turning hither and thither in hesitant and doubtful striving has often made his very strength to lose effectiveness, to seem like absence of power, like weakness. And yet it is not weakness—it is the contradiction of double aims. The double-aimed struggle of the black artisan—on the one hand to escape white contempt for a nation of mere hewers of wood and drawers of water, and on the other hand to plough and nail and dig for a poverty-stricken horde—could only result in making him a poor craftsman, for he had but half a heart in either cause. By the poverty and ignorance of his people, the Negro minister or doctor was tempted toward quackery and demagogy; and by the criticism of the other world, toward ideals that made him ashamed of his lowly tasks. The would-be black *savant* was confronted by the paradox that the knowledge his people needed was a twice-told tale to his white neighbors, while the knowledge which would teach the white world was Greek to his own flesh and blood. The innate love of harmony and beauty that set the ruder souls of his people a-dancing and a-singing raised but confusion and doubt in the soul of the black artist; for the beauty revealed to him was the soul-beauty of a race which his larger audience despised, and he could not articulate the message of another people. This waste of double aims, this seeking to satisfy two unreconciled ideals, has wrought sad havoc with the courage and faith and deeds of ten thousand thousand people—has sent them often wooing false gods and invoking false means of salvation, and at times has even seemed about to make them ashamed of themselves.

Away back in the days of bondage they thought to see in one divine event the end of all doubt and disappointment; few men ever worshipped Freedom with half such unquestioning faith as did the American Negro for two centuries. To him, so far as he thought and dreamed, slavery was indeed the sum of all villainies, the cause of all sorrow, the root of all prejudice; Emancipation was the key to a promised land of sweeter beauty than ever stretched before the eyes of wearied Israelites. In song and exhortation swelled one refrain—Liberty; in his tears and curses the God he implored had Freedom in his right hand. At last it came—suddenly, fearfully, like a dream. With one wild carnival of blood and passion came the message in his own plaintive cadences:

> "Shout, O children!
> Shout, you're free!
> For God has bought your liberty!"

Years have passed away since then—ten, twenty, forty; forty years of national life, forty years of renewal and development, and yet the swarthy spectre sits in its accustomed seat at the Nation's feast. In vain do we cry to this our vastest social problem:

> "Take any shape but that, and my firm nerves
> Shall never tremble!"

The Nation has not yet found peace from its sins; the freedman has not yet found in freedom his promised land. Whatever of good may have come in these years of change, the shadow of a deep disappointment rests upon the Negro people—a disappointment all the more bitter because the unattained ideal was unbounded save by the simple ignorance of a lowly people.

The first decade was merely a prolongation of the vain search for freedom, the boon that seemed ever barely to elude their grasp—like a tantalizing will-o'-the-wisp, maddening and misleading the headless host. The holocaust of war, the terrors of the Ku-Klux Klan, the lies of carpet-baggers, the disorganization of industry, and the contradictory advice of friends and foes, left the bewildered serf with no new watchword beyond the old cry for freedom. As the time flew, however, he began to grasp a new idea. The ideal of liberty demanded for its attainment powerful means, and these the Fifteenth Amendment gave him. The ballot, which before he had looked upon as a visible sign of freedom, he now regarded as the chief means of gaining and perfecting the liberty with which war had partially endowed him. And why not? Had not votes made war and emancipated millions? Had not votes enfranchised the freedmen? Was anything impossible to a power that had done all this? A million black men started with renewed zeal to vote themselves into the kingdom. So the decade flew away, the revolution of 1876 came, and left the half-free serf weary, wondering, but still inspired. Slowly but steadily, in the following years, a new vision began gradually to replace the dream of political power—a powerful movement, the rise of another ideal to guide the unguided, another pillar of fire by night after a clouded day. It was the ideal of "book-learning"; the curiosity, born of compulsory ignorance, to know and test the power of the cabalistic letters of the white man, the longing to know. Here at last seemed to have been discovered the mountain path to Canaan; longer than the highway of Emancipation and law, steep and rugged, but straight, leading to heights high enough to overlook life.

Up the new path the advance guard toiled, slowly, heavily, doggedly; only those who have watched and guided the faltering feet, the misty minds, the dull understandings, of the dark pupils of these schools know how faithfully, how piteously, this people strove to learn. It was weary work. The cold statistician wrote down the inches of progress here and there, noted also where here and there a foot had slipped or some one had fallen. To the tired climbers, the horizon was ever dark, the mists were often cold, the Canaan was always dim and far away. If, however, the vistas disclosed as yet no goal, no resting-place, little but flattery and criticism, the journey at least gave leisure for reflection and self-examination; it changed the child of Emancipation to the youth with dawning self-consciousness, self-realization, self-respect. In those sombre forests of his striving his own soul rose before him, and he saw himself—darkly as through a veil; and yet he saw in himself some faint revelation of his power, of his mission. He began to have a dim feeling that, to attain his place in the world, he must be himself, and not another. For the first time he sought to analyze the burden he bore upon his back, that dead-weight of social degradation partially masked behind a half-named Negro problem. He felt his poverty; without a cent, without a home, without land, tools, or savings, he had entered into competition with rich, landed, skilled neighbors. To be a poor man is hard, but to be a poor race in a land of dollars is the very bottom of hardships. He felt the weight of his ignorance—not simply of letters, but of life, of business, of the humanities; the accumulated sloth and shirking and awkwardness of decades and centuries shackled his hands and feet. Nor was his burden all poverty and ignorance. The red stain of bastardy, which two centuries of systematic legal defilement of Negro women had stamped upon his race, meant not only the loss of ancient African chastity, but also the hereditary weight of a mass of corruption from white adulterers, threatening almost the obliteration of the Negro home.

A people thus handicapped ought not to be asked to race with the world, but rather allowed to give all its time and thought to its own social problems. But alas! while sociologists gleefully count his bastards and his prostitutes, the very soul of the toiling, sweating black man is darkened by the shadow of a vast despair. Men call the shadow prejudice, and learnedly explain it as the natural defence of culture against barbarism, learning against ignorance, purity against crime, the "higher" against the "lower" races. To which the Negro cries Amen! and

swears that to so much of this strange prejudice as is founded on just homage to civilization, culture, righteousness, and progress, he humbly bows and meekly does obeisance. But before that nameless prejudice that leaps beyond all this he stands helpless, dismayed, and well-nigh speechless; before that personal disrespect and mockery, the ridicule and systematic humiliation, the distortion of fact and wanton license of fancy, the cynical ignoring of the better and the boisterous welcoming of the worse, the all-pervading desire to inculcate disdain for everything black, from Toussaint to the devil—before this there rises a sickening despair that would disarm and discourage any nation save that black host to whom "discouragement" is an unwritten word.

But the facing of so vast a prejudice could not but bring the inevitable self-questioning, self-disparagement, and lowering of ideals which ever accompany repression and breed in an atmosphere of contempt and hate. Whisperings and portents came borne upon the four winds: Lo! we are diseased and dying, cried the dark hosts; we cannot write, our voting is vain; what need of education, since we must always cook and serve? And the Nation echoed and enforced this self-criticism, saying: Be content to be servants, and nothing more; what need of higher culture for half-men? Away with the black man's ballot, by force or fraud—and behold the suicide of a race! Nevertheless, out of the evil came something of good—the more careful adjustment of education to real life, the clearer perception of the Negroes' social responsibilities, and the sobering realization of the meaning of progress.

So dawned the time of *Sturm und Drang:* storm and stress to-day rocks our little boat on the mad waters of the world-sea; there is within and without the sound of conflict, the burning of body and rending of soul; inspiration strives with doubt, and faith with vain questionings. The bright ideals of the past— physical freedom, political power, the training of brains and the training of hands—all these in turn have waxed and waned, until even the last grows dim and overcast. Are they all wrong—all false? No, not that, but each alone was over-simple and incomplete—the dreams of a credulous race-childhood, or the fond imaginings of the other world which does not know and does not want to know our power. To be really true, all these ideals must be melted and welded into one. The training of the schools we need today more than ever—the training of deft hands, quick eyes and ears, and above all the broader, deeper, higher culture of gifted minds and pure hearts. The power of the ballot we need in sheer self-defence—else what shall save us from a second slavery? Freedom, too, the long-sought, we still seek—the freedom of life and limb, the freedom to work and think, the freedom to love and aspire. Work, culture, liberty—all these we need, not singly but together, not successively but together, each growing and aiding each, and all striving toward that vaster ideal that swims before the Negro people, the ideal of human brotherhood, gained through the unifying ideal of Race; the ideal of fostering and developing the traits and talents of the Negro, not in opposition to or contempt for other races, but rather in large conformity to the greater ideals of the American Republic, in order that some day on American soil two world-races may give each to each those characteristics both so sadly lack. We the darker ones come even now not altogether empty-handed: there are today no truer exponents of the pure human spirit of the Declaration of Independence than the American Negroes; there is no true American music but the wild sweet melodies of the Negro slave; the American fairy tales and folklore are Indian and African; and, all in all, we black men seem the sole oasis of simple faith and reverence in a dusty desert of dollars and smartness. Will America be poorer if she replace her brutal dyspeptic blundering with light-hearted but determined Negro humility? or her coarse and cruel wit with loving jovial good-humor? or her vulgar music with the soul of the Sorrow Songs?

Merely a concrete test of the underlying principles of the great republic is the Negro Problem, and the spiritual striving of the freedmen's sons is the travail of souls whose burden is almost beyond the measure of their strength, but who bear it in the name of an historic race, in the name of this the land of their fathers' fathers, and in the name of human opportunity.

And now what I have briefly sketched in large outline let me on coming pages tell again in many ways, with loving emphasis and deeper detail, that men may listen to the striving in the souls of black folk.

Further Readings: The Classic Tradition

KARL MARX

AVINERI, SHLOMO: *The social and political thought of Karl Marx.* Cambridge University Press, 1968.

BERLIN, ISAIAH, SIR: *Karl Marx: his life and environment.* 4th ed. Oxford; New York: Oxford University Press, 1978, 1979 printing.

LICHTHEIM, GEORGE: *Marxism; an historical and critical study.* New York, Praeger, 1961.

MARX, KARL: *Capital: a critique of political economy;* introduced by Ernest Mandel; translated by Ben Fowkes. 1977.

MARX, KARL: *Economic and philosophic manuscripts of 1844.* Edited with an introduction by Dirk J. Struik. Translated by Martin Milligan. 1st American ed. New York, International Publishers, 1973.

MARX, KARL: *The eighteenth Brumaire of Louis Bonaparte;* with explanatory notes. New York, International Publishers, 1935.

MARX, KARL and FREDERICK ENGELS: *The communist manifesto.* Authorized English translation, edited and annotated by Frederick Engels. New York, New York Labor News Co., 1933.

MARX, KARL and FREDERICK ENGELS: *The German ideology.* Part one, with selections from parts two and three, together with Marx's "Introduction to a critique of political economy." Edited, and with introduction, by C. J. Arthur. New York, International Publishers, 1972.

MCLELLAN, DAVID: *The thought of Karl Marx;* with an introduction [by] David McLellan. New York, Harper & Row, 1972.

MEHRING, FRANZ: *Karl Marx; the story of his life;* with illustrations and facsimile reproductions, notes by the author, an appendix prepared under the direction of Eduard Fuchs based on researches of the Marx-Engels institute, a bibliography and an index. Translated by Edward Fitzgerald, edited by Ruth & Heinz Norden. New York, Covici, Friede, 1935.

MÉSZÁROS, ISTVÁN: *Marx's theory of alienation.* 4th ed. London, Merlin Press, 1975.

OLLMAN, BERTELL: *Alienation: Marx's conception of man in capitalist society.* 2d ed. Cambridge, New York, Cambridge University Press, 1976.

EMILE DURKHEIM

ALEXANDER, JEFFREY C. (ed.) *Durkheimian sociology: cultural studies,* Cambridge University Press, 1988.

CLADIS, MARK Sydney: *A communitarian defense of liberalism: Emile Durkheim and contemporary social theory.* Stanford, Calif., Stanford University Press, 1992.

DOUGLAS, JACK D.: *The social meanings of suicide.* Princeton, N.J., Princeton University Press, 1967.

DURKHEIM, EMILE: *On morality and society; selected writings.* Edited and with an introduction by Robert N. Bellah. Chicago, University of Chicago Press, 1973.

DURKHEIM, EMILE: *Suicide, a study in sociology.* Translated by John A. Spaulding and George Simpson; edited with an introduction by George Simpson. London, Routledge & K. Paul, 1952.

DURKHEIM, EMILE: *The division of labor in society;* with an introduction by Lewis A. Coser; translated by W. D. Halls. New York, Free Press, 1997.

DURKHEIM, EMILE: *The elementary forms of the religious life.* Translated from the French by Joseph Ward Swain. New York, Free Press, 1965.

DURKHEIM, EMILE: *The rules of sociological method;* edited, with an introduction, by Steven Lukes; translated by W. D. Halls. New York, Free Press, 1982.

GIDDENS, ANTHONY: *Capitalism and modern social theory; an analysis of the writings of Marx, Durkheim and Max Weber.* Cambridge [Eng.] University Press, 1971.

LACAPRA, DOMINICK: *Émile Durkheim: sociologist and philosopher.* Ithaca, N.Y., Cornell University Press, 1972.

LUKES, STEVEN: *Émile Durkheim, his life and work: a historical and critical study.* Harmondsworth, Penguin, 1975.

TIRYAKIAN, EDWARD A.: *Sociologism and existentialism, two perspectives on the individual and society.* Englewood Cliffs, N.J., Prentice-Hall, 1962.

MAX WEBER

BENDIX, REINHARD: *Max Weber; an intellectual portrait.* Garden City, N.Y., Doubleday 1962.

GIDDENS, ANTHONY: *Capitalism and modern social theory; an analysis of the writings of Marx, Durkheim and Max Weber.* Cambridge [Eng.] University Press, 1971.

LÖWITH, KARL: *Max Weber and Karl Marx;* edited with an introduction by Tom Bottomore and William Outhwaite; translated by Hans Fantel. London; Boston, George Allen & Unwin, 1982.

MITZMAN, ARTHUR: *The iron cage: an historical interpretation of Max Weber.* 1st ed. New York, Knopf, 1970.

MOMMSEN, WOLFGANG J.: *The age of bureaucracy; perspectives on the political sociology of Max Weber.* Oxford, Blackwell, 1974.

ROTH, GUENTHER and WOLFGANG SCHLUCHTER: *Max Weber's vision of history: ethics and methods.* Berkeley, University of California Press, 1979.

TURNER, BRYAN S.: *Weber and Islam: a critical study.* London; Boston, Routledge & Kegan Paul, 1974.

WEBER, MARIANNE: *Max Weber: a biography;* translated from the German and edited by Harry Zohn. New York, Wiley, 1975.

WEBER, MAX: *Economy and society: an outline of interpretive sociology,* edited by Guenther Roth and Claus Wittich; translators, Ephraim Fischoff, et al. Berkeley, University of California Press, 1978.

WEBER, MAX: *From Max Weber: essays in sociology,* translated, edited and with an introduction by H. H. Gerth and C. Wright Mills. New York, Oxford University Press, 1958.

WEBER, MAX: *Max Weber on the methodology of the social sciences,* translated and edited by Edward A. Shils and Henry A. Finch. With a foreword by Edward A. Shils. Glencoe, Ill., Free Press, 1949.

WEBER, MAX: *The Protestant ethic and the spirit of capitalism.* Translated by Talcott Parsons. With a foreword by R. H. Tawney. New York, Scribner, 1958.

WEBER, MAX: *The sociology of religion.* Translated by Ephraim Fischoff. Introduction by Talcott Parsons. Boston, Beacon Press, 1963.

WEBER, MAX: *The theory of social and economic organization,* tr. by A. M. Henderson and Talcott Parsons, ed., with an introduction by Talcott Parsons. 1st American ed. New York, Oxford University Press, 1947.

GEORGE HERBERT MEAD

BALDWIN, JOHN C.: *George Herbert Mead: A Unifying Theory for Sociology.* Newbury Park, Calif., Sage.

COOK, GARY A.: *George Herbert Mead: The Making of a Social Pragmatist.* Urbana, University of Illinois Press, 1993.

JOAS, HANS: *G. H. Mead: A Contemporary Re-examination of His Thought,* Cambridge: Polity Press, 1985.

MORRIS, CHARLES W., ed.: *Mind, Self, and Society from the Standpoint of a Social Behaviorist.* Chicago, University of Chicago Press, 1967.

MORRIS, CHARLES W., in collaboration with J. M. Brewster, A. M. Dunham, and D. L. Miller, eds.: *The Philosophy of the Act.* Chicago, University of Chicago Press, 1938.

STRAUSS, ANSELM L., ed.: *The Social Psychology of George Herbert Mead.* Introduced (pp. iv–xvi) by Anselm L. Strauss. Chicago, University of Chicago Press, 1956.

W. E. B. DU BOIS

ANDREWS, WILLIAM L., editor: *Critical Essays on W. E. B. Du Bois.* Boston, G. K. Hall, 1985.

LEWIS, DAVID L.: *W. E. B. Du Bois: Biography of a Race, 1868–1919.* New York, H. Holt, 1993.

MARABLE, MANNING: *W. E. B. Du Bois: Black Radical Democrat.* Boston, Twayne, 1986.

ZAMIR, SHAMOON: *Dark Voices: W. E. B. Du Bois and American Thought, 1888–1903.* Chicago, The University of Chicago Press, 1995.

Contemporary Sociological Theory

Chapter 7

Functionalism

Introduction

Functionalism reigned as the dominant paradigm in sociology for a brief period from the early 1950s to the late 1960s. Through the work of Talcott Parsons and Robert Merton, among others, the earlier insights of Auguste Comte, Herbert Spencer, and Émile Durkheim were refined and developed. In general, the major distinctive contribution of functionalism has been its view of social order as a consensual agreement reflecting shared values and norms that bind a community together. From this perspective the reason people obey rules, follow codes of behavior, and abide by the laws of a society, is that they accept the fundamental values of their society and see its authority structures as legitimate expressions of this consensus. Rules and regulations are understood, by the functionalist, as codes and enactments designed to benefit the totality rather than the expressions of a dominant class or particular interest with privileged access to decision-making power. Functionalism in this respect is set apart from Marxian explanations of social order, in which coercion is seen as the ultimate reason that people obey rules and abide by codes and laws.

Functionalists generally adhere to the view that society can be understood in its totality as an entity unto itself. Among the earlier functionalist thinkers it was not uncommon to view society as an organism with differentiated parts that function together in order for it to adapt and survive in its environment. Although contemporary functionalists are not as crude, they nevertheless tend to look at society as an integrated system of functionally interrelated structures, at times suggesting that societies have a life of their own and that their survival demands that particular needs of the system have to be met.

Kingsley Davis, Wilbert Moore, Robert Merton, and Talcott Parsons have made significant contributions to the development of functionalist theory. Davis and Moore (1945) have together authored a pathbreaking and controversial article, "Some Principles of Stratification," in which they argue that stratification is a functionally necessary structure that every society must develop in order to ensure that appropriate individuals with the requisite talents and skills assume the roles and positions in society for which they are best suited. Because individuals are born with vastly different talents, because the positions in society most necessary to social survival require the most capable people to do the job, and, furthermore, because these positions may also be among the most demanding, a method has to be developed whereby the most capable wind up in the top positions in the social order. Moore and Davis argue that the differential reward structure of society is the mechanism that functions to bring about this match between talent and social position.

The contributions of Talcott Parsons to the theory of functionalism are the record of a lifetime of writing in the area of social theory. Parsons attempted in his several works to develop concepts that would help organize our perceptions of social reality. In recasting the functional imperatives of a social system, Parsons developed a fourfold classification scheme with the acronym AGIL. *Adaptation* refers to the fact that systems are embedded in physical and sociopolitical environments to which they must adapt if they are to survive. *Goal Attainment* refers to the need in any system to define its primary goals and the methods by which individuals accept those goals as their own and strive to achieve them. *Integration* refers to the need to coordinate the component parts of the system so that they contribute to the maintenance of the whole. *Latency* refers to those structures that serve to maintain and revitalize the motivation of individuals to perform their roles according to social expectations.

Parsons further elaborated his conceptual scheme to a fourfold action system. Each of the action systems, namely social, cultural, personality, and the behavioral organism, is tied to the functional imperatives of a total system. Thus, the complex of institutions that we group under the rubric of socialization and social control perform the integrative functions of the system, whereas the values and norms that serve to motivate social action are grouped as part of the cultural system. The personality system functions to attain the goals of the system and the behavioral organism provides the energy for adaptation and transformation of the system in relation to its environment.

An early essay of Talcott Parsons is reproduced in the following pages in which he explains how a functionalist views sex roles and age in the context of American social structure. The piece is of interest for several reasons. First, it demonstrates how a functionalist applies these abstract ideas to concrete problems in American society. Second, because the piece was written in the 1940s, it invites the student to discuss the changes that have taken place in the way in which we define sex roles today. Finally, the student should attempt to apply a functional way of thinking to discuss the reasons for the changes, that is, why have the older definitions become dysfunctional, or alternatively, what are the functions served by the new ones? How have these changes been implemented in the socialization processes that Parsons describes?

The final excerpt in this section is taken from Robert K. Merton's essay on manifest and latent functions. What is important here is not only Merton's theoretical elaboration and extension of functional categories but his excellent discussion of the Hawthorne studies, Veblen's discussion of conspicuous consumption, and the function of political machines in the recent past. The reader should keep in mind the following questions when reading the Merton selection. What was the impact of the "experimental situation" on the workers in the Hawthorne studies? Why did it take a "sociological" perspective rather than an "engineering" one to ferret out the latent functions of the experiment? Are there any contemporary applications of these discoveries? What is the latent function of consumption as Merton recounts Veblen's thesis, and why is this function no longer latent? Finally, what does a functional analysis of political machines reveal about how they work and for whom? How does this approach to political machines avoid ideological and moral arguments and engage in sociological analysis? Is this desirable?

Functionalism and its emphasis on stability, equilibrium, integration, and adaptation came in for severe criticism during the 1960s, when American society was engaged in convulsive protest movements, dissension, conflict, disorder, and change. Reality and theory were out of synchrony. As many abandoned functionalism, supported by the trenchant critiques of C. Wright Mills (1959) and Alvin Gouldner (1970), some declared functionalism dead whereas others embraced alternative theoretical approaches. Conflict theory, discussed in the next chapter, emerged as a corrective to functionalism, and Neo-functionalism has recently come forth as a theoretical interest among those who have accepted many of the criticisms leveled against functionalism. Specifically, Neo-functionalism acknowledges the imbalance in functionalism's key orientation toward stability and equilibrium, its sparse attention to the dynamic of social change, and its exclusive concern with order in large-scale social systems.

KINGSLEY DAVIS AND WILBERT E. MOORE: SOME PRINCIPLES OF STRATIFICATION

In a previous paper some concepts for handling the phenomena of social inequality were presented.[1] In the present paper a further step in stratification theory is undertaken—an attempt to show the relationship between stratification and the rest of the social order.[2] Starting from the proposition that no society is "classless," or unstratified, an effort is made to explain, in functional terms, the universal necessity which calls forth stratification in any social system. Next, an attempt is made to explain the roughly uniform distribution of prestige as between the major types of positions in every society. Since, however, there occur between one society and another great differences in the degree and kind of stratification, some attention is also given to the varieties of social inequality and the variable factors that give rise to them.

Clearly, the present task requires two different lines of analysis—one to understand the universal, the other to understand the variable features of stratification. Naturally each line of inquiry aids the other and is indispensable, and in the treatment that follows the two will be interwoven, although, because of space limitations, the emphasis will be on the universals.

Throughout, it will be necessary to keep in mind one thing—namely, that the discussion relates to the system of positions, not to the individuals occupying those positions. It is one thing to ask why different positions carry different degrees of prestige, and quite another to ask how certain individuals get into those positions. Although, as the argument will try to show, both questions are related, it is essential to keep them separate in our thinking. Most of the literature of stratification has tried to answer the second question (particularly with regard to the ease or difficulty of mobility between strata) without tackling the first. The first question, however, is logically prior and, in the case of any particular individual or group factually prior.

The Functional Necessity of Stratification

Curiously, however, the main functional necessity explaining the universal presence of stratification is precisely the requirement faced by any society of placing and motivating individuals in the social structure. As a functioning mechanism a society must somehow distribute its members in social positions and induce them to perform the duties of these positions. It must thus concern itself with motivation at two different levels: to instill in the proper individuals the desire to fill certain positions, and, once in these positions, the desire to perform the duties attached to them. Even though the social order may be relatively static in form, there is a continuous process of metabolism as new individuals are born into it, shift with age, and die off. Their absorption into the positional system must somehow be arranged and motivated. This is true whether the system is competitive or non-competitive. A competitive system gives greater importance to the motivation to achieve positions, whereas a non-competitive system gives perhaps greater importance to the motivation to perform the duties of the positions; but in any system both types of motivation are required.

Kingsley Davis and Wilbert E. Moore, "Some Principles of Stratification," *American Sociological Review,* Vol. 10, pp. 242–249, 1945.
[1] Kingsley Davis, "A Conceptual Analysis of Stratification," *American Sociological Review.* 7:309–321, June 1942.
[2] The writers regret (and beg indulgence) that the present essay, a condensation of a longer study, covers so much in such short space that adequate evidence and qualificaiton cannot be given and that as a result what is actually very tentative is presented in an unfortunately dogmatic manner.

If the duties associated with the various positions were all equally pleasant to the human organism, all equally important to societal survival, and all equally in need of the same ability or talent, it would make no difference who got into which positions, and the problem of social placement would be greatly reduced. But actually it does make a great deal of difference who gets into which positions, not only because some positions are inherently more agreeable than others, but also because some require special talents or training and some are functionally more important than others. Also, it is essential that the duties of the positions be performed with the diligence that their importance requires. Inevitably, then, a society must have first, some kind of rewards that it can use as inducements, and, second, some way of distributing these rewards differentially according to positions. The rewards and their distribution become a part of the social order, and thus give rise to stratification.

One may ask what kind of rewards a society has at its disposal in distributing its personnel and securing essential services. It has, first of all, the things that contribute to sustenance and comfort. It has, second, the things that contribute to humor and diversion. And it has, finally, the things that contribute to self respect and ego expansion. The last, because of the peculiarly social character of the self, is largely a function of the opinion of others, but it nonetheless ranks in importance with the first two. In any social system all three kinds of rewards must be dispensed differentially according to positions.

In a sense the rewards are "built into" the position. They consist in the "rights" associated with the position, plus what may be called its accompaniments or perquisites. Often the rights, and sometimes the accompaniments, are functionally related to the duties of the position. (Rights as viewed by the incumbent are usually duties as viewed by other members of the community.) However, there may be a host of subsidiary rights and perquisites that are not essential to the function of the position and have only an indirect and symbolic connection with its duties, but which still may be of considerable importance in inducing people to seek the positions and fulfill the essential duties.

If the rights and perquisites of different positions in a society must be unequal then the society must be stratified, because that is precisely what stratification means. Social inequality is thus an unconsciously evolved device by which societies insure that the most important positions are conscientiously filled by the most qualified persons. Hence every society, no matter how simple or complex, must differentiate persons in terms of both prestige and esteem, and must therefore possess a certain amount of institutionalized inequality.

It does not follow that the amount or type of inequality need be the same in all societies. This is largely a function of factors that will be discussed presently.

The Two Determinants of Positional Rank

Granting the general function that inequality subserves, one can specify the two factors that determine the relative rank of different positions. In general those positions convey the best reward, and hence have the highest rank, which (a) have the greatest importance for the society and (b) require the greatest training or talent. The first factor concerns function and is a matter of relative significance; the second concerns means and is a matter of scarcity.

Differential Functional Importance   Actually a society does not need to reward positions in proportion to their functional importance. It merely needs to give sufficient reward to them to insure that they will be filled competently. In other words, it must see that less essential positions do not compete successfully with more essential ones. If a position is easily filled, it need not be heavily rewarded, even though important. On the other hand, if it is important but hard to fill, the reward must be high enough to get it filled anyway. Functional importance is therefore a necessary but not a sufficient cause of high rank being assigned to a position.[3]

Differential Scarcity of Personnel Practically all positions, no matter how acquired, require some form of skill or capacity for performance. This is implicit in the very notion of position, which implies that the incumbent must, by virtue of his incumbency, accomplish certain things.

There are, ultimately, only two ways in which a person's qualifications come about: through inherent capacity or through training. Obviously, in concrete activities both are always necessary, but from a practical standpoint the scarcity may lie primarily in one or the other, as well as in both. Some positions require innate talents of such high degree that the persons who fill them are bound to be rare. In many cases, however, talent is fairly abundant in the population but the training process is so long, costly, and elaborate that relatively few can qualify. Modern medicine, for example, is within the mental capacity of most individuals, but a medical education is so burdensome and expensive that virtually none would undertake

---

[3] Unfortunately, functional importance is difficult to establish. To use the position's prestige to establish it, as is often unconsciously done, constitutes circular reasoning from our point of view. There are, however, two independent clues: (a) the degree to which a position is functionally unique, there being no other positions that can perform the same function satisfactorily; (b) the degree to which other positions are dependent on the one in question. Both clues are best exemplified in organized systems of positions built around one major function. Thus, in most complex societies the religious, political, economic, and educational functions are handled by distinct structures not easily interchangeable. In addition, each structure possesses many different positions, some clearly dependent on, if not subordinate to, others. In sum, when an institutional nucleus becomes differentiated around one main function, and at the same time organizes a large portion of the population into its relationships, the *key* positions in it are of the highest functional importance. The absence of such specialization does not prove functional unimportance, for the whole society may be relatively unspecialized; but it is safe to assume that the more important functions receive the first and clearest structural differentiation.

it if the position of the M.D. did not carry a reward commensurate with the sacrifice.

If the talents required for a position are abundant and the training easy, the method of acquiring the position may have little to do with its duties. There may be, in fact, a virtually accidental relationship. But if the skills required are scarce by reason of the rarity of talent or the costliness of training the position, if functionally important, must have an attractive power that will draw the necessary skills in competition with other positions. This means, in effect, that the position must be high in the social scale—must command great prestige, high salary, ample leisure, and the like.

How Variations Are to Be Understood In so far as there is a difference between one system of stratification and another, it is attributable to whatever factors affect the two determinants of differential reward—namely, functional importance and scarcity of personnel. Positions important in one society may not be important in another because the conditions faced by the societies or their degree of internal development, may be different. The same conditions, in turn may affect the question of scarcity; for in some societies the stage of development, or the external situation, may wholly obviate the necessity of certain kinds of skill or talent. Any particular system of stratification, then, can be understood as a product of the special conditions affecting the two aforementioned grounds of differential reward.

Major Societal Functions and Stratification

Religion The reason why religion is necessary is apparently to be found in the fact that human society achieves its unity primarily through the possession by its members of certain ultimate values and ends in common. Although these values and ends are subjective, they influence behavior, and their integration enables the society to operate as a system. Derived neither from inherited nor from external nature, they have evolved as a part of culture by communication and moral pressure. They must, however, appear to the members of the society to have some reality, and it is the role of religious belief and ritual to supply and reinforce this appearance of reality. Through belief and ritual the common ends and values are connected with an imaginary world symbolized by concrete sacred objects, which world in turn is related in a meaningful way to the facts and trials of the individual's life. Through the worship of the sacred objects and the beings they symbolize, and the acceptance of supernatural prescriptions that are at the same time codes of behavior, a powerful control over human conduct is exercised, guiding it along lines sustaining the institutional structure and conforming to the ultimate ends and values.

If this conception of the role of religion is true, one can understand why in every known society the religious activities tend to be under the charge of particular persons, who tend thereby to enjoy greater rewards than the ordinary societal member. Certain of the rewards and special privileges may attach to only the highest religious functionaries, but others usually apply, if such exists, to the entire sacerdotal class.

Moreover, there is a peculiar relation between the duties of the religious official and the special privileges he enjoys. If the supernatural world governs the destinies of men more ultimately than does the real world, its earthly representative, the person through whom one may communicate with the supernatural, must be a powerful individual. He is a keeper of sacred tradition, a skilled performer of the ritual, and an interpreter of lore and myth. He is in such close contact with the gods that he is viewed as possessing some of their characteristics. He is, in short, a bit sacred, and hence free from some of the more vulgar necessities and controls.

It is no accident, therefore, that religious functionaries have been associated with the very highest positions of power, as in theocratic regimes. Indeed, looking at it from this point of view, one may wonder why it is that they do not get *entire* control over their societies. The factors that prevent this are worthy of note.

In the first place, the amount of technical competence necessary for the performance of religious duties is small. Scientific or artistic capacity is not required. Anyone can set himself up as enjoying an intimate relation with deities, and nobody can successfully dispute him. Therefore, the factor of scarcity of personnel does not operate in the technical sense.

One may assert, on the other hand, that religious ritual is often elaborate and religious lore abstruse, and that priestly ministrations require tact, if not intelligence. This is true, but the technical requirements of the profession are for the most part adventitious, not related to the end in the same way that science is related to air travel. The priest can never be free from competition, since the criteria of whether or not one has genuine contact with the supernatural are never strictly clear. It is this competition that debases the priestly position below what might be expected at first glance. That is why priestly prestige is highest in those societies where membership in the profession is rigidly controlled by the priestly guild itself. That is why, in part at least, elaborate devices are utilized to stress the identification of the person with his office—spectacular costume, abnormal conduct, special diet, segregated residence, celibacy, conspicuous leisure, and the like. In fact, the priest is always in danger of becoming somewhat discredited—as happens in a secularized society—because in a world of stubborn fact, ritual and sacred knowledge alone will not grow crops or build houses. Furthermore, unless he is protected by a professional guild, the priest's identification with the supernatural tends to preclude his acquisition of abundant wordly goods.

As between one society and another it seems that the highest general position awarded the priest occurs in the medieval type of social order.

Here there is enough economic production to afford a surplus, which can be used to support a numerous and highly organized priesthood; and yet the populace is unlettered and therefore credulous to a high degree. Perhaps the most extreme example is to be found in the Buddhism of Tibet, but others are encountered in the Catholicism of feudal Europe, the Inca regime of Peru, the Brahminism of India, and the Mayan priesthood of Yucatan. On the other hand, if the society is so crude as to have no surplus and little differentiation, so that every priest must be also a cultivator or hunter, the separation of the priestly status from the others has hardly gone far enough for priestly prestige to mean much. When the priest actually has high prestige under these circumstances, it is because he also performs other important functions (usually political and medical).

In an extremely advanced society built on scientific technology, the priesthood tends to lose status, because sacred tradition and supernaturalism drop into the background. The ultimate values and common ends of the society tend to be expressed in less anthropomorphic ways, by officials who occupy fundamentally political, economic, or educational rather than religious positions. Nevertheless, it is easily possible for intellectuals to exaggerate the degree to which the priesthood in a presumably secular milieu has lost prestige. When the matter is closely examined the urban proletariat, as well as the rural citizenry, proves to be surprisingly god-fearing and priest-ridden. No society has become so completely secularized as to liquidate entirely the belief in transcendental ends and supernatural entities. Even in a secularized society some system must exist for the integration of ultimate values, for their ritualistic expression, and for the emotional adjustments required by disappointment, death, and disaster.

Government   Like religion, government plays a unique and indispensable part in society. But in contrast to religion, which provides integration in terms of sentiments, beliefs, and rituals, it organizes the society in terms of law and authority. Furthermore, it orients the society to the actual rather than the unseen world.

The main functions of government are, internally, the ultimate enforcement of norms, the final arbitration of conflicting interests, and the overall planning and direction of society; and externally, the handling of war and diplomacy. To carry out these functions it acts as the agent of the entire people, enjoys a monopoly of force, and controls all individuals within its territory.

Political action, by definition, implies authority. An official can command because he has authority, and the citizen must obey because he is subject to that authority. For this reason stratification is inherent in the nature of political relationships.

So clear is the power embodied in political position that political inequality is sometimes thought to comprise all inequality. But it can be shown that there are other bases of stratification, that the following controls operate in practice to keep political power from becoming complete: (a) The fact that the actual holders of political office, and especially those determining top policy must necessarily be few in number compared to the total population. (b) The fact that the rulers represent the interest of the group rather than of themselves, and are therefore restricted in their behavior by rules and mores designed to enforce this limitation of interest. (c) The fact that the holder of political office has his authority by virtue of his office and nothing else, and therefore any special knowledge, talent, or capacity he may claim is purely incidental, so that he often has to depend upon others for technical assistance.

In view of these limiting factors, it is not strange that the rulers often have less power and prestige than a literal enumeration of their formal rights would lead one to expect.

Wealth, Property, and Labor   Every position that secures for its incumbent a livelihood is, by definition, economically rewarded. For this reason there is an economic aspect to those positions (e.g. political and religious) the main function of which is not economic. It therefore becomes convenient for the society to use unequal economic returns as a principal means of controlling the entrance of persons into positions and stimulating the performance of their duties. The amount of the economic return therefore becomes one of the main indices of social status.

It should be stressed, however, that a position does not bring power and prestige *because* it draws a high income. Rather, it draws a high income because it is functionally important and the available personnel is for one reason or another scarce. It is therefore superficial and erroneous to regard high income as the cause of a man's power and prestige, just as it is erroneous to think that a man's fever is the cause of his disease.[4]

The economic source of power and prestige is not income primarily, but the ownership of capital goods (including patents, goodwill, and professional reputation). Such ownership should be distinguished from the possession of consumers' goods, which is an index rather than a cause of social standing. In other words, the ownership of producers' goods is properly speaking, a source of income like other positions, the income itself remaining an index. Even in situations where social values are widely commercialized and earnings are the readiest method of judging social position, income does not confer prestige on a position so much as it induces people to compete for the position. It is true that a man who has a high income as a result of one position may find this money helpful in climbing into another position as well, but this again reflects the effect of his initial, economically advantageous status, which exercises its influence through the medium of money.

In a system of private property in productive enterprise, an income above what an individual spends can give rise to possession of capital wealth. Presumably such possession is a reward for the proper management of one's finances originally and of the productive enterprise later. But as social differentiation becomes highly advanced and yet the institution of inheritance persists, the phenomenon of pure ownership, and reward for pure ownership, emerges. In such a case it is difficult to prove that the position is functionally important or that the scarcity involved is anything other than extrinsic and accidental. It is for this reason, doubtless, that the institution of private property in productive goods becomes more subject to criticism as social development proceeds toward industrialization. It is only this pure, that is, strictly legal and functionless ownership, however, that is open to attack; for some form of active ownership, whether private or public, is indispensable.

One kind of ownership of production goods consists in rights over the labor of others. The most extremely concentrated and exclusive of such rights are found in slavery, but the essential principle remains in serfdom, peonage, encomienda, and indenture. Naturally this kind of ownership has the greatest significance for stratification, because it necessarily entails an unequal relationship.

But property in capital goods inevitably introduces a compulsive element even into the nominally free contractual relationship. Indeed, in some respects the authority of the contractual employer is greater than that of the feudal landlord, inasmuch as the latter is more limited by traditional reciprocities. Even the classical economics recognized that competitors would fare unequally, but it did not pursue this fact to its necessary conclusion that, however it might be acquired, unequal control of goods and services must give unequal advantage to the parties to a contract.

---

[4] The symbolic rather than intrinsic role of income in social stratification has been succinctly summarized by Talcott Parsons, "An Analytical Approach to the Theory of Social Stratification," *American Journal of Sociology.* 45:841–862, May 1940.

Technical Knowledge   The function of finding means to single goals, without any concern with the choice between goals, is the exclusively technical sphere. The explanation of why positions requiring great technical skill receive fairly high rewards is easy to see, for it is the simplest case of the rewards being so distributed as to draw talent and motivate training. Why they seldom if ever receive the highest rewards is also clear: the importance of technical knowledge from a societal point of view is never so great as the integration of goals, which take place on the religious, political, and economic levels. Since the technological level is concerned solely with means, a purely technical position must ultimately be subordinate to other positions that are religious, political, or economic in character.

Nevertheless, the distinction between expert and layman in any social order is fundamental, and cannot be entirely reduced to other terms. Methods of recruitment, as well as of reward, sometimes lead to the erroneous interpretation that technical positions are economically determined. Actually, however, the acquisition of knowledge and skill cannot be accomplished by purchase, although the opportunity to learn may be. The control of the avenues of training may inhere as a sort of property right in certain families or classes, giving them power and prestige in consequence. Such a situation adds an artificial scarcity to the natural scarcity of skills and talents. On the other hand, it is possible for an opposite situation to arise. The rewards of technical position may be so great that a condition of excess supply is created, leading to at least temporary devaluation of the rewards. Thus "unemployment in the learned professions" may result in a debasement of the prestige of those positions. Such adjustments and readjustments are constantly occurring in changing societies; and it is always well to bear in mind that the efficiency of a stratified structure may be affected by the modes of recruitment of positions. The social order itself, however, sets limits to the inflation or deflation of the prestige of experts: an over-supply tends to debase the rewards and discourage recruitment or produce revolution, whereas an under-supply tends to increase the rewards or weaken the society in competition with other societies.

Particular systems of stratification show a wide range with respect to the exact position of technically competent persons. This range is perhaps most evident in the degree of specialization. Extreme division of labor tends to create many specialists without high prestige since the training is short and the required native capacity relatively small. On the other hand it also tends to accentuate the high position of the true experts—scientists, engineers, and administrators—by increasing their authority relative to other functionally important positions. But the idea of a technocratic social order or a government or priesthood of engineers or social scientists neglects the limitations of knowledge and skills as a basic for performing social functions. To the extent that the social structure is truly specialized the prestige of the technical person must also be circumscribed.

Variation in Stratified Systems

The generalized principles of stratification here suggested form a necessary preliminary to a consideration of types of stratified systems, because it is in terms of these principles that the types must be described. This can be seen by trying to delineate types according to certain modes of variation. For instance, some of the most important modes (together with the polar types in terms of them) seem to be as follows:

(a) The Degree of Specialization   The degree of specialization affects the fineness and multiplicity of the gradations in power and prestige. It also influences the extent to which particular functions may be emphasized in the invidious system, since a given function cannot receive much emphasis in the hierarchy until it has

achieved structural separation from the other functions. Finally, the amount of specialization influences the bases of selection. Polar types: *Specialized, Unspecialized.*

(b) The Nature of the Functional Emphasis   In general when emphasis is put on sacred matters, a rigidity is introduced that tends to limit specialization and hence the development of technology. In addition, a brake is placed on social mobility, and on the development of bureaucracy. When the preoccupation with the sacred is withdrawn, leaving greater scope for purely secular preoccupations, a great development, and rise in status, of economic and technological positions seemingly takes place. Curiously, a concomitant rise in political position is not likely, because it has usually been allied with the religious and stands to gain little by the decline of the latter. It is also possible for a society to emphasize family functions—as in relatively undifferentiated societies where high mortality requires high fertility and kinship forms the main basis of social organization. Main types: *Familistic, Authoritarian* (*Theocratic* or sacred, and *Totalitarian* or secular), *Capitalistic.*

(c) The Magnitude of Invidious Differences. What may be called the amount of social distance between positions, taking into account the entire scale, is something that should lend itself to quantitative measurement. Considerable differences apparently exist between different societies in this regard, and also between parts of the same society. Polar types: *Equalitarian, Inequalitarian.*

(d) The Degree of Opportunity   The familiar question of the amount of mobility is different from the question of the comparative equality or inequality of rewards posed above, because the two criteria may vary independently up to a point. For instance, the tremendous divergences in monetary income in the United States are far greater than those found in primitive societies, yet the equality of opportunity to move

from one rung to the other in the social scale may also be greater in the United States than in a hereditary tribal kingdom. Polar types: *Mobile* (open), *Immobile* (closed).

(e) The Degree of Stratum Solidarity   Again, the degree of "class solidarity" (or the presence of specific organizations to promote class interests) may vary to some extent independently of the other criteria, and hence is an important principle in classifying systems of stratification. Polar types: *Class organized, Class unorganized.*

External Conditions

What state any particular system of stratification is in with reference to each of these modes of variation depends on two things: (1) its state with reference to the other ranges of variation, and (2) the conditions outside the system of stratification which nevertheless influence that system. Among the latter are the following:

(a) The Stage of Cultural Development   As the cultural heritage grows, increased specialization becomes necessary, which in turn contributes to the enhancement of mobility, a decline of stratum solidarity, and a change of functional emphasis.

(b) Situation with Respect to Other Societies   The presence or absence of open conflict with other societies, of free trade relations or cultural diffusion, all influence the class structure to some extent. A chronic state of warfare tends to place emphasis upon the military functions, especially when the opponents are more or less equal. Free trade, on the other hand, strengthens the hand of the trader at the expense of the warrior and priest. Free movement of ideas generally has an equalitarian effect. Migration and conquest create special circumstances.

(c) Size of the Society.   A small society limits the degree to which functional specialization can go, the degree of segregation of different strata, and the magnitude of inequality.

Composite Types

Much of the literature on stratification has attempted to classify concrete systems into a certain number of types. This task is deceptively simple, however, and should come at the end of an analysis of elements and principles, rather than at the beginning. If the preceding discussion has any validity, it indicates that there are a number of modes of variation between different systems, and that any one system is a composite of the society's status with reference to all these modes of variation. The danger of trying to classify whole societies in such rubrics as *caste, feudal,* or *open class* is that one or two criteria are selected and others ignored, the result being an unsatisfactory solution to the problem posed. The present discussion has been offered as a possible approach to the more systematic classification of composite types.

TALCOTT PARSONS: AGE AND SEX IN THE SOCIAL STRUCTURE OF THE UNITED STATES

In our society age grading does not to any great extent, except for the educational system, involve formal age categorization, but is interwoven with other structural elements. In relation to these, however, it constitutes an important connecting link and organizing point of reference in many respects. The most important of these for present purposes are kinship structure, formal education, occupation and community participation. In most cases the age lines are not rigidly specific, but approximate; this does not, however, necessarily lessen their structural significance.[1]

In all societies the initial status of every normal individual is that of child in a given kinship unit. In our society, however, this universal starting point is used in distinctive ways. Although in early childhood the sexes are not usually sharply differentiated, in many kinship systems a relatively sharp segregation of children begins

Reprinted from Talcott Parsons, "Age and Sex in the Social Structure of the United States," *American Sociological Review,* Vol. 7, 1942. The substance of this paper was presented to the American Sociological Society on December 27, 1941, at New York City.

The attempt to embark on this analysis was suggested to the writer largely by Professor Ralph Linton, through his paper, "A Neglected Aspect of Social Structure," *American Journal of Sociology,* May 1940, and through personal conversation. Both the general analytical significance of age and sex categories in social structure, and the main outline of the cultural variability of particular modes of organization of age and sex roles are taken for granted in the present paper. Professor Linton has amplified his treatment of these subjects in the preceding article in this issue of the *Review.*

The present paper will not embody the results of systematic research but constitutes rather a tentative statement of certain major aspects of the role of age and sex in our society and of their bearing on a variety of problems. It will not attempt to treat adequately the important variations according to social class, rural-urban differences, and so on, but will concentrate particularly on the urban middle and upper middle classes.

[1] The problem of organization of this material for systematic presentation is, in view of this fact, particularly difficult. It would be possible to discuss the subject in terms of the above four principal structures with which age and sex are most closely interwoven, but there are serious disadvantages involved in this procedure. Age and sex categories constitute one of the main links of structural continuity in terms of which structures are differentiated in other respects which are articulated with each other; and in isolating the treatment of these categories there is danger that this extremely important aspect of the problem will be lost sight of. The least objectionable method, at least within the limits of space of such a paper, seems to be to follow the sequence of the life cycle.

very early. Our own society is conspicuous for the extent to which children of both sexes are in many fundamental respects treated alike. This is particularly true of both privileges and responsibilities. The primary distinctions within the group of dependent siblings are those of age. Birth order as such is notably neglected as a basis of discrimination; a child of eight and a child of five have essentially the privileges and responsibilities appropriate to their respective age levels without regard to what older, intermediate, or younger siblings there may be. The preferential treatment of an older child is not to any significant extent differentiated if and because he happens to be the first born.

There are, of course, important sex differences in dress and in approved play interest and the like, but if anything, it may be surmised that in the urban upper middle classes these are tending to diminish. Thus, for instance, play overalls are essentially similar for both sexes. What is perhaps the most important sex discrimination is more than anything else a reflection of the differentiation of adult sex roles. It seems to be a definite fact that girls are more apt to be relatively docile, to conform in general according to adult expectations, to be "good," whereas boys are more apt to be recalcitrant to discipline and defiant of adult authority and expectations. There is really no feminine equivalent of the expression "bad boy." It may be suggested that this is at least partially explained by the fact that it is possible from an early age to initiate girls directly into many important aspects of the adult feminine role. Their mothers are continually about the house and the meaning of many of the things they are doing is relatively tangible and easily understandable to a child. It is also possible for the daughter to participate actively and usefully in many of these activities. Especially in the urban middle classes, however, the father does not work in the home and his son is not able to observe his work or to participate in it from an early age. Furthermore many of the masculine functions are of a

relatively abstract and intangible character, such that their meaning must remain almost wholly inaccessible to a child. This leaves the boy without a tangible meaningful model to emulate and without the possibility of a gradual initiation into the activities of the adult male role. An important verification of this analysis could be provided through the study in our own society of the rural situation. It is my impression that farm boys tend to be "good" in a sense in which that is not typical of their urban brothers.

The equality of privileges and responsibilities, graded only by age but not by birth order, is extended to a certain degree throughout the whole range of the life cycle. In full adult status, however, it is seriously modified by the asymmetrical relation of the sexes to the occupational structure. One of the most conspicuous expressions and symbols of the underlying equality, however, is the lack of sex differentiation in the process of formal education, so far, at least, as it is not explicitly vocational. Up through college differentiation seems to be primarily a matter on the one hand of individual ability, on the other hand of class status, and only to a secondary degree of sex differentiation. One can certainly speak of a strongly established pattern that all children of the family have a "right" to a good education, rights which are graduated according to the class status of the family but also to individual ability. It is only in post-graduate professional education, with its direct connection with future occupational careers, that sex discrimination becomes conspicuous. It is particularly important that this equality of treatment exists in the sphere of liberal education since throughout the social structure of our society there is a strong tendency to segregate the occupational sphere from one in which certain more generally human patterns and values are dominant, particularly in informal social life and the realm of what will here be called community participation.

Although this pattern of equality of treatment is present in certain fundamental respects at all age levels, at the transition from childhood to adolescence new features appear which disturb the symmetry of sex roles while still a second set of factors appears with marriage and the acquisition of full adult status and responsibilities.

An indication of the change is the practice of chaperonage, through which girls are given a kind of protection and supervision by adults to which boys of the same age group are not subjected. Boys, that is, are chaperoned only in their relations with girls of their own class. This modification of equality of treatment has been extended to the control of the private lives of women students in boarding schools and colleges. Of undoubted significance is the fact that it has been rapidly declining not only in actual effectiveness but as an ideal pattern. Its prominence in our recent past, however, is an important manifestation of the importance of sex role differentiation. Important light might be thrown upon its functions by systematic comparison with the related phenomena in Latin countries where this type of asymmetry has been far more sharply accentuated than in this country in the more modern period.

It is at the point of emergence into adolescence that there first begins to develop a set of patterns and behavior phenomena which involve a highly complex combination of age grading and sex role elements. These may be referred to together as the phenomena of the "youth culture." Certain of its elements are present in pre-adolescence and others in the adult culture. But the peculiar combination in connection with this particular age level is unique and highly distinctive for American society.

Perhaps the best single point of reference for characterizing the youth culture lies in its contrast with the dominant pattern of the adult male role. By contrast with the emphasis on responsibility in this role, the orientation of the youth culture is more or less specifically irresponsible. One of its dominant notes is "having a good time" in relation to which there is a particularly strong emphasis on social activities in company with the opposite sex. A second predominant characteristic on the male side lies in the prominence of athletics, which is an avenue of achievement and competition which stands in sharp contrast to the primary standards of adult achievement in professional and executive capacities. Negatively, there is a strong tendency to repudiate interest in adult things and to feel at least a certain recalcitrance to the pressure of adult expectations and discipline. In addition to, but including, athletic prowess the typical pattern of the male youth culture seems to lay emphasis on the value of certain qualities of attractiveness, especially in relation to the opposite sex. It is very definitely a rounded humanistic pattern rather than one of competence in the performance of specified functions. Such stereotypes as the "swell guy" are significant of this. On the feminine side there is correspondingly a strong tendency to accentuate sexual attractiveness in terms of various versions of what may be called the "glamor girl" pattern.[2]

---

[2] Perhaps the most dramatic manifestation of this tendency lies in the prominence of the patterns of "dating," for instance among college women. As shown by an unpublished participant-observer study made at one of the Eastern Women's colleges, perhaps the most important single basis of informal prestige rating among the residents of a dormitory lies in their relative dating success—though this is by no means the only basis. One of the most striking features of the pattern is the high publicity given to the "achievements" of the individual in a sphere where traditionally in the culture a rather high level of privacy is sanctioned—it is interesting that once an engagement has occurred a far greater amount of privacy is granted. The standards of rating cannot be said to be well integrated, though there is an underlying consistency in that being in demand by what the group regards as desirable men is perhaps the main standard.

It is true that the "dating" complex need not be exclusively bound up with the "glamor girl" stereotype of ideal feminine personality—the "good companion" type may also have a place. Precisely, however, where the competitive aspect of dating is most prominent the glamor pattern seems heavily to predominate, as does, on the masculine side, a somewhat comparable glamorous type. On each side at the same time there is room for considerable difference as to just where the emphasis is placed—for example as between "voluptuous" sexuality and more decorous "charm."

Although these patterns defining roles tend to polarize sexually—for instance, as between star athlete and socially popular girl—yet on a certain level they are complementary, both emphasizing certain features of a total personality in terms of the direct expression of certain values rather than of instrumental significance.

One further feature of this situation is the extent to which it is crystallized about the system of formal education.[3] One might say that the principal centers of prestige dissemination are the colleges, but that many of the most distinctive phenomena are to be found in high schools throughout the country. It is of course of great importance that liberal education is not primarily a matter of vocational training in the United States. The individual status on the curricular side of formal education is, however, in fundamental ways linked up with adult expectations, and doing "good work" is one of the most important sources of parental approval. Because of secondary institutionalization this approval is extended into various spheres distinctive of the youth culture. But it is notable that the youth culture has a strong tendency to develop in directions which are either on the borderline of parental approval or beyond the pale, in such matters as sex behavior, drinking and various forms of frivolous and irresponsible behavior. The fact that adults have attitudes to these things which are often deeply ambivalent and that on such occasions as college reunions they may outdo the younger generation, as, for instance, in drinking, is of great significance, but probably structurally secondary to the youth-versus-adult differential aspect. Thus the youth culture is not only, as is true of the curricular aspect of formal education, a matter of age status as such but also

shows strong signs of being a product of tensions in the relationship of younger people and adults.

From the point of view of age grading perhaps the most notable fact about this situation is the existence of definite pattern distinctions from the periods coming both before and after. At the line between childhood and adolescence "growing up" consists precisely in ability to participate in youth culture patterns, which are not for either sex, the same as the adult patterns practiced by the parental generation. In both sexes the transition to full adulthood means loss of a certain "glamorous" element. From being the athletic hero or the lion of college dances, the young man becomes a prosaic business executive or lawyer. The more successful adults participate in an important order of prestige symbols but these are of a very different order from those of the youth culture. The contrast in the case of the feminine role is perhaps equally sharp, with at least a strong tendency to take on a "domestic" pattern with marriage and the arrival of young children.

The symmetry in this respect must, however, not be exaggerated. It is of fundamental significance to the sex role structure of the adult age levels that the normal man has a "job" which is fundamental to his social status in general. It is perhaps not too much to say that only in very exceptional cases can an adult man be genuinely self-respecting and enjoy a respected status in the eyes of others if he does not "earn a living" in an approved occupational role. Not only is this a matter of his own economic support but, generally speaking, his occupational status is the primary source of the income and class status of his wife and children.

In the case of the feminine role the situation is radically different. The majority of married women, of course, are not employed, but even of those that are a very large proportion do not have jobs which are in basic competition for status with those of their husbands.[4] The majority

---

[3] A central aspect of this focus of crystallization lies in the element of tension, sometimes of direct conflict, between the youth culture patterns of college and school life, and the "serious" interests in and obligations toward curricular work. It is of course the latter which defines some at least of the most important foci of adult expectations of doing "good" work and justifying the privileges granted. It is not possible here to attempt to analyze the interesting, ambivalent attitudes of youth toward curricular work and achievement.

[4] The above statement, even more than most in the present paper, needs to be qualified in relation to the problem of class. It is above all to the upper middle class that it applies.

of "career" women whose occupational status is comparable with that of men in their own class, at least in the upper middle and upper classes, are unmarried, and in the small proportion of cases where they are married the result is a profound alteration in family structure.

This pattern, which is central to the urban middle classes, should not be misunderstood. In rural society, for instance, the operation of the farm and the attendant status in the community may be said to be a matter of the joint status of both parties to a marriage. Whereas a farm is operated by a family, an urban job is held by an individual and does not involve other members of the family in a comparable sense. One convenient expression of the difference lies in the question of what would happen in case of death. In the case of a farm it would at least be not at all unusual for the widow to continue operating the farm with the help of a son or even of hired men. In the urban situation the widow would cease to have any connection with the organization which had employed her husband and he would be replaced by another man without reference to family affiliations.

In this urban situation the primary status-carrying role is in a sense that of housewife. The woman's fundamental status is that of her husband's wife, the mother of his children, and traditionally the person responsible for a complex of activities in connection with the management of the household, care of children, etc.

For the structuring of sex roles in the adult phase the most fundamental considerations seem to be those involved in the interrelations of the occupational system and the conjugal family. In a certain sense the most fundamental basis of the family's status is the occupational status of the husband and father. As has been pointed out, this is a status occupied by an individual by virtue of his individual qualities and achievements. But both directly and indirectly, more than any other single factor, it determines the status of the family in the social structure, directly because of the symbolic significance of the office or occupation as a symbol of prestige, indirectly because as the principal source of family income it determines the standard of living of the family. From one point of view the emergence of occupational status into this primary position can be regarded as the principal source of strain in the sex role structure of our society since it deprives the wife of her role as a partner in a common enterprise. The common enterprise is reduced to the life of the family itself and to the informal social activities in which husband and wife participate together. This leaves the wife a set of utilitarian functions in the management of the household which may be considered a kind of "pseudo-" occupation. Since the present interest is primarily in the middle classes, the relatively unstable character of the role of housewife as the principal content of the feminine role is strongly illustrated by the tendency to employ domestic servants wherever financially possible. It is true that there is an American tendency to accept tasks of drudgery with relative willingness, but it is notable that in middle class families there tends to be a dissociation of the essential personality from the performance of these tasks. Thus, advertising continually appeals to such desires as to have hands which one could never tell had washed dishes or scrubbed floors.[5] Organization about the function of housewife, however, with the addition of strong affectional

---

Here probably the great majority of "working wives" are engaged in some form of secretarial work which would, on an independent basis, generally be classed as a lower middle class occupation. The situation at lower levels of the class structure is quite different since the prestige of the jobs of husband and wife is then much more likely to be nearly equivalent. It is quite possible that this fact is closely related to the relative instability of marriage which Davis and Gardner *(Deep South)* find, at least for the community they studied, to be typical of lower class groups. The relation is one which deserves careful study.

---

[5] This type of advertising appeal undoubtedly contains an element of "snob appeal" in the sense of an invitation to the individual by her appearance and ways to identify herself with a higher social class than that of her actual status. But it is almost certainly not wholly explained by this element. A glamorously feminine appearance which is specifically dissociated from physical work is undoubtedly a genuine part of an authentic personality ideal of the middle class, and not only evidence of a desire to belong to the upper class.

devotion to husband and children, is the primary focus of one of the principal patterns governing the adult feminine role—what may be called the "domestic" pattern. It is, however, a conspicuous fact, that strict adherence to this pattern has become progressively less common and has a strong tendency to a residual status—that is, to be followed most closely by those who are unsuccessful in competition for prestige in other directions.

It is, of course, possible for the adult woman to follow the masculine pattern and seek a career in fields of occupational achievement in direct competition with men of her own class. It is, however, notable that in spite of the very great progress of the emancipation of women from the traditional domestic pattern only a very small fraction have gone very far in this direction. It is also clear that its generalization would only be possible with profound alterations in the structure of the family.

Hence it seems that concomitant with the alteration in the basic masculine role in the direction of occupation there have appeared two important tendencies in the feminine role which are alternative to that of simple domesticity on the one hand, and to a full-fledged career on the other. In the older situation there tended to be a very rigid distinction between respectable married women and those who were "no better than they should be." The rigidity of this line has progressively broken down through the infiltration into the respectable sphere of elements of what may be called again the glamor pattern, with the emphasis on a specifically feminine form of attractiveness which on occasion involves directly sexual patterns of appeal. One important expression of this trend lies in the fact that many of the symbols of feminine attractiveness have been taken over directly from the practices of social types previously beyond the pale of respectable society. This would seem to be substantially true of the practice of women smoking and of at least the modern version of the use of cosmetics. The same would seem to be true of many of the modern versions of women's dress. "Emancipation" in this connection means primarily emancipation from traditional and conventional restrictions on the free expression of sexual attraction and impulses, but in a direction which tends to segregate the element of sexual interest and attraction from the total personality and in so doing tends to emphasize the segregation of sex roles. It is particularly notable that there has been no corresponding tendency to emphasize masculine attraction in terms of dress and other such aids. One might perhaps say that in a situation which strongly inhibits competition between the sexes on the same plane the feminine glamor pattern has appeared as an offset to masculine occupational status and to its attendant symbols of prestige. It is perhaps significant that there is a common stereotype of the association of physically beautiful, expensively and elaborately dressed women with physically unattractive but rich and powerful men.

The other principal direction of emancipation from domesticity seems to lie in emphasis on what has been called the common humanistic element. This takes a wide variety of forms. One of them lies in a relatively mature appreciation and systematic cultivation of cultural interests and educated tastes, extending all the way from the intellectual sphere to matters of art, music and house furnishings. A second consists in cultivation of serious interests and humanitarian obligations in community welfare situations and the like. It is understandable that many of these orientations are most conspicuous in fields where through some kind of tradition there is an element of particular suitability for feminine participation. Thus, a woman who takes obligations to social welfare particularly seriously will find opportunities in various forms of activity which traditionally tie up with women's relation to children, to sickness and so on. But this may be regarded as secondary to the underlying orientation which would seek an outlet in work useful to the community following the most favorable opportunities which happen to be available.

This pattern, which with reference to the character of relationship to men may be called that of the "good companion," is distinguished from the others in that it lays far less stress on the exploitation of sex role as such and more on that which is essentially common to both sexes. There are reasons, however, why cultural interests, interest in social welfare and community activities are particularly prominent in the activities of women in our urban communities. On the one side the masculine occupational role tends to absorb a very large proportion of the man's time and energy and to leave him relatively little for other interests. Furthermore, unless his position is such as to make him particularly prominent his primary orientation is to those elements of the social structure which divide the community into occupational groups rather than those which unite it in common interests and activities. The utilitarian aspect of the role of housewife, on the other hand, has declined in importance to the point where it scarcely approaches a full-time occupation for a vigorous person. Hence the resort to other interests to fill up the gap. In addition, women, being more closely tied to the local residential community are more apt to be involved in matters of common concern to the members of that community. This peculiar role of women becomes particularly conspicuous in middle age. The younger married woman is apt to be relatively highly absorbed in the care of young children. With their growing up, however, her absorption in the household is greatly lessened, often just at the time when the husband is approaching the apex of his career and is most heavily involved in its obligations. Since to a high degree this humanistic aspect of the feminine role is only partially institutionalized it is not surprising that its patterns often bear the marks of strain and insecurity, as perhaps has been classically depicted by Helen Hokinson's cartoons of women's clubs.

The adult roles of both sexes involve important elements of strain which are involved in certain dynamic relationships, especially to the youth culture. In the case of the feminine role marriage is the single event toward which a selective process, in which personal qualities and effort can play a decisive role, has pointed up. That determines a woman's fundamental status, and after that her role patterning is not so much status determining as a matter of living up to expectations and finding satisfying interests and activities. In a society where such strong emphasis is placed upon individual achievement it is not surprising that there should be a certain romantic nostalgia for the time when the fundamental choices were still open. This element of strain is added to by the lack of clear-cut definition of the adult feminine role. Once the possibility of a career has been eliminated there still tends to be a rather unstable oscillation between emphasis in the direction of domesticity or glamor or good companionship. According to situational pressures and individual character the tendency will be to emphasize one or another of these more strongly. But it is a situation likely to produce a rather high level of insecurity. In this state the pattern of domesticity must be ranked lowest in terms of prestige but also, because of the strong emphasis in community sentiment on the virtues of fidelity and devotion to husband and children, it offers perhaps the highest level of a certain kind of security. It is no wonder that such an important symbol as Whistler's mother concentrates primarily on this pattern.

The glamor pattern has certain obvious attractions since to the woman who is excluded from the struggle for power and prestige in the occupational sphere it is the most direct path to a sense of superiority and importance. It has, however, two obvious limitations. In the first place, many of its manifestations encounter the resistance of patterns of moral conduct and engender conflicts not only with community opinion but also with the individual's own moral standards. In the second place, it is a pattern the highest manifestations of which are inevitably associated with a rather early age level—in fact, overwhelmingly with the courtship period. Hence, if strongly entered upon serious strains result from the problem of adaptation to increasing age.

The one pattern which would seem to offer the greatest possibilities for able, intelligent, and emotionally mature women is the third— the good companion pattern. This, however, suffers from a lack of fully institutionalized status and from the multiplicity of choices of channels of expression. It is only those with the strongest initiative and intelligence who achieve fully satisfactory adaptations in this direction. It is quite clear that in the adult feminine role there is quite sufficient strain and insecurity so that wide-spread manifestations are to be expected in the form of neurotic behavior.

The masculine role at the same time is itself by no means devoid of corresponding elements of strain. It carries with it to be sure the primary prestige of achievement, responsibility and authority. By comparison with the role of the youth culture, however, there are at least two important types of limitations. In the first place, the modern occupational system has led to increasing specialization of role. The job absorbs an extraordinarily large proportion of the individual's energy and emotional interests in a role the content of which is often relatively narrow. This in particular restricts the area within which he can share common interests and experiences with others not in the same occupational specialty. It is perhaps of considerable significance that so many of the highest prestige statuses of our society are of this specialized character. There is in the definition of roles little to bind the individual to others in his community on a comparable status level. By contrast with this situation, it is notable that in the youth culture common human elements are far more strongly emphasized. Leadership and eminence are more in the role of total individuals and less of competent specialists. This perhaps has something to do with the significant tendency in our society for

all age levels to idealize youth and for the older age groups to attempt to imitate the patterns of youth behavior.

It is perhaps as one phase of this situation that the relation of the adult man to persons of the opposite sex should be treated. The effect of the specialization of occupational role is to narrow the range in which the sharing of common human interests can play a large part. In relation to his wife the tendency of this narrowness would seem to be to encourage on her part either the domestic or the glamorous role, or community participation somewhat unrelated to the marriage relationship. This relationship between sex roles presumably introduces a certain amount of strain into the marriage relationship itself since this is of such overwhelming importance to the family and hence to a woman's status and yet so relatively difficult to maintain on a level of human companionship. Outside the marriage relationship, however, there seems to be a notable inhibition against easy social intercourse, particularly in mixed company.[6] The man's close personal intimacy with other women is checked by the danger of the situation being defined as one of rivalry with the wife, and easy friendship without sexual-emotional involvement seems to be inhibited by the specialization of interests in the occupational sphere. It is notable that brilliance of conversation of the "salon" type seems to be associated with aristocratic society and is not prominent in ours.

Along with all this goes a certain tendency for middle-aged men, as symbolized by the "bald-headed row," to be interested in the physical aspect of sex—that is, in women precisely as dissociated from those personal considerations

---

[6] In the informal social life of academic circles with which the writer is familiar there seems to be a strong tendency in mixed gatherings—as after dinner—for the sexes to segregate. In such groups the men are apt to talk either shop subjects or politics whereas the women are apt to talk about domestic affairs, schools, their children etc., or personalities. It is perhaps on personalities that mixed conversation is apt to flow most freely.

which are important to relationships of companionship or friendship, to say nothing of marriage. In so far as it does not take this physical form, however, there seems to be a strong tendency for middle-aged men to idealize youth patterns—that is, to think of the ideal inter-sex friendship as that of their pre-marital period.[7]

In so far as the idealization of the youth culture by adults is an expression of elements of strain and insecurity in the adult roles it would be expected that the patterns thus idealized would contain an element of romantic unrealism. The patterns of youthful behavior thus idealized are not those of actual youth so much as those which older people wish their own youth might have been. This romantic element seems to coalesce with a similar element derived from certain strains in the situation of young people themselves.

The period of youth in our society is one of considerable strain and insecurity. Above all, it means turning one's back on the security both of status and of emotional attachment which is engaged in the family of orientation. It is structurally essential to transfer one's primary emotional attachment to a marriage partner who is entirely unrelated to the previous family situation. In a system of free marriage choice this applies to women as well as men. For the man there is in addition the necessity to face the hazards of occupational competition in the determination of a career. There is reason to believe that the youth culture has important positive functions in easing the transition from the security of childhood in the family of orientation to that of full adult in marriage and occupational status. But precisely because the transition is a period of strain it is to be expected that it involves elements of unrealistic romanticism. Thus significant features in the status of youth patterns in our society would seem to derive from the coincidence of

the emotional needs of adolescents with those derived from the strains of the situation of adults.

A tendency to the romantic idealization of youth patterns seems in different ways to be characteristic of modern western society as a whole.[8] It is not possible in the present context to enter into any extended comparative analysis, but it may be illuminating to call attention to a striking difference between the patterns associated with this phenomenon in Germany and in the United States. The German "youth movement," starting before the first World War, has occasioned a great deal of comment and has in various respects been treated as the most notable instance of the revolt of youth. It is generally believed that the youth movement has an important relation to the background of National Socialism, and this fact as much as any suggests the important difference. While in Germany as everywhere there has been a generalized revolt against convention and restrictions on individual freedom as embodied in the traditional adult culture, in Germany particular emphasis has appeared on the community of male youth. "Comradeship" in a sense which strongly suggests that of soldiers in the field has from the beginning been strongly emphasized as the ideal social relationship. By contrast with this, in the American youth culture and its adult romantization a much stronger emphasis has been placed on the cross-sex relationship. It would seem that this fact, with the structural factors which underlie it, have much to do with the failure of the youth culture to develop any considerable political significance in this country. Its predominant pattern has been that of the idealization of the isolated couple in romantic love. There have, to be sure, been certain tendencies among radical youth to a political orientation but in this case there has been a notable absence of emphasis on the solidarity of the

---

[7] This, to be sure, often contains an element of romanticization. It is more nearly what he wishes these relations had been than what they actually were.

[8] *Cf.* E. Y. Hartshorne, "German Youth and the Nazi Dream of Victory," *America in a World at War*, Pamphlet, No. 12, New York, 1941.

members of one sex. The tendency has been rather to ignore the relevance of sex difference in the interest of common ideals.

The importance of youth patterns in contemporary American culture throws into particularly strong relief the status in our social structure of the most advanced age groups. By comparison with other societies the United States assumes an extreme position in the isolation of old age from participation in the most important social structures and interests. Structurally speaking, there seem to be two primary bases of this situation. In the first place, the most important single distinctive feature of our family structure is the isolation of the individual conjugal family. It is impossible to say that with us it is "natural" for any other group than husband and wife and their dependent children to maintain a common household. Hence, when the children of a couple have become independent through marriage and occupational status the parental couple is left without attachment to any continuous kinship group. It is, of course, common for other relatives to share a household with the conjugal family but this scarcely ever occurs without some important elements of strain. For independence is certainly the preferred pattern for an elderly couple, particularly from the point of view of the children.

The second basis of the situation lies in the occupational structure. In such fields as farming and the maintenance of small independent enterprises there is frequently no such thing as abrupt "retirement," rather a gradual relinquishment of the main responsibilities and functions with advancing age. So far, however, as an individual's occupational status centers in a specific "job," he either holds the job or does not, and the tendency is to maintain the full level of functions up to a given point and then abruptly to retire. In view of the very great significance of occupational status and its psychological correlates, retirement leaves the older

man in a peculiarly functionless situation, cut off from participation in the most important interests and activities of the society. There is a further important aspect of this situation. Not only status in the community but actual place of residence is to a very high degree a function of the specific job held. Retirement not only cuts the ties to the job itself but also greatly loosens those to the community of residence. Perhaps in no other society is there observable a phenomenon corresponding to the accumulation of retired elderly people in such areas as Florida and Southern California in the winter. It may be surmised that this structural isolation from kinship, occupational, and community ties is the fundamental basis of the recent political agitation for help to the old. It is suggested that it is far less the financial hardship[9] of the position of elderly people than their social isolation which makes old age a "problem." As in other connections we are here very prone to rationalize generalized insecurity in financial and economic terms. The problem is obviously of particularly great significance in view of the changing age distribution of the population with the prospect of a far greater proportion in the older age groups than in previous generations. It may also be suggested, that through well-known psychosomatic mechanisms, the increased incidence of the disabilities of older people, such as heart disease, cancer, etc., may be at least in part attributed to this structural situation.

---

[9] That the financial difficulties of older people are in a very large proportion of cases real is not to be doubted. This, however, is at least to a very large extent a consequence rather than a determinant of the structural situation. Except where it is fully taken care of by pension schemes, the income of older people is apt to be seriously reduced, but, even more important, the younger conjugal family usually does not feel an obligation to contribute to the support of aged parents. Where as a matter of course both generations shared a common household, this problem did not exist.

ROBERT K. MERTON: MANIFEST AND LATENT FUNCTIONS

As has been implied in earlier sections, the distinction between manifest and latent functions was devised to preclude the inadvertent confusion, often found in the sociological literature, between conscious *motivations* for social behavior and its *objective consequences*. Our scrutiny of current vocabularies of functional analysis has shown how easily, and how unfortunately, the sociologist may identify *motives* with *functions*. It was further indicated that the motive and the function vary independently and that the failure to register this fact in an established terminology has contributed to the unwitting tendency among sociologists to confuse the subjective categories of motivation with the objective categories of function. This, then, is the central purpose of our succumbing to the not-always-commendable practice of introducing new terms into the rapidly growing technical vocabulary of sociology, a practice regarded by many laymen as an affront to their intelligence and an offense against common intelligibility.

As will be readily recognized, I have adapted the terms "manifest" and "latent" from their use in another context by Freud (although Francis Bacon had long ago spoken of "latent process" and "latent configuration" in connection with processes which are below the threshold of superficial observation).

The distinction itself has been repeatedly drawn by observers of human behavior at irregular intervals over a span of many centuries.[64]

Indeed, it would be disconcerting to find that a distinction which we have come to regard as central to functional analysis had not been made by any of that numerous company who have in effect adopted a functional orientation. We need mention only a few of those who have, in recent decades, found it necessary to distinguish in their specific interpretations of behavior between the end-in-view and the functional consequences of action.

> George H. Mead:[65] "... that attitude of hostility toward the law breaker has the unique advantage [read: latent function] of uniting all members of the community in the emotional solidarity of aggression. While the most admirable of humanitarian efforts are sure to run counter to the individual interests of very many in the community, or fail to touch the interest and imagination of the multitude and to leave the community divided or indifferent, the cry of thief or murderer is attuned to profound complexes, lying below the surface of competing individual efforts, and citizens who have [been] separated by divergent interests stand together against the common enemy."

Emile Durkheim's[66] similar analysis of the social functions of punishment is also focused on its latent functions (consequences for the community) rather than confined to manifest functions (consequences for the criminal).

Editor's note The abridgement of the original article for our current purposes included deletion of text and corresponding footnotes 1–63.
Reprinted with the permission of The Free Press, a Division of Simon & Schuster Adult Publishing Group, from *Social Theory and Social Structure* by Robert K. Merton. Copyright © 1957 by The Free Press; copyright renewed 1985 by Robert K. Merton.
[64] References to some of the more significant among these earlier appearances of the distinction will be found in Merton, "Unanticipated consequences . . .," *op. cit.*

[65] George H. Mead, "The psychology of punitive justice," *American Journal of Sociology*, 1918, 23, 577–602, esp. 591.
[66] As suggested earlier in this chapter, Durkheim adopted a functional orientation throughout his work, and he operates, albeit often without explicit notice, with concepts equivalent to that of latent function in all of his researches. The reference in the text at this point is to his "Deux lois de l'évolution penale," *L'année sociologique*, 1899–1900, 4, 55–95, as well as to his *Division of Labor in Society* (Glencoe, Illinois: The Free Press, 1947).

W. G. Sumner:[67] ". . . from the first acts by which men try to satisfy needs, each act stands by itself, and looks no further than the immediate satisfaction. From recurrent needs arise habits for the individual and customs for the group, but these results are consequences which were never conscious, and never foreseen or intended. They are not noticed until they have long existed, and it is still longer before they are appreciated." Although this fails to locate the latent functions of standardized social actions for a designated social structure, it plainly makes the basic distinction between ends-in-view and objective consequences.

R. M. MacIver:[68] In addition to the direct effects of institutions, "there are further effects by way of control which lie outside the direct purposes of men . . . this type of reactive form of control . . . may, though unintended, be of profound service to society."

W. I. Thomas and F. Znaniecki:[69] "Although all the new [Polish peasant cooperative] institutions are thus formed with the definite purpose of satisfying certain specific needs, their social function is by no means limited to their explicit and conscious purpose . . .

every one of these institutions—commune or agricultural circle, loan and savings bank, or theater—is not merely a mechanism for the management of certain values but also an association of people, each member of which is supposed to participate in the common activities as a living, concrete individual. Whatever is the predominant, official common interest upon which the institution is founded, the association as a concrete group of human personalities unofficially involves many other interests; the social contacts between its members are not limited to their common pursuit, though the latter, of course, constitutes both the main reason for which the association is formed and the most permanent bond which holds it together. Owing to this combination of an abstract political, economic, or rather rational mechanism for the satisfaction of specific needs with the concrete unity of a social group, the new institution is also the best intermediary link between the peasant primary-group and the secondary national system."

These and numerous other sociological observers have, then, from time to time distinguished between categories of subjective disposition ("needs, interests, purposes") and categories of generally unrecognized but objective functional consequences ("unique advantages," "never conscious" consequences, "unintended . . . service to society," "function not limited to conscious and explicit purpose").

Since the occasion for making the distinction arises with great frequency, and since the purpose of a conceptual scheme is to direct observations toward salient elements of a situation and to prevent the inadvertent oversight of these elements, it would seem justifiable to designate this distinction by an appropriate set of terms. This is the rationale for the distinc- tion between manifest functions and latent functions; the first referring to those objective consequences for a

---

[67] This one of his many such observations is of course from W. G. Sumner's *Folkways* (Boston: Ginn & Co., 1906), 3. His collaborator, Albert G. Keller retained the distinction in his own writings; see, for example, his *Social Evolution,* (New York: Macmillan, 1927), at 93–95.

[68] This is advisedly drawn from one of MacIver's earlier works, *Community* (London: Macmillan, 1915). The distinction takes on greater importance in his later writings, becoming a major element in his *Social Causation* (Boston: Ginn & Co., 1942), esp. at 314–321, and informs the greater part of his *The More Perfect Union* (New York: Macmillan, 1948).

[69] The single excerpt quoted in the text is one of scores which have led to *The Polish Peasant in Europe and America* being deservedly described as a "sociological classic." See pages 1426–7 and 1523 ff. As will be noted later in this chapter, the insights and conceptual distinctions contained in this one passage, and there are many others like it in point of richness of content, were forgotten or never noticed by those industrial sociologists who recently came to develop the notion of "informal organization" in industry.

specified unit (person, subgroup, social or cultural system) which contribute to its adjustment or adaptation and were so intended; the second referring to unintended and unrecognized consequences of the same order.

There are some indications that the christening of this distinction may serve a heuristic purpose by becoming incorporated into an explicit conceptual apparatus, thus aiding both systematic observation and later analysis. In recent years, for example, the distinction between manifest and latent functions has been utilized in analyses of racial intermarriage,[70] social stratification,[71] affective frustration,[72] Veblen's sociological theories,[73] prevailing American orientations toward Russia,[74] propaganda as a means of social control,[75] Malinowski's anthropological theory,[76] Navajo witchcraft,[77] problems in the sociology of knowledge,[78] fashion,[79] the dynamics of personality,[80] national security measures,[81] the internal social dynamics of bureaucracy,[82] and a great variety of other sociological problems.

The very diversity of these subject-matters suggests that the theoretic distinction between manifest and latent functions is not bound up with a limited and particular range of human behavior. But there still remains the large task of ferreting out the specific uses to which this distinction can be put, and it is to this large task that we devote the remaining pages of this chapter.

Heuristic Purposes of the Distinction

Clarifies the analysis of seemingly irrational social patterns. In the first place, the distinction aids the sociological interpretation of many social practices which persist even though their manifest purpose is clearly not achieved. The time-worn procedure in such instances has been for diverse, particularly lay, observers to refer to these practices as "superstitions," "irrationalities," "mere inertia of tradition," *etc.* In other words, when group behavior does not—and, indeed, often cannot—attain its ostensible purpose there is an inclination to attribute its occurrence to lack of intelligence, sheer ignorance, survivals, or so-called inertia. Thus, the Hopi ceremonials designed to produce abundant rainfall may be labelled a superstitious practice of primitive folk and that is assumed to conclude the matter. It should be noted that this in no sense accounts for the group behavior. It is simply a case of name-calling; it substitutes the epithet "superstition" for an analysis of the actual role of this behavior in the life of the group. Given the concept of latent function, however, we are reminded that this behavior *may* perform

---

[70] Merton, "Intermarriage and the social structure," *op. cit.*
[71] Kingsley Davis, "A conceptual analysis of stratification," *American Sociological Review*, 1942, 7, 309–321.
[72] Thorner, *op. cit.*, esp. at 165.
[73] A. K. Davis, *Thorstein Veblen's Social Theory*, Harvard Ph.D. dissertation, 1941 and "Veblen on the decline of the Protestant Ethic," *Social Forces*, 1944, 22, 282–86; Louis Schneider, *The Freudian Psychology and Veblen's Social Theory* (New York: King's Crown Press, 1948), esp. chapter 2.
[74] A. K. Davis, "Some sources of American hostility to Russia," *American Journal of Sociology*, 1947, 53, 174–183.
[75] Talcott Parsons, "Propaganda and social control," in his *Essays in Sociological Theory*.
[76] Clyde Kluckhohn, "Bronislaw Malinowski, 1884–1942," *Journal of American Folklore*, 1943, 56, 208–219.
[77] Clyde Kluckhohn, *Navaho Witchcraft, op. cit.*, esp. at 46–47 and ff.
[78] Merton, Chapter XII of this volume.
[79] Bernard Barber and L. S. Lobel, "'Fashion' in women's clothes and the American social system," *Social Forces*, 1952, 31, 124–131.
[80] O. H. Mowrer and C. Kluckhohn, "Dynamic theory of personality," in J. M. Hunt, ed., *Personality and the Behavior Disorders* (New York: Ronald Press, 1944), 1, 69–135, esp. at 72.
[81] Marie Jahoda and S. W. Cook, "Security measures and freedom of thought: an exploratory study of the impact of loyalty and security programs," *Yale Law Journal*, 1952, 61, 296–333.

---

[82] Philip Selznick, *TVA and the Grass Roots* (University of California Press, 1949); A. W. Gouldner, *Patterns of Industrial Bureaucracy* (Glencoe, Illinois: The Free Press, 1954); P. M. Blau, *The Dynamics of Bureaucracy* (University of Chicago Press, 1955); A. K. Davis, "Bureaucratic patterns in Navy officer corps," *Social Forces*, 1948, 27, 142–153.

a function for the group, although this function may be quite remote from the avowed purpose of the behavior.

The concept of latent function extends the observer's attention beyond the question of whether or not the behavior attains its avowed purpose. Temporarily ignoring these explicit purposes, it directs attention *toward* another range of consequences: those bearing, for example, upon the individual personalities of Hopi involved in the ceremony and upon the persistence and continuity of the larger group. Were one to confine himself to the problem of whether a manifest (purposed) function occurs, it becomes a problem, not for the sociologist, but for the meteorologist. And to be sure, our meteorologists agree that the rain ceremonial does not produce rain; but this is hardly to the point. It is merely to say that the ceremony does not have this technological use; that this purpose of the ceremony and its actual consequences do not coincide. But with the concept of latent function, we continue our inquiry, examining the consequences of the ceremony not for the rain gods or for meteorological phenomena, but for the groups which conduct the ceremony. And here it may be found, as many observers indicate, that the ceremonial does indeed have functions—but functions which are non-purposed or latent.

Ceremonials may fulfill the latent function of reinforcing the group identity by providing a periodic occasion on which the scattered members of a group assemble to engage in a common activity. As Durkheim among others long since indicated, such ceremonials are a means by which collective expression is afforded the sentiments which, in a further analysis, are found to be a basic source of group unity. Through the systematic application of the concept of latent function, therefore, *apparently* irrational behavior may *at times* be found to be positively functional for the group. Operating with the concept of latent function, we are not too quick to conclude that if an activity of a group does not achieve its nominal purpose, then its persistence can be described only as an instance of "inertia,"

"survival," or "manipulation by powerful subgroups in the society."

In point of fact, some conception like that of latent function has very often, almost invariably, been employed by social scientists observing *a standardized practice designed to achieve an objective which one knows from accredited physical science cannot be thus achieved*. This would plainly be the case, for example, with Pueblo rituals dealing with rain or fertility. *But with behavior which is not directed toward a clearly unattainable objective, sociological observers are less likely to examine the collateral or latent functions of the behavior.*

Directs attention to theoretically fruitful fields of inquiry. The distinction between manifest and latent functions serves further to direct the attention of the sociologist to precisely those realms of behavior, attitude and belief where he can most fruitfully apply his special skills. For what is his task if he confines himself to the study of manifest functions? He is then concerned very largely with determining whether a practice instituted for a particular purpose does, in fact, achieve this purpose. He will then inquire, for example, whether a new system of wage-payment achieves its avowed purpose of reducing labor turnover or of increasing output. He will ask whether a propaganda campaign has indeed gained its objective of increasing "willingness to fight" or "willingness to buy war bonds," or "tolerance toward other ethnic groups." Now, these are important, and complex, types of inquiry. But, so long as sociologists *confine* themselves to the study of manifest functions, their inquiry is set for them by practical men of affairs (whether a captain of industry, a trade union leader, or, conceivably, a Navaho chieftain, is for the moment immaterial), rather than by the theoretic problems which are at the core of the discipline. By dealing primarily with the realm of manifest functions, with the key problem of whether deliberately instituted practices or organizations succeed in achieving their objectives, the sociologist becomes converted into an industrious and skilled recorder of the altogether familiar pattern of behavior. *The terms of appraisal are fixed and limited by the question put to him by the non-theoretic men of affairs,* e.g., has the new wage-payment program achieved such-and-such purposes?

But armed with the concept of latent function, the sociologist extends his inquiry in those very directions which promise most for the theoretic development of the discipline. He examines the familiar (or planned) social practice to ascertain the latent, and hence generally unrecognized, functions (as well, of course, as the manifest functions). He considers, for example, the consequences of the new wage plan for, say, the trade union in which the workers are organized or the consequences of a propaganda program, not only for increasing its avowed purpose of stirring up patriotic fervor, but also for making large numbers of people reluctant to speak their minds when they differ with official policies, *etc.* In short, it is suggested that the *distinctive* intellectual contributions of the sociologist are found primarily in the study of unintended consequences (among which are latent functions) of social practices, as well as in the study of anticipated consequences (among which are manifest functions).[83]

There is some evidence that it is precisely at the point where the research attention of sociologists has shifted from the plane of manifest to the plane of latent functions that they have made their *distinctive* and major contributions. This can be extensively documented but a few passing illustrations must suffice.

The Hawthorne Western Electric Studies[84]

As is well known, the early stages of this inquiry were concerned with the problem of the relations of "illumination to efficiency" of industrial workers. For some two and a half years, attention was focused on problems such as this: do variations in the intensity of lighting affect production? The initial results showed that within wide limits there was no uniform relation between illumination and output. Production output increased *both* in the experimental group where illumination was increased (or *decreased*) *and* in the control group where no changes in illumination were introduced. In short, the investigators confined themselves wholly to a search for the manifest functions. Lacking a concept of latent social function, no attention whatever was initially paid to the social consequences *of the experiment* for relations among members of the test and control groups or for relations between workers and the test room authorities. In other words, the investigators lacked a sociological frame of reference and operated merely as "engineers" (just as a group of meteorologists might have explored the "effects" upon rainfall of the Hopi ceremonial).

Only after continued investigation, did it occur to the research group to explore the consequences of the new "experimental situation" for the self-images and self-conceptions of the workers taking part in the experiment, for the interpersonal relations among members of the group, for the coherence and unity of the group. As Elton Mayo reports it, "the illumination fiasco had made them alert to the need that very careful records should be kept of everything that happened in the room in addition to the obvious engineering and industrial devices. Their observations therefore included not only records of industrial and engineering changes but also records of physiological or medical changes, and, *in a sense,* of social and anthropological. This last took the form of a 'log' that gave as full an account as possible of the actual events of every day. . . ."[85] In short, it was only

---

[83] For a brief illustration of this general proposition, see Robert K. Merton, Marjorie Fiske and Alberta Curtis, *Mass Persuasion* (New York: Harper, 1946). 185–189; Jahoda and Cook, *op. cit.*

[84] This is cited as a case study of how *an elaborate research was wholly changed in theoretic orientation and in the character of its research findings by the introduction of a concept approximating the concept of latent function.* Selection of the case for this purpose does not, of course, imply full

acceptance of the *interpretations* which the authors give their findings. Among the several volumes reporting the Western Electric research, see particularly F. J. Roethlisberger and W. J. Dickson, *Management and the Worker* (Harvard University Press, 1939).

[85] Elton Mayo, *The Social Problems of an Industrial Civilization* (Harvard University Press, 1945), 70.

after a long series of experiments which wholly neglected the latent social functions of the experiment (as a contrived social situation) that this distinctly sociological framework was introduced. "With this realization," the authors write, "the inquiry changed its character. No longer were the investigators interested in testing for the effects of single variables. In the place of a controlled experiment, they substituted the notion of a social situation which needed to be described and understood as a system of interdependent elements." Thereafter, as is now widely known, inquiry was directed very largely toward ferreting out the latent functions of standardized practices among the workers, of informal organization developing among workers, of workers' games instituted by "wise administrators," of large programs of worker counselling and interviewing, etc. The new conceptual scheme entirely altered the range and types of data gathered in the ensuing research.

One has only to return to the previously quoted excerpt from Thomas and Znaniecki in their classical work of some thirty years ago, to recognize the correctness of Shils' remark:

> . . . indeed the history of the study of primary groups in American sociology is a supreme instance of the *discontinuities of the development of this discipline:* a problem is stressed by one who is an acknowledged founder of the discipline, the problem is left unstudied, then, some years later, it is taken up with enthusiasm as if no one had ever thought of it before.[86]

For Thomas and Znaniecki had repeatedly emphasized the sociological view that, whatever its major purpose, "the association as a concrete group of human personalities unofficially involves many other interests; the social contacts between its members are not limited to their

common pursuit. . . ." In effect, then, it had taken years of experimentation to turn the attention of the Western Electric research team to the latent social functions of primary groups emerging in industrial organizations. It should be made clear that this case is not cited here as an instance of defective experimental design; that is not our immediate concern. It is considered only as an illustration of the pertinence for *sociological* inquiry of the concept of latent function, and the associated concepts of functional analysis. It illustrates how the inclusion of this concept (whether the term is used or not is inconsequential) can sensitize sociological investigators to a range of significant social variables which are otherwise easily overlooked. The explicit ticketing of the concept may perhaps lessen the frequency of such occasions of discontinuity in future sociological research.

The discovery of latent functions represents significant increments in sociological knowledge. There is another respect in which inquiry into latent functions represents a distinctive contribution of the social scientist. It is precisely the latent functions of a practice or belief which are *not* common knowledge, for these are unintended and generally unrecognized social and psychological consequences. As a result, findings concerning latent functions represent a greater increment in knowledge than findings concerning manifest functions. They represent, also, greater departures from "common-sense" knowledge about social life. Inasmuch as the latent functions depart, more or less, from the avowed manifest functions, the research which uncovers latent functions very often produces "paradoxical" results. The seeming paradox arises from the sharp modification of a familiar popular preconception which regards a standardized practice or belief *only* in terms of its manifest functions by indicating some of its subsidiary or collateral latent functions. The introduction of the concept of latent function in social research leads to conclusions which show that "social life is not as simple as it first seems."

---

[86] Edward Shils, *The Present State of American Sociology* (Glencoe, Illinois: The Free Press, 1948), 42 [italics supplied].

For as long as people confine themselves to *certain* consequences (e.g. manifest consequences), it is comparatively simple for them to pass moral judgments upon the practice or belief in question. Moral evaluations, generally based on these manifest consequences, tend to be polarized in terms of black or white. But the perception of further (latent) consequences often complicates the picture. Problems of moral evaluation (which are not our immediate concern) and problems of social engineering (which are our concern[87]) both take on the additional complexities usually involved in responsible social decisions.

An example of inquiry which implicitly uses the notion of latent function will illustrate the sense in which "paradox"—discrepancy between the apparent, merely manifest, function and the actual, which also includes latent functions—tends to occur as a result of including this concept. Thus, to revert to Veblen's well-known analysis of conspicuous consumption, it is no accident that he has been recognized as a social analyst gifted with an eye for the paradoxical, the ironic, the satiric. For these are frequent, if not inevitable, outcomes of applying the concept of latent function (or its equivalent).

The Pattern of Conspicuous Consumption

The manifest purpose of buying consumption goods is, of course, the satisfaction of the needs for which these goods are explicitly designed. Thus, automobiles are obviously intended to provide a certain kind of transportation; candles, to provide light; choice articles of food to provide sustenance; rare art products to provide aesthetic pleasure. Since these products *do* have these uses, it was largely assumed that these encompass the range of socially significant functions. Veblen indeed suggests that this was ordinarily the prevailing view (in the pre-Veblenian era, of course): "The end of acquisition and accumulation is conventionally held to be the consumption of the goods accumulated. . . . This is at least felt to be the economically legitimate end of acquisition, *which alone it is incumbent on the theory to take account of.*"[88]

However, says Veblen in effect, as sociologists we must go on to consider the latent functions of acquisition, accumulation and consumption, and these latent functions are remote indeed from the manifest functions. "But, it is only when taken in a sense far removed from its naive meaning [*i.e.,* manifest function] that the consumption of goods can be said to afford the incentive from which accumulation invariably proceeds." And among these latent functions, which help explain the persistence and the social location of the pattern of conspicuous consumption, is its symbolization of "pecuniary strength and so of gaining or retaining a good name." The exercise of "punctilious discrimination" in the excellence of "food, drink, shelter, service, ornaments, apparel, amusements" results not merely in direct gratifications derived from the consumption of "superior" to "inferior" articles, but also, and Veblen argues, more importantly, it results in a *heightening or reaffirmation of social status.*

The Veblenian paradox is that people buy expensive goods not so much because they are superior but because they are expensive. For it is the latent equation ("costliness = mark of higher social status") which he singles out in his functional analysis, rather than the manifest equation ("costliness = excellence of the goods"). Not that he denies manifest functions *any* place in buttressing the pattern of conspicuous consumption. These, too, are operative. "What has just been said must not be taken to mean that

---

[87] This is not to deny that social engineering has direct moral implications or that technique and morality are inescapably intertwined, but I do not intend to deal with this range of problems in the present chapter. For some discussion of these problems see chapters VI, XV and XVII; also Merton, Fiske and Curtis, *Mass Persuasion,* chapter 7.

[88] Veblen, *Theory of Leisure Class, op. cit.,* p. 25.

there are no other incentives to acquisition and accumulation than this desire to excel in pecuniary standing and so gain the esteem and envy of one's fellowmen. The desire for added comfort and security from want is present as a motive at every stage. . . ." Or again: "It would be hazardous to assert that a useful purpose is ever absent from the utility of any article or of any service, however obviously its prime purpose and chief element is conspicuous waste" and derived social esteem.[89] It is only that *these direct, manifest functions do not fully account for the prevailing patterns of consumption. Otherwise put, if the latent functions of status-enhancement or status-reaffirmation were removed from the patterns of conspicuous consumption, these patterns would undergo severe changes of a sort which the "conventional" economist could not foresee.*

In these respects, Veblen's analysis of latent functions departs from the common-sense notion that the end-product of consumption is "of course, the direct satisfaction which it provides": "People eat caviar because they're hungry; buy Cadillacs because they want the best car they can get; have dinner by candlelight because they like the peaceful atmosphere." The common-sense interpretation in terms of selected manifest motives gives way, in Veblen's analysis, to the collateral latent functions which are also, and perhaps more significantly, fulfilled by these practices. To be sure, the Veblenian analysis has,

_____
[89] *Ibid.*, 32, 101. It will be noted throughout that Veblen is given to loose terminology. In the marked passages (and repeatedly elsewhere) he uses "incentive," "desire," "purpose," and "function" interchangeably. Since the context usually makes clear the denotation of these terms, no great harm is done. But it is clear that the expressed purposes of conformity to a culture pattern are by no means identical with the latent functions of the conformity. Veblen occasionally recognizes this. For example, "In strict accuracy nothing should be included under the head of conspicuous waste but such expenditure as is incurred on the ground of an invidious pecuniary comparison. But in order to bring any given item or element in under this head *it is not necessary that it should be recognized as waste in this sense by the person incurring the expenditure.*" (*Ibid.* 99; italics supplied). *Cf.* A. K. Davis, "Veblen on the decline of the Protestant Ethic," *op. cit.*

in the last decades, entered so fully into popular thought, that these latent functions are now widely recognized. [This raises the interesting problem of the changes occurring in a prevailing pattern of behavior when its *latent* functions become generally recognized (and are thus no longer latent). There will be no occasion for discussing this important problem in the present publication.]

The discovery of latent functions does not merely render conceptions of the functions served by certain social patterns more precise (as is the case also with studies of manifest functions), but introduces a *qualitatively different increment in the previous state of knowledge.*

Precludes the substitution of naive moral judgments for sociological analysis. Since moral evaluations in a society tend to be largely in terms of the manifest consequences of a practice or code, we should be prepared to find that analysis in terms of latent functions at times runs counter to prevailing moral evaluations. For it does not follow that the latent functions will operate in the same fashion as the manifest consequences which are ordinarily the basis of these judgments. Thus, in large sectors of the American population, the political machine or the "political racket" are judged as unequivocally "bad" and "undesirable." The grounds for such moral judgment vary somewhat, but they consist substantially in pointing out that political machines violate moral codes: political patronage violates the code of selecting personnel on the basis of impersonal qualifications rather than on grounds of party loyalty or contributions to the party war-chest; bossism violates the code that votes should be based on individual appraisal of the qualifications of candidates and of political issues, and not on abiding loyalty to a feudal leader; bribery, and "honest graft" obviously offend the proprieties of property; "protection" for crime clearly violates the law and the mores; and so on.

In view of the manifold respects in which political machines, in varying degrees, run counter to the mores and at times to the law, it becomes pertinent to inquire how they manage to continue in operation. The familiar "explanations" for the continuance of the political machine are not here in point. To be sure, it may well be that if "respectable citizenry" would live up to their political obligations, if the electorate were to be alert and enlightened; if the number of elective officers were substantially reduced from the dozens, even hundreds, which the average voter is now expected to appraise in the course of town, county, state and national elections; if the electorate were activated by the "wealthy and educated classes without whose participation," as the not-always democratically oriented Bryce put it, "the best-framed government must speedily degenerate"—if these and a plethora of similar changes in political structure were introduced, perhaps the "evils" of the political machine would indeed be exorcised.[90] But it should be noted that these changes are often not introduced, that political machines have had the phoenix-like quality of arising, strong and unspoiled from their ashes, that, in short, this structure has exhibited a notable vitality in many areas of American political life.

Proceeding from the functional view, therefore, that we should *ordinarily* (not invariably) expect persistent social patterns and social structures to perform positive functions *which are at the time not adequately fulfilled by other existing patterns and structures*, the thought occurs that perhaps this publicly maligned organization is, *under present conditions*, satisfying basic latent functions.[91]

A brief examination of current analyses of this type of structure may also serve to illustrate additional problems of functional analysis.

Some Functions of the Political Machine

Without presuming to enter into the variations of detail marking different political machines—a Tweed, Vare, Crump, Flynn, Hague are by no means identical types of bosses—we can briefly examine the functions more or less common to the political machine, as a generic type of social organization. We neither attempt to itemize all the diverse functions of the political machine nor imply that all these functions are similarly fulfilled by each and every machine.

The key structural function of the Boss is to organize, centralize and maintain in good working condition "the scattered fragments of power" which are at present dispersed through our political organization. By this centralized organization of political power, the boss and his apparatus can satisfy the needs of diverse subgroups in the larger community which are not adequately satisfied by legally devised and culturally approved social structures.

To understand the role of bossism and the machine, therefore, we must look at two types of sociological variables: (1) the *structural context* which makes it difficult, if not impossible, for morally approved structures to fulfill essential social functions, thus leaving the door open for political machines (or their structural equivalents) to fulfill these functions and (2) the subgroups whose distinctive needs are left

---

[90] These "explanations" are "causal" in design. They profess to indicate the social conditions under which political machines come into being. In so far as they are empirically confirmed, these explanations of course add to our knowledge concerning the problem: how is it that political machines operate in certain areas and not in others? How do they manage to continue? *But these causal accounts are not sufficient.* The functional consequences of the machine, as we shall see, go far toward supplementing the causal interpretation.

[91] I trust it is superfluous to add that this hypothesis is not "in support of the political machine." The question whether the dysfunctions of the machine outweigh its functions, the question whether alternative structures are not

---

available which may fulfill its functions without necessarily entailing its social dysfunctions, still remain to be considered at an appropriate point. We are here concerned with documenting the statement that moral judgments based *entirely* on an appraisal of manifest functions of a social structure are "unrealistic" in the strict sense, i.e., they do not take into account other actual consequences of that structure, consequences which may provide basic social support for the structure. As will be indicated later, "social reforms" or "social engineering" which ignore latent functions do so on pain of suffering acute disappointments and boomerang effects.

unsatisfied, except for the latent functions which the machine in fact fulfills.[92]

Structural Context   The constitutional framework of American political organization specifically precludes the legal possibility of highly centralized power and, it has been noted, thus "discourages the growth of effective and responsible leadership. The framers of the Constitution, as Woodrow Wilson observed, set up the check and balance system 'to keep government at a sort of mechanical equipoise by means of a standing amicable contest among its several organic parts.' They distrusted power as dangerous to liberty: and therefore they spread it thin and erected barriers against its concentration." This dispersion of power is found not only at the national level but in local areas as well. "As a consequence," Sait goes on to observe, "when *the people or particular groups* among them demanded positive action, no one had adequate authority to act. The machine provided an antidote."[93]

The constitutional dispersion of power not only makes for difficulty of effective decision and action but when action does occur it is defined and hemmed in by legalistic considerations. In consequence, there developed "a much *more human system* of partisan government, whose chief object soon became the circumvention of government by law. . . . The lawlessness of the extra-official democracy was merely the counterpoise of the legalism of the official democracy. The lawyer having been permitted to subordinate democracy to the Law, the Boss had to be called in to extricate the victim, which he did after a fashion and for a consideration."[94]

Officially, political power is dispersed. Various well-known expedients were devised for this manifest objective. Not only was there the familiar separation of powers among the several branches of the government but, in some measure, tenure in each office was limited, rotation in office approved. And the scope of power inherent in each office was severely circumscribed. Yet, observes Sait in rigorously functional terms, "Leadership is necessary; and *since* it does not develop readily within the constitutional framework, the Boss provides it in a crude and irresponsible form from the outside."[95]

Put in more generalized terms, *the functional deficiencies of the official structure generate an alternative (unofficial) structure to fulfill existing needs somewhat more effectively.* Whatever its specific historical origins, the political machine persists as an apparatus for satisfying otherwise unfulfilled needs of diverse groups in the population. By turning to a few of these subgroups and their characteristic needs, we shall be led at once to a range of latent functions of the political machine.

Functions of the Political Machine for Diverse Subgroups   It is well known that one source of strength of the political machine derives from its roots in the local community and the neighborhood. The political machine does not regard the electorate as an amorphous, undifferentiated mass of voters. With a keen sociological intuition, the machine recognizes that the voter is a person living in a specific neighborhood, with specific personal problems and personal wants. Public issues are abstract and remote; private problems are extremely concrete and immediate. It is not through the generalized appeal to large public concerns that the machine operates, but through the direct, quasi-feudal relationships between local representatives of the machine and voters in their neighborhood. Elections are won in the precinct.

---

[92] Again, as with preceding cases, we shall not consider the possible dysfunctions of the political machine.
[93] Edward M. Sait, "Machine, Political," *Encyclopedia of the Social Sciences*, IX, 658 b [italics supplied]; cf. A. F. Bentley, *The Process of Government* (Chicago, 1908), chap. 2.
[94] Herbert Croly, *Progressive Democracy* (New York, 1914), p. 254, cited by Sait, *op. cit.*, 658 b.

---

[95] Sait, *op. cit.*, 659 a. [italics supplied].

The machine welds its link with ordinary men and women by elaborate networks of personal relations. Politics is transformed into personal ties. The precinct captain "must be a friend to every man, assuming if he does not feel sympathy with the unfortunate, and utilizing in his good works the resources which the boss puts at his disposal."[96] The precinct captain is forever a friend in need. In our prevailingly impersonal society, the machine, through its local agents, fulfills the important social *function of humanizing and personalizing all manner of assistance* to those in need. Foodbaskets and jobs, legal and extra-legal advice, setting to rights minor scrapes with the law, helping the bright poor boy to a political scholarship in a local college, looking after the bereaved—the whole range of crises when a feller needs a friend, and, above all, a friend who knows the score and who can do something about it,—all these find the ever-helpful precinct captain available in the pinch.

To assess this function of the political machine adequately, it is important to note not only that aid *is* provided but *the manner in which it is provided*. After all, other agencies do exist for dispensing such assistance. Welfare agencies, settlement houses, legal aid clinics, medical aid in free hospitals, public relief departments, immigration authorities—these and a multitude of other organizations are available to provide the most varied types of assistance. But in contrast to the professional techniques of the welfare worker which may typically represent in the mind of the recipient the cold, bureaucratic dispensation of limited aid following upon detailed investigation of *legal* claims to aid of the "client" are the unprofessional techniques of the precinct captain who asks no questions, exacts no compliance with legal rules of eligibility and does not "snoop" into private affairs.[97]

For many, the loss of "self-respect" is too high a price for legalized assistance. In contrast to the gulf between the settlement house workers who so often come from a different social class, educational background and ethnic group, the precinct worker is "just one of us," who understands what it's all about. The condescending lady bountiful can hardly compete with the understanding friend in need. In *this struggle between alternative structures for fulfilling the nominally same function* of providing aid and support to those who need it, it is clearly the machine politician who is better integrated with the groups which he serves than the impersonal, professionalized, socially distant and legally constrained welfare worker. And since the politician can at times influence and manipulate the official organizations for the dispensation of assistance, whereas the welfare worker has practically no influence on the political machine, this only adds to his greater effectiveness. More colloquially and also, perhaps, more incisively, it was the Boston ward-leader, Martin Lomasny, who described this essential function to the curious Lincoln Steffens: "I think," said Lomasny, "that there's got to be in every ward somebody that any bloke can come to—no matter what he's done—and get help. *Help, you understand; none of your law and justice, but help.*"[98]

The "deprived classes," then, constitute one subgroup for whom the political machine satisfies

---

[96] *Ibid.*, 659 a.

[97] Much the same contrast with official welfare policy is found in Harry Hopkins' open-handed and non-political distribution of unemployment relief in New York State under the governorship of Franklin Delano Roosevelt. As Sherwood reports: "Hopkins was harshly criticized for these irregular activities by the established welfare agencies, which claimed it was 'unprofessional conduct' to hand out work tickets without thorough investigation of each applicant, his own or his family's financial resources and probably his religious affiliations. 'Harry told the agency to go to hell,' said [Hopkins' associate, Dr. Jacob A.] Goldberg." Robert E. Sherwood, *Roosevelt and Hopkins, An Intimate History* (New York: Harper, 1948), 30.

[98] *The Autobiography of Lincoln Steffens* (Chautauqua, New York: Chautauqua Press, 1931), 618. Deriving largely from Steffens, as he says, F. Stuart Chapin sets forth these functions of the political machine with great clarity. See his *Contemporary American Institutions* (New York: Harper, 1934), 40–54.

wants not adequately satisfied in the same fashion by the legitimate social structure.

For a second subgroup, that of business (primarily "big" business but also "small"), the political boss serves the function of providing those political privileges which entail immediate economic gains. Business corporations, among which the public utilities (railroads, local transportation and electric light companies, communications corporations) are simply the most conspicuous in this regard, seek special political dispensations which will enable them to stabilize their situation and to near their objective of maximizing profits. Interestingly enough, corporations often want to avoid a chaos of uncontrolled competition. They want the greater security of an economic czar who controls, regulates and organizes competition, providing that this czar is not a public official with his decisions subject to public scrutiny and public control. (The latter would be "government control," and hence taboo.) The political boss fulfills these requirements admirably.

Examined for a moment apart from any moral considerations, the political apparatus operated by the Boss is effectively designed to perform these functions with a minimum of inefficiency. Holding the strings of diverse governmental divisions, bureaus and agencies in his competent hands, the Boss rationalizes the relations between public and private business. He serves as the business community's ambassador in the otherwise alien (and sometimes unfriendly) realm of government. And, in strict business-like terms, he is well-paid for his economic services to his respectable business clients. In an article entitled, "An Apology to Graft," Lincoln Steffens suggested that "Our economic system, which held up riches, power and acclaim as prizes to men bold enough and able enough to buy corruptly timber, mines, oil fields and franchises and 'get away with it,' was at fault."[99] And, in a

conference with a hundred or so of Los Angeles business leaders, he described a fact well known to all of them: the Boss and his machine were an *integral part* of the organization of the economy. "You cannot build or operate a railroad, or a street railway, gas, water, or power company, develop and operate a mine, or get forests and cut timber on a large scale, or run any privileged business, without corrupting or joining in the corruption of the government. You tell me privately that you must, and here I am telling you semi-publicly that you must. And that is so all over the country. And that means that we have an organization of society in which, *for some reason*, you and your kind, the ablest, most intelligent, most imaginative, daring, and resourceful leaders of society, are and must be against society and its laws and its all-around growth."[100]

Since the demand for the services of special privileges are built into the structure of the society, the Boss fulfills diverse functions for this second subgroup of business-seeking-privilege. These "needs" of business, as presently constituted, are not adequately provided for by conventional and culturally approved social structures; consequently, the extra-legal but more-or-less efficient organization of the political machine comes to provide these services. To adopt an *exclusively* moral attitude toward the "corrupt political machine" is to lose sight of the very structural conditions which generate the "evil" that is so bitterly attacked. To adopt a functional outlook is to provide not an apologia for the political machine but a more solid basis for modifying or eliminating the machine, *providing* specific structural arrangements are introduced either for eliminating these effective demands of the business community or, if that is the objective, of satisfying these demands through alternative means.

---

[99] *Autobiography of Lincoln Steffens*, 570.

[100] *Ibid.*, 572–3 [italics supplied]. This helps explain, as Steffens noted after Police Commissioner Theodore Roosevelt, "the prominence and respectability of the men and women who intercede for crooks" when these have been apprehended in a periodic effort to "clean up the political machine." *Cf.* Steffens, 371, and *passim*.

A third set of distinctive functions fulfilled by the political machine for a special subgroup is that of providing alternative channels of social mobility for those otherwise excluded from the more conventional avenues for personal "advancement." Both the sources of this special "need" (for social mobility) and the respect in which the political machine comes to help satisfy this need can be understood by examining the structure of the larger culture and society. As is well known, the American culture lays enormous emphasis on money and power as a "success" goal legitimate for all members of the society. By no means alone in our inventory of cultural goals, it still remains among the most heavily endowed with positive affect and value. However, certain subgroups and certain ecological areas are notable for the relative absence of opportunity for achieving these (monetary and power) types of success. They constitute, in short, sub-populations where "the cultural emphasis upon pecuniary success has been absorbed, but where there is *little access to conventional and legitimate* means for attaining such success. The conventional occupational opportunities of persons in (such areas) are almost completely limited to manual labor. Given our cultural stigmatization of manual labor,[101] and its correlate, the prestige of white-collar work, it is clear that the result is a

tendency to achieve these culturally approved objectives *through whatever means are possible.* These people are on the one hand, "asked to orient their conduct toward the prospect of accumulating wealth [and power] and, on the other, they are largely denied effective opportunities to do so institutionally."

It is within this context of social structure that the political machine fulfills the basic function of providing avenues of social mobility for the otherwise disadvantaged. Within this context, even the corrupt political machine and the racket "represent the triumph of amoral intelligence over morally prescribed 'failure' when the channels of vertical mobility are closed or narrowed *in a society which places a high premium on economic affluence, [power] and social ascent for all its members.*"[102] As one sociologist has noted on the basis of several years of close observation in a slum area:

> The sociologist who dismisses racket and political organizations as deviations from desirable standards thereby neglects some of the major elements of slum life. . . . *He does not discover the functions they perform for the members* [of the groupings in the slum]. The Irish and later immigrant peoples have had the greatest difficulty in finding places for themselves in our urban social and economic structure. Does anyone believe that the immigrants and their children could have achieved their present degree of social mobility without gaining control of the political organization of some of our largest cities? The same is true of the racket organization. *Politics and the rackets have furnished an important means of social mobility for individuals,*

---

[101] See the National Opinion Research Center survey of evaluation of occupations which firmly documents the general impression that the manual occupations rate very low indeed in the social scale of values, *even among those who are themselves engaged in manual labor.* Consider this latter point in its full implications. In effect, the cultural and social structure exacts the values of pecuniary and power success even among those who find themselves confined to the stigmatized manual occupations. Against this background, consider the powerful motivation for achieving this type of "success" by any means whatsoever. A garbage-collector who joins with other Americans in the view that the garbage-collector is "the lowest of the low" occupations can scarcely have a self-image which is pleasing to him; he is in a "pariah" occupation in the very society where he is assured that "all who have genuine merit can get ahead." Add to this, his occasional recognition that "he didn't have the same chance as others, no matter what they say," and one perceives the

enormous psychological pressure upon him for "evening up the score" by finding some means, whether strictly legal or not, for moving ahead. All this provides the structural and derivatively psychological background for the "socially induced need" in *some* groups to find some accessible avenue for social mobility.

[102] Merton, "Social structure and anomie," chapter IV of this volume.

who, because of ethnic background and low class position, are blocked from advancement in the "respectable" channels.[103]

This, then, represents a third type of function performed for a distinctive subgroup. This function, it may be noted in passing, is fulfilled by the *sheer* existence and operation of the political machine, for it is in the machine itself that these individuals and subgroups find their culturally induced needs more or less satisfied. It refers to the services which the political apparatus provides for its own personnel. But seen in the wider social context we have set forth, it no longer appears as *merely* a means of self-aggrandizement for profit-hungry and power-hungry *individuals*, but as an organized provision for *subgroups* otherwise excluded from or handicapped in the race for "getting ahead."

Just as the political machine performs services for "legitimate" business, so it operates to perform not dissimilar services for "illegitimate" business: vice, crime and rackets. Once again, the basic sociological role of the machine in this respect can be more fully appreciated only if one temporarily abandons attitudes of

---

[103] William F. Whyte, "Social organization in the slums," *American Sociological Review*, Feb. 1943, 8, 34–39 (italics supplied). Thus, the political machine and the racket represent a special case of the type of organizational adjustment to the conditions described in chapter IV. It represents, note, an *organizational* adjustment: definite structures arise and operate to reduce somewhat the acute tensions and problems of individuals caught up in the described conflict between the "cultural accent on success-for-all" and the "socially structured fact of unequal opportunities for success." As chapter IV indicates, other types of *individual* "adjustment" are possible: lone-wolf crime, psychopathological states, rebellion, retreat by abandoning the culturally approved goals, etc. Likewise, other types of *organizational adjustment* sometimes occur; the racket or the political machine are not alone available as organized means for meeting this socially induced problem. Participation in revolutionary organizations, for example, can be seen within this context, as an alternative mode of organizational adjustment. All this bears theoretic notice here, since we might otherwise overlook the basic functional concepts of functional substitutes and functional equivalents, which are to be discussed at length in a subsequent publication.

moral indignation, to examine in all moral innocence the actual workings of the organization. In this light, it at once appears that the subgroup of the professional criminal, racketeer or gambler has basic similarities of organization, demands and operation to the subgroup of the industrialist, man of business or speculator. If there is a Lumber King or an Oil King, there is also a Vice King or a Racket King. If expansive legitimate business organizes administrative and financial syndicates to "rationalize" and to "integrate" diverse areas of production and business enterprise, so expansive rackets and crime organize syndicates to bring order to the otherwise chaotic areas of production of illicit goods and services. If legitimate business regards the proliferation of small business enterprises as wasteful and inefficient, substituting, for example, the giant chain stores for hundreds of corner groceries, so illegitimate business adopts the same businesslike attitude and syndicates crime and vice.

Finally, and in many respects, most important, is the basic similarity, if not near-identity, of the economic role of "legitimate" business and of "illegitimate" business. *Both are in some degree concerned with the provision of goods and services for which there is an economic demand.* Morals aside, they are both business, industrial and professional enterprises, dispensing goods and services which some people want, for which there is a market in which goods and services are transformed into commodities. And, in a prevalently market society, we should expect appropriate enterprises to arise whenever there is a market demand for certain goods or services.

As is well known, vice, crime and the rackets *are* "big business." Consider only that there have been estimated to be about 500,000 professional prostitutes in the United States in 1950, and compare this with the approximately 200,000 physicians and 350,000 professional registered nurses. It is difficult to estimate which have the larger clientele: the professional men and women of medicine or the professional men and women of vice. It is, of course, difficult to estimate the economic assets, income, profits and dividends of illicit gambling in this country and to compare it with the economic assets, income, profits and dividends of, say, the shoe industry, but it is altogether possible that the two industries are about on a par. No precise figures exist on the annual expenditures on illicit narcotics, and it is probable that these are less than the expenditures on candy, but it is also probable that they are larger than the expenditure on books.

It takes but a moment's thought to recognize that, *in strictly economic terms*, there is no relevant difference between the provision of licit and of illicit goods and services. The liquor traffic illustrates this perfectly. It would be peculiar to argue that prior to 1920 (when the 18th amendment became effective), the provision of liquor constituted an economic service, that from 1920 to 1933, its production and sale no longer constituted an economic service dispensed in a market, and that from 1934 to the present, it once again took on a serviceable aspect. Or, it would be *economically* (not morally) absurd to suggest that the sale of bootlegged liquor in the dry state of Kansas is less a response to a market demand than the sale of publicly manufactured liquor in the neighboring wet state of Missouri. Examples of this sort can of course be multiplied many times over. Can it be held that in European countries, with registered and legalized prostitution, the prostitute contributes an economic service, whereas in this country, lacking legal sanction, the prostitute provides no such service? Or that the professional abortionist is in the economic market where he has approved legal status and that he is out of the economic market where he is legally taboo? Or that gambling satisfies a specific demand for entertainment in Nevada, where it constitutes the largest business enterprise of the larger cities in the state, but that it differs essentially in this respect from motion pictures in the neighboring state of California?[104]

The failure to recognize that these businesses are only *morally* and not *economically* distinguishable from "legitimate" businesses has led to badly scrambled analysis. Once the economic identity of the two is recognized, we may anticipate that if the political machine performs functions for "legitimate big business" it will be all the more likely to perform not dissimilar functions for "illegitimate big business." And, of course, such is often the case.

The distinctive function of the political machine for their criminal, vice and racket clientele is to enable them to operate in satisfying the economic demands of a large market without due interference from the government. Just as big business may contribute funds to the political party war-chest to ensure a minimum of governmental interference, so with big rackets and big crime. In both instances, the political machine can, in varying degrees, provide "protection." In both instances, many features of the structural context are identical: (1) market demands for goods and services; (2) the operators' concern with maximizing gains from their enterprises; (3) the need for partial control of government which might otherwise interfere with these activities of businessmen; (4) the need for an efficient, powerful and centralized agency to provide an effective liaison of "business" with government.

Without assuming that the foregoing pages exhaust either the range of functions or the range of subgroups served by the political machine, we can at least see that *it presently fulfills some functions for these diverse subgroups which are not adequately fulfilled by culturally approved or more conventional structures.*

---

[104] Perhaps the most perceptive statement of this view has been made by Hawkins and Waller. "The prostitute, the pimp, the peddler of dope, the operator of the gambling hall, the vendor of obscene pictures, the bootlegger, the abortionist, all are productive, all produce services or goods which people desire and for which they are willing to pay. It happens that society has put these goods and services under the ban, but people go on producing them and people go on consuming them, and an act of the legislature does not make them any less a part of the economic system." "Critical notes on the cost of crime," *Journal of Criminal Law and Criminology,* 1936, 26, 679–94, at 684.

Several additional implications of the functional analysis of the political machine can be mentioned here only in passing, although they obviously require to be developed at length. First, the foregoing analysis has direct implications for *social engineering*. It helps explain why the periodic efforts at "political reform," "turning the rascals out" and "cleaning political house" are typically (though not necessarily) short-lived and ineffectual. It exemplifies a basic theorem: *any attempt to eliminate an existing social structure without providing adequate alternative structures for fulfilling the functions previously fulfilled by the abolished organization is doomed to failure.* (Needless to say, this theorem has much wider bearing than the one instance of the political machine.) When "political reform" confines itself to the manifest task of "turning the rascals out," it is engaging in little more than sociological magic. The reform may for a time bring new figures into the political limelight; it may serve the casual social function of re-assuring the electorate that the moral virtues remain intact and will ultimately triumph; it may actually effect a turnover in the personnel of the political machine; it may even, for a time, so curb the activities of the machine as to leave unsatisfied the many needs it has previously fulfilled. But, inevitably, unless the reform also involves a "re-forming" of the social and political structure such that the existing needs are satisfied by alternative structures or unless it involves a change which eliminates these needs altogether, the political machine will return to its integral place in the social scheme of things. *To seek social change, without due recognition of the manifest and latent functions performed by the social organization undergoing change, is to indulge in social ritual rather than social engineering.* The concepts of manifest and latent functions (or their equivalents) are indispensable elements in the theoretic repertoire of the social engineer. In this crucial sense, these concepts are not "merely" theoretical (in the abusive sense of the term), but are eminently practical. In the deliberate enactment of

social change, they can be ignored only at the price of considerably heightening the risk of failure.

A second implication of this analysis of the political machine also has a bearing upon areas wider than the one we have considered. The paradox has often been noted that the supporters of the political machine include both the "respectable" business class elements who are, of course, opposed to the criminal or racketeer and the distinctly "unrespectable" elements of the underworld. And, at first appearance, this is cited as an instance of very strange bedfellows. The learned judge is not infrequently called upon to sentence the very racketeer beside whom he sat the night before at an informal dinner of the political bigwigs. The district attorney jostles the exonerated convict on his way to the back room where the Boss has called a meeting. The big business man may complain almost as bitterly as the big racketeer about the "extortionate" contributions to the party fund demanded by the Boss. Social opposites meet—in the smoke-filled room of the successful politician.

In the light of a functional analysis all this of course no longer seems paradoxical. Since the machine serves both the businessman and the criminal man, the two seemingly antipodal groups intersect. This points to a more general theorem: *the social functions of an organization help determine the structure (including the recruitment of personnel involved in the structure), just as the structure helps determine the effectiveness with which the functions are fulfilled.* In terms of social status, the business group and the criminal group are indeed poles apart. But status does not fully determine behavior and the inter-relations between groups. Functions modify these relations. Given their distinctive needs, the several subgroups in the large society are "integrated," whatever their personal desires or intentions, by the centralizing structure which serves these several needs. In a phrase with many implications which require further study, *structure affects function and function affects structure.*

Concluding Remarks

This review of some salient considerations in structural and functional analysis has done little more than indicate some of the principal problems and potentialities of this mode of sociological interpretation. Each of the items codified in the paradigm require sustained theoretic clarification and cumulative empirical research. But it is clear that in functional theory, stripped of those traditional postulates which have fenced it in and often made it little more than a latter-day rationalization of existing practices, sociology has one beginning of a systematic and empirically relevant mode of analysis. It is hoped that the direction here indicated will suggest the feasibility and the desirability of further codification of functional analysis. In due course each section of the paradigm will be elaborated into a documented, analyzed and codified chapter in the history of functional analysis.

Chapter 8

Conflict Theory

Introduction

The roots of conflict theory are to be found in the works of Marx and Weber, both of whom recognize that ultimately it is coercion rather than consensus that maintains social order. Although Marx and Weber envisioned different forms and degrees of social stratification, both argued that conflict was the fundamental dynamic that operated between these strata. Marx saw capitalist society dichotomized into two major economic classes, the proletariat and the bourgeoisie. These two classes were pitted in inexorable opposition. Weber acknowledged that economy was one of the determinant forces in society but asserted that political power and status were also important. Social groups would identify themselves not merely according to wealth, but more deeply by ethnic and cultural backgrounds, and by shared "styles of life." Hence, whereas Marx and Weber viewed different groups competing for different social rewards, they agreed that society was fundamentally unstable, and that the operative force behind change was the conflict which inevitably arose between various social groups in competition for social scarcities.

The resurgence of interest in conflict theory was a consequence of the increasing skepticism in the explanatory power of functionalism as a paradigm of social analysis. The intense conflicts that marked the 1960s and the inability of functionalism to account for these developments given its commitment to stability, equilibrium, and consensus, intensified the quest for an alternative.

These concerns were forcefully spelled out in several works by Ralf Dahrendorf. In his *Class and Class Conflict in Industrial Society* a portion of which is reproduced in the following pages, Dahrendorf analyzed in some detail what he termed the "two faces" of society. The structural functionalists held that every society is relatively persistent and consists of elements that are stable and integrated into the system. Each element has a function and contributes to the maintenance of the total system, and the social system is based on the consensus of its members. By contrast, Dahrendorf developed the conflict model, in which society is depicted as constantly engaged in the process of change resulting from the social conflict and dissent that are pervasive in the system. Rather than equilibrium and consensus, this model focuses on disintegration and coercion, as some dominate others in the struggle for power. Furthermore, consensus theorists, and particularly Talcott Parsons, viewed power as a medium of exchange, in which power holders enjoyed the trust of others to perform their duties and enlarge their scope of operation. Conflict theorists saw power as a zero-sum game in which there are winners and losers and where those with power dominate and control those who are powerless.

In further developing his conflict model, Dahrendorf argues that the sources of conflict in modern society stem from authority relations of domination and subordination that are ubiquitous in the system. "Imperatively coordinated associations" is the term he uses to describe associations in which those with authority roles dominate and control others. These associations, defined as basic social units which designate a specific organization of hierarchical roles can be of any size, and roles within them may tend to overlap. Rather than describe the structural composition of these groups, like Marx and Weber, Dahrendorf sought to characterize the conflict around them. All roles within these associations, he states, can be described as either ruling or ruled. Each set of roles competes for power, which is legitimized by the very structure of the group. When one subset succeeds in appropriating authority, it establishes new structures of integration to help maintain its control.

In a departure from Marx, however, Dahrendorf claims that authority positions in society are widely distributed and that it is possible to exercise authority in one setting but not in another. A corporation executive does not exercise his authority at a PTA meeting but does do so when he presides over the board of directors of the corporation. This position of Dahrendorf's leads him away from the class model of economic and political power that underlies so much of Marx's social theory.

In "Out of Utopia," an essay published in 1958, Dahrendorf characterizes Parsonian structural functionalism as utopian because real societies do not operate in the way in which Parsons claims they do. Utopian societies are characterized by the absence of change, the uniformity of their people, the universality of their consensus, and the absence of power struggles or intense conflicts of interest. Point by point, Dahrendorf demonstrates the affinity between consensus models and utopia. We have already noted the emphasis on equilibrium and consensus: in addition, Dahrendorf notes that deviant behavior is regarded as a temporary aberration, a failure of the socialization process rather than an expression of difference and dissent. Everything is too neatly laid out: the family performs the reproductive function and replenishes the society with fresh births; the educational system secures conformity and adherence to the rules through its function as an agent of socialization;

and the division of labor allocates the different roles that people must play in a complex economic system. However, he argues, there is one significant difference between the two: whereas utopias are generally critical of society and attempt to stimulate change, Parsonianism is a celebration and affirmation of the status quo.

It is important to note that although Dahrendorf did see dialectical social conflict as the fundamental ingredient of social dynamics, he did not think that conflict theory alone adequately described society. Rather, he chose to regard both functional or integration theory and conflict theory as conceptual tools which can be applied to illuminate the complexities of social systems. Dahrendorf accepted Marx's dichotomy of superstructure and substructure; he understood how both the political and ideological relations in the former and the economic relations in the latter can be detailed by either the functional or the conflict perspective. Dahrendorf also described how the concepts of integration and conflict can only be understood in contradistinction to each other; he thus asserts that society maintains tension between stasis and change, between consensus and coercion, and between function and conflict.

In *The Power Elite,* written in the mid-1950s, C. Wright Mills challenged the pluralistic and consensual model of American democracy. Influenced by Marx, Weber, and Pareto, Mills rejected the idea of a "ruling class" because it failed to capture the complexity of the American power structure and access to it. As the reader will note from the extract printed herein, Mills locates power within the corporate, military, and executive decision-making structures. The top echelons in the major corporations, the military establishment, and the executive branch of government make the key decisions affecting American society. Writing as he was during the Cold War, Mills saw a confluence of interest among these strategic elites in their definition of the national interest as requiring a strong military arsenal to repel and deter a Soviet adversary.

At the middle levels of power Mills describes the activities of pluralistic democracy at work, in Congress, in the parties, and in the conflict of interest groups. But he notes that the framework for their decisions is defined by the power elite and is given concrete expression in the privileged position of the military budget, which Congress accepts, and which is endorsed by the Executive and the Joint Chiefs of Staff and supported by the corporate elite.

At the base of this power pyramid is a manipulated mass society whose images of politics and whose information are conveyed by the mass media of communication. This is seen by Mills as supportive of the power elite and the consumer values of corporate capitalism. Democracy is thus frustrated by the lack of choice between parties, the consensus among the power elite about the national interest, and the collusive support of the mass media.

Mills's ideas were a powerful challenge to the consensus theories of the fifties and to the functionalist approaches to understanding social reality. Mills projected the emergence of a committed intelligentsia, operating out of the universities, that would challenge the dominant views of the power elite and bring the public into closer touch with its real interests.

In reading this essay by Mills, it is not only important to understand the model of power that he is developing but also to inquire as to its relevance to our contemporary politics. Has the end of the Cold War brought any changes to challenge the Mills analysis? What percentage of the federal budget now goes for military expenditures as opposed to social benefits like medicare, social welfare, and education? In an age of interactive computers, cable networks, radio and television talk shows, National Public Radio, and the Public Broadcasting Corporation, is the image of a passive and manipulated mass society still credible? And what can be said about the vitality of American democracy with the explosion of social movements such as the civil rights movement, the feminist movement, the gay liberation movement, and the environmental movement? Finally, has a "cultural elite" or a "knowledge elite" emerged, as some claim, to become the adversary of the "power elite"?

Richard L. Zweigenhaft and G. William Domhoff's updated study of the composition of the power elite, excerpted and printed below, brings to light a number of changes that have taken place in American society since the publication of Mills's original study. In particular, Zweigenhaft and Domhoff document significant changes in the composition of the power elite, particularly in respect to the inclusion of women and African-Americans and other minorities. Despite these changes, they nevertheless maintain that "class" continues to be a critically important feature of American society and politics. The student should bear in mind the following questions when reading this selection: Is diversity in the power elite an important development? What did the authors expect to be the consequences of this diversity and why are they disappointed? In what sense do the authors claim that "class" is still very significant?

RALF DAHRENDORF: SOCIAL STRUCTURE, GROUP INTERESTS, AND CONFLICT GROUPS

Integration and Values Versus Coercion and Interests: The Two Faces of Society

Throughout the history of Western political thought, two views of society have stood in conflict. Both these views are intended to explain what has been, and will probably continue to be, the most puzzling problem of social philosophy: how is it that human societies cohere? There is one large and distinguished school of thought according to which social order results from a general agreement of values, a *consensus omnium* or *volonté générale* which outweighs all possible or actual differences of opinion and interest. There is another equally distinguished school of thought which holds that coherence and order in society are founded on force and constraint, on the domination of some and the subjection of others. To be sure, these views are not at all points mutually exclusive. The Utopian (as we shall call those who insist on coherence by consensus) does not deny the existence of differences of interest; nor does the Rationalist (who believes in coherence by constraint and domination) ignore such agreements of value as are required for the very establishment of force. But Utopian and Rationalist alike advance claims of primacy for their respective standpoints. For the Utopian, differences of interest are subordinated to agreements of value, and for the Rationalist these agreements are but a thin, and as such ineffective, coating of the primary reality of differences that

have to be precariously reconciled by constraint. Both Utopians and Rationalists have shown much ingenuity and imagination in arguing for their respective points of view. This has not, however, led them more closely together. There is a genuine conflict of approach between Aristotle and Plato, Hobbes and Rousseau, Kant and Hegel, and this conflict has grown in intensity as the history of thought has advanced. Unless one believes that all philosophical disputes are spurious and ultimately irrelevant, the long history of the particular dispute about the problem of social order has exposed—if not solved—what appear to be fundamental alternatives of knowledge, moral decision, and political orientation.

Conflicting philosophical positions must inevitably, it seems to me, reappear constantly in theories of science. Even if this should not generally be the case, I would claim that the philosophical alternative of a Utopian or a Rational solution of the problem of order pervades modern sociological thinking even in its remotest manifestations. Here, as elsewhere, philosophical positions do not enter into scientific theories unchanged. Here, as elsewhere, they pass through the filter of logical supposition before they become relevant for testable explanations of problems of experience. The sociological Utopian does not claim that order *is based on* a general consensus of values, but that it *can be conceived of in terms of* such consensus, and that, if it is conceived of in these terms, certain propositions follow which are subject to the test of specific observations. Analogously, for the sociological Rationalist the assumption of the coercive nature of social order is a heuristic principle rather than a judgment of fact. But this obvious reservation does not prevent the Utopians and the Rationalists of sociology from engaging in disputes which are hardly less intense (if often rather less imaginative and ingenious) than those of their philosophical antecedents. The subject matter of our concern in this study demands that we take a stand with respect to this dispute.

Twice in our earlier considerations we have been faced with differences in the image of society—as I then called it—which correspond very closely to the conflicting views of Utopians and Rationalists. I have tried to show that, at least in so far as historical societies are concerned, Marx subscribed to an image of society of the Rational variety. He assumed the ubiquity of change and conflict as well as domination and subjection, and I suggest that this view seems particularly appropriate for the analysis of problems of conflict. In any case, it seems more appropriate than the Utopian view implicit in the works of Drucker and Mayo, according to which happy cooperation is the normal state of social life. Marx, or Drucker and Mayo, may not be especially convincing representatives of these views,[1] but the distinction with which we are concerned here is, in any case, not tied to their names. Generally speaking, it seems to me that two (meta-) theories can and must be distinguished in contemporary sociology. One of these, the *integration theory of society*, conceives of social structure in terms of a functionally integrated system held in equilibrium by certain patterned and recurrent processes. The other one, the *coercion theory of society*, views social structure as a form of organization held together by force and constraint and reaching continuously beyond itself in the

sense of producing within itself the forces that maintain it in an unending process of change. Like their philosophical counterparts, these theories are mutually exclusive. But—if I may be permitted a paradoxical formulation that will be explained presently—in sociology (as opposed to philosophy) a decision which accepts one of these theories and rejects the other is neither necessary nor desirable. There are sociological problems for the explanation of which the integration theory of society provides adequate assumptions; there are other problems which can be explained only in terms of the coercion theory of society; there are, finally, problems for which both theories appear adequate. For sociological analysis, society is Janus-headed, and its two faces are equivalent aspects of the same reality.

In recent years, the integration theory of society has clearly dominated sociological thinking. In my opinion, this prevalence of one partial view has had many unfortunate consequences. However, it has also had at least one agreeable consequence, in that the very one-sidedness of this theory gave rise to critical objections which enable us today to put this theory in its proper place. Such objections have been stimulated with increasing frequency by the works of the most eminent sociological theorist of integration, Talcott Parsons. It is not necessary here to attempt a comprehensive exposition of Parsons' position; nor do we have to survey the sizable literature concerned with a critical appraisal of this position. To be sure, much of this criticism is inferior in subtlety and insight to Parsons' work, so that it is hardly surprising that the sociological climate of opinion has remained almost unaffected by Parsons' critics. There is one objection to Parson's position, however, which we have to examine if we are to make a systematic presentation of a theory of group conflict. In a remarkable essay, D. Lockwood claims "that Parsons' array of concepts is heavily weighted by assumptions and categories which relate to the role of *normative* elements in social action, and especially to the processes

---

[1] This would be true, of course, for rather different reasons. Drucker and Mayo are rather lacking in subtlety, and it is therefore too easy to polemicize against their positions. Marx, on the other hand, is certainly subtle, but his notions of the "original" and the "terminal" societies of (imaginary) history demonstrate that he was but a limited Rationalist with strong Utopian leanings. Such mixtures of views really quite incompatible are in fact not rare in the history of social thought.

whereby motives are structured normatively to ensure social stability. On the other hand, what may be called the *substratum* of social action, especially as it conditions interests which are productive of social conflict and instability, tends to be ignored as a general determinant of the dynamics of social systems" (1, p. 136). Lockwood's claim touches on the core of our problem of the two faces of society—although his formulation does not, perhaps, succeed in exposing the problem with sufficient clarity.

It is certainly true that the work of Parsons displays a conspicuous bias in favor of analysis in terms of values and norms. It is equally true that many of those who have been concerned with problems of conflict rather than of stability have tended to emphasize not the normative but the institutional aspects of social structure. The work of Marx is a case in point. Probably, this difference in emphasis is no accident. It is nevertheless as such irrelevant to an understanding of or adoption of the alternative images of society which pervade political thought and sociological theory. The alternative between "normative elements in social action" and a factual "substratum of social action," which Lockwood takes over from the work of Renner, in fact indicates two levels of the analysis of social structure which are in no way contradictory. There is no theoretical reason why Talcott Parsons should not have supplemented (as indeed he occasionally does) his analysis of normative integration by an analysis of the integration of social systems in terms of their institutional substratum. However we look at social structure, it always presents itself as composed of a moral and a factual, a normative and an institutional, level or, in the doubtful terms of Marx, a superstructure and a substratum. The investigator is free to choose which of these levels he wants to emphasize more strongly—although he may be well-advised, in the interest of clarity as well as of comprehensiveness of his analysis, not to stress one of these levels to the exclusion of the other.

At the same time, there is an important element of genuine critique in Lockwood's objection to Parsons. When Lockwood contrasts stability and instability, integration and conflict, equilibrium and disequilibrium, values and interests, he puts his finger on a real alternative of thought, and one of which Parsons has apparently not been sufficiently aware. For of two equivalent models of society, Parsons has throughout his work recognized only one, the Utopian or integration theory of society. His "array of concepts" is therefore incapable of coping with those problems with which Lockwood is concerned in his critical essay, and which constitute the subject matter of the present study.

For purposes of exposition it seems useful to reduce each of the two faces of society to a small number of basic tenets, even if this involves some degree of oversimplification as well as overstatement. The integration theory of society, as displayed by the work of Parsons and other structural-functionalists, is founded on a number of assumptions of the following type:

1. Every society is a relatively persistent, stable structure of elements.
2. Every society is a well-integrated structure of elements.
3. Every element in a society has a function, i.e., renders a contribution to its maintenance as a system.
4. Every functioning social structure is based on a consensus of values among its members.

In varying forms, these elements of (1) stability, (2) integration, (3) functional coordination, and (4) consensus recur in all structural-functional approaches to the study of social structure. They are, to be sure, usually accompanied by protestations to the effect that stability, integration, functional coordination, and consensus are only "relatively" generalized. Moreover, these assumptions are not metaphysical propositions about the essence of society; they are merely assumptions for purposes of scientific analysis.

As such, however, they constitute a coherent view of the social process[2] which enables us to comprehend many problems of social reality.

However, it is abundantly clear that the integration approach to social analysis does not enable us to comprehend all problems of social reality. Let us look at two undeniably sociological problems of the contemporary world which demand explanation. (1) In recent years, an increasing number of industrial and commercial enterprises have introduced the position of personnel manager to cope with matters of hiring and firing, advice to employees, etc. Why? And: what are the consequences of the introduction of this new position? (2) On the 17th of June, 1953, the building workers of East Berlin put down their tools and went on a strike that soon led to a generalized revolt against the Communist regime of East Germany. Why? And: what are the consequences of this uprising? From the point of view of the integration model of society, the first of these problems is susceptible of a satisfactory solution. A special position to cope with personnel questions is functionally required by large enterprises in an age of rationalization and "social ethic"; the introduction of this position adapts the enterprise to the values of the surrounding society; its consequence is therefore of an integrative and stabilizing nature. But what about the second problem? Evidently, the uprising of the 17th of June is neither due to nor productive of integration in East German society. It documents and produces not stability, but instability. It contributes to the disruption, not the maintenance, of the existing system. It testifies to dissensus rather than consensus. The integration model tells us little more than that there are certain "strains" in the "system." In fact, in order to cope with problems of this kind we have to replace the integration theory of society by a different and, in many ways, contradictory model.

What I have called the coercion theory of society can also be reduced to a small number of basic tenets, although here again these assumptions oversimplify and overstate the case:

1. Every society is at every point subject to processes of change; social change is ubiquitous.
2. Every society displays at every point dissensus and conflict; social conflict is ubiquitous.
3. Every element in a society renders a contribution to its disintegration and change.
4. Every society is based on the coercion of some of its members by others.

If we return to the problem of the German workers' strike, it will become clear that this latter model enables us to deal rather more satisfactorily with its causes and consequences. The revolt of the building workers and their fellows in other industries can be explained in terms of coercion.[3] The revolting groups are engaged in a conflict which "functions" as an agent of change by disintegration. A ubiquitous phenomenon is expressed, in this case, in an exceptionally intense and violent way, and further explanation will have to account for this violence on the basis of the acceptance of conflict and change as universal features of social life. I need hardly add that, like the integration model, the coercion theory of society constitutes but a set of assumptions for purposes of

---

[2] It is important to emphasize that "stability" as a tenet of the integration theory of society does not mean that societies are "static." It means, rather, that such processes as do occur (and the structural-functional approach is essentially concerned with processes) serve to maintain the patterns of the system as a whole. Whatever criticism I have of this approach, I do not want to be misunderstood as attributing to it a "static bias" (which has often been held against this approach without full consideration of its merits).

[3] For purposes of clarity, I have deliberately chosen an example from a totalitarian state. But coercion is meant here in a very general sense, and the coercion model is applicable to all societies, independent of their specific political structure.

scientific analysis and implies no claim for philosophical validity—although, like its counterpart, this model also provides a coherent image of social organization.

Now, I would claim that, in a sociological context, neither of these models can be conceived as exclusively valid or applicable. They constitute complementary, rather than alternative, aspects of the structure of total societies as well as of every element of this structure. We have to choose between them only for the explanation of specific problems; but in the conceptual arsenal of sociological analysis they exist side by side. Whatever criticism one may have of the advocates of one or the other of these models can therefore be directed only against claims for the exclusive validity of either.[4] Strictly speaking, both models are "valid" or, rather, useful and necessary for sociological analysis. We cannot conceive of society unless we realize the dialectics of stability and change, integration and conflict, function and motive force, consensus and coercion. In the context of this study, I regard this point as demonstrated by the analysis of the exemplary problems sketched above.

It is perhaps worth emphasizing that the thesis of the two faces of social structure does not require a complete, or even partial, revision of the conceptual apparatus that by now has become more or less generally accepted by sociologists in all countries. Categories like role, institution, norm, structure, even function are as useful in terms of the coercion model as they are for the analysis of social integration. In fact, the dichotomy of aspects can be carried through all levels of sociological analysis; that is, it can be shown that, like social structure itself, the notions of role and institution, integration and function, norm and substratum have two faces which may be expressed by two terms, but which may also in many cases be indicated by an extension of concepts already in use. "Interest and value," Radcliffe-Brown once remarked, "are correlative terms, which refer to the two sides of an asymmetrical relation" (2, p. 199). The notions of interest and value indeed seem to describe very well the two faces of the normative superstructure of society: what appears as a consensus of values on the basis of the integration theory can be regarded as a conflict of interests in terms of the coercion theory. Similarly, what appears on the level of the factual substratum as integration from the point of view of the former model presents itself as coercion or constraint from the point of view of the latter. We shall presently have occasion to explore these two faces of societies and their elements rather more thoroughly with reference to the two categories of power and of role.

While logically feasible,[5] the solution of the dilemma of political thought which we have offered here for the more restricted field of sociological analysis nevertheless raises a number of serious problems. It is evidently virtually impossible to think of society in terms of either model without positing its opposite number at the same time. There can be no conflict, unless this conflict occurs within a context of meaning, i.e., some kind of coherent "system." No conflict is conceivable between French housewives and Chilean chess players, because these groups are not united by, or perhaps "integrated into," a common frame of reference. Analogously, the notion of integration makes little sense unless it presupposes the existence of different elements that are integrated. Even Rousseau derived his

---

[4] This, it seems to me, is the only—if fundamental—legitimate criticism that can be raised against Parsons' work on this general level. In *The Social System,* Parsons repeatedly advances, for the integration theory of society, a claim that it is the nucleus of "the general" sociological theory—a claim which I regard as utterly unjustified. It is Lockwood's main concern also, in the essay quoted above, to reject this claim to universal validity.

[5] As is demonstrated most clearly by the fact that a similar situation can be encountered in physics with respect to the theory of light. Here, too, there are two seemingly incompatible theories which nevertheless exist side by side, and each of which has its proper realm of empirical phenomena: the wave theory and the quantum theory of light.

volonté générale from a modified *bellum omnium contra omnes.* Using one or the other model is therefore a matter of emphasis rather than of fundamental difference; and there are, as we shall see, many points at which a theory of group conflict has to have recourse to the integration theory of social structure.

Inevitably, the question will be raised, also, whether a unified theory of society that includes the tenets of both the integration and the coercion models of society is not at least conceivable—for as to its desirability there can be little doubt. Is there, or can there be, a general point of view that synthesizes the unsolved dialectics of integration and coercion? So far as I can see, there is no such general model; as to its possibility, I have to reserve judgment. It seems at least conceivable that unification of theory is not feasible at a point which has puzzled thinkers ever since the beginning of Western philosophy.

For the explanation of the formation of conflict groups out of conditions of social structure, we shall employ a model that emphasizes the ugly face of society. In the following sections of this chapter I shall try to show how, on the assumption of the coercive nature of social structure, relations of authority become productive of clashes of role interest which under certain conditions lead to the formation of organized antagonistic groups within limited social organizations as well as within total societies. By proceeding step by step along these lines, we shall eventually be in a position to contrast the rudiments of a sociological theory of group conflict with such earlier approaches as have been discussed in the first part of this study, and to decide whether the category of class is still a useful tool of sociological analysis.

Power and Authority

From the point of view of the integration theory of social structure, units of social analysis ("social systems") are essentially voluntary associations of people who share certain values and set up institutions in order to ensure the smooth functioning of cooperation. From the point of view of coercion theory, however, the units of social analysis present an altogether different picture. Here, it is not voluntary cooperation or general consensus but enforced constraint that makes social organizations cohere. In institutional terms, this means that in every social organization some positions are entrusted with a right to exercise control over other positions in order to ensure effective coercion; it means, in other words, that there is a differential distribution of power and authority. One of the central theses of this study consists in the assumption that this differential distribution of authority invariably becomes the determining factor of systematic social conflicts of a type that is germane to class conflicts in the traditional (Marxian) sense of this term. The structural origin of such group conflicts must be sought in the arrangement of social roles endowed with expectations of domination or subjection. Wherever there are such roles, group conflicts of the type in question are to be expected. Differentiation of groups engaged in such conflicts follows the lines of differentiation of roles that are relevant from the point of view of the exercise of authority. Identification of variously equipped authority roles is the first task of conflict analysis;[6] conceptually and empirically all further steps of analysis follow from the investigation of distributions of power and authority.

"Unfortunately, the concept of power is not a settled one in the social sciences, either in political science or in sociology" (Parsons: 3, p. 139). Max Weber, Pareto, Mosca, later Russell, Bendix, Lasswell, and others have explored some of the dimensions of this category; they have not, however, reached such a degree of consensus as

---

[6] To facilitate communication, I shall employ in this study a number of abbreviations. These must not however be misunderstood. Thus, "conflict analysis" in this context stands for "analysis of group conflict of the class type, class being understood in the traditional sense." At no point do I want to imply a claim for a generalized theory of social conflict.

would enable us to employ the categories of power and authority without at least brief conceptual preliminaries. So far as the terms "power" and "authority" and their distinction are concerned, I shall follow in this study the useful and well-considered definitions of Max Weber. For Weber, power is the "probability that one actor within a social relationship will be in a position to carry out his own will despite resistance, regardless of the basis on which this probability rests"; whereas authority *(Herrschaft)* is the "probability that a command with a given specific content will be obeyed by a given group of persons" (3, p. 28). The important difference between power and authority consists in the fact that whereas power is essentially tied to the personality of individuals, authority is always associated with social positions or roles. The demagogue has power over the masses to whom he speaks or whose actions he controls; but the control of the officer over his men, the manager over his workers, the civil servant over his clientele is authority, because it exists as an expectation independent of the specific person occupying the position of officer, manager, civil servant. It is only another way of putting this difference if we say—as does Max Weber—that while power is merely a factual relation, authority is a legitimate relation of domination and subjection. In this sense, authority can be described as legitimate power.

In the present study we are concerned exclusively with relations of authority, for these alone are part of social structure and therefore permit the systematic derivation of group conflicts from the organization of total societies and associations within them. The significance of such group conflicts rests with the fact that they are not the product of structurally fortuitous relations of power but come forth wherever authority is exercised—and that means in all societies under all historical conditions. (1) Authority relations are always relations of super- and subordination. (2) Where there are authority relations, the superordinate element is socially expected to control, by orders and commands, warnings and

prohibitions, the behavior of the subordinate element. (3) Such expectations attach to relatively permanent social positions rather than to the character of individuals; they are in this sense legitimate. (4) By virtue of this fact, they always involve specification of the persons subject to control and of the spheres within which control is permissible.[7] Authority, as distinct from power, is never a relation of generalized control over others. (5) Authority being a legitimate relation, noncompliance with authoritative commands can be sanctioned; it is indeed one of the functions of the legal system (and of course of quasi-legal customs and norms) to support the effective exercise of legitimate authority.

Alongside the term "authority," we shall employ (and have employed) in this study the terms "domination" and "subjection." These will be used synonymously with the rather clumsy expressions "endowed with authority" or "participating in the exercise of authority" (domination), and "deprived of authority" or "excluded from the exercise of authority" (subjection).

It seems desirable for purposes of conflict analysis to specify the relevant unit of social organization in analogy to the concept of social system in the analysis of integration. To speak of specification here is perhaps misleading. "Social system" is a very general concept applicable to all types of organization; and we shall want to employ an equally general concept which differs from that of social system by emphasizing a different aspect of the same organizations. It seems to me that Max Weber's category "imperatively

---

[7] This element of the definition of authority is crucial. It implies that the manager who tries to control people outside his firm, or the private lives of people inside his firm, trespasses the borderline between authority and power. Although he has authority over people in his firm, his control assumes the form of power as soon as it goes beyond the specified persons and spheres of legitimate control. This type of trespassing is of course frequent in every authority relation; and an empirical phenomenon well worth investigating is to what extent the fusion of authority and power tends to intensify group conflicts.

coordinated association" *(Herrschaftsverband)* serves this purpose despite its clumsiness.[8]

In conflict analysis we are concerned *inter alia* with the generation of conflict groups by the authority relations obtaining in imperatively coordinated associations. Since imperative coordination, or authority, is a type of social relation present in every conceivable social organization, it will be sufficient to describe such organizations simply as associations. Despite prolonged terminological discussions, no general agreement has been attained by sociologists on the precise meaning of the categories "organization," "association," and "institution." If I am not mistaken in my interpretation of the trend of terminological disputes, it appears justifiable to use the term "association" in such a way as to imply the coordination of organized aggregates of roles by domination and subjection. The state, a church, an enterprise, but also a political party, a trade union, and a chess club are associations in this sense. In all of them, authority relations exist; for all of them, conflict analysis is therefore applicable. If at a later stage we shall suggest restriction to the two great associations of the state and the industrial enterprise, this suggestion is dictated merely by considerations of empirical significance, not logical (or definitional) difference. In looking at social organizations not in terms of their integration and coherence but from the point of view of their structure of coercion and constraint, we regard them as (imperatively coordinated) associations rather than as social systems. Because social organizations are also associations, they generate conflicts of interest and become the birthplace of conflict groups.

I have assumed in the preceding remarks that authority is a characteristic of social organizations as general as society itself. Despite the assertion of Renner—and other modern sociologists—that in some contemporary societies the exercise of authority has been eliminated and replaced by the more anonymous "rule of the law" or other nonauthoritative relations, I should indeed maintain that authority is a universal element of social structure. It is in this sense more general than, for example, property, or even status. With respect to postcapitalist industrial society, I hope to establish this position more unambiguously in the final chapters of this study. Generally speaking, however, the universality of authority relations would seem evident as soon as we describe these relations in a "passive" rather than in an "active" sense. Authority relations exist wherever there are people whose actions are subject to legitimate and sanctioned prescriptions that originate outside them but within social structure. This formulation, by leaving open who exercises what kind of authority, leaves little doubt as to the omnipresence of some kind of authority somehow exercised. For it is evident that there are many forms and types of authority in historical societies. There are differences of a considerable order of magnitude between the relations of the citizen of classical Athens and his slaves, the feudal landlord and his villains and serfs, the nineteenth-century capitalist and his workers, the secretary of a totalitarian state party and its members, the appointed manager of a modern enterprise and its employees, or the elected prime minister of a democratic country and the electorate. No attempt will be made in this study to develop a typology of authority. But it is assumed throughout that the existence of domination and subjection is a common feature of all possible types of authority and, indeed, of all possible types of association and organization.

The notion of power and authority employed in the present study represents what Parsons in a critical review of C. W. Mill's book

---

[8] Parsons, in his translation of Weber's *Wirtschaft und Gesellschaft,* suggests "imperatively coordinated group." Any translation of Weber's term is bound to be somewhat awkward, but it seems to me that the word "group" in Parsons' translation is false. Weber uses *Verband,* e.g., to describe the state, or a church—units of organization which can hardly be called "groups." "Association" is probably as precise an English equivalent of *Verband* as is likely to be found.

on the American power elite calls the "zero-sum" concept of authority. Parsons objects to this concept, and his argument provides a welcome opportunity to clarify our notion somewhat further and relate it to the two models distinguished above. "The essential point at present is that, to Mills [and of course to us in this study—R. D.], power is not a facility for the performance of function in and on behalf of the society as a system, but is interpreted exclusively as a facility for getting what one group, the holders of power, wants by preventing another group, the 'outs,' from getting what it wants" (4, p. 139). This statement is unobjectionable, and in so far as Mills really uses power "exclusively" in the "zero-sum" sense, I should tend to agree also with Parsons' critique. But then Parsons continues, in the same passage, to make the same mistake in the opposite direction, and to make it deliberately and consideredly: "What this conception does is to elevate *a secondary and derived aspect of a total phenomenon* into the central place" [italics mine]. Not surprisingly, Parsons continues to point out what is presumably the primary and original aspect of the total phenomenon: "It is the capacity to mobilize the resources of the society for the attainment of goals for which a general 'public' commitment has been made, or may be made. It is mobilization, above all, of the action of persons and groups, which is binding on them by virtue of their position in the society" (4, p. 140). A clearer exposition of the two faces of society, and of the untenable and dangerous one-sidedness of Parsons' position, is hardly conceivable.

It is certainly true that for many purposes of analysis, power or—as I should prefer to say—authority, both realizes and symbolizes the functional integration of social systems. To use a pertinent illustration: in many contexts, the elected president or prime minister of democratic countries[9] represents his country as a whole; his position expresses therefore the unity and integration of a nation. In other contexts, however, the chief of government is but the representative of the majority party, and therefore exponent of sectional interests. I suggest that as in the position of the prime minister neither of these elements is primary or secondary, thus neither the integrative nor the disruptive aspect of authority in social analysis is primary or secondary. Like all other elements of social structure, authority has two faces—those, so to speak, of Mills and Parsons—and on the highest level of abstraction it is illegitimate to emphasize either of these to the exclusion of the other. Authority is certainly not *only* productive of conflict; but neither is it *only* (or even primarily) "a facility for the performance of function in and on behalf of the society as a system." If we are concentrating in this study on what Parsons would call the "negative functions" of authority, we do so because this aspect is more appropriate and useful for the analysis of structurally generated systematic social conflicts.

In referring to the ugly face of authority as a "zero-sum" concept, Parsons brings out one further aspect of this category which is essential for our considerations. By zero-sum, Parsons evidently means that from the point of view of the disruptive "functions" of authority there are two groups or aggregates of persons, of which one possesses authority to the extent to which the other one is deprived of it.[10] This implies—for us, if not for Parsons—that in terms of the coercion theory of society we can always observe a dichotomy of positions in imperatively coordinated associations with respect to the distribution of authority. Parsons, in his critique of Mills, compares the distribution of authority to the distribution of wealth. It

---

[9] This illustration is unambiguous with respect to the president of the United States. Elsewhere, the representative and the governmental functions are usually separated; in these cases I mean not the head of state (king, president), but the chief of government (prime minister, chancellor).

[10] There is one implication of the expression "zero-sum" which would be contrary to my thesis. Mathematically, it would be possible for both groups to have no authority in the sense of a complete absence of authority. I have argued above that under all conditions the authority of one aggregate is, so to speak, greater than zero, and that of the other aggregate correspondingly smaller than zero. The presence of authority, and its unequal distribution, are universal features of social structure.

seems to me that this comparison is misleading. However unequally wealth may be distributed, there always is a continuum of possession ranging from the lowest to the highest rank. Wealth is not and cannot be conceived as a zero-sum concept. With respect to authority, however, a clear line can at least in theory be drawn between those who participate in its exercise in given associations and those who are subject to the authoritative commands of others. Our analysis of modern societies in later chapters will show that empirically it is not always easy to identify the border line between domination and subjection. Authority has not remained unaffected by the modern process of division of labor. But even here, groups or aggregates can be identified which do not participate in the exercise of authority other than by complying with given commands or prohibitions. Contrary to all criteria of social stratification, authority does not permit the construction of a scale. So-called hierarchies of authority (as displayed, for example, in organization charts) are in fact hierarchies of the "plus-side" of authority, i.e., of the differentiation of domination; but there is, in every association, also a "minus-side" consisting of those who are subjected to authority rather than participate in its exercise.

In two respects this analysis has to be specified, if not supplemented. First, for the individual incumbent of roles, domination in one association does not necessarily involve domination in all others to which he belongs, and subjection, conversely, in one association does not mean subjection in all. The dichotomy of positions of authority holds for specific associations only. In a democratic state, there are both mere voters and incumbents of positions of authority such as cabinet ministers, representatives, and higher civil servants. But this does not mean that the "mere voter" cannot be incumbent of a position of authority in a different context, say, in an industrial enterprise; conversely, a cabinet minister may be, in his church, a mere member, i.e., subject to the authority of others. Although empirically a certain correlation of the authority positions of individuals in different associations

seems likely, it is by no means general and is in any case a matter of specific empirical conditions. It is at least possible, if not probable, that if individuals in a given society are ranked according to the sum total of their authority positions in all associations, the resulting pattern will not be a dichotomy but rather like scales of stratification according to income or prestige. For this reason it is necessary to emphasize that in the sociological analysis of group conflict the unit of analysis is always a specific association and the dichotomy of positions within it.

As with respect to the set of roles associated with an individual, total societies, also, do not usually present an unambiguously dichotomic authority structure. There are a large number of imperatively coordinated associations in any given society. Within every one of them we can distinguish the aggregates of those who dominate and those who are subjected. But since domination in industry does not necessarily involve domination in the state, or a church, or other associations, total societies can present the picture of a plurality of competing dominant (and, conversely, subjected) aggregates. This, again, is a problem for the analysis of specific historical societies and must not be confounded with the clearer lines of differentiation within any one association. Within the latter, the distribution of authority always sums up to zero, i.e., there always is a division involving domination and subjection.[11]

I need hardly emphasize that from the point of view of "settling" the concepts of power and

---

[11] Inevitably, the qualifications introduced in the two preceding paragraphs are rather vague if stated merely in the abstract. They are, however, of the utmost importance for empirical analysis. By strictly postulating imperatively coordinated associations as units of conflict analysis, we are able to consider, e.g., the relations between industry and society as an empirical problem which allows of varying solutions in different historical contexts. Similarly we can, by this emphasis, regard subjection (and consequent deprivation) in several associations as a condition strengthening and intensifying conflict, but by no means necessary in historical situations. These and similar problems will become increasingly crucial as our investigation proceeds.

authority, the preceding discussion has raised more problems than it has solved. I believe, however, that for the purposes of this study, and of a sociological theory of conflict, little needs to be added to what has been stated here. In order somewhat to substantiate this perhaps rather bold assertion, it seems useful to recapitulate briefly the heuristic purpose and logical status of the considerations of this section.

I have introduced, as a structural determinant of conflict groups, the category of authority as exercised in imperatively coordinated associations. While agreeing with Marx that source and level of income—even socioeconomic status—cannot usefully be conceived as determinants of conflict groups, I have added to this list of erroneous approaches Marx's own in terms of property in the means of production. Authority is both a more general and a more significant social relation. The former has been shown in our critique of Marx; the latter will have to be demonstrated by subsequent considerations and analyses. The concept of authority is used, in this context, in a specific sense. It is differentiated from power by what may roughly be referred to as the element of legitimacy; and it has to be understood throughout in the restricted sense of authority as distributed and exercised in imperatively coordinated associations. While its "disruptive" or conflict-generating consequences are not the only aspect of authority, they are the one relevant in terms of the coercion model of society. Within the frame of reference of this model, (1) the distribution of authority in associations is the ultimate "cause" of the formation of conflict groups, and (2), being dichotomous, it is, in any given association, the cause of the formation of two, and only two, conflict groups.

The first of these statements is logically an assumption, since it underlies scientific theories. It cannot as such be tested by observation; its validity is proven, rather, by its usefulness for purposes of explanation. We shall derive from this assumption certain more specific hypotheses which, if refuted, would take the assumption

with them into the waste-paper basket of scientific theories. We assume in this sense that if we manage to identify the incumbents of positions of domination and subjection in any given association, we have identified the contenders of one significant type of conflicts—conflicts which occur in this association at all times.

As to the second statement, the one concerned with the dichotomy of authority positions in imperatively coordinated associations, it is not, I suggest, either an assumption or an empirical hypothesis, but an analytical statement. It follows from and is implicit in the very concept of authority that within specified contexts some have authority and others not. If either nobody or everybody had authority, the concept would lose its meaning. Authority implies both domination and subjection, and it therefore implies the existence of two distinct sets of positions or persons. This is not to say, of course, that there is no difference between those who have a great deal and those who have merely a little authority. Among the positions of domination there may be, and often is, considerable differentiation. But such differentiation, while important for empirical analysis, leaves unaffected the existence of a border line somewhere between those who have whatever little authority and the "outs." Strictly speaking, an analytical statement which states that there is a dichotomy of authority positions is tautological; but as this example shows, there are tautologies which are worth stating.

Having thus established the frame of reference and basic assumptions of a sociological theory of conflict, we now turn to its more specific elements—first with respect to patterns of conflicts between these groups.

* * *

"Elites" and "Ruling Classes"

Our model of conflict group formation stipulates the existence of two opposed groupings in any given association. Each of these groups shares certain features, and each differs from the other by contradictory orientations of interest. Before concluding the abstract discussion of the model and the examination of some of its empirical consequences we may ask what, if anything, can be stated in general about the two groups thus distinguished. Independent of particular empirical conditions, are there any features that characterize or otherwise distinguish the occupants of positions of domination and their interest groups from those of positions of subjection? It appears useful to discuss this problem with reference to the theories of three sociologists whose work is here representative and has heretofore in this discussion deliberately been mentioned only occasionally. I mean Pareto, Mosca, and Aron, whose conceptions resemble ours in several points. Of the three, Mosca takes the most explicit stand on the problem at hand, and his conception will therefore require particular attention.

The chief element of the model of class formation consists in the explanation of conflicts of interest groups in terms of quasi-groups determined by the distribution of authority in imperatively coordinated associations. We share this emphasis on authority structures with all three authors mentioned, whose work might therefore be described as the proximate origin of a theory of conflict of the type here proposed.[12] Since they argue in terms of authority, Pareto, Mosca, and Aron also operate with a two-class model. It is characteristic of all of them, however, that they concentrate their attention—unlike Marx, Weber, and many others—on the group possessing authority, the members of which occupy, in other words, positions of domination. We shall presently consider some of the implications of this emphasis on dominating groups for the

analysis of subjected groups and of group conflict in general. In describing dominating conflict groups the authors in question use primarily two concepts. Mosca refers almost exclusively to the "political class" which, in the German and English translations of his *Elementi di Scienza Politica*, has become a "ruling class." Pareto introduces for this group the much-disputed category of "elite"; however, he distinguishes "governing" and "nongoverning" elites (5, p. 222) and devotes as much attention to the latter as to the former. Aron has narrowed down the notion of "elite" to the "minority" that "exercises power" (6, p. 567); elsewhere, he speaks of "ruling classes." Without entering into terminological disputes, I propose to examine the general characteristics ascribed by these three authors to dominating groups and the validity of their analyses.

In their way of posing the problem, the approaches of Pareto, Mosca, and Aron entail at many points indications of the sociological theory of group conflict as we understand it. All three authors deal with the problem of inertia, i.e., the tendency of dominating groups to maintain and defend their domination. They also deal with the role of legitimacy in the maintenance or change of authority structures. Mosca and Pareto, in particular, emphasize the problem of social mobility to which we shall have to return. As to the psychology of conflict groups, their works contain many a useful suggestion. They discuss in some detail the formation and disintegration of "aristocracies" as well as other types of social change, basing their analyses on thorough historical documentation. If for the discussion of this section I select only five aspects of the theories of Pareto, Mosca, and Aron, it is because this selection is guided by the intention to combine a critical examination of these theories with some discussion of the general characteristics of dominating conflict groups.

(1) Even in his definition of dominating groups, Aron refers to these as "minorities." Mosca does not hesitate to elaborate this into the

---

[12] To this list other names would obviously have to be added, among them, above all, Max Weber. However, Weber has failed to connect his theory of power and authority with the analysis of conflict. Contrary to Aron's, Pareto's, and Mosca's, his work is suggestive rather than directly indicative of the approach of the present study.

general thesis that the ruling class is "always the less numerous" group. The notion of an elite appears to evoke almost automatically the idea of the "chosen few," of a small ruling stratum. Thus, even Marx describes the action of the proletariat as the "independent movement of the overwhelming majority in the interest of the overwhelming majority" (7, pp. 20 f.), and almost as a matter of course Geiger, in his graphical schema of class structure (8, p. 43), represents the ruling class by a segment of the whole (circle) much smaller than the subjected class. That dominating groups are by comparison with their subjected counterpart often insignificantly small groupings is an assumption which to my knowledge has never been contested in the literature. Not all authors state as clearly as Machiavelli how small, exactly, these groups are: "In any city, however it may be organized politically, no more than 40 or 50 men attain real power" (9, p. 271). Mosca, in particular, supplements his political class by "another, much more numerous stratum including all those who are suited for leading position" (9, p. 329); but by this extension he merely obliterates his analysis without abandoning the minority character of elites. In fact, the assumption that in any association the number of those subjected to authority is larger than the number of those in possession of authority does seem capable of generalization. It seems hard to imagine an association in which the "rulers" outweigh the "ruled" in number. In every state, the number of cabinet ministers is smaller than the number of citizens; in every enterprise there are fewer executives than employees. However, this seemingly general statement requires qualification for industrial societies at an advanced stage of development. Today, one is hardly surprised to find that in many modern industrial enterprises almost one-third of all employees exercise superordinate functions. Delegation of authority in industry, in the state, and in other associations makes possible in industrial societies dominating groups which are no longer small minorities but which in size hardly fall short of subjected

groups. We have earlier examined some of the problems of delegated authority and we shall return to this point. By way of generalization, these phenomena justify at least the negative statement that it seems to be one of the characteristics of industrial societies that those who are plainly subjected to authority in imperatively coordinated associations of many types not only do not any longer amount to the "overwhelming majority" but actually decrease steadily. Pareto's, Mosca's, and Aron's thesis of a small ruling minority requires correction. Legitimate power may be distributed, if with considerable gradations of spheres of authority, over a large number of positions.

(2) Pareto and Mosca characterize dominating groups by a number of peculiar properties which are alleged to be necessary for a group to attain and successfully defend its position of power. Pareto emphasizes "energy" and "superiority" (5, p. 230), an "instinct of combination," concentration on the proximate, and similar "properties" (e.g., pp. 242 f.). Mosca goes even further; for him "the ruling minorities usually consist of individuals who are superior to the mass of the ruled in material, intellectual, and even moral respects, or they are at least the descendants of individuals who had such virtues. To put it differently, the members of the ruling minority generally have real or apparent properties which are highly esteemed and convey great influence in their societies" (9, p. 55). This kind of thesis illustrates that pre-sociological character of Mosca's analyses, i.e., the speculative recourse from social structures and roles to individuals and their "properties," which hardly helps our insight into social relations. Without the full consistency of the Aristotelian argument, Mosca approximates the notion that certain people are "by nature" rulers or ruled, freemen or slaves. This notion, however, in whatever variant it may appear, has to be banned radically and finally from the sociological theory of group conflict.

Whether dominating conflict groups are characterized by attributes and patterns of behavior other than common manifest interests is a question that can be answered only by empirical observation and in relation to specific social conditions. This is in fact the question with which we have dealt above in terms of "class culture." It is certainly possible that there are societies in which dominating groups are also distinguished by patterns of behavior crystallized hypothetically in "properties"; but it is at least equally possible that the coherence of such groups is confined to the defense of common interests within well-defined units of social organization without significantly affecting other spheres of the behavior of the members of ruling groups. From the point of view of the theory of group conflict, the "properties" of individual group members are in principle indeterminate and variable.

(3) Mosca consistently derives from two untenable postulates—the minority character of ruling groups and the existence of a common culture among them—the conclusion that dominating conflict groups are always better organized than subjected groups. "The minority is organized simply because it is the minority" (9, p. 55). Like its premises, this conclusion can by no means be assumed; it is, rather, an empirical generalization, and one demonstrably false. Within the association of industry, for example, it would appear that there are greater obstacles to the formation of an interest group on behalf of the incumbents of positions of domination (because of the far-going internal differentiation of this quasi-group?) than is the case for the subjected workers. At the very least, we can say that we know of no point of view that would permit the postulate that a transition from quasi-groups to interest groups is easier for dominating than for subjected groups.[13]

---

[13] To clarify this problem fully one would have to consider all the conditions of organization. Thus it might be feasible to make an empirical generalization to the effect that in pre-industrial societies ruling groups were (above all because of easier communication) provided with better conditions than subjected groups. In industrial societies, however, this clearly does not hold.

(4) Mosca, and to some extent Pareto, means by the name "ruling class" only the incumbents of positions of domination in the political society. Pareto recognizes elites in all spheres and associations of society, but "governing elites" are for him politically governing elites. Mosca limits the field of his analyses by the very concept of "political class." It is only Aron who intimates an extension of this approach by emphasizing "the distinction between the political power of classes, founded on the position occupied in the state by their representatives, and their economic power, determined by their place in the process of production" (6, p. 572). Yet Aron also presupposes the unity of a class ruling in all spheres in which authority is exercised. In so far as this presupposition implies a restriction of conflict analysis to the association of the political state, it is unnecessary and, indeed, disadvantageous; in so far as it implies the assertion that the "political class" is *eo ipso* the ruling group in all other spheres of society, it is once again an untenable empirical generalization. One of the shortcomings of the theories of Mosca, of Pareto, and, to some extent, of Aron is that although these authors derive conflict groups from relations of authority, they fail to relate these to the crucial category of imperatively coordinated associations.

Ruling groups are, in the first place, no more than ruling groups within defined associations. In theory, there can be as many competing, conflicting, or coexisting dominating conflict groups in a society as there are associations. Whether and in what way certain associations—such as industry and society—are connected in given societies is a subject for empirical analysis. Without doubt, such analysis is of considerable significance for a theory of conflict. Nevertheless, it is analytically necessary and empirically fruitful to retain the possibility of a competition or even conflict between the ruling groups of different associations. In this sense, the expression "ruling class" is, in the singular, quite misleading.

(5) Of the three authors under discussion, Mosca in particular has fallen victim to a Marxian overestimation of class analysis. If Pareto claims that history is "a cemetery of aristocracies" (5, p. 229), he leaves it open whether group conflicts or other forces caused the death of ruling elites. But Mosca is quite explicit: "One could explain the whole history of civilized mankind in terms of the conflict between the attempt of the rulers to monopolize and bequeath political power and the attempt of new forces to change the relations of power" (9, p. 64 f.). This is hardly more than a reformulation of the Marxian thesis "the history of all hitherto society is the history of class struggles" (7, p. 6). Mosca's statement is therefore subject to the same objections. Ruling groups in the sense of the theory here advanced do by no means determine the entire "level of culture of a people" (9, p. 54). As coercion theory emphasizes but one aspect of social structure, thus the distinction between ruling and subjected groups is but one element of society. It would be false to identify the upper stratum of a society unequivocally with its ruling conflict group. There is no need for these two to be identical with respect to their personnel, nor do these categories, even if the personnel of upper stratum and ruling conflict groups are the same, describe the same aspect of social behavior. In any case, ruling classes or conflict groups decide not so much the "level of civilization" of a society as the dynamics of the associations in which they originated.

"Masses" and "Suppressed Classes"

It is a significant if confusing trait of the theories of Pareto and Mosca that both of them are concerned less with the explanation of social change than with that of stability or, as Pareto explicitly says at many points, of "equilibrium." By concentrating their attention primarily on the "elite" or "ruling class," they tend to reduce

all changes to changes in the composition of the ruling class, i.e., to one type of social mobility.[14] Pareto's "circulation of elites" and Mosca's emphasis on the "ability" of a people "to produce in its womb new forces suited for leadership" (9, p. 227) aim at the same phenomenon, i.e., the regeneration of a leading stratum which is assumed to be universally procured by individual mobility. By virtue of this emphasis the theories of Pareto and Mosca take a strange turn of which their authors are probably not aware. Although both of them originally refer to two classes (5, p. 226; 9, p. 52), their approach gradually and barely noticeably reduces itself to a "one-class model," in which only the ruling group functions as a class proper. Pareto characteristically speaks, by way of introducing the notion of "circulation of elites," of "two groups, the elite and the *rest of the population*" (5, p. 226), and Mosca similarly distinguishes at one point "the subjected *masses*" and "the political class" (9, p. 53).[15] Both notions, however—that of a "rest of the population" and that of "masses"— are basically residual categories defined by privation and not considered as independently operative forces. It need hardly be mentioned that this procedure robs any theory of conflict of its substance. At this point we see the crucial difference between elite theories and conflict theories in the sense of the present study.

The almost unnoticed transition from conflict theory to elite theory in the works of Pareto and Mosca has one aspect of some significance for our context. This becomes apparent if we contrast this modification with Marx's approach (which at times almost appears to commit the opposite mistake and to recognize only the proletariat as a class). The thesis might be advanced that in post-classical history of Europe the

---

[14] Quite consistently, then, revolutions are, for Pareto and Mosca, abnormal events which betray the weakness of an elite, namely its inability to rejuvenate by absorbing new members.

[15] Italics in both quotations mine.

industrial workers of the nineteenth century constituted, indeed, the first subjected group that managed to establish itself as such, i.e., that left the stage of quasi-group and organized itself as an interest group. Thus, earlier "suppressed classes" could quite properly be described as "masses" or "rest of the population," that is, as quasi-groups such as the French peasants of Marx's "18th Brumaire," who provided—as Mosca argues along lines similar to Marx's in his study of Louis Bonaparte—merely a basis of legitimacy and "support" of competing "groups within the political class." We need not settle this question here. But the fact that it can be raised provides a further reason why I have chosen to limit this study—contrary to Pareto and Mosca as well as Marx—to industrial societies. Perhaps it is feasible to make the general assertion that, in principle, ruling and suppressed classes have, in industrial societies, equal chances of organization, because in these societies one obstacle to the organization of subjected groups characteristic for most earlier societies is removed: the impossibility of communication. Although I suspect that the theory formulated in this study might be extended in such a way as to apply to pre-industrial societies also, I shall confine myself to applying it to societies in which manifest conflicts of organized interest groups are empirically possible.

Subjected conflict groups must therefore not be visualized as essentially unorganized masses without effective force. In analogy to the characteristics of ruling groups we can state (a) that they do not necessarily comprise the majority of the members of an association, (b) that their members are not necessarily connected by "properties" or a "culture" beyond the interests that bind them into groups, and (c) that their existence is always related to particular associations, so that one society may display several subjected conflict groups. Beyond these, one distinguishing feature of subjected groups must be emphasized. The Marxian expression "suppressed classes" might appear to mean that any

such group is characterized by the attributes which Marx ascribed to, or found present in, the proletariat of his time. However, this implication is by no means intended here. "Pauperism," "slavery," absolute exclusion from the wealth and liberty of society is a possible but unnecessary attribute of the incumbents of roles of subjection. Here, again, the connection is indeterminate, i.e., variable, and its particular pattern can be established only by empirical observation and for particular associations. It is not only conceivable that members of the subjected group of one association belong to the dominating group of another association, it is above all possible that "suppressed classes" enjoy, despite their exclusion from legitimate power, an (absolutely) high measure of social rewards without this fact impeding their organization as interest groups or their participation in group conflicts. Even a "bourgeoisified proletariat" can function as a subjected conflict group, for conflict groups and group conflicts are solely based on the one criterion of participation in or exclusion from the exercise of authority in imperatively coordinated associations. Difficult as it may be for minds schooled in Marx to separate the category of "suppressed class" from the ideas of poverty and exploitation, a well-formulated theory of group conflict requires the radical separation of these spheres.

Classes or Conflict Groups?

Up to this point I have postponed and at times avoided the question whether the concept of class is a useful concept to employ and, if so, what its precise meaning is in the context of the theory of conflict group formation. The reader will not have failed to notice that I have in fact strenuously avoided the word "class" in the present chapter wherever possible. Before turning now to an attempt to settle this rather disturbing question, I want to emphasize one point. In my opinion, the problem of the applicability of the concept of class is a purely terminological problem. In positive terms, this means that it is in part a matter of arbitrary decision, and in part a matter of convenience. Logically, there is no reason why we should not call quasi-groups and interest groups classes or anything else. Pragmatically, of course, the usage and history of words has to be considered; it is unwise to provoke misunderstandings by choosing words which carry associations that are not intended. In negative terms, the terminological nature of this problem means that I see no meaning in the statement that class is a "historical concept" in the sense of being inseparably tied to a definite historical entity such as the industrial proletariat of the nineteenth century. "Historical concepts" of this kind are fictions of Hegelianism or, more generally, conceptual realism. If I shall therefore try to bring together, in the following pages, the arguments that can be advanced for and against using the concept of class for conflict groups other than those described by Marx, the ensuing discussion is concerned exclusively with problems of pragmatic convenience, and the conclusion it reaches remains reversible.

So far in our considerations there have emerged four main reasons why the concept of class should not be applied to the analysis of conflicts in post-capitalist societies. The first of these is of a historical nature. We have seen that the changes which have occurred since Marx's time have in several ways affected the classes with which he was concerned. Bourgeoisie and proletariat are no longer uniform blocs of identically situated and oriented people if, indeed, they can be said to exist at all in post-capitalist society. The progressive institutionalization of the values of achievement and equality has removed many barriers which for Marx were associated with the concept of class. Without anticipating the results of empirical analysis we can already conclude that conflict groups in modern society are likely to be rather loose aggregations combined for special purposes

and within particular associations. In view of factual developments of this kind, it seems certainly questionable whether it is useful to employ for the conflict groups of advanced industrial society the concept used for the Marxian classes of the nineteenth century.

This doubt is strengthened by a second argument accruing from our theoretical considerations in the present chapter. We have deliberately restricted our model of group formation to elementary and highly formal features of the phenomenon. Most of the empirical characteristics of conflict groups are subject to a wide range of variability the limits of which may be fixed in terms of a constructed model but the substance of which needs to be determined by observation and experience. Conflict groups may, but need not be, immobile entities; they may, but need not be, characterized by a "class culture"; they may, but need not, engage in violent conflicts. Moreover, we have endeavored to detach the category of conflict groups and the whole notion of social conflicts from economic determinants both in the Marxian sense of relations of production and ownership and in the Weberian sense of socioeconomic class situations. Conceptually, the similarity between Marx's and even Weber's concepts of class and our concept of conflict group is but slight. There is reasonable doubt as to whether there is a chance for the concept of class not to be misunderstood if it is applied to conflict groups in the sense of this study.

Third, in addition to these general conceptual difficulties, the question must be raised: what precisely do we mean by class even if we decide to apply this term to conflict groups? Are we to follow Ginsberg and conceive of classes as quasi-groups, i.e., unorganized aggregates of the occupants of positions endowed with role interests? Or are we to follow Marx in calling classes only such groups as have attained political organization and coherence, and which are interest groups? Distinctions such as those between "collectivity" and "class," or "class," and "party," or "class in itself" and "class for itself" are necessary, but they do not exactly help to render the concept of class unambiguous.

Finally, the history of the concept in sociological literature has to be considered. One may deplore the fact that the terms "class" and "stratum" have tended to become interchangeable categories in sociological studies, but it remains a fact. While the existence of a difference between the study of social conflict and the study of social stratification is probably plausible to anybody, the concepts of "class" and "stratum," as they are often used today, fail to express this difference. Under these conditions, it may not be wise to try to restore to the concept of class a meaning which for many it lost long ago.

There are, on the other hand, three arguments that might be held against these doubts about the applicability of the concept of class to conflict groups in the sense of our model. First, the alternative category of conflict group is so general as to be almost embarrassing. We have explicitly distinguished from other conflicts those conflicts arising out of the distribution of authority in associations. Yet there is no conceivable reason, other than an inconveniently narrow definition, why the contestants in conflicts between Protestants and Catholics, Negroes and whites, town and country should not be called conflict groups. Short of using a more specific, but extremely clumsy, expression (such as "conflict groups arising from authority structures in associations"), the concept of class seems to provide a convenient tool for emphasizing the limitations of scope of the theory advanced in this study.

This is, secondly, all the more plausible, since the heuristic purpose originally associated with the concept of class is also the heuristic purpose of this study. When Marx adapted the word "class" to the requirements of his theories, he used this word as a term for structurally generated groups that engage in conflicts over existing arrangements of social structure. It is true that before Marx the term "class" was used

by a number of authors in a rather less specific sense; but it is probably fair to say that it was Marx's category which became germinal for later students in the field and which therefore represents its original version. The essential importance of this heuristic purpose has been emphasized at many points in our considerations. Since there is no other concept that expresses this purpose with equal clarity, one might consider it reasonable to retain the concept of class despite all qualifications necessitated by the arguments against it.

One of these arguments has referred to the history of the concept in sociological literature. Thirdly, however, there is one not entirely insignificant branch of sociological thinking which has consistently used (and uses) the term "class" in the form, if not the substance, assigned to it by Marx. This is true not only for many Marxist scholars whose work is, as we have seen, often pitifully barren and fruitless, but also for eminent non-Marxist (although possibly Marxian) sociologists such as Renner and Geiger, Aron and Gurvitch, Pareto and Mosca, Marshall and Ginsberg, Lipset and Bendix, and many others. We might go even further and assert that the trend of conceptual development in the work of these scholars anticipates in many ways the theses advanced in the present study. Many of them have tried to refine the concept of class by maintaining its heuristic purpose while altering its substance; quite often, this altering of substance meant a shift from property to power as a determinant, or other attempts at generalization. In using the concept of class for Marx's bourgeoisie and proletariat as well as for modern and utterly different conflict groups, one could refer not only to the origin of this concept with Marx, but also to a great and unbroken tradition in sociological analysis.

It is hard to weigh the "pros and cons" of the preceding argument entirely rationally; an element of personal preference will probably enter into any decision. Without trying to argue for this decision at any length, I will therefore state immediately that in my opinion the case in favor of retaining the concept of class is still sufficiently strong to warrant its application to even the most advanced industrial societies. This decision does involve, of course, a polemical stand against all those who "falsify" the term "class" by applying it to what should properly be called social strata. It also involves considerable extensions of the concept as it was used by Marx as well as by all Marxists and Marxians. But it emphasizes that in class analysis we are concerned (a) with systematic social conflicts and their structural origin, and (b) with but one specific type of such conflicts.

In terms of our model, the term "class" signifies conflict groups that are generated by the differential distribution of authority in imperatively coordinated associations. This definition implies no assumption as to the looseness or rigidity of their coherence, the presence or absence of a common culture or ideology (beyond specific interests) among their members, and the intensity or lack of intensity of their engagement in social conflicts.

It will be noted that this definition is inconclusive with respect to the differentiation of quasi-groups and interest groups. I would suggest that it is useful to leave it so. The category of class is a general term for groupings of the kind described more specifically in our model of conflict group formation. For all particular purposes of analysis, it is necessary to abandon this general category in favor of the more specific concepts of quasi-group and interest group. The attempt to confine the concept of class to either of these is bound, indeed, to provoke misunderstandings. Classes, like conflict groups, indicate an area and type of sociological analysis rather than its substance. Both terms are more

useful in compounds such as "class analysis," "class structure," or "class conflict" than on their own. This is but one further illustration of the essential insignificance of a terminological dispute about these matters. For purposes of the present study, and without any dogmatic insistence on terms, I propose to dissolve the alternative "classes or conflict groups" into the definition "classes as conflict groups."

Bibliography

1. David Lockwood, "Some Remarks on 'The Social System,'" *British Journal of Sociology*, Vol. VII, No. 2 (1956).

2. A. R. Radcliffe-Brown, "On Social Structure," in *Structure and Function in Primitive Society*. London, 1952.

3. Talcott Parsons, "The Distribution of Power in American Society," *World Politics*, Vol. X, No. 1 (October 1957).

4. Max Weber, *Wirtschaft und Gesellschaft* (Grundriss der Sozialökonomik, section III). 4th ed. Tübingen, 1947.

5. Vilfredo Pareto, *Allgemeine Soziologie*. Transl. and ed. by C. Brinkmann. Tübingen, 1955.

6. Raymond Aron, "Social Structure and the Ruling Class," in Reinhord Bendix and S. N. Lipset, eds., *Class, Stature and Power: A Reader in Social Stratification*. Glencoe, 1953.

7. Karl Marx, *Manifest der kommunistischen Partei*. New ed. Berlin, 1953.

8. Theodor Geiger, *Die Klassengesellschaft im Schmelztiegel*. Cologne and Hagen, 1949.

9. Gaetano Mosca, *Die herrschende Klasse*. Bern, 1950.

C. WRIGHT MILLS: THE STRUCTURE OF POWER IN AMERICA

Crit de Durkheim?

I

Power has to do with whatever decisions men make about the arrangements under which they live, and about the events which make up the history of their times. Events that are beyond human decision do happen; social arrangements do change without benefit of explicit decision. But in so far as such decisions are made, the problem of who is involved in making them is the basic problem of power. In so far as they could be made but are not, the problem becomes who fails to make them?

We cannot today merely assume that in the last resort men must always be governed by their own consent. For among the means of power which now prevail is the power to manage and to manipulate the consent of men. That we do not know the limits of such power, and that we hope it does have limits, does not remove the fact that much power today is successfully employed without the sanction of the reason or the conscience of the obedient.

Surely nowadays we need not argue that, in the last resort, coercion is the "final" form of power. But then, we are by no means constantly at the last resort. Authority (power that is justified by the beliefs of the voluntarily obedient) and manipulation (power that is wielded unbeknown to the powerless)—must also be considered, along with coercion. In fact, the three types must be sorted out whenever we think about power.

In the modern world, we must bear in mind, power is often not so authoritative as it seemed to be in the medieval epoch: ideas which justify

Reprinted with permission of Routledge and Taylor & Francis Ltd. (http://www.tandf.co.uk/journals from C. Wright Mills, "The Structure of Power in American Society," *The British Journal of Sociology*, Vol. IX, no. 1, March 1958.

rulers no longer seem so necessary to their exercise of power. At least for many of the great decisions of our time—especially those of an international sort—mass "persuasion" has not been "necessary"; the fact is simply accomplished. Furthermore, such ideas as are available to the powerful are often neither taken up nor used by them. Such ideologies usually arise as a response to an effective debunking of power; in the United States such opposition has not been effective enough recently to create the felt need for new ideologies of rule.

There has, in fact, come about a situation in which many who have lost faith in prevailing loyalties have not aquired new ones, and so pay no attention to politics of any kind. They are not radical, not liberal, not conservative, not reactionary. They are inactionary. They are out of it. If we accept the Greek's definition of the idiot as an altogether private man, then we must conclude that many American citizens are now idiots. And I should not be surprised, although I do not know, if there were not some such idiots even in Germany. This—and I use the word with care—this spiritual condition seems to me the key to many modern troubles of political intellectuals, as well as the key to much political bewilderment in modern society. Intellectual "conviction" and moral "belief" are not necessary, in either the rulers or the ruled, for a ruling power to persist and even to flourish. So far as the role of ideologies is concerned, their frequent absences and the prevalence of mass indifference are surely two of the major political facts about the western societies today.

How large a role any explicit decisions do play in the making of history is itself an historical problem. For how large that role may be depends very much upon the means of power that are available at any given time in any given society. In some societies, the innumerable actions of innumerable men modify their milieux, and so gradually modify the structure itself. These modifications—the course of history—go on behind the backs of men. History is drift, although in total "men make it." Thus, innumerable entrepreneurs and innumerable consumers by ten-thousand decisions per minute may shape and re-shape the free-market economy. Perhaps this was the chief kind of limitation Marx had in mind when he wrote, in *The 18th Brumaire:* that "Men make their own history, but they do not make it just as they please; they do not make it under circumstances chosen by themselves. . . ."

But in other societies—certainly in the United States and in the Soviet Union today—a few men may be so placed within the structure that by their decisions they modify the milieux of many other men, and in fact nowadays the structural conditions under which most men live. Such elites of power also make history under circumstances not chosen altogether by themselves, yet compared with other men, and compared with other periods of world history, these circumstances do indeed seem less limiting.

I should contend that "men are free to make history," but that some men are indeed much freer than others. For such freedom requires access to the means of decision and of power by which history can now be made. It has not always been so made; but in the later phases of the modern epoch it is. It is with reference to this epoch that I am contending that if men do not make history, they tend increasingly to become the utensils of history-makers as well as the mere objects of indeed seem less limiting.

The history of modern society may readily be understood as the story of the enlargement and the centralization of the means of power—in economic, in political, and in military institutions. The rise of industrial society has involved these developments in the means of economic production. The rise of the nation-state has involved similar developments in the means of violence and in those of political administration.

In the western societies, such transformations have generally occurred gradually, and many cultural traditions have restrained and shaped them. In most of the Soviet societies, they are happening very rapidly indeed and without the great discourse of western civilization, without the Renaissance and without the Reformation, which so greatly strengthened and gave political focus to the idea of freedom. In those societies, the enlargement and the coordination of all the means of power has occurred more brutally, and from the beginning under tightly centralized authority. But in both types, the means of power have now become international in scope and similar in form. To be sure, each of them has its own ups and downs; neither is as yet absolute; how they are run differs quite sharply.

Yet so great is the reach of the means of violence, and so great the economy required to produce and support them, that we have in the immediate past witnessed the consolidation of these two world centres, either of which dwarfs the power of Ancient Rome. As we pay attention to the awesome means of power now available to quite small groups of men we come to realize that Caesar could do less with Rome than Napoleon with France; Napoleon less with France than Lenin with Russia. But what was Caesar's power at its height compared with the power of the changing inner circles of Soviet Russia and the temporary administrations of the United States? We come to realize—indeed they continually remind us—how a few men have access to the means by which in a few days continents can be turned into thermonuclear wastelands. That the facilities of power are so enormously enlarged and so decisively centralized surely means that the powers of quite small groups of men, which we may call elites, are now of literally inhuman consequence.

My concern here is not with the international scene but with the United States in the middle of the twentieth century. I must emphasize "in the middle of the twentieth century" because in our attempt to understand any society we come upon images which have been drawn from its past and which often confuse our attempt to confront its present reality. That is one minor reason why history is the shank of any social science: we must study it if only to rid ourselves of it. In the United States, there are indeed many such images and usually they have to do with the first half of the nineteenth century. At that time the economic facilities of the United States were very widely dispersed and subject to little or to no central authority.

The state watched in the night but was without decisive voice in the day.

One man meant one rifle and the militia were without centralized orders.

Any American as old-fashioned as I can only agree with R. H. Tawney that "Whatever the future may contain, the past has shown no more excellent social order than that in which the mass of the people were the masters of the holdings which they ploughed and the tools with which they worked, and could boast . . . 'It is a quietness to a man's mind to live upon his own and to know his heir certain.'"

But then we must immediately add: all that is of the past and of little relevance to our understanding of the United States today. Within this society three broad levels of power may now be distinguished. I shall begin at the top and move downward.

II

The power to make decisions of national and international consequence is now so clearly seated in political, military, and economic institutions that other areas of society seem off to the side and, on occasion, readily subordinated to these. The scattered institutions of religion, education and family are increasingly shaped by the big three, in which history-making decisions now regularly occur. Behind this fact there is all the push and drive of a fabulous technology; for these three institutional orders have incorporated this technology and now guide it, even as it shapes and paces their development.

As each has assumed its modern shape, its effects upon the other two have become greater, and the traffic between the three has increased. There is no longer, on the one hand, an economy, and, on the other, a political order, containing a military establishment unimportant to politics and to money-making. There is a political economy numerously linked with military order and decision. This triangle of power is now a structural fact, and it is the key to any understanding of the higher circles in America today. For as each of these domains has coincided with the others, as decisions in each have become broader, the leading men of each—the high military, the corporation executives, the political directorate—have tended to come together to form the power elite of America.

The political order, once composed of several dozen states with a weak federal-centre, has become an executive apparatus which has taken up into itself many powers previously scattered, legislative as well as administrative, and which now reaches into all parts of the social structure. The long-time tendency of business and government to become more closely connected has since World War II reached a new point of explicitness. Neither can now be seen clearly as a distinct world. The growth of executive government does not mean merely the "enlargement of government" as some kind of autonomous bureaucracy: under American conditions, it has meant the ascendency of the corporation man into political eminence. Already during the New Deal, such men had joined the political directorate; as of World War II they came to dominate it. Long involved with government, now they have moved into quite full direction of the economy of the war effort and of the post-war era.

The economy, once a great scatter of small productive units in somewhat automatic balance, has become internally dominated by a few hundred corporations, administratively and politically interrelated, which together hold the keys to economic decision. This economy is at once a permanent-war economy and a private-corporation economy. The most important relations of the corporation to the state now rest on the coincidence between military and corporate interests, as defined by the military and the corporate rich, and accepted by politicians and public. Within the elite as a whole, this coincidence of military domain and corporate realm strengthens both of them and further subordinates the merely political man. Not the party politician, but the corporation executive, is now more likely to sit with the military to answer the question: what is to be done?

The military order, once a slim establishment in a context of civilian distrust, has become the largest and most expensive feature of government; behind smiling public relations, it has all the grim and clumsy efficiency of a great and sprawling bureaucracy. The high military have gained decisive political and economic relevance. The seemingly permanent military threat places a premium upon them and virtually all political and economic actions are now judged in terms of military definitions of reality: the higher military have ascended to a firm position within the power elite of our time.

In part at least this is a result of an historical fact, pivotal for the years since 1939: the attention of the elite has shifted from domestic problems—centered in the 'thirties around slump—to international problems—centered in the 'forties and 'fifties around war. By long historical usage, the government of the United States has been shaped by domestic clash and balance; it does not have suitable agencies and traditions for the democratic handling of international affairs. In considerable part, it is in this vacuum that the power elite has grown.

(i) To understand the unity of this power elite, we must pay attention to the psychology of its several members in their respective milieux. In so far as the power elite is composed of men of similar origin and education, of similar career and style of life, their unity may be said to rest upon the fact that they are of similar social type,

and to lead to the fact of their easy intermingling. This kind of unity reaches its frothier apex in the sharing of that prestige which is to be had in the world of the celebrity. It achieves a more solid culmination in the fact of the interchangeability of positions between the three dominant institutional orders. It is revealed by considerable traffic of personnel within and between these three, as well as by the rise of specialized go-betweens as in the new style high-level lobbying.

(ii) Behind such psychological and social unity are the structure and the mechanics of those institutional hierarchies over which the political directorate, the corporate rich, and the high military now preside. How each of these hierarchies is shaped and what relations it has with the others determine in large part the relations of their rulers. Were these hierarchies scattered and disjointed, then their respective elites might tend to be scattered and disjointed; but if they have many interconnections and points of coinciding interest, then their elites tend to form a coherent kind of grouping. The unity of the elite is not a simple reflection of the unity of institutions, but men and institutions are always related; that is why we must understand the elite today in connection with such institutional trends as the development of a permanent-war establishment, alongside a privately incorporated economy, inside a virtual political vacuum. For the men at the top have been selected and formed by such institutional trends.

(iii) Their unity, however, does not rest solely upon psychological similarity and social intermingling, nor entirely upon the structural blending of commanding positions and common interests. At times it is the unity of a more explicit coordination.

To say that these higher circles are increasingly coordinated, that this is *one* basis of their unity, and that at times—as during open war—such coordination is quite wilful, is not to say that the coordination is total or continuous, or even that it is very surefooted. Much less is it to say that the power elite has emerged as the realization of a plot. Its rise cannot be adequately explained in any psychological terms.

Yet we must remember that institutional trends may be defined as opportunities by those who occupy the command posts. Once such opportunities are recognized, men may avail themselves of them. Certain types of men from each of these three areas, more far-sighted than others, have actively promoted the liaison even before it took its truly modern shape. Now more have come to see that their several interests can more easily be realized if they work together, in informal as well as in formal ways, and accordingly they have done so.

The idea of the power elite is of course an interpretation. It rests upon and it enables us to make sense of major institutional trends, the social similarities and psychological affinities of the men at the top. But the idea is also based upon what has been happening on the middle and lower levels of power, to which I now turn.

III

There are of course other interpretations of the American system of power. The most usual is that it is a moving balance of many competing interests. The image of balance, at least in America, is derived from the idea of the economic market: in the nineteenth century, the balance was thought to occur between a great scatter of individuals and enterprises; in the twentieth century, it is thought to occur between great interest blocs. In both views, the politician is the key man of power because he is the broker of many conflicting powers.

I believe that the balance and the compromise in American society—the "countervailing powers" and the "veto groups," of parties and associations, of strata and unions—must now be seen as having mainly to do with the middle levels of power. It is these middle levels that the political journalist and the scholar of politics are most likely to understand and to write about—if

only because, being mainly middle class themselves, they are closer to them. Moreover these levels provide the noisy content of most "political" news and gossip; the images of these levels are more or less in accord with the folklore of how democracy works; and, if the master-image of balance is accepted, many intellectuals, especially in their current patrioteering, are readily able to satisfy such political optimism as they wish to feel. Accordingly, liberal interpretations of what is happening in the United States are now virtually the only interpretations that are widely distributed.

But to believe that the power system reflects a balancing society is, I think, to confuse the present era with earlier times, and to confuse its top and bottom with its middle levels.

By the top levels, as distinguished from the middle, I intend to refer, first of all, to the scope of the decisions that are made. At the top today, these decisions have to do with all the issues of war and peace. They have also to do with slump and poverty which are now so very much problems of international scope. I intend also to refer to whether or not the groups that struggle politically have a chance to gain the positions from which such top decisions are made, and indeed whether their members do usually hope for such top national command. Most of the competing interests which make up the clang and clash of American politics are strictly concerned with their slice of the existing pie. Labour unions, for example, certainly have no policies of an international sort other than those which given unions adopt for the strict economic protection of their members. Neither do farm organizations. The actions of such middle-level powers may indeed have consequence for top-level policy; certainly at times they hamper these policies. But they are not truly concerned with them, which means of course that their influence tends to be quite irresponsible.

The facts of the middle levels may in part be understood in terms of the rise of the power elite. The expanded and centralized and interlocked hierarchies over which the power elite preside have encroached upon the old balance and relegated it to the middle level. But there are also independent developments of the middle levels. These, it seems to me, are better understood as an affair of intrenched and provincial demands than as a centre of national decision. As such, the middle level often seems much more of a stalemate than a moving balance.

(i) The middle level of politics is not a forum in which there are debated the big decisions of national and international life. Such debate is not carried on by nationally responsible parties representing and clarifying alternative policies. There are no such parties in the United States. More and more, fundamental issues never come to any point or decision before the Congress, much less before the electorate in party campaigns. In the case of Formosa, in the spring of 1955, the Congress abdicated all debate concerning events and decisions which surely bordered on war. The same is largely true of the 1957 crisis in the Middle East. Such decisions now regularly bypass the Congress, and are never clearly focused issues for public decision.

The American political campaign distracts attention from national and international issues, but that is not to say that there are no issues in these campaigns. In each district and state, issues are set up and watched by organized interests of sovereign local importance. The professional politician is of course a party politician, and the two parties are semi-feudal organizations: they trade patronage and other favours for votes and for protection. The differences between them, so far as national issues are concerned, are very narrow and very mixed up. Often each seems to be forty-eight parties, one to each state; and accordingly, the politician as campaigner and as Congressman is not concerned with national party lines, if any are discernible. Often he is not subject to any effective national party discipline. He speaks for the interests of his own constituency, and he is concerned with national issues only in so far as they

affect the interests effectively organized there, and hence his chances of re-election. That is why, when he does speak of national matters, the result is so often such an empty rhetoric. Seated in his sovereign locality, the politician is not at the national summit. He is on and of the middle levels of power.

(ii) Politics is not an arena in which free and independent organizations truly connect the lower and middle levels of society with the top levels of decision. Such organizations are not an effective and major part of American life today. As more people are drawn into the political arena, their associations become mass in scale, and the power of the individual becomes dependent upon them; to the extent that they are effective, they have become larger, and to that extent they have become less accessible to the influence of the individual. This is a central fact about associations in any mass society: it is of most consequence for political parties and for trade unions.

In the 'thirties, it often seemed that labour would become an insurgent power independent of corporation and state. Organized labour was then emerging for the first time on an American scale, and the only political sense of direction it needed was the slogan, "organize the unorganized." Now without the mandate of the slump, labour remains without political direction. Instead of economic and political struggles it has become deeply entangled in administrative routines with both corporation and state. One of its major functions, as a vested interest of the new society, is the regulation of such irregular tendencies as may occur among the rank and file.

There is nothing, it seems to me, in the make up of the current labour leadership to allow us to expect that it can or that it will lead, rather than merely react. In so far as it fights at all it fights over a share of the goods of a single way of life and not over that way of life itself. The typical labour leader in the U.S.A. today is better understood as an adaptive creature of the main business drift than as an independent actor in a truly national context.

(iii) The idea that this society is a balance of powers requires us to assume that the units in balance are of more or less equal power and that they are truly independent of one another. These assumptions have rested, it seems clear, upon the historical importance of a large and independent middle class. In the latter nineteenth century and during the Progressive Era, such a class of farmers and small businessmen fought politically—and lost—their last struggle for a paramount role in national decision. Even then, their aspirations seemed bound to their own imagined past.

This old, independent middle class has of course declined. On the most generous count, it is now 40 percent of the total middle class (at most 20 percent of the total labour force). Moreover, it has become politically as well as economically dependent upon the state, most notably in the case of the subsidized farmer.

The *new* middle class of white-collar employees is certainly not the political pivot of any balancing society. It is in no way politically unified. Its unions, such as they are, often serve merely to incorporate it as hanger-on of the labour interest. For a considerable period, the old middle class *was* an independent base of power; the new middle class cannot be. Political freedom and economic security *were* anchored in small and independent properties; they are not anchored in the worlds of the white-collar job. Scattered property holders were economically united by more or less free markets; the jobs of the new middle class are integrated by corporate authority. Economically, the white-collar classes are in the same condition as wage workers; politically, they are in a worse condition, for they are not organized. They are no vanguard of historic change; they are at best a rearguard of the welfare state.

The agrarian revolt of the 'nineties, the small-business revolt that has been more or less continuous since the 'eighties, the labour revolt of the 'thirties—each of these has failed as an independent movement which could countervail against the powers that be; they have failed as politically autonomous third parties. But they have succeeded, in varying degree, as interests vested in the expanded corporation and state; they have succeeded as parochial interests seated in particular districts, in local divisions of the two parties, and in the Congress. What they would become, in short, are well-established features of the *middle* levels of balancing power, on which we may now observe all those strata and interests which in the course of American history have been defeated in their bids for top power or which have never made such bids.

Fifty years ago many observers thought of the American state as a mask behind which an invisible government operated. But nowadays, much of what was called the old lobby, visible or invisible, is part of the quite visible government. The 'governmentalization of the lobby' has proceeded in both the legislative and the executive domain, as well as between them. The executive bureaucracy becomes not only the centre of decision but also the arena within which major conflicts of power are resolved or denied resolution. 'Administration' replaces electoral politics; the manœuvring of cliques (which include leading Senators as well as civil servants) replaces the open clash of parties.

The shift of corporation men into the political directorate has accelerated the decline of the politicians in the Congress to the middle levels of power; the formation of the power elite rests in part upon this relegation. It rests also upon the semi-organized stalemate of the interests of sovereign localities, into which the legislative function has so largely fallen; upon the virtually complete absence of a civil service that is a politically neutral but politically relevant, depository of brain-power and executive skill; and it rests upon the increased official secrecy behind which great decisions are made without benefit of public or even of Congressional debate.

IV

There is one last belief upon which liberal observers everywhere base their interpretations and rest their hopes. That is the idea of the public and the associated idea of public opinion. Conservative thinkers, since the French Revolution, have of course Viewed With Alarm the rise of the public, which they have usually called the masses, or something to that effect. "The populace is sovereign," wrote Gustave Le Bon, "and the tide of barbarism mounts." But surely those who have supposed the masses to be well on their way to triumph are mistaken. In our time, the influence of publics or of masses within political life is in fact decreasing, and such influence as on occasion they do have tends, to an unknown but increasing degree, to be guided by the means of mass communication.

In a society of publics, discussion is the ascendant means of communication, and the mass media, if they exist, simply enlarge and animate this discussion, linking one face-to-face public with the discussions of another. In a mass society, the dominant type of communication is the formal media, and publics become mere markets for these media: the "public" of a radio programme consists of all those exposed to it. When we try to look upon the United States today as a society of publics, we realize that it has moved a considerable distance along the road to the mass society.

In official circles, the very term, "the public," has come to have a phantom meaning, which dramatically reveals its eclipse. The deciding elite can identify some of those who clamour publicly as "Labour," others as "Business," still others as "Farmer." But these are not the public. "The public" consists of the unidentified and the non-partisan in a world of defined and partisan interests. In this faint echo of the classic notion, the public is composed of these remnants of the old and new middle classes whose interests are not explicitly defined, organized, or clamorous. In a curious adaptation, "the public" often becomes, in administrative fact, "the disengaged expert," who, although ever so well informed, has never taken a clear-cut and public stand on controversial issues. He is the "public" member of the board, the commission, the committee. What "the public" stands for, accordingly, is often a vagueness of policy (called "open-mindedness"), a lack of involvement in public affairs (known as "reasonableness"), and a professional disinterest (known as "tolerance").

All this is indeed far removed from the eighteenth-century idea of the public of public opinion. That idea parallels the economic idea of the magical market. Here is the market composed of freely competing entrepreneurs; there is the public composed of circles of people in discussion. As price is the result of anonymous, equally weighted, bargaining individuals, so public opinion is the result of each man's having thought things out for himself and then contributing his voice to the great chorus. To be sure, some may have more influence on the state of opinion than others, but no one group monopolizes the discussion, or by itself determines the opinions that prevail.

In this classic image, the people are presented with problems. They discuss them. They formulate viewpoints. These viewpoints are organized, and they compete. One viewpoint "wins out." Then the people act on this view, or their representatives are instructed to act it out, and this they promptly do.

Such are the images of democracy which are still used as working justifications of power in America. We must now recognize this description as more a fairy tale than a useful approximation. The issues that now shape man's fate are neither raised nor decided by any public at large. The idea of a society that is at bottom composed of publics is not a matter of fact; it is the proclamation of an ideal, and as well the assertion of a legitimation masquerading as fact.

I cannot here describe the several great forces within American society as well as elsewhere which have been at work in the debilitation of the public. I want only to remind you that publics, like free associations, can be deliberately and suddenly smashed, or they can more slowly wither away. But whether smashed in a week or withered in a generation, the demise of the public must be seen in connection with the rise of centralized organizations, with all their new means of power, including those of the mass media of distraction. These, we now know, often seem to expropriate the rationality and the will of the terrorized or—as the case may be—the voluntarily indifferent society of masses. In the more democratic process of indifference the remnants of such publics as remain may only occasionally be intimidated by fanatics in search of "disloyalty." But regardless of that, they lose their will for decision because they do not possess the instruments for decision; they lose their sense of political belonging because they do not belong; they lose their political will because they see no way to realize it.

The political structure of a modern democratic state requires that such a public as is projected by democratic theorists not only exist but that it be the very forum within which a politics of real issues is enacted.

It requires a civil service that is firmly linked with the world of knowledge and sensibility, and which is composed of skilled men who, in their careers and in their aspirations, are truly independent of any private, which is to say, corporation, interests.

It requires nationally responsible parties which debate openly and clearly the issues which the nation, and indeed the world, now so rigidly confronts.

It requires an intelligentsia, inside as well as outside the universities, who carry on the big discourse of the western world, and whose work is relevant to and influential among parties and movements and publics.

And it certainly requires, as a fact of power, that there be free associations standing between families and smaller communities and publics, on the one hand, and the state, the military, the corporation, on the other. For unless these do exist, there are no vehicles for reasoned opinion, no instruments for the rational exertion of public will.

Such democratic formations are not now ascendant in the power structure of the United States, and accordingly the men of decision are not men selected and formed by careers within such associations and by their performance before such publics. The top of modern American society is increasingly unified, and often seems wilfully coordinated: at the top there has emerged an elite whose power probably exceeds that of any small group of men in world history. The middle levels are often a drifting set of stalemated forces: the middle does not link the bottom with the top. The bottom of this society is politically fragmented, and even as a passive fact, increasingly powerless: at the bottom there is emerging a mass society.

These developments, I believe, can be correctly understood neither in terms of the liberal nor the marxian interpretation of politics and history. Both these ways of thought arose as guidelines to reflection about a type of society which does not now exist in the United States. We confront there a new kind of social structure, which embodies elements and tendencies of all modern society, but in which they have assumed a more naked and flamboyant prominence.

That does not mean that we must give up the ideals of these classic political expectations. I believe that both have been concerned with the problem of rationality and of freedom: liberalism, with freedom and rationality as supreme facts about the individual; Marxism, as supreme facts about man's role in the political making of history. What I have said here, I suppose, may be taken as an attempt to make evident why the ideas of freedom and of rationality now so often seem so ambiguous in the new society of the United States of America.

RICHARD L. ZWEIGENHAFT AND G. WILLIAM DOMHOFF: THE IRONIES OF DIVERSITY

As the preceding chapters have shown in detail, the power elite and Congress are more diverse than they were before the social movements that emerged in the 1960s brought pressure to bear on corporations, politicians, and government. Although the power elite is still composed primarily of Christian white men, there are now Jews, women, blacks, Latinos, and Asian Americans on the boards of the country's largest corporations; presidential cabinets are far more diverse than was the case forty years ago; and the highest ranks of the military are no longer filled solely by white men. In the case of elected officials in Congress, the trend toward diversity is even greater for women and all of the minority groups that we have studied. At the same time, we have shown that the assimilation of the different groups has been uneven. In this final chapter, we explain the successful assimilation by women and minorities into the power elite and Congress in terms of four factors: identity management; the importance of class; the importance of education; and the importance of light skin. We conclude that class origin is the most important factor for all groups except blacks and "Indian-appearing" Latinos, and we offer a general explanation for the continuing exclusion of people with darker skins.

Ultimately we suggest that the increase in diversity at the top contains several ironies, the most important of which is related to what is perhaps the major unresolved tension in American life, between liberal individualism and the class structure. The diversification of the power

From *Diversity in the Power Elite* by Richard L. Zweigenhaft and G. William Domhoff. Yale University Press, 1998. Reprinted with permission of Yale University Press. Copyright © 1998 by Richard L. Zweigenhaft and G. William Domhoff.

elite has been celebrated, but this celebration ignores the continuing importance of the class structure. The movements that led to diversity in the power elite have succeeded to some extent, especially for women and minorities from privileged social backgrounds, but there has been no effect on the way the power elite functions or on the class structure itself.

Identity Management

We have seen that newcomers who seek to join the power elite have to find ways to demonstrate their loyalty to those who dominate American institutions—straight white Christian males. We can recall, for example, Cecily Cannan Selby's decision to reduce tension at a dinner meeting with the previously all-male Avon Products board by lighting up a cigar, or Hazel O'Leary's realization that she had to learn to play golf if she expected to advance in her corporate career. We can envision William T. Coleman demonstrating his elite educational background by reciting great poetry with his fellow law clerk Elliot Richardson. Reading between the lines of traditional stereotypes, we can imagine Jewish and black executives being properly reserved, Asian-American executives acting properly assertive, gay executives behaving in traditionally masculine ways and lesbian executives in traditionally feminine ways. Thus we have seen the importance of identity management. As Terrie Miyamoto of U.S. West put it, the challenge is to move into a "comfort zone" with those who decide who is and is not acceptable for inclusion.

At the same time, in Chapter 2 we drew on the work of sociologist Rosabeth Kanter to stress that the demand for demonstrations of outward conformity by established leaders is not primarily a matter of personal prejudice or cultural heritage. It is, instead, the need for trust and smooth working relationships within complex organizations that leads to the marked preference for women and minorities who think and act like the straight Christian males running those organizations. The social movements that arose in the 1960s were able to rock the boat enough to open up some space for nontraditional leaders, but not enough to change the way in which institutions are managed. Unless and until such changes are made in institutional governance, women and minorities will be at a disadvantage in climbing the managerial hierarchy even though they are now allowed to enter the competition.

Identity management, however, is only the final step, the icing on the cake, so to speak. Before atypical candidates for acceptance into the higher circles can even think about making adjustments in their personas, they have to meet prerequisites that are attainable by only a small percentage of the population whatever their race, ethnicity, gender, or sexual orientation. It is to these prerequisites that we now turn.

The Importance of Class

Those who brought diversity to the power elite tended to come from business and professional backgrounds, like the white Christian males whom Mills studied more than forty years ago. Fully one-third of the women who have become corporate directors are from the upper class, and many others are from the middle and upper middle classes. Most of the Cuban Americans and Chinese Americans who have risen to the top have come from displaced ruling classes, a far cry from the conventional image of the immigrant. The Jews and Japanese Americans in high positions have mostly been the products of two- and three-generational climbs up the social ladder. The first black members of the corporate elite and the cabinet tended to come

from the small black middle class that predated the civil rights movement. Although there is no systematic information on the social backgrounds of gay and lesbian leaders, who are treated in most studies as if they had no class origins, our anecdotal information suggests that many visible activists and professionals come from business and professional families as well.

A high-level social background, of course, makes it easier to acquire the values, attitudes, and styles that are necessary to hire, fire, and manage the work lives of employees with blue, white, and pink collars. This point can be extended to include even those from more modest circumstances, like Lauro Cavazos, whose father was a ranch foreman, or Katherine Ortega, Sue Ginn, and David Geffen, whose families owned small businesses, or David Mixner, whose father was in charge of minority farmhands on a farm he did not own. Most of those we studied, in other words, learned firsthand that a few people boss the majority or have independent professions based on academic credentials, and that they were expected to be part of this managerial and professional stratum.

When we compare women and minority members of the power elite with their counterparts in Congress, however, two further generalizations emerge. First, members of the power elite tend to come from more privileged social backgrounds than the elected officials. Second, the elected women and minorities are more likely to be Democrats than Republicans. These two findings suggest that there are class and political dimensions to our findings on the differences between the power elite and Congress that cut across gender and ethnic lines. If the power elite comes to be housed almost exclusively in the Republican Party as well-to-do southerners leave the Democrats and as the liberal-labor coalition becomes more important within the Democratic Party, then the country's traditional regional, racal, and ethnic politics may be replaced by a more clear-cut class-and-values politics, with both the Republicans and

Democrats being able to say that they are multicultural in terms of gender and minority representation.[1]

The Importance of Education

Class by no means explains all of our findings, however. Education also matters a great deal. The women and minorities who make it to the power elite are typically better educated than the white males who are already a part of it. This was seen with the European-American women and African Americans on corporate boards and in presidential cabinets, as well as the successful Asian-American immigrants. Education seems to have given them the edge needed to be accepted into the power elite.

Moreover, it is not merely academic degrees that matter but also where those degrees are from. Again and again, we saw that a significant minority were from the same few schools that educate Christian white male leaders—Harvard, Yale, Princeton, and MIT on the East Coast, the University of Chicago in the Midwest, Stanford and the University of California on the West

Coast. Three of the five Asian-American appointees to the executive branch, for example, have at least one degree from Harvard (Julia Chang Bloch, Elaine Chao, and Lon Hatamiya). The other two attended the University of Chicago (Patsy Mink) and the University of California (Dennis Hayashi).

These elite schools not only confer status on their graduates but also provide contacts with white male elites that are renewed throughout life at alumni gatherings and other special occasions. School connections in turn lead to invitations to attend exclusive social events and join expensive social clubs, which extend the newcomers' social networks even further. With success in business or a profession comes invitations to serve on boards of trustees of elite foundations and universities, and the circle is completed. The newcomers become part of the ongoing institutional framework that defines and shapes the power elite in the United States, even though they are unlikely to reach the very top. The individuals in the power elite may come and go, and they may diversify in gender, ethnicity, and sexual orientation, but there is stability and continuity within the overall power structure.

As was true of social class origins, there is a difference in educational attainment between those in the power elite and those in Congress: the men and women elected to Congress are not as likely as those in the power elite to have attended elite colleges and universities or to have earned postgraduate degrees.

The Importance of Color

Just as class alone cannot explain all of our findings, neither can the combination of class and education: color also matters. African Americans and darker-skinned Latinos find it more difficult than others to use their educational credentials as a passport to occupational success. This can be seen poignantly in our skin-color comparisons of successful blacks and Latinos.

[1] On the continuing importance of class voting in the United States, contrary to recent claims based on weak methods, see Michael Hout, Clem Brooks, and Jeff Manza, "The Democratic Class Struggle in the United States, 1948–1992," *American Sociological Review* 60, no. 6 (1995), 805–828; Jeff Manza and Clem Brooks, "Continuity and Change in the Social Bases of U.S. Political Alignments, 1960–1992," paper presented at the American Sociological Association Meetings, New York, August 1996.

On class voting by Latinos, see Barry Kosmin and Ariela Keysar, "Party Political Preferences of U.S. Hispanics: The Varying Impact of Religion, Social Class and Demographic Factors," *Ethnic and Racial Studies* 18, no. 2 (1995), 236–347. In surveys of the CEOs of the largest Hispanic-owned businesses in 1989 and 1996, *Hispanic Business* found that 78 percent of them voted Republican in 1988 and that 67 percent said they were Republicans in 1996. See "CEOs and the Entrepreneurial 80s," *Hispanic Business*, April 1989, p. 30; "HB 500 CEOs Opt for Dole," *Hispanic Business*, June 1996, p. 34. On class voting by Chinese Americans, see Wendy Tam, "Asians—a Monolithic Voting Bloc?" *Political Behavior* 17, no. 2 (1995), 223–249.

Even among those who had achieved some level of prominence (measured by inclusion in *Ebony's* fiftieth anniversary issue or the *Hispanic Business* listing of "Hispanic influentials"), those who had made it into the power elite were lighter skinned than those who had not. On this score, our data simply reinforce earlier work by others. As the Glass Ceiling Commission reported, "Our society has developed an extremely sophisticated, and often denied, acceptability index based on gradations in skin color."[2]

There is another side of the coin: darker-skinned blacks may have a harder time finding jobs and may, if convicted of crimes, receive stiffer jail sentences.[3] Furthermore, both blacks and Latinos in the United States understand (and sometimes indulge in) the discrimination against those who are darkest. Blacks speak openly of the advantage lighter-skinned blacks have, and surveys of Latinos reveal that those who are described as "Indian" in appearance report greater discrimination than do Latinos who are described as more Caucasian in appearance.[4]

These findings on color discrimination may be useful in explaining why the assimilation of blacks into the power elite may be slowing down. The failure of American society to accept darker-skinned citizens—especially blacks—is the single most important issue that needs to be understood by social scientists.

Explaining Discrimination

How is the greater discrimination against blacks and against Latinos who are "Indian" in appearance to be explained? We think it hinges on a distinction between immigrant minorities, whose migration to a country was voluntary, and subjugated minorities, who have been defeated by groups with superior military technology or brought to a country against their will as slaves.

A distinction between immigrant and subjugated minorities, as opposed to a focus on race, is compatible with the general patterns of assimilation and integration in the United States. This can be seen most clearly through what social psychologist Thomas F. Pettigrew, perhaps the leading authority on race and ethnic relations of the past thirty-five years, sees as the two most important and revealing indicators of integration: residential patterns and intermarriage.[5] Asian Americans, Latinos, and African Americans are designated as "people of color," but when we look at the extent to which those in each group live among and marry people from other groups, the importance of immigration rather than race becomes apparent.

The best data on residential patterns demonstrate that blacks continue to live in predominantly black neighborhoods, but this is not the

---

[2] *Good for Business: Making Full Use of the Nation's Human Capital, a Fact-Finding Report of the Federal Glass Ceiling Commission* (Washington, D.C.: U.S. Government Printing Office, 1995), 95.

[3] James H. Johnson Jr. and Walter C. Farrell Jr., "Race Still Matters," *The Chronicle of Higher Education,* July 7, 1995, p. A48.

[4] Carlos H. Arce, Edward Marguia, and W. Parker Frisbie, "Phenotype and Life Chances Among Chicanos," *Hispanic Journal of Behavioral Sciences* 9, no. 1 (1987), 19–32; E. A. Telles and Edward Murguia, "Phenotypic Discrimination and Income Differences Among Mexican Americans," *Social Science Quarterly* 71 (1990), 682–696; Aida Hurtado, "Does Similarity Breed Respect? Interviewer Evaluations of Mexican-Descent Respondents in a Bilingual Survey," *Public Opinion Quarterly* 58 (1994), 77–95.

---

[5] Thomas F. Pettigrew, "Integration and Pluralism," in Phyllis A. Katz and Dalmas A. Taylor, eds., *Modern Racism: Profiles in Controversy* (New York: Plenum, 1988), 19–30. As noted in Chapter 2, intermarriage as an indicator of "assimilation" is stressed by Milton Gordon (*Assimilation in American Life* [New York: Oxford University Press, 1964]) and by Seymour Martin Lipset and Earl Raab (*Jews and the New American Scene* [Cambridge: Harvard University Press, 1995]), but here the emphasis is on "integration," which highlights the fact that African Americans have faced distinct barriers to acceptance. "*Assimilation,*" concludes Pettigrew, is a concept "used in North America largely in reference to *national* groups that have arrived over the past 150 years with distinctive non-anglo cultures. *Integration* is a concept shaped by black-white relations in the United States to refer to inclusion processes for a *racial* group that has a unique history of rigorous exclusion" (20).

TABLE 8.1 Intermarriage by U.S.-Born Members of Ethnic and Racial Minorities

	% Married to Non-Hispanic Whites			
	Male	(N)	Female	(N)
Filipino Americans	61%	(106)	66%	(103)
Native Americans	57	(1,212)	58	(1,234)
Cuban Americans	61	(92)	47	(137)
Chinese Americans	47	(140)	52	(152)
Japanese Americans	44	(216)	54	(266)
Puerto Rican Americans	42	(528)	35	(602)
Mexican Americans	31	(4,793)	28	(5,261)
African Americans	5	(9,804)	2	(9,581)

Note: The table includes only individuals under age forty and excludes war brides and grooms.

Source: Adapted from Jacobs and Labov, "Asian Brides, Anglo Grooms," p. 23, table 4.

case for Latinos or Asian Americans. In *American Apartheid: Segregation and the Making of the Underclass*, the sociologists Douglas Massey and Nancy Denton demonstrate just how persistent residential segregation has been in the United States. Using computerized data from the U.S. census of 1970 and 1980, they looked at the thirty metropolitan areas with the largest black populations. Based on two different measures ("black-white segregation" and "spatial isolation"), they conclude that the 1970s showed virtually no increase in integration, "despite what whites said on opinion polls and despite the provisions of the Fair Housing Act."[6] Moreover, they found that degree of segregation was not the case for Hispanics and Asians. "In fact," Massey and Denton conclude, "within most metropolitan areas, Hispanics and Asians are more likely to share a neighborhood with whites than with another member of their own group." In the final chapter of their book, Massey and Denton update their work to include 1990 census data. They conclude that "there is little in recent data

to suggest that processes of racial segregation have moderated much since 1980. . . . Racial segregation still constitutes a fundamental cleavage in American society."[7]

There have been dozens of studies focusing on the recent marriage patterns of minority groups. All of them point to increasing intermarriage occurring between the large white population and each minority group except blacks. The exact percentage of "outmarriage" varies with a number of factors, including country of birth, years of residency in the United States, region of residence, educational level, and income. For our emphasis on intermarriage as a sensitive indicator of integration and acceptance, two papers by sociologists Jerry Jacobs and Teresa Labov using a 1 percent sample from the 1990 census (539,279 marriages) provide an ideal test case. The findings of their analysis of marriages to non-Hispanic white partners by American-born minorities under the age of forty are summarized in table 8.1.[8]

---

[6] Douglas S. Massey and Nancy A. Denton, *American Apartheid: Segregation and the Making of the Underclass* (Cambridge: Harvard University Press, 1993), 61.

[7] Ibid., 67, 223.

[8] Jerry A. Jacobs and Teresa Labov, "Asian Brides, Anglo Grooms: Asian Exceptionalism in Intermarriage," Department of Sociology, University of Pennsylvania, October 1995; Jerry A. Jacobs and Teresa Labov, "Sex Differences in Intermarriage: Exchange Theory Reconsidered," Department of Sociology, University of Pennsylvania, September 1995.

For similar findings based on 1990 survey data with native-born Latinos that are slightly lower due to a wider age range, see Rodolfo de la Garza, Louis DeSipio, F. Chris Garcia, John Garcia, and Angelo Falcon, *Latino Voices: Mexican, Puerto Rican, and Cuban Perspectives on American Politics* (Boulder, Colo.: Westview, 1992), 25, table 2.6. Jacobs and Labov find low rates of intermarriage among subgroups of Latinos, and de la Garza et al. report similarly low rates among Latino groups in the table cited. There is, however, evidence for a growing number of intermarriages among Asian Americans in California, with the rate being higher than intermarriage with whites when the size of the population is taken into account. See Larry Hajima Shinagawa and Gin Yong Pang, "Intraethnic, Interethnic, and Interracial Marriages Among Asian Americans in California, 1980," *Berkeley Journal of Sociology* 13 (1988), 95–114. Inter-Asian marriages are also high in Hawaii; see Morrison G. Wong, "A Look at Intermarriage Among the Chinese in the U.S. in 1980," *Sociological Perspectives* 32, no. 1 (1989), 87–107.

There are many dramatic findings in this table, including the very high percentage of native-born Asian Americans marrying non-Hispanic whites, but none is more important to our point than the continuing low levels of inter-marriage by African Americans to non-Hispanic whites. In a sample that focuses only on married couples, thereby excluding any distortion by the high percentage of unmarried males and females in the African-American community, only 5 percent of married African-American males and 2 percent of married African-American females under age forty were married to non-Hispanic whites. This is less than one-sixth the percentage for the next-lowest group, Mexican Americans, and far below the 44–46 percent figure for Asian Americans. Even among African-American college graduates, only 11 percent of the males and 3 percent of the females had married whites, whereas the percentages for all married Asian-American college graduates as a group were 51 percent for males and 59 percent for females.[9]

As might be deduced from the higher percentage of Asian-American college graduates marrying whites, there is a strong tendency for affluent immigrant minorities to marry affluent whites and for less affluent minorities, like Native Americans, Mexican Americans, and Puerto Ricans, to marry less affluent whites. The same pattern holds for marriages between African Americans and whites—the partners usually have similar education and occupational levels.[10]

Based on these findings, it seems likely to us that, over time, the overwhelming majority of the children and grandchildren of new immigrants to the United States will blend together with non-Hispanic whites into a common cultural pool and then sort themselves out along class and educational lines, using ethnic and racial identities for mostly symbolic and strategic purposes. This mix will include the 79 percent of self-identified American Indians who do not live on reservations (few of whom have pure Native American ancestry).[11] Such a sorting along class and educational lines would reinforce the tendency to class-and-values politics that we noted as a possibility in an earlier section of this chapter.

Put more strongly, class is going to be the factor most affecting the likelihood of reaching the highest levels of the institutional structure for all Americans except blacks and darker-skinned Latinos. Blacks, as Pettigrew has argued, have been treated very differently from all other minority groups. Pettigrew is fully aware that other groups "have suffered discrimination in many forms," and neither he nor we wish to diminish the depth of personal anguish that such discrimination has caused, but he also points out that the situation is different for blacks because they are "the only group to experience the confluence of race, slavery, and segregation."[12] They also have been by far the largest minority in the country for centuries, constituting 18.9 percent of the population in 1800, 11.6 percent in 1900, and 12.3 percent in 1990, and they have always been

---

[9] Jacobs and Labov, "Sex Differences in Intermarriage," 11.

[10] On black-white marriages and socioeconomic similarities, see also James H. Gadberry and Richard A. Dodder, "Educational Homogamy in Interracial Marriages: An Update," *Journal of Social Behavior and Personality* 8, no. 6 (1993), 155–163; Matthijs Kalmijn, "Trends in Black/White Intermarriage," *Social Forces* 72, no. 1 (1993), 119–146; Kristyan M. Kouri and Marcia Lasswell, "Black-White Marriages: Social Change and Intergenerational Mobility," *Marriage and Family Review* 19, no. 34 (1993), 241–255.

[11] Stephen Steinberg, *The Ethnic Myth: Race, Ethnicity, and Class in America* (New York: Atheneum, 1981); Mary C. Waters, *Ethnic Options: Choosing Identities in America* (Berkeley: University of California Press, 1990).

In making this claim, we are aware that the Hmong, Laotians, Cambodians, and many Vietnamese are more accurately described as refugees fleeing war-ravaged countries and that they may be exceptions to our general statement.

[12] Pettigrew, "Integration and Pluralism," 24–26. For detailed evidence on the difficulties still faced by black Americans, including members of the middle class, see Lois Benjamin, *The Black Elite* (Chicago: Nelson Hall, 1991); Joe R. Feagin and Melvin P. Sikes, *Living with Racism* (Boston: Beacon, 1994).

concentrated in specific areas, first in the rural South, then in large cities.

In our view, blacks are still seen as a subjugated minority that remains a potential threat to the white system of power relations, which is why many of the stigmas built into the culture over the course of U.S. history continue to be used by many white Americans, even if the communication of these stigmas is now more subtle.

Blacks have resisted this subjugation and its attendant indignities to self-esteem by developing a "resistance culture" that defies white culture and authority. In the past, when violence was so readily and easily used by whites on assertive blacks, this resistance most often manifested itself in a seeming conformity, passivity, and inarticulateness that slowed the pace of work.[13] Since the Civil Rights Movement the resistance has very often taken the form of an "oppositional culture" that challenges white culture and is communicated through such varied forms as rap music, style of walking, and use of language, although there are regional, class, and individual variations in the degree of acceptance of this culture. The oppositional culture, which is a response to white prejudices, is annoying and even frightening to many white adults, who in turn use it as evidence that blacks are "different," unemployable, and untrustworthy. Further complicating the picture, the oppositional culture is often attractive to privileged white adolescents, who pick up on its defiance of authority and use aspects of it for their own purposes in gaining independence from their parents.

For our purposes, the clash between the dominant and oppositional cultures expresses itself most pertinently in the school setting, leading young blacks to have great ambivalence about doing well in school. Historically, whites did everything they could to deprive blacks of adequate education, fearing that the ability to read and write might aid them in their attempts to escape enslavement and segregation. Conversely, blacks put an enormous value on education for the same reason—as an avenue to liberation. More recently, however, as blacks have come to see that a good education does not necessarily lead to respect and occupational levels commensurate with their efforts, many lower-income blacks have begun to doubt its worth. Education came to be seen as a "white man's thing," and those who continued to work hard in school were accused of "acting white." Defying school authorities and refusing to do homework became part of the oppositional culture, and those who ignored the code became subject to rejection by their peers, a combination of social isolation and hazing that few adolescents of any group—or adults, for that matter—are able to endure. The result is that many black students who attend predominantly black public schools, including some children of middle-class parents, are underachievers.[14] Poor performance in school is then used by whites as further evidence for black inferiority, and the lack of proper educational credentials is used to disqualify blacks from job opportunities. The

---

[13] See, for example, Signithia Fordham, *Blacked Out: Dilemmas of Race, Identity, and Success at Capital High* (Chicago: University of Chicago Press, 1996), chapter 1. See also Bonnie L. Mitchell and Joe R. Feagin, "America's Racial-Ethnic Cultures: Opposition Within a Mythical Melting Pot," Benjamin P. Bowser, Terry Jones, and Gale Auletta Young, eds., *Toward the Multicultural University* (Westport, Conn.: Praeger, 1995), 65–86.

[14] John U. Ogbu, "Class Stratification, Racial Stratification, and Schooling," in L. Weis, ed., *Race, Class, and Schooling: Special Studies in Comparative Education* (Albany: State University of New York Press, 1988). For some evidence that challenges some of the assumptions of oppositional culture, see James W. Ainsworth-Darnell and Douglas B. Downey, "Assessing the Oppositional Culture Explanation for Racial/Ethnic Differences in School Performance," *American Sociological Review* 63, no. 4 (1998), 536–553. For an article that extols the success of immigrant children, comparing their academic performance and their attitudes toward education to their peers with American-born parents, see Andrew J. Fuligni, "The Adjustment of Children from Immigrant Families," *Current Directions in Psychological Research* 7, no. 4 (1998), 99–103.

cycle of white and black separation is thereby perpetuated.[15]

To make matters more complex, the unique oppositional identity created by blacks to protect their dignity is not well understood by the immigrant minorities, who are often assumed to be potential allies of blacks because they too are "people of color." In fact, most of these immigrants of color have a very different attitude toward the society than African Americans do and often are puzzled that African Americans do not see the "opportunities" that lie before them and therefore "work harder." Sometimes they are as bothered as whites by the boisterous expressive behaviors that are part of the oppositional culture. Thus most immigrants come to share the stereotypes and prejudices of the dominant white majority.

Perhaps the most painful evidence of this point is an interview study of second-generation West Indians and African Americans conducted by Mary Waters. Her Caribbean interviewees claimed that African Americans are lazy, loud, and impolite. Indeed, their views often sound like those of southern whites in the past, when open expression of prejudice was common. African Americans, in turn, told Waters of their contempt for what they saw as the obsequious behavior of many immigrant blacks, and their skepticism about the immigrants' self-respect and understanding of the obstacles in white American society. The result is a complex relationship between immigrant and native-born blacks, with the immigrants emphasizing their foreign origins to whites and masking their origins to African Americans.[16]

As the sociologist Philip Kasinitz notes, some West Indians in New York City have created ways to educate and socialize their children so as to protect them from adopting certain characteristics prevalent among their African-American peers. Earlier generations of West Indian immigrants sent their children back to the Caribbean to be educated. Shirley Chisholm, for example, who served in Congress from 1969 until 1983, wrote in her 1970 memoir:

> Years later I would know what an important gift my parents had given me by seeing to it that I had my early education in the strict, traditional, British-style schools of Barbados. If I speak and write easily now, that early education is the main reason. . . . It's an inescapable fact, but one I have never liked to discuss because of the bad feeling it can cause, that a surprising number of successful black politicians are of West Indian descent. . . . I think that blacks from the islands tend to have less fear of whites, and therefore less hatred of them. They can meet whites as equals; this is harder for American blacks who tend to overreact by jumping from the feeling that whites are superior to looking down on them as inferior.[17]

---

[15] We recognize that many children of the white working class also develop negative attitudes toward school and authority figures that lead to discouragement and underachievement. We also recognize that low-income Latinos of the second and third generations may develop negative attitudes toward school as they come to see themselves less as immigrants and more as members of the working class (see Carola Suarez-Orozco and Marcelo Suarez-Orozco, *Transformations: Migration, Family Life, and Achievement Motivation Among Latino Adolescents* [Stanford: Stanford University Press, 1995]). But we are not focusing in this book on the way the educational system reproduces the class structure. For our views on this issue, see Richard L. Zweigenhaft and G. William Domhoff, *Blacks in the White Establishment? A Study of Race and Class in America* (New Haven: Yale University Press, 1981), 159–162.

[16] Mary C. Waters, "Ethnic and Racial Identities of Second-Generation Black Immigrants in New York City," *International Migration Review* 28, no. 4 (1994), 795–820.

[17] Cited in Philip Kasinitz, *Caribbean New York: Black Immigrants and the Politics of Race* (Ithaca, N.Y.: Cornell University Press, 1992), 76, 220–221. Both Sidney Poitier, the actor, and Harry Belafonte, the singer, spent portions of their childhoods in the West Indies. As Poitier observed, "I firmly believe that we both had the opportunity to arrive at the formation of a sense of ourselves without having it fucked with by racism as it existed in the United States." Henry Louis Gates Jr., "Belafonte's Balancing Act," *New Yorker*, August 26–September 2, 1996, pp. 133–143. The quotation appears on p. 134.

More recently, West Indian New Yorkers have founded many private schools that provide "back home"–style education. These schools often emphasize that their teachers have been trained in the West Indies, the curricula are rigorous, the students wear British-style school uniforms, and there is strict discipline. Kasinitz notes that the demand for such schools "did not arise solely from cultural norms about what constitutes a 'good' education" but stemmed from the hope on the part of West Indian parents that they could help their children avoid feelings of inferiority.[18]

On the basis of this analysis, we can see why some of the most prominent black Americans are those who were able to bypass or overcome an oppositional identity. Some have done so because they were immigrants or the children of immigrants; some have done so by attending Catholic schools, where the stringent academic and social requirements provide an alternative identity, or by participating in special programs, like A Better Chance, that also provide new empowered identities; some have done so as a result of the rigorous resocialization provided by the military; and some have been raised in part by a white parent who did not share the oppositional identity of the black culture.[19] The African American who has reached the most powerful position in the power elite, Colin Powell, not only is light-skinned but is the son of Jamaican immigrants and moved up through (and was shaped by) the military, starting with his involvement in ROTC as a college student.[20]

This framework also explains the somewhat greater success of black women than of black men in school. Maintaining the subjugated state of a minority group involves constant vigilance against organized resistance by its male members, so whites have always had a greater fear of black men than of black women and have dealt with the slightest hint of organized resistance by them with deadly force. True enough, many black women have been abused physically and sexually by whites, and we are not minimizing the negative psychological consequences of such mistreatment, but it is nonetheless the case that whites have been far more likely to kill, maim, and exclude black men than black women. Most dramatically, less than 1 percent of known lynching victims were women. The legacies of this long historical power confrontation between white and black males are very great.

White fear of black males then interacts with the form of resistance to discrimination that is more often practiced everywhere by males than by females—opposition and defiance. Black males are more likely to defy school authorities and to be disciplined and suspended. They are more likely to come into conflict with their bosses at work and thus lose their jobs. Black women, on the other hand, are less likely to express open resistance because of the way most women are socialized in societies throughout the world. They therefore have fewer open conflicts with authority figures and are more likely to do well in school and hold onto a job.

A related factor reinforces these gender differences: the earnings gap is narrower between black women and white women than it is between black men and white men. Because

---

[18] Kasinitz, *Caribbean New York*, 75.

[19] See, for example, James McBride, *The Color of Water: A Black Man's Tribute to His White Mother* (New York: Riverhead, 1996). As a teenager in the 1970s, McBride confronted the oppositional identity and resisted it, in no small part because of his white, Jewish mother. He and all eleven of his black siblings went to college, and eight of the twelve earned graduate or professional degrees. For another exceptionally fine book about the Jewish mother of two black sons educated at Brown and Columbia, see Jane Lazarre, *Beyond the Whiteness of Whiteness: Memoir of a White Mother of Black Sons* (Durham, N.C.: Duke University Press, 1996).

[20] Charles C. Moskos and John Sibley Butler, *All That We Can Be: Black Leadership and Racial Integration the Army Way* (New York: Basic, 1996); Henry Louis Gates Jr., "Powell and the Black Elite," *New Yorker*, September 25, 1995, 63–80.

TABLE 8.2   Median Annual Full-Time Earnings, 1994

	Men		Women	
	High School	*College*	*High School*	*College*
Black	$25,349	$36,000	$17,750	$31,890
White	29,321	48,600	20,050	33,700
B/W[a]	86%	78%	89%	95%

Source: Drawn from Ramon G. McLeod, "Elite Black Women Closing Income Gap," *San Francisco Chronicle,* June 11, 1996; see also *Black Population in the U.S.,* U.S. Bureau of the Census, January 1995.
[a]Earnings of blacks expressed as a percentage of earnings of whites in the same category.

black women use gender as one of their reference points and realize that some of the discrimination against them is based on gender, they are more hopeful about their future and therefore more willing to put up with school. Information on black and white earning differences for men and women is presented in table 8.2. Among other things, it shows that the gap is even greater between college-educated black and white males than it is for men with less education, a fact not easily explained by conventional theories.

Support for this analysis can be found in a detailed attitudinal survey in Los Angeles high schools by sociologist Roslyn Mickelson, who showed that blacks were just as positive as whites in their abstract belief in the value and importance of education but far less likely to trust that education would have any practical value for people such as themselves. She also found that the gap between these abstract and concrete attitudes was smaller for middle-class black women than for either middle- or working-class black men. Concrete attitudes were better predictors of school achievement than abstract attitudes for all the students she studied, and being female was "much more important in achievement for blacks than for whites." These findings, Mickelson argues, reflect the different occupational realities that black men and women

face, for "middle-class black women receive the best returns on higher education of any black cohort."[21]

If our overall analysis of the power relationship between whites and blacks is correct, then we are not hopeful that there will be a gradual integration of African Americans without the strong support of laws and programs at the federal level advocated by the sociologist Sharon Collins.[22] It is the need for such laws that is likely to keep African Americans of all income and educational levels as part of the liberal-labor coalition in the Democratic Party. Contrary to those who say that race is no longer important—by pointing to immigrant blacks or Asian Americans—we believe that the gap between African Americans and all others remains the sharpest divide in U.S. society. Indeed, as we argued in *Blacks in the White Establishment? A Study of Race and Class in America*, this divide is wider than all others, including class.

The Ironies of Diversity

The impetus for greater diversity, as we have stressed, did not come from within the power elite but was the result of external pressures. Generally speaking, members of the power elite reluctantly accepted diversification as a goal for themselves only because they had little choice. This point is best demonstrated in the case of one aspect of diversity called affirmative action, a set of programs originally designed to create more job opportunities for African Americans.

As John Skrentny argues, the idea of affirmative action as a policy was adopted by business

---

[21] Roslyn Arlin Mickelson, "The Attitude-Achievement Paradox Among Black Adolescents," *Sociology of Education* 63 (1990), 44–61. The quotations appear on pp. 56, 69.
[22] See our discussion of Collins's work in Chapter 3. For a systematic empirical demonstration of the importance of such government policies using time series data, see Martin Carnoy, *Faded Dreams: The Politics and Economics of Race in America* (New York: Cambridge University Press, 1994).

and political elites very hurriedly in the face of the 290 serious urban disturbances that occurred between 1963 and 1968. These elites quickly legitimized what they saw as preferential hiring through a series of special commissions and government hearings, before the concept was widely discussed, because they feared that even greater unrest might develop. Job programs were seen not only as the quickest and surest way to restore domestic tranquility but as a means of avoiding larger government programs and expanded welfare benefits as well. Moreover, it was the Nixon administration that created the stringent guidelines later attacked as a "quota" system. Once the fear of urban unrest subsided, however, the elite origins of the plan were ignored, and conservatives began to attack affirmative action as unfair to whites and unconstitutional. In the first of many ironies, liberals and minorities ended up defending a plan endorsed by white male elites in a time of crisis.[23]

Moreover, the diversity forced upon the power elite may have helped to strengthen it, at least in the short run. Diversity has given the power elite buffers, ambassadors, tokens, and legitimacy. This is an unintended consequence that few insurgents or social scientists foresaw. One who did was the late E. Digby Baltzell, who argued in the early 1960s that the acceptance of successful Jews would strengthen what he called the establishment. Baltzell believed that the exclusion of successful newcomers, whatever their social origins, would cause the establishment to become castelike and hence vulnerable.[24] But even Baltzell missed the bigger picture. As the power elite diversified far beyond the inclusion of Jews, he joined the long parade of those who lamented the alleged death of the establishment. By the late 1980s and into the 1990s, rather than praising the establishment for taking in new members, Baltzell was bemoaning the "decline of traditional class authority."[25]

The power elite has been strengthened because diversity has been achieved primarily by the selection of women and minorities who share the prevailing perspectives and values of those already in power. The power elite is not "multicultural" in any full sense of the concept, but only in terms of ethnic or racial origins. This process has been helped along by those who have called for the inclusion of women and minorities without any consideration of criteria other than sex, race, or ethnicity. Because the demand was strictly for a woman on the Supreme Court, President Reagan could comply by choosing a conservative upper-class corporate lawyer, Sandra Day O'Connor. When pressure mounted to have more black justices, President Bush could respond by appointing Clarence Thomas, a conservative black Republican with a law degree from Yale University. It is yet another irony that appointments like these served to undercut the liberal social movements that caused them to happen.[26]

[23] John David Skrentny, *The Ironies of Affirmative Action: Politics, Culture, and Justice in America* (Chicago: University of Chicago Press, 1996), 78–91. Although he concludes that affirmative action was an "elite" response to a possible loss of societal control, Skrentny abandons any consideration of class. For a critical analysis of the return to a classless paradigm in American social science, see G. William Domhoff, *State Autonomy or Class Dominance?* (Hawthorne, N.Y.: Aldine de Gruyter, 1996).

[24] E. Digby Baltzell, *The Protestant Establishment: Aristocracy and Caste in America* (New York: Vintage, 1964; New Haven: Yale University Press, 1987).

[25] E. Digby Baltzell, *Sporting Gentlemen: Men's Tennis from the Age of Honor to the Cult of the Superstar* (New York: Free Press, 1995), 388. At the time of his death, in August 1996, Baltzell was in the early stages of research for a book on what he called "the end of the Protestant establishment." See Eric Pace, "E. Digby Baltzell Dies at 80; Studied WASP's," *New York Times,* August 120, 1996.

[26] In addition, evidence from experimental work in social psychology suggests that tokenism has the effect of undercutting the impetus for collective action by the excluded group. See, for example, Stephen C. Wright, Donald M. Taylor, and Fathali M. Moghaddam, "Responding to Membership in a Disadvantaged Group: From Acceptance to Collective Protest," *Journal of Personality and Social Psychology* 58, no. 6 (1990), 994–1003. See also Bruce R. Hare, "On the Desegregation of the Visible Elite; or, Beware of the Emperor's New Helpers: He or She May Look Like You or Me," *Sociological Forum* 10, no. 4 (1995), 673–678.

It is not surprising, therefore, that when we look at the business practices of the women and minorities who have risen to the top of the corporate world, we find that their perspectives and values do not differ markedly from those of their white male counterparts. When Linda Wachner, one of the few women to become CEO of a *Fortune*-level company, the Warnaco Group, concluded that one of Warnaco's many holdings, the Hathaway Shirt Company, was unprofitable, she decided to stop making Hathaway shirts and to sell or close down the factory. It did not matter to Wachner that Hathaway, which started making shirts in 1837, was one of the oldest companies in Maine, that almost all of the five hundred employees at the factory were working-class women, or even that the workers had given up a pay raise to hire consultants to teach them to work more effectively and, as a result, had doubled their productivity. The bottom-line issue was that the company was considered unprofitable, and the average wage of the Hathaway workers, $7.50 an hour, was thought to be too high. (In 1995 Wachner was paid $10 million in salary and stock, and Warnaco had a net income of $46.5 million.) "We did need to do the right thing for the company and the stockholders," explained Wachner.[27]

Nor did ethnic background matter to Thomas Fuentes, a senior vice president at a consulting firm in Orange County, California, a director of Fleetwood Enterprises, and chairman of the Orange County Republican Party. Fuentes targeted fellow Latinos who happened to be Democrats when he sent uniformed security guards to twenty polling places in 1988 "carrying signs in Spanish and English warning people not to vote if they were not U.S. citizens."

The security firm ended up paying $60,000 in damages when it lost a lawsuit stemming from this intimidation.[28]

We also recall that the Fanjuls, the Cuban-American sugar barons, have had no problem ignoring labor laws in dealing with their migrant labor force, and that the Sakioka family illegally gave short-handled hoes to its migrant farm workers. These people were acting as employers, not as members of ethnic groups. That is, members of the power elite of both genders and all ethnicities have practiced class politics, making it possible for the power structure to weather the challenge created by the social movements that began in the 1960s.

Those who challenged Christian white male homogeneity in the power structure during the 1960s not only sought to create civil rights and new job opportunities for men and women who had previously been mistreated, important though these goals were. They also hoped that new perspective in the boardrooms and the halls of government would bring greater openness throughout the society. The idea was both to diversify the power elite and to shift some of its power to previously excluded groups and social classes. The social movements of the 1960s were strikingly successful in increasing the individual rights and freedoms available to all Americans, especially African Americans. As we have shown, they also created pressures that led to openings at the top for individuals from groups that had previously been excluded.

But as the concerns of social movements, political leaders, and the courts came to focus more and more on individual rights, the emphasis on social class and "distributive justice" was lost. The age-old American commitment to individualism, reinforced at every turn by members of the power elite, won out over the commitment to greater equality of income and wealth

---

[27] Sara Rimer, "Fall of a Shirtmaking Legend Shakes its Maine Hometown," *New York Times*, May 15, 1996. See also Floyd Norris, "Market Place," *New York Times*, June 7, 1996; Stephanie Strom, "Double Trouble at Linda Wachner's Twin Companies," *New York Times*, August 4, 1996. Strom's article reveals that Hathaway Shirts "got a reprieve" when an investor group stepped in to save it.

[28] Claudia Luther and Steven Churm, "GOP Official Says He OK'd Observers at Polls," *Los Angeles Times*, November 12, 1988; Jeffrey Perlman, "Firm Will Pay $60,000 in Suit Over Guards at Polls," *Los Angeles Times*, May 31, 1989.

that had been one strand of New Deal liberalism and a major emphasis of left-wing activists in the 1960s.

We therefore have to conclude on the basis of our findings that the diversification of the power elite did not generate any changes in an underlying class system in which the top 1 percent have 45.6 percent of all financial wealth, the next 19 percent have 46.7 percent, and the bottom 80 percent have 7.8 percent.[29] The values of liberal individualism embedded in the Declaration of Independence, the Bill of Rights, and the civic culture were renewed by vigorous and courageous activists, but despite their efforts the class structure remains a major obstacle to individual fulfillment for the overwhelming majority of Americans. This fact is more than an irony. It is a dilemma. It combines with the dilemma of race to create a nation that celebrates equal opportunity but is, in reality, a bastion of class privilege and conservatism.

---

[29] Edward N. Wolff, *Top Heavy* (New York: New Press, 1996), 67.

Chapter 9

Exchange Theory and Rational Choice

Introduction

Exchange theory, which has its roots in utilitarianism and psychological behaviorism, emerged in the 1960s as yet another paradigm of social theory to challenge functionalism. The rudimentary ideas of exchange theory are also to be found in certain notions developed by Georg Simmel as he sought to capture the fundamental nature of human life as an interactive process involving reciprocal relations, or exchange, within social associations. However, the work of George Homans is most strongly tied to the psychological behaviorism of the Harvard psychologist B. F. Skinner, while Peter Blau has been more heavily influenced by the work of Simmel.

Both Homans and Blau express serious reservations about functionalism's reliance on values and norms in the explanation of social behavior. For Homans, in particular, the work of Durkheim and later of Parsons ascribed too much to the play of external social forces that impinge on behavior and too little on the individual. When Homans speaks of these sociological theories, there is a sense in which he views them as ideological, a betrayal of western ideals. For Homans, Durkheim's theory of society is an attack on the liberal ideal of individual autonomy and on the idea that individuals are unique entities who ultimately give meaning to society.

Homans' sociology is therefore individualistic and attempts to build a theory about social life from the basic behavioristic propositions derived from B. F. Skinner's psychology of operant conditioning. What this means is that, extrapolating from the study of pigeons, Skinner and Homans formulate propositions about human behavior. In everyday social interaction, Homans maintains that individuals will act to secure rewards and avoid punishment. Social relationships are seen as exchange relationships in the sense that rewards, such as approval or recognition, are attendant on certain behaviors. When these behaviors are rewarded an individual is likely to repeat them in similar situations. If those behaviors elicit negative reactions then they are not likely to be repeated. This leads to a view of human behavior in terms of costs and benefits and of rational individuals who can calculate the consequences of their actions before taking them. However, it is highly problematic whether these formulations lead Homans to a theory of society or to an adequate explanation of social structures and social institutions, as well as of social behavior beyond the face-to-face interaction.

In response to Homans' theories, Peter Blau further developed exchange theory by extending his analysis to more complex social structures, exploring the development of social structures and the reciprocal relationship between these larger structures and social interaction on the individual level.

Born in Vienna, Austria, in 1918, Blau emigrated to the United States in 1939. In 1943, he acquired American citizenship, and after serving in the military during World War II, he completed his Ph.D. at Columbia University in 1952. In 1968, Blau won the Sorokin Award from the American Sociological Association for a book which he and Otis Dudley coauthored, entitled *The American Occupational Structure*. However, it is for his work in *Exchange and Power in Social Life* that Blau has gained his reputation as a theorist of considerable stature.

In the excerpt from Blau that follows, his devotion to Simmel's idea of exchange and his rejection of the Parsonian views of values and cultural norms as explanations for individual action are evident. Yet Blau was interested in moving beyond the Homans model in order to account for large social structures. Inevitably, Blau returns to values and norms as media of social life that impact directly upon social exchange and affect the processes of social integration and differentiation.

Blau's interest in and criticism of the theories of social behaviorism and value theory compelled him to develop his own theory of social exchange, one that recognized the importance of face-to-face interaction on an individual level but also explored exchange in the larger social realm. Like Homans, Blau saw the value of studying face-to-face interaction in order to explain social phenomena, but he wanted to explore more complex structures and the social forces that surround and determine their form.

Blau defines a four-step sequence, which leads from interpersonal exchange to determination of status and power to legitimation and organization, and culminates in opposition and social change. He believes that the main force which draws and ties people together is social attraction. A person or institution which can offer rewards to individuals is highly attractive socially. Rewards granted serve to strengthen social ties. Inadequate rewards lead to a deterioration of social ties. Two types of rewards are described by Blau: *extrinsic rewards,* which are tangible things, such as money, and *intrinsic rewards,* which are intangible, such as love or respect.

In his attempt to understand exchange in complex social formations, Blau turns to a study of social groups. He believes that social interaction develops initially in social groups, which attract individuals by the rewards they offer.

Blau discusses problems of power and legitimation as they impact on face-to-face relations and macro-structures or large-scale social organizations. Social integration results from commonly shared values.

Blau establishes two categories of social groups: emergent social groups, which evolve according to the above principles, and established groups, which exist to achieve a specific goal, such as selling a product.

It is important to differentiate between small groups and large collective structures. In a small group, face-to-face exchange occurs between most members, whereas in large groups, direct contact between all members is rare. There is therefore a need for some mediating force to tie members together. Blau argues that this demonstrates the inability of social behaviorism, based as it is on studies of face-to-face interaction, to explain social exchange in large structures. Although the behaviorists might argue that the same principles which apply to exchange on an individual scale apply on a larger scale, Blau asserts that these micro-interactions do not occur in the macro sphere. He argues that values and norms serve as mediators in large collectivities, because they facilitate indirect social exchange and determine social differentiation and integration. The reward for conformity to social values and norms is acceptance and approval as well as the maintenance of structures.

Rational choice theory, represented here in a 1988 article by James S. Coleman, follows in the tradition of Homans and Blau. Coleman's writings in the area of social theory are informed by a critique of the deterministic emphasis of classical European theory at the expense of the rational purposive actions of individuals. In this sense, the individual is seen as overdetermined by social structures such as class, or as a role player in a complex of corporate entities. Part of Coleman's mission as a social theorist is to bring the individual back into social theory, to demonstrate that social relationships, or "social capital," provide significant benefits to individuals in the form of "human capital," or resources that can benefit the individual. Thus, instead of conceiving social structure as a purely exogenous force that constrains behavior beyond the capacity of individuals to control, Coleman theorizes that individuals engage in social relations because they rationally calculate or understand the benefits to be derived from them. The article reprinted below provides several illustrations of what Coleman means by "social capital" and "human capital," how and why individuals engage in behaviors that provide them with "social capital," and the circumstances under which "human capital" can be created.

Coleman's broader view, later expressed in his presidential address before the ASA Meetings (1993), is that sociology should become a discipline concerned with the rational redesign of society. In the article excerpted below, Coleman picks up this theme as he describes the social conditions that have eroded the creation of "human capital" in the decline of "social capital" within the family and the community. Readers should be able to trace out the policy implications of these discussions as Coleman moves these questions into the arena of "public goods." Were sociologists to engage actively in the social reconstruction of society using Coleman's formulations, what kinds of public policies would be required to restore the creation of "human capital"?

Blau's departure from the earlier views espoused by Homans should be evident, as is his attempt to integrate face-to-face interaction with the large-scale social structures and to account for their existence. Whether Blau has succeeded where Homans failed is still open to question.

PETER BLAU: THE STRUCTURE OF SOCIAL ASSOCIATIONS

Of course the elementary qualities of which the social fact consists are present in germ in individual minds. But the social fact emerges from them only when they have been transformed by association since it is only then that it appears. Association itself is also an active factor productive of special effects. In itself it is therefore something new. When the consciousness of individuals, instead of remaining isolated, becomes grouped and combined, something in the world has been altered.

ÉMILE DURKHEIM, *Suicide*

To speak of social life is to speak of the associations between people—their associating together in work and in play, in love and in war, to trade or to worship, to help or to hinder. It is in the social relations men establish that their interests find expression and their desires become realized. As Simmel put it: "Social association refers to the widely varying forms that are generated as the diverse interests of individuals prompt them to develop social units in which they realize these—sensual or ideal, lasting or fleeting, conscious or unconscious, casually impelling or teleologically inducing—interests."[1] Simmel's fundamental postulate, and also that of this book, is that the analysis of social associations,

[1] Georg Simmel, *Soziologie,* Leipzig: Duncker and Humblot, 1908, p. 6 (my translation).

of the processes governing them, and of the forms they assume is the central task of sociology. The title of this first chapter can be considered a free translation *of* Simmel's basic concept, "Die Formen der Vergesellschaftung."

People's associations proliferate through social space and time. Social relations unite not only individuals in groups but also groups in communities and societies. The associations between individuals tend to become organized into complex social structures, and they often become institutionalized to perpetuate the form of organization far beyond the life span of human beings. The main sociological purpose of studying processes of face-to-face interaction is to lay the foundation for an understanding of the social structures that evolve and the emergent social forces that characterize their development.

The objectives of our investigation are to analyze social associations, the processes that sustain them and the forms they attain, and to proceed to inquire into the complex social forces and structures to which they give rise. Broad as this topic is, it is intended to provide a specific focus that explicitly excludes many sociological problems from consideration. Sociology is defined by Weber as "a science which attempts the interpretative understanding of social action in order thereby to arrive at a causal explanation of its course and effects. . . . Action is social insofar as, by virtue of the subjective meaning attached to it by the acting individual (or individuals), it takes account of the behavior of others and is thereby oriented in its course."[2] A concern with social action, broadly conceived as any conduct that derives its impetus and meaning from social values, has characterized contemporary theory in sociology for some years. The resulting preoccupation with value orientations has diverted theoretical attention from the study of the actual associations between people and the structures of their associations. While structures of social relations are, of course, profoundly influenced by common values, these structures have a significance of their own, which is ignored if concern is exclusively with the underlying values and norms. Exchange transactions and power relations, in particular, constitute social forces that must be investigated in their own right, not merely in terms of the norms that limit and the values that reinforce them, to arrive at an understanding of the dynamics of social structures. If one purpose of the title of this chapter is to indicate a link with the theoretical tradition of Simmel, another purpose is to distinguish the theoretical orientation in this monograph from that of Weber and Parsons; not "the structure of social action"[3] but the structure of social associations is the focal point of the present inquiry.

After illustrating the concept of social exchange and its manifestations in various social relations, this chapter presents the main theme of how more complex processes of social association evolve out of simpler ones. Forces of social attraction stimulate exchange transactions. Social exchange, in turn, tends to give rise to differentiation of status and power. Further processes emerge in a differentiated status structure that lead to legitimation and organization, on the one hand, and to opposition and change, on the other. Whereas the conception of reciprocity in exchange implies the existence of balancing forces that create a strain toward equilibrium, the simultaneous operations of diverse balancing forces recurrently produce imbalances in social life, and the resulting dialectic between reciprocity and imbalance gives social structures their distinctive nature and dynamics.

[2] Max Weber, *The Theory of Social and Economic Organization,* New York: Oxford University Press, 1947, p. 88.

[3] The title of Talcott Parsons' first major work, *The Structure of Social Action,* New York: McGraw-Hill, 1937, would also be appropriate for some of his later theoretical writings, as he himself has noted in *The Social System,* Glencoe: Free Press, 1951, p. ix.

The Exchange of Social Rewards

By Honour, in its proper and genuine Significa-
tion, we mean nothing else but the good Opinion
of others. . . .

> The Reason why there are so few Men of
> real Virtue, and so many of real Honour, is,
> because all the Recompence a Man has of a
> virtuous Action, is the Pleasure of doing it,
> which most People reckon but poor Pay;
> but the Self-denial a Man of Honour sub-
> mits to in one Appetite, is immediately
> rewarded by the Satisfaction he receives
> from another, and what he abates of his
> Avarice, or any other Passion, is doubly
> repaid to his Pride. . . .

MANDEVILLE, *The Fable of the Bees*

Most human pleasures have their roots in social
life. Whether we think of love or power, professional recognition or sociable companionship,
the comforts of family life or the challenge of
competitive sports, the gratifications experienced by individuals are contingent on actions of
others. The same is true for the most selfless and
spiritual satisfactions. To work effectively for a
good cause requires making converts to it. Even
the religious experience is much enriched by
communal worship. Physical pleasures that can
be experienced in solitude pale in significance by
comparison. Enjoyable as a good dinner is, it is
the social occasion that gives it its luster. Indeed,
there is something pathetic about the person
who derives his major gratification from food or
drink as such, since it reveals either excessive
need or excessive greed; the pauper illustrates
the former, the glutton, the latter. To be sure,
there are profound solitary enjoyments—reading
a good book, creating a piece of art, producing a
scholarly work. Yet these, too, derive much of
their significance from being later communicated
to and shared with others. The lack of such anticipation makes the solitary activity again somewhat pathetic: the recluse who has nobody to talk

to about what he reads; the artist or scholar
whose works are completely ignored, not only by
his contemporaries but also by posterity.

Much of human suffering as well as much of
human happiness has its source in the actions of
other human beings. One follows from the other,
given the facts of group life, where pairs do not
exist in complete isolation from other social relations. The same human acts that cause pleasure
to some typically cause displeasure to others.
For one boy to enjoy the love of a girl who has
committed herself to be his steady date, other
boys who had gone out with her must suffer the
pain of having been rejected. The satisfaction a
man derives from exercising power over others
requires that they endure the deprivation of
being subject to his power. For a professional to
command an outstanding reputation in his field,
most of his colleagues must get along without
such pleasant recognition, since it is the lesser
professional esteem of the majority that defines
his as outstanding. The joy the victorious team
members experience has its counterpart in the
disappointment of the losers. In short, the
rewards individuals obtain in social associations
tend to entail a cost to other individuals. This
does not mean that most social associations
involve zero-sum games in which the gains of
some rest on the losses of others. Quite the contrary, individuals associate with one another
because they all profit from their association. But
they do not necessarily all profit equally, nor do
they share the cost of providing the benefits
equally, and even if there are no direct costs to
participants, there are often indirect costs born
by those excluded from the association, as the
case of the rejected suitors illustrates.

Some social associations are intrinsically
rewarding. Friends find pleasure in associating
with one another, and the enjoyment of whatever they do together—climbing a mountain,
watching a football game—is enhanced by the
gratification that inheres in the association
itself. The mutual affection between lovers or
family members has the same result. It is not

what lovers do together but their doing it *together* that is the distinctive source of their special satisfaction—not seeing a play but sharing the experience of seeing it. Social interaction in less intimate relations than those of lovers, family members, or friends, however, may also be inherently rewarding. The sociability at a party or among neighbors or in a work group involves experiences that are not especially profound but are intrinsically gratifying. In these cases, all associates benefit simultaneously from their social interaction, and the only cost they incur is the indirect one of giving up alternative opportunities by devoting time to the association.

Social associations may also be rewarding for a different reason. Individuals often derive specific benefits from social relations because their associates deliberately go to some trouble to provide these benefits for them. Most people like helping others and doing favors for them— to assist not only their friends but also their acquaintances and occasionally even strangers, as the motorist who stops to aid another with his stalled car illustrates. Favors make us grateful, and our expressions of gratitude are social rewards that tend to make doing favors enjoyable, particularly if we express our appreciation and indebtedness publicly and thereby help establish a person's reputation as a generous and competent helper. Besides, one good deed deserves another. If we feel grateful and obligated to an associate for favors received, we shall seek to reciprocate his kindness by doing things for him. He in turn is likely to reciprocate, and the resulting mutual exchange of favors strengthens, often without explicit intent, the social bond between us.

A person who fails to reciprocate favors is accused of ingratitude. This very accusation indicates that reciprocation is expected, and it serves as a social sanction that discourages individuals from forgetting their obligations to associates. Generally, people are grateful for favors and repay their social debts, and both their gratitude and their repayment are social rewards for

the associate who has done them favors.[4] The fact that furnishing benefits to others tends to produce these social rewards is, of course, a major reason why people often go to great trouble to help their associates and enjoy doing so. We would not be human if these advantageous consequences of our good deeds were not important inducements for our doing them.[5] There are, to be sure, some individuals who selflessly work for others without any thought of reward and even without expecting gratitude, but these are virtually saints, and saints are rare. The rest of us also act unselfishly sometimes, but we require some incentive for doing so, if it is only the social acknowledgement that we are unselfish.

An apparent "altruism" pervades social life; people are anxious to benefit one another and to reciprocate for the benefits they receive. But beneath this seeming selflessness an underlying "egoism" can be discovered; the tendency to help others is frequently motivated by the expectation that doing so will bring social rewards. Beyond this self-interested concern with profiting from social associations, however, there is again an "altruistic" element or, at least, one that removes social transactions from simple egoism or psychological hedonism. A basic reward people seek in their associations is social approval and selfish disregard for others makes it impossible to obtain this important reward.[6]

---

[4] "We rarely meet with ingratitude, so long as we are in a position to confer favors." François La Rochefoucauld, *The Maxims,* London: Oxford University Press, 1940, p. 101 (#306).
[5] Once a person has become emotionally committed to a relationship, his identification with the other and his interest in continuing the association provide new independent incentives for supplying benefits to the other. Similarly, firm commitments to an organization lead members to make recurrent contributions to it without expecting reciprocal benefits in every instance. The significance of these social attachments is further elaborated in subsequent chapters.
[6] Bernard Mandeville's central theme is that private vices produce public benefits because the importance of social approval prompts men to contribute to the welfare of

The social approval of those whose opinions we value is of great significance to us, but its significance depends on its being genuine. We cannot force others to give us their approval, regardless of how much power we have over them, because coercing them to express their admiration or praise would make these expressions worthless. "Action can be coerced, but a coerced show of feeling is only a show."[7] Simulation robs approval of its significance, but its very importance makes associates reluctant to withhold approval from one another and, in particular, to express disapproval, thus introducing an element of simulation and dissimulation into their communications. As a matter of fact, etiquette prescribes that approval be simulated in disregard of actual opinions under certain circumstances. One does not generally tell a hostess, "Your party was boring," or a neighbor, "What you say is stupid." Since social conventions require complimentary remarks on many occasions, these are habitually discounted as not reflecting genuine approbation, and other evidence that does reflect it is looked for, such as whether guests accept future invitations or whether neighbors draw one into further conversations.

In matters of morality, however, individuals have strong convictions that constrain them to voice their actual judgments more freely. They usually do not hesitate to express disapproval of or, at least, withhold approval from associates who have violated socially accepted standards of conduct. Antisocial disregard for the welfare of the in group meets universally with disapprobation regardless of how immoral, in terms of the mores of the wider community, the norms of a particular group may be The significance of social approval, therefore, discourages conduct that is utterly and crudely selfish. A more pro-

found morality must rest not merely on group pressure and long-run advantage but primarily on internalized normative standards. In the ideal case, an individual unerringly follows the moral commands of his conscience whatever the consequences. While such complete morality is attained only by the saint and the fool, and most men make some compromises,[8] moral standards clearly do guide and restrain human conduct. Within the rather broad limits these norms impose on social relations, however, human beings tend to be governed in their associations with one another by the desire to obtain social rewards of various sorts, and the resulting exchanges of benefits shape the structure of social relations.

The question that arises is whether a rationalistic conception of human behavior underlies this principle that individuals pursue social rewards in their social associations. The only assumption made is that human beings choose between alternative potential associates or courses of action by evaluating the experiences or expected experiences with each in terms of a preference ranking and then selecting the best alternative. Irrational as well as rational behavior is governed by these considerations, as Boulding has pointed out:

> All behavior, in so far as the very concept of behavior implies doing one thing rather than another, falls into the above pattern, even the behavior of the lunatic and the irrational or irresponsible or erratic person. The distinction between rational and irrational behavior lies in the degree of self-consciousness and the stability of the images involved rather than in any distinction of the principle of optimum.[9]

---

others in their own self-interest. As he put it tersely at one point, "Moral Virtues are the Political Offspring which Flattery begot upon Pride." *The Fable of the Bees*, Oxford: Clarendon, 1924, Vol. I, 51; see also pp. 63–80.

[7] Erving Goffman, *Asylums*, Chicago: Aldine, 1962, p. 115.

[8] Heinrich von Kleist's story "Michael Kohlhaas" is a pathetic illustration of the foolishness inherent in the insistence on rigid conformity with moral standards in complete disregard of consequences.

[9] Kenneth Boulding, *Conflict and Defense*, New York: Harper, 1962, p. 151.

What is explicitly *not* assumed here is that men have complete information, that they have no social commitments restricting their alternatives, that their preferences are entirely consistent or remain constant, or that they pursue one specific ultimate goal to the exclusion of all others. These more restrictive assumptions, which are not made in the present analysis, characterize rationalistic models of human conduct, such as that of game theory.[10] Of particular importance is the fact that men strive to achieve diverse objectives. The statement that men select the most preferred among available alternatives does not imply that they always choose the one that yields them the greatest material profit.[11] They may, and often do, choose the alternative that requires them to make material sacrifices but contributes the most to the attainment of some lofty ideal, for *this* may be their objective. Even in this choice they may err and select an alternative that actually is not the best means to realize their goal. Indeed, the need to anticipate in advance the social rewards with which others will reciprocate for favors in exchange relations inevitably introduces uncertainty and recurrent errors of judgment that make perfectly rational calculations impossible. Granted these qualifications, the assumption that men seek to adjust social conditions to achieve their ends seems to be quite realistic, indeed inescapable.

---

[10] For a discussion of game theory which calls attention to its limitations, see R. Duncan Luce and Howard Raiffa, *Games and Decisions,* New York: Wiley, 1957, esp. chapters iii and vii. For other criticisms of game theory, notably its failure to utilize empirical research, and an attempt to incorporate some of its principles into a substantive theory of conflict, see Thomas C. Schelling, *The Strategy of Conflict,* Cambridge: Harvard University Press, 1960, esp. chapters iv and vi.

[11] See on this point George C. Homans, *Social Behavior,* New York: Harcourt, Brace and World, 1961, pp.79–80; and Anatol Rapoport, *Fights, Games, and Debates,* Ann Arbor: University of Michigan Press, 1960, p. 122.

Basic Processes

> To reward, is to recompense, to remunerate, to return good for good received. To punish, too, is to recompense, to remunerate, though in a different manner; it is to return evil for evil that has been done.
>
> ADAM SMITH, *The Theory of Moral Sentiments*

The basic social processes that govern associations among men have their roots in primitive psychological processes, such as those underlying the feelings of attraction between individuals and their desires for various kinds of rewards. These psychological tendencies are primitive only in respect to our subject matter, that is, they are taken as given without further inquiry into the motivating forces that produce them, for our concern is with the social forces that emanate from them.

The simpler social processes that can be observed in interpersonal associations and that rest directly on psychological dispositions give rise to the more complex social processes that govern structures of interconnected social associations, such as the social organization of a factory or the political relations in a community. New social forces emerge in the increasingly complex social structures that develop in societies, and these dynamic forces are quite removed from the ultimate psychological base of all social life. Although complex social systems have their foundation in simpler ones, they have their own dynamics with emergent properties. In this section, the basic processes of social associations will be presented in broad strokes, to be analyzed subsequently in greater detail, with special attention to their wider implications.

Social attraction is the force that induces human beings to establish social associations on their own initiative and to expand the scope of their associations once they have been formed. Reference here is to social relations into which men enter of their own free will rather than to either those into which they are born (such as kinship groups) or those imposed on them by forces beyond their control (such as the combat teams to which soldiers are assigned), although even in these involuntary relations the extent and intensity of the association depend on the degree of mutual attraction. An individual is attracted to another if he expects associating with him to be in some way rewarding for himself, and his interest in the expected social rewards draws him to the other. The psychological needs and dispositions of individuals determine which rewards are particularly salient for them and thus to whom they will be attracted. Whatever the specific motives, there is an important difference between the expectation that the association will be an intrinsically rewarding experience and the expectation that it will furnish extrinsic benefits, for example, advice. This difference calls attention to two distinct meanings of the term "attraction" and its derivatives. In its narrower sense, social attraction refers to liking another person *intrinsically* and having positive feelings toward him; in the broader sense, in which the term is now used, social attraction refers to being drawn to another person for any reason whatsoever. The customer is attracted in this broader sense to the merchant who sells goods of a given quality at the lowest price, but he has no intrinsic feelings of attraction for him, unless they happen to be friends.

A person who is attracted to others is interested in proving himself attractive to them, for his ability to associate with them and reap the benefits expected from the association is contingent on their finding him an attractive associate and thus wanting to interact with him. Their attraction to him, just as his to them, depends on the anticipation that the association will be rewarding. To arouse this anticipation, a person tries to impress others. Attempts to appear impressive are pervasive in the early stages of acquaintance and group formation. Impressive qualities make a person attractive and promise that associating with him will be rewarding. Mutual attraction prompts people to

establish an association, and the rewards they provide each other in the course of their social interaction, unless their expectations are disappointed, maintain their mutual attraction and the continuing association.

Processes of social attraction, therefore, lead to processes of social exchange. The nature of the exchange in an association experienced as intrinsically rewarding, such as a love relationship, differs from that between associates primarily concerned with extrinsic benefits, such as neighbors who help one another with various chores, but exchanges do occur in either case. A person who furnishes needed assistance to associates, often at some cost to himself, obligates them to reciprocate his kindness. Whether reference is to instrumental services or to such intangibles as social approval, the benefits each supplies to the others are rewards that serve as inducements to continue to supply benefits, and the integrative bonds created in the process fortify the social relationship.

A situation frequently arises, however, in which one person needs something another has to offer, for example, help from the other in his work, but has nothing the other needs to reciprocate for the help. While the other may be sufficiently rewarded by expressions of gratitude to help him a few times, he can hardly be expected regularly to devote time and effort to providing help without receiving any return to compensate him for his troubles. (In the case of intrinsic attraction, the only return expected is the willingness to continue the association.) The person in need of recurrent services from an associate to whom he has nothing to offer has several alternatives. First, he may force the other to give him help. Second, he may obtain the help he needs from another source. Third, he may find ways to get along without such help.[12] If he is unable or unwilling to choose any of

---

[12] The last two of these alternatives are noted by Parsons (*op. cit.,* p. 252) in his discussion of a person's reactions to having his expectations frustrated by another.

these alternatives, however, there is only one other course of action left for him; he must subordinate himself to the other and comply with his wishes, thereby rewarding the other with power over himself as an inducement for furnishing the needed help. Willingness to comply with another's demands is a generic social reward, since the power it gives him is a generalized means, parallel to money, which can be used to attain a variety of ends. The power to command compliance is equivalent to credit, which a man can draw on in the future to obtain various benefits at the disposal of those obligated to him.[13] The unilateral supply of important services establishes this kind of credit and thus is a source of power.

Exchange processes, then, give rise to differentiation of power. A person who commands services others need, and who is independent of any at their command, attains power over others by making the satisfaction of their need contingent on their compliance. This principle is held to apply to the most intimate as well as the most distant social relations. The girl with whom a boy is in love has power over him, since his eagerness to spend much time with her prompts him to make their time together especially pleasant for her by acceding to her wishes. The employer can make workers comply with his directives because they are dependent on his wages. To be sure, the superior's power wanes if subordinates can resort to coercion, have equally good alternatives, or are able to do without the benefits at his disposal. But given these limiting conditions, unilateral services that meet basic needs are the penultimate source of power. Its ultimate source, of course, is physical coercion. While the power that rests on coercion is more absolute, however, it is also more limited in scope than the power that derives from met needs.

A person on whom others are dependent for vital benefits has the power to enforce his demands. He may make demands on them that they consider fair and just in relation to the benefits they receive for submitting to his power. On the other hand, he may lack such restraint and make demands that appear excessive to them, arousing feelings of exploitation for having to render more compliance than the rewards received justify. Social norms define the expectations of subordinates and their evaluations of the superior's demands. The fair exercise of power gives rise to approval of the superior, whereas unfair exploitation promotes disapproval. The greater the resources of a person on which his power rests, the easier it is for him to refrain from exploiting subordinates by making excessive demands, and consequently the better are the chances that subordinates will approve of the fairness of his rule rather than disapprove of its unfairness.

There are fundamental differences between the dynamics of power in a collective situation and the power of one individual over another. The weakness of the isolated subordinate limits the significance of his approval or disapproval of the superior. The agreement that emerges in a collectivity of subordinates concerning their judgment of the superior, on the other hand, has far-reaching implications for developments in the social structure.

Collective approval of power legitimates that power. People who consider that the advantages they gain from a superior's exercise of power outweigh the hardships that compliance with his demands imposes on them tend to communicate to each other their approval of the ruler and their feelings of obligation to him. The consensus that develops as the result of these communications finds expression in group pressures that promote compliance with the ruler's directives, thereby strengthening his power of control and legitimating his authority. "A feeling of obligation to obey the commands of the established public authority is found, varying in

---

[13] See Parsons, "On the Concept of Influence," *Public Opinion Quarterly,* 27 (1963), 37–62, esp. pp. 59–60.

liveliness and effectiveness from one individual to another, among the members of any political society."[14] Legitimate authority is the basis of organization. It makes it possible to organize collective effort to further the achievement of various objectives, some of which could not be attained by individuals separately at all and others that can be attained more effectively by coordinating efforts. Although power that is not legitimated by the approval of subordinates can also be used to organize them, the stability of such an organization is highly precarious.

Collective disapproval of power engenders opposition. People who share the experience of being exploited by the unfair demands of those in positions of power, and by the insufficient rewards they receive for their contributions, are likely to communicate their feelings of anger, frustration, and aggression to each other. There tends to arise a wish to retaliate by striking down the existing powers. "As every man doth, so shall it be done to him, and retaliation seems to be the great law that is dictated to us by nature."[15] The social support the oppressed give each other in the course of discussing their common grievances and feelings of hostility justifies and reinforces their aggressive opposition against those in power. It is out of such shared discontent that opposition ideologies and movements develop—that men organize a union against their employer or a revolutionary party against their government.

In brief, differentiation of power in a collective situation evokes contrasting dynamic forces: legitimating processes that foster the organization of individuals and groups in common endeavors; and countervailing forces that deny legitimacy to existing powers and promote opposition and cleavage. Under the influence of these forces, the scope of legitimate organization expands to include ever larger collectivities, but opposition and conflict recurrently redivide these collectivities and stimulate reorganization along different lines.

The distinctive characteristic of complex social structures is that their constituent elements are also social structures. We may call these structures of interrelated groups "macrostructures" and those composed of interacting individuals "microstructures." There are some parallels between the social processes in microstructures and macrostructures. Processes of social attraction create integrative bonds between associates, and integrative processes also unite various groups in a community. Exchange processes between individuals give rise to differentiation among them, and intergroup exchanges further differentiation among groups. Individuals become incorporated in legitimate organizations, and these in turn become part of broader bodies of legitimate authority. Opposition and conflict occur not only within collectivities but also between them. These parallels, however, must not conceal the fundamental differences between the processes that govern the interpersonal associations in microstructures and the forces characteristic of the wider and more complex social relations in macrostructures.

First, value consensus is of crucial significance for social processes that pervade complex social structures, because standards commonly agreed upon serve as mediating links for social transactions between individuals and groups without any direct contact. Sharing basic values creates integrative bonds and social solidarity among millions of people in a society, most of whom have never met, and serves as functional equivalent for the feelings of personal attraction that unite pairs of associates and small groups. Common standards of valuation produce media of exchange—money being the prototype but not the only one—which alone make it possible to transcend personal transactions and develop complex networks of indirect exchange. Legitimating values expand the scope of centralized

---

[14] Bertrand de Jouvenel, *Sovereignty*, University of Chicago Press, 1957, p. 87.
[15] Adam Smith, *The Theory of Moral Sentiments* (2d ed.), London: A. Millar, 1761, p. 139.

control far beyond the reach of personal influence, as exemplified by the authority of a legitimate government. Opposition ideals serve as rallying points to draw together strangers from widely dispersed places and unite them in a common cause. The study of these problems requires an analysis of the significance of social values and norms that must complement the analysis of exchange transactions and power relations but must not become a substitute for it.

A second emergent property of macrostructures is the complex interplay between the internal forces within substructures and the forces that connect the diverse substructures, some of which may be microstructures composed of individuals while others may themselves be macrostructures composed of subgroups. The processes of integration, differentiation, organization, and opposition formation in the various substructures, which often vary greatly among the substructures, and the corresponding processes in the macrostructure all have repercussions for each other. A systematic analysis of these intricate patterns, which will only be adumbrated in chapters ten and eleven, would have to constitute the core of a general theory of social structures.

Finally, enduring institutions typically develop in macrostructures. Established systems of legitimation raise the question of their perpetuation through time. The strong identification of men with the highest ideals and most sacred beliefs they share makes them desirous to preserve these basic values for succeeding generations. The investments made in establishing and expanding a legitimate organization create an interest in stabilizing it and assuring its survival in the face of opposition attacks. For this purpose, formalized procedures are instituted that make the organization independent of any individual member and permit it to persist beyond the life span or period of tenure of its members. Institutionalization refers to the emergence of social mechanisms through which social values and norms, organizing principles,

and knowledge and skills are transmitted from generation to generation. A society's institutions constitute the social matrix in which individuals grow up and are socialized, with the result that some aspects of institutions are reflected in their own personalities, and others appear to them as the inevitable external conditions of human existence. Traditional institutions stabilize social life but also introduce rigidities that make adjustment to changing conditions difficult. Opposition movements may arise to promote such adjustment, yet these movements themselves tend to become institutionalized and rigid in the course of time, creating needs for fresh oppositions.

Reciprocity and Imbalance

Now in these unequal friendships the benefits that one party receives and is entitled to claim from the other are not the same on either side; . . . the better of the two parties, for instance, or the more useful or otherwise superior as the case may be, should receive more affection than he bestows; since when the affection rendered is proportionate to desert, this produces equality in a sense between the parties, and equality is felt to be an essential element of friendship.

ARISTOTLE, *The Nicomachean Ethics*

There is a strain toward imbalance as well as toward reciprocity in social associations. The term "balance" itself is ambiguous inasmuch as we speak not only of balancing our books but also of a balance in our favor, which refers, of course, to a lack of equality between inputs and outputs. As a matter of fact, the balance of the accounting sheet merely rests, in the typical case, on an underlying imbalance between income and outlays, and so do apparent balances in social life. Individuals and groups are interested in, at least, maintaining a balance between inputs and outputs and staying out of debt in their social transactions; hence the strain toward reciprocity. Their aspirations, however, are to achieve a balance in their favor and accumulate credit that makes their status superior to that of others; hence the strain toward imbalance.

Arguments about equilibrium—that all scientific theories must be conceived in terms of equilibrium models or that any equilibrium model neglects the dynamics of real life—ignore the important point that the forces sustaining equilibrium on one level of social life constitute disequilibrating forces on other levels. For supply and demand to remain in equilibrium in a market, for example, forces must exist that continually disturb the established patterns of exchange. Similarly, the circulation of the elite, an equilibrium model, rests on the operation of forces that create imbalances and disturbances in the various segments of society. The principle suggested is that balanced social states depend on imbalances in other social states; forces that restore equilibrium in one respect do so by creating disequilibrium in others. The processes of association described illustrate this principle.

A person who is attracted to another will seek to prove himself attractive to the other. Thus a boy who is very much attracted to a girl, more so than she is to him, is anxious to make himself more attractive to her. To do so, he will try to impress her and, particularly, go out of his way to make associating with him an especially rewarding experience for her. He may devote a lot of thought to finding ways to please her, spend much money on her, and do the things she likes on their dates rather than those he would prefer. Let us assume that he is successful and she becomes as attracted to him as he is to her, that is, she finds associating with him as rewarding as he finds associating with her, as indicated by the fact that both are equally eager to spend time together.

Attraction is now reciprocal, but the reciprocity has been established by an imbalance in the exchange. To be sure, both obtain satisfactory rewards from the association at this stage,

the boy as the result of her willingness to spend as much time with him as he wants, and the girl as the result of his readiness to make their dates enjoyable for her. These reciprocal rewards are the sources of their mutual attraction. The contributions made, however, are in imbalance. Both devote time to the association, which involves giving up alternative opportunities, but the boy contributes in addition special efforts to please her. Her company is sufficient reward by itself, while his is not, which makes her "the more useful or otherwise superior" in terms of their own evaluations, and he must furnish supplementary rewards to produce "equality in a sense between the parties." Although two lovers may, of course, be equally anxious to spend time together and to please one another, it is rare for a perfect balance of mutual affection to develop spontaneously. The reciprocal attraction in most intimate relations—marriages and lasting friendships as well as more temporary attachments—is the result of some imbalance of contributions that compensates for inequalities in spontaneous affection, notably in the form of one partner's greater willingness to defer to the other's wishes.

The relationship between this conception and balance theory in psychology may be briefly indicated. Thus, Newcomb's ABX scheme is concerned with an individual A, who is attracted to another individual B, has a certain attitude toward an object X, and perceives B to have a certain attitude toward X.[16] Discrepancies between any of these elements produce a strain toward balance both in individual systems, that is, internal psychological states, and in collective systems, that is, interpersonal relations. For example, if A prefers the Democrats and B the Republicans, there are several ways for A to restore balance: he may become more

---

[16] Theodore M. Newcomb, *The Acquaintance Process*, New York: Holt, Rinehart and Winston, 1961, esp. chapter ii. See also Fritz Heider, *The Psychology of Interpersonal Relations*, New York: Wiley, 1958.

favorable toward the Republicans; he may misperceive B's attitude as being really not Republican; he may lose interest in politics, making the disagreement inconsequential; or he may cease to associate with B and search for other associates whose opinions he finds more congenial. The focus here is on the implications that imbalances in interpersonal relations have for psychological processes that restore balance in the mental states of individuals,[17] on the one hand, and for changes in interpersonal relations on the other. Initially, however, individuals tend to cope with impending imbalances of attraction by seeking to prove themselves attractive to associates they find attractive in order to establish friendly relations and become integrated among them. These processes, rather than those to which Newcomb calls attention, are the main concern of the preceding discussion and of the more extensive one in the next chapter.

The theoretical principle that has been advanced is that a given balance in social associations is produced by imbalances in the same associations in other respects. This principle, which has been illustrated with the imbalances that underlie reciprocal attraction, also applies to the process of social differentiation. A person who supplies services in demand to others obligates them to reciprocate. If some fail to reciprocate, he has strong inducements to withhold the needed assistance from them in order to supply it to others who do repay him for his troubles in some form. Those who have nothing else to offer him that would be a satisfactory return for his services, therefore, are under pressure to defer to his wishes and comply with his requests in repayment for his assistance. Their compliance with his demands gives him the power to utilize their resources at his discretion

to further his own ends. By providing unilateral benefits to others, a person accumulates a capital of willing compliance on which he can draw whenever it is to his interest to impose his will upon others, within the limits of the significance the continuing supply of his benefits has for them. The general advantages of power enable men who cannot otherwise repay for services they need to obtain them in return for their compliance; although in the extreme case of the person who has much power and whose benefits are in great demand, even an offer of compliance may not suffice to obtain them.

Here, an imbalance of power establishes reciprocity in the exchange. Unilateral services give rise to a differentiation of power that equilibrates the exchange. The exchange balance, in fact, rests on two imbalances: unilateral services and unilateral power. Although these two imbalances make up a balance or equilibrium in terms of one perspective, in terms of another, which is equally valid, the exchange equilibrium reinforces and perpetuates the imbalances of dependence and power that sustain it. Power differences not only are an imbalance by definition but also are actually experienced as such, as indicated by the tendency of men to escape from domination if they can. Indeed, a major impetus for the eagerness of individuals to discharge their obligations and reciprocate for services they receive, by providing services in return, is the threat of becoming otherwise subject to the power of the supplier of the services. While reciprocal services create an interdependence that balances power, unilateral dependence on services maintains an imbalance of power.

Differentiation of power evidently constitutes an imbalance in the sense of an inequality of power; but the question must be raised whether differentiation of power also necessarily constitutes an imbalance in the sense of a strain toward change in the structure of social relations. Power differences as such, analytically conceived and abstracted from other considerations, create such a pressure toward change,

---

[17] Processes that restore the psychological balance of individuals by reducing dissonance, that is, by decreasing the significance of an unattainable object or person, are the central focus in Leon Festinger, *A Theory of Cognitive Dissonance*, Evanston: Row, Peterson, 1957.

because it can be assumed that men experience having to submit to power as a hardship from which they would prefer to escape. The advantages men derive from their ruler or government, however, may outweigh the hardships entailed in submitting to his or its power, with the result that the analytical imbalance or disturbance introduced by power differences is neutralized. The significance of power imbalances for social change depends, therefore, on the reactions of the governed to the exercise of power.

Social reactions to the exercise of power reflect once more the principle of reciprocity and imbalance, although in a new form. Power over others makes it possible to direct and organize their activities. Sufficient resources to command power over large numbers enable a person or group to establish a large organization. The members recruited to the organization receive benefits, such as financial remuneration, in exchange for complying with the directives of superiors and making various contributions to the organization. The leadership exercises power within the organization and it derives power from the organization for use in relation with other organizations or groups. The clearest illustration of this double power of organizational leadership is the army commander's power over his own soldiers and, through the force of their arms, over the enemy. Another example is the power business management exercises over its own employees and, through the strength of the concern, in the market. The greater the external power of an organization, the greater are its chances of accumulating resources that put rewards at the disposal of the leadership for possible distribution among the members.

The normative expectations of those subject to the exercise of power, which are rooted in their social experience, govern their reactions to it. In terms of these standards, the benefits derived from being part of an organization or political society may outweigh the investments required to obtain them, or the demands made on members may exceed the returns they receive for fulfilling these demands. The exercise of power, therefore, may produce two different kinds of imbalance, a positive imbalance of benefits for subordinates or a negative imbalance of exploitation and oppression.

If the members of an organization, or generally those subject to a governing leadership, commonly agree that the demands made on them are only fair and just in view of the ample rewards the leadership delivers, joint feelings of obligation and loyalty to superiors will arise and bestow legitimating approval on their authority. A positive imbalance of benefits generates legitimate authority for the leadership and thereby strengthens and extends its controlling influence. By expressing legitimating approval of, and loyalty to, those who govern them subordinates reciprocate for the benefits their leadership provides, but they simultaneously fortify the imbalance of power in the social structure.

If the demands of the men who exercise power are experienced by those subject to it as exploitative and oppressive, and particularly if these subordinates have been unsuccessful in obtaining redress for their grievances, their frustrations tend to promote disapproval of existing powers and antagonism toward them. As the oppressed communicate their anger and aggression to each other, provided there are opportunities for doing so, their mutual support and approval socially justify and reinforce the negative orientation toward the oppressors, and their collective hostility may inspire them to organize an opposition. The exploitative use of coercive power that arouses active opposition is more prevalent in the relations between organizations and groups than within organizations. Two reasons for this are that the advantages of legitimating approval restrain organizational superiors and that the effectiveness of legitimate authority, once established, obviates the need for coercive measures. But the exploitative use of power also occurs within organizations, as unions organized in opposition to exploitative employers show. A negative imbalance for the subjects of power stimulates opposition. The opposition negatively reciprocates, or retaliates, for excessive demands in an attempt to even the score, but it simultaneously creates conflict, disequilibrium, and imbalance in the social structure.[18]

Even in the relatively simple structures of social association considered here, balances in one respect entail imbalances in others. The interplay between equilibrating and disequilibrating forces is still more evident, if less easy to unravel, in complex macrostructures with their cross-cutting substructures, where forces that sustain reciprocity and balance have disequilibrating and imbalancing repercussions not only on other levels of the same substructure but also on other substructures. As we shall see, disequilibrating and re-equilibrating forces generate a dialectical pattern of change in social structures.

Conclusions

In this chapter the basic processes underlying the structure of social associations were outlined, and some of the emergent forces characteristic of complex social structures were briefly indicated. The principles presented in simplified form to convey an overall impression of the theoretical scheme in this book will be elaborated and refined in subsequent chapters. After discussing processes of social integration, support, and exchange in interpersonal associations in some detail, various aspects of social differentiation in groups will be analyzed, and finally attention will be centered on the implication of these social forces as well as of newly emergent ones for organization and change in complex social structures.

The discussion will proceed, therefore, from the basic processes that govern the social interaction between individuals in microstructures to the increasingly complex processes in macrostructures composed of several layers of intersecting substructures. We shall be concerned with the changes in social processes that occur as one moves from simpler to more complex social structures and with the new social forces that emerge in the latter. Entire countries, for example, cannot rely for social control primarily on social approval and personal obligations, as small groups of friends can, and must consequently give formalized procedures and coercive powers, such as law courts and police forces, a more prominent role. While progressing from the simpler to the more complex seems to be the only logical sequence, it does pose some problems in the study of social life.

The pattern of association between two individuals is of course, strongly influenced by the social context in which it occurs. Even the analysis of social interaction in dyads, therefore, must not treat these pairs as if they existed in isolation from other social relations. The mutual attraction of two persons and the exchanges between them, for example, are affected by the alternative opportunities of each, with the result that competitive processes arise that include wider circles and that complement and modify the processes of exchange and attraction in this pair and in other pairs. The power of an individual over another depends entirely on the social alternatives or lack of alternatives of the subjected individual, and this fact, as well as some others, makes it mandatory to examine power relations in a wider context than the isolated pair. Simmel's perceptive discussion of the dyad and the triad is instructive in this connection.[19]

Simmel's analysis of the dyad seems to be conceived as a polar case that highlights, by contrast, the distinctive characteristics of group life. To cite only one example, the death or withdrawal of one individual destroys the dyad,

---

[18] Organized opposition gives expression to latent conflicts and makes them manifest.

[19] Georg Simmel, *The Sociology of Georg Simmel*, Glencoe: Free Press, 1950, chapters iii and iv.

whereas groups are not completely dependent on any single member. His discussion of the triad is explicitly concerned with the significance of a multiplicity of social relations in social life, and his use of the triad for this purpose is apparently intended to emphasize the crucial distinction between a pair and any group of more than two.[20] Power can be strengthened by dividing the opposition (*divide et impera*); it can be resisted by forming coalitions (*tertius gaudens*); and power conflicts can be mediated by third parties. All these distinctive processes of the dynamics of power cannot be manifest in a dyad. The legitimation of the power of a superior and the mobilization of opposition to him also do not occur in dyads but only if a superior is confronted by a group of subordinates in communication with each other.

It is essential, in the light of these considerations, to conceptualize processes of social association between individuals realistically as finding expression in networks of social relations in groups and not to abstract artificially isolated pairs from this group context. Crusoe and Friday were a dyad that existed in isolation, but most associations are part of a broad matrix of social relations. Although the analysis of complex structures will be postponed until after interpersonal processes have been examined, the group structures within which the associations between individuals occur will be taken into account from the very beginning.

GEORGE C. HOMANS: SOCIAL BEHAVIOR AS EXCHANGE

Abstract

To consider social behavior as an exchange of goods may clarify the relations among four bodies of theory: behavioral psychology, economics, propositions about the dynamics of influence, and propositions about the structure of small groups.

The Problems of Small-Group Research

This essay will hope to honor the memory of Georg Simmel in two different ways. So far as it pretends to be suggestive rather than conclusive, its tone will be Simmel's; and its subject,

---

[20] See *ibid.*, pp. 138–139, 141, 145.
George C. Homans, "Social Behavior as Exchange," *American Journal of Sociology*, vol. 63, pp. 597–606, 1958. Reprinted with permission of the University of Chicago Press, copyright © 1958.

too, will be one of his. Because Simmel, in essays such as those on sociability, games, coquetry, and conversation, was an analyst of elementary social behavior, we call him an ancestor of what is known today as small-group research. For what we are really studying in small groups is elementary social behavior: what happens when two or three persons are in a position to influence one another, the sort of thing of which those massive structures called "classes," "firms," "communities," and "societies" must ultimately be composed.

As I survey small-group research today, I feel that, apart from just keeping on with it, three sorts of things need to be done. The first is to show the relation between the results of experimental work done under laboratory conditions and the results of *quasi-* anthropological field research on what those of us who do it are pleased to call "real-life" groups in industry and elsewhere. If the experimental work has anything to do with real life—and I am persuaded that it has everything to do—its propositions cannot be inconsistent with those discovered through the field work. But the consistency has not yet been demonstrated in any systematic way.

The second job is to pull together in some set of general propositions the actual results, from the laboratory and from the field, of work on small groups—propositions that at least sum up, to an approximation, what happens in elementary social behavior, even though we may not be able to explain why the propositions should take the form they do. A great amount of work has been done, and more appears every day, but what it all amounts to in the shape of a set of propositions from which, under specified conditions, many of the observational results might be derived, is not at all clear—and yet to state such a set is the first aim of science.

The third job is to begin to show how the propositions that empirically hold good in small groups may be derived from some set of still more general propositions. "Still more general" means only that empirical propositions other than ours may also be derived from the set. This derivation would constitute the explanatory stage in the science of elementary social behavior, for explanation *is* derivation. (I myself suspect that the more general set will turn out to contain the propositions of behavioral psychology. I hold myself to be an "ultimate psychological reductionist," but I cannot know that I am right so long as the reduction has not been carried out.)

I have come to think that all three of these jobs would be furthered by our adopting the view that interaction between persons is an exchange of goods, material and non-material. This is one of the oldest theories of social behavior, and one that we still use every day to interpret our own behavior, as when we say, "I found so-and-so rewarding"; or "I got a great deal out of him"; or, even, "Talking with him took a great deal out of me." But, perhaps just because it is so obvious, this view has been much neglected by social scientists. So far as I know, the

only theoretical work that makes explicit use of it is Marcel Mauss's *Essai sur le don*, published in 1925, which is ancient as social science goes. It may be that the tradition of neglect is now changing and that, for instance, the psychologists who interpret behavior in terms of transactions may be coming back to something of the sort I have in mind.

An incidental advantage of an exchange theory is that it might bring sociology closer to economics—that science of man most advanced, most capable of application, and, intellectually, most isolated. Economics studies exchange carried out under special circumstances and with a most useful built-in numerical measure of value. What are the laws of the general phenomenon of which economic behavior is one class?

In what follows I suggest some reasons for the usefulness of a theory of social behavior as exchange and suggest the nature of the propositions such a theory might contain.

An Exchange Paradigm

I start with the link to behavioral psychology and the kind of statement it makes about the behavior of an experimental animal such as the pigeon. As a pigeon explores its cage in the laboratory, it happens to peck a target, whereupon the psychologist feeds it corn. The evidence is that it will peck the target again; it has learned the behavior, or, as my friend Skinner says, the behavior has been reinforced, and the pigeon has undergone *operant conditioning*. This kind of psychologist is not interested in how the behavior was learned: "learning theory" is a poor name for his field. Instead, he is interested in what determines changes in the rate of emission of learned behavior, whether pecks at a target or something else.

The more hungry the pigeon, the less corn or other food it has gotten in the recent past, the more often it will peck. By the same token, if the behavior is often reinforced, if the pigeon is given much corn every time it pecks, the rate of emission will fall off as the pigeon gets *satiated.* If, on the other hand, the behavior is not reinforced at all, then, too, its rate of emission will tend to fall off, though a long time may pass before it stops altogether, before it is *extinguishe* In the emission of many kinds of behavior t pigeon incurs *aversive stimulation,* or what I sh call "cost" for short, and this, too, will lead in time to a decrease in the emission rate. Fatigue is an example of a "cost." Extinction, satiation, and cost, by decreasing the rate of emission of a particular kind of behavior, render more probable the emission of some other kind of behavior, including doing nothing. I shall only add that even a hard-boiled psychologist puts "emotional" behavior, as well as such things as pecking, among the unconditioned responses that may be reinforced in operant conditioning. As a statement of the propositions of behavioral psychology, the foregoing is, of course, inadequate for any purpose except my present one.

We may look on the pigeon as engaged in an exchange—pecks for corn—with the psychologist, but let us not dwell upon that, for the behavior of the pigeon hardly determines the behavior of the psychologist at all. Let us turn to a situation where the exchange is real, that is, where the determination is mutual. Suppose we are dealing with two men. Each is emitting behavior reinforced to some degree by the behavior of the other. How it was in the past that each learned the behavior he emits and how he learned to find the other's behavior reinforcing we are not concerned with. It is enough that each does find the other's behavior reinforcing, and I shall call the reinforcers—the equivalent of the pigeon's corn—*values,* for this, I think, is what we mean by this term. As he emits behavior, each man may incur costs, and each man has more than one course of behavior open to him.

This seems to me the paradigm of elementary social behavior, and the problem of the elementary sociologist is to state propositions relating the variations in the values and costs of each man to his frequency distribution of behavior among alternatives, where the values (in the mathematical sense) taken by these variable for one man determine in part their values for the other.

I see no reason to believe that the propositions of behavioral psychology do not apply to this situation, though the complexity of their implications in the concrete case may be great indeed. In particular, we must suppose that, with men as with pigeons, an increase in extinction, satiation, or aversive stimulation of any one kind of behavior will increase the probability of emission of some other kind. The problem is not, as it is often stated, merely, what a man's values are, what he has learned in the past to find reinforcing, but how much of any one value his behavior is getting him now. The more he gets, the less valuable any further unit of that value is to him, and the less often he will emit behavior reinforced by it.

The Influence Process

We do not, I think, possess the kind of studies of two-person interaction that would either bear out these propositions or fail to do so. But we do have studies of larger numbers of persons that suggest that they may apply, notably the studies by Festinger, Schachter, Back, and their associates on the dynamics of influence. One of the variables they work with they call *cohesiveness,* defined as anything that attracts people to take part in a group. Cohesiveness is a value variable; it refers to the degree of reinforcement people find in the activities of the group. Festinger and his colleagues consider two kinds of reinforcing activity: the symbolic behavior we call "social approval" (sentiment) and activity valuable in other ways, such as doing something interesting.

The other variable they work with they call *communication* and others call *interaction.* This is a frequency variable; it is a measure of the frequency of emission of valuable and costly verbal behavior. We must bear in mind that, in general, the one kind of variable is a function of the other.

Festinger and his co-workers show that the more cohesive a group is, that is, the more valuable the sentiment or activity the members exchange with one another, the greater the average frequency of interaction of the members. With men, as with pigeons, the greater the reinforcement, the more often is the reinforced behavior emitted. The more cohesive a group, too, the greater the change that members can produce in the behavior of other members in the direction of rendering these activities more valuable. That is, the more valuable the activities that members get, the more valuable those that they must give. For if a person is emitting behavior of a certain kind, and other people do not find it particularly rewarding, these others will suffer their own production of sentiment and activity, in time, to fall off. But perhaps the first person has found their sentiment and activity rewarding, and, if he is to keep on getting them, he must make his own behavior more valuable to the others. In short, the propositions of behavioral psychology imply a tendency toward a certain proportionality between the value to others of the behavior a man gives them and the value to him of the behavior they give him.

Schachter also studied the behavior of members of a group toward two kinds of other members, "conformers" and "deviates." I assume that conformers are people whose activity the other members find valuable. For conformity is behavior that coincides to a degree with some group standard or norm, and the only meaning I can assign to *norm* is "a verbal description of behavior that many members find it valuable for the actual behavior of themselves and others to conform to." By the same token, a deviate is a member whose behavior is not particularly valuable. Now Schachter shows that, as the members of a group come to see another member as a deviate, their interaction with him—communication

addressed to getting him to change his behavior—goes up, the faster the more cohesive the group. The members need not talk to the other conformers so much; they are relatively satiated by the conformers' behavior: they have gotten what they want out of them. But if the deviate, by failing to change his behavior, fails to reinforce the members, they start to withhold social approval from him: the deviate gets low sociometric choice at the end of the experiment. And in the most cohesive groups—those Schachter calls "high cohesive-relevant"—interaction with the deviate also falls off in the end and is lowest among those members that rejected him most strongly, as if they had given him up as a bad job. But how plonking can we get? These findings are utterly in line with everyday experience.

Practical Equilibrium

At the beginning of this paper I suggested that one of the tasks of small-group research was to show the relation between the results of experimental work done under laboratory conditions and the results of field research on real-life small groups. Now the latter often appear to be in practical equilibrium, and by this I mean nothing fancy. I do not mean that all real-life groups are in equilibrium. I certainly do not mean that all groups must tend to equilibrium. I do not mean that groups have built-in antidotes to change: there is no homeostasis here. I do not mean that we assume equilibrium. I mean only that we sometimes *observe* it, that for the time we are with a group—and it is often short—there is no great change in the values of the variables we choose to measure. If, for instance, person A is interacting with B more than with C both at the beginning and at the end of the study, then at least by this crude measure the group is in equilibrium.

Many of the Festinger-Schachter studies are experimental, and their propositions about the process of influence seem to me to imply the kind of proposition that empirically holds good of real-life groups in practical equilibrium. For instance, Festinger *et al.* find that, the more cohesive a group is, the greater the change that members can produce in the behavior of other members. If the influence is exerted in the direction of conformity to group norms, then, when the process of influence has accomplished all the change of which it is capable, the proposition should hold good that, the more cohesive a group is, the larger the number of members that conform to its norms. And it does hold good.

Again, Schachter found, in the experiment I summarized above, that in the most cohesive groups and at the end, when the effort to influence the deviate had failed, members interacted little with the deviate and gave him little in the way of sociometric choice. Now two of the propositions that hold good most often of real-life groups in practical equilibrium are precisely that the more closely a member's activity conforms to the norms the more interaction he receives from other members and the more liking choices he gets from them too. From these main propositions a number of others may be derived that also hold good.

Yet we must ever remember that the truth of the proposition linking conformity to liking may on occasion be masked by the truth of other propositions. If, for instance, the man that conforms to the norms most closely also exerts some authority over the group, this may render liking for him somewhat less than it might otherwise have been.

Be that as it may, I suggest that the laboratory experiments on influence imply propositions about the behavior of members of small groups, when the process of influence has worked itself out, that are identical with propositions that hold good of real-life groups in equilibrium. This is hardly surprising if all we mean by equilibrium is that all the change of which the system is, under present conditions, capable has been effected, so that no further change occurs. Nor would this be the first time that statics has turned out to be a special case of dynamics.

Profit and Social Control

Though I have treated equilibrium as an observed fact, it is a fact that cries for explanation. I shall not, as structural-functional sociologists do, use an assumed equilibrium as a means of explaining, or trying to explain, why the other features of a social system should be what they are. Rather, I shall take practical equilibrium as something that is itself to be explained by the other features of the system.

If every member of a group emits at the end of, and during, a period of time much the same kinds of behavior and in much the same frequencies as he did at the beginning, the group is for that period in equilibrium. Let us then ask why any one member's behavior should persist. Suppose he is emitting behavior of value A_1. Why does he not let his behavior get worse (less valuable or reinforcing to the others) until it stands at $A_1 - \Delta A$? True, the sentiments expressed by others toward him are apt to decline in value (become less reinforcing to him), so that what he gets from them may be $S_1 - \Delta S$. But it is conceivable that, since most activity carries cost, a decline in the value of what he emits will mean a reduction in cost to him that more than offsets his losses in sentiment. Where, then, does he stabilize his behavior? This is the problem of social control.

Mankind has always assumed that a person stabilizes his behavior, at least in the short run, at the point where he is doing the best he can for himself under the circumstances, though his best may not be a "rational" best, and what he can do may not be at all easy to specify, except that he is not apt to think like one of the theoretical antagonists in the *Theory of Games*. Before a sociologist rejects this answer out of hand for its horrid profit-seeking implications, he will do well to ask himself if he can offer any other answer to the question posed. I think he will find that he cannot. Yet experiments designed to test the truth of the answer are extraordinarily rare.

I shall review one that seems to me to provide a little support for the theory, though it was not meant to do so. The experiment is reported by H. B. Gerard, a member of the Festinger-Schachter team, under the title "The Anchorage of Opinions in Face-to-Face Groups." The experimenter formed artificial groups whose members met to discuss a case in industrial relations and to express their opinions about its probable outcome. The groups were of two kinds: high-attraction groups, whose members were told that they would like one another very much, and low-attraction groups, whose members were told that they would not find one another particularly likable.

At a later time the experimenter called the members in separately, asked them again to express their opinions on the outcome of the case, and counted the number that had changed their opinions to bring them into accord with those of other members of their groups. At the same time, a paid participant entered into a further discussion of the case with each member, always taking, on the probable outcome of the case, a position opposed to that taken by the bulk of the other members of the group to which the person belonged. The experimenter counted the number of persons shifting toward the opinion of the paid participant.

The experiment had many interesting results, from which I choose only those summed up in Tables 1 and 2. The three different agreement classes are made up of people who, at the original sessions, expressed different degrees of agreement with the opinions of other members of their groups. And the figure 44, for instance, means that, of all members of high-attraction groups whose initial opinions were strongly in disagreement with those of other members, 44 percent shifted their opinion later toward that of others.

In these results the experimenter seems to have been interested only in the differences in the sums of the rows, which show that there is more shifting toward the group, and less shifting

TABLE 1   Percentage of Subjects Changing toward Someone in the Group

	Agree-ment	Mild Disagree-ment	Strong Disagree-ment
High attraction	0	12	44
Low attraction	0	15	9

TABLE 2   Percentage of Subjects Changing toward The Paid Participant

	Agree-ment	Mild Disagree-ment	Strong Disagree-ment
High attraction	7	13	25
Low attraction	20	38	8

toward the paid participant, in the high-attraction than in the low-attraction condition. This is in lien with a proposition suggested earlier. If you think that the members of a group can give you much—in this case, liking—you are apt to give them much—in this case, a change to an opinion in accordance with their views—or you will not get the liking. And, by the same token, if the group can give you little of value, you will not be ready to give it much of value. Indeed, you may change your opinion so as to depart from agreement even further, to move, that is, toward the view held by the paid participant.

So far so good, but, when I first scanned these tables, I was less struck by the difference between them than by their similarity. The same classes of people in both tables showed much the same relative propensities to change their opinions, no matter whether the change was toward the group or toward the paid participant. We see, for instance, that those who change least are the high-attraction, agreement people and the low-attraction, strong-disagreement ones. And those who change most are the high-attraction, strong-disagreement people and the low-attraction, mild-disagreement ones.

How am I to interpret these particular results? Since the experimenter did not discuss them, I am free to offer my own explanation. The behavior emitted by the subjects is opinion and changes in opinion. For this behavior they have learned to expect two possible kinds of reinforcement. Agreement with the group gets the subject favorable sentiment (acceptance) from it, and the experiment was designed to give this reinforcement a higher value in the high-attraction condition than in the low-attraction one. The second kind of possible reinforcement is what I shall call the "maintenance of one's personal integrity," which a subject gets by sticking to his own opinion in the face of disagreement with the group. The experimenter does not mention this reward, but I cannot make sense of the results without something much like it. In different degrees for different subjects, depending on their initial positions, these rewards are in competition with one another: they are alternatives. They are not absolutely scarce goods, but some persons cannot get both at once.

Since the rewards are alternatives, let me introduce a familiar assumption from economics—that the cost of a particular course of action is the equivalent of the foregone value of an alternative—and then add the definition: Profit = Reward – Cost.

Now consider the persons in the corresponding cells of the two tables. The behavior of the high-attraction, agreement people gets them much in the way of acceptance by the group, and for it they must give up little in the way of personal integrity, for their views are from the start in accord with those of the group. Their profit is high, and they are not prone to change their behavior. The low-attraction, strong-disagreement people are getting much in integrity, and they are not giving up for it much in valuable acceptance, for they are members of low-attraction groups. Reward less cost is high for them, too, and they change little. The high-attraction, strong-disagreement people are getting much in

the way of integrity, but their costs in doing so are high, too, for they are in high-attraction groups and thus foregoing much valuable acceptance by the group. Their profit is low, and they are very apt to change, either toward the group or toward the paid participant, from whom they think, perhaps, they will get some acceptance while maintaining some integrity. The low-attraction, mild-disagreement people do not get much in the way of integrity, for they are only in mild disagreement with the group, but neither are they giving up much in acceptance, for they are members of low-attraction groups. Their rewards are low; their costs are low too, and their profit—the difference between the two—is also low. In their low profit they resemble the high-attraction, strong-disagreement people, and, like them, they are prone to change their opinions, in this case, more toward the paid participant. The subjects in the other two cells, who have medium profits, display medium propensities to change.

If we define profit as reward less cost, and if cost is value foregone, I suggest that we have here some evidence for the proposition that change in behavior is greatest when perceived profit is least. This constitutes no direct demonstration that change in behavior is least when profit is greatest, but if, whenever a man's behavior brought him a balance of reward and cost, he changed his behavior away from what got him, under the circumstances, the less profit, there might well come a time when his behavior would not change further. That is, his behavior would be stabilized, at least for the time being. And, so far as this were true for every member of a group, the group would have a social organization in equilibrium.

I do not say that a member would stabilize his behavior at the point of greatest conceivable profit to himself, because his profit is partly at the mercy of the behavior of others. It is a commonplace that the short-run pursuit of profit by several persons often lands them in positions where all are worse off than they might conceivably be.

I do not say that the paths of behavioral change in which a member pursues his profit under the condition that others are pursuing theirs too are easy to describe or predict; and we can readily conceive that in jockeying for position they might never arrive at any equilibrium at all.

Distributive Justice

Yet practical equilibrium is often observed, and thus some further condition may make its attainment, under some circumstance, more probable than would the individual pursuit of profit left to itself. I can offer evidence for this further condition only in the behavior of subgroups and not in that of individuals. Suppose that there are two subgroups, working close together in a factory, the job of one being somewhat different from that of the other. And suppose that the members of the first complain and say: "We are getting the same pay as they are. We ought to get just a couple of dollars a week more to show that our work is more responsible." When you ask them what they mean by "more responsible," they say that, if they do their work wrong, more damage can result, and so they are under more pressure to take care. Something like this is a common feature of industrial behavior. It is at the heart of disputes not over absolute wages but over wage differentials—indeed, at the heart of disputes over rewards other than wages.

In what kind of proposition may we express observations like these? We may say that wages and responsibility give status in the group, in the sense that a man who takes high responsibility and gets high wages is admired, other things equal. Then, if the members of one group score higher on responsibility than do the members of another, there is a felt need on the part of the first to score higher on pay too. There is a pressure, which shows itself in complaints, to bring the *status factors,* as I have called them, into line with one another. If they are in line, a condition of *status congruence* is said to exist. In this condition the workers may find their jobs dull or irksome, but they will not complain about the relative position of groups.

But there may be a more illuminating way of looking at the matter. In my example I have considered only responsibility and pay, but these may be enough, for they represent the two kinds of thing that come into the problem. Pay is clearly a reward; responsibility may be looked on, less clearly, as a cost. It means constraint and worry—or peace of mind foregone. Then the proposition about status congruence becomes this: If the costs of the members of one group are higher than those of another, distributive justice requires that their rewards should be higher too. But the thing works both ways: If the rewards are higher, the costs should be higher too. This last is the theory of *noblesse oblige,* which we all subscribe to, though we all laugh at it, perhaps because the *noblesse* often fails to *oblige.* To put the matter in terms of profit: though the rewards and costs of two persons or the members of two groups may be different, yet the profits of the two—the excess of reward over cost—should tend to equality. And more than "should." The less-advantaged group will at least try to attain greater equality, as, in the example I have used, the first group tried to increase its profit by increasing its pay.

I have talked of distributive justice. Clearly, this is not the only condition determining the actual distribution of rewards and costs. At the same time, never tell me that notions of justice are not a strong influence on behavior, though we sociologists often neglect them. Distributive justice may be one of the conditions of group equilibrium.

Exchange and Social Structure

I shall end by reviewing almost the only study I am aware of that begins to show in detail how a stable and differentiated social structure in a real-life group might arise out of a process of exchange between members. This is Peter Blau's description of the behavior of sixteen agents in a federal law-enforcement agency.

The agents had the duty of investigating firms and preparing reports on the firms' compliance with the law. Since the reports might lead to legal action against the firms, the agents had to prepare them carefully, in the proper form, and take strict account of the many regulations that might apply. The agents were often in doubt what they should do, and then they were supposed to take the question to their supervisor. This they were reluctant to do, for they naturally believed that thus confessing to him their inability to solve a problem would reflect on their competence, affect the official ratings he made of their work, and so hurt their chances for promotion. So agents often asked other agents for help and advice, and, though this was nominally forbidden, the supervisor usually let it pass.

Blau ascertained the ratings the supervisor made of the agents, and he also asked the agents to rate one another. The two opinions agreed closely. Fewer agents were regarded as highly competent than were regarded as of middle or low competence; competence, or the ability to solve technical problems, was a fairly scarce good. One or two of the more competent agents would not give help and advice when asked, and so received few interactions and little liking. A man that will not exchange, that will not give you what he has when you need it, will not get from you the only thing you are, in this case, able to give him in return, your regard.

But most of the more competent agents were willing to give help, and of them Blau says:

A consultation can be considered an exchange of values: both participants gain something, and both have to pay a price. The questioning agent is enabled to perform better than he could otherwise have done, without exposing his difficulties to his supervisor. By asking for advice, he implicitly pays his respect to the superior proficiency of his colleague. This acknowledgment of inferiority is the cost of receiving assistance. The consultant gains prestige, in return for which he is willing to devote some time to the consultation and permit it to disrupt his own work. The following remark of an agent illustrates this: "I like giving advice. It's flattering, I suppose, if you feel that others come to you for advice."

Blau goes on to say: "All agents liked being consulted, but the value of any one of very many consultations became deflated for experts, and the price they paid in frequent interruptions became inflated." This implies that, the more prestige an agent received, the less was the increment of value of that prestige; the more advice an agent gave, the greater was the increment of cost of that advice, the cost lying precisely in the foregone value of time to do his own work. Blau suggests that something of the same sort was true of an agent who went to a more competent colleague for advice: the more often he went, the more costly to him, in feelings of inferiority, became any further request. "The repeated admission of his inability to solve his own problems . . . undermined the self-confidence of the worker and his standing in the group."

The result was that the less competent agents went to the more competent ones for help less often than they might have done if the costs of repeated admissions of inferiority had been less high and that, while many agents sought out the few highly competent ones, no single agent sought out the latter much. Had they done so (to look at the exchange from the other side), the costs to the highly competent in interruptions to their own work would have become exorbitant. Yet the need of the less competent for help was still not fully satisfied. Under these circumstances they tended to turn for help to agents more nearly like themselves in competence. Though the help they got was not the most valuable, it was of a kind they could themselves return on occasion. With such agents they could exchange help and liking, without the exchange becoming on either side too great a confession of inferiority.

The highly competent agents tended to enter into exchanges, that is, to interact with many others. But, in the more equal exchanges I have just spoken of, less competent agents tended to pair off as partners. That is, they interacted with a smaller number of people, but interacted often with these few. I think I could show why pair relations in these more equal exchanges would be more economical for an agent than a wider distribution of favors. But perhaps I have gone far enough. The final pattern of this social structure was one in which a small number of highly competent agents exchanged advice for prestige with a large number of others less competent and in which the less competent agents exchanged, in pairs and in trios, both help and liking on more nearly equal terms.

Blau shows, then, that a social structure in equilibrium might be the result of a process of exchanging behavior rewarding and costly in different degrees, in which the increment of reward and cost varied with the frequency of the behavior, that is, with the frequency of interaction. Note that the behavior of the agents seems also to have satisfied my second condition of equilibrium: the more competent agents took more responsibility for the work, either their own or others', than did the less competent ones, but they also got more for it in the way of prestige. I suspect that the same kind of explanation could be given for the structure of many "informal" groups.

Summary

The current job of theory in small-group research is to make the connection between experimental and real-life studies, to consolidate the propositions that empirically hold good in the two fields, and to show how these propositions might be derived from a still more general set. One way of doing this job would be to revive and make more rigorous the oldest of theories of social behavior—social behavior as exchange.

Some of the statements of such a theory might be the following. Social behavior is an exchange of goods, material goods but also nonmaterial ones, such as the symbols of approval or prestige. Persons that give much to others try to get much from them, and persons that get much from others are under pressure to give much to them. This process of influence tends to work out at equilibrium to a balance in the exchanges. For a person engaged in exchange, what he gives may be a cost to him, just as what he gets may be a reward, and his behavior changes less as profit, that is, reward less cost, tends to a maximum. Not only does he seek a maximum for himself, but he tries to see to it that no one in his group makes more profit than he does. The cost and the value of what he gives and of what he gets vary with the quantity of what he gives and gets. It is surprising how familiar these propositions are; it is surprising, too, how propositions about the dynamics of exchange can begin to generate the static thing we call "group structure" and, in so doing, generate also some of the propositions about group structure that students of real-life groups have stated.

In our unguarded moments we sociologists find words like "reward" and "cost" slipping into what we say. Human nature will break in upon even our most elaborate theories. But we seldom let it have its way with us and follow up systematically what these words imply. Of all our many "approaches" to social behavior, the one that sees it as an economy is the most neglected, and yet it is the one we use every moment of our lives—except when we write sociology.

JAMES S. COLEMAN: SOCIAL CAPITAL IN THE CREATION OF HUMAN CAPITAL[1]

There are two broad intellectual streams in the description and explanation of social action. One, characteristic of the work of most sociologists, sees the actor as socialized and action as governed by social norms, rules, and obligations. The principal virtues of this intellectual stream lie in its ability to describe action in social context and to explain the way action is shaped, constrained, and redirected by the social context.

The other intellectual stream, characteristic of the work of most economists, sees the actor as having goals independently arrived at, as acting independently, and as wholly self-interested. Its principal virtue lies in having a principle of action, that of maximizing utility. This principle of action, together with a single empirical generalization (declining marginal utility) has generated the extensive growth of neoclassical economic theory, as well as the growth of political philosophy of several varieties: utilitarianism, contractarianism, and natural rights. . . .

In earlier works (Coleman 1986a, 1986b), I have argued for and engaged in the development of a theoretical orientation in sociology that includes components from both these intellectual streams. It accepts the principle of rational or purposive action and attempts to show how that principle, in conjunction with particular social contexts, can account not only for the actions of individuals in particular contexts but also for the development of social

organization. In the present paper, I introduce a conceptual tool for use in this theoretical enterprise: social capital . . .

Social Capital

Elements for these two intellectual traditions cannot be brought together in a pastiche. It is necessary to begin with a conceptually coherent framework from one and introduce elements from the other without destroying that coherence. . . .

If we begin with a theory of rational action, in which each actor has control over certain resources and interests in certain resources and events, then social capital constitutes a particular kind of resource available to an actor.

Social capital is defined by its function. It is not a single entity but a variety of different entities, with two elements in common: they all consist of some aspect of social structures, and they facilitate certain actions of actors—whether persons or corporate actors—within the structure. Like other forms of capital, social capital is productive, making possible the achievement of certain ends that in its absence would not be possible. Like physical capital and human capital, social capital is not completely fungible but may be specific to certain activities. A given form of social capital that is valuable in facilitating certain actions may be useless or even harmful for others.

Unlike other forms of capital, social capital inheres in the structure of relations between actors and among actors. It is not lodged either in the actors themselves or in physical implements of production. Because purposive organizations can be actors ("corporate actors") just as persons can, relations among corporate actors can constitute social capital for them as well (with perhaps the best-known example

From James S. Coleman, "Social Capital in the Creation of Human Capital," *American Journal of Sociology*, vol. 94 Supplement, 1988. Reprinted with permission of the University of Chicago Press, copyright © 1988.
[1] I thank Mark Granovetter, Susan Shapiro, and Christopher Winship for criticisms of an earlier draft, which aided greatly in revision. Requests for reprints should be sent to James S. Coleman, Department of Sociology, University of Chicago, Chicago, Illinois 60637.

being the sharing of information that allows price-fixing in an industry). However, in the present paper, the examples and area of application to which I will direct attention concern social capital as a resource for persons.

Before I state more precisely what social capital consists of, it is useful to give several examples that illustrate some of its different forms.

1. Wholesale diamond markets exhibit a property that to an outsider is remarkable. In the process of negotiating a sale, a merchant will hand over to another merchant a bag of stones for the latter to examine in private at his leisure, with no formal insurance that the latter will not substitute one or more inferior stones or a paste replica. The merchandise may be worth thousands, or hundreds of thousands, of dollars. Such free exchange of stones for inspection is important to the functioning of this market. In its absence, the market would operate in a much more cumbersome, much less efficient fashion.

Inspection shows certain attributes of the social structure. A given merchant community is ordinarily very close, both in the frequency of interaction and in ethnic and family ties. The wholesale diamond market in New York City, for example, is Jewish, with a high degree of intermarriage, living in the same community in Brooklyn, and going to the same synagogues. It is essentially a closed community.

Observation of the wholesale diamond market indicates that these close ties, through family, community, and religious affiliation, provide the insurance that is necessary to facilitate the transactions in the market. If any member of this community defected through substituting other stones or through stealing stones in his temporary possession, he would lose family, religious, and community ties. The strength of these ties makes possible transactions in which trustworthiness is taken for granted and trade can occur with ease. In the absence of these ties, elaborate and expensive bonding and insurance devices would be necessary—or else the transactions could not take place.

2. The *International Herald Tribune* of June 21–22, 1986, contained an article on page 1 about South Korean student radical activists. It describes the development of such activism: "Radical thought is passed on in clandestine 'study circles,' groups of students who may come from the same high school or hometown or church. These study circles . . . serve as the basic organizational unit for demonstrations and other protests. To avoid detection, members of different groups never meet, but communicate through an appointed representative."

This description of the basis of organization of this activism illustrates social capital of two kinds. The "same high school or hometown or church" provides social relations on which the "study circles" are later built. The study circles themselves constitute a form of social capital—a cellular form of organization that appears especially valuable for facilitating opposition in any political system intolerant of dissent. Even where political dissent is tolerated, certain activities are not, whether the activities are politically motivated terrorism or simple crime. The organization that makes possible these activities is an especially potent form of social capital.

3. A mother of six children, who recently moved with husband and children from suburban Detroit to Jerusalem, described as one reason for doing so the greater freedom her young children had in Jerusalem. She felt safe in letting her eight year old take the six year old across town to school on the city bus and felt her children to be safe in playing without supervision in a city park, neither of which she felt able to do where she lived before.

The reason for this difference can be described as a difference in social capital available in Jerusalem and suburban Detroit. In Jerusalem, the normative structure ensures that unattended children will be "looked after" by adults in the vicinity, while no such normative structure exists in most metropolitan areas of the United States. One can say that families have available to them in Jerusalem social capital that does not exist in metropolitan areas of the United States.

4. In the Kahn El Khalili market of Cairo, the boundaries between merchants are difficult for an outsider to discover. The owner of a shop that specializes in leather will, when queried about where one can find a certain kind of jewelry, turn out to sell that as well— or, what appears to be nearly the same thing, to have a close associate who sells it, to whom he will immediately take the customer. Or he will instantly become a money changer, although he is not a money changer, merely by turning to his colleague a few shops down. For some activities, such as bringing a customer to a friend's store, there are commissions; for others, such as money changing, merely the creation of obligations. Family relations are important in the market, as is the stability of proprietorship. The whole market is so infused with relations of the sort I have described that it can be seen as an organization, no less so than a department store. Alternatively, one can see the market as consisting of a set of individual merchants, each having an extensive body of social capital on which to draw, through the relationships of the market.

The examples above have shown the value of social capital for a number of outcomes, both economic and noneconomic. There are, however, certain properties of social capital that are important for understanding how it comes into being and how it is employed in the creation of human capital. First, a comparison with human capital, and then an examination of different forms of social capital, will be helpful for seeing these.

Human Capital and Social Capital

Probably the most important and most original development in the economics of education in the past 30 years has been the idea that the concept of physical capital as embodied in tools,

machines, and other productive equipment can be extended to include human capital as well (see Schultz 1961;l Becker 1964). Just as physical capital is created by changes in materials to form tools that facilitate production, human capital is created by changes in persons that bring about skills and capabilities that make them able to act in new ways.

Social capital, however, comes about through changes in the relations among persons that facilitate action. If physical capital is wholly tangible, being embodied in observable material form, and human capital is less tangible, being embodied in the skills and knowledge acquired by an individual, social capital is less tangible yet, for it exists in the *relations* among persons. Just as physical capital and human capital facilitate productive activity, social capital does as well. For example, a group within which there is extensive trustworthiness and extensive trust is able to accomplish much more than a comparable group without that trustworthiness and trust.

Forms of Social Capital

The value of the concept of social capital lies first in the fact that it identifies certain aspects of social structure by their functions, just as the concept "chair" identifies certain physical objects by their function, despite differences in form, appearance, and construction. The function identified by the concept of "social capital" is the value of these aspects of social structure to actors as resources that they can use to achieve their interests. . . .

Obligations, Expectations, and Trustworthiness of Structures

If *A* does something for *B* and trusts *B* to reciprocate in the future, this establishes an expectation in *A* and an obligation on the part of *B*. This obligation can be conceived as a credit slip held by *A* for performance by *B*. If *A* holds a large number of these credit slips, for a number of persons with whom *A* has relations, then the analogy to financial capital is direct. These credit slips constitute a large body of credit that *A* can call in if necessary—unless, of course, the placement of trust has been unwise, and these are bad debts that will not be repaid.

In some social structures, it is said that "people are always doing things for each other." There are a large number of these credit slips outstanding, often on both sides of a relation (for these credit slips appear often not to be completely fungible across areas of activity, so that credit slips of *B* held by *A* and those of *A* held by *B* are not fully used to cancel each other out). The El Khalili market in Cairo, described earlier, constitutes an extreme case of such a social structure. In other social structures where individuals are more self-sufficient and depend on each other less, there are fewer of these credit slips outstanding at any time.

This form of social capital depends on two elements: trustworthiness of the social environment, which means that obligations will be repaid, and the actual extent of obligations held. Social structures differ in both these dimensions, and actors within the same structure differ in the second. A case that illustrates the value of the trustworthiness of the environment is that of the rotating-credit associations of Southeast Asia and elsewhere. These associations are groups of friends and neighbors who typically meet monthly, each person contributing to a central fund that is then given to one of the members (through bidding or by lot), until, after a number of months, each of the *n* persons has made *n* contributions and received one payout. As Geertz (1962) points out, these associations serve as efficient institutions for amassing savings for small capital expenditures, an important aid to economic development.

But without a high degree of trustworthiness among the members of the group, the institution could not exist—for a person who receives a payout early in the sequence of meetings could abscond and leave the others with a loss. For example, one could not imagine a rotating-credit association operating successfully in urban areas marked by a high degree of social disorganization—or, in other words, by a lack of social capital.

Differences in social structures in both dimensions may arise for a variety of reasons. There are differences in the actual needs that persons have for help, in the existence of other sources of aid (such as government welfare services), in the degree of affluence (which reduces aid needed from others), in cultural differences in the tendency to lend aid and ask for aid (see Banfield 1967) in the closure of social networks, in the logistics of social contacts (see Festinger, Schachter, and Back 1963), and other factors. Whatever the source, however, individuals in social structures with high levels of obligations outstanding at any time have more social capital on which they can draw. The density of outstanding obligations means, in effect, that the overall usefulness of the tangible resources of that social structure is amplified by their availability to others when needed.

Individual actors in a social system also differ in the number of credit slips outstanding on which they can draw at any time. The most extreme examples are in hierarchically structured extended family settings, in which a patriarch (or "godfather") holds an extraordinarily large set of obligations that he can call in at any time to get what he wants done. Near this extreme are villages in traditional settings that are highly stratified, with certain wealthy families who, because of their wealth, have built up extensive credits that they can call in at any time.

Similarly, in political settings such as a legislature, a legislator in a position with extra resources (such as the Speaker of the House of Representatives or the Majority Leader of the Senate in the U.S. Congress) can, by effective use of resources, build up a set of obligations from other legislators that makes it possible to get legislation passed that would otherwise be stymied. This concentration of obligations constitutes social capital that is useful not only for this powerful legislator but useful also in getting an increased level of action on the part of a legislature. Thus, those members of legislatures among whom such credits are extensive should be more powerful than those without extensive credits and debits because they can use the credits to produce bloc voting on many issues. It is well recognized, for example, that in the U.S. Senate, some senators are members of what is called "the Senate Club," while others are not. This in effect means that some senators are embedded in the system of credits and debits, while others, outside the "Club," are not. It is also well recognized that those in the Club are more powerful than those outside it.

Information Channels

An important form of social capital is the potential for information that inheres in social relations. Information is important in providing a basis for action. But acquisition of information is costly. At a minimum, it requires attention, which is always in scarce supply. One means by which information can be acquired is by use of social relations that are maintained for other purposes. Katz and Lazarsfeld (1955) showed how this operated for women in several areas of life in a midwestern city around 1950. They showed that a woman with an interest in being in fashion, but no interest in being on the leading edge of fashion, used friends who she knew kept up with fashion as sources of information. Similarly, a person who is not greatly interested in current events but who is interested in being informed about important developments can save the time of reading a newspaper by depending on spouse or friends who pay attention to such matters. A social scientist who is interested in being up-to-date on research in related fields can make use of everyday interactions with colleagues to do so, but only in a university in which most colleagues keep up-to-date.

All these are examples of social relations that constitute a form of social capital that provides information that facilitates action. The relations in this case are not valuable for the "credit slips" they provide in the form of obligations that one holds for others' performances or for the trustworthiness of the other party but merely for the information they provide.

Norms and Effective Sanctions

When a norm exists and is effective, it constitutes a powerful, though sometimes fragile, form of social capital. Effective norms that inhibit crime make it possible to walk freely outside at night in a city and enable old persons to leave their houses without fear for their safety. Norms in a community that support and provide effective rewards for high achievement in school greatly facilitate the school's task.

A prescriptive norm within a collectivity that constitutes an especially important form of social capital is the norm that one should forgo self-interest and act in the interests of the collectivity. A norm of this sort, reinforced by social support, status, honor, and other rewards, is the social capital that builds young nations (and then dissipates as they grow older), strengthens families by leading family members to act selflessly in "the family's" interest, facilitates the development of nascent social movements through a small group of dedicated, inward-looking, and mutually rewarding members, and in general leads persons to work for the public good. In some of these cases, the norms are internalized; in others, they are largely supported through external rewards for selfless actions and disapproval for selfish actions. But, whether supported by internal or external sanctions, norms of this sort are important in overcoming the public goods problem that exists in collectivities.

As all these examples suggest, effective norms can constitute a powerful form of social capital. This social capital, however, like the forms described earlier, not only facilitates certain actions; it constrains others. A community with strong and effective norms about young persons' behavior can keep them from "having a good time." Norms that make it possible to walk alone at night also constrain the activities of criminals (and in some cases of noncriminals as well). Even prescriptive norms that reward certain actions, like the norm in a community that says that a boy who is a good athlete should go out for football, are in effect directing energy away from other activities. Effective norms in an area can reduce innovativeness in an area, not only deviant actions that harm others but also deviant actions that can benefit everyone. (See Merton [1968, pp. 195–203] for a discussion of how this can come about.)

Social Structure that Facilitates Social Capital

All social relations and social structures facilitate some forms of social capital; actors establish relations purposefully and continue them when they continue to provide benefits. Certain kinds of social structure, however, are especially important in facilitating some forms of social capital.

Closure of Social Networks

One property of social relations on which effective norms depend is what I will call closure. In general, one can say that a necessary but not sufficient condition for the emergence of effective norms is action that imposes external effects on others (see Ullmann-Margalit 1977; Coleman 1987). Norms arise as attempts to limit negative external effects or encourage positive ones. But, in many social structures where these conditions exist, norms do not come into existence. The reason is what can be described as lack of closure of the social structure. . . .

Closure of the social structure is important not only for the existence of effective norms but also for another form of social capital: the trustworthiness of social structures that allows the

proliferation of obligations and expectations. Defection from an obligation is a form of imposing a negative externality or another. Yet, in a structure without closure, it can be effectively sanctioned, if at all, only by the person to whom the obligation is owed. Reputation cannot arise in an open structure, and collective sanctions that would ensure trustworthiness cannot be applied. Thus, we may say that closure creates trustworthiness in a social structure. . . .

Social Capital in the Creation of Human Capital

The preceding pages have been directed toward defining and illustrating social capital in general. But there is one effect of social capital that is especially important: its effect on the creation of human capital in the next generation. Both social capital in the family and social capital in the community play roles in the creation of human capital in the rising generation. I will examine each of these in turn.

Social Capital in the Family

Ordinarily, in the examination of the effects of various factors on achievement in school, "family background" is considered a single entity, distinguished from schooling in its effects. But there is not merely a single "family background"; family background is analytically separable into at least three different components: financial capital, human capital, and social capital. Financial capital is approximately measured by the family's wealth or income. It provides the physical resources that can aid achievement: a fixed place in the home for studying, materials to aid learning, the financial resources that smooth family problems. Human capital is approximately measured by parents' education and provides the potential for a cognitive environment for the child that aids learning. Social capital within the family is different from either of these. Two examples will give a sense of what it is and how it operates.

John Stuart Mill, at an age before most children attend school, was taught Latin and Greek by his father, James Mill, and later in childhood would discuss critically with his father and with Jeremy Bentham drafts of his father's manuscripts. John Stuart Mill probably had no extraordinary genetic endowments, and his father's learning was no more extensive than that of some other men of the time. The central difference was the time and effort spent by the father with the child on intellectual matters.

In one public school district in the United States where texts for school use were purchased by children's families, school authorities were puzzled to discover that a number of Asian immigrant families purchased *two* copies of each textbook needed by the child. Investigation revealed that the family purchased the second copy for the mother to study in order to help her child do well in school. Here is a case in which the human capital of the parents, at least as measured traditionally by years of schooling, is low, but the social capital in the family available for the child's education is extremely high.

These examples illustrate the importance of social capital within the family for a child's intellectual development. It is of course true that children are strongly affected by the human capital possessed by their parents. But this human capital may be irrelevant to outcomes for children if parents are not an important part of their children's lives, if their human capital is employed exclusively at work or elsewhere outside the home. The social capital of the family is the relations between children and parents (and, when families include other members, relationships with them as well). That is, if the human capital possessed by parents is not complemented by social capital embodied in family relations, it is irrelevant to the child's educational growth that the parent has as great deal, or a small amount, of human capital. . . .

Social capital within the family that gives the child access to the adult's human capital depends both on the physical presence of adults in the family and on the attention given by the adults to the child. The physical absence of adults may be described as a structural deficiency in family social capital. The most prominent element of structural deficiency in modern families is the single-parent family. However, the nuclear family itself, in which one or both parents work outside the home, can be seen as structurally deficient, lacking the social capital that comes with the presence of parents during the day, or with grandparents or aunts and uncles in or near the household.

Even if adults are physically present, there is a lack of social capital in the family if there are not strong relations between children and parents. The lack of strong relations can result from the child's embeddedness in a youth community, from the parents' embeddedness in relationships with other adults that do not cross generations, or from other sources. Whatever the source, it means that whatever *human* capital exists in the parents, the child does not profit from it because the *social* capital is missing.

The effects of a lack of social capital within the family differ for different educational outcomes. One for which it appears to be especially important is dropping out of school. With the *High School and Beyond* sample of students in high schools, table 1 shows the expected dropout rates for students in different types of families when various measures of social and human capital in the family and a measure of social capital in the community are controlled statistically. An explanation is necessary for the use of number of siblings as a measure of lack of social capital. The number of siblings represents, in this interpretation, a dilution of adult attention to the child. This is consistent with research results for measures of achievement and IQ, which show that test scores decline with sib position, even when total family size is controlled, and that scores decline with number of

TABLE 1   Dropout Rates between Spring, Grade 10, and Spring, Grade 12, for Students Whose Families Differ in Social Capital, Controlling for Human Capital and Financial Capital in the Family[a]

	Percentage Dropping Out	Difference in Percentage Points
1. Parents' presence:		
Two parents	13.1	6.0
Single parent	19.1	
2. Additional children:		
One sibling	10,.8	6.4
Four siblings	17.2	
3. Parents and children:		
Two parents, one sibling	10.1	12.5
One parent, four siblings	22.6	
4. Mother's expectation for child's education:		
Expectation of college	11.6	8.6
No expectation of college	20.2	
5. Three factors together:		
Two parents, one sibling, mother expects college	8.1	22.5
One parent, four siblings, no college expectation	30.6	

[a]Estimates taken from logistic regression reported more fully in App. table A1.

children in the family. Both results are consistent with the view that younger sibs and children in large families have less adult attention, which produces weaker educational outcomes.

Item 1 of table 1 shows that, when other family resources are controlled, the percentage of students who drop out between spring of the sophomore year and spring of the senior year is 6 percentage points higher for children from single-parent families. Item 2 of table 1 shows that the rate is 6.4 percentage points higher for sophomores with four siblings than for those with otherwise equivalent family resources but only one sibling. Or, taking these two together, we can think of the ratio of adults to children as a measure of the social capital in the family available for the education of any one of them. Item 3 of table 1 shows that for a sophomore with four siblings and one parent, and an otherwise average background, the rate is 22.6%; with one sibling and two parents, the rate is 10.1%—a difference of 12.5 percentage points.

Another indicator of adult attention in the family, although not a pure measure of social capital, is the mother's expectation of the child's going to college. Item 4 of the table shows that, for sophomores without this parental expectation, the rate is 8.6 percentage points higher than for those with it. With the three sources of family social capital taken together, item 5 of the table shows that sophomores with one sibling, two parents, and a mother's expectation for college (still controlling on other resources of family) have an 8.1% dropout rate; with four siblings, one parent, and no expectation of the mother for college, the rate is 30.6%. . . .

Social Capital outside the Family

The social capital that has value for a young person's development does not reside solely within the family. It can be found outside as well in the community consisting of the social relationships that exist among parents, in the closure exhibited by this structure of relations, and in the parents' relations with the institutions of the community.

The effect of this social capital outside the family on educational outcomes can be seen by

TABLE 2 Dropout Rates between Spring, Grade 10, and Spring, Grade 12, for Students from Schools with Differing Amounts of Social Capital in the Surrounding Community

	Public	Catholic	Other Private Schools
1. Raw dropout rates	14.4	3.4	11.9
2. Dropout rates standardized to average public school sophomore[a]	14.4	5.2	11.7

	Non-Catholic Religious	Independent
3. Raw dropout rates for students[b] from independent and non-Catholic religious private schools	3.7	10.0

[a]The standardization is based on separate logistic regressions for these two sets of schools, using the same variables listed in n. 5. Coefficients and means for the standardization are in Hoffer (1986), tables 5 and 24).
[b]This tabulation is based on unweighted data, which is responsible for the fact that both rates are lower than the rate for other private schools in item 1 of the table, which is based on weighted data.

examining outcomes for children whose parents differ in the particular source of social capital discussed earlier, intergenerational closure. There is not a direct measure of intergenerational closure in the data, but there is a proximate indicator. This is the number of times the child has changed schools because the family moved. For families that have moved often, the social relations that constitute social capital are broken at each move. Whatever the degree of intergenerational closure available to others in the community, it is not available to parents in mobile families. . . .

In the *High School and Beyond* data set, another variation among the schools constitutes a useful indicator of social capital. This is the distinctions among public high schools, religiously based private high schools, and nonreligiously based private high schools. It is the religiously based high schools that are surrounded by a community based on the religious organization. These families have intergenerational closure that is based on a multiplex relation: whatever other relations they have, the adults are members of the same religious body and parents of children in the same school.

In contrast, it is the independent private schools that are typically least surrounded by a community, for their student bodies are collections of students, most of whose families have no contact. The choice of private school for most of these parents is an individualistic one, and, although they back their children with extensive human capital, they send their children to these schools denuded of social capital.

In the *High School and Beyond* data set, there are 893 public schools, 84 Catholic schools, and 27 other private schools. Most of the other private schools are independent schools, though a minority have religious foundations. In this analysis, I will at the outset regard the other private schools as independent private schools to examine the effects of social capital outside the family.

The results of these comparisons are shown in table 2. Item 1 of the table shows that the dropout rates between sophomore and senior years are 14.4% in public schools, 3.4% in Catholic schools, and 11.9% in other private schools. What is most striking is the low dropout rate in Catholic schools. The rate is a fourth of that in the public schools and a third of that in the other private schools.

Adjusting the dropout rates for differences in student-body financial, human, and social capital among the three sets of schools by standardizing the population of the Catholic schools and other private schools to the student-body backgrounds of the public schools shows that the differences are affected only slightly. Furthermore, the differences are not due to the religion of the students or to the degree of religious observance. Catholic students in public school are only slightly less likely to drop out than non-Catholics. Frequency of attendance at religious services, which is itself a measure of social capital through intergenerational closure, is strongly related to dropout rate, with 19.5% of public school students who rarely or never attend dropping out compared with 9.1% of those who attend often. But this effect exists apart from, and in addition to, the effect of the school's religious affiliation. Comparable figures for Catholic school students are 5.9% and 2.6%, respectively (Coleman and Hoffer 1987, p. 138).

The low dropout rates of the Catholic schools, the absence of low dropout rates in the other private schools, and the independent effect of frequency of religious attendance all provide evidence of the importance of social capital outside the school, in the adult community surrounding it, for this outcome of education.

A further test is possible, for there were eight schools in the sample of non-Catholic private schools ("other private" in the analysis above) that have religious foundations and over 50% of the student body of that religion. Three were Baptist schools, two were Jewish, and three from three other denominations. If the inference is correct about the religious community's providing intergenerational closure and thus social capital and about the importance of social capital in depressing the chance of dropping out of high school, these schools also should show a lower dropout rate than the independent private schools. Item 3 of table 2 shows that their dropout rate is lower, 3.7%, essentially the same as that of the Catholic schools.

The data presented above indicate the importance of social capital for the education of youth, or, as it might be put, the importance of social capital in the creation of human capital. Yet there is a fundamental difference between social capital and most other forms of capital that has strong implications for the development of youth. It is this difference to which I will turn in the next section.

Public Goods Aspects of Social Capital

Physical capital is ordinarily a private good, and property rights make it possible for the person who invests in physical capital to capture the benefits it produces. Thus, the incentive to invest in physical capital is not depressed; there is not a suboptimal investment in physical capital because those who invest in it are able to capture the benefits of their investments. For human capital also—at least human capital of the sort that is produced in schools—the person who invests the time and resources in building up this capital reaps its benefits in the form of a higher-paying job, more satisfying or higher-status work, or even the pleasure of greater understanding of the surrounding world—in short, all the benefits that schooling brings to a person.

But most forms of social capital are not like this. For example, the kinds of social structures that make possible social norms and the sanctions that enforce them do not benefit primarily the person or persons whose efforts would be necessary to bring them about, but benefit all those who are part of such a structure. For example, in some schools where there exists a dense set of associations among some parents, these are the result of a small number of persons, ordinarily mothers who do not hold full-time jobs outside the home. Yet these mothers themselves experience only a subset of the benefits of this social capital surrounding the school. If one of them decides to abandon these activities—for example, to take a full-time job—this may be an entirely reasonable action from a personal point of view and even from the point of view of that household with its children. The benefits of the new activity may far outweigh the losses that arise from the decline in associations with other parents whose children are in the school. But the withdrawal of these activities constitutes a loss to all those other parents whose associations and contacts were dependent on them.

Similarly, the decision to move from a community so that the father, for example, can take a better job may be entirely correct from the point of view of that family. But, because social capital consists of relations among persons, other persons may experience extensive losses by the severance of those relations, a severance over which they had no control. A part of those losses is the weakening of norms and sanctions that aid the school in its task. For each family, the total cost it experiences as a consequence of the decisions it and other families make may outweigh the benefits of those few decisions it has control over. Yet the beneficial consequences to the family of those decisions made by the family may far outweigh the minor losses it experiences from them alone.

It is not merely voluntary associations, such as a PTA, in which underinvestment of this sort occurs. When an individual asks a favor from another, thus incurring an obligation, he does so because it brings him a needed benefit; he does not consider that it does the other a benefit as well by adding to a drawing fund of social capital available in a time of need. If the first individual can satisfy his need through self-sufficiency, or through aid from some official source without incurring an obligation, he will do so–and thus fail to add to the social capital outstanding in the community.

Similar statements can be made with respect to trustworthiness as social capital. An actor choosing to keep trust or not (or choosing whether to devote resources to an attempt to keep trust) is doing so on the basis of costs and benefits he himself will experience. That his

trustworthiness will facilitate others' actions or that his lack of trustworthiness will inhibit others' actions does not enter into his decision. A similar but more qualified statement can be made for information as a form of social capital. An individual who serves as a source of information for another because he is well informed ordinarily acquires that information for his own benefit, not for the others who make use of him. (This is not always true. As Katz and Lazarsfeld [1955] show, "opinion leaders" in an area acquire information in part to maintain their position as opinion leaders.)

For norms also, the statement must be qualified. Norms are intentionally established, indeed as means of reducing externalities, and their benefits are ordinarily captured by those who are responsible for establishing them. But the capability of establishing and maintaining effective norms depend on properties of the social structure (such as closure) over which one actor does not have control yet are affected by one actor's action. These are properties that affect the structure's capacity to sustain effective norms, yet properties that ordinarily do not enter into an individual's decision that affects them.

Some forms of social capital have the property that their benefits can be captured by those who invest in them; consequently, rational actors will not underinvest in this type of social capital. Organizations that produce a private good constitute the outstanding example. The result is that there will be in society an imbalance in the relative investment in organizations that produce private goods for a market and those associations and relationships in which the benefits are not captured—an imbalance in the sense that, if the positive externalities created by the latter form of social capital could be internalized, it would come to exist in greater quantity.

The public goods quality of most social capital means that it is in a fundamentally different position with respect to purposive action than are most other forms of capital. It is an important resource for individuals and may affect greatly their ability to act and their perceived quality of life. They have the capability of bringing it into being. Yet, because the benefits of actions that bring social capital into being are largely experienced by persons other than the actor, it is often not in his interest to bring it into being. The result is that most forms of social capital are created or destroyed as by-products of other activities. This social capital arises or disappears without anyone's willing it into or out of being and is thus even less recognized and taken account of in social action than its already intangible character would warrant.

There are important implications of this public goods aspect of social capital that play a part in the development of children and youth. Because the social structural conditions that overcome the problems of supplying these public goods—that is, strong families and strong communities—are much less often present now than in the past, and promise to be even less present in the future, we can expect that, ceteris paribus, we confront a declining quantity of human capital embodied in each successive generation. The obvious solution appears to be to attempt to find ways of overcoming the problem of supply of these public goods, that is, social capital employed for the benefit of children and youth. This very likely means the substitution of some kind of formal organization for the voluntary and spontaneous social organization that has in the past been the major source of social capital available to the young.

Conclusion

In this paper, I have attempted to introduce into social theory a concept, "social capital," paralleling the concepts of financial capital, physical capital, and human capital—but embodied in relations among persons. This is part of a theoretical strategy that involves use of the paradigm of rational action but without the

assumption of atomistic elements stripped of social relationships. I have shown the use of this concept through demonstrating the effect of social capital in the family and in the community in aiding the formation of human capital. The single measure of human capital formation used for this was one that appears especially responsive to the supply of social capital, remaining in high school until graduation versus dropping out. Both social capital in the family and social capital outside it, in the adult community surrounding the school, showed evidence of considerable value in reducing the probability of dropping out of high school.

In explicating the concept of social capital, three forms were identified: obligations and expectations, which depend on trustworthiness of the social environment, information-flow capability of the social structure, and norms accompanied by sanctions. A property shared by most forms of social capital that differentiates it from other forms of capital is its public good aspect: the actor or actors who generate social capital ordinarily capture only a small part of its benefits, a fact that leads to underinvestment in social capital.

References

Baker, Wayne. 1983. "Floor Trading and Crowd Dynamics." Pp. 107–28 in *Social Dynamics of Financial Markets*, edited by Patricia Adler and Peter Adler. Greenwich, Conn.: JAI.

Banfield, Edward. 1967. *The Moral Basis of a Backward Society.* New York: Free Press.

Becker, Gary. 1964. *Human Capital.* New York: National Bureau of Economic Research.

Ben-Porath, Yoram. 1980. "The *F*-Connection: Families, Friends, and Firms and the Organization of Exchange." *Population and Development Review* 6:1–30.

Black, R. D. C., A. W. Coats, and C. D. W. Goodwin, eds. 1973. *The Marginal Revolution in Economics.* Durham, N.C.: Duke University Press.

Blau, Peter. 1964. *Exchange and Power in Social Life.* New York: Wiley.

Coleman, James S. 1986*a*. "Social Theory, Social Research, and a Theory of Action." *American Journal of Sociology* 91:1309–35.

———. 1986*b*. *Individual Interests and Collective Action*. Cambridge: Cambridge University Press.

———. 1987. "Norms as Social Capital." Pp. 133–55 in *Economic Imperialism*, edited by Gerard Radnitzky and Peter Bernholz. New York: Paragon.

Coleman, J. S., and T. B. Hoffer. 1987. *Public and Private Schools: The Impact of Communities*. New York: Basic.

DeGraaf, Nan Dirk, and Hendrik Derk Flap. 1988. "With a Little Help from My Friends." *Social Forces* vol. 67 (in press).

Festinger, Leon, Stanley Schachter, and Kurt Back. 1963. *Social Pressures in Informal Groups*. Stanford, Calif.: Stanford University Press.

Geertz, Clifford, 1962. "The Rotating Credit Association: A 'Middle Rung' in Development." *Economic Development and Cultural Change* 10:240–63.

Gluckman, Max. 1967. *The Judicial Process among the Barotse of Northern Rhodesia*, 2nd ed. Manchester: Manchester University Press.

Gouldner, Alvin. 1960. "The Norm of Reciprocity: A Preliminary Statement." *American Sociological Review* 25:161–78.

Granovetter, Mark. 1985. "Economic Action, Social Structure, and Embeddedness." *American Journal of Sociology* 91:481–510.

Hoffer, T. B. 1986. *Educational Outcomes in Public and Private High Schools*. Ph.D. dissertation. University of Chicago, Department of Sociology.

Homans, George. 1974. *Social Behavior: Its Elementary Forms*, rev. ed. New York: Harcourt, Brace & World.

Katz, E., and P. Lazarsfeld. 1955. *Personal Influence*. New York: Free Press.

Lenin, V. I. (1902) 1973. *What Is To Be Done*. Peking: Foreign Language Press.

Lin, Nan. 1988. "Social Resources and Social Mobility: A Structural Theory of Status Attainment." In *Social Mobility and Social Structure*, edited by Ronald Breiger. Cambridge: Cambridge University Press.

Lipset, Seymour, M. Trow, and J. Coleman. 1956. *Union Democracy*. New York: Free Press.

Merry, Sally, E. 1984. "Rethinking Gossip and Scandal." Pp. 271–302 in *Toward a General Theory of Social Control*. Vol. 1, *Fundamentals*, edited by Donald Black. New York: Academic.

Merton, Robert K. 1968. *Social Theory and Social Structure*, 2d ed. New York: Free Press.

———. n.d. "Study of World War II Housing Projects." Unpublished manuscript. Columbia University, Department of Sociology.

Schultz, Theodore. 1961. "Investment in Human Capital." *American Economic Review* 51 (March): 1–17.

Ullmann-Margalit, Edna. 1977. *The Emergence of Norms*. Oxford: Clarendon.

Williamson, Oliver. 1975. *Markets and Hierarchies*. New York: Free Press.

———. 1981. "The Economics of Organization: The Transaction Cost Approach." *American Journal of Sociology* 87:548–77.

Wrong, Dennis. 1961. "The Oversocialized Conception of Man in Modern Sociology." *American Sociological Review* 26:183–93.

Chapter 10

Phenomenological Sociology and Ethnomethodology
Garfinkel

Introduction

Phenomenological sociology is an attempt on the part of Alfred Schutz (1899–1959) to make the basic ideas of the philosopher Edmund Husserl, the founder of phenomenology, relevant to the study of society. At the heart of the matter is the impact of natural science methodology on our perception and understanding of social reality. For it is the contention of Husserl and others that the understanding of the social world is fundamentally distorted when we come to our knowledge of it using the methods of the natural sciences. As we shall see below, phenomenological sociology endorses and employs observational techniques to secure empirical data. But the critical questions for phenomenology are how relevance is determined in scientific study, and what assumptions must be made about social reality before one can proceed to gain knowledge about it.

Phenomenological sociology is characterized as a subjective or creative sociology because it seeks to understand the world from the point of view of the acting subject and not from the perspective of the scientific observer. Initially then, the relevant world of study for the sociologist is the world that is inhabited by ordinary people and defined as their commonsense reality. The everyday life of ordinary people is lived in this social reality, and people share a culture, a language, and a set of meaning structures that allow them to negotiate their everyday lives. People come to understand their social world as a natural order. It exists prior to their emergence on the scene and will exist after they depart.

They have no doubts about its reality or its objective facticity. That world which we all occupy has an order and a structure, and the question for the phenomenologist is the content of our consciousness about that social reality and how it comes to be what it is.

Historically, the natural sciences have challenged commonsense understanding of reality, yet Schutz is arguing that the commonsense world is precisely what must be taken as problematic. The natural sciences freely create models of reality that assist in the quest to know more about the natural world. But the social world already has a structure, and people who occupy that world share meaning structures that make social interaction possible. The sociologist therefore cannot simply create abstract models as does the natural scientist because he or she is bound to address the already existing commonsense world of everyday life. What concerns phenomenologists is that the abstract constructions by intellectuals will contain deductively derived truth claims about human action but ignore the understandings and meaning structures that are brought to the interaction by the actors themselves. In short, sociologists who take the life world for granted are missing the central problematic of their discipline: to analyze the life world and its structure, and to ascertain how it has come to be what it is. Moreover, because the life world is shared and actively constructed rather than a natural occurrence, the sociologist is obliged to recount how that social construction process transpires. From these brief comments, the potentially radical challenge to mainstream sociology can be discerned. The excerpt by

Alfred Schutz in the following pages details the distinctions between the natural scientific and the phenomenological approach.

Peter Berger and Thomas Luckmann were both students of Alfred Schutz, and their book, *The Social Construction of Reality,* is a careful and systematic explanation of the processes that Schutz pioneered. Berger and Luckmann draw upon Marx, Durkheim, and Weber in setting upon this task. From Marx they preserve the dialectical idea that human beings create their institutions; from Durkheim they draw the idea that institutions become objectified and constrain human action; from Weber they take subjective meaning and attempt to show how institutions develop and how they are legitimated. Ultimately, Berger and Luckmann demonstrate their thesis that social reality is constructed, but that people forget their role in creating and maintaining that reality. In bringing this social amnesia to light, Berger and Luckmann realize the radical potential of phenomenology: that people may reconstruct their social institutions with will and consciousness in the future.

Berger and Luckmann begin with a rejection of the traditional view of the sociology of knowledge as developed by Marx and Mannheim. That discourse is seen as intellectual history. Sociology must address the question of knowledge that ordinary people share in their everyday life world. How does that fabric of meanings arise, and how does it become institutionalized, objectified, and legitimated?

When social theorists discuss the problem of social order and how it is possible, they frame it in terms of Marx, who sees force as the ultimate basis of order, and Durkheim, who sees consensus as the foundation of society. The phenomenologist views these as abstract intellectual concerns based on theorists' value assumptions, that is, the ideas of an elite group of thinkers who have ignored the experiences of individuals and how they behave to create and maintain social order. However, whereas Berger and Luckmann write more theoretically and abstractly about the life world and its legitimization, ethnomethodologists such as Harold Garfinkel have developed an intriguing experimental approach called *breaching* that demonstrates empirically the existence of the taken-for-granted meaning structures by observing the reactions of people in various settings when these meanings are violated or expectations are denied. What becomes clear from this work is that social reality is based on tacit assumptions that are shared by participants in everyday interaction situations. These unspoken rules guide behavior and make discourse and action possible. If they are violated, interaction is difficult, if not impossible, and the social definition of reality breaks down. The fragility of social order becomes evident and contrasts starkly with the structuralist view of an external, objective, and determinative institutional order.

ALFRED SCHUTZ: COMMON-SENSE AND
SCIENTIFIC INTERPRETATION OF HUMAN ACTION

I. Introduction: Content of Experience and Thought Objects

1) The Constructs of Common-Sense and of Scientific Thinking

"Neither common sense nor science can proceed without departing from the strict consideration of what is actual in experience." This statement by A. N. Whitehead is at the foundation of his analysis of the Organization of Thought.[1] Even the thing perceived in everyday life is more than a simple sense presentation.[2] It is a thought object, a construct of a highly complicated nature, involving not only particular forms of time-successions in order to constitute it as an object of one single sense, say of sight,[3] and of space relations in order to constitute it as a sense-object of several senses, say of sight and touch,[4] but also a contribution of imagination of hypothetical sense presentations in order to complete it.[5] According to Whitehead, it is precisely the last-named factor, the imagination of hypothetical sense presentation, "which is the rock upon which the whole structure of common-sense thought is erected"[6] and it is the effort of

reflective criticism "to construe our sense presentation as actual realization of the hypothetical thought object of perceptions."[7] In other words, the so-called concrete facts of common-sense perception are not so concrete as it seems. They already involve abstractions of a highly complicated nature, and we have to take account of this situation lest we commit the fallacy of misplaced concreteness.[8]

Science always, according to Whitehead, has a twofold aim: First, the production of a theory which agrees with experience, and second, the explanation of common-sense concepts of nature at least in their outline; this explanation consists in the preservation of these concepts in a scientific theory of harmonized thought.[9] For this purpose physical science (which, in this context, is alone of concern to Whitehead) has to develop devices by which the thought objects of common-sense perception are superseded by the thought objects of science.[10] The latter, such as molecules, atoms, and electrons have shed all qualities capable of direct sense presentation in our consciousness and are known to us only by the series of events in which they are implicated, events, to be sure, which are represented in our consciousness by sense presentations. By this device a bridge is formed between the fluid vagueness of sense and the exact definition of thought.[11]

It is not our concern to follow here step by step the ingenious method by which Whitehead uses the principle briefly outlined for his

---

Reprinted with permission of Kluwer Academic Publishers from Alfred Schutz, *Collected Papers*, Vol. 1., pp. 7–47. Copyright © Philosophy & Phenomenological Research XIV (1953)/ © Schutz (1974).

[1] Alfred North Whitehead: *The Organization of Thought*, London, 1917, now partially republished in *The Aims of Education*, New York, 1929, also as "Mentor-Book," New York, 1949. The quotations refer to this edition. For the first quotation see p. 110.
[2] *Ibid.*, Chapter 9, "The Anatomy of Some Scientific Ideas, I Fact, II Objects."
[3] *Ibid.*, p. 128f. and 131.
[4] *Ibid.*, p. 131 and 136.
[5] *Ibid.*, p. 133.
[6] *Ibid.*, p. 134.

[7] *Ibid.*, p. 135.
[8] Alfred North Whitehead: *Science and the Modern World*, New York, 1925, reprinted as "Mentor-Book," New York, 1948, p. 52 ff.
[9] *The Aims of Education*, p. 126.
[10] *Ibid.*, p. 135.
[11] *Ibid.*, p. 136.

analysis of the organization of thought, starting from the "anatomy of scientific ideas" and ending with the mathematically formulated theories of modern physics and the procedural rules of symbolic logic.[12] We are, however, highly interested in the basic view which Whitehead shares with many other prominent thinkers of our time such as William James,[13] Dewey,[14] Bergson,[15] and Husserl.[16] This view can be, very roughly, formulated as follows:

All our knowledge of the world, in common-sense as well as in scientific thinking, involves constructs, i.e., a set of abstractions, generalizations, formalizations, idealizations specific to the respective level of thought organization. Strictly speaking, there are no such things as facts, pure and simple. All facts are from the outset facts selected from a universal context by the activities of our mind. They are, therefore, always interpreted facts, either facts looked at as detached from their context by an artificial abstraction or facts considered in their particular setting. In either case, they carry along their interpretational inner and outer horizon. This does not mean that, in daily life or in science, we are unable to grasp the reality of the world. It just means that we grasp merely certain aspects of it, namely those which are relevant to us either for carrying on our business of living or

from the point of view of a body of accepted rules of procedure of thinking called the method of science.

2) *Particular Structure of the Constructs of the Social Sciences*

If, according to this view, all scientific constructs are designed to supersede the constructs of common-sense thought, then a principal difference between the natural and the social sciences becomes apparent. It is up to the natural scientists to determine which sector of the universe of nature, which facts and events therein, and which aspects of such facts and events are topically and interpretationally relevant to their specific purpose. These facts and events are neither preselected nor preinterpreted; they do not reveal intrinsic relevance structures. Relevance is not inherent in nature as such, it is the result of the selective and interpretative activity of man within nature or observing nature. The facts, data, and events with which the natural scientist has to deal are just facts, data, and events within his observational field but this field does not "mean" anything to the molecules, atoms, and electrons therein.

But the facts, events, and data before the social scientist are of an entirely different structure. His observational field, the social world, is not essentially structureless. It has a particular meaning and relevance structure for the human beings living, thinking, and acting therein. They have preselected and preinterpreted this world by a series of common-sense constructs of the reality of daily life, and it is these thought objects which determine their behavior, define the goal of their action, the means available for attaining them—in brief, which help them to find their bearings within their natural and socio-cultural environment and to come to terms with it. The thought objects constructed by the social scientists refer to and are founded upon the thought objects constructed by the common-sense thought of man living his everyday life among his fellow-men. Thus, the constructs used by the social scientist

[12] *Ibid.*, pp. 112–123 and 136–155.

[13] William James, *Principles of Psychology*, Vol. I, Chapter IX, "The Stream of Thought," p. 224f; especially p. 239f.

[14] John Dewey, *Logic, The Theory of Inquiry*, New York, 1938, especially Chs. III, IV, VII, VIII, XII; See also the essay, "The Objectivism-Subjectivism of Modern Philosophy" (1941) now in the collection *Problems of Men*, New York, 1946, p. 316f.

[15] Henri Bergson, *Matière et mémoire*, Ch. I, "La Sélection des Images par la Représentation."

[16] See for instance Edmund Husserl, *Logische Untersuchungen*, IIBd., II, "Die ideale Einheit der Species und die neuen Abstraktions Theorien"; rendered excellently by Marvin Farber, *The Foundation of Phenomenology*, Cambridge, 1943, Ch. IX, esp. p. 251f; Husserl, *Ideen zu einer reinen Phänomenologie*, English translation by Boyce Gibson, London, 1931, First Section; *Formale und transzendentale Logik*, Halle, 1929, Secs. 82–86, 94–96 (cf. Farber. l.c., p. 501ff.); *Erfahrung und Urteil*, Prague, 1939, Secs. 6–10, 16–24, 41–43, and *passim*.

are, so to speak, constructs of the second degree, namely constructs of the constructs made by the actors on the social scene, whose behavior the scientist observes and tries to explain in accordance with the procedural[17] rules of his science.

Modern social sciences find themselves faced with a series dilemma. One school of thought feels that there is a basic difference in the structure of the social world and of the world of nature. This insight leads, however, to the erroneous conclusion that the social sciences are *toto coelo* different from the natural sciences, a view which disregards the fact that certain procedural rules relating to correct thought organization are common to all empirical sciences. The other school of thought tries to look at the behavior of man in the same way in which the natural scientist looks at the "behavior" of his thought objects, taking it for granted that the methods of the natural sciences (above all, mathematical physics), which have achieved such magnificent results, are the only scientific methods. On the other hand, it takes for granted that the very adoption of the methods of the natural sciences for establishing constructs will lead to reliable knowledge of social reality. Yet these two assumptions are incompatible with each other. An ideally refined and fully developed behavioristic system, for example, would lead far away from the constructs in terms of which men in the reality of daily life experience their own and their fellow-men's behavior.

To overcome this difficulty particular methodological devices are required, among them the constructs of patterns of rational action. For the purpose of further analysis of the specific nature of the thought objects of social sciences we have to characterize some of the common-sense constructs used by men in everyday life. It is upon the latter that the former are founded.

II. Constructs of Thought Objects in Common-Sense Thinking

1) *The Individual's Common-Sense Knowledge of the World Is a System of Constructs of Its Typicality*

Let us try to characterize the way in which the wide-awake[18] grown-up man looks at the intersubjective world of daily life within which and upon which he acts as a man amidst his fellowmen. This world existed before our birth, experienced and interpreted by others, our predecessors, as an organized world. Now it is given to our experience and interpretation. All interpretation of this world is based on a stock of previous experiences of it, our own or those handed down to us by parents or teachers; these experiences in the form of "knowledge at hand" function as a scheme of reference.

To this stock of knowledge at hand belongs our knowledge that the world we live in is a world of more or less well circumscribed objects with more or less definite qualities, objects among which we move, which resist us and upon which we may act. Yet none of these objects is perceived as insulated. From the outset it is an object within a horizon of familiarity and pre-acquaintanceship which is, as such, just taken for granted until further notice as the unquestioned, though at anytime questionable stock of knowledge at hand. The unquestioned pre-experiences are, however, also from the outset, at hand as *typical*, that is, as carrying open horizons of anticipated similar experiences. For example, the outer world is not experienced as an arrangement of individual unique objects, dispersed in space and time, but as "mountains," "trees," "animals," "fellow-men." I may have never seen an Irish setter but if I see one, I know that it is an animal and in particular a

---

[17] On the concept of procedural rules, see Felix Kaufmann, *Methodology of the Social Sciences,* New York, 1944, esp. Chs. III and IV; on the divergent views of the relationship between the natural and the social sciences, *ibid.,* Ch. X.

[18] As to the precise meaning of this term, see "On Multiple Realities," p. 213. (Note: where articles are cited without further indication of source, as in this instance, the reference is to the present volume.) (M.N.)

dog, showing all the familiar features and the typical behavior of a dog and not, say, of a cat. I may reasonably ask: "What kind of dog is this?" The question presupposes that the dissimilarity of this particular dog from all other kinds of dogs which I know stands out and becomes questionable merely by reference to the similarity it has to my unquestioned experiences of typical dogs. In the more technical language of Husserl, whose analysis of the typicality of the world of daily life we have tried to sum up,[19] what is experienced in the actual perception of an object is apperceptively transferred to any other similar object, perceived merely as to its type. Actual experience will or will not confirm my anticipation of the typical conformity with other objects. If confirmed, the content of the anticipated type will be enlarged; at the same time the type will be split up into sub-types; on the other hand the concrete real object will prove to have its individual characteristics, which, nevertheless, have a form of typicality.

Now, and this seems to be of special importance, I *may* take the typically apperceived object as an *exemplar* of the general type and allow myself to be led to this concept of the type, but I do not *need* by any means to think of the concrete dog as an exemplar of the general concept of "dog." "In general" my Irish setter Rover shows all the characteristics which the type "dog," according to my previous experience, implies. Yet exactly what he has in common with other dogs is of no concern to me. I look at him as my friend and companion Rover, as such distinguished from all the other Irish setters with which he shares certain typical characteristics of appearance and behavior. I am, without a special motive, not induced to look at Rover as a mammal, an animal, an object of the outer world, although I know that he is all this too.

Thus, in the natural attitude of daily life we are concerned merely with certain objects standing out over against the unquestioned field of pre-experienced other objects, and the result of the selecting activity of our mind is to determine which particular characteristics of such an object are individual and which typical ones. More generally, we are merely concerned with some aspects of this particular typified object. Asserting of this object S that it has the characteristic property p, in the form "S is p," is an elliptical statement. For S, taken without any question as it appears to me, is not merely p but also q and r and many other things. The full statement should read: "S is, among many other things, such as q and r, also p." If I assert with respect to an element of the world as taken for granted: "S is p," I do so because under the prevailing circumstances I am interested in the p-being of S, disregarding as not relevant its being also q and r.[20]

The terms "interest" and "relevant" just used are, however, merely headings for a series of complicated problems which cannot be elaborated upon within the frame of the present discussion. We have to restrict ourselves to a few remarks.

Man finds himself at any moment of his daily life in a biographically determined situation, that is, in a physical and sociocultural environment as defined by him,[21] within which he has his position, not merely his position in terms of physical space and outer time or of his status and role within the social system but also his moral and ideological position.[22] To say that this definition of the situation is biographically

---

[19] Edmund Husserl, *Erfahrung und Urteil*, Secs. 18–21 and 82–85; cf. also "Language, Language Disturbances and the Texture of Consciousness," esp. pp. 277–283.

[20] See literature referred to in footnote 19.
[21] As to the concept of "Defining the Situation," see the various pertinent papers of W. I. Thomas, now collected in the volume, *Social Behavior and Personality, Contributions of W. I. Thomas to Theory and Social Research*, ed. by Edmund H. Volkart, New York, 1951. Consult index and the valuable introductory essay by the editor.
[22] Cf. Maurice Merleau-Ponty, *Phénoménologie de la perception*, Paris, 1945, p. 158.

determined is to say that it has its history; it is the sedimentation of all man's previous experiences, organized in the habitual possessions of his stock of knowledge at hand, and as such his unique possession, given to him and to him alone.* This biographically determined situation includes certain possibilities of future practical or theoretical activities which shall be briefly called the "purpose at hand." It is this purpose at hand which defines those elements among all the others contained in such a situation which are relevant for this purpose. This system of relevances in turn determines what elements have to be made a substratum of generalizing typification, what traits of these elements have to be selected as characteristically typical, and what others as unique and individual, that is, how far we have to penetrate into the open horizon of typicality. To return to our previous example: A change in my purpose at hand and the system of relevances attached thereto, the shifting of the "context" within which S is interesting to me, may induce me to become concerned with the q-being of S, its being also p having become irrelevant to me.

2) The Intersubjective Character of Common-Sense Knowledge and Its Implication

In analyzing the first constructs of common-sense thinking in everyday life we proceeded, however, as if the world were my private world and as if we were entitled to disregard the fact that it is from the outset an intersubjective world of culture. It is intersubjective because we live in it as men among other men, bound to them through common influence and work, understanding others and being understood by them. It is a world of culture because, from the outset, the world of everyday life is a universe of significance to us, that is, a texture of meaning which we have to interpret in order to find our bearings within it and come to terms with it. This texture of meaning, however—and this distinguishes the realm of culture from that of nature—originates in and has been instituted by human actions, our own and our fellow-men's, contemporaries and predecessors. All cultural objects—tools, symbols, language systems, works of art, social institutions, etc.—point back by their very origin and meaning to the activities of human subjects. For this reason we are always conscious of the historicity of culture which we encounter in traditions and customs. This historicity is capable of being examined in its reference to human activities of which it is the sediment. For the same reason I cannot understand a cultural object without referring it to the human activity from which it originates. For example, I do not understand a tool without knowing the purpose for which it was designed, a sign or symbol without knowing what it stands for in the mind of the person who uses it, an institution without understanding what it means for the individuals who orient their behavior with regard to its existence. Here is the origin of the so-called postulate of subjective interpretation of the social sciences which will call for our attention later on.

Our next task is, however, to examine the additional constructs which emerge in common-sense thinking if we take into account that this world is not my private world but an intersubjective one and that, therefore, my knowledge of it is not my private affair but from the outset intersubjective or socialized. For our purpose we have briefly to consider three aspects of the problem of the socialization of knowledge:

a. The reciprocity of perspectives or the structural socialization of knowledge;

b. The social origin of knowledge or the genetic socialization of knowledge;

c. The social distribution of knowledge.

a) The Reciprocity of Perspectives   In the natural attitude of common-sense thinking in daily

---

* See "Choosing among Projects of Action," pp. 76–77. (M.N.)

life I take it for granted that intelligent fellow-men exist. This implies that the objects of the world are, as a matter of principle, accessible to their knowledge, i.e., either known to them or knowable by them. This I know and take for granted beyond question. But I know also and take for granted that, strictly speaking, the "same" object must mean something different to me and to any of my fellow-men. This is so because

i. I, being "here," am at another distance from and experience other aspects as being typical of the objects than he, who is "there." For the same reason, certain objects are out of my reach (of my seeing, hearing, my manipulatory sphere, etc.) but within his, and vice versa.

ii. My and my fellow-man's biographically determined situations, and therewith our respective purposes at hand and our respective systems of relevances originating in such purposes, must differ, at least to a certain extent.

Common-sense thinking overcomes the differences in individual perspectives resulting from these factors by two basic idealizations:

i. The idealization of the interchangeability of the standpoints: I take it for granted—and assume my fellow-man does the same—that if I change places with him so that his "here" becomes mine, I shall be at the same distance from things and see them with the same typicality as he actually does; moreover, the same things would be in my reach which are actually in his. (The reverse is also true.)

ii. The idealization of the congruency of the system of relevances: Until counterevidence I take it for granted—and assume my fellow-man does the same—that the differences in perspectives originating in our unique biographical situations are irrelevant for the purpose at hand of either of us and that he

and I, that "We" assume that both of us have selected and interpreted the actually or potentially common objects and their features in an identical manner or at least an "empirically identical" manner, i.e., one sufficient for all practical purposes.

It is obvious that both idealizations, that of the interchangeability of the standpoints and that of the congruency of relevances—together constituting the *general thesis of reciprocal perspectives*—are typifying constructs of objects of thought which supersede the thought objects of my and my fellow-man's private experience. By the operation of these constructs of common-sense thinking it is assumed that the sector of the world taken for granted by me is also taken for granted by you, my individual fellow-man, even more, that it is taken for granted by "Us." But this "We" does not merely include you and me but "everyone who is one of us," i.e., everyone whose system of relevances is substantially (sufficiently) in conformity with yours and mine. Thus, the general thesis of reciprocal perspectives leads to the apprehension of objects and their aspects actually known by me and potentially known by you as everyone's knowledge. Such knowledge is conceived to be objective and anonymous, i.e., detached from and independent of my and my fellow-man's definition of the situation, our unique biographical circumstances and the actual and potential purposes at hand involved therein.

We must interpret the terms "objects" and "aspect of objects" in the broadest possible sense as signifying objects of knowledge taken for granted. If we do so, we shall discover the importance of the constructs of intersubjective thought objects, originating in the structural socialization of knowledge just described, for many problems investigated, but not thoroughly analyzed, by eminent social scientists. What is supposed to be known in common by everyone who shares our system of relevances is the way of life considered to be the natural, the good, the right one by the members of the "in-group";[23] as such, it is at the origin of the many recipes for handling things and men in order to come to terms with typified situations, of the folkways and mores, of "traditional behavior," in Max Weber's sense,[24] of the "of-course statements" believed to be valid by the in-group in spite of their inconsistencies,[25] briefly, of the "relative natural aspect of the world."[26] All these terms refer to constructs of a typified knowledge of a highly socialized structure which supersede the thought objects of my and my fellow-man's private knowledge of the world as taken for granted. Yet this knowledge has its history, it is a part of our "social heritage," and this brings us to the second aspect of the problem of socialization of knowledge, its genetic structure.

b) The Social Origin of Knowledge   Only a very small part of my knowledge of the world originates within my personal experience. The greater part is socially derived, handed down to me by my friends, my parents, my teachers and the teachers of my teachers. I am taught not only how to define the environment (that is, the typical features of the relative natural aspect of the world prevailing in the in-group as the unquestioned but always questionable sum total of things taken for granted until further notice), but also how typical constructs have to be formed

in accordance with the system of relevances accepted from the anonymous unified point of view of the in-group. This includes ways of life, methods of coming to terms with the environment, efficient recipes for the use of typical means for bringing about typical ends in typical situations. The typifying medium *par excellence* by which socially derived knowledge is transmitted is the vocabulary and the syntax of everyday language. The vernacular of everyday life is primarily a language of named things and events, and any name includes a typification and generalization referring to the relevance system prevailing in the linguistic in-group which found the named thing significant enough to provide a separate term for it. The pre-scientific vernacular can be interpreted as a treasure house of ready made pre-constituted types and characteristics, all socially derived and carrying along an open horizon of unexplored content.[27]

c) The Social Distribution of Knowledge   Knowledge is socially distributed. The general thesis of reciprocal perspectives, to be sure, overcomes the difficulty that my actual knowledge is merely the potential knowledge of my fellow-men and vice versa. But the stock of *actual* knowledge at hand differs from individual to individual, and common-sense thinking takes this fact into account. Not only *what* an individual knows differs from what his neighbor knows, but also *how* both know the "same" facts. Knowledge has manifold degrees of clarity, distinctness, precision, and familiarity. To take as an example William James'[28] well known distinction between "knowledge of acquaintance" and "knowledge-about," it is obvious that many things are known to me just in the dumb way of mere acquaintance, whereas *you* have knowledge "about" what makes them

---

[23] William Graham Sumner, *Folkways, A Study of the Sociological Importance of Manners, Customs, Mores, and Morals,* New York, 1906.

[24] Max Weber, *The Theory of Social and Economic Organization,* translated by A. M. Henderson and Talcott Parsons, New York, 1947, pp. 115ff; see also Talcott Parsons, *The Structure of Social Action,* New York, 1937, Ch. XVI.

[25] Robert S. Lynd, *Middletown in Transition,* New York, 1937, Ch. XII, and *Knowledge for What?* Princeton, 1939, pp. 38–63.

[26] Max Scheler, *Die Wissensformen und die Gesellschaft, Probleme einer Soziologie des Wissens,* Leipzig, 1926, pp. 58ff. Cf. Howard Becker and Helmut Dahlke, "Max Scheler's Sociology of Knowledge," *Philosophy and Phenomenological Research,* Vol. II, 1942, pp. 310–22, esp. 315.

[27] See "Language, Language Disturbances, and the Texture of Consciousness," p. 285f.

[28] William James, l.c., Vol. I, p. 221f.

what they are and vice versa. I am an "expert" in a small field and "layman" in many others, and so are you.[29] Any individual's stock of knowledge at hand is at any moment of his life structured as having zones of various degrees of clarity, distinctness and precision. This structure originates in the system of prevailing relevances and is thus biographically determined. The knowledge of these individual differences is itself an element of common-sense experience: I know whom and under what typical circumstances I have to consult as a "competent" doctor or lawyer. In other words, in daily life I construct types of the Other's field of acquaintance and of the scope and texture of his knowledge. In doing so, I assume that he will be guided by certain relevance structures, expressing themselves in a set of constant motives leading to a particular pattern of action and even co-determining his personality. But this statement anticipates the analysis of the common-sense constructs related to the understanding of our fellow-men, which is our next task.[29a]

3) The Structure of the Social World and Its Typification by Common-Sense Constructs

I, the human being, born into the social world, and living my daily life in it, experience it as built around my place in it, as open to my interpretation and action, but always referring to my actual biographically determined situation. Only in reference to me does a certain kind of my relations with others obtain the specific meaning which I designate with the word "We"; only with reference to "Us," whose center I am, do others stand out as "You," and in reference to "You," who refer back to me, third parties stand out as "They." In the dimension of time there are with reference to me in my actual biographical moment "contemporaries," with whom a mutual interplay of action and reaction can be established; "predecessors," upon whom I cannot act, but whose past actions and their outcome are open to my interpretation and may influence my own actions; and "successors," of whom no experience is possible but toward whom I may orient my actions in a more or less empty anticipation. All these relations show the most manifold forms of intimacy and anonymity, of familiarity and strangeness, of intensity and extensity.[30]

In the present context we are restricting ourselves to the interrelationship prevailing among contemporaries. Still dealing with common-sense experience we may just take for granted that man can understand his fellow-man and his actions and that he can communicate with others because he assumes they understand his actions; also, that this mutual understanding has certain limits but is sufficient for many practical purposes.

Among my contemporaries are some with whom I share, as long as the relation lasts, not only a community of time but also of space. We shall, for the sake of terminological convenience, call such contemporaries "consociates" and the relationship prevailing among them a "face-to-face" relationship, this term being understood in

---

[29] Alfred Schutz, "The Well-Informed Citizen, an Essay on the Social Distribution of Knowledge," *Social Research,* Vol. 13, 1946, pp. 463–472.

[29a] With the exception of some economists (e.g., F. A. Hayek, "Economics and Knowledge," *Economica*, February 1937, now reprinted in *Individualism and Economic Order,* Chicago 1948) the problem of the social distribution of knowledge has not attracted the attention of the social scientists it merits. It opens a new field for theoretical and empirical research which would truly deserve the name of a sociology of knowledge, now reserved for an ill-defined discipline which just takes for granted the social distribution of knowledge, upon which it is founded. It may be hoped that the systematic investigation of this field will yield significant contributions to many problems of the social sciences such as those of social role, of social stratification, of institutional or organizational behavior, of the sociology of occupations and professions, of prestige and status, etc.

[30] Alfred Schutz, *Der sinnhafte Aufbau der sozialen Welt,* Vienna, 1932, 2nd edition 1960. See also Alfred Stonier and Karl Bode, "A New Approach to the Methodology of the Social Sciences," *Economica,* Vol. V, November, 1937, pp. 406–424, esp. pp. 416ff.

a sense other than that used by Cooley[31] and his successors; we designate by it merely a purely formal aspect of social relationship equally applicable to an intimate talk between friends and the co-presence of strangers in a railroad car.

Sharing a community of space implies that a certain sector of the outer world is equally within the reach of each partner, and contains objects of common interest and relevance. For each partner the other's body, his gestures, his gait and facial expressions, are immediately observable, not merely as things or events of the outer world but in their physiognomical significance, that is, as symptoms of the other's thoughts. Sharing a community of time—and this means not only of outer (chronological) time, but of inner time—implies that each partner participates in the on-rolling life of the other, can grasp in a vivid present the other's thoughts as they are built up step by step. They may thus share one another's anticipations of the future as plans, or hopes or anxieties. In brief, consociates are mutually involved in one another's biography; they are growing older together; they live, as we may call it, in a pure We-relationship.

In such a relationship, fugitive and superficial as it may be, the Other is grasped as a unique individuality (although merely one aspect of his personality becomes apparent) in its unique biographical situation (although revealed merely fragmentarily). In all the other forms of social relationship (and even in the relationship among consociates as far as the unrevealed aspects of the Other's self are concerned) the fellow-man's self can merely be grasped by a "contribution of imagination of hypothetical meaning presentation" (to allude to Whitehead's statement quoted earlier), that is, by forming a construct of a typical way of behavior, a typical pattern of underlying motives, of typical attitudes of a personality

type, of which the Other and his conduct under scrutiny, both outside of my observational reach, are just instances or exemplars. We cannot here[32] develop a full taxonomy of the structuredness of the social world and of the various forms of constructs of course-of-action types and personality types needed for grasping the Other and his behavior. Thinking of my absent friend A, I form an ideal type of his personality and behavior based on my past experience of A as my consociate. Putting a letter in the mailbox, I expect that unknown people, called postmen, will act in a typical way, not quite intelligible to me, with the result that my letter will reach the addressee within typically reasonable time. Without ever having met a Frenchman or a German, I understand "Why France fears the rearmament of Germany." Complying with a rule of English grammar, I follow a socially approved behavior pattern of contemporary English-speaking fellow-men to which I have to adjust my own behavior in order to make myself understandable. And, finally, any artifact or utensil refers to the anonymous fellow-man who produced it to be used by other anonymous fellow-men for attaining typical goals by typical means.[*]

These are just a few examples but they are arranged according to the degree of increasing anonymity of the relationship among contemporaries involved and therewith of the construct needed to grasp the Other and his behavior. It becomes apparent that an increase in anonymity involves a decrease of fullness of content. The more anonymous the typifying construct is, the more detached it is from the uniqueness of the individual fellow-man involved and the fewer aspects of his personality and behavior pattern enter the typification as being relevant for the purpose at hand, for the sake of which the type has been constructed. If we distinguish between

[31] Charles H. Cooley, *Social Organization*, New York, 1909, Chs. III–V; and Alfred Schutz, "The Homecomer," *American Journal of Sociology*, Vol. 50, 1945, p. 371.

[32] See footnote 30.
[*] See Alfred Schutz, "The Problem of Rationality in the Social World," *Economica*, Vol. X, May 1943, (M.N.).

(subjective) personal types and (objective) course-of-action types, we may say that increasing anonymization of the construct leads to the superseding of the former by the latter. In complete anonymization the individuals are supposed to be interchangeable and the course-of-action type refers to the behavior of "whomsoever" acting in the way defined as typical by the construct.

Summing up, we may say that, except in the pure We-relation of consociates, we can never grasp the individual uniqueness of our fellow-man in his unique biographical situation. In the constructs of common-sense thinking the Other appears at best as a partial self, and he enters even the pure We-relation merely with a part of his personality. This insight seems to be important in several respects. It helped Simmel[33] to overcome the dilemma between individual and collective consciousness, so clearly seen by Durkheim[34]; it is at the basis of Cooley's[35] theory of the origin of the Self by a "looking glass effect"; it led George H. Mead[36] to his ingenious concept of the "generalized other"; it is, finally, decisive for the clarification of such concepts as "social functions," "social role," and, last but not least, "rational action."*

---

[33] Georg Simmel: "Note on the Problem: How Is Society Possible?" translated by Albion W. Small, *The American Journal of Sociology,* Vol. XVI, 1910, pp. 372–391; see also, *The Sociology of Georg Simmel,* translated, edited and with an introduction by Kurt H. Wolff, Glencoe, Ill. 1950, and consult Index under "Individual and Group."
[34] An excellent presentation of Durkheim's view in Georges Gurvitch, *La Vocation Actuelle de la Sociologie,* Paris, 1950, Ch. VI, pp. 351–409; see also Talcott Parsons, *The Structure of Social Action,* Ch. X; Émile Benoit-Smullyan: "The Sociologism of Émile Durkheim and his School," in Harry Elmer Barnes: *An Introduction to the History of Sociology,* Chicago, 1948, pp. 499–537, and Robert K. Merton: *Social Theory and Social Structure,* Glencoe, Ill. 1949, Ch. IV, pp. 125–150.
[35] Charles H. Cooley, *Human Nature and the Social Order,* rev. ed., New York, 1922, p. 184.
[36] George H. Mead: *Mind, Self, and Society,* Chicago, 1934, pp. 152–163.
* For critical clarification of this concept, see "The Problem of Rationality in the Social World," *Economica,* Vol. X, May 1943. (M.N.)

But this is merely half the story. My constructing the Other as a partial self, as the performer of typical roles or functions, has a corollary in the process of self-typification which takes place if I enter into interaction with him. I am not involved in such a relationship with my total personality but merely with certain layers of it. In defining the role of the Other I am assuming a role myself. In typifying the Other's behavior I am typifying my own, which is interrelated with his, transforming myself into a passenger, consumer, taxpayer, reader, bystander, etc. It is this self-typification which is at the bottom of William James'[37] and of George H. Mead's[38] distinction between the "I" and the "Me" in relation to the social self.

We have, however, to keep in mind that the common-sense constructs used for the typification of the Other and of myself are to a considerable extent socially derived and socially approved. Within the in-group the bulk of personal types and course-of-action types is taken for granted (until counter-evidence appears) as a set of rules and recipes which have stood the test so far and are expected to stand it in the future. Even more, the pattern of typical constructs is frequently institutionalized as a standard of behavior, warranted by traditional and habitual mores and sometimes by specific means of so-called social control, such as the legal order.

4) Course-of-Action Types and Personal Types

We have now briefly to investigate the pattern of action and social interaction which underlies the construction of course-of-action and personal types in common-sense thinking.

---

[37] William James, *op. cit.,* Vol. I, Ch. X.
[38] George H. Mead, *op. cit.,* pp. 173–175, 196–198, 203; "The Genesis of the Self," reprinted in *The Philosophy of the Present,* Chicago, 1932, pp. 176–195; "What Social Objects Must Psychology Presuppose?" *Journal of Philosophy,* Vol. X, 1913, pp. 374–380.

a) Action, Project, Motive   The term "action" as used in this paper shall designate human conduct devised by the actor in advance, that is, conduct based upon a preconceived project. The term "act" shall designate the outcome of this ongoing process, that is, the accomplished action. Action may be covert (for example, the attempt to solve a scientific problem mentally) or overt, gearing into the outer world; it may take place by commission or omission, purposive abstention from acting being considered an action in itself.

All projecting consists in anticipation of future conduct by way of phantasying, yet it is not the ongoing process of action but the phantasied act as having been accomplished which is the starting point of all projecting. I have to visualize the state of affairs to be brought about by my future action before I can draft the single steps of such future acting from which this state of affairs will result. Metaphorically speaking, I must have some idea of the structure to be erected before I can draft the blueprints. Thus I have to place myself in my phantasy at a future time, when this action *will* already *have been* accomplished. Only then may I reconstruct in phantasy the single steps which *will have* brought forth this future act. In the terminology suggested, it is not the future action but the future act that is anticipated in the project, and it is anticipated in the Future Perfect Tense, *modo futuri exacti*. This time perspective peculiar to the project has rather important consequences.

i. All projects of my forthcoming acts are based upon my knowledge at hand at the time of projecting. To this knowledge belongs my experience of previously performed acts which are typically similar to the projected one. Consequently all projecting involves a particular idealization, called by Husserl the idealization of "I-can-do-it-again,"[39] i.e., the

assumption that I may under typically similar circumstances act in a way typically similar to that in which I acted before in order to bring about a typically similar state of affairs. It is clear that this idealization involves a construction of a specific kind. My knowledge at hand at the time of projecting must, strictly speaking, be different from my knowledge at hand after having performed the projected act, if for no other reason than because I "grew older" and at least the experiences I had while carrying out my project have modified my biographical circumstances and enlarged my stock of experience. Thus, the "repeated" action will be something else than a mere re-performance. The first action A' started within a set of circumstances C' and indeed brought about the state of affairs S'; the repeated action A'' starts in a set of circumstances C'' and is expected to bring about the state of affairs S''. By necessity C'' will differ from C' because the experience that A' succeeded in bringing about S' belongs to my stock of knowledge, which is an element of C'', whereas, to my stock of knowledge, which was an element of C', belonged merely the empty anticipation that this would be the case. Similarly S'' will differ from S' as A'' will from A'. This is so because all the terms—C', C'', A', A'', S', S''— are as such unique and irretrievable events. Yet exactly those features which make them unique and irretrievable in the strict sense are—to my common-sense thinking— eliminated as being irrelevant for my purpose at hand. When making the idealization of "I-can-do-it-again" I am merely interested in the typicality of A, C, and S, all of them without primes. The construction consists, figuratively speaking, in the suppression of the primes as being irrelevant, and this, incidentally, is characteristic of typifications of all kinds.

This point will become especially important for the analysis of the concept of so-called rational action. It is obvious that in the habitual and routine actions of daily life

[39] Edmund Husserl, *Formale und transzendentale Logik*, Halle, 1929, Sec. 74, p. 167; *Erfahrung und Urteil*, Sec. 24, Sec. 51b.

we apply the construction just described in following recipes and rules of thumb which have stood the test so far and in frequently stringing together means and ends without clear knowledge "about" their real connections. Even in common-sense thinking we construct a world of supposedly interrelated facts containing exclusively elements deemed to be relevant for our purpose at hand.

ii. The particular time perspective of the project sheds some light on the relationship between project and motive. In ordinary speech the term "motive" covers two different sets of concepts which have to be distinguished.

a. We may say that the motive of a murderer was to obtain the money of the victim. Here "motive" means the state of affairs, the end, which is to be brought about by the action undertaken. We shall call this kind of motive the "in-order-to motive." From the point of view of the actor this class of motives refers to the future. The state of affairs to be brought about by the future action, prephantasied in its project, is the in-order-to motive for carrying out the action.

b. We may say that the murderer has been motivated to commit his deed because he grew up in this or that environment, had these or those childhood experiences, etc. This class of motives, which we shall call "(genuine)[39a] because-motives" refers from the point of view of the actor to his past experiences which have determined him to act as he did. What is motivated in an action in the form of "because" is the project of the action itself (for

instance, to satisfy his need for money by killing a man).

We cannot enter here[40] into a more detailed analysis of the theory of motives. But it should be pointed out that the actor who lives in his ongoing process of acting has merely the in-order-to motive of his ongoing action in view, that is, the projected state of affairs to be brought about. Only by turning back to his accomplished act or to the past initial phases of his still ongoing action or to the once established project which anticipates the act *modo futuri exacti* can the actor grasp retrospectively the because-motive that determined him to do what he did or what he projected to do. But then the actor is not acting any more; he is an observer of himself.

The distinction between the two kinds of motives becomes of vital importance for the analysis of human interaction to which we now turn.

b) Social Interaction   Any form of social interaction is founded upon the constructs already described relating to the understanding of the Other and the action pattern in general. Take as an example the interaction of consociates involved in questioning and answering. In projecting my question, I anticipate that the Other will understand my action (for instance my uttering an interrogative sentence) as a question and that this understanding will induce him to act in such a way that I may understand his behavior as an adequate response. (I: "Where is the ink?" The Other points at a table.) The in-order-to motive of my action is to obtain adequate information which, in this particular situation, presupposes that the understanding of my in-order-to motive will become the Other's because-motive to perform an action in-order-to furnish me this information—provided he is able and willing to do so, which I assume he is. I anticipate that he understands English, that he knows where the ink is, that he will tell me if

---

[39a] Linguistically in-order-to motives may be expressed in modern languages also by "because" *sentences*. Genuine because-motives, however, cannot be expressed by "in-order-to" *sentences*. This distinction between the two possibilities of linguistic expressions relating to the in-order-to motive, important as it is in another context, will be disregarded in the following and the term "because-motive" or "because-sentence" will be exclusively reserved for the genuine because-motive and its linguistic expression.

[40] See footnote 30.

he knows, etc. In more general terms, I anticipate that he will be guided by the same types of motives by which in the past, according to my stock of knowledge at hand, I myself and many others were guided under typically similar circumstances. Our example shows that even the simplest interaction in common life presupposes a series of common-sense constructs—in this case constructs of the Other's anticipated behavior—all of them based on the idealization that the actor's in-order-to motives will become because-motives of his partner and vice versa. We shall call this *idealization* that *of the reciprocity of motives.* It is obvious that this idealization depends upon the general thesis of the reciprocity of perspectives, since it implies that the motives imputed to the Other are typically the same as my own or that of others in typically similar circumstances; all this is in accordance with my genuine or socially derived knowledge at hand.

Suppose now that I want to find some ink in order to refill my fountain pen so that I can write this application to the fellowship committee which, if granted, will change my entire way of life. I, the actor (questioner), and I alone know of this plan of mine to obtain the fellowship which is the ultimate in-order-to motive of my actual action, the state of affairs to be brought about. Of course, this can be done merely by a series of steps (writing an application, bringing writing tools within my reach, etc.) each of them to be materialized by an "action" with its particular project and its particular in-order-to motive. Yet all these "sub-actions" are merely phases of the total action and all intermediary steps to be materialized by them are merely means for attaining my final goal as defined by my original project. It is the span of this original project which welds together the chain of sub-projects into a unit. This becomes clear if we consider that in this chain of interrelated partial actions, designed to materialize states of affairs which are merely "means" for attaining the projected end, certain links can be replaced by others or even drop out without any change in the original project. If I

cannot find some ink I may turn to the typewriter in order to prepare my application.

In other words, only the actor knows "when his action starts and where it ends," that is, why it will have been performed. It is the span of his projects which determines the unit of his action. His partner has neither knowledge of the projecting preceding the actor's action nor of the context of a higher unit in which it stands. He knows merely that fragment of the actor's action which has become manifest to him, namely, the performed act observed by him or the past phases of the still ongoing action. If the addressee of my question were asked later on by a third person what I wanted from him he would answer that I wanted to know where to find some ink. That is all he knows of my projecting and its context, and he has to look at it as a selfcontained unit action. In order to "understand" what I, the actor, meant by my action he would have to start from the observed act and to construct from there my underlying in-order-to motive for the sake of which I did what he observed.

It is now clear that the meaning of an action is necessarily a different one (a) for the actor; (b) for his partner involved with him in interaction and having, thus, with him a set of relevances and purposes in common; and (c) for the observer not involved in such relationship. This fact leads to two important consequences: First, that in common-sense thinking we have merely a *chance* to understand the Other's action sufficiently for our purpose at hand; secondly, that to increase this chance we have to search for the meaning the action has for the actor. Thus, the postulate of the "subjective interpretation of meaning," as the unfortunate term goes, is not a particularity of Max Weber's[41] sociology or of

---

[41] Max Weber, *op. cit.,* pp. 9, 18, 22, 90, esp. p. 88: "In 'action' is included all human behavior when and insofar as the acting individual attaches a subjective meaning to it . . . Action is social insofar as, by virtue of the subjective meaning attached to it by the acting individual (or individuals), it takes account of the behavior of others and is thereby oriented in its course." See Talcott Parsons, *op. cit.,* esp. pp. 82ff, 345–47, and 484ff; Felix Kaufmann, *op. cit.,* pp. 166f.

the methodology of the social sciences in general but a principle of constructing course-of-action types in common-sense experience.[*]

But subjective interpretation of meaning is merely possible by revealing the motives which determine a given course of action. By referring a course-of-action type to the underlying typical motives of the actor we arrive at the construction of a personal type. The latter may be more or less anonymous and, therewith, more or less empty of content. In the We-relationship among consociates the Other's course of action, its motives (insofar as they become manifest) and his person (insofar as it is involved in the manifest action) can be shared in immediacy and the constructed types, just described, will show a very low degree of anonymity and a high degree of fullness. In constructing course-of-action types of contemporaries other than consociates, we impute to the more or less anonymous actors a set of supposedly invariant motives which govern their actions. This set is itself a construct of typical expectations of the Other's behavior and has been investigated frequently in terms of social role or function or institutional behavior. In common-sense thinking such a construct has a particular significance for projecting actions which are oriented upon my contemporaries' (not my consociates') behavior. Its functions can be described as follows:

1) I take it for granted that my action (say putting a stamped and duly addressed envelope in a mailbox) will induce anonymous fellow-men (postmen) to perform typical actions (handling the mail) in accordance with typical in-order-to motives (to live up to their occupational duties) with the result that the state of affairs projected by me (delivery of the letter to the addressee within reasonable time) will be achieved. 2) I also take it for granted that my construct of the Other's course-of-action

type corresponds substantially to his own self-typification and that to the latter belongs a typified construct of my, his anonymous partner's, typical way of behavior based on typical and supposedly invariant motives. ("Whoever puts a duly addressed and stamped envelope in the mailbox is assumed to intend to have it delivered to the addressee in due time.") 3) Even more, in my own self-typification—that is by assuming the role of a customer of the mail service—I have to project my action in such a typical way as I suppose the typical post office employee expects a typical customer to behave. Such a construct of mutually interlocked behavior patterns reveals itself as a construct of mutually interlocked in-order-to and because-motives which are supposedly invariant. The more institutionalized or standardized such a behavior pattern is, that is, the more typified it is in a socially approved way by laws, rules, regulations, customs, habits, etc., the greater is the chance that my own self-typifying behavior will bring about the state of affairs aimed at.

c) The Observer   We have still to characterize the special case of the observer who is not a partner in the interaction patterns. His motives are not interlocked with those of the observed person or persons; he is "tuned in" upon them but not they upon him. In other words, the observer does not participate in the complicated mirror-reflexes involved by which in the interaction pattern among contemporaries, the actor's in-order-to motives become understandable to the partner as his own because-motives and vice versa. Precisely this fact constitutes the so-called "disinterestedness" or detachment of the observer. He is not involved in the actor's hopes and fears whether or not they will understand one another and achieve their end by the interlocking of motives. Thus, his system of relevances differs from that of the interested parties and permits him to see at the same time more and less than what is seen by them. But under all circumstances, it is merely the manifested

---

[*] Cf. "Concept and Theory Formation in the Social Sciences," p. 56f. (M.N.).

fragments of the actions of *both* partners that are accessible to his observation. In order to understand them the observer has to avail himself of his knowledge of typically similar patterns of interaction in typically similar situational settings and has to construct the motives of the actors from that sector of the course of action which is patent to his observation. The constructs of the observer are, therefore, different ones than those used by the participants in the interaction, if for no other reason than the fact that the purpose of the observer is different from that of the interactors and therewith the systems of relevances attached to such purposes are also different. There is a mere chance, although a chance sufficient for many practical purposes, that the observer in daily life can grasp the subjective meaning of the actor's acts. This chance increases with the degree of anonymity and standardization of the observed behavior. The scientific observer of human interrelation patterns, the social scientist, has to develop specific methods for the building of his constructs in order to assure their applicability for the interpretation of the subjective meaning the observed acts have for the actors. Among these devices we are here especially concerned with the constructs of models of so-called rational actions. Let us consider first the possible meaning of the term "rational action" within the common-sense experience of everyday life.

III. Rational Action Within Common-Sense Experience*

Ordinary language does not sharply distinguish among a sensible, a reasonable, and a rational way of conduct. We may say that a man acted sensibly if the motive and the course of his action is understandable to us, his partners or observers. This will be the case if his action is in accordance with a socially approved set of rules

---

* Cf. "The Problem of Rationality in the Social World," *Economica*, Vol. X, May, 1943. (M.N.).

and recipes for coming to terms with typical problems by applying typical means for achieving typical ends. If I, if We, if "Anybody who is one of us" found himself in typically similar circumstances he would act in a similar way. Sensible behavior, however, does not presuppose that the actor is guided by insight into his motives and the means-ends context. A strong emotional reaction against an offender might be sensible and refraining from it foolish. If an action seems to be sensible to the observer and is, in addition, supposed to spring from a judicious choice among different courses of action, we may call it reasonable even if such action follows traditional or habitual patterns just taken for granted. Rational action, however, presupposes that the actor has clear and distinct insight[41a] into the ends, the means, and the secondary results, which "involves rational consideration of alternative means to the end, of the relations of the end to other prospective results of employment of any given means and, finally, of the relative importance of different possible ends. Determination of action, either in affectual or in traditional terms, is thus incompatible with this type."[42]

[41a] This postulate of Leibniz obviously underlies the concept of rationality used by many students of this topic. Pareto, distinguishing between logical and nonlogical actions, requires that the former have logically to conjoin means to ends not only from the standpoint of the subject performing the action but also from the standpoint of other persons who have a more extensive knowledge, that is, of the scientist, [Vilfredo Pareto, *Trattato de Sociologia Generale*, English translation under the title *The Mind and Society*, ed. by Arthur Livingston, New York 1935 and 1942; see especially Volume I, Secs. 150ff.] Objective and subjective purpose have to be identical. Professor Talcott Parsons (*The Structure of Social Action*, p. 58) develops a similar theory. Pareto admits, however, (l.c., sect. 150) that from the subjective point of view nearly all human actions belong to the logical class. Professor Howard Becker (*Through Values to Social Interpretation*, Durham, 1950, pp. 23–27) is of the opinion that action may be found (expediently) rational where it is completely centered upon means viewed by the actor as adequate for the attainment of ends which he conceives as unambiguous.

[42] Max Weber, *op. cit.*, p. 117. The characterization of "rational action" follows Max Weber's definition of one of

These very preliminary definitions for sensible, reasonable, and rational actions are stated in terms of common-sense interpretations of other people's actions in daily life but, characteristically, they refer not only to the stock of knowledge taken for granted in the in-group to which the observer of this course of action belongs but also to the subjective point of view of the actor, that is, to his stock of knowledge at hand at the time of carrying out the action. This involves several difficulties. First, it is, as we have seen, our biographical situation which determines the problem at hand and, therewith, the systems of

relevances under which the various aspects of the world are constructed in the form of types. Of necessity, therefore, the actor's stock of knowledge will differ from that of the observer. Even the general thesis of the reciprocity of perspectives is not sufficient to eliminate this difficulty because it presupposes that both the observed and the observer are sharing a system of relevances sufficiently homogeneous in structure and content for the practical purpose involved. If this is not the case, then a course of action which is perfectly rational from the point of view of the actor may appear as non-rational to the partner or observer and vice versa. Both attempts, to induce rain by performing the rain-dance or by seeding clouds with silver iodine, are subjectively seen, rational actions from the point of view of the Hopi Indian or the modern meteorologist respectively, but both would have been judged as non-rational by a meteorologist twenty years ago.

Secondly, even if we restrict our investigation to the subjective point of view, we have to ascertain whether there is a difference in the meaning of the term "rational," in the sense of reasonable, if applied to my own past acts or to the determination of a future course of my actions. At first glance, it seems that the difference is considerable. What I did has been done and cannot be undone, although the state of affairs brought about by my actions might be modified or eliminated by countermoves. I do not have, with respect to past actions, the possibility of choice. Anything anticipated in an empty way in the project which had preceded my past action has been fulfilled or not by the outcome of my action. On the other hand, all future action is projected under the idealization of "I can do it again," which may or may not stand the test.

Closer analysis shows, however, that even in judging the reasonableness of our own past action we refer always to our knowledge at hand at the time of projecting such action. If we find, retrospectively, that what we had formerly

---

the two types of rational actions distinguished by him, (*op. cit.*, p. 115) namely, the so-called *"zweckrationales Handeln"* (rendered in Parsons' translation by "rational orientation to a system of discrete ends"). We disregard here Weber's second type of rational action, the *"wertrationales Handeln,"* (rendered by "rational orientation to an absolute value") since the distinction between both types can be reduced in the terms of the present discussion to a distinction between two types of "because-motives" leading to the project of an action as such. "Zweckrationales Handeln" implies that within the system of hierarchical projects, which we have called the "plans," several courses of action stand to choice and that this choice has to be a rational one; "wertrationales Handeln" cannot choose among several projects of action equally open to the actor within the system of his plan. The project is taken for granted, but there are alternatives open for bringing about the projected state of affairs, and they have to be determined by rational selection. Parsons has rightly pointed out (l.c., p. 115, footnote 38) that it is nearly impossible to find English terms for *"zweckrational"* and *"Wertrational,"* but the circumscription chosen by him for their translation already implies an interpretation of Weber's theory and obfuscates an important issue: Neither is, in the case of *"Zweckrationalität,"* a system of *discrete* ends presupposed nor, in the case of *"Wertrationalität,"* an absolute value. (For Parson's own theory, see pp. 16ff. of his introduction to the Weber volume.)

Far more important for our problem than the distinction of two types of rational action is the distinction between rational actions of both types, on the one hand, and traditional and affectual actions on the other. The same holds good for the modifications suggested by Howard Becker (*op. cit.*, p. 22ff) between "four types of means" followed by the members of any society in attaining their ends: (1) expedient rationality; (2) sanctioned rationality; (3) traditional non-rationality; (4) affective non-rationality. Whereas Weber and Parsons include the ends in their concept of rationality, Becker speaks of types of means.

projected as a reasonable course of action under the then known circumstances proved to be a failure, we may accuse ourselves of various mistakes: of an error in judgment if the then prevailing circumstances were incorrectly or incompletely ascertained; or of a lack of foresight if we failed to anticipate future developments, etc. We will, however, not say that we acted unreasonably.

Thus, in both cases, that of the past and of the future action, our judgment of reasonableness refers to the project determining the course of action and, still more precisely, to the choice among several projects of action involved. As has been shown elsewhere,[43] any projecting of future action involves a choice between at least two courses of conduct, namely, to carry out the projected action or to refrain from doing so.

Each of the alternatives standing to choice has, as Dewey says,[44] to be rehearsed in phantasy in order to make choice and decision possible. If this deliberation is to be strictly a rational one then the actor must have a clear and distinct knowledge of the following elements of each projected course-of-action standing to choice:

a. of the particular state of affairs within which his projected action has to start. This involves a sufficiently precise definition of his biographical situation in the physical and socio-cultural environment;

b. of the state of affairs to be brought about by his projected action, that is, its end. Yet since there is no such thing as an isolated project or end, (all my projects, present to my mind at a given time, being integrated into systems of projects, called my plans and all my plans being integrated into my plan of life), there are also no isolated ends. They are interconnected in a hierarchical

order, and the attaining of one might have repercussions on the other. I have, therefore, to have clear and distinct knowledge of the place of my project within the hierarchical order of my plans (or the interrelationship of the end to be achieved with other ends), the compatibility of one with the other, and the possible repercussions of one upon another, briefly: of the secondary results of my future actions, as Max Weber calls it.[45]

c. of the various means necessary for attaining the established end, of the possibility of bringing them within my reach, of the degree of the expediency of their application, of the possible employment of these same means for the attainment of other potential ends, and of the compatibility of the selected means with other means needed for the materialization of other projects.

The complication increases considerably if the actor's project of a rational action involves the rational action or reaction of a fellow-man, say of a consociate. Projecting rationally such a kind of action involves sufficiently clear and distinct knowledge of the situation of departure not only as defined by me but also as defined by the Other. Moreover, there has to be sufficient likelihood that the Other will be tuned in upon me and consider my action as relevant enough to be motivated by my in-order-to motive. If this is the case, then there has to be a sufficient chance that the Other will understand me, and this means in the case of a rational interrelationship that he will interpret my action rationally as being a rational one and that he will react in a rational way. To assume that the Other will do so implies, however, on the one hand, that he will have sufficiently clear and distinct knowledge of my project and of its place in the hierarchy of my plans (at least as far as my overt action make them manifest to him) and of my system of relevances attached thereto; and, on

---

[43] "Choosing Among Projects of Action."
[44] John Dewey, *Human Nature and Conduct,* Modern Library edition, p. 190.

---

[45] See quotation from Max Weber on p. 279.

the other hand, that the structure and scope of his stock of knowledge at hand will be in its relevant portion substantially similar to mine and that his and my system of relevances will, if not overlap, be at least partially congruent. If, furthermore, I assume in my projecting that the Other's reaction to my projected action will be a rational one, I suppose that he, in projecting his response, knows all the aforementioned elements (a), (b), (c) of his reaction in a clear and distinct way. Consequently, if I project a rational action which requires an interlocking of my and the Other's motives of action to be carried out (e.g., I want the Other to do something for me), I must, by a curious mirror-effect, have sufficient knowledge of what he, the Other, knows (and knows to be relevant with respect to my purpose at hand), and this knowledge of his is supposed to include sufficient acquaintance with what I know. This is a condition of *ideally* rational interaction because without such mutual knowledge I could not "rationally" project the attainment of my goal by means of the Other's co-operation or reaction. Moreover, such mutual knowledge has to be clear and distinct; merely a more or less empty expectation of the Other's behavior is not sufficient.

It seems that under these circumstances rational social interaction becomes impracticable even among consociates. And yet we receive reasonable answers to reasonable questions, our commands are carried out, we perform in factories and laboratories and offices highly "rationalized" activities, we play chess together, briefly, we come conveniently to terms with our fellow-men. How is this possible?

Two different answers seem to offer themselves. First, if interaction among consociates is involved we may assume that the mutual participation in the consociate's onrolling life, the sharing of his anticipations so characteristic of the pure We-relation establishes the prerequisites for rational interaction just analyzed. Yet it is precisely this pure We-relation which is the irrational element of any interrelationship among consociates. The second answer refers

not only to the interrelationship among consociates but among contemporaries in general. We may explain the rationality of human interaction by the fact that both actors orient their actions on certain standards which are socially approved as rules of conduct by the in-group to which they belong: norms, mores of good behavior, manners, the organizational framework provided for this particular form of division of labor, the rules of the chess game, etc. But neither the origin nor the import of the socially approved standard is "rationally" understood. Such standards might be traditionally or habitually accepted as just being taken for granted, and, within the meaning of our previous definitions, behavior of this kind will be sensible or even reasonable but not necessarily rational. At any rate, it will not be "ideally" rational, that is, meeting all the requirements worked out in the analysis of this concept.

We come, therefore, to the conclusion that "rational action" on the common-sense level is always action within an unquestioned and undetermined frame of constructs of typicalities of the setting, the motives, the means and ends, the courses of action and personalities involved and taken for granted. They are, however, not merely taken for granted by the actor but also supposed as being taken for granted by the fellow-man. From this frame of constructs, forming their undetermined horizon, merely particular sets of elements stand out which are clearly and distinctly determinable. To these elements refers the common-sense concept of rationality. Thus we may say that on this level actions are at best partially rational and that rationality has many degrees. For instance, our assumption that our fellow-man who is involved with us in a pattern of interaction knows its rational elements will never reach "empirical certainty" (certainty "until further notice" or "good until counter-evidence")[46] but will always bear the character of plausibility, that is, of subjective likelihood (in

---

[46] Edmund Husserl, *Erfahrung und Urteil*, Sec. 77, p. 370.

contradistinction to mathematical probability). We always have to "take chances" and to "run risks," and this situation is expressed by our hopes and fears which are merely the subjective corollaries of our basic uncertainty as to the outcome of our projected interaction.

To be sure, the more standardized the prevailing action pattern is, the more anonymous it is, the greater is the subjective chance of conformity and, therewith, of the success of intersubjective behavior. Yet—and this is the paradox of rationality on the common-sense level—the more standardized the pattern is, the less the underlying elements become analyzable for common-sense thought in terms of rational insight.

All this refers to the criterion of rationality as applicable to the thinking of everyday life and its constructs. Only on the level of models of interaction patterns constructed by the social scientist in accordance with certain particular requirements defined by the methods of his science does the concept of rationality obtain its full significance. In order to make this clear we have first to examine the basic character of such scientific constructs and their relationship to the "reality" of the social world, as such reality presents itself to the common-sense thought of everyday life.

IV. Constructs of Thought Objects by the Social Sciences

1) *The Postulate of Subjective Interpretation*

There will be hardly any issue among social scientists that the object of the social sciences is human behavior, its forms, its organization, and its products. There will be, however, different opinions about whether this behavior should be studied in the same manner in which the natural scientist studies his object or whether the goal of the social sciences is the explanation of the "social reality" as experienced by man living

his everyday life within the social world. The introductory section of the present discussion attempted to show that both principles are incompatible with each other. In the following pages we take the position that the social sciences have to deal with human conduct and its common-sense interpretation in the social reality, involving the analysis of the whole system of projects and motives, of relevances and constructs dealt with in the preceding sections. Such an analysis refers by necessity to the subjective point of view, namely, to the interpretation of the action and its settings in terms of the actor. Since this postulate of the subjective interpretation is, as we have seen, a general principle of constructing course-of-action types in common-sense experience, any social science aspiring to grasp "social reality" has to adopt this principle also.

Yet, at first glance, it seems that this statement is in contradiction to the well-established method of even the most advanced social sciences. Take as an example modern economics. Is it not the "behavior of prices" rather than the behavior of men in the market situation which is studied by the economist, the "shape of demand curves" rather than the anticipations of economic subjects symbolized by such curves? Does not the economist investigate successfully subject matters such as "savings," "capital," "business cycle," "wages" and "unemployment," "multipliers" and "monopoly" as if these phenomena were entirely detached from any activity of the economic subjects, even less without entering into the subjective meaning structure such activities may have for them? The achievements of modern economic theories would make it preposterous to deny that an abstract conceptual scheme can be used very successfully for the solution of many problems. And similar examples could be given from the field of almost all the other social sciences. Closer investigation, however, reveals that this abstract conceptual scheme is nothing else than a kind of intellectual shorthand and that the underlying subjective elements of human actions involved are either taken for granted or deemed to be irrelevant with respect to the scientific purpose at hand—the problem under scrutiny—and are, therefore, disregarded. Correctly understood, the postulate of subjective interpretation as applied to economics as well as to all the other social sciences means merely that we always *can*—and for certain purposes *must*—refer to the activities of the subjects within the social world and their interpretation by the actors in terms of systems of projects, available means, motives, relevances, and so on.[47]

But if this is true, two other questions have to be answered. First, we have seen from the previous analyses that the subjective meaning an action has for an actor is unique and individual because it originates in the unique and individual biographical situation of the actor. How is it then possible to grasp subjective meaning scientifically? Secondly, the meaning context of any system of scientific knowledge is objective knowledge but accessible equally to all his fellow scientists and open to their control, which means capable of being verified, invalidated, or falsified by them. How is it, then, possible to grasp by a system of objective knowledge subjective meaning structures? Is this not a paradox?

Both questions can be satisfactorily met by a few simple considerations. As to the first question, we learned from Whitehead that all sciences have to construct thought objects of their own which supersede the thought objects of common-sense thinking.[48] The thought objects constructed by the social sciences do not refer to unique acts of unique individuals occurring within a unique situation. By particular methodological devices, to be described presently, the social scientist replaces the thought objects of common-sense thought relating to unique

events and occurrences by constructing a model of a sector of the social world within which merely those typified events occur that are relevant to the scientist's particular problem under scrutiny. All the other happenings within the social world are considered as being irrelevant, as contingent "data," which have to be put beyond question by appropriate methodological techniques as, for instance, by the assumption "all other things being equal."[49] Nevertheless, it is possible to construct a model of a sector of the social world consisting of typical human interaction and to analyze this typical interaction pattern as to the meaning it might have for the personal types of actors who presumptively originated them.

The second question has to be faced. It is indeed the particular problem of the social sciences to develop methodological devices for attaining objective and verifiable knowledge of a subjective meaning structure. In order to make this clear we have to consider very briefly the particular attitude of the scientist to the social world.

2) The Social Scientist as Disinterested Observer

This attitude of the social scientist is that of a mere disinterested observer of the social world. He is not involved in the observed situation, which is to him not of practical but merely of cognitive interest. It is not the theater of his activities but merely the object of his contemplation. He does not act within it, vitally interested in the outcome of his actions, hoping or fearing what their consequences might be but he looks at it with the same detached equanimity with which the natural scientist looks at the occurrences in his laboratory.

A word of caution is necessary here to prevent possible misunderstandings. Of course, in

---

[47] Ludwig Von Mises rightly calls his "Treatise on Economics" *Human Action*, New Haven, 1949. See also F. A. Hayek, *The Counter-Revolution of Science*, Glencoe, 1952, pp. 25–36.
[48] See above, pp. 265–266.

[49] On this concept see Felix Kaufmann, *op. cit.,* p. 84ff and 213ff, on the concept "scientific situation" p. 52 and 251 n. 4.

his daily life the social scientist remains a human being, a man living among his fellow-men, with whom he is interrelated in many ways. And, surely, scientific activity itself occurs within the tradition of socially derived knowledge, is based upon co-operation with other scientists, requires mutual corroboration and criticism and can only be communicated by social interaction. But insofar as scientific activity is socially founded, it is one among all the other activities occurring within the social world. Dealing with science and scientific matters within the social world is one thing, the specific scientific attitude which the scientist has to adopt toward his object is another, and it is the latter which we propose to study in the following.

Our analysis of the common-sense interpretation of the social world of everyday life has shown how the biographical situation of man within the natural attitude determines at any given moment his purpose at hand. The system of relevances involved selects particular objects and particular typical aspects of such objects as standing out over against an unquestioned background of things just taken for granted. Man in daily life considers himself as the center of the social world which he groups around himself in layers of various degrees of intimacy and anonymity. By resolving to adopt the disinterested attitude of a scientific observer—in our language, by establishing the life-plan for scientific work—the social scientist detaches himself from his biographical situation within the social world. What is taken for granted in the biographical situation of daily life may become questionable for the scientist, and vice versa; what seems to be of highest relevance on one level may become entirely irrelevant on the other. The center of orientation has been radically shifted and so has the hierarchy of plans and projects. By making up his mind to carry out a plan for scientific work governed by the disinterested quest for truth in accordance with preestablished rules, called the scientific method, the scientist has entered a field of preorganized

knowledge, called the corpus of his science.[50] He has either to accept what is considered by his fellow-scientist as established knowledge or to "show cause" why he cannot do so. Merely within this frame may he select his particular scientific problem and make his scientific decisions. This frame constitutes his "being in a scientific situation" which supersedes his biographical situation as a human being within the world. It is henceforth the scientific problem once established which determines alone what is and what is not relevant to its solution, and thus what has to be investigated and what can be taken for granted as a "datum," and, finally, the level of research in the broadest sense, that is, the abstractions, generalizations, formalizations, idealizations, briefly, the constructs required and admissible for considering the problem as being solved. In other words, the scientific problem is the "locus" of all possible constructs relevant to its solution, and each construct carries along—to borrow a mathematical term—a subscript referring to the problem for the sake of which it has been established. It follows that any shifting of the problem under scrutiny and the level of research involves a modification of the structures of relevance and of the constructs formed for the solution of another problem or on another level; a great many misunderstandings and controversies, especially in the social sciences, originate from disregarding this fact.

3) Differences Between Common-Sense and Scientific Constructs of Action Patterns

Let us consider very briefly (and very incompletely) some of the more important differences between common-sense constructs and scientific constructs of interaction patterns originating in the transition from the biographically determined to the scientific situation. Common-sense constructs are formed from a "Here" within the world which determines the presupposed

---

[50] *Ibid.*, pp. 42 and 232.

reciprocity of perspectives. They take a stock of socially derived and socially approved knowledge for granted. The social distribution of knowledge determines the particular structure of the typifying construct, for instance, the assumed degree of anonymity of personal roles, the standardization of course-of-action patterns, and the supposed constancy of motives. Yet this social distribution itself depends upon the heterogeneous composition of the stock of knowledge at hand which itself is an element of common-sense experience. The concepts of "We," "You," "They," of "in-group" and "out-group," of consociates, contemporaries, predecessors, and successors, all of them with their particular structurization of familiarity and anonymity are at least implied in the common-sense typifications or even co-constitutive for them. All this holds good not only for the participants in a social interaction pattern but also for the mere observer of such interaction who still makes his observations from his biographical situation within the social world. The difference between both is merely that the participant in the interaction pattern, guided by the idealization of reciprocity of motives, assumes his own motives as being interlocked with that of his partners, whereas to the observer merely the manifest fragments of the actors' actions are accessible. Yet both, participants and observer, form their common-sense constructs relatively to their biographical situation. In either case, these constructs have a particular place within the chain of motives originating in the biographically determined hierarchy of the constructor's plans.

The constructs of human interaction patterns formed by the social scientist, however, are of an entirely different kind. The social scientist has no "Here" within the social world or, more precisely, he considers his position within it and the system of relevances attached thereto as irrelevant for his scientific undertaking. His stock of knowledge at hand is the corpus of his science, and he has to take it for granted—which means, in this context, as scientifically

ascertained—unless he makes explicit why he cannot do so. To this corpus of science belong also the rules of procedure which have stood the test, namely, the methods of his science, including the methods of forming constructs in a scientifically sound way. This stock of knowledge is of quite another structure than that which man in everyday life has at hand. To be sure, it will also show manifold degrees of clarity and distinctness. But this structurization will depend upon knowledge of problems solved, of their still hidden implications and open horizons of other still not formulated problems. The scientist takes for granted what he defines to be a datum, and this is independent of the beliefs accepted by any in-group in the world of everyday life.[51] The scientific problem, once established, determines alone the structure of relevances.

Having no "Here" within the social world the social scientist does not organize this world in layers around himself as the center. He can never enter as a consociate in an interaction pattern with one of the actors on the social scene without abandoning, at least temporarily, his scientific attitude. The participant observer or field worker establishes contact with the group studied as a man among fellow-men; only his system of relevances which serves as the scheme of his selection and interpretation is determined by the scientific attitude, temporarily dropped in order to be resumed again.

Thus, adopting the scientific attitude, the social scientist observes human interaction patterns or their results insofar as they are accessible to his observation and open to his interpretation. These interaction patterns, however, he has to interpret in terms of their subjective meaning structure lest he abandon any hope of grasping "social reality."

In order to comply with this postulate, the scientific observer proceeds in a way similar to

---

[51] We intentionally disregard the problems of the so-called sociology of knowledge here involved.

that of the observer of a social interaction pattern in the world of everyday life, although guided by an entirely different system of relevances.

4) *The Scientific Model of the Social World*[52]

He begins to construct typical course-of-action patterns corresponding to the observed events. Thereupon he coordinates to these typical course-of-action patterns a personal type, a model of an actor whom he imagines as being gifted with consciousness. Yet it is a consciousness restricted to containing nothing but all the elements relevant to the performance of the course-of-action patterns under observation and relevant, therewith, to the scientist's problem under scrutiny. He ascribes, thus, to this fictitious consciousness a set of typical in-order-to motives corresponding to the goals of the observed course-of-action patterns and typical because-motives upon which the in-order-to motives are founded. Both types of motives are assumed to be invariant in the mind of the imaginary actor-model.

Yet these models of actors are not human beings living within their biographical situation in the social world of everyday life. Strictly speaking, they do not have any biography or any history, and the situation into which they are placed is not a situation defined by them but defined by their creator, the social scientist. He has created these puppets or homunculi to manipulate them for his purpose. A merely specious consciousness is imputed to them by the scientist, which is constructed in such a way that its presupposed stock of knowledge at hand (including the ascribed set of invariant motives) would make actions originating from it subjectively understandable, provided that these actions were performed by real actors within the social world. But the puppet and his artificial consciousness is not subjected to the ontological conditions of human beings. The homunculus was not born, he does not grow up, and he will not die. He has no hopes and no fears; he does not know anxiety as the chief motive of all his deeds. He is not free in the sense that his acting could transgress the limits his creator, the social scientist, has predetermined. He cannot, therefore, have other conflicts of interests and motives than those the social scientist has imputed to him. He cannot err, if to err is not his typical destiny. He cannot choose, except among the alternatives the social scientist has put before him as standing to his choice. Whereas man, as Simmel has clearly seen,[53] enters any social relationship merely with a part of his self and is, at the same time, always within and outside of such a relationship, the homunculus, placed into a social relationship is involved therein in his totality. He is nothing else but the originator of his typical function because the artificial consciousness imputed to him contains merely those elements which are necessary to make such functions subjectively meaningful.

Let us very briefly examine some of the implications of this general characterization. The homunculus is invested with a system of relevances originating in the scientific problem of his constructor and not in the particular biographically determined situation of an actor within the world. It is the scientist who defines what is to his puppet a Here and a There, what is within his reach, what is to him a We and a You or a They. The scientist determines the stock of knowledge his model has supposedly at hand. This stock of knowledge is not socially derived and, unless especially designed to be so, without reference to social approval. The relevance system pertinent to the scientific problem

---

[52] To this section cf. in addition to the literature mentioned in footnotes 30 and 43, Alfred Schutz: "The Problem of Rationality in the Social World," *Economica*, Vol. X, May 1943, pp. 130–149.

[53] See footnote 33 above.

under scrutiny alone determines its intrinsic structure, namely, the elements "about" which the homunculus is supposed to have knowledge, those of which he has a mere knowledge of acquaintance and those others which he just takes for granted. With this is determined what is supposed to be familiar and what anonymous to him and on what level the typification of the experiences of the world imputed to him takes place.

If such a model of an actor is conceived as interrelated and interacting with others—they, too, being homunculi—then the general thesis of reciprocal perspectives, their interlocking, and, therewith, the correspondence of motives is determined by the constructor. The course-of-action and personal types supposedly formed by the puppet of his partners, including the definition of their systems of relevances, roles, motives, have not the character of a mere chance which will or will not be fulfilled by the supervening events. The homunculus is free from empty anticipations of the Other's reactions to his own actions and also from self-typifications. He does not assume a role other than that attributed to him by the director of the puppet show, called the model of the social world. It is he, the social scientist, who sets the stage, who distributes the roles, who gives the cues, who defines when an "action" starts and when it ends and who determines, thus, the "span of projects" involved. All standards and institutions governing the behavioral pattern of the model are supplied from the outset by the constructs of the scientific observer.

In such a simplified model of the social world pure rational acts, rational choices from rational motives are possible because all the difficulties encumbering the real actor in the everyday life-world have been eliminated. Thus, the concept of rationality in the strict sense already defined does not refer to actions within the common-sense experience of everyday life in the social world; it is the expression for a *particular* type of constructs of *certain specific* models of the social

world made by the social scientist for certain specific methodological purposes.

Before, discussing the particular functions of "rational" models of the social world, however, we have to indicate some principles governing the construction of scientific models of human action in general.

5) Postulates for Scientific Model Constructs of the Social World

We said before that it is the main problem of the social sciences to develop a method in order to deal in an objective way with the subjective meaning of human action and that the thought objects of the social sciences have to remain consistent with the thought of objects of common sense, formed by men in everyday life in order to come to terms with social reality. The model constructs as described before fulfill these requirements if they are formed in accordance with the following postulates:

a) The Postulate of Logical Consistency   The system of typical constructs designed by the scientist has to be established with the highest degree of clarity and distinctness of the conceptual framework implied and must be fully compatible with the principles of formal logic. Fulfillment of this postulate warrants the objective validity of the thought objects constructed by the social scientist, and their strictly logical character is one of the most important features by which scientific thought objects are distinguished from the thought objects constructed by common-sense thinking in daily life which they have to supersede.

b) The Postulate of Subjective Interpretation   In order to explain human actions the scientist has to ask what model of an individual mind can be constructed and what typical contents must be attributed to it in order to explain the observed facts as the result of the activity of such a mind in an understandable relation. The compliance with this postulate warrants the possibility of referring all kinds of human action or their result to the subjective meaning such action or result of an action had for the actor.

c) The Postulate of Adequacy   Each term in a scientific model of human action must be constructed in such a way that a human act performed within the life-world by an individual actor in the way indicated by the typical construct would be understandable for the actor himself as well as for his fellow-men in terms of common-sense interpretation of everyday life. Compliance with this postulate warrants the consistency of the constructs of the social scientist with the constructs of common-sense experience of the social reality.

V. Scientific Model Constructs of Rational Action Patterns

All model constructs of the social world in order to be scientific have to fulfill the requirements of these three postulates. But is not any construct complying with the postulate of logical consistency, is not any scientific activity by definition a rational one?

This is certainly true but here we have to avoid a dangerous misunderstanding. We have to distinguish between rational constructs of models of human actions on the one hand, and constructs of models of rational human actions on the other. Science may construct rational models of irrational behavior, as a glance in any textbook of psychiatry shows. On the other hand, common-sense thinking frequently constructs irrational models of highly rational behavior, for example, in explaining economic, political, military and even scientific decisions by referring them to sentiments or ideologies presupposed to govern the behavior of the participants. The rationality of the construction of the model is one thing and in this sense all properly constructed models of the sciences—not merely of the social sciences—are rational; the construction of models of rational behavior is quite another thing. It would be a serious misunderstanding to believe that it is the purpose of model constructs in the social sciences or a criterion for their scientific character that irrational behavior patterns be interpreted as if they were rational.

In the following we are mainly interested in the usefulness of scientific—therefore rational—models of rational behavior patterns. It can easily be understood that the scientific construct of a perfect rational course-of-action type, of its corresponding personal type and also of rational interaction patterns is, as a matter of principle, possible. This is so because in constructing a model of a fictitious consciousness the scientist may select as relevant for his problem merely those elements which make rational actions or reactions of his homunculi possible. The postulate of rationality which such a construct would have to meet can be formulated as follows:

The rational course-of-action and personal types have to be constructed in such a way that an actor in the life-world would perform the typified action if he had a perfectly clear and distinct knowledge of all the elements, and only of the elements, assumed by the social scientist as being relevant to this action and the constant tendency to use the most appropriate means assumed to be at his disposal for achieving the ends defined by the construct itself.

The advantage of the use of such models of rational behavior in the social sciences can be characterized as follows:

1. The possibility of constructing patterns of social interaction under the assumption that all participants in such interaction act rationally within a set of conditions, means, ends, motives defined by the social scientist and supposed to be either common to all participants or distributed among them in a specific manner. By this arrangement standardized behavior such as so-called social roles, institutional behavior, etc., can be studied in isolation.

2. Whereas the behavior of individuals in the social life-world is not predictable unless in empty anticipations, the rational behavior of a constructed personal type is by definition supposed to be predictable, within the limits of the elements typified in the construct. The model of rational action can, therefore, be used as a device for ascertaining deviating behavior in the real social world and for referring it to "problem-transcending data," that is, to non-typified elements.

3. By appropriate variations of some of the elements several models or even sets of models of rational actions can be constructed for solving the same scientific problem and compared with one another.

The last point, however, seems to require some comment. Did we not state earlier that all constructs carry along a "subscript" referring to the problem under scrutiny and have to be revised if a shift in the problem occurs? Is there not a certain contradiction between this insight and the possibility of constructing several competing models for the solution of one and the same scientific problem?

The contradiction disappears if we consider that any problem is merely a locus of implications which can be made explicit or, to use a term of Husserl's,[54] that it carries along its inner horizon of unquestioned but questionable elements.*

In order to make the inner horizon of the problem explicit we may vary the conditions within which the fictitious actors are supposed to act, the elements of the world of which they are supposed to have knowledge, their assumed interlocked motives, the degree of familiarity or anonymity in which they are assumed to be interrelated, etc. For example, as an economist concerned with the theory of oligopoly,[55] I may construct models of a single firm or of an industry or of the economic system as a whole. If restricting myself to the theory of the individual firm (say, if analyzing the effects of a cartel agreement on the output of the commodity concerned), I may construct a model of a producer acting under conditions of unregulated competition, another of a producer with the same cost-conditions acting under the cartel restrictions imposed upon him and with the knowledge of similar restrictions imposed on the other suppliers of the "same" commodity. We can then compare the output of "the" firm in the two models.

All these models are models of rational actions but not of actions performed by living human beings in situations defined by them. They are assumed to be performable by the personal types constructed by the economist within the artificial environment in which he has placed his homunculi.

VI. Concluding Remarks

The relationship between the social scientist and the puppet he has created reflects to a certain extent an age-old problem of theology and metaphysics, that of the relationship between God and his creatures. The puppet exists and acts merely by the grace of the scientist; it cannot act otherwise than according to the purpose which the scientist's wisdom has determined it to carry out. Nevertheless, it is supposed to act as if it were not determined but could determine itself. A total harmony has been pre-established between the determined consciousness bestowed

---

54 As to the concept of horizon, see Helmut Kuhn, "The Phenomenological Concept of Horizon" in *Philosophical Essays in Memory of Edmund Husserl,* edited by Marvin Farber, Cambridge, 1940, pp. 106–124 and Ludwig Landgrebe in Husserl, *Erfahrung und Urteil,* secs. 8–10.
* See, for example, "Concept and Theory Formation in the Social Sciences," pp. 63–65. (M.N.).

---

55 I gratefully acknowledge the permission of my friend, Professor Fritz Machlup, to borrow the following examples from his book *The Economics of Seller's Competition Model Analysis of Seller's Conduct,* Baltimore, 1952, p. 4ff.

upon the puppet and the pre-constituted environment within which it is supposed to act freely, to make rational choices and decisions. This harmony is possible only because both, the puppet and its reduced environment, are the creation of the scientist. And by keeping to the principles which guided him, the scientist succeeds, indeed, in discovering within the universe, thus created, the perfect harmony established by himself.

PETER BERGER AND THOMAS LUCKMANN: FOUNDATIONS OF KNOWLEDGE IN EVERYDAY LIFE

1. The Reality of Everyday Life

Since our purpose in this treatise is a sociological analysis of the reality of everyday life, more precisely, of knowledge that guides conduct in everyday life, and we are only tangentially interested in how this reality may appear in various theoretical perspectives to intellectuals, we must begin by a clarification of that reality as it is available to the common-sense of the ordinary members of society. How that common-sense reality may be influenced by the theoretical constructions of intellectuals and other merchants of ideas is a further question. Ours is thus an enterprise that, although theoretical in character, is geared to the understanding of a reality that forms the subject matter of the empirical science of sociology, that is, the world of everyday life.

It should be evident, then, that our purpose is *not* to engage in philosophy. All the same, if the reality of everyday life is to be understood, account must be taken of its intrinsic character before we can proceed with sociological analysis proper. Everyday life presents itself as a reality interpreted by men and subjectively meaningful

to them as a coherent world. As sociologists we take this reality as the object of our analyses. Within the frame of reference of sociology as an empirical science it is possible to take this reality as given, to take as data particular phenomena arising within it, without further inquiring about the foundations of this reality, which is a philosophical task. However, given the particular purpose of the present treatise, we cannot completely bypass the philosophical problem. The world of everyday life is not only taken for granted as reality by the ordinary members of society in the subjectively meaningful conduct of their lives. It is a world that originates in their thoughts and actions, and is maintained as real by these. Before turning to our main task we must, therefore, attempt to clarify the foundations of knowledge in everyday life, to wit, the objectivations of subjective processes (and meanings) by which the *inter*subjective commonsense world is constructed.

For the purpose at hand, this is a preliminary task, and we can do no more than sketch the main features of what we believe to be an adequate solution to the philosophical problem—adequate, let us hasten to add, only in the sense that it can serve as a starting point for sociological analysis. The considerations immediately following are, therefore, of the nature of philosophical prolegomena and, in themselves, pre-sociological. The method we consider best suited to clarify the foundations of knowledge in everyday life is that of phenomenological analysis, a purely descriptive method and, as such, "empirical" but not "scientific"—as we understand the nature of the empirical sciences.[1]

The phenomenological analysis of everyday life, or rather of the subjective experience of everyday life, refrains from any causal or genetic hypotheses, as well as from assertions about the ontological status of the phenomena analyzed. It is important to remember this. Commonsense contains innumerable pre- and quasi-scientific interpretations about everyday reality, which it takes for granted. If we are to describe the reality of commonsense we must refer to these interpretations, just as we must take account of its taken-for-granted character—but we do so within phenomenological brackets.

Consciousness is always intentional; it always intends or is directed toward objects. We can never apprehend some putative substratum of consciousness as such, only consciousness of something or other. This is so regardless of whether the object of consciousness is experienced as belonging to an external physical world or apprehended as an element of an inward subjective reality. Whether I (the first person singular, here as in the following illustrations, standing for ordinary self-consciousness in everyday life) am viewing the panorama of New York City or whether I become conscious of an inner anxiety, the process of consciousness involved are intentional in both instances. The point need not be belabored that the consciousness of the Empire State Building differs from the awareness of anxiety. A detailed phenomenological analysis would uncover the various layers of experience, and the different structures of meaning involved in, say, being bitten by a dog, remembering having been bitten by a dog, having a phobia about all dogs, and so forth. What interests us here is the common intentional character of all consciousness.

Different objects present themselves to consciousness as constituents of different spheres of reality. I recognize the fellowmen I must deal with in the course of everyday life as pertaining to a reality quite different from the disembodied figures that appear in my dreams. The two sets of objects introduce quite different tensions into my consciousness and I am attentive to them in quite different ways. My consciousness, then, is capable of moving through different spheres of reality. Put differently, I am conscious of the world as consisting of multiple realities. As I move from one reality to another, I experience the transition as a kind of shock. This shock is to be understood as caused by the shift in attentiveness that the transition entails. Waking up from a dream illustrates this shift most simply.

Among the multiple realities there is one that presents itself as the reality par excellence. This is the reality of everyday life. Its privileged position entitles it to the designation of paramount reality. The tension of consciousness is highest in everyday life, that is, the latter imposes itself upon consciousness in the most massive, urgent and intense manner. It is impossible to ignore, difficult even to weaken in its imperative presence. Consequently, it forces me to be attentive to it in the fullest way. I experience everyday life in the state of being wide-awake. This wide-awake state of existing in and apprehending the reality of everyday life is taken by me to be normal and self-evident, that is, it constitutes my natural attitude.

I apprehend the reality of everyday life as an ordered reality. Its phenomena are prearranged in patterns that seem to be independent of my apprehension of them and that impose themselves upon the latter. The reality of everyday life appears already objectified, that is, constituted by an order of objects that have been designated *as* objects before my appearance on the scene. The language used in everyday life continuously provides me with the necessary objectifications and posits the order within which these make sense and within which everyday life has meaning for me. I live in a place that is geographically designated; I employ tools, from can openers to sports cars, which are designated in the technical vocabulary of my society; I live within a web of human relationships, from my chess club to the United States of America, which are also ordered by means of vocabulary. In this manner language marks the coordinates of my life in society and fills that life with meaningful objects.

The reality of everyday life is organized around the "here" of my body and the "now" of my present. This "here and now" is the focus of my attention to the reality of everyday life. What is "here and now" presented to me in everyday life is the *realissimum* of my consciousness. The reality of everyday life is not, however, exhausted by these immediate presences, but embraces phenomena that are not present "here and now." This means that I experience everyday life in terms of differing degrees of closeness and remoteness, both spatially and temporally. Closest to me is the zone of everyday life that is directly accessible to my bodily manipulation. This zone contains the world within my reach, the world in which I act so as to modify its reality, or the world in which I work. In this world of working my consciousness is dominated by the pragmatic motive, that is, my attention to this world is mainly determined by what I am doing, have done or plan to do in it. In this way it is *my* world par excellence. I know, of course, that the reality of everyday life contains zones that are not accessible to me in this manner. But either I have no pragmatic interest in these zones or my interest in them is indirect insofar as they may be, potentially, manipulative zones for me. Typically, my interest in the far zones is less intense and certainly less urgent. I am intensely interested in the cluster of objects involved in my daily occupation—say, the world of the garage, if I am a mechanic. I am interested, though less directly, in what goes on in the testing laboratories of the automobile industry in Detroit—I am unlikely ever to be in one of these laboratories, but the work done there will eventually affect my everyday life. I may also be interested in what goes on at Cape Kennedy or in outer space, but this interest is a matter of private, "leisure-time" choice rather than an urgent necessity of my everyday life.

The reality of everyday life further presents itself to me as an intersubjective world, a world that I share with others. This intersubjectivity sharply differentiates everyday life from other realities of which I am conscious. I am alone in the world of my dreams, but I know that the world of everyday life is as real to others as it is to myself. Indeed, I cannot exist in everyday life without continually interacting and communicating with others. I know that my natural attitude to this world corresponds to the natural attitude of others, that they also comprehend the objectifications by which this world is ordered, that they also organize this world around the "here and now" of *their* being in it and have projects for working in it. I also know, of course, that the others have a perspective on this common world that is not identical with mine. My "here" is their "there." My "now" does not fully overlap with theirs. My projects differ from and may even conflict with theirs. All the same, I know that I live with them in a common world. Most importantly, I know that there is an ongoing correspondence between *my* meanings and *their* meanings in this world, that we share a common sense about its reality. The natural attitude is the attitude of commonsense consciousness precisely because it refers to a world that is common to many men. Commonsense knowledge is the knowledge I share with others in the normal, self-evident routines of everyday life.

The reality of everyday life is taken for granted *as* reality. It does not require additional verification over and beyond its simple presence. It is simply *there*, as self-evident and compelling facticity. I *know* that it is real. While I am capable of engaging in doubt about its reality, I am obliged to suspend such doubt as I routinely exist in everyday life. This suspension of doubt is so firm that to abandon it, as I might want to do, say, in theoretical or religious contemplation, I have to make an extreme transition. The world of everyday life proclaims itself and, when I want to challenge the proclamation, I must engage in a deliberate, by no means easy effort. The transition from the natural attitude to the theoretical attitude of the philosopher or scientist illustrates this point. But not all aspects of this reality are equally unproblematic. Everyday life is divided into sectors that are apprehended routinely, and others that present me with problems of one kind or another. Suppose that I am an automobile mechanic who is highly knowledgeable about all American-made cars. Everything that pertains to the latter is a routine, unproblematic facet of my everyday life. But one day someone appears in the garage and asks me to repair his Volkswagen. I am now compelled to enter the problematic world of foreign-made cars. I may do so reluctantly or with professional curiosity, but in either case I am now faced with problems that I have not yet routinized. At the same time, of course, I do not leave the reality of everyday life. Indeed, the latter becomes enriched as I begin to incorporate into it the knowledge and skills required for the repair of foreign-made cars. The reality of everyday life encompasses both kinds of sectors, as long as what appears as a problem does not pertain to a different reality altogether (say, the reality of theoretical physics, or of nightmares). As long as the routines of everyday life continue without interruption they are apprehended as unproblematic.

But even the unproblematic sector of everyday reality is so only until further notice, that is, until its continuity is interrupted by the appearance of a problem. When this happens, the reality of everyday life seeks to integrate the problematic sector into what is already unproblematic. Commonsense knowledge contains a variety of instructions as to how this is to be done. For instance, the others with whom I work are unproblematic to me as long as they perform their familiar, taken-for-granted routines—say, typing away at desks next to mine in my office. They become problematic if they interrupt these routines—say, huddling together in a corner and talking in whispers. As I inquire about the meaning of this unusual activity, there is a variety of possibilities that my commonsense knowledge is capable of reintegrating into the unproblematic routines of everyday life: they may be consulting on how to fix a broken typewriter, or one of them may have some urgent instructions from the boss, and so on. On the other hand, I may find that they are discussing a union directive to go on strike, something as yet outside my experience but still well within the range of problems with which my commonsense knowledge can deal. It will deal with it, though, *as* a problem, rather than simply reintegrating it into the unproblematic sector of everyday life. If, however, I come to the conclusion that my colleagues have gone collectively mad, the problem that presents itself is of yet another kind. I am now faced with a problem that transcends the boundaries of the reality of everyday life and points to an altogether different reality. Indeed, my conclusion that my colleagues have gone mad implies *ipso facto* that they have gone off into a world that is no longer the common world of everyday life.

Compared to the reality of everyday life, other realities appear as finite provinces of meaning, enclaves within the paramount reality marked by circumscribed meanings and modes of experience. The paramount reality envelops them on all sides, as it were, and consciousness always returns to the paramount reality as from an excursion. This is evident from the illustrations already given, as in the reality of dreams or that of theoretical thought. Similar "commutations" take place between the world of everyday life and the world of play, both the playing of children and, even more sharply, of adults. The theater provides an excellent illustration of such playing on the part of adults. The transition between realities is marked by the rising and falling of the curtain. As the curtain rises, the spectator is "transported to another world," with its own meanings and an order that may or may not have much to do with the order of everyday life. As the curtain falls, the spectator "returns to reality," that is, to the paramount reality of everyday life by comparison with which the reality presented on the stage now appears tenuous and ephemeral, however vivid the presentation may have been a few moments previously. Aesthetic and religious experience is rich in producing transitions of this kind, inasmuch as art and religion are endemic producers of finite provinces of meaning.

All finite provinces of meaning are characterized by a turning away of attention from the reality of everyday life. While there are, of course, shifts in attention *within* everyday life, the shift to a finite province of meaning is of a much more radical kind. A radical change takes place in the tension of consciousness. In the context of religious experience this has been aptly called "leaping." It is important to stress, however, that the reality of everyday life retains its paramount status even as such "leaps" take place. If nothing else, language makes sure of this. The common language available to me for the objectification of my experiences is grounded in everyday life and keeps pointing back to it even as I employ it to interpret experiences in finite provinces of meaning. Typically, therefore, I "distort" the reality of the latter as soon as I begin to use the common language in interpreting them, that is, I "translate" the non-everyday experiences back into the paramount reality of everyday life. This may be readily seen in terms of dreams, but is also typical of those trying to report about theoretical, aesthetic or religious worlds of meaning. The theoretical physicist tells us that his concept of space cannot be conveyed linguistically, just as the artist does with regard to the meaning of his creations and the mystic with regard to his encounters with the divine. Yet all these—dreamer, physicist, artist and mystic—*also* live in the reality of everyday

life. Indeed, one of their important problems is to interpret the coexistence of this reality with the reality enclaves into which they have ventured.

The world of everyday life is structured both spatially and temporally. The spatial structure is quite peripheral to our present considerations. Suffice it to point out that it, too, has a social dimension by virtue of the fact that my manipulatory zone intersects with that of others. More important for our present purpose is the temporal structure of everyday life.

Temporality is an intrinsic property of consciousness. The stream of consciousness is always ordered temporally. It is possible to differentiate between different levels of this temporality as it is intrasubjectively available. Every individual is conscious of an inner flow of time, which in turn is founded on the physiological rhythms of the organism though it is not identical with these. It would greatly exceed the scope of these prolegomena to enter into a detailed analysis of these levels of intrasubjective temporality. As we have indicated, however, intersubjectivity in everyday life also has a temporal dimension. The world of everyday life has its own standard time, which is intersubjectively available. This standard time may be understood as the intersection between cosmic time and its socially established calendar, based on the temporal sequences of nature, and inner time, in its aforementioned differentiations. There can never be full simultany between these various levels of temporality, as the experience of waiting indicates most clearly. Both my organism and my society impose upon me, and upon my inner time, certain sequences of events that involve waiting. I may want to take part in a sports event, but I must wait for my bruised knee to heal. Or again, I must wait until certain papers are processed so that my qualification for the event may be officially established. It may readily be seen that the temporal structure of everyday life is exceedingly complex, because the different levels of empirically present temporality must be ongoingly correlated.

The temporal structure of everyday life confronts me as a facticity with which I must reckon, that is, with which I must try to synchronize my own projects. I encounter time in everyday reality as continuous and finite. All my existence in this world is continuously ordered by its time, is indeed enveloped by it. My own life is an episode in the externally factitious stream of time. It was there before I was born and it will be there after I die. The knowledge of my inevitable death makes this time finite *for me*. I have only a certain amount of time available for the realization of my projects, and the knowledge of this affects my attitude to these projects. Also, since I do not want to die, this knowledge injects an underlying anxiety into my projects. Thus I cannot endlessly repeat my participation in sports events. I know that I am getting older. It may even be that this is the last occasion on which I have the chance to participate. My waiting will be anxious to the degree in which the finitude of time impinges upon the project.

The same temporal structure, as has already been indicated, is coercive. I cannot reverse at will the sequences imposed by it—"first things first" is an essential element of my knowledge of everyday life. Thus I cannot take a certain examination before I have passed through certain educational programs, I cannot practice my profession before I have taken this examination, and so on. Also, the same temporal structure provides the historicity that determines my situation in the world of everyday life. I was born on a certain date, entered school on another, started working as a professional on another, and so on. These dates, however, are all "located" within a much more comprehensive history, and this "location" decisively shapes my situation. Thus I was born in the year of the great bank crash in which my father lost his wealth, I entered school just before the revolution, I began to work just after the great war broke out, and so forth. The temporal structure of everyday life not only imposes prearranged sequences upon the "agenda" of any single day but also imposes itself upon my biography as a whole. Within the coordinates set by this temporal structure I apprehend both daily "agenda" and overall biography. Clock and calendar ensure that, indeed, I am a "man of my time." Only within this temporal structure does everyday life retain for me its accent of reality. Thus in cases where I may be "disoriented" for one reason or another (say, I have been in an automobile accident in which I was knocked unconscious), I feel an almost instinctive urge to "reorient" myself within the temporal structure of everyday life. I look at my watch and try to recall what day it is. By these acts alone I reenter the reality of everyday life.

2. Social Interaction in Everyday Life

The reality of everyday life is shared with others. But how are these others themselves experienced in everyday life? Again, it is possible to differentiate between several modes of such experience.

The most important experience of others takes place in the face-to-face situation, which is the prototypical case of social interaction. All other cases are derivatives of it.

In the face-to-face situation the other is appresented to me in a vivid present shared by both of us. I know that in the same vivid present I am appresented to him. My and his "here and now" continuously impinge on each other as long as the face-to-face situation continues. As a result, there is a continuous interchange of my expressivity and his. I see him smile, then react to my frown by stopping the smile, then smiling again as I smile, and so on. Every expression of mine is oriented toward him, and vice versa, and this continuous reciprocity of expressive acts is simultaneously available to both of us. This means that, in the face-to-face situation, the other's subjectivity is available to me through a maximum of symptoms. To be sure, I may misinterpret some of these symptoms. I may think that the other is smiling while in fact he is smirking. Nevertheless, no other form of social relating can reproduce the plenitude of symptoms of subjectivity present in the face-to-face situation. Only here is the other's subjectivity emphatically "close." All other forms of relating to the other are, in varying degrees, "remote."

In the face-to-face situation the other is fully real. This reality is part of the overall reality of everyday life, and as such massive and compelling. To be sure, another may be real to me without my having encountered him face to face—by reputation, say, or by having corresponded with him. Nevertheless, he becomes real to me in the fullest sense of the word only when I meet him face to face. Indeed, it may be argued that the other in the face-to-face situation is more real to me than I myself. Of course I "know myself better" than I can ever know him. My subjectivity is accessible to me in a way his can never be, no matter how "close" our relationship. My past is available to me in memory in a fullness with which I can never reconstruct his, however much he may tell me about it. But this "better knowledge" of myself requires reflection. It is not immediately appresented to me. The other, however, *is* so appresented in the face-to-face situation. "What he is," therefore, is ongoingly available to me. This availability is continuous and prereflective. On the other hand, "What I am" is *not* so available. To make it available requires that I stop, arrest the continuous spontaneity of my experience, and deliberately turn my attention back upon myself. What is more, such reflection about myself is typically occasioned by the attitude toward me that *the other* exhibits. It is typically a "mirror" response to attitudes of the other.

It follows that relations with others in the face-to-face situation are highly flexible. Put negatively, it is comparatively difficult to impose rigid patterns upon face-to-face interaction. Whatever patterns are introduced will be continuously modified through the exceedingly variegated and subtle interchange of subjective meanings that goes on. For instance, I may view the other as someone inherently unfriendly to me and act toward him within a pattern of "unfriendly relations" as understood by me. In the face-to-face situation, however, the other may confront me with attitudes and acts that contradict this pattern, perhaps up to a point where I am led to abandon the pattern as inapplicable and to view him as friendly. In other words, the pattern cannot sustain the massive evidence of the other's subjectivity that is available to me in the face-to-face situation. By contrast, it is much easier for me to ignore such evidence as long as I do not encounter the other face to face. Even in such a relatively "close" relation as may be maintained by correspondence I can more successfully dismiss the other's protestations of friendship as not actually representing his subjective attitude to me, simply because in correspondence I lack the immediate, continuous and massively real presence of his expressivity. It is, to be sure, possible for me to misinterpret the other's meanings even in the face-to-face situation, as it is possible for him "hypocritically" to hide his meanings. All the same, both misinterpretation and "hypocrisy" are more difficult to sustain in face-to-face interaction than in less "close" forms of social relations.

On the other hand, I apprehend the other by means of typificatory schemes even in the face-to-face situation, although these schemes are more "vulnerable" to his interference than in "remoter" forms of interaction. Put differently, while it is comparatively difficult to impose rigid patterns on face-to-face interaction, even it is patterned from the beginning if it takes place within the routines of everyday life. (We can leave aside for later consideration cases of interaction between complete strangers who have no common background of everyday life.) The reality of everyday life contains typificatory schemes in terms of which others are apprehended and "dealt with" in face-to-face encounters. Thus I apprehend the other as "a man," "a European," "a buyer," "a jovial type," and so on. All these typifications ongoingly affect my interaction with him as, say, I decide to show him a good time on the town before trying to sell him my product. Our face-to-face interaction will be patterned by these typifications as long as they do not become problematic through interference on his part. Thus, he may come up with evidence that, although "a man," "a European" and "a buyer," he is also a self-righteous moralist, and that what appeared first as joviality is actually an expression of contempt for Americans in general and American salesmen in particular. At this point, of course, my typificatory scheme will have to be modified, and the evening planned differently in accordance with this modification. Unless thus challenged, though, the typifications will hold until further notice and will determine my actions in the situation.

The typificatory schemes entering into face-to-face situations are, of course, reciprocal. The other also apprehends me in a typified way— as "a man," "an American," "a salesman," "an ingratiating fellow," and so on. The other's typifications are as susceptible to my interference as mine are to his. In other words, the two typificatory schemes enter into an ongoing "negotiation" in the face-to-face situation. In everyday life such "negotiation" is itself likely to be pre-arranged in a typical manner—as in the typical bargaining process between buyers and salesmen. Thus, most of the time, my encounters with others in everyday life are typical in a double sense—I apprehend the other *as* a type and I interact with him in a situation that is itself typical.

The typifications of social interaction become progressively anonymous the farther away they are from the face-to-face situation. Every typification, of course, entails incipient anonymity. If I typify my friend Henry as a member of category X (say, as an Englishman), I *ipso facto* interpret at least certain aspects of his conduct as resulting from this typification—for instance, his tastes in food are typical of Englishmen as are his manners, certain of his emotional reactions, and so on. This implies, though, that these characteristics and actions of my friend Henry appertain to *anyone* in the category of Englishman, that is, I apprehend these aspects of his being in anonymous terms. Nevertheless, as long as my friend Henry is available in the plenitude of expressivity of the face-to-face situation, he will constantly break through my type of anonymous Englishman and manifest himself as a unique and therefore atypical individual—to wit, as my friend Henry. The anonymity of the type is obviously less susceptible to this kind of individualization when face-to-face interaction is a matter of the past (my friend Henry, *the Englishman*, whom I knew when I was a college student), or is of a superficial and transient kind (the Englishman with whom I have a brief conversation on a train), or has never taken place (my business competitors in England).

An important aspect of the experience of others in everyday life is thus the directness or indirectness of such experience. At any given time it is possible to distinguish between consociates with whom I interact in face-to-face situations and others who are mere contemporaries of whom I have only more or less detailed recollections, or of whom I know merely by hearsay. In face-to-face situations I have direct evidence of my fellowman, of his actions, his attributes, and so on. Not so in the case of contemporaries—of them I have more or less reliable knowledge. Furthermore, I must take account of my fellowmen in face-to-face situations, while I may, but need not, turn my thoughts to mere contemporaries. Anonymity increases as I go from the former to the latter, because the anonymity of the typifications by means of which I apprehend fellowmen in face-to-face situations is constantly "filled in" by the multiplicity of vivid symptoms referring to a concrete human being.

This, of course, is not the whole story. There are obvious differences in my experiences of mere contemporaries. Some I have experienced again and again in face-to-face situations and expect to meet again regularly (my friend Henry); others I *recollect* as concrete human beings from a past meeting (the blonde I passed on the street), but the meeting was brief and, most likely, will not be repeated. Still others *I know of* as concrete human beings, but I can apprehend them only by means of more or less anonymous intersecting typifications (my British business competitors, the Queen of England). Among the latter one could again distinguish between likely partners in face-to-face situations (my British business competitors), and potential but unlikely partners (the Queen of England).

The degree of anonymity characterizing the experience of others in everyday life depends, however, upon another factor too. I see the newspaper vendor on the street corner as regularly as I see my wife. But he is less important to me and I am not on intimate terms with him. He may remain relatively anonymous to me. The degree of interest and the degree of intimacy may combine to increase or decrease anonymity of experience. They may also influence it independently. I can be on fairly intimate terms with a number of the fellow-members of a tennis club and on very formal terms with my boss. Yet the former, while by no means completely anonymous, may merge into "that bunch at the courts" while the latter stands out as a unique individual. And finally, anonymity may become near-total with certain typifications that are not intended ever to become individualized—such as the "typical reader of the London Times." Finally, the "scope" of the typification—and thereby its anonymity—can be further increased by speaking of "British public opinion."

The social reality of everyday life is thus apprehended in a continuum of typifications, which are progressively anonymous as they are removed from the "here and now" of the face-to-face situation. At one pole of the continuum are those others with whom I frequently and intensively interact in face-to-face situations—my "inner circle," as it were. At the other pole are highly anonymous abstractions, which by their very nature can never be available in face-to-face interaction. Social structure is the sum total of these typifications and of the recurrent patterns of interaction established by means of them. As such, social structure is an essential element of the reality of everyday life.

One further point ought to be made here, though we cannot elaborate it. My relations with others are not limited to consociates and contemporaries. I also relate to predecessors and successors, to those others who have preceded and will follow me in the encompassing history of my society.

NOTES

1. This entire section of our treatise is based on Alfred Schutz and Thomas Luckmann, *Die Strukturen der Lebenswelt,* now being prepared for publication. In view of this, we have refrained from providing individual references to the places in Schutz's published work where the same problems are discussed. Our argument here is based on Schutz, as developed by Luckmann in the afore-mentioned work, *in toto.* The reader wishing to acquaint himself with Schutz's work published to date may consult Alfred Shutz, *Der sinnhafte Aufbau der sozialen Welt* (Vienna, Springer, 1960); *Collected Papers,* Vols. I and II. The reader interested in Schutz's adaptation of the phenomenological method to the analysis of the social world may consult especially his *Collected Papers,* Vol. I, pp. 99 ff., and Maurice Natanson (ed.), *Philosophy of the Social Sciences* (New York, Random House, 1963), pp. 183 ff.

HAROLD GARFINKEL: STUDIES OF THE
ROUTINE GROUNDS OF EVERYDAY ACTIVITIES

The Problem

For Kant the moral order "within" was an awesome mystery, for sociologists the moral order "without" is a technical mystery. From the point of view of sociological theory the moral order consists of the rule governed activities of everyday life. A society's members encounter and know the moral order as perceivedly normal courses of action—familiar scenes of everyday affairs, the world of daily life known in common with others and with others taken for granted.

They refer to this world as the "natural facts of life" which, for members, are through and through moral facts of life. For members not only are matters so about familiar scenes, but they are so because it is morally right or wrong that they are so. Familiar scenes of everyday activities, treated by members as the "natural facts of life," are massive facts of the members' daily existence both as a real world and as the product of activities in a real world. They furnish the "fix," the "this is it" to which the waking state returns one, and are the points of departure and return for every modification of the world of daily life that is achieved in play, dreaming, trance, theater, scientific theorizing, or high ceremony.

In every discipline, humanistic or scientific, the familiar common sense world of everyday life is a matter of abiding interest. In the social sciences, and in sociology particularly, it is a matter of essential preoccupation. It makes up sociology's problematic subject matter, enters the very constitution of the sociological attitude, and exercises an odd and obstinate sovereignty over sociologists' claims to adequate explanation.

Despite the topic's centrality, an immense literature contains little data and few methods with which the essential features of socially recognized "familiar scenes" may be detected and related to dimensions of social organization. Although sociologists take socially structured scenes of everyday life as a point of departure they rarely see,[1] as a task of sociological inquiry in its own right, the general question of how any such common sense world is possible. Instead, the possibility of the everyday world is either settled by theoretical representation or merely assumed. As a topic and methodological ground for sociological inquiries, the definition of the common sense world of everyday life, though it is appropriately a project of sociological inquiry, has been neglected. My purposes in this paper are to demonstrate the essential relevance, to sociological inquiries, of a concern for common sense activities as a topic of inquiry in its own right and, by reporting a series of studies, to urge its "rediscover."

Making Commonplace Scenes Visible

In accounting for the stable features of everyday activities sociologists commonly select familiar settings such as familial households or work places and ask for the variables that contribute to their stable features. Just as commonly, one set of considerations are unexamined: the socially standardized and standardizing, "seen but unnoticed," expected, background features of everyday scenes. The member of the society uses background expectancies as a scheme of interpretation. With their use actual appearances

[1] The work of Alfred Schutz, cited in footnote 2, is a magnificent exception. Readers who are acquainted with his writings will recognize how heavily this paper is indebted to him.

are for him recognizable and intelligible as the appearances-of-familiar-events. Demonstrably he is responsive to this background, while at the same time he is at a loss to tell us specifically of what the expectancies consist. When we ask him about them he has little or nothing to say.

For these background expectancies to come into view one must either be a stranger to the "life as usual" character of everyday scenes, or become estranged from them. As Alfred Schutz pointed out, a "special motive" is required to make them problematic. In the sociologists' case this "special motive" consists in the programmatic task of treating a societal member's practical circumstances, which include from the member's point of view the morally necessary character of many of its background features, as matters of theoretic interest. The seen but unnoticed backgrounds of everyday activities are made visible and are described from a perspective in which persons live out the lives they do, have the children they do, feel the feelings, think the thoughts, enter the relationships they do, all in order to permit the sociologist to solve his theoretical problems.

Almost alone among sociological theorists, the late Alfred Schutz, in a series of classical studies[2] of the constitutive phenomenology of the world of everyday life, described many of these seen but unnoticed background expectancies. He called them the "attitude of daily life." He referred to their scenic attributions as the "world known in common and taken for granted." Schutz' fundamental work makes it possible to pursue further the tasks of clarifying their nature and operation, of relating them to the processes of concerted actions, and assigning them their palce in an empirically imaginable society.

The studies reported in this paper attempt to detect some expectancies that lend commonplace

scenes their familiar, life-as-usual character, and to relate these to the stable social structures of everyday activities. Procedurally it is my preference to start with familiar scenes and ask what can be done to make trouble. The operations that one would have to perform in order to multiply the senseless features of perceived environments; to produce and sustain bewilderment, consternation, and confusion; to produce the socially structured affects of anxiety, shame, guilt, and indignation; and to produce disorganized interaction should tell us something abut how the structures of everyday activities are ordinarily and routinely produced and maintained.[3]

A word of reservation. Despite their procedural emphasis, my studies are not properly speaking experimental. They demonstrations, designed, in Herbert Spiegelberg's phrase, as "aids to a sluggish imagination." I have found that they produce reflections through which the strangeness of an obstinately familiar world can be detected.

Some Essential Features of Common Understandings

Various considerations dictate that common understandings cannot possibly consist of a measured amount of shared agreement among persons on certain topics. Even if the topics are limited in the number and scope and every practical difficulty of assessment is forgiven, the notion that we are dealing with an amount of shared agreement remains essentially incorrect. This may be demonstrated as follows.

Students were asked to report common conversations by writing on the left side of a sheet what the parties actually said and on the right side what they and their partners understood that they were talking about. A student reported the following colloquy between himself and his wife.

[2] Afred Schutz, *Der Sinnhafte Aufbau Der Sozialen Welt* (Wein: Verlag von Julius Springer, 1932); *Collected Papers I: The Problem of Social Reality*, ed. Maurice Natanson (The Hague: Martinus Nijhoff, 1962); *Collected Papers II: Studies in Social Theory*, ed. Arvid Broderson (The Hague: Martinus Nihjoff, 1964); *Collected Papers III: Studies in Phenomenological Philosophy*, ed. I. Schutz (The Hague: Martinus Nihjoff, 1966).

[3] Obversely, a knowledge of how the structures of everyday activities are routinely produced should permit us to tell how we might proceed for the effective production of desired disturbances.

HUSBAND: Dana succeeded in putting a penny in a parking meter today without being picked up.	This afternoon as I was bringing Dana, our four-year-old son, home from the nursery school, he succeeded in reaching high enough to put a penny in a parking meter when we parked in a meter parking zone, whereas before he has always had to be picked up to reach that high.
WIFE: Did you take him to the record store?	Since he put a penny in a meter that means that you stopped while he was with you. I know that you stopped at the record store either on the way to get him or on the way back. Was it on the way back, so that he was with you or did you stop there on the way to get him and somewhere else on the way back?
HUSBAND: No, to the shoe repair shop.	No, I stopped at the record store on the way to get him and stopped at the shoe repair shop on the way home when he was with me.
WIFE: What for?	I know of one reason why you might have stopped at the shoe repair shop. Why did you in fact?
HUSBAND: I got some new shoe laces for my shoes.	As you will remember I broke a shoe lace on one of my brown oxfords the other day so I stopped to get some new laces.
WIFE: Your loafers need new heels badly.	Something else you could have gotten that I was thinking of. You could have taken in your black loafers which need heels badly. You'd better get them taken care of pretty soon.

An examination of the colloquy reveals the following. (a) There were many matters that the partners understood they were talking about that they did not mention. (b) Many matters that the partners understood were understood on the basis not only of what was actually said but what was left unspoken. (c) Many matters were understood through a process of attending to the temporal series of utterances as documentary evidences of a developing conversation rather than as a string of terms. (d) Matters that the two understood in common were understood only in and through a course of understanding work that consisted of treating an actual linguistic event as "the document of," as "pointing to," as standing on behalf of an underlying pattern of matters that each already supposed to be the matters that the person, by his speaking, could be telling the other about. The underlying pattern was not only derived from a course of individual documentary evidences but the documentary evidences in their turn were interpreted on the basis of "what was known" and anticipatorily knowable about the underlying patterns.[4] Each was used to elaborate the other. (e) In attending to the utterances as events-in-the-conversation

---

[4] Karl Mannheim, in his essay "On the Interpretation of 'Weltanschauung'" (in *Essays on the Sociology of Knowledge*, trans. and ed. Paul Kecskemeti [New York: Oxford University Press, 1952], pp. 33–83), referred to this work as the "documentary method of interpretation." Its features are detailed in Chapter Three.

each party made references to the biography and prospects of the present interaction which each used and attributed to the other as a common scheme of interpretation and expression. (f) Each waited for something more to be said in order to hear what had previously been talked about, and each seemed willing to wait.

Common understandings would consist of a measured amount of shared agreement if the common understandings consisted of events coordinated with the successive positions of the hands of the clock, i.e., of events in standard time. The foregoing results, because they deal with the exchanges of the colloquy as events-in-a-conversation, urge that one more time parameter, at least, is required: the role of time as it is constitutive of "the matter talked about" as a developing and developed event over the course of action that produced it, as both the process and product were known *from within* this development by both parties, each for himself as well as on behalf of the other.

The colloquy reveals additional features. (1) Many of its expressions are such that their sense cannot be decided by an auditor unless he knows or assumes something about the biography and the purposes of the speaker, the circumstances of the utterance, the previous course of the conversation, or the particular relationship of actual or potential interaction that exists between user and auditor. The expressions do not have a sense that remains identical through the changing occasions of their use. (2) The events that were talked about were specifically vague. Not only do they not frame a clearly restricted set of possible determinations but the depicted events include as their essentially intended and sanctioned features an accompanying "fringe" of determinations that are open with respect to internal relationships, relationships to other events, and relationships to retrospective and prospective possibilities (3) For the sensible character of an expression, upon its occurrence each of the conversationalists as auditor of his own as well as

the other's productions had to assume as of any present accomplished point in the exchange that by waiting for what he or the other person might have said at a later time the present significance of what had already been said would have been clarified. Thus many expressions had the property of being progressively realized and realizable through the further course of the conversation. (4) It hardly needs to be pointed out that the sense of the expressions depended upon where the expression occurred in serial order, the expressive character of the terms that comprised it, and the importance to the conversationalists of the events depicted.

These properties of common understandings stand in contrast to the features they would have if we disregarded their temporally constituted character and treated them instead as precoded entries on a memory drum, to be consulted as a definite set of alternative meanings from among which one was to select, under predecided conditions that specified in which of some set of alternative ways one was to understand the situation upon the occasion that the necessity for a decision arose. The latter properties are those of strict rational discourse as these are idealized in the rules that define an adequate logical proof.

For the purposes of *conducting their everyday affairs* persons refuse to permit each other to understand "what they are really talking about" in this way. The anticipation that persons *will* understand, the occasionality of expressions, the specific vagueness of references, the retrospective-prospective sense of a present occurrence, waiting for something late in order to see what was meant before, are sanctioned properties of common discourse. They furnish a background of seen but unnoticed features of common discourse whereby actual utterances are recognized as events of common, reasonable, understandable, plain talk. Persons require these properties of discourse as conditions under which they are themselves entitled and entitle others to claim that they know what they are talking about, and that what they are saying is understandable and ought to be understood. In short, their seen but unnoticed presence is used to entitle persons to conduct their common conversational affairs without interference. Departures from such usages call forth immediate attempts to restore a right state of affairs.

The sanctioned character of these properties is demonstrable as follows. Students were instructed to engage an acquaintance or a friend in an ordinary conversation and, without indicating that what the experimenter was asking was in any way unusual, to insist that the person clarify the sense of his commonplace remarks. Twenty-three students reported twenty-five instances of such encounters. The following are typical excerpts from their accounts.

CASE 1

The subject was telling the experimenter, a member of the subject's car pool, about having had a flat tire while going to work the previous day.

(S) I had a flat tire.
(E) What do you mean, you had a flat tire?

She appeared momentarily stunned. Then she answered in a hostile way: "What do you mean, 'What do you mean?' A flat tire is a flat tire. That is what I meant. Nothing special. What a crazy question!"

CASE 2

(S) Hi, Ray. How is your girlfriend feeling?
(E) What do you mean, "How is she feeling?" Do you mean physical or mental?
(S) I mean how is she feeling? What's the matter with you? (He looked peeved.)
(E) Nothing. Just explain a little clearer what do you mean?
(S) Skip it. How are your Med School applications coming?
(E) What do you mean, "How are they?"
(S) You know what I mean.
(E) I really don't.
(S) What's the matter with you? Are you sick?

CASE 3

"On Friday night my husband and I were watching television. My husband remarked that he was tired. I asked, 'How are you tired? Physically, mentally, or just bored?'"

(S) I don't know, I guess physically, mainly.
(E) You mean that your muscles ache or your bones?
(S) I guess so. Don't be so technical. (*After more watching*)
(S) All these old movies have the same kind of old iron bedstead in them.
(E) What do you mean? Do you mean all old movies, or some of them, or just the ones you have seen?
(S) What's the matter with you? You know what I mean.
(E) I wish you would be more specific.
(S) You know what I mean! Drop dead!

CASE 4

During a conversation (with the E's female fiancee) the E questioned the meaning of various words used by the subject . . .

> For the first minute and a half the subject responded to the questions as if they were legitimate inquiries. Then she responded with "Why are you asking me those questions?" and repeated this two or three times after each question. She became nervous and jittery, her face and hand movements . . . uncontrolled. She appeared bewildered and complained that I was making her nervous and demanded that I "Stop it". . . . The subject picked up a magazine and covered her face. She put down the magazine and pretended to be engrossed. When asked why she was looking at the magazine she closed her mouth and refused any further remarks.

CASE 5

My friend said to me, "Hurry or we will be late." I asked him what did he mean by late and from what point of view did it have reference. There was a look of perplexity and cynicism on his face. "Why are you asking me such silly questions? Surely I don't have to explain such a statement. What is wrong with you today? Why should I have to stop to analyze such a statement? Everyone understands my statements and you should be no exception!"

CASE 6

The victim waved his hand cheerily.

(S) How are you?
(E) How am I in regard to what? My health, my finances, my school work, my peace of mind, my . . . ?
(S) (*Red in the face and suddenly out of control.*) Look! I was just trying to be polite. Frankly, I don't give a damn how you are.

CASE 7

My friend and I were talking about a man whose overbearing attitude annoyed us. My friend expressed his feeling.

(S) I'm sick of him.
(E) Would you explain what is wrong with you that you are sick?
(S) Are you kidding me? You know what I mean.
(E) Please explain your ailment.
(S) (*He listened to me with a puzzled look.*) What came over you? We never talk this way, do we?

Background Understandings and "Adequate" Recognition of Commonplace Events

What kinds of expectancies make up a "seen but unnoticed" background of common understandings, and how are they related to persons' recognition of stable courses of interpersonal

transactions? Some information can be obtained if we first ask how a person will look at an ordinary and familiar scene and what will he see in it if we require of him that he do no more than look at it as something that for him it "obviously" and "really" is not.

Undergraduate students were assigned the task of spending from fifteen minutes to an hour in their homes viewing its activities while assuming that they were boarders in the household. They were instructed not to act out the assumption. Thirty-three students reported their experiences.

In their written reports students "behaviorized" the household scenes. Here is an excerpt from one account to illustrate my meaning.

> A short, stout man entered the house, kissed me on the cheek and asked, "How was school?" I answered politely. He walked into the kitchen, kissed the younger of the two women, and said hello to the other. The younger woman asked me, "What do you want for dinner, honey?" I answered, "Nothing." She shrugged her shoulders and said no more. The older woman shuffled around the kitchen muttering. The man washed his hands, sat down at the table, and picked up the paper. He read until the two women had finished putting the food on the table. The three sat down. They exchanged idle chatter about the day's events. The older woman said something in a foreign language which made the others laugh.

Persons, relationships, and activities were described without respect for their history, for the place of the scene in a set of developing life circumstances, or for the scenes as texture of relevant events for the parties themselves. References to motives, propriety, subjectivity generally, and the socially standardized character of the events were omitted. Descriptions might be thought of as those of a keyhole observer who puts aside much of what he knows in common with subjects about the scenes he is looking at, as if the writer had witnessed the scenes under a mild amnesia for his common sense knowledge of social structures.

Students were surprised to see the ways in which members' treatments of each other were personal. The business of one was treated as the business of the others. A person being criticized was unable to stand on dignity and was prevented by the others from taking offense. One student reported her surprise at how freely she had the run of the house. Displays of conduct and feeling occurred without apparent concern for the management of impressions. Table manners were bad, and family members showed each other little politeness. An early casualty in the scene was the family news of the day which turned into trivial talk.

Students reported that this way of looking was difficult to sustain. Familiar objects—persons obviously, but furniture and room arrangements as well—resisted students' efforts to think of themselves as strangers. Many became uncomfortably aware of how habitual movements were being made; of *how* one was handling the silverware, or *how* one opened a door or greeted another member. Many reported that the attitude was difficult to sustain because with it quarreling, bickering, and hostile motivations became discomfitingly visible. Frequently an account that recited newly visible troubles was accompanied by the student's assertion that his account of family problems was not a "true" picture; the family was *really* a very happy one. Several students reported a mildly oppressive feeling of "conforming to a part." Several students attempted to formulate the "real me" as activities governed by rules of conduct but gave it up as a bad job. They found it more convincing to think of themselves in "usual" circumstances as "being one's real self." Nevertheless one student was intrigued with how deliberately and successfully he could predict the other's responses to his actions. He was not troubled by this feeling.

Many accounts reported a variation on the theme: "I was glad when the hour was up and I could return to the real me."

Students were convinced that the view from the boarder's attitude was not their real home environment. The boarder's attitude produced appearances which they discounted as interesting incongruities of little and misleading practical import. How had the familiar ways of looking at their home environments been altered? How did their looking differ from usual?

Several contrasts to the "usual" and "required" way of looking are detectable from their accounts. (1) In looking at their homes as boarders they replaced the mutually recognized texture of events with a rule of interpretation which required that this mutual texture be *temporarily* disregarded. (2) The mutually recognized texture was brought under the jurisdiction of the new attitude as a definition of the essential structures of this texture. (3) This was done by engaging in interaction with others with an attitude whose nature and purpose only the user knew about, that remained undisclosed, that could be either adopted or put aside at a time of the user's own choosing, and was a matter of willful election. (4) The attitude as an intention was sustained as a matter of personal and willed compliance with an explicit and single rule, (5) in which, like a game, the goal of the intention was identical with looking at things under the auspices of the single rule itself. (6) Above all, looking was not bound by any necessity for gearing one's interest within the attitude to the actions of others. These were the matters that students found strange.

When students used these background expectancies not only as ways of looking at familial scenes but as grounds for acting in them, the scenes exploded with the bewilderment and anger of family members.

In another procedure students were asked to spend from fifteen minutes to an hour in their homes imagining that they were boarders and acting out this assumption. They were instructed to conduct themselves in a circumspect and polite fashion. They were to avoid getting personal, to use formal address, to speak only when spoken to.

In nine of forty-nine cases students either refused to do the assignment (five cases) or the try was "unsuccessful" (four cases). Four of the "no try" students said they were afraid to do it; a fifth said she preferred to avoid the risk of exciting her mother who had a heart condition. In two of the "unsuccessful" cases the family treated it as a joke from the beginning and refused despite the continuing actions of the student to change. A third family took the view that something undisclosed was the matter, but what it might be was of no concern to them. In the fourth family the father and mother remarked that the daughter was being "extra nice" and undoubtedly wanted something that she would shortly reveal.

In the remaining four-fifths of the cases family members were stupefied. They vigorously sought to make the strange actions intelligible and to restore the situation to normal appearances. Reports were filled with accounts of astonishment, bewilderment, shock, anxiety, embarrassment, and anger, and with charges by various family members that the student was mean, inconsiderate, selfish, nasty, or impolite. Family members demanded explanations: What's the matter? What's gotten into you? Did you get fired? Are you sick? What are you being so superior about? Why are you mad? Are you out of your mind or are you just stupid? One student acutely embarrassed his mother in front of her friends by asking if she minded if he had a snack from the refrigerator. "Mind if you have a little snack? You've been eating little snacks around here for years without asking me. What's gotten into you?" One mother, infuriated when her daughter spoke to her only when she was spoken to, began to shriek in angry denunciation of the daughter for her disrespect and insubordination and refused to be calmed by the student's sister. A father berated his daughter for being insufficiently concerned for the welfare of others and of acting like a spoiled child.

Occasionally family members would first treat the student's action as a cue for a joint comedy routine which was soon replaced by irritation and exasperated anger at the student for not knowing when enough was enough. Family members mocked the "politeness" of the students—"Certainly Mr. Herzberg!"—or charged the student with acting like a wise guy and generally reported the "politeness" with sarcasm.

Explanations were sought in previous, understandable motives of the student: the student was "working too hard" in school; the student was "ill"; there had been "another fight" with a financee. When offered explanations by family members went unacknowledged, there followed withdrawal by the offended member, attempted isolation of the culprit retaliation, and denunciation. "Don't bother with him, he's in one of his moods again"; "Pay no attention buy just wait until he asks me for something"; "You're cutting me, okay I'll cut you and then some"; Why must you always create friction in our family harmony?" Many accounts reported versions of the following confrontation. A father followed his son into the bedroom. "Your Mother is right. You don't look well and you're not talking sense. You had better get another job that doesn't require such late hours." To this the student replied that he appreciated the consideration, but that he felt fine and only wanted a little privacy. The father responded in a high rage, "I don't want any more of *that* out of *you* and if you can't treat your mother decently you'd better move out!"

There were no cases in which the situation was not restorable upon the student's explanation. Nevertheless, for the most part family members were not amused and only rarely did they find the experience instructive as the student argued that it was supposed to have been. After hearing the explanation a sister replied coldly on behalf of a family of four, "Please, no more of these experiments. We're not rats, you know." Occasionally an explanation was accepted but still it added offense. In several cases students reported that the explanations left them, their families, or both wondering how much of what the student had said was "in character" and how much the student "really meant."

Students found the assignment difficult to complete. But in contrast with on-lookers' accounts students were likely to report that difficulties consisted in not being treated as if they were in the role that they were attempting to play, and of being confronted with situations but not knowing how a boarder would respond.

There were several entirely unexpected findings. (1) Although many students reported extensive rehearsals in imagination, very few mentioned anticipatory fears or embarrassment. (2) On the other hand, although unanticipated and nasty developments frequently occurred, in only one case did a student report serious regrets. (3) Very few students reported heartfelt relief when the hour was over. They were much more likely to report partial relief. They frequently reported that in response to the anger of others they became angry in return and slipped easily into subjectively recognizable feelings and actions.

In contrast to the reports of the on-looking "boarders" very few reports "behaviorized" the scene.

Chapter 11

Symbolic Interaction

Introduction

We discussed the ideas of George Herbert Mead in an earlier chapter. It will be recalled that Mead's contribution to sociological understanding was his theory concerning the self as a social product and his attempt to capture the interactive and dynamic process by which the self is formed. In rejecting Watsonian behaviorism, Mead was not only setting aside an overly simplistic view of human behavior as a conditioned response but introducing an active and reflective social actor whose consciousness could be understood by analyzing the social processes that contribute to its construction.

Herbert Blumer (1900–1987) was a student of Mead's at the University of Chicago. Although Mead was a philosopher, his courses in social psychology attracted a number of sociology graduate students, Blumer among them. He became a major interpreter of Mead's work and first used the term *symbolic interactionism* in 1937 in an article explaining how active involvement in the life of a group affects the social development of an individual. Blumer's own work built upon that of Mead but extended it into a critique of reductionist theories in psychology and deterministic theories in sociology. Blumer's writings attempt to capture the fluidity of social action, the reflexivity of the self, and the negotiated character of much of everyday life. Instead of focusing on social structure as the antecedent cause of human action, Blumer emphasizes the social and interactive processes that allow individuals to construct their actions. In this respect, Blumer rejects the notion that human action is a

response to internal drives or external forces that play upon the individual. Rather it is Blumer's contention that human actions are best understood as a consequence of reflexive and deliberative processes in which the individual is able to note and determine the relevance of objects in the environment, calculate whether and how to respond in particular situations, and reject certain courses of action and choose among alternatives. In this way, Blumer challenges the prevailing explanations of human action in the the social sciences and brings to the fore a conscious and reflective actor in place of the passive and determined object.

Blumer views symbolic interaction as a uniquely human process in that it requires the definition and interpretation of language and gestures and the determination of the meaning of the actions of others as well. For humans to interact, they must be able to understand the meaning of the remarks and the actions of others and shape an appropriate response. Individuals thus attempt to fit their actions and mesh their behaviors with those of others with whom they interact. As a result, social life is a fluid and negotiated process rather than one that is determined by macro-structures like economic class or bureaucratic organization. Blumer's discussion of "joint action" captures this view of social life as process rather than structure, and projects a view of society as a complex web of collaborative actions in which participants are constantly reflecting, negotiating, and fitting their actions to others in order to achieve common objectives. In place of the view that society is a fixed and definable structure with predictable outcomes and severely constrained lines of action for individuals, Blumer stresses the uncertainty, the contingency, and the transformation that characterizes everyday life.

As we have seen, the ideas of Mead and their further development by Blumer provide the foundation for the school of thought known as symbolic interactionism. Two important criticisms have emerged with respect to this perspective. First, symbolic interactionism is faulted for placing too much emphasis on everyday life and the social formation of the self while virtually ignoring social structure. There are times when symbolic interactionists write as if the poor, the homeless, and the victims of economic dislocations were not a part of everyday life. Class relations and the constraints they place on the lines of action open to individual actors are ignored or overlooked in favor of a more optimistic view of an open society in which negotiated joint action is the relevant characteristic of human action.

Second, some have found in the perspective of symbolic interactionism a departure from the canons of scientific methodology and its quest for objectively verifiable generalizations in sociology. Symbolic interactionism places great emphasis on a methodology which focuses on subjective meanings, symbols, and interpretations in the determination of how actors arrive at their courses of action. Because the processes are mental and internal, some interactionists rely on subjective and introspective insights rather than readily observable and objective data. This critique has caused a rupture from within symbolic interactionism: some have claimed that Blumer has not been faithful to Mead's commitment to scientific behaviorism, and that Blumer's version of the field has not led to the development of useful concepts or the formulation of generalizations based on the observation of overt behavior.

Another voice in the field of symbolic interactionism is Erving Goffman's (1922–1982). A Canadian by birth, Goffman studied at the University of Toronto but took his advanced degrees at the University of Chicago, where he studied with Herbert Blumer. Goffman accepted an appointment at the University of California at Berkeley, where he taught sociology in the same department as Blumer. In 1969 he left Berkeley for the University of Pennsylvania, where he taught until 1982.

Goffman's approach to sociology is heavily influenced by Mead and Blumer although he strikes a somewhat different chord in the various works that he has produced. His early work, *The Presentation of Self in Everyday Life* (1959), is very much in the tradition of symbolic interactionism, because Goffman focuses on the individual as an active and reflective self capable of making a wide range of choices in determining how it should be presented in the varied social spaces in which it must perform. In his other works, such as *Stigma* (1963) and *Asylums* (1961), Goffman continued the focus on the creativity of the self and its tenacity to survive against all odds. Unlike his mentors, Goffman paid significantly more attention to social structures and, particularly in *Asylums*, developed the concept of "total institutions" and the ways in which inmates develop strategies to circumvent their keepers.

Dramaturgy is the novel twist given to traditional Meadian thought by Goffman, and the term most often associated with his name. Goffman asks that we view our actions and those of others through the prism of a dramatic stage play. Social action does not simply entail playing a role, but also involves a "back stage" and a "front stage." In the back stage, always hidden from the audience as in the theater, actors prepare themselves for their performances, which take place in the front stage. The selection of "props"; the clothing to be worn; the use, disuse, or abuse of make-up; and whatever other aids are deemed appropriate by the actor to project the appropriate image, are all carefully determined out of view of the audience before whom the performance is to take place. All actors engaged in social interaction partake of this selection of the appropriate mask in order to play the role convincingly. In each instance, Goffman argues, a different self is projected; and what and how it is projected is a conscious decision on the part of the actor; moreover, and here Goffman moves beyond Mead and Blumer, just as the actor in a stage play performs a role so as to be credible to the audience, so too, in everyday life, individuals play their roles with conscious attention to those details that will make them believable. Finally, in everyday life, as in the theater, there is an element of manipulation that is entailed in the relationship between actor and audience. In both instances the actor attempts to gauge the reaction of the audience and thus shapes the performance, or the presentation of the self, in order to elicit the desired reaction from the other.

In the excerpt below, Goffman summarizes his views on the meaning of the self and concludes with some striking observations. The self is not singular but multiple, not a morally coherent source of action but a repertoire of acts. It does not exist except as credible performances, as an illusion that is considered real by the observer or the audience. Although these conclusions may be difficult, or perhaps unacceptable to some, they do speak to the prescience of Goffman's ideas, not to speak of Simmel, Mead, and Blumer before him, in that they anticipate notions of the decentered self, popularized by contemporary post-modernist theorists. For Goffman as with Simmel, contemporary social life involves us in a multiplicity of heterodox interactions in different social spaces. To interact with others successfully, to achieve individual or collective objectives, entails the ability to play a variety of roles and to manipulate the self in order to get from others the desired reactions, responses, or rewards. The self thus becomes an object to itself in a somewhat different fashion than assumed by Mead and Blumer as Goffman introduces considerations of manipulation and power to symbolic interactionism. More important, the ideologically liberal view of the individual as the central source of action, of will, intention, and moral consistency and integrity, is replaced by the sociological conception of the social actor operating in many contexts, which call forth different acts to meet new and varied situations. Whether this is a morally reprehensible or an emancipated condition is not for Goffman to decide. His role as sociologist is to present us with the realities that we confront in our everyday lives even though we tend to deny them.

HERBERT BLUMER: SOCIETY AS SYMBOLIC INTERACTION

A view of human society as symbolic interaction has been followed more than it has been formulated. Partial, usually fragmentary, statements of it are to be found in the writings of a

From Herbert Blumer, "Society as Symbolic Interaction," in *Human Behavior and Social Processes: An Interactionist Approach,* edited by Arnold M. Rose. Reprinted with permission of Houghton-Mifflin Co. Copyroght © 1962.

number of eminent scholars, some inside the field of sociology and some outside. Among the former we may note such scholars as Charles Horton Cooley, W. I. Thomas, Robert E. Park, E. W. Burgess, Florian Znaniecki, Ellsworth Faris, and James Mickel Williams. Among those outside the discipline we may note William James, John Dewey, and George Herbert Mead. None of these scholars, in my judgment, has presented a systematic statement of the nature of human group life from the standpoint of symbolic interaction. Mead stands out among all of them in laying bare the fundamental premises of the approach, yet he did little to develop its methodological implications for sociological study. Students who seek to depict the position of symbolic interaction may easily give different pictures of it. What I have to present should be regarded as my personal version. My aim is to present the basic premises of the point of view and to develop their methodological consequences for the study of human group life.

The term "symbolic interaction" refers, of course, to the peculiar and distinctive character of interaction as it takes place between human beings. The peculiarity consists in the fact that human beings interpret or "define" each other's actions instead of merely reacting to each other's actions. Their "response" is not made directly to the actions of one another but instead is based on the meaning which they attach to such actions. Thus, human interaction is mediated by the use of symbols, by interpretation, or by ascertaining the meaning of one another's actions. This mediation is equivalent to inserting a process of interpretation between stimulus and response in the case of human behavior.

The simple recognition that human beings interpret each other's actions as the means of acting toward one another has permeated the thought and writings of many scholars of human conduct and of human group life. Yet few of them have endeavored to analyze what such interpretation implies about the nature of the human being or about the nature of human association. They are usually content with a mere recognition that "interpretation" should be caught by the student, or with a simple realization that symbols, such as cultural norms or values, must be introduced into their analyses. Only G. H. Mead, in my judgment, has sought to think through what the act of interpretation implies for an understanding of the human being, human action, and human association. The essentials of his analysis are so penetrating

and profound and so important for an understanding of human group life that I wish to spell them out, even though briefly.

The key feature in Mead's analysis is that the human being has a self. This idea should not be cast aside as esoteric or glossed over as something that is obvious and hence not worthy of attention. In declaring that the human being has a self, Mead had in mind chiefly that the human being can be the object of his own actions. He can act toward himself as he might act toward others. Each of us is familiar with actions of this sort in which the human being gets angry with himself, rebuffs himself, takes pride in himself, argues with himself, tries to bolster his own courage, tells himself that he should "do this" or not "do that," sets goals for himself, makes compromises with himself, and plans what he is going to do. That the human being acts toward himself in these and countless other ways is a matter of easy empirical observation. To recognize that the human being can act toward himself is no mystical conjuration.

Mead regards this ability of the human being to act toward himself as the central mechanism with which the human being faces and deals with his world. This mechanism enables the human being to make indication to himself of things in his surroundings and thus to guide his actions by what he notes. Anything of which a human being is conscious is something which he is indicating to himself—the ticking of a clock, a knock at the door, the appearance of a friend, the remark made by a companion, a recognition that he has a task to perform, or the realization that he has a cold. Conversely, anything of which he is not conscious is, *ipso facto*, something which he is not indicating to himself. The conscious life of the human being, from the time that he awakens until he falls asleep, is a continual flow of self-indications—notations of the things with which he deals and takes into account. We are given, then, a picture of the human being as an organism which confronts its world with a mechanism for making indications to itself. This is the mechanism that is involved in interpreting the actions of others. To interpret the actions of another is to point out to oneself that the action has this or that meaning or character.

Now, according to Mead, the significance of making indications to oneself is of paramount importance. The importance lies along two lines. First, to indicate something is to extricate it from its setting, to hold it apart, to give it a meaning or, in Mead's language, to make it into an object. An object—that is to say, anything that an individual indicates to himself—is different from a stimulus; instead of having an intrinsic character which acts on the individual and which can be identified apart from the individual, its character or meaning is conferred on it by the individual. The object is a product of the individual's disposition to act instead of being an antecedent stimulus which evokes the act. Instead of the individual being surrounded by an environment of pre-existing objects which play upon him and call forth his behavior, the proper picture is that he constructs his objects on the basis of his ongoing activity. In any of his countless acts—whether minor, like dressing himself, or major, like organizing himself for a professional career—the individual is designating different objects to himself, giving them meaning, judging their suitability to his action, and making decisions on the basis of the judgment. This is what is meant by interpretation or acting on the basis of symbols.

The second important implication of the fact that the human being makes indications to himself is that his action is constructed or built up instead of being a mere release. Whatever the action in which he is engaged, the human individual proceeds by pointing out to himself the divergent things which have to be taken into account in the course of his action. He has to note what he wants to do and how he is to do it; he has to point out to himself the various conditions which may be instrumental to his action and those which may obstruct his action; he has to take account of the demands, the expecta-

tions, the prohibitions, and the threats as they may arise in the situation in which he is acting. His action is built up step by step through a process of such self-indication. The human individual pieces together and guides his action by taking account of different things and interpreting their significance for his prospective action. There is no instance of conscious action of which this is not true.

The process of constructing action through making indications to oneself cannot be swallowed up in any of the conventional psychological categories. This process is distinct from and different from what is spoken of as the "ego"—just as it is different from any other conception which conceives of the self in terms of composition or organization. Self-indication is a moving communicative process in which the individual notes things, assesses them, gives them a meaning, and decides to act on the basis of the meaning. The human being stands over against the world, or against "alters," with such a process and not with a mere ego. Further, the process of self-indication cannot be subsumed under the forces, whether from the outside or inside, which are presumed to play upon the individual to produce his behavior. Environmental pressures, external stimuli, organic drives, wishes, attitudes, feelings, ideas, and their like do not cover or explain the process of self-indication. The process of self-indication stands over against them in that the individual points out to himself and interprets the appearance or expression of such things, noting a given social demand that is made on him, recognizing a command, observing that he is hungry, realizing that he wishes to buy something, aware that he has a given feeling, conscious that he dislikes eating with someone he despises, or aware that he is thinking of doing some given thing. By virtue of indicating such things to himself, he places himself over against them and is able to act back against them, accepting them, rejecting them, or transforming them in accordance with how he defines or interprets them. His behavior, accordingly, is not a result of such things as environmental pressures, stimuli, motives, attitudes, and ideas but arises instead from how he interprets and handles these things in the action which he is constructing. The process of self-indication by means of which human action is formed cannot be accounted for by factors which precede the act. The process of self-indication exists in its own right and must be accepted and studied as such. It is through this process that the human being constructs his conscious action.

Now Mead recognizes that the formation of action by the individual through a process of self-indication always takes place in a social context. Since this matter is so vital to an understanding of symbolic interaction it needs to be explained carefully. Fundamentally, group action takes the form of a fitting together of individual lines of action. Each individual aligns his action to the action of others by ascertaining what they are doing or what they intend to do—that is, by getting the meaning of their acts. For Mead, this is done by the individual "taking the role" of others—either the role of a specific person or the role of a group (Mead's "generalized other"). In taking such roles the individual seeks to ascertain the intention or direction of the acts of others. He forms and aligns his own action on the basis of such interpretation of the acts of others. This is the fundamental way in which group action takes place in human society.

The foregoing are the essential features, as I see them, in Mead's analysis of the bases of symbolic interaction. They presuppose the following: that human society is made up of individuals who have selves (that is, make indications to themselves); that individual action is a construction and not a release, being built up by the individual through noting and interpreting features of the situations in which he acts; that group or collective action consists of the aligning of individual actions, brought about by the individual's interpreting or taking into account each other's actions. Since my purpose is to

present and not to defend the position of symbolic interaction I shall not endeavor in this essay to advance support for the three premises which I have just indicated. I wish merely to say that the three premises can be easily verified empirically. I know of no instance of human group action to which the three premises do not apply. The reader is challenged to find or think of a single instance which they do not fit.

I wish now to point out that sociological views of human society are, in general, markedly at variance with the premises which I have indicated as underlying symbolic interaction. Indeed, the predominant number of such views, especially those in vogue at the present time, do not see or treat human society as symbolic interaction. Wedded, as they tend to be, to some form of sociological determinism, they adopt images of human society, of individuals in it, and of group action which do not square with the premises of symbolic interaction. I wish to say a few words about the major lines of variance.

Sociological thought rarely recognizes or treats human societies as composed of individuals who have selves. Instead, they assume human beings to be merely organisms with some kind of organization, responding to forces which play upon them. Generally, although not exclusively, these forces are lodged in the make-up of the society, as in the case of "social system," "social structure," "culture," "status position," "social role," "custom," "institution," "collective representation," "social situation," "social norm," and "values." The assumption is that the behavior of people as members *of a society* is an expression of the play on them of these kinds of factors or forces. This, of course, is the logical position which is necessarily taken when the scholar explains their behavior or phases of their behavior in terms of one or other of such social factors. The individuals who compose a human society are treated as the media through which such factors operate, and the social action of such individuals is regarded as an expression of such factors. This approach or point of view denies, or at least ignores, that human beings have selves—that they act by making indications to themselves. Incidentally, the "self" is not brought into the picture by introducing such items as organic drives, motives, attitudes, feelings, internalized social factors, or psychological components. Such psychological factors have the same status as the social factors mentioned: they are regarded as factors which play on the individual to produce his action. They do not constitute the process of self-indication. The process of self-indication stands over against them, just as it stands over against the social factors which play on the human being. Practically all sociological conceptions of human society fail to recognize that the individuals who compose it have selves in the sense of spoken of.

Correspondingly, such sociological conceptions do not regard the social actions of individuals in human society as being constructed by them through a process of interpretation. Instead, action is treated as a product of factors which play on and through individuals. The social behavior of people is not seen as built up by them through an interpretation of objects, situations, or the actions of others. If a place is given to "interpretation," the interpretation is regarded as merely an expression of other factors (such as motives) which precede the act, and accordingly disappears as a factor in its own right. Hence, the social action of people is treated as an outward flow or expression of forces playing on them rather than as acts which are built up by people through their interpretation of the situations in which they are placed.

These remarks suggest another significant line of difference between general sociological views and the position of symbolic interaction. These two sets of views differ in where they lodge social action. Under the perspective of symbolic interaction, social action is lodged in acting individuals who fit their respective lines of action to one another through a process of interpretation; group action is the collective action of such individuals. As opposed to this view, sociological conceptions generally lodge social action in the action of society or in some unit of society. Examples of this are legion. Let me cite a few. Some conceptions, in treating societies or human groups as "social systems," regard group action as an expression of a system, either in a state of balance or seeking to achieve balance. Or group action is conceived as an expression of the "functions" of a society or of a group. Or group action is regarded as the outward expression of elements lodged in society or the group, such as cultural demands, societal purposes, social values, or institutional stresses. These typical conceptions ignore or blot out a view of group life or of group action as consisting of the collective or concerted actions of individuals seeking to meet their life situations. If recognized at all, the efforts of people to develop collective acts to meet their situations are subsumed under the play of underlying or transcending forces which are lodged in society or its parts. The individuals composing the society or the group become "carriers," or media for the expression of such forces; and the interpretative behavior by means of which people form their actions is merely a coerced link in the play of such forces.

The indication of the foregoing lines of variance should help to put the position of symbolic interaction in better perspective. In the remaining discussion I wish to sketch somewhat more fully how human society appears in terms of symbolic interaction and to point out some methodological implications.

Human society is to be seen as consisting of acting people, and the life of the society is to be seen as consisting of their actions. The acting units may be separate individuals, collectives whose members are acting together on a common quest, or organizations acting on behalf of a constituency. Respective examples are individual purchasers in a market, a play group or missionary band, and a business corporation or a national professional association. There is no empirically observable activity in a human society that does not spring from some acting unit.

This banal statement needs to be stressed in light of the common practice of sociologists of reducing human society to social units that do not act—for example, social classes in modern society. Obviously, there are ways of viewing human society other than in terms of the acting units that compose it. I merely wish to point out that in respect to concrete or empirical activity human society must necessarily be seen in terms of the acting units that form it. I would add that any scheme of human society claiming to be a realistic analysis has to respect and be congruent with the empirical recognition that a human society consists of acting units.

Corresponding respect must be shown to the conditions under which such units act. One primary condition is that action takes place in and with regard to a situation. Whatever be the acting unit—an individual, a family, a school, a church, a business firm, a labor union, a legislature, and so on—any particular action is formed in the light of the situation in which it takes place. This leads to the recognition of a second major condition, namely, that the action is formed or constructed by interpreting the situation. The acting unit necessarily has to identify the things which it has to take into account— tasks, opportunities, obstacles, means, demands, discomforts, dangers, and the like; it has to assess them in some fashion and it has to make decisions on the basis of the assessment. Such interpretative behavior may take place in the individual guiding his own action, in a collectivity of individuals acting in concert, or in "agents" acting on behalf of a group or organization. Group life consists of acting units developing acts to meet the situations in which they are placed.

Usually, most of the situations encountered by people in a given society are defined or "structured" by them in the same way. Through previous interaction they develop and acquire common understandings or definitions of how to act in this or that situation. These common definitions enable people to act alike. The common repetitive behavior of people in such situations should not mislead the student into believing that no process of interpretation is in play; on the contrary, even though fixed, the actions of the participating people are constructed by them through a process of interpretation. Since readymade and commonly accepted definitions are at hand, little strain is placed on people in guiding and organizing their acts. However, many other situations may not be defined in a single way by the participating people. In this event, their lines of action do not fit together readily and collective action is blocked. Interpretations have to be developed and effective accommodation of the participants to one another has to be worked out. In the case of such "undefined" situations, it is necessary to trace and study the emerging process of definition which is brought into play.

Insofar as sociologists or students of human society are concerned with the behavior of acting units, the position of symbolic interaction requires the student to catch the process of interpretation through which they construct their actions. This process is not to be caught merely by turning to conditions which are antecedent to the process. Such antecedent conditions are helpful in understanding the process insofar as they enter into it, but as mentioned previously they do not constitute the process. Nor can one catch the process merely by inferring its nature from the overt action which is its product. To catch the process, the student must take the role of the acting unit whose behavior he is studying. Since the interpretation is being made by the acting unit in terms of objects designated and appraised, meanings acquired, and decisions made, the process has to be seen from the standpoint of the acting unit. It is the recognition of this fact that makes the research work of such scholars as R. E. Park and W. I. Thomas so notable. To try to catch the interpretative process by remaining aloof as a so-called "objective" observer and refusing to take the role of the acting unit is to risk the worst kind of subjectivism—the objective observer is likely to fill in the process of interpretation with his own sur-mises in place of catching the process as it occurs in the experience of the acting unit which uses it.

By and large, of course, sociologists do not study human society in terms of its acting units. Instead, they are disposed to view human society in terms of structure or organization and to treat social action as an expression of such structure or organization. Thus, reliance is placed on such structural categories as social system, culture, norms, values, social stratification, status positions, social roles and institutional organization. These are used both to analyze human society and to account for social action within it. Other major interests of sociological scholars center around this focal theme of organization. One line of interest is to view organization in terms of the functions it is supposed to perform. Another line of interest is to study societal organization as a system seeking equilibrium; here the scholar endeavors to detect mechanisms which are indigenous to the system. Another line of interest is to identify forces which play upon organization to bring about changes in it; here the scholar endeavors, especially through comparative study, to isolate a relation between causative factors and structural results. These various lines of sociological perspective and interest, which are so strongly entrenched today, leap over the acting units of a society and bypass the interpretative process by which such acting units build up their actions.

These respective concerns with organization on one hand and with acting units on the other hand set the essential difference between conventional views of human society and the view of it implied in symbolic interaction. The latter view recognizes the presence of organization in human society and respects its importance. However, it sees and treats organization differently. The difference is along two major lines. First, from the standpoint of symbolic interaction the organization of a human society is the framework inside of which social action takes place and is not the determinant of that action. Second, such organization and changes in it are the product of the activity of acting units and not of "forces" which leave such acting units out of account. Each of these two major lines of difference should be explained briefly in order to obtain a better understanding of how human society appears in terms of symbolic interaction.

From the standpoint of symbolic interaction, social organization is a framework inside of which acting units develop their actions. Structural features, such as "culture," "social systems," "social stratification," or "social roles," set conditions for their action but do not determine their action. People—that is, acting units—do not act toward culture, social structure or the like; they act toward situations. Social organization enters into action only to the extent to which it shapes situations in which people act, and to the extent to which it supplies fixed sets of symbols which people use in interpreting their situations. These two forms of influence of social organization are important. In the case of settled and stabilized societies, such as isolated primitive tribes and peasant communities, the influence is certain to be profound. In the case of human societies, particularly modern societies, in which streams of new situations arise and old situations become unstable, the influence of organization decreases. One should bear in mind that the most important element confronting an acting unit in situations is the actions of other acting units. In modern society, with its increasing criss-crossing of lines of action, it is common for situations to arise in which the actions of participants are not previously regularized and standardized. To this extent, existing social organization does not shape the situations. Correspondingly, the symbols or tools of interpretation used by acting units in such situations may vary and shift considerably. For these reasons, social action may go beyond, or depart from, existing organization in any of its structural dimensions. The organization of a human society is not to be identified with the process of interpretation used by its acting units; even though it affects that process, it does not embrace or cover the process.

Perhaps the most outstanding consequence of viewing human society as organization is to overlook the part played by acting units in social change. The conventional procedure of sociologists is *(a)* to identify human society (or some part of it) in terms of an established or organized form, *(b)* to identify some factor or condition of change playing upon the human society or the given part of it, and *(c)* to identify the new form assumed by the society following upon the play of the factor of change. Such observations permit the student to couch propositions to the effect that a given factor of change playing upon a given organization form results in a given new organized form. Examples ranging from crude to refined statements are legion, such as that an economic depression increases solidarity in the families of workingmen or that industrialization replaces extended families by nuclear families. My concern here is not with the validity of such propositions but with the methodological position which they presuppose. Essentially, such propositions either ignore the role of the interpretative behavior of acting units in the given instance of change, or else regard the interpretative behavior as coerced by the factor of change. I wish to point out that any line of social change, since it involves change in human action, is necessarily mediated by interpretation on the part of the people caught up in the change—the change appears in the form of new situations in which people have to construct new forms of action. Also, in line with what has been said previously, interpretations of new situations are not predetermined by conditions antecedent to the situations but depend on what is taken into account and assessed in the actual situations in which behavior is formed. Variations in interpretation may readily occur as different acting units cut out different objects in the situation, or give different weight to the objects which they note, or piece objects together in different patterns. In formulating propositions of social change, it would be wise to recognize that any given line of such change is mediated by acting units interpreting the situations with which they are confronted.

Students of human society will have to face the question of whether their preoccupation with categories of structure and organization can be squared with the interpretative process by means of which human beings, individually and collectively, act in human society. It is the discrepancy between the two which plagues such students in their efforts to attain scientific propositions of the sort achieved in the physical and biological sciences. It is this discrepancy, further, which is chiefly responsible for their difficulty in fitting hypothetical propositions to new arrays of empirical data. Efforts are made, of course, to overcome these shortcomings by devising new structural categories, by formulating new structural hypotheses, by developing more refined techniques of research, and even by formulating new methodological schemes of a structural character. These efforts continue to ignore or to explain away the interpretative process by which people act, individually and collectively, in society. The question remains whether human society or social action can be successfully analyzed by schemes which refuse to recognize human beings as they are, namely, as persons constructing individual and collective action through an interpretation of the situations which confront them.

ERVING GOFFMAN: THE PRESENTATION OF SELF IN EVERYDAY LIFE

The Framework

A social establishment is any place surrounded by fixed barriers to perception in which a particular kind of activity regularly takes place. I have suggested that any social establishment may be studied profitably from the point of view of impression management. Within the walls of a social establishment we find a team of performers who cooperate to present to an audience a given definition of the situation. This will include the conception of own team and of audience and assumptions concerning the ethos that is to be maintained by rules of politeness and decorum. We often find a division into back region, where the performance of a routine is prepared, and front region, where the performance is presented. Access to these regions is controlled in order to prevent the audience from seeing back-stage and to prevent outsiders from coming into a performance that is not addressed to them. Among members of the team we find that familiarity prevails, solidarity is likely to develop, and that secrets that could give the show away are shared and kept. A tacit agreement is maintained between performers and audience to act as if a given degree of opposition and of accord existed between them. Typically, but not always, agreement is stressed and opposition is underplayed. The resulting working consensus tends to be contradicted by the attitude toward the audience which the performers express in the absence of the audience and by carefully controlled communication out of character conveyed by the performers while the audience is present. We find that discrepant roles develop: some of the

individuals who are apparently teammates, or audience, or outsiders acquire information about the performance and relations to the team which are not apparent and which complicate the problem of putting on a show. Sometimes disruptions occur through unmeant gestures, faux pas, and scenes, thus discrediting or contradicting the definition of the situation that is being maintained. The mythology of the team will dwell upon these disruptive events. We find that performers, audience, and outsiders all utilize techniques for saving the show, whether by avoiding likely disruptions or by correcting for unavoided ones, or by making it possible for others to do so. To ensure that these techniques will be employed, the team will tend to select members who are loyal, disciplined, and circumspect, and to select an audience that is tactful.

These features and elements, then, comprise the framework I claim to be characteristic of much social interaction as it occurs in natural settings in our Anglo-American society. This framework is formal and abstract in the sense that it can be applied to any social establishment; it is not, however, merely a static classification. The framework bears upon dynamic issues created by the motivation to sustain a definition of the situation that has been projected before others.

The Analytical Context

This report has been chiefly concerned with social establishments as relatively closed systems. It has been assumed that the relation of one establishment to others is itself an intelligible area of study and ought to be treated analytically as part of a different order of fact—the order of institutional integration. It might be well here to try to place the perspective taken in this report in the context of other perspectives which seem to be the ones currently employed, implicitly or explicitly, in the study of social establishments as closed systems. Four such perspectives may be tentatively suggested.

An establishment may be viewed "technically," in terms of its efficiency and inefficiency as an intentionally organized system of activity for the achievement of predefined objectives. An establishment may be viewed "politically," in terms of the actions which each participant (or class of participants) can demand of other participants, the kinds of deprivations and indulgences which can be meted out in order to enforce these demands, and the kinds of social controls which guide this exercise of command and use of sanctions. An establishment may be viewed "structurally," in terms of the horizontal and vertical status divisions and the kinds of social relations which relate these several groupings to one another. Finally, an establishment may be viewed "culturally," in terms of the moral values which influence activity in the establishment—values pertaining to fashions, customs, and matters of taste, to politeness and decorum, to ultimate ends and normative restrictions on means, etc. It is to be noted that all the facts that can be discovered about an establishment are relevant to each of the four perspectives but that each perspective gives its own priority and order to these facts.

It seems to me that the dramaturgical approach may constitute a fifth perspective, to be added to the technical, political, structural, and cultural perspectives.[1] The dramaturgical perspective, like each of the other four, can be employed as the end-point of analysis, as a final way of ordering facts. This would lead us to describe the techniques of impression manage-

ment employed in a given establishment, the principal problems of impression management in the establishment, and the identity and inter-relationships of the several performance teams which operate in the establishment. But, as with the facts utilized in each of the other perspectives, the facts specifically pertaining to impression management also play a part in the matters that are a concern in all the other perspectives. It may be useful to illustrate this briefly.

The technical and dramaturgical perspectives intersect most clearly, perhaps, in regard to standards of work. Important for both perspectives is the fact that one set of individuals will be concerned with testing the unapparent characteristics and qualities of the work-accomplishments of another set of individuals, and this other set will be concerned with giving the impression that their work embodies these hidden attributes. The political and dramaturgical perspectives intersect clearly in regard to the capacities of one individual to direct the activity of another. For one thing, if an individual is to direct others, he will often find it useful to keep strategic secrets from them. Further, if one individual attempts to direct the activity of others by means of example, enlightenment, persuasion, exchange, manipulation, authority, threat, punishment, or coercion, it will be necessary, regardless of his power position, to convey effectively what he wants done, what he is prepared to do to get it done and what he will do if it is not done. Power of any kind must be clothed in effective means of displaying it, and will have different effects depending upon how it is dramatized. (Of course, the capacity to convey effectively a definition of the situation may be of little use if one is not in a position to give example, exchange, punishment, etc.) Thus the most objective form of naked power, i.e., physical coercion, is often neither objective nor naked but rather functions as a display for persuading the audience; it is often a means of communication, not merely a means of action. The structural and dramaturgical perspectives seem

---

[1] Compare the position taken by Oswald Hall in regard to possible perspectives for the study of closed systems in his "Methods and Techniques of Research in Human Relations" (April 1952), reported in E. C. Hughes *et al., Cases on Field Work* (forthcoming).

to intersect most clearly in regard to social distance. The image that one status grouping is able to maintain in the eyes of an audience of other status groupings will depend upon the performers' capacity to restrict communicative contact with the audience. The cultural and dramaturgical perspectives intersect most clearly in regard to the maintenance of moral standards. The cultural values of an establishment will determine in detail how the participants are to feel about many matters and at the same time establish a framework of appearances that must be maintained, whether or not there is feeling behind the appearances.

Personality-Interaction-Society

In recent years there have been elaborate attempts to bring into one framework the concepts and findings derived from three different areas of inquiry: the individual personality, social interaction, and society. I would like to suggest here a simple addition to these interdisciplinary attempts.

When an individual appears before others, he knowingly and unwittingly projects a definition of the situation, of which a conception of himself is an important part. When an event occurs which is expressively incompatible with this fostered impression, significant consequences are simultaneously felt in three levels of social reality, each of which involves a different point of reference and a different order of fact.

First, the social interaction, treated here as a dialogue between two teams, may come to an embarrassed and confused halt; the situation may cease to be defined, previous positions may become no longer tenable, and participants may find themselves without a charted course of action. The participants typically sense a false note in the situation and come to feel awkward, flustered, and, literally, out of countenance. In other words, the minute social system created and sustained by orderly social interaction

becomes disorganized. These are the consequences that the disruption has from the point of view of social interaction.

Second, in addition to these disorganizing consequences for action at the moment, performance disruptions may have consequences of a more far-reaching kind. Audiences tend to accept the self projected by the individual performer during any current performance as a responsible representative of his colleague-grouping, of his team, and of his social establishment. Audiences also accept the individual's particular performance as evidence of his capacity to perform the routine and even as evidence of his capacity to perform any routine. In a sense these larger social units—teams, establishments, etc.—become committed every time the individual performs his routine; with each performance the legitimacy of these units will tend to be tested anew and their permanent reputation put at stake. This kind of commitment is especially strong during some performances. Thus, when a surgeon and his nurse both turn from the operating table and the anesthetized patient accidentally rolls off the table to his death, not only is the operation disrupted in an embarrassing way, but the reputation of the doctor, as a doctor and as a man, and also the reputation of the hospital may be weakened. These are the consequences that disruptions may have from the point of view of social structure.

Finally, we often find that the individual may deeply involve his ego in his identification with a particular part establishment, and group, and in his self-conception as someone who does not disrupt social interaction or let down the social units which depend upon that interaction. When a disruption occurs, then, we may find that the self-conceptions around which his personality has been built may become discredited. These are consequences that disruptions may have from the point of view of individual personality.

Performance disruptions, then, have consequences at three levels of abstraction: personality, interaction, and social structure. While the likelihood of disruption will vary widely from interaction to interaction, and while the social importance of likely disruptions will vary from interaction to interaction, still it seems that there is no interaction in which the participants do not take an appreciable chance of being slightly embarrassed or a slight chance of being deeply humiliated. Life may not be much of a gamble, but interaction is. Further, in so far as individuals make efforts to avoid disruptions or to correct for ones not avoided, these efforts, too, will have simultaneous consequences at the three levels. Here, then, we have one simple way of articulating three levels of abstraction and three perspectives from which social life has been studied.

Comparisons and Study

In this report, use has been made of illustrations from societies other than our Anglo-American one. In doing this I did not mean to imply that the framework presented here is culture-free or applicable in the same areas of social life in non-Western societies as in our own. We lead an indoor social life. We specialize in fixed settings, in keeping strangers out, and in giving the performer some privacy in which to prepare himself for the show. Once we begin a performance, we are inclined to finish it, and we are sensitive to jarring notes which may occur during it. If we are caught out in a misrepresentation we feel deeply humiliated. Given our general dramaturgical rules and inclinations for conducting action, we must not overlook areas of life in other societies in which other rules are apparently followed. Reports by Western travelers are filled with instances in which their dramaturgical sense was offended or surprised, and if we are to generalize to other cultures we must consider these instances as well as more favorable ones. We must be ready to see in China that while actions and décor may be wonderfully harmonious and coherent in a private tearoom,

extremely elaborate meals may be served in extremely plain restaurants, and shops that look like hovels staffed with surly, familiar clerks may contain within their recesses, wrapped in old brown paper, wonderfully delicate bolts of silk.[2] And among a people said to be careful to save each other's face, we must be prepared to read that:

> Fortunately the Chinese do not believe in the privacy of a home as we do. They do not mind having the whole details of their daily experience seen by everyone that cares to look. How they live, what they eat, and even the family jars that we try to hush up from the public are things that seem to be common property, and not to belong exclusively to this particular family who are most concerned.[3]

And we must be prepared to see that in societies with settled inequalitarian status systems and strong religious orientations, individuals are sometimes less earnest about the whole civic drama than we are, and will cross social barriers with brief gestures that give more recognition to the man behind the mask than we might find permissible.

Furthermore, we must be very cautious in any effort to characterize our own society as a whole with respect to dramaturgical practices. For example, in current management-labor relations, we know that a team may enter joint consultation meetings with the opposition with the knowledge that it may be necessary to give the appearance of stalking out of the meeting in a huff. Diplomatic teams are sometimes required to stage a similar show. In other words, while teams in our society are usually obliged to suppress their rage behind a working consensus, there are times when teams are obliged to suppress the appearance of sober opposition behind a demonstration of outraged feelings. Similarly, there are occasions when individuals, whether

---

[2] Macgowan, *op. cit.,* pp. 178–79.
[3] *Ibid.,* pp. 180–81.

they wish to or not, will feel obliged to destroy an interaction in order to save their honor and their face. It would be more prudent, then, to begin with smaller units, with social establishments or classes of establishments, or with particular statuses, and document comparisons and changes in a modest way by means of the case-history method. For example, we have the following kind of information about the shows that businessmen are legally allowed to put on:

> The last half-century has seen a marked change in the attitude of the courts toward the question of justifiable reliance. Earlier decisions, under the influence of the prevalent doctrine of "caveat emptor," laid great stress upon the plaintiff's "duty" to protect himself and distrust his antagonist, and held that he was not entitled to rely even upon positive assertions of fact made by one with whom he was dealing at arms length. It was assumed that anyone may be expected to overreach another in a bargain if he can, and that only a fool will expect common honesty. Therefore the plaintiff must make a reasonable investigation, and form his own judgment. The recognition of a new standard of business ethics, demanding that statements of fact be at least honestly and carefully made, and in many cases that they be warranted to be true, has led to an almost complete shift in this point or view.

> It is now held that assertions of fact as to the quantity or quality of land or goods sold, the financial status of the corporations, and similar matters inducing commercial transactions, may justifiably be relied on without investigation, not only where such investigation would be burdensome and difficult, as where land which is sold lies at a distance, but likewise where the falsity of the representation might be discovered with little effort by means easily at hand.[4]

And while frankness may be increasing in business relations, we have some evidence that marriage counselors are increasingly agreed that an individual ought not to feel obliged to tell his or her spouse about previous "affairs," as this might only lead to needless strain. Other examples may be cited. We know, for example, that up to about 1830 pubs in Britain provided a backstage setting for workmen, little distinguishable from their own kitchens, and that after that date the gin palace suddenly burst upon the scene to provide much the same clientele with a fancier front region than they could dream of.[5] We have records of the social history of particular American towns, telling us of the recent decline in the elaborateness of domestic and avocational fronts of the local upper classes. In contrast, some material is available which describes the recent increase in elaborateness of the setting that union organizations employ,[6] and the increasing tendency to "stock" the setting with academically-trained experts who provide an aura of thought and respectability.[7] We can trace changes in the plant layout of specific industrial and commercial organizations and show an increase in front, both as regards the exterior of the head-office building and as regards the conference rooms, main halls, and waiting rooms of these buildings. We can trace in a particular crofting community how the barn for animals, once backstage to the kitchen and accessible by a small door next the stove, has lately been removed a distance from the house, and how the house itself, once set down in an unprotected way in the midst of garden, croft equipment, garbage, and grazing stock, is becoming, in a sense, public-relations oriented, with a front yard fenced off and kept somewhat clean, presenting a dressed-up side to the community

---

[4] Prosser, *op. cit.*, pp. 749–50.

[5] M. Gorham and H. Dunnett, *Inside the Pub* (London: the Architectural Press, 1950), pp. 23–24.
[6] See, for example, Hunter, *op. cit.*, p. 19.
[7] See Wilensky, *op. cit.*, chap. iv, for a discussion of the "window-dressing" function of staff experts. For reference to the business counterpart of this movement see Riesman, *op. cit.*, pp. 138–39.

while debris is strewn at random in the unfenced back regions. And as the connected byre disappears, and the scullery itself starts to become less frequent, we can observe the upgrading of domestic establishments, wherein the kitchen, which once possessed its own back regions, is now coming to be the least presentable region of the house while at the same time becoming more and more presentable. We can also trace that peculiar social movement which led some factories, ships, restaurants, and households to clean up their backstages to such an extent that, like monks, Communists, or German aldermen, their guards are always up and there is no place where their front is down, while at the same time members of the audience become sufficiently entranced with the society's id to explore the places that had been cleaned up for them. Paid attendance at symphony orchestra rehearsals is only one of the latest examples. We can observe what Everett Hughes calls collective mobility, through which the occupants of a status attempt to alter the bundle of tasks performed by them so that no act will be required which is expressively inconsistent with the image of self that these incumbents are attempting to establish for themselves. And we can observe a parallel process, which might be called "role enterprise," within a particular social establishment, whereby a particular member attempts not so much to move into a higher position already established as to create a new position for himself, a position involving duties which suitably express attributes that are congenial to him. We can examine the process of specialization, whereby many performers come to make brief communal use of very elaborate social settings, being content to sleep alone in a cubicle of no pretension. We can follow the diffusion of crucial fronts—such as the laboratory complex of glass, stainless steel, rubber gloves, white tile, and lab coat—which allow an increasing number of persons connected with unseemly tasks a way of self-purification. Starting with the

tendency in highly authoritarian organizations for one team to be required to spend its time infusing a rigorously ordered cleanliness in the setting the other team will perform in, we can trace, in establishments such as hospitals, air force bases, and large households, a current decline in the hypertrophic strictness of such settings. And finally, we can follow the rise and diffusion of the jazz and "West Coast" cultural patterns, in which terms such as bit, goof, scene, drag, dig, are given currency, allowing individuals to maintain something of a professional stage performer's relation to the technical aspects of daily performances.

The Role of Expression is Conveying Impressions of Self

Perhaps a moral note can be permitted at the end. In this report the expressive component of social life has been treated as a source of impressions given to or taken by others. Impression, in turn, has been treated as a source of information about unapparent facts and as a means by which the recipients can guide their response to the informant without having to wait for the full consequences of the informant's actions to be felt. Expression, then, has been treated in terms of the communicative role it plays during social interaction and not, for example, in terms of consummatory or tension-release function it might have for the expresser.[8]

Underlying all social interaction there seems to be a fundamental dialectic. When one individual enters the presence of others, he will want to discover the facts of the situation. Were he to possess this information, he could know, and make allowances for, what will come to

---

[8] A recent treatment of this kind may be found in Talcott Parsons, Robert F. Bales, and Edward A. Shils, *Working Papers in the Theory of Action* (Glencoe, Ill.: The Free Press, 1953), Chap. II, "The Theory of Symbolism in Relation to Action."

happen and he could give the others present as much of their due as is consistent with his enlightened self-interest. To uncover fully the factual nature of the situation, it would be necessary for the individual to know all the relevant social data about the others. It would also be necessary for the individual to know the actual outcome or end product of the activity of the others during the interaction, as well as their innermost feelings concerning him. Full information of this order is rarely available; in its absence, the individual tends to employ substitutes—cues, tests, hints, expressive gestures, status symbols, etc.—as predictive devices. In short, since the reality that the individual is concerned with is unperceivable at the moment, appearances must be relied upon in its stead. And, paradoxically, the more the individual is concerned with the reality that is not available to perception, the more must he concentrate his attention on appearances.

The individual tends to treat the others present on the basis of the impression they give now about the past and the future. It is here that communicative acts are translated into moral ones. The impressions that the others give tend to be treated as claims and promises they have implicitly made, and claims and promises tend to have a moral character. In his mind the individual says: "I am using these impressions of you as a way of checking up on you and your activity, and you ought not to lead me astray." The peculiar thing about this is that the individual tends to take this stand even though he expects the others to be unconscious of many of their expressive behaviors and even though he may expect to exploit the others on the basis of the information he gleans about them. Since the sources of impression used by the observing individual involve a multitude of standards pertaining to politeness and decorum, pertaining both to social intercourse and task-performance, we can appreciate afresh how daily life is enmeshed in moral lines of discrimination.

Let us shift now to the point of view of the others. If they are to be gentlemanly, and play the individual's game, they will give little conscious heed to the fact that impressions are being formed about them but rather act without guile or contrivance, enabling the individual to receive valid impressions about them and their efforts. And if they happen to give thought to the fact that they are being observed, they will not allow this to influence them unduly, content in the belief that the individual will obtain a correct impression and give them their due because of it. Should they be concerned with influencing the treatment that the individual gives them, and this is properly to be expected, then a gentlemanly means will be available to them. They need only guide their action in the present so that its future consequences will be the kind that would lead a just individual to treat them now in a way they want to be treated; once this is done, they have only to rely on the perceptiveness and justness of the individual who observes them.

Sometimes those who are observed do, of course, employ these proper means of influencing the way in which the observer treats them. But there is another way, a shorter and more efficient way, in which the observed can influence the observer. Instead of allowing an impression of their activity to arise as an incidental by-product of their activity, they can reorient their frame of reference and devote their efforts to the creation of desired impressions. Instead of attempting to achieve certain ends by acceptable means, they can attempt to achieve the impression that they are achieving certain ends by acceptable means. It is always possible to manipulate the impression the observer uses as a substitute for reality because a sign for the presence of a thing, not being that thing, can be employed in the absence of it. The observer's need to rely on representations of things itself creates the possibility of misrepresentation.

There are many sets of persons who feel they could not stay in business, whatever their business, if they limited themselves to the gentlemanly means of influencing the individual who observes them. At some point or other in the round of their activity they feel it is necessary to band together and directly manipulate the impression that they give. The observed become a performing team and the observers become the audience. Actions which appear to be done on objects become gestures addressed to the audience. The round of activity becomes dramatized.

We come now to the basic dialectic. In their capacity as performers, individuals will be concerned with maintaining the impression that they are living up to the many standards by which they and their products are judged. Because these standards are so numerous and so pervasive, the individuals who are performers dwell more than we might think in a moral world. But, *qua* performers, individuals are concerned not with the moral issue of realizing these standards, but with the amoral issue of engineering a convincing impression that these standards are being realized. Our activity, then, is largely concerned with moral matters, but as performers we do not have a moral concern with them. As performers we are merchants of morality. Our day is given over to intimate contact with the goods we display and our minds are filled with intimate understandings of them; but it may well be that the more attention we give to these goods, then the more distant we feel from them and from those who are believing enough to buy them. To use a different imagery, the very obligation and profitability of appearing always in a steady moral light, of being a socialized character, forces one to be the sort of person who is practiced in the ways of the stage.

Staging and the Self

The general notion that we make a presentation of ourselves to others is hardly novel; what ought to be stressed in conclusion is that the very structure of the self can be seen in terms of how we arrange for such performances in our Anglo-American society.

In this report, the individual was divided by implication into two basic parts: he was viewed as a *performer*, a harried fabricator of impressions involved in the all-too-human task of staging a performance; he was viewed as a *character*, a figure, typically a fine one, whose spirit, strength, and other sterling qualities the performance was designed to evoke. The attributes of a performer and the attributes of a character are of a different order, quite basically so, yet both sets have their meaning in terms of the show that must go on.

First, character. In our society the character one performs and one's self are somewhat equated, and this self-as-character is usually seen as something housed within the body of its possessor, especially the upper parts thereof, being a nodule, somehow, in the psychobiology of personality. I suggest that this view is an implied part of what we are all trying to present, but provides, just because of this, a bad analysis of the presentation. In this report the performed self was seen as some kind of image, usually creditable, which the individual on stage and in character effectively attempts to induce others to hold in regard to him. While this image is entertained *concerning* the individual, so that a self is imputed to him, this self itself does not derive from its possessor, but from the whole scene of his action, being generated by that attribute of local events which renders them interpretable by witnesses. A correctly staged and performed scene leads the audience to impute a self to a performed character, but this imputation—this self—is a *product* of a scene that comes off, and is not a *cause* of it. The self, then, as a performed character, is not an organic thing that has a specific location, whose fundamental fate is to be born, to mature, and to die; it is a dramatic effect arising diffusely from a scene that is presented, and the characteristic issue, the crucial concern, is whether it will be credited or discredited.

In analyzing the self then we are drawn from its possessor, from the person who will profit or lose most by it, for he and his body merely provide the peg on which something of collaborative manufacture will be hung for a time. And the means for producing and maintaining selves do not reside inside the peg; in fact these means are often bolted down in social establishments. There will be a back region with its tools for shaping the body, and a front region with its fixed props. There will be a team of persons whose activity on stage in conjunction with available props will constitute the scene from which the performed character's self will emerge, and another team, the audience, whose interpretive activity will be necessary for this emergence. The self is a product of all of these arrangements, and in all of its parts bears the marks of this genesis.

The whole machinery of self-production is cumbersome, of course, and sometimes breaks down, exposing its separate components: back region control; team collusion; audience tact; and so forth. But, well oiled, impressions will flow from it fast enough to put us in the grips of one of our types of reality—the performance will come off and the firm self accorded each performed character will appear to emanate intrinsically from its performer.

Let us turn now from the individual as character performed to the individual as performer. He has a capacity to learn, this being exercised in the task of training for a part. He is given to having fantasies and dreams, some that pleasurably unfold a triumphant performance, others full of anxiety and dread that nervously deal with vital discreditings in a public front region. He often manifests a gregarious desire for teammates and audiences, a tactful considerateness for their concerns; and he has a capacity for deeply felt shame, leading him to minimize the chances he takes of exposure.

These attributes of the individual *qua* performer are not merely a depicted effect of particular performances; they are psychobiological in nature, and yet they seem to arise out of intimate interaction with the contingencies of staging performances.

And now a final comment. In developing the conceptual framework employed in this report, some language of the stage was used. I spoke of performers and audiences; of routines and parts; of performances coming off or falling flat; of cues, stage settings and backstage; of dramaturgical needs, dramaturgical skills, and dramaturgical strategies. Now it should be admitted that this attempt to press a mere analogy so far was in part a rhetoric and a maneuver.

The claim that all the world's a stage is sufficiently commonplace for readers to be familiar with its limitations and tolerant of its presentation, knowing that at any time they will easily be able to demonstrate to themselves that it is not to be taken too seriously. An action staged in a theater is a relatively contrived illusion and an admitted one; unlike ordinary life, nothing real or actual can happen to the performed characters—although at another level of course something real and actual can happen to the reputation of performers *qua* professionals whose everyday job is to put on theatrical performances.

And so here the language and mask of the stage will be dropped. Scaffolds, after all, are to build other things with, and should be erected with an eye to taking them down. This report is not concerned with aspects of theater that creep into everyday life. It is concerned with the structure of social encounters—the structure of those entities in social life that come into being whenever persons enter one another's immediate physical presence. The key factor in this structure is the maintenance of a single definition of the situation, this definition having to be expressed, and this expression sustained in the face of a multitude of potential disruptions.

A character staged in a theater is not in some ways real, nor does it have the same kind of real consequences as does the thoroughly contrived character performed by a confidence man; but the *successful* staging of either of these types of false figures involves use of *real* techniques—the same techniques by which everyday persons sustain their real social situations. Those who conduct face to face interaction on a theater's stage must meet the key requirement of real situations; they must expressively sustain a definition of the situation: but this they do in circumstances that have facilitated their developing an apt terminology for the interactional tasks that all of us share.

Chapter 12

Feminist Theory

Introduction

Despite a substantial history of protest literature, feminism was not a strong or widespread movement until the 1960s, although a few periods of mobilization for the feminist cause existed, primarily around issues of suffrage and employment. Ideas of importance to women can be found in classical social theory (in Marx, Durkheim, Weber, and Simmel), but the issue of gender as a variable in the analyses of social phenomena came into its own with the advent of the contemporary women's movement.

Feminism draws on the work of early sociological and psychological theorists, most particularly Marx, Engels, and Freud. Reworking the ideas of these writers, contemporary feminists analyze gender differences, inequality, and oppression. The discussion of gender explores the ways in which men and women construct and perceive reality and social relations differently. Social psychological theories discuss gender differences in two ways. The phenomenological view sees the everyday experiences of the individual as defined by typifications which are maintained by the collective action of individuals and which ultimately shape the psyches of the actors. Socialization theory examines how sex roles and expectations of men and women are transmitted and internalized. In each instance, the argument is that one's embodiment affects how one comes to know the world.

Theories of gender inequality go beyond the definition of differences between men and women to explore economic and social inequalities. These theories assert that inequality is the result of social organization, not of biology. They reject biological differences as a significant cause of gender inequality and maintain that the way in which gender is esteemed or regarded as well as changes in women's disadvantaged situation are a political project to be realized by a social movement.

Liberal feminism finds sexism to be the fundamental attitude that causes gender inequality. Sexism, the prejudice and discrimination against women, legitimates the belief in biological predetermination of women's roles. Liberal feminists (e.g., Sylvia Hewlett and Cynthia Fuchs Epstein) believe that sexist attitudes disadvantage women through socialization into submissive gender roles. They argue that the role that women are forced to play—that of the emotional, sexual, and household servant—renders them mindless, dependent, and subconsciously depressed. Liberal feminists argue that this oppressive situation for women is not easily changed because of women's isolation in private households and exclusion from the public sphere.

Liberal feminism is popular in the United States and serves as a fundamental philosophy for the National Organization of Women (NOW). The goal for which the liberal feminists are striving is a society in which all individuals have the opportunity to realize their potential. To this end, liberal feminists seek changes in the social position of women through legal and political channels, an equalization of economic opportunities for women, changes in family structure, and an increase in individual awareness of and action against sexism.

Marxist feminists (e.g., Clare Burton and Nancy Hartsock) draw their inspiration from Marxist social theory and particularly from Engels' *The Origins of the Family, Private Property, and the State*, where it is argued that the status of women is not biologically determined but results from the economic system of ownership and private property. Contemporary Marxist feminist theory concentrates on gender relations within the class system in capitalist society. Women within the bourgeois and working classes serve indispensable functions in maintaining the capitalist system. Bourgeois women are not propertied but are kept by propertied men as possessions to perform services that perpetuate the class interests of the bourgeoisie. They produce the heirs to property and provide the emotional support, the nurturing family, and the sexual gratification for the men of property.

Working class women may be hired more cheaply than their male counterparts and provide recruits to the reserve army of labor. They are reproducers of the work force needed to sustain production in capitalist society and, in their roles as mothers, inculcate their children with the appropriate values that sustain class relations. Only a revolutionary restructuring of property relations would eliminate these conditions and allow women to take their place as equals in a democratic and communal system. Efforts to unite women across class lines are counterproductive in that they divide the working class and undermine its revolutionary potential in the destruction of capitalist property relations.

Radical feminists (e.g., Mary Daly and Catherine MacKinnon) view social institutions as tools of male domination which support patriarchy and the oppression of women. All associations of social groups are characterized by domination and submission, and this is especially apparent in gender associations. The system of patriarchy teaches women how to subjugate themselves and teaches men how to dominate, and this knowledge of sexist domination is carried over into other spheres. Radical feminists

believe that patriarchy is all-pervasive in our culture and in our social institutions and that violence, such as rape and domestic abuse, and more subtle means of control, such as beauty standards and emotional harassment, are symptoms of the ills of patriarchy. The solution to this subordination offered by the radical feminists is women's recognition of their strength and value, the unification of women regardless of differences, and the empowerment of women through organized efforts within institutions where patriarchical values prevail.

Socialist feminists (e.g., Alison Jaggar and Nancy Fraser) combine Marxian and radical feminism in an attempt at theoretical synthesis, breadth, and precision, and an explicit method for social analysis and change. Among those who call themselves socialist feminists, there are those who focus on capitalist patriarchy and those who wish to study domination in a wide range of contexts, including race, class, and gender, as well as forms of domination among nations in the world system. Although both types of socialist feminist theory have been greatly influenced by Marx, they depart from his emphasis on a linkage between materialism and production and seek to include consciousness and knowledge as important factors that shape and sustain structures of domination. Change can be achieved through increased consciousness of these structures and how they impact on social and individual levels and through the appropriate action to achieve the goals of the movement.

Dorothy Smith, whose latest work, *The Conceptual Practices of Power: A Feminist Sociology of Knowledge* (1990), is excerpted in the following pages, was born in Great Britain in 1926, received her degree from the University of London, and went on to complete a Ph.D. in sociology at the University of California at Berkeley in 1963. Since then, Smith has published several important works relating to questions in feminist social theory.

Smith asks the question, How would sociology look from a woman's standpoint? In doing so, she wishes to raise questions about the claims to objective knowledge that characterize mainstream sociology. What Smith argues is that all knowledge is knowledge from a particular standpoint and that what has been claimed as objective knowledge of society conceals a male bias. Moreover, as a discipline sociology functions within a larger social system with structures of economic and political power. Smith contends that this framework of power, whose domain assumptions are widely accepted within mainstream sociology, make it a discipline that shares a standpoint consonant with that of the prevailing network of power. In short, sociology is situated within a context and is not an objective discipline.

A central theme in Dorothy Smith's work is her theory of *bifurcation*. What she means to convey by that term is a conceptual distinction between the world as we experience it and the world as we come to know it through the conceptual frameworks that science invents. In formulating the problem in these terms, Smith is adopting the phenomenological perspective articulated by Alfred Schutz in his distinction between the scientific and the commonsense ways of knowing the world. Smith argues for a restructuring of the sociological method of inquiry so that the direct experience of women's reality, hitherto repressed, becomes an active and critical voice. In reading the excerpt, the reader may wish to ask about the meaning of the concept of "standpoint" and "bifurcation." If all knowledge is situated, then is all knowledge biased? Which women's voices are to be heard? Will they speak of their experiences with one voice or many, and with what consequences for a political movement?

Michele Barrett's article, "Words and Things: Materialism and Method in Contemporary Feminist Analysis," raises a number of important questions regarding new directions in feminist thought. Barrett's focus is on the shift away from "modernist" assumptions about social structure or material things that constitute the reality of social life to the "post-structuralist" emphasis on "words" or the ways in which our discourses create rather than reflect the meaning of social reality. These issues and the ways in which Barrett carefully analyzes them anticipate the discussions which follow in the next chapter on "Modernism and Post-Modernism."

According to Barrett, the feminist embrace of Foucault and other postmodern thinkers has moved research and discussion away from liberal and socialist formulations about patriarchy, sexism, male power and emancipation as objective conditions analyzed in the social sciences. Instead, it is personal narratives, reflecting differences among women, and concerns about identity and the formation of self, that define the new directions in feminist thought and find their support in the literary and humanities disciplines. This is the "paradigm shift" that interests Barrett, and its implications are the focus of her article.

What is at stake here is the question of how we are to know "social reality" and whether the methods of the social sciences or the humanities are best suited to the task. Furthermore, there are political and practical consequences that follow from each of these perspectives and the assumptions on which they are based. Ideals of equality and social justice emanate from the Enlightenment. In this view, reason and emancipation are seen as universal human values, as is the belief that rational inquiry in the social sciences empowers people to question authority, challenge dogma, and act politically and collectively. By contrast, the post-structuralists, or postmodernists, challenge these ideals on two grounds: (a) as discourses, these ideals arrogantly presuppose moral universal truths in the presence of vastly different multicultural experiences and perspectives, and (b) as discourses, these ideals of scientific method claim to discover rational and objective truths, while genealogical and other studies expose the hidden value assumptions and biases of purported scientific and objectives studies.

DOROTHY SMITH: WOMEN'S EXPERIENCE AS A RADICAL CRITIQUE OF SOCIOLOGY

Relations of Ruling and Objectified Knowledge

When I speak here of governing or ruling I mean something more general than the notion of government as political organization. I refer rather to that total complex of activities, differentiated into many spheres, by which our kind of society is ruled, managed, and administered. It includes what the business world calls *management*, it includes the professions, it includes government and the activities of those who are selecting, training, and indoctrinating those who will be its governors. The last includes those who provide and elaborate the procedures by which it is governed and develop methods for accounting for how it is done—namely, the business schools, the sociologists, the economists. These are the institutions through which we are ruled and through which we, and I emphasize this *we*, participate in ruling.

Sociology, then, I conceive as much more than a gloss on the enterprise that justifies and rationalizes it, and at the same time as much less than "science." The governing of our kind of society is done in abstract concepts and symbols, and sociology helps create them by transposing the actualities of people's lives and experience into the conceptual currency with which they can be governed.

Thus the relevances of sociology are organized in terms of a perspective on the world, a view from the top that takes for granted the

From *The Conceptual Practices of Power: A Feminist Sociology of Knowledge* by Dorothy E. Smith. Copyright © 1990 by Dorothy E. Smith. Reprinted with the permission of Northeastern University Press.

pragmatic procedures of governing as those that frame and identify its subject matter. Issues are formulated because they are administratively relevant, not because they are significant first in the experience of those who live them. The kinds of facts and events that matter to sociologists have already been shaped and given their character and substance by the methods and practice of governing. Mental illness, crimes, riots, violence, work satisfaction, neighbors and neighborhoods, motivation, and so on—these are the constructs of the practice of government. Many of these constructs, such as mental illness, crimes, or neighborhoods, are constituted as discrete phenomena in the institutional contexts of ruling; others arise as problems in relation to the actual practice of government or management (for example, concepts of violence, motivation, or work satisfaction).

The governing processes of our society are organized as social entities external to those persons who participate in and perform them. Sociologists study these entities under the heading of formal organization. They are objectified structures with goals, activities, obligations, and so on, separate from those of the persons who work for them. The academic professions are similarly constituted. Members of a discipline accumulate knowledge that is then appropriated by the discipline as its own. The work of members aims at contributing to that body of knowledge.

As graduate students learning to become sociologists, we learn to think sociology as it is thought and to practice it as it is practiced. We learn that some topics are relevant and others are not. We learn to discard our personal experience as a source of reliable information about the character of the world and to confine and focus our insights within the conceptual frameworks and relevances of the discipline. Should we think other kinds of thoughts or experience the world in a different way or with horizons that pass beyond the conceptual, we must discard them or find some way to sneak them in. We learn a way of thinking about the world that is recognizable to its practitioners as the sociological way of thinking.

We learn to practice the sociological subsumption of the actualities of ourselves and of other people. We find out how to treat the world as instances of a sociological body of knowledge. The procedure operates as a sort of conceptual imperialism. When we write a thesis or a paper, we learn that the first thing to do is to latch it on to the discipline at some point. This may be by showing how it is a problem within an existing theoretical and conceptual framework. The boundaries of inquiry are thus set within the framework of what is already established. Even when this becomes, as it happily often does, a ceremonial authorization of a project that has little to do with the theory used to authorize it, we still work within the vocabularies and within the conceptual boundaries of "the sociological perspective."

An important set of procedures that serve to separate the discipline's body of knowledge from its practitioners is known as *objectivity*. The ethic of objectivity and the methods used in its practice are concerned primarily with the separation of knowers from what they know and in particular with the separation of what is known from knowers' interests, "biases," and so forth, that are not authorized by the discipline. In the social sciences the pursuit of objectivity makes it possible for people to be paid to pursue a knowledge to which they are otherwise indifferent. What they feel and think about society can be kept out of what they are professionally or academically interested in. Correlatively, if they are interested in exploring a topic sociologically, they must find ways of converting their private interest into an objectified, unbiased form.

Sociology Participates in the Extralocal Relations of Ruling

Sociologists, when they go to work, enter into the conceptually ordered society they are investigating. They observe, analyze, explain, and examine that world as if there were no problem in how it becomes observable to them. They move among the doings of organizations, governmental processes, and bureaucracies as people who are at home in that medium. The nature of that world itself, how it is known to them, the conditions of its existence, and their relation to it are not called into question. Their methods of observation and inquiry extend into it as procedures that are essentially of the same order as those that bring about the phenomena they are concerned with. Their perspectives and interests may differ, but the substance is the same. They work with facts and information that have been worked up from actualities and appear in the form of documents that are themselves the product of organizational processes, whether their own or those of some other agency. They fit that information back into a framework of entities and organizational processes which they take for granted as known, without asking how it is that they know them or by what social processes the actual events—what people do or utter—are construed as the phenomena known.

Where a traditional gender division of labor prevails, men enter the conceptually organized world of governing without a sense of transition. The male sociologist in these circumstances passes beyond his particular and immediate setting (the office he writes in, the libraries he consults, the streets he travels, the home he returns to) without attending to the shift in consciousness. He works in the very medium he studies.

But, of course, like everyone else, he also exists in the body in the place in which it is. This is also then the place of his sensory organization of immediate experience; the place where his coordinates of here and now, before and after, are organized around himself as center; the place where he confronts people face to face in the physical mode in which he expresses himself to them and they to him as more and other than either can speak. This is the place where things smell, where the irrelevant birds fly away in front of the window, where he has indigestion, where he dies. Into this space must come as actual material events—whether as sounds of speech, scratchings on the surface of paper, which he constitutes as text, or directly—anything he knows of the world. It has to happen here somehow if he is to experience it at all.

Entering the governing mode of our kind of society lifts actors out of the immediate, local, and particular place in which we are in the body. What becomes present to us in the governing mode is a means of passing beyond the local into the conceptual order. This mode of governing creates, at least potentially, a bifurcation of consciousness. It establishes two modes of knowing and experiencing and doing, one located in the body and in the space it occupies and moves in, the other passing beyond it. Sociology is written in and aims at the latter mode of action. Robert Bierstedt writes, "Sociology can liberate the mind from time and space themselves and remove it to a new and transcendental realm where it no longer depends upon these Aristotelian categories."[1] Even observational work aims at description in the categories and hence conceptual forms of the "transcendental realm." Yet the local and particular site of knowing that is the other side of the bifurcated consciousness has not been a site for the development of systematic knowledge.

Women's Exclusion from the Governing Conceptual Mode

The suppression of the local and particular as a site of knowledge has been and remains gender organized. The domestic sites of women's work, traditionally identified with women, are outside and subservient to this structure. Men have functioned as subjects in the mode of governing; women have been anchored in the local and particular phase of the bifurcated world. It has been a condition of a man's being able to enter and become absorbed in the conceptual mode, and to forget the dependence of his being in that mode upon his bodily existence, that he does not have to focus his activities and interests upon his bodily existence. Full participation in the abstract mode of action requires liberation from attending to needs in the concrete and particular. The organization of work in managerial and professional circles depends upon the alienation of subjects from their bodily and local existence. The structure of work and the structure of career take for granted that these matters have been provided for in such a way that they will not interfere with a man's action and participation in that world. Under the traditional gender regime, providing for a man's liberation from Bierstedt's Aristotelian categories is a woman who keeps house for him, bears and cares for his children, washes his clothes, looks after him when he is sick, and generally provides for the logistics of his bodily existence.

Women's work in and around professional and managerial settings performs analogous functions. Women's work mediates between the abstracted and conceptual and the material form in which it must travel to communicate. Women do the clerical work, the word processing, the interviewing for the survey; they take messages, handle the mail, make appointments, and care for patients. At almost every point women mediate for men at work the relationship between the conceptual mode of action and the actual concrete forms in which it is and must be realized, and the actual material conditions upon which it depends.

Marx's concept of alienation is applicable here in a modified form. The simplest formulation of alienation posits a relation between the work individuals do and an external order oppressing them in which their work contributes to the strength of the order that oppresses them. This is the situation of women in this relation. The more successful women are in mediating the world of concrete particulars so that men do not have to become engaged with (and therefore conscious of) that world as a condition to their abstract activities, the more complete men's absorption in it and the more effective its authority. The dichotomy between the two worlds organized on the basis of gender separates the dual forms of consciousness; the governing consciousness dominates the primary world of a locally situated consciousness but cannot cancel it; the latter is a subordinated, suppressed, absent, but absolutely essential ground of the governing consciousness. The gendered organization of subjectivity dichotomizes the two worlds, estranges them, and silences the locally situated consciousness by silencing women.

Women Sociologists and the Contradiction Between Sociology and Experience

Bifurcation of consciousness is experienced as women move between these two modes with a working consciousness active in both. We are situated as sociologists across a contradiction in our discipline's relationship to our experience of the world. Traditional gender roles deny the existence of the contradiction; suppression makes it invisible, as it has made other contradictions between women and men invisible. Recognizing, exploring, and working within it means finding alternative ways of thinking and inquiry to those that would implicate us in the sociological practice of the relations of ruling.

The theories, concepts, and methods of our discipline claim to be capable of accounting for the world we experience directly. But they have been organized around and built up from a way of knowing the world that takes for granted and subsumes without examining the conditions of its own existence. It is not capable of analyzing

its relation to its conditions because the sociological subject as an actual person in an actual concrete setting has been canceled in the procedures that objectify and separate her from her knowledge. Thus the linkage that points back to its conditions is obliterated.

For women those conditions are a direct practical problem to be somehow solved in doing sociological work and following a sociological career. How are we to manage career and children (including of course negotiating sharing that work with a man)? How is domestic work to get done? How is career time to be coordinated with family caring time? How is the remorseless structure of the children's school schedule to be coordinated with the equally exigent scheduling of professional and managerial work? Rarely are these problems solved by the full sharing of responsibilities between women and men. But for the most part these claims, these calls, these somehow unavoidable demands, are still ongoingly present and pressing for women, particularly, of course, for those with children. Thus the relation between ourselves as practicing sociologists and ourselves as working women is always there for us as a practical matter, an ordinary, unremarked, yet pervasive aspect of our experience of the world. The bifurcation of consciousness becomes for us a daily chasm to be crossed, on the one side of which is this special conceptual activity of thought, research, teaching, and administration, and on the other the world of localized activities oriented toward particular others, keeping things clean, managing somehow the house and household and the children—a world in which the particularities of persons in their full organic immediacy (feeding, cleaning up the vomit, changing the diapers) are inescapable. Even if this isn't something that currently preoccupies us, as it no longer preoccupies me, our present is given shape by a past that was thus.

We have learned, as women in sociology, that the discipline has not been one that we could enter and occupy on the same terms as men. We do not fully appropriate its authority, that is, the right to author and authorize the acts of knowing and thinking that are the knowing and thinking of the discipline. Feminist theory in sociology is still *feminist* theory and not just plain sociological theory. The inner principles of our theoretical work remain lodged outside us. The frames of reference that order the terms upon which inquiry and discussion are conducted have originated with men. The subjects of sociological sentences (if they have a subject) are still male, even though protocol now calls for a degendering of pronouns. Even before we became conscious of our sex as the basis of an exclusion (they have not been talking about us), we nonetheless could not fully enter ourselves as the subjects of its statements. The problem remains; we must suspend our sex and suspend our knowledge of who we are as well as who it is that in fact is speaking and of whom. Even now, we do not fully participate in the declarations and formulations of its mode of consciousness. The externalization of sociology as a profession is for women an estrangement both in suppressing dimensions of our experience as women and in creating for our use systems of interpreting and understanding our society that enforce that suppression.

Women who move between these two worlds have access to an experience that displays for us the structure of the bifurcated consciousness. For those of us who are sociologists, it undermines our commitment to a sociology aimed at an externalized body of knowledge based on an organization of experience that excludes ours.

Knowing a Society from within: A Woman's Perspective

An alternative sociological approach must somehow transcend this contradiction without reentering Bierstedt's "transcendental realm."

Women's standpoint, as I am analyzing it here, discredits sociology's claim to constitute an objective knowledge independent of the sociologist's situation. Sociology's conceptual procedures, methods, and relevances organize its subject matter from a determinate position in society. This critical disclosure is the basis of an alternative way of thinking sociology. If sociology cannot avoid being situated, then it should take that as its beginning and build it into its methodological and theoretical strategies. As it is now, these strategies separate a sociologically constructed world from that of direct experience; it is precisely that separation that must be undone.

I am not proposing an immediate and radical transformation of the subject matter and methods of the discipline nor the junking of everything that has gone before. What I am suggesting is more in the nature of a reorganization of the relationship of sociologists to the object of our knowledge and of our problematic. This reorganization involves first placing sociologists where we are actually situated, namely, at the beginning of those acts by which we know or will come to know, and second, making our direct embodied experience of the everyday world the primary ground of our knowledge.

A sociology worked on in this way would not have as its objective a body of knowledge subsisting in and of itself; inquiry would not be justified by its contribution to the heaping up of such a body. We would reject a sociology aimed primarily at itself. We would not be interested in contributing to a body of knowledge whose uses are articulated to relations of ruling in which women participate only marginally, if at all. The professional sociologist is trained to think in the objectified modes of sociological discourse, to think sociology as it has been and is thought; that training and practice has to be discarded. Rather, as sociologists we would be constrained by the actualities of how things come about in people's direct experience, including our own. A sociology for women would offer a knowledge of the social organization and determinations of the properties and events of our directly experienced world.[2] Its analyses would become part of our ordinary interpretations of the experienced world, just as our experience of the sun's sinking below the horizon is transformed by our knowledge that the world turns away from a sun that seems to sink.

The only way of knowing a socially constructed world is knowing it from within. We can never stand outside it. A relation in which sociological phenomena are objectified and presented as external to and independent of the observer is itself a special social practice also known from within. The relation of observer and object of observation, of sociologist to "subject," is a specialized social relationship. Even to be a stranger is to enter a world constituted from within as strange. The strangeness itself is the mode in which it is experienced.

When Jean Briggs[3] made her ethnographic study of the ways in which an Eskimo people structure and express emotion, what she learned emerged for her in the context of the actual developing relations between her and the family with whom she lived and other members of the group. Her account situates her knowledge in the context of those relationships and in the actual sites in which the work of family subsistence was done. Affections, tensions, and quarrels, in some of which she was implicated, were the living texture in which she learned what she describes. She makes it clear how this context structured her learning and how what she learned and can speak of became observable to her.

Briggs tells us what is normally discarded in the anthropological or sociological telling. Although sociological inquiry is necessarily a social relation, we have learned to dissociate our own part in it. We recover only the object of our knowledge as if it stood all by itself. Sociology does not provide for seeing that there are always two terms to this relation. An alternative sociology must preserve in it the presence, concerns, and experience of the sociologist as knower and discoverer.

To begin from direct experience and to return to it as a constraint or "test" of the adequacy of a systematic knowledge is to begin from where we are located bodily. The actualities of our everyday world are already socially organized. Settings, equipment, environment, schedules, occasions, and so forth, as well as our enterprises and routines, are socially produced and concretely and symbolically organized prior to the moment at which we enter and at which inquiry begins. By taking up a standpoint in our original and immediate knowledge of the world, sociologists can make their discipline's socially organized properties first observable and then problematic.

When I speak of *experience* I do not use the term as a synonym for *perspective*. Nor in proposing a sociology grounded in the sociologist's actual experience am I recommending the self-indulgence of inner exploration or any other enterprise with self as sole focus and object. Such subjectivist interpretations of *experience* are themselves an aspect of that organization of consciousness that suppresses the locally situated side of the bifurcated consciousness and transports us straight into mind country, stashing away the concrete conditions and practices upon which it depends. We can never escape the circles of our own heads if we accept that as our territory. Rather, sociologists' investigation of our directly experienced world as a problem is a mode of discovering or rediscovering the society from within. We begin from our own original but tacit knowledge and from within the acts by which we bring it into our grasp in making it observable and in understanding how it works. We aim not at a reiteration of what we already (tacitly) know, but at an exploration of what passes beyond that knowledge and is deeply implicated in how it is.

Sociology as Structuring Relations Between Subject and Object

Our knowledge of the world is given to us in the modes by which we enter into relations with the object of knowledge. But in this case the object of our knowledge is or originates in the co-ordering of activities among "subjects." The constitution of an objective sociology as an authoritative version of how things are is done from a position in and as part of the practices of ruling in our kind of society. Our training as sociologists teaches us to ignore the uneasiness at the junctures where multiple and diverse experiences are transformed into objectified forms. That juncture shows in the ordinary problems respondents have of fitting their experience of the world to the questions in the interview schedule. The sociologist who is a woman finds it hard to preserve this exclusion, for she discovers, if she will, precisely that uneasiness in her relation to her discipline as a whole. The persistence of the privileged sociological version (or versions) relies upon a substructure that has already discredited and deprived of authority to speak the voices of those who know the society differently. The objectivity of a sociological version depends upon a special relationship with others that makes it easy for sociologists to remain outside the others' experience and does not require them to recognize that experience as a valid contention.

Riding a train not long ago in Ontario I saw a family of Indians—woman, man, and three children—standing together on a spur above a river watching the train go by. I realized that I could tell this incident—the train, those five people seen on the other side of the glass—as it was, but that my description was built on my position and my interpretations. I have called them "Indians" and a family; I have said they were watching the train. My understanding has already subsumed theirs. Everything may have been quite different for them. My description is privileged to stand as what actually happened because theirs is not heard in the contexts in which I may speak. If we begin from the world as we actually experience it, it is at least possible to see that we are indeed located and that what we know of the other is conditional upon that location. There are and must be different experiences of the world and different bases of experience. We must not do away with them by taking advantage of our privileged speaking to construct a sociological version that we then impose upon them as their reality. We may not rewrite the other's world or impose upon it a conceptual framework that extracts from it what fits with ours. Their reality, their varieties of experience, must be an unconditional datum. It is the place from which inquiry begins.

A Bifurcation of Consciousness

My experience in the train epitomizes a sociological relation. I am already separated from the world as it is experienced by those I observe. That separation is fundamental to the character of that experience. Once I become aware of how my world is put together as a practical everyday matter and of how my relations are shaped by its concrete conditions (even in so simple a matter as that I am sitting in the train and it travels, but those people standing on the spur do not), I am led into the discovery that I cannot understand the nature of my experienced world by staying within its ordinary boundaries of assumption and knowledge. To account for that moment on the train and for the relation between the two experiences (or more) and the two positions from which those experiences begin I must posit a larger socioeconomic order in back of that moment. The coming together that makes the observation possible as well as how we were separated and drawn apart as well as how I now make use of that here—these properties are determined elsewhere than in that relation itself.

Furthermore, how our knowledge of the world is mediated to us becomes a problem of knowing how that world is organized for us prior to our participation in it. As intellectuals we ordinarily receive it as a media world, a world of texts, images, journals, books, talk, and other symbolic modes. We discard as an essential focus of our practice other ways of knowing. Accounting for that mode of knowing and the social organization that sets it up for us again leads us back into an analysis of the total socioeconomic order of which it is part. Inquiry remaining within the circumscriptions of the directly experienced cannot explore and explicate the relations organizing the everyday matrices of direct experience.

If we address the problem of the conditions as well as the perceived forms and organization of immediate experience, we should include in it the events as they actually happen and the ordinary material world we encounter as a matter of fact: the urban renewal project that uproots four hundred families; how it is to live on welfare as an ordinary daily practice; cities as the actual physical structures in which we move; the organization of academic occasions such as that in which this chapter originated. When we examine them, we find that there are many aspects of how these things come about of which we, as sociologists, have little to say. We have a sense that the events entering our experience originate somewhere in a human intention, but we are unable to track back to find it and to find out how it got from there to here.

Or take this room in which I work or that room in which you are reading and treat that as a problem. If we think about the conditions of our activity here, we can trace how these chairs, this table, the walls, our clothing, our presence come to be here; how these places (yours and mine) are cleaned and maintained; and so forth. There are human activities, intentions, and relations that are not apparent as such in the actual material conditions of our work. The social organization of the setting is not wholly available

to us in its appearance. We bypass in the immediacy of the specific practical activity a complex division of labor that is an essential precondition to it. Such preconditions are fundamentally mysterious to us and present us with problems in grasping social relations with which sociology is ill equipped to deal. We experience the world as largely incomprehensible beyond the limits of what we know in a common sense. No amount of observation of face-to-face relations, no amount of commonsense knowledge of everyday life, will take us beyond our essential ignorance of how it is put together. Our direct experience of it makes it (if we will) a problem, but it does not offer any answers. We experience a world of "appearances," the determinations of which lie beyond it.

We might think of the appearances of our direct experience as a multiplicity of surfaces, the properties and relations among which are generated by social organizations not observable in their effects. The relations underlying and generating the characteristics of our own directly experienced world bring us into unseen relations with others. Their experience is necessarily different from ours. If we would begin from our experienced world and attempt to analyze and account for how it is, we must posit others whose experience is not the same as ours.

Women's situation in sociology discloses to us a typical bifurcate structure with the abstracted, conceptual practices on the one hand and the concrete realizations, the maintenance routines, and so forth, on the other. Taking each for granted depends upon being fully situated in one or the other so that the other does not appear in contradiction to it. Women's direct experience places us a step back, where we can recognize the uneasiness that comes from sociology's claim to be about the world we live in, and, at the same time, its failure to account for or even describe the actual features we experience. Yet we cannot find the inner principle of our own activity through exploring what is directly experienced. We do not see how it is put together because it is determined elsewhere. The very organization of the world that has been assigned to us as the primary locus of our being, shaping other projects and desires, is determined by and subordinate to the relations of society founded in a capitalist mode of production. The aim of an alternative sociology would be to explore and unfold the relations beyond our direct experience that shape and determine it. An alternative sociology would be a means to anyone of understanding how the world comes about for us and how it is organized so that it happens to us as it does in our experience. An alternative sociology, from the standpoint of women, makes the everyday world its problematic.

The Standpoint of Women as a Place to Start

The standpoint of women situates the inquirer in the site of her bodily existence and in the local actualities of her working world. It is a standpoint that positions inquiry but has no specific content. Those who undertake inquiry from this standpoint begin always from women's experience as it is for women. We are the authoritative speakers of our experience. The standpoint of women situates the sociological subject prior to the entry into the abstracted conceptual mode, vested in texts, that is the order of the relations of ruling. From this standpoint, we know the everyday world through the particularities of our local practices and activities, in the actual places of our work and the actual time it takes. In making the everyday world problematic we also problematize the everyday localized practices of the objectified forms of knowledge organizing our everyday worlds.

A bifurcated consciousness is an effect of the actual social relations in which we participate as part of a daily work life. Entry as subject into the social relations of an objectified consciousness is itself an organization of actual everyday practices. The sociology that objectifies society and social relations and transforms the actualities of people's experience into the synthetic objects of its discourse is an organization of actual practices and activities. We know and use practices of thinking and inquiring sociologically that sever our knowledge of society from the society we know as we live and practice it. The conceptual practices of an alienated knowledge of society are also in and of the everyday world. In and through its conceptual practices and its everyday practices of reading and writing, we enter a mode of consciousness outside the everyday site of our bodily existence and experiencing. The standpoint of women, or at least, *this* standpoint of women at work, in the traditional ways women have worked and continue to work, exposes the alienated knowledge of the relations of ruling as the everyday practices of actual individuals. Thus, though an alienated knowledge also alienates others who are not members of the dominant white male minority, the standpoint of women distinctively opens up for exploration the conceptual practices and activities of the extralocal, objectified relations of ruling as what actual people do.

NOTES

1. Robert Bierstedt, "Sociology and general education," in *Sociology and contemporary education,* ed. Charles H. Page (New York: Random House, 1966).

2. Dorothy E. Smith, *The everyday world as problematic: A feminist sociology* (Boston: Northeastern University Press, 1987).

3. Jean Briggs, *Never in anger* (Cambridge: Harvard University Press, 1970).

MICHÈLE BARRETT: WORDS AND THINGS: MATERIALISM AND METHOD IN CONTEMPORARY FEMINIST ANALYSIS

Introduction: Dispensing with 'Things'

What, in short, we wish to do is to dispense with 'things' . . . To substitute for the enigmatic treasure of 'things' anterior to discourse, the regular formation of objects that emerge only in discourse.

(MICHAEL FOUCAULT)

The ambition to dispense with 'things'—and to value 'words' more—has caused some general perplexity and irritation. Many feminists, in particular, have traditionally tended to see 'things'—be they low pay, rape or female foeticide—as more significant than, for example, the discursive construction of marginality in a text or document. In this essay I want to explore how the issue of the relative status of things and words has become a central one in contemporary social theory and philosophy, and why feminists have a particularly strong investment in this question.

Where has this movement of ideas come from? One source would be the group of thinkers and theories often loosely referred to as 'post-structuralism'. In many ways this is a very unsatisfactory label, lumping together a diverse and often contradictory group of ideas on the specious basis of what preceded them in a chronology of Parisian thought. Yet the key thinkers of 'post-structuralism'—Derrida, Foucault and Lacan—have, in combination as well

Michéle Barrett and Anne Phillips (eds.), *Destabilizing Theory: Contemporary Feminist Debates.* Reprinted with permission from Stanford University Press, www.sup.org. Collection and Introduction copyright 1992 Michéle Barrett and Anne Phillips. Each chapter copyright the author.

as individually, mounted a devastating critique of the main assumptions on which much social and feminist theory was previously based, and it has proved to be a critique from which neither has emerged unscathed. In social science generally, such unexceptionable concepts as 'social structure', 'role', 'individual' or 'labour market' have become contentious in terms of what they assume about a social totality or infrastructure, or the presumed characteristics of social actors. In cultural theory and the humanities, the critical assumptions about authors, readers and, most important of all, the 'human subject' as such have come under fundamental scrutiny. Contemporary western feminism, confident for several years about its 'sex–gender distinction', analysis of 'patriarchy' or postulation of 'the male gaze' has found all of these various categories radically undermined by the new 'deconstructive' emphasis on fluidity and contingency. These uncertainties of terminology are the effect of the popularization of some central themes, however distorted, of the work of Derrida, Lacan and Foucault.

Post-structuralism

These post-structuralists offer a critique of both mainstream liberal social theory and philosophy (including psychology, political science and so on), but a perhaps more intimate blow to the working assumptions of Marxist and radical thought. In particular, the claims of materialism—the doctrine seeing consciousness as dependent on matter and the more general assumption that economic relations are dominant—have been decimated. The 'words and things' quotation from Foucault aptly illustrates this point. It is not that Foucault wished to dispense with things altogether: he was not 'denying reality' or some such inanity. But Foucault challenged the familiar hierarchy of value of the materialist perspective, counterposing the 'dumb existence of a reality' with the ability of groups of signs (discourses) to act as 'practices that systematically form the objects of which they speak'.[1] This critique of the importance ascribed to matter, and the corresponding insistence that the importance of meaning has gone unrecognized, has—where it has been heard had far-ranging effects.

A second thesis worth noting is post-structuralism's challenge to assumptions about causality. The problem of causality is here linked to criticisms of teleological thought and the retrospective assignation of epistemological power to the past. Thus in both Derrida and Foucault we find an extended critique of the search for the origin, for the founding moment that will explain everything. For feminism, which has from time to time been preoccupied with the question of the origins or cause of women's oppression, any side-stepping of the question of cause is both momentous and contentious. Echoes of the critique of an originary, founding cause can also be found in contemporary understanding of Lacan. Instead of the search for a 'real event' in the psychic past that would explain the causes of neurosis or pathology, one looks for meaning to the ongoing inner representation of experience, with current repetitions being seen as more significant than any 'original' moment.

A third element of 'post-structuralism' with an obvious and crucial bearing on the words/things relationship is the approach taken to language. The working assumption about language in social and feminist theory tended to be that language was a vehicle for the expression of ideas. This is most easily illustrated in the issue of translation. Somebody writes a book containing various ideas and propositions, and this can unproblematically be rendered as the 'same book' in another language. If this is a caricature of the innocent pre-post-structuralist view, it was none the less a commonly assumed

one in both social and feminist theory until recently. The Saussurian revolution has, at the very least, knocked out this view of language as merely a vehicle of expression, and the attribution to language itself of the power to construct rather than simply convey meaning has been growing. This can be seen in a variety of different ways, some relatively theoretical and others more pragmatic. Roland Barthes opened up this question in relation to varying degrees of 'writerliness' in texts, and his work has made it clear that—to take one example—the classical French ideal of *clarté* (lucidity) was one of various available writing styles. Clarity is a discursive *style* rather than an essential attribute of an author or a text.[2] Central to this view of language is the understanding that meaning is constructed, within language, through a process of differentiation. Meaning is not absolute or fixed in relation to a referent, but is arbitrary in that respect. Meaning is constructed through the counterposition of differing elements, whose definition lies precisely in their difference from each other.

People have accepted to varying degrees the view that meaning is constructed in rather than expressed by language. The strong position has been taken by Jacques Derrida for whom, logically, there can be no such thing as a 'summary' or a 'translation'. Each new text will construct meaning from its constituent elements in a different way and will not be a vehicle—it will be no more and no less than another text. Another influential approach is that of Michel Foucault, for whom the central question was 'What can be said?' The Foucauldian concept of discourse allows us to think about the epistemological power of discursive regimes and how important it is to understand what can be articulated when. As Foucault put it himself: 'It's a problem of verbalisation.'[3] The implications of these views are obviously far-reaching. Before discussing them, however, I want to indicate another, and related aspect of the relationship of 'words and things', and this is one within feminism.

Feminism's Own Turn to Culture

In the past ten years we have seen an extensive 'turn to culture' in feminism.[4] Academically, the social sciences have lost their purchase within feminism and the rising star lies with the arts, humanities and philosophy. Within this general shift we can see a marked interest in analyzing processes of symbolization and representation—the field of 'culture'—and attempts to develop a better understanding of subjectivity, the psyche and the self. The type of feminist sociology that has a wider audience, for example, has shifted away from a determinist model of 'social structure' (be it capitalism, or patriarchy, or a gender-segmented labour market or whatever) and deals with questions of culture, sexuality or political agency—obvious counterbalances to an emphasis on social structure.

Such academic developments are part of a much more general shift within feminism, at least in Britain and in Europe generally. In publishing, for instance, the sales of fiction have rocketed and non-fiction plummeted. Feminism sells beset as fiction, and attempts to write and market modern versions of the classic feminist non-fiction blockbusters have been notably unsuccessful. Interestingly, too, feminist cultural commentary and discussion has often tended to draw on the pleasures of fiction: the things we want to write and read about are romance, crime, melodrama and so on.

These developments raise some complex questions, not least that of the disillusionment and critique that presaged this new direction. In this chapter I shall not explore the political why or the historical when of these changes, although these are highly significant questions. I want to focus instead on the implications, and on the issues at stake, in this move from one cluster of disciplines to another. At the outset, I would suggest that it will not be adequate simply to shift attention in one direction rather than another, or even to apply the critical tools of one discipline to another's traditional subject matter (the economic or the aesthetic, for example) will eventually have to be rethought. Meanwhile, we can certainly say that the words/things balance has been shifted away from the social sciences' preoccupation with things and towards a more cultural sensibility of the salience of words.

Finally, we might ask what it signifies that the post-modern term 'meta-narrative' has become so appealing. Many who do not really agree with the arguments of Jean-François Lyotard are none the less happy to describe large-scale political and intellectual projects as the 'meta-narratives' of feminism, democratism and so on. The interest here lies in our willingness to fictionalize these entities and to regard them as stories (narrative: to tell a tale, give an account). To say this is not to pose a crude antithesis between 'politics' and 'fiction', but it is to remark on how helpful many have found it to use a metaphorical fictionalizing as a critical tool for unlocking the objectivist pretensions of things like rationality, the Enlightenment or even feminism. In what follows I shall be discussing some of the general implications of these changes.

A Paradigm Shift in Feminist Theory?

I have opened with a discussion of a from-things-to-words move, but there can be no doubt that this forms part of a broader sea change within contemporary social thought. Feminist thought both contributes to and is influenced by these larger developments. As Anne Phillips and I have commented in the introduction to this book, the changes within feminist thought could be seen as something of a 'paradigm shift'. Another way of thinking about this is to cast the question in terms of whether any given problem can be rethought within the terms of reference of one's existing theory, or whether—in order to proceed—one has to develop a new framework altogether.

Ernesto Laclau has written about this in terms of whether one can ever, strictly speaking, 'solve' a theoretical problem within the original paradigm. Laclau suggests that one can't: that if a problem is a genuinely 'theoretical' problem (rather than a matter of how you apply a theory, or the empirical support for it) it cannot be solved but can only be 'superseded' in a new theory.[5] It is, of course, quite easy to suggest that the influence of post-structuralism, and the fundamental critique of Enlightenment rationality and classical Marxism, is establishing a new frame of reference that could be described as a shift of paradigmatic order. Seyla Benhabib, for example, refers decisively to a 'paradigm shift in contemporary philosophy from consciousness to language, from the denotative to the performative, from the proposition to the speech-act.'[6] Many feminists might regard the shift from 'equality' to 'difference' models of feminism, which has characterized the past decade of western feminism, as a shift of that order; on the other hand, one might conceptualize the equality–difference debate as itself a paradigm *within* which either position can be taken without undue strain on the model.

Post-Modernism

To explore the question of the relationship between contemporary feminist and social theory is, of course, to address 'post-modernist' as well as post-structuralist arguments. Although there is less confusion in the use of this term than when it first appeared on the scene, it might be worth recapitulating the different contexts in which it is used. In terms of aesthetic strategies and cultural forms, post-modernism refers to an interest in surface rather than depth, to pastiche and parody, to reference to the past and to self-reference, and it focuses attention on a plurality of styles. In terms of philosophy, post-modernism entails a rejection of the grand projects of the rationalist Enlightenment, including Marxist as

well as liberal systems of thought. In terms of sociological analysis, post-modernity is a phenomenon of post-industrial capitalism, crucially determined by the micro-electronic revolution and the globalization of communication and information systems. But since most sociology owes much to rationalism, sociologists must choose between a sociology of post-modernity and a post-modern sociology.[7] A different source of confusion operates within the arts and critical humanities disciplines, and this is what the 'modernism' invoked by post-modern critics is much more like nineteenth-century realism than it is like the 'avant-garde' or 'high modernist' experiments that used to be associated with the term modernism in the arts. A further complication lies in the matter of dates, as unfortunately modernity stars at different times in the different academic disciplines. For philosophy and political theory modernity is under full steam by the end of the eighteenth century; in the arts and humanities the modern world starts no earlier than 1890 and, according to Virginia Woolf, as late as 1910. Since Baudelaire's *flâneur*—the mid-nineteenth-century metropolitan loafer—is such a popular trope of post-modernism, one might legitimately observe that in philosophical terms he was inhabiting modernity and in literary terms was distinctively pre-modernist. In addition, as Janet Wolff's question about 'the invisible flaneuse' indicated at an early stage in these debates, the concepts of post-modernism were urgently in need of some gendering.[8]

Elements of the Current Theoretical Conjuncture

It is as well, then, to use the notion of post-modernism with respectful caution. Notwithstanding this, and the comparable problems associated with the term 'post-structuralism', these generic labels direct us to some very important broad trends in contemporary thought. It might be helpful to identify these at this point, in the following terms.

(1) First, we can see a general critique of *theoretical universalism*. It is not necessary to reiterate here the major political impact t of the recognition that western feminism of the 1970s spoke in a falsely universalized voice. The need to register and engage with the implications of differences among women has been the subject of considerable debate. Elizabeth Spelman has quoted the poet Gwendolyn Brooks in this context: 'The juice from tomatoes is not called merely *juice*. It is always called TOMATO juice.' Spelman observes that 'Even the most literal reading of Brooks ought to make us ask whether we're more careful about what we order in a restaurant than we are in thinking of women as the particular women they are.'[9] I'm not sure how far one can push this metaphor for the problem of difference in feminism. Aren't there situations in which one might opt for 'juice' generically, if offered that or alcohol? (Isn't there even something *very* particular about tomato juice that illustrates the commonality of other fruit juices?)

These debates within feminism form part of a much broader current of contemporary thought in which universalistic theoretical discourses have been subjected to sustained and profound critique. The two clearest cases to take are Marxism and psychoanalysis, both of which can be shown to operate in a strongly universalistic mode in terms of their explanatory claims.[10]

(2) Second, there has been an extensive critique of two central aspects of what is usually referred to as 'Enlightenment' thought, or philosophical 'liberalism': the doctrine of *rationalism* and the *'Cartesian'* concept of a human subject. Feminist political theorists and philosophers have built up a considerable body of work on the masculine character of 'rationalism', and these debates are represented elsewhere in this volume.[11] The so-called 'Cartesian subject' is a topic of complex debate, and much of what is written within post-structuralist and post-modern thought touches on this question. At the heart of the issue is the model of the rational, centered, purposive (and in practice modern European and male) subject for whom Descartes deduced *'cogito ergo sum'*. There are so many things wrong with this model of subjectivity, one scarcely knows where to begin. It displaces and marginalizes other subjects and other forms of subjectivity. It also denies what many would now accept as a central contribution of psychoanalysis—that the self is built on conflict and tension rather than being an essential or given. Yet the critique of this model of subjectivity has brought in its train a whole set of new problems, neatly captured in the title of Kate Soper's article 'Constructa Ergo Sum?' If we replace the given self with a constructed, fragmented self, this poses not only the obvious political question of who is the I that acts and on what basis, but the more teasing conundrum of who is the I that is so certain of its fragmented and discursively constructed nature.[12] Hence the critique of the Cartesian subject has posed a new set of questions about identity and experience, well developed in the arguments of, for example, Chandra Talpade Mohanty and Biddy Martin.[13]

(3) Third, we can speak of *the gendering of modernity* as a new critical enterprise. One can increasingly identify a debate on the implications, for feminism, of the various critiques of modernism and modernity. Griselda Pollock's discussion of the artist, iconic for the modernist project, has illuminated in great detail the cultural meaning of the masculinity inscribed within that figure.[14] The problem remains, however, that feminism is itself too indebted to 'modernist values' and an emancipatory, liberal project to be able to cut loose from the culture and discourse within which it was formed. Susan Hekman points out that one cannot 'simply' suggest that 'the feminist critique extends the post-modern critique of rationalism by revealing its gendered character'.[15] This is because one cannot readily

separate out the constituent elements of an integrated theoretical and political 'package'. Hence one may object to Enlightenment dualisms in which the feminine, or women, are always cast as inferior to the masculine, or men, but a thorough-going post-modern abandonment (in so far as this is possible) of these binary structures would be rejected by many feminists.

(4) Fortunately, we can see a new *critique of materialism* in these debates, and it is to these issues that I want to turn in more detail.

The critique of materialism

Modern critiques of (philosophical) materialism have attracted a great deal of attention and other hostile responses. The greatest anxiety has been generated from those who see what they call 'discourse theory' as an ideologically suspect attempt to deny material reality— which, presumably, would be as futile an enterprise as Canute's if the materialist perspective is, itself, correct. In so far as ideas are powerful, mechanical materialism is wrong. There is no doubt, however, that these responses are the result of the intellectual provocation offered by 'performative' statements such as Derrida's famous *'il n'y a pas d'hors texte'* (there is nothing outside the text). This statement does not literally mean that railway trains do not exist other than as numbers in timetables, but that all knowledge is discursively apprehended. Erneseto Laclau and Chantal Mouffe have explained the general point very clearly in a reply to their critics, giving the prosaic example of a football. The spherical object exists, but it has no significant *meaning* outside the systems of rules and conventions (discourse) by which it is constituted as a football.[16]

Arguments about materialism have a very different purchase in different academic subjects. Materialist assumptions, whether Marxist or not, are common in the social sciences, and flourish particularly in the notion of a deter-

mining 'social structure' on which culture and beliefs, as well as subjectivity and agency, rest. Nevertheless, there has long been what one might regard as an alternative tradition within social theory, emphasizing experience and attempting to understand society without the aid of a social structural model. Phenomenology is an obvious case here, as is the work of Simmel. Recent years have seen a rise of interest in various traditions of social theory—phenomenology, hermeneutics, subjectivist sociology and so on—previously somewhat neglected. The materialist model with the greatest epistemological power is the paradigm of classical Marxism, a formative influence within European social theory.

On the other side of the social sciences/arts divide, the problem of materialism has not had an undue impact on disciplines that have taken the text as by definition constituting the object of study. In history, however, the ramifications of a critique of materialist premises have proved extensive. History's ambiguous position has rested on the fact that what was traditionally sought was a reconstitution or reconstruction of 'social reality', but one necessarily based methodologically on a reading of textual evidence. Thus the question of how historiography adjusts to a rethinking of the balance between text and reality is a particularly acute one.

The implications of post-structuralism for feminist historiography have been much debated. The incorporation of Foucault's work had already taken root (for instance, in the work of Judith Walkowitz and Jeffrey Weeks on sexuality), and the methodological orientation of Mary Poovey's readings is clearly influenced by Derrida. Joan Scott has taken the lead in explicating the new trend, suggesting that Derridian insights could lead to a feminist history that 'undermines claims for authority based on totalising explanations, essentialised categories of analysis (be they human nature, race, class, sex, or "the oppressed"), or synthetic narratives that assume an inherent unity for the past'.[17]

In this context Derrida's ideas can be used to shore up further an already far-reaching critique of conventional historiography developed by Michel Foucault. As he explained in the opening sections of *The Archaeology of Knowledge,* Foucault's ambition was to replace the old linear and teleological history with an approach that sought for such systematicity as might be found in a general context of dispersal and particularity.[18]

It is a moot point how far some of the theoretical refusals characteristic of post-structuralism can be taken in the accomplishment of specific researches. Without offending anyone we can consider this by looking at a statement which appears on the jacket of a book about Foucault. It reads: 'In the most obvious sense Foucault's analyses of the birth of the clinic, the asylum and the prison are historical and raise problems of historical interpretation. But he makes no attempt to reconstitute the past historically and accurately.'[19] This is a slight exaggeration of the book's authors' view that Foucault's relationship to history was 'eccentric', but it illustrates the point in question. How can history dispense with historicality and accuracy? Of course, despite disclaimers that there is no such thing as truth, only effects of truth that are discursively secured, Foucault's substantive analyses themselves propose a *better account* of the history of mental illness, or punishment, or sexuality, than previous histories, and in this sense are loaded with epistemological claims.

Derrida, particularly, of the post-structuralists, has focused attention on the impossibility of escaping intellectual constraints we may object to. To point to the covert reintroduction of metaphysics, or idealism, in his work is thus not likely to surprise him. Nevertheless, there is tension between the highly particularistic and relativistic view of knowledge adopted in post-structuralism and the epistemological claims necessarily made in substantive instances. This is clearest in the domain of history, where social reality is always in play, but is a problem too in more philosophical discussions that are none

the less always historically located. Yet in these writers one often finds a coy hesitation about actually pinning a date on to something.[20]

Such uneasiness is symptomatic of a more general uncertainty about the implication of post-structuralism's critique of materialism. Such a critique has taken many forms: it is played out in debates about the place of evidence, texts and archives in historical research, in debates about social structure or 'interests' as determinants of behaviour and so on. A critique of the mechanical assumptions of materialism underlies the continued 'turn to culture' in feminism, as witness to a concern with representation and symbolization rather than more classically sociological approaches. In this context perhaps one might add that the contestation of cultural meaning is every bit as important as other feminist projects. Foucault's analysis of the exclusions and prohibitions of discourse is extremely pertinent to a feminism that has pioneered understanding of the power of naming and the efficacy of language.[21]

Disciplinary Considerations

Debates in philosophy and social theory, and the parallel discussions in the humanities, take place in an institutional context. I want next to focus on some of the disciplinary aspects of these debates. In the first place, one can note that feminist scholarship has always had the ambition to transcend disciplinary boundaries. Like Marxism, it has tended to regard them as constructions of an unenlightened system that are better ignored. The philosophy of 'women's studies' is very clearly based on this recognition. In practice, however, there are two widely recognized limitations of working under the rubric of 'women's studies': that it leaves the mainstream definition of the academic subjects unchallenged and even denuded of feminist scholars (an aspect of 'ghettoization') and that it militates against developing an understanding of men, masculinity and the interaction of the sexes (the subject matter of the alternative rubric of 'gender'). I am not interested here in these issues, important though they are. I want to focus instead on some of the problems that arise in relation to feminist concerns and the academic disciplines—outside women's studies—in more general terms.

It is not too banal to observe that most feminist scholars have been trained within the conventions of one or the other of the academic disciplines in the arts and social sciences. The marks of these specific trainings are often indelible. They are particularly visible in feminist work, in that one discipline after the next has historically gained a certain 'influence' within contemporary feminism. This often comes up in the context of accusations of using 'jargon', which usually means using another discipline's accepted terminology: I tend not to perceive my own disciplinary vocabulary as jargon.

Disciplines do not simply generate jargon, though; they rest on distinctive assumptions and conventions as to what their objects of study are and what methods are appropriate to study them. Academic debate can reduce itself, on occasion, to a simple trading of assumptions across disciplinary divides. Foucault developed ideas of disciplinary apparatus and discursive policing to describe the practices that regulate what can be said within a discipline, and has shown how Canguilheim's idea of knowledge being 'in the true' can be applied. 'Within its own limits, each discipline recognizes true and false propositions; but it pushes back a whole teratology of knowledge beyond its margins.' So unless a proposition is 'within the true' of these requirements at the time, it cannot be accepted as true. Foucault gives the example of Mendel, whose theories were rejected in the nineteenth century, because he spoke of objects and used methods that were alien to the biology of his time. Foucault concludes (surprisingly to those who insist on regarding him as a complete relativist) that 'Mendel spoke the truth, but he was not "within the true" of the biological discourse of his time.'[22]

To speak 'within the true' of a particular discipline is to speak within a complex web of inclusions and exclusions. Differences of time and space are crucial in understanding these requirements in specific contexts. In contemporary western feminist theory there are clearly different conventions of reference as between, say, Australian, European and US feminists—the sense of what you need to know about to be up with your field is very different.[23] Similarly, for instance, there are significant differences between the different disciplines as to how far interdisciplinarity is desirable or necessary, and significant differences between national and regional disciplinary development of subjects in various parts of the world. To understand these patterns in their complexity would require extensive knowledge and—not least—would require an insight into the educational aspects of colonization in the past and the effects of these on the present distribution of academic power.

Another way of thinking about Foucault's notion of the boundaries of particular disciplines might be to consider a license to ignore. There is, if you like, an informal division of labour in which certain questions are assigned to one subject and can thus legitimately be ignored by another. In particular, I think one can see this process in the informal division of labour between the arts/humanities critical disciplines and the social sciences. One effect of what I have called here a shift from 'things' to 'words' is a destabilization of this informal disciplinary division of labour. However, it seems to me that the form this has taken has been to open up new substantive areas, or topics, of study to scholars from disciplines that had previously regarded them as beyond the range of what could be studied. The more ambitious task of rethinking the appropriate *methods* of study, and developing ways of genuinely working across disciplines, has lagged behind. The kinds of example that one might give here are obviously contentious, and I will try to present them in a constructive spirit.

The 'post-colonial subject', for example, is better known as a phenomenon of the archive or psyche than as an agent in labour migration or a victim of globalizing managerial strategies.[24] The reasons for this are complex. Feminist economists and sociologists have taken up these issues but the lines of communication between them and literary readers and scholars are institutionally poor.[25] There has also been an evident vacuum within feminist social science on these issues, in my view because the social structural model has proved particularly unwieldy in the face of a triple interaction of disadvantage. Ideally, we would be able to complement knowledge of post-coloniality drawn from textual and archival sources and often focusing on subjective and symbolic questions with a richer social, economic and political treatment of this historical theme. These various aspects of the subject are not in competition with each other, and nor should any aspect be given, in the abstract, greater epistemological significance. But they call for a variety of competences, training and knowledges.

In practice, the recent shifting of disciplinary definitions of appropriate subject matter has often meant an export of methods and techniques. The redefinition of 'literary criticism' is a very important case in point. Certainly one can say that the traditional 'canon fodder' approach has been destabilized, although with complex consequences. Barbara Christian, for example, clearly struck a nerve in pointing to the pursuit of theory for its own sake in literary study and the consequent neglect of reading texts of feeling as well as thought.[26] I want to focus here on a different aspect of this destabilization—the relation between critical reading method and the text or object of study.

One development in the intellectual 'crisis' of literary criticism has been to turn critical attention to texts way outside the previously accepted 'literary' range. The school of thought known as 'new historicism' took a lead in reading social, medical, legal and political documents alongside literary texts; Derridian techniques of reading have played an important part in this development. More generally, one can hear at any up-to-date literary critical meeting (the MLA being the ideal type) many a paper in which the most mundanely social of sources are decoded, deconstructed and 'read' using the critical armoury of modern textual interpretation. The question to be asked, however, is whether these exercises are more than a method bored by its usual stamping ground. How, in particular, does the knowledge gained by such readings interact with what we know from social history, or sociology, about Victorian drains or 1950s cross-dressing practices?

If all this is to say that one trend has been the application of literary critical techniques to social historical documents and archives, read as 'texts', another important trend has been to retain the canon of classical literary texts but to 'read' them through a completely different interpretive grid. The most influential example of this at present is the application of psychoanalytic concepts as a method of literary criticism. This, too, raises some complex questions. Given that psychoanalysis has a history of being one of the most 'reductive' of perspectives, in that its strong explanatory claims, exclusion of other factors and incipient theoretical universalism are legendary, it is perhaps ironic that (from the point of view of its practitioners) in this process its epistemological status is dramatically altered. It is increasingly apparent that the working assumptions of those who use psychoanalytic concepts as a method of reading texts are strongly at variance with the assumptions of those who practise psychoanalysis in a therapeutic context. Although there is a certain amount of movement from one to the other, there is none the less a distance and sometimes outright conflict between free-floating cultural analysis and the clinical institution. One might pose this as a breach between 'psychoanalysis'. where certain assumptions hold true across the schools of Freudians, Kleinians, Lacanians and

390 Part 2 Contemporary Sociological Theory

others, and a *post-psychoanalysis* whose object is exclusively symbolic.[27]

Psychoanalysis is poised at a complex conjunction of 'words and things', some variants facing exclusively towards the symbolic realm of language and representation while others (though stopping short of the 'real event' mentality) would endorse claims that psychic experience carries some sort of causal power in a subjective history.

To refer to these differences of method and epistemology is to raise the question of how objects of study are constituted within the various disciplines. To ignore this question is to work within very narrow confines. There may be some apprehension that to pose the question is itself to endorse or imply a search for a 'general theory' or 'integrated perspective', but I do not think that this is the likely outcome. On the contrary, to address the specific 'truths' of the different disciplines is to discover not the controlling modernism of a fully integrated general theory of knowledge, but precisely the reverse— an incommensurability of knowledges that provokes interesting reflection.

In Conclusion

It would, I believe, be useful to consider further the implications of what in Foucauldian vein one might regard as 'disciplinary truth apparatuses'. In the examples I have raised here I have tended to focus on the questions of which I have some experience (sociology and literary studies), and this is inevitable since one cannot speak outside these conventions altogether. It is worth noting, however, that these disciplinary apparatuses are not simply relics of the bad old disciplines, but are powerful and living developments within the good new ones too. 'Women's studies', 'cultural studies', 'lesbian and gay studies' have quickly lost their initial openness of perspective and developed highly distinctive assumptions and conventions (disciplinary paradigms) within

which each operates. In feminist studies ambivalence about academic privilege may have marginalized these problems. Yet we might perhaps be in a better position politically if the institutional context of particular knowledges, and the varying powers that go with them, were more openly addressed.

As far as the issue of materialism is concerned, it seems likely that it will take a long time before the far-reaching influence and effects of the structure–culture and base–superstructure dichotomies have been registered, still more worked through. Certainly this is true for feminists working within the disciplinary bases of the social sciences and history. In the arts and humanities the impact of post-structuralism, albeit still highly contentious, has been much greater. Feminist theory has been able to take up a number of issues outside that classically 'materialist' perspective: in particular the analysis of corporeality and of the psyche. 'Post-structuralist' theories, notably Derridian deconstructive reading, Lacanian psychoanalysis and Foucault's emphasis on the material body and the discourses of power, have proved very important in this. Feminists have appropriated these theories rather than others for good reasons: these theorists address the issues of sexuality, subjectivity and textuality that feminists have put at the top of the agenda. In considering the debates that now ramify around feminism and post-structuralism, it is clear that the classic materialist presuppositions are increasingly harder to apply usefully.

To say that is not, however, to endorse a wholesale conversion to 'post-structuralism'. The many post-structuralist and post-modernist critiques of liberal and Marxist thought have decisively exposed the fundamental flaws of those earlier theories. Whether, however, they can promise a more useful alternative is a much more vexed question. In the meantime, there are losses attached to a wholesale abandonment of the areas of study traditionally denoted by the academic disciplines of sociology, political economy, economics and politics.

There is another, paradoxical, aspect of modern feminist deployment of the status historically attributed to materiality in an economic sense. While social class is definitely *non grata* as a topic, one may creditably speak of 'proletarianization' and 'exploitation' in the context of global capitalism and racially driven disadvantage (rather like the legal class discrimination that continues in Britain, in education and housing, for example, where analogous cases of sex and race discrimination would be at risk of prosecution). This is surely something of an anomaly, if a politically explicable one.

Finally, I want to conclude with a point about the issue of materialism and the theoretical 'grounding' of political practice. In the debates around feminism and post-modernism some have argued for a 'modernist' conception of rationalism, egalitarianism and autonomy as the basis of an emancipatory practice, in feminism as elsewhere. On this model, the work of Habermas and critical theory, for example, could be seen to rescue feminism from the irrationalism and political limitations of post-modern perspectives. Clearly this discussion is part of a broader debate as to whether feminism is 'essentially' a modernist or a post-modernist enterprise. There are some good reasons for holding either position on this and, indeed, for the third position that feminism straddles and thus destabilizes the modern–post-modern binary divide.[28] It seems to me, however, that we do not necessarily need more and better theories legitimating or justifying feminist political practice. Such a need is based on an assumption that political values are produced by scientific analysis (the type case being the classical 'scientific' as opposed to utopian definition of Marxism). This 'scientism', taken to its extreme, strips values from politics, and this has also been the effect of the blanket anti-humanism that has characterized post-structuralism and certain schools of feminist thought. Debates about ideology and subjectivity have shown that we need a better conception of agency and identity than has been available in either (anti-humanist) post-structuralist thought or its (humanist) modernist predecessors. It may well be that to develop a better account of subjective political motivation we shall have to reopen in new and imaginative ways the issue of humanism. Meanwhile, perhaps, it will be important to assert that political objectives are in an important sense constituted on the basis of values and principles—that they cannot be grounded in a scientific social analysis but spring from aspiration rather than proof.

NOTES

I am grateful to Isobel Armstrong for commissioning the article ('Feminism's Turn to Culture') which set me off down this track, and to all the members of the discussion group on post-structuralism and feminist historiography that I have gained so much from. Particular thanks to Catherine Hall, Anne Phillips and Ruthie Petrie.

1. Michael Foucault, *The Archaeology of Knowledge* (Routledge, London, 1989), p. 49.
2. It is a pleasure to acknowledge my debt to Gayatri Spivak (Alabama, 1986) for this point.
3. Michel Foucault, 'The Minimalist Self', in *Michel Foucault: Politics, Philosophy, Culture. Interviews and Other Writings 1977–1984*, ed. Lawrence Kritzman (Routledge, London, 1990), pp. 3–16; p. 8.
4. See Michèle Barrett, 'Feminism's Turn to Culture', in *Woman: A Cultural Review*, 1 (1990), pp. 22–4.
5. Ernesto Laclau, *Politics and Ideology in Marxist Theory* (Verso, London, 1977), pp. 60–1.
6. Seyla Benhabib, 'Epistemologies of Postmodernism: A Rejoinder to Jean-François Lyotard', in Linda J. Nicholson (ed.), *Feminism/Postmodernism* (Routledge, New York and London, 1990), p. 125.

7. This telegraphic formulation signals a complex debate on the extent to which sociology, and the social sciences in general, were born of the modernist 'moment'. For discussion of these issues see Roy Boyne and Ali Rattansi (eds), *Post-modernism and Society* (Macmillan, London, 1990); Scott Lash, *Sociology of Postmodernism* (Routledge, London, 1990), ch. 5; Bryan Turner (ed.), *Theories of Modernity and Postmodernity* (Sage, London, 1990); David Frisby's significant study *Fragments of Modernity* (Polity, Cambridge, 1985); Zygmunt Bauman, *Legislators and Interpreters: On Modernity, Post-Modernity and Intellectuals* (Polity, Cambridge, 1989).

8. Janet Wolff, 'The Invisible Flâneuse: Women and the Literature of Modernity', *Theory, Culture and Society*, 2 (1985), pp. 37–48.

9. Elizabeth V. Spelman, *Inessential Woman: Problems of Exclusion in Feminist Thought* (The Women's Press, London, 1990), p. 186.

10. These issues are discussed in some detail in my *The Politics of Truth: From Marx to Foucault* (Polity, Cambridge, 1991).

11. See also, for example, the collection by Carole Pateman and Elizabeth Gross (eds), *Feminist Challenges: Social and Political Theory* (Allen and Unwin, Sydney, 1986).

12. Kate Soper, 'Constructa Ergo Sum?', in Soper, *Troubled Pleasures: Writings on Politics, Gender and Hedonism* (Verso, London, 1990), pp. 146–61.

13. See Biddy Martin and Chandra Talpade Mohanty, 'Feminist Politics: What's Home Got to Do with It?', in Teresa de Lauretis (eds), *Feminist Studies/Critical Studies* (Indiana University Press, Bloomington, Ind., 1986), and their essays in this volume.

14. See the essay by Griselda Pollock in this volume; also Pollock, *Vision and Difference:*

Femininity, Feminism and the Histories of Art (Routledge, New York and London, 1988); Pollock, 'Feminism and Modernism', in Roszika Parker and Griselda Pollock (eds), *Framing Feminism: Art and the Women's Movement 1970–1985* (Pandora/Routledge, London, 1987).

15. Susan Hekman, *Gender and Knowledge: Elements of a Postmodern Feminism* (Polity, Cambridge, 1990), p. 5.

16. Ernesto Laclau and Chantal Mouffe, 'Post-Marxism Without Apologies', in Ernesto Laclau (ed.), *New Reflections on the Revolution in Our Time* (Verso, London, 1990, p. 100.

17. Joan Wallach Scott, *Gender and the Politics of History* (Columbia University Press, New York, 1988), pp. 7–8; Mary Poovey, *Uneven Developments: The Ideological Work of Gender in Mid-Victorian England* (Virago, London, 1989/Chicago University Press, Chicago, 1988).

18. Foucault, *The Archaeology of Knowledge*, pp. 3–39. Foucault later declared himself 'flabbergasted' at being described one-sidedly as a philosopher of discontinuity and took for the title of his chair at the Collège de France 'Professor of the History of Systems of Thought'.

19. Mark Cousins and Athar Hussain, *Michel Foucault* (Macmillan, London, 1984), jacket copy.

20. See, for example, Derrida's essay 'Structure, Sign and Play in the Discourse of the Human Sciences', which eventually discloses the 'where and when' of a central thesis by choosing the names ('as indications only') Nietzsche, Freud and Heidegger—enabling us to locate it in late nineteenth-century/early twentieth-century Europe: Jacques Derrida, *Writing and Difference* (Routledge, London, 1978), p. 280.

21. Michel Foucault, 'The Order of Discourse', in Robert Young (ed.), *Untying the Text: A*

Post-Structuralist Reader (Routledge, London and New York, 1987), pp. 48–78. On feminism and the power of naming see Adrienne Rich, *On Lies, Secrets and Silence* (Virago, London, 1980).

22. Foucault, 'The Order of Discourse', pp. 60–1.

23. The usual gripe here is that feminists in the USA see much less need to read what Australian or British feminists write (until it attracts a US publisher) than vice versa.

24. Gayatri Spivak, whose work has been crucial for the development of understanding of post-coloniality, provides an exception to this general observation in that her interests and knowledges range across matters of technology, economics and so on. 'We cannot ask the economists and the sociologists to attend to our speculations about the subject-constitution of the woman in post-modern neo-colonialism if we do it as charming primitivists' (Gayatri Chakravorty Spivak, 'The Political Economy of Women as Seen by a Literary Critic', in Elizabeth Weed [ed.], *Coming to Terms: Feminism, Theory, Politics* [Routledge, New York, 1989], p. 228). See also Spivak, 'Scattered Speculations on the Question of Value', in her *In Other Worlds: Essays in Cultural Politics* (Routledge, London and New York, 1987), pp. 154–75.

25. For two examples, see Maria Mies, *Patriarchy and Accumulation on a World Scale* (Zed Press, London and New Jersey, 1986); Haleh Afshar (eds), *Women, Work and Ideology in the Third World* (Tavistock/Routledge, London and New York, 1985).

26. Barbara Christian, 'The Race for Theory', *Cultural Critique*, 6 (1987), pp. 51–64.

27. Barrett, *The Politics of Truth*, ch. 5; see also Richard Feldstein and Henry Sussman (eds), *Psychoanalysis and . . .* (Routledge, New York and London, 1990), pp. 1–8.

28. The most useful anthology in this debate is Linda Nicholson (ed.), *Feminism/Postmodernism* (Routledge, London and New York, 1990). Feminists sympathetically critical of 'critical theory' can be found in Seyla Benhabib and Drucilla Cornell (eds), *Feminism as Critique* (Polity, Cambridge, 1987); see also Nancy Fraser, *Unruly Practices: Power, Discourse and Gender in Contemporary Social Theory* (Polity, Cambridge, 1989). Susan Hekman's *Gender and Knowledge* gives an excellent account from a position sympathetic to post-modernism. See also Rita Felski, *Beyond Feminist Aesthetics* (Harvard University Press, Cambridge, Mass., 1989), ch. 2.

Further Readings: Contemporary Sociological Theory

FUNCTIONALISM

ALEXANDER, JEFFREY C.: *Theoretical logic in sociology,* Vol. 4, *The modern reconstruction of classical thought: Talcott Parsons.* Berkeley: University of California Press, 1984.

ALEXANDER, JEFFREY C.: *Neofunctionalism.* Beverly Hills, Sage, 1985.

ALEXANDER, JEFFREY C., and PAUL COLOMY: "Toward neo-functionalism," *Sociological Theory* 3:11–23, 1985.

MERTON, ROBERT K.: *Social theory and social structure.* New York, Free Press 1957. Talcott Parsons: *the social system.* Glencoe, Free Press, 1951.

CONFLICT THEORY

COLLINS, RANDALL: *Conflict sociology: Toward explanatory science.* New York, Academic Press, 1975.

DAHRENDORF, RALF: *Class and class conflict in industrial society.* Stanford, Stanford University Press, 1958.

MILLS, C. WRIGHT: *The power elite.* New York, Oxford University Press, 1956.

LENSKI, GERHARD: *Power and privilege: A theory of social stratification.* (Chapel Hill: University of North Carolina Press), 1984.

EXCHANGE THEORY AND RATIONAL CHOICE

BLAU, PETER: *Exchange and power in social life.* New York, Wiley, 1964.

COLEMAN, JAMES S.: *Foundations of social theory.* Cambridge, Harvard University Press, 1990.

COOK, KAREN, RICHARD EMERSON, MARY GILLMORE, and TOSHIO YAMAGISHI: "The distribution of power in exchange networks," *American Journal of Sociology,* 1983.

HOMANS, GEORGE C.: *Social behavior: Its elementary forms.* New York, Harcourt Brace, 1961.

SHUBIK, MARTIN: *Game theory in the social sciences.* Cambridge, MIT Press, 1957.

SIMON, HERBERT A.: *Models of man.* New York, Wiley, 1957.

PHENOMENOLOGICAL SOCIOLOGY AND ETHNOMETHODOLOGY

BERGER, PETER, and THOMAS LUCKMANN: *The social construction of reality.* New York, Doubleday, 1966.

BODEN, DEIDRE, and DON ZIMMERMAN, eds.: *Talk and social structure. Studies in ethnomethodology and conversation analysis.* Berkeley, University of California Press, 1991.

CICOUREL, AARON: *Cognitive sociology.* Baltimore, Penguin, 1973.

GARFINKEL, HAROLD: *Studies in ethnomethodology.* Englewood Cliffs, N.J., Prentice-Hall, 1967.

SCHUTZ, ALFRED: *Collected papers.* The Hague, Martinus Nijoff, 1962–66.

SYMBOLIC INTERACTION

BLUMER, HERBERT: *Symbolic interactionism; perspective and method.* Englewood Cliffs, NJ, Prentice-Hall, 1969.

DEEGAN, MARY JO: *American ritual dramas: social rules and cultural meanings.* New York, Greenwood Press, 1989.

DEEGAN, MARY JO, and MICHAEL R. HILL, eds., *Women and symbolic interaction.* Boston, Allen & Unwin, 1987.

GOFFMAN, ERVING: *The presentation of self in everyday life.* Garden City, N.Y., Doubleday, 1959.

————: *Asylums.* Garden City, N.Y., Doubleday, 1961.

————: *Interaction ritual.* Garden City, N.Y., Doubleday, 1967.

————: *Relations in public.* N.Y., Basic Books, 1971.

HEWITT, JOHN P: *Dilemmas of the American self.* Philadelphia, Temple University Press, 1989.

LEWIS, J. DAVID, and RICHARD L. SMITH: *American sociology and pragmatism: Mead, Chicago sociology, and symbolic interaction.* Chicago, University of Chicago Press, 1980.

FEMINIST THEORY

BARRETT, MICHÈLE, and ANNE PHILLIPS, eds.: *Destabilizing theory: contemporary feminist debates.* Stanford, Stanford University Press, 1992.

BENHABIB, SEYLA: *Situating the self: gender, community, and postmodernism in contemporary ethics.* New York, Routledge, 1992.

BENHABIB, SEYLA, et al.: *Feminist contentions: a philosophical exchange;* introduction by Linda Nicholson. New York, Routledge, 1995.

BUTLER, JUDITH: *Bodies that matter: on the discursive limits of "sex."* New York, Routledge, 1993.

CORNELL, DRUCILLA: *At the heart of freedom: feminism, sex, and equality.* Princeton, N.J., Princeton University Press, c1998.

NICHOLSON, LINDA J., ed.: *Feminism/postmodernism;* with an introduction by Linda J. Nicholson. New York, Routledge, 1990.

SAWICKI, JANA: *Disciplining Foucault: feminism, power, and the body.* New York, Routledge, 1991.

SMITH, DOROTHY E.: *The conceptual practices of power: A feminist sociology of knowledge.* Boston, Northeastern University Press, c1990.

YOUNG, IRIS MARION: *Throwing like a girl and other essays in feminist philosophy and social theory.* Bloomington, Ind., Indiana University Press, c1990.

Modernity and Post-Modernism

Chapter 13

Critical Theory

Introduction

Critical theory is the name given to that school of thought that emerged from the writings of the members of the Frankfurt School, among them T. W. Adorno, Max Horkheimer, Herbert Marcuse, and Friedrich Pollock. They were among a group of German intellectuals at the Institute for Social Research at the University of Frankfurt who continued their association from the 1930s through the period of the Second World War and on into the postwar era. They were drawn together by a common interest in Marxism and its relevance to a world dominated by Stalinism in the East and by emerging Fascism in Europe. Critical theory was distinguished from traditional, i.e, scientific social theory, by its commitment to a moral concept of progress and emancipation that would form the foundation for all its studies. It was multidisciplinary in its approach, drawing upon psychology, sociology, economics, and politics to develop its unique standpoint, and it was committed, finally, to the idea that knowledge should be put to use to achieve a just and democratic social order.

This chapter presents excerpts from works by Herbert Marcuse (1898–1979) and Jürgen Habermas. Marcuse was an early member of the Institute in Frankfurt and after the rise of Nazi power in Germany, he came to the United States in 1934 to join Max Horkheimer and to continue the work of the Institute, which had by then found a new home at Columbia University.

Jürgen Habermas is the most prominent "second generation" critical theorist. A student

of Adorno's, Habermas was a teenager during Hitler's reign. That, and the subsequent experience of Germany in the postwar period underlies much of Habermas's concern about the future prospects of a humane and rational democratic society.

Herbert Marcuse was a student of philosophy and studied at the great universities of Berlin and Freiburg. His work reflects the powerful influence of Marx and Weber, but also those of Hegel, Husserl, and Heidegger and to some extent Nietzsche.

During the 1960's Herbert Marcuse achieved great fame among American and European university students because his theoretical writings provided a broadly historical and sociopolitical context for understanding the protest movements here and abroad. In that sense he was the most widely known social theorist on the American scene. He gave intellectual support to the anti-war movement and joined the growing ranks of protesters against the Vietnam War.

The social movements of the 1960s emerging around issues such as civil rights, feminism, gay rights, as well as the counterculture also found support in Marcuse's later writings. In his view, these social movements were a sign of great hope for the future of advanced industrial society because they demonstrated, contrary to his own pessimistic formulations in *One-Dimensional Man*, that there were extant sources of negativity and resistance to the new forms of social control he saw enveloping American society.

Marcuse published a number of important works in social theory and political sociology.

Among them are *Reason and Revolution* (1941), *Eros and Civilization* (1955), *Soviet Marxism* (1958), *One-Dimensional Man* (1964), *A Critique of Pure Tolerance* (1965), *Negations: Essays in Critical Theory* (1968), *An Essay on Liberation* (1969), *Counterrevolution and Revolt* (1972), *Studies in Critical Philosophy* (1973), *The Aesthetic Dimension* (1978).

In *One-Dimensional Man*, Marcuse gave full and popular expression to the idea of dialectical thinking and demonstrated its continuing relevance as a mode of social analysis. At the same time, there is an important sense in which Marcuse's analysis extends Weber's idea of rationalization by employing the concept of "technological rationality." Weber, it will be recalled, sought to capture the end point of the centuries-long process in which science had come to dominate the Western intellectual viewpoint by characterizing modern society as an "iron cage." The rationalization process not only manifested itself in the rational behavior of individuals in bureaucratic settings, but also referred to their method of thinking. Instrumental rationality, a calculating and *means*-oriented mode of thought, had gradually come to replace substantive rationality, or thought dealing with morality, with the validity of the *ends* of action.

In Marcuse's view, advanced industrial society has become a society without opposition, dominated by "technological rationality." Moreover, his analysis leads him to reject the traditional Marxist formulations on the sources of conflict in the class structure of capitalism. Instead he sees a working class that has steadily embraced middle-class values (embourgeoisment) and has become absorbed into the mainstream of capitalist consumer culture. No longer the negation of capitalism, the working class has become its vocal supporter and defender.

Thus Marcuse projects a society that appears open and tolerant but is closed to fundamental criticism and radical change. Advanced industrial society is capable of absorbing all manner of dissent by co-opting the dissenters and using their platforms for political or commercial profit.

The student should think of several examples from the world of media advertising, popular culture, and politics that might illustrate how issues begin as negation and end up as co-option. Is this the inevitable way of democratic politics?

Nevertheless, the social movements of the 1960s appeared to Marcuse to have revolutionary potential. In the last few pages of *One-Dimensional Man* he refers to the potential for opposition among "the outcasts and the outsiders, the exploited and persecuted of other races and other colors." Clearly these are not the radical students of the 1960s, but history is never a neat fit with social theory. Marcuse later anticipated social change as the long march through the institutions of advanced capitalist society to bring about a just and more democratic society.

Jürgen Habermas, who studied with T. W. Adorno, one of the major figures of the Frankfurt School, is considered the foremost contemporary exponent of critical theory. Generally regarded as the leading German social theorist of our time, and quite possibly the most important since Max Weber, Habermas has written extensively in the areas of philosophy and sociology. Born in 1929, Habermas studied in Germany and has taught philosophy and sociology at the Universities of Heidelberg and Frankfurt. Among his writings are the following: *Towards a Rational Society* (1970), *Knowledge and Human Interests* (1971), *Legitimation Crisis* (1976), *Communication and the Evolution of Society* (1979), *Reason and the Rationalization of Society* (1984), *Between Facts and Norms: Contributions to a Discourse Theory of Law and Democracy* (1996), *The Inclusion of the Other: Studies in Political Theory* (1998).

The major focus of Habermas's work is the survival of democracy in a world that is increasingly transformed by science and technology. Habermas engages the great thinkers of the classical tradition in a reconstructive dialogue in which he develops and creates new formulations. He is faithful to the emancipatory project of Marx yet mindful of the rationalization thesis developed by Weber, and his project is to demonstrate how and why the "iron cage" need not be our destiny in spite of the fact that the rationalization process continues. Moreover, it is his intention to demonstrate how effective social change in the direction of a substantively just democratic order is possible in the absence of the proletariat as a revolutionary force.

These questions had focused the work of the critical theorists of the Frankfurt School, particularly Adorno, Horkheimer, and Marcuse. In *Dialectic of Enlightenment* (1972), Horkheimer and Adorno had reached their most pessimistic conclusions about the prospects of achieving the progressive goals of the Enlightenment. Similarly, Herbert Marcuse had argued in *One-Dimensional Man* (1964) that all sources of critical negation had been effectively absorbed into the established framework of values and power.

Rather than succumb to this pessimism, Habermas has challenged the formulations of his erstwhile teachers and colleagues on the grounds that they have too readily accepted Marx's deterministic view of the relationship between substructure and superstructure, or in Weber's terms, between state and society. In both instances the autonomous potential of the life-world, with its indigenous forms of symbolic and communicative action, has been undermined or unappreciated, resulting in the view of the totally administered society, directed by technocratic elites and legitimated by an ideology that emerges from the widespread acceptance of science and instrumental rationality.

In Habermas's view the integrative needs of the social system do not entail the absorption and direction of the life-world. The mode of communication in the life-world preserves conceptions of justice and freedom, even as these values are leached from the vocabulary of technocratic elites whose language is wholly couched in the instrumental terms of cost-benefit analysis. As the social system evolves in its political and economic institutions in the direction of greater efficiency, predictability, coordination, and control, the life-world evolves in the direction of greater reflexivity and more understanding of the common fate of all peoples. The life-world is thus characterized as having a logic of its own that does not automatically succumb to the influences of money and power as these emanate from the economic and political subsystems of the social system.

Habermas is well aware of the pressures to absorb the life-world of communicative action into the amoral system of instrumental or purposive action. The dangers are extensively developed in much of his work. However, Habermas does more than his predecessors when he opens up options for action that were foreclosed to them because of the limitations of their conceptual analyses. The consequences of these reconstructive dialogues with past and present thinkers in which Habermas is engaged are to be found in his formulation of alternatives that more accurately portray the historical moment that we occupy. In simple terms, Habermas sees two possible directions that confront our society in the future: a technocratic solution, called the colonization of the life-world, or a democratic solution, envisioning a revitalization of democratic public life.

If the life-world is colonized, then it gradually loses its cultural and moral purpose, which is to articulate and formulate a vision of the just social order that is consonant with the evolutionary progress of the human race. Instead an increasingly apathetic and disinterested public succumbs to the material inducements of money and power and adapts itself to the integrative demands of the technocratic system. If, on the other hand, the democratic option is forthcoming, then the life-world of communicative action may be able to impose its moral framework onto the economic and political system and reintegrate the public into the cultural system that will provide it with substantive meaning and purpose.

What this means is that as advanced industrial societies develop they release resources for cultural development and education. A more enlightened population becomes increasingly conscious of the structures of power that dominate the present system and of the historical development and evolution of the social order. They likewise become more aware of global, environmental, and universalistic issues of human rights. This increased consciousness leads to the formation of new social movements that articulate the more general or universalistic values rather than the special interests that have dominated the politics of the past. The new social movements express concerns about the environment, about human rights, and about fairness in treatment of minorities of race, gender, and sexual preference. This is the new cultural politics that is expressive of life-world concerns and engages in a moral discourse that cannot readily be absorbed into the framework of instrumental politics. For Habermas, the new social movements are the harbingers of a new moral consensus, that will provide the basis for a revitalized democratic order.

In rejecting the necessity of the technocratic solution, Habermas resurrects the ideals of the Enlightenment and reminds us that this is a project that has yet to be completed. It is in this sense that Habermas is deemed a "modernist," namely as one who continues with the Enlightenment vision of the modern world as one in which progress, reason, truth, and justice eventually triumph.

HERBERT MARCUSE: ONE-DIMENSIONAL MAN

The Paralysis of Criticism: Society Without Opposition

Does not the threat of an atomic catastrophe which could wipe out the human race also serve to protect the very forces which perpetuate this danger? The efforts to prevent such a catastrophe overshadow the search for its potential causes in contemporary industrial society. These causes remain unidentified, unexposed, unattacked by the public because they recede before the all too obvious threat from without—to the West from the East, to the East from the West. Equally obvious is the need for being prepared, for living on the brink, for facing the challenge. We submit to the peaceful production of the means of destruction, to the perfection of waste, to being educated for a defense which deforms the defenders and that which they defend.

If we attempt to relate the causes of the danger to the way in which society is organized and organizes its members, we are immediately confronted with the fact that advanced industrial society becomes richer, bigger, and better as it perpetuates the danger. The defense structure makes life easier for a greater number of people and extends man's mastery of nature. Under these circumstances, our mass media have little difficulty in selling particular interests as those of all sensible men. The political needs of society become individual needs and aspirations, their satisfaction promotes business and the commonweal, and the whole appears to be the very embodiment of Reason.

And yet this society is irrational as a whole. Its productivity is destructive of the free development of human needs and faculties, its peace maintained by the constant threat of war, its growth dependent on the repression of the real possibilities for pacifying the struggle for existence—individual, national, and international. This repression, so different from that which characterized the preceding, less developed stages of our society, operates today not from a position of natural and technical immaturity but rather from a position of strength. The capabilities (intellectual and material) of contemporary society are immeasurably greater than ever before—which means that the scope of society's domination over the individual is immeasurably greater than ever before. Our society distinguishes itself by conquering the centrifugal social forces with Technology rather that Terror, on the dual basis of an overwhelming efficiency and an increasing standard of living.

To investigate the roots of these developments and examine their historical alternatives is part of the aim of a critical theory of contemporary society, a theory which analyzes society in the light of its used and unused or abused capabilities for improving the human condition. But what are the standards for such a critique?

Certainly value judgments play a part. The established way of organizing society is measured against other possible ways, ways which are held to offer better chances for alleviating man's struggle for existence; a specific historical practice is measured against its own historical alternatives. From the beginning, any critical theory of society is thus confronted with the problem of historical objectivity, a problem which arises at the two points where the analysis implies value judgments:

1. the judgment that human life is worth living, or rather can be and ought to be made worth living. This judgment underlies all intellectual effort; it is the *a priori* of social theory, and its rejection (which is perfectly logical) rejects theory itself;
2. the judgment that, in a given society, specific possibilities exist for the amelioration

of human life and specific ways and means of realizing these possibilities. Critical analysis has to demonstrate the objective validity of these judgments, and the demonstration has to proceed on empirical grounds. The established society has available an ascertainable quantity and quality of intellectual and material resources. How can these resources be used for the optimal development and satisfaction of individual needs and faculties with a minimum of toil and misery? Social theory is historical theory, and history is the realm of chance in the realm of necessity. Therefore, among the various possible and actual modes of organizing and utilizing the available resources, which ones offer the greatest chance of an optimal development?

The attempt to answer these questions demands a series of initial abstractions. In order to identify and define the possibilities of an optimal development, the critical theory must abstract from the actual organization and utilization of society's resources, and from the results of this organization and utilization. Such abstraction which refuses to accept the given universe of facts as the final context of validation, such "transcending" analysis of the facts in the light of their arrested and denied possibilities, pertains to the very structure of social theory. It is opposed to all metaphysics by virtue of the rigorously historical character of the transcendence.[1] The "possibilities" must be within the reach of the respective society; they must be definable goals of practice. By the same token, the abstraction from the established institutions must be expressive of an actual tendency—that is, their transformation must be the real need of the underlying population. Social theory is concerned with the historical alternatives which

---

[1] The terms "transcend" and "transcendence" are used throughout in the empirical, critical sense: they designate tendencies in theory and practice which, in a given society, "overshoot" the established universe of discourse and action toward its historical alternatives (real possibilities).

haunt the established society as subversive tendencies and forces. The values attached to the alternatives do become facts when they are translated into reality by historical practice. The theoretical concepts terminate with social change.

But here, advanced industrial society confronts the critique with a situation which seems to deprive it of its very basis. Technical progress, extended to a whole system of domination and coordination, creates forms of life (and of power) which appear to reconcile the forces opposing the system and to defeat or refute all protest in the name of the historical prospects of freedom from toil and domination. Contemporary society seems to be capable of containing social change—qualitative change which would establish essentially different institutions, a new direction of the productive process, new modes of human existence. This containment of social change is perhaps the most singular achievement of advanced industrial society; the general acceptance of the National Purpose, bipartisan policy, the decline of pluralism, the collusion of Business and Labor within the strong State testify to the integration of opposites which is the result as well as the prerequisite of this achievement.

A brief comparison between the formative stage of the theory of industrial society and its present situation may help to show how the basis of the critique has been altered. At its origins in the first half of the nineteenth century, when it elaborated the first concepts of the alternatives, the critique of industrial society attained concreteness in a historical mediation between theory and practice, values and facts, needs and goals. This historical mediation occurred in the consciousness and in the political action of the two great classes which faced each other in the society: the bourgeoisie and the proletariat. In the capitalist world, they are still the basic classes. However, the capitalist development has altered the structure and function of these two classes in such a way that they no longer appear to be agents of historical transformation. An overriding interest in the preservation and improvement of the institutional status quo unites the former antagonists in the most advanced areas of contemporary society. And to the degree to which technical progress assures the growth and cohesion of communist society, the very idea of qualitative change recedes before the realistic notions of a non-explosive evolution. In the absence of demonstrable agents and agencies of social change, the critique is thus thrown back to a high level of abstraction. There is no ground on which theory and practice, thought and action meet. Even the most empirical analysis of historical alternatives appears to be unrealistic speculation, and commitment to them a matter of personal (or group) preference.

And yet: does this absence refute the theory? In the face of apparently contradictory facts, the critical analysis continues to insist that the need for qualitative change is as pressing as ever before. Needed by whom? The answer continues to be the same: by the society as a whole, for every one of its members. The union of growing productivity and growing destruction; the brinkmanship of annihilation; the surrender of thought, hope, and fear to the decisions of the powers that be; the preservation of misery in the face of unprecedented wealth constitute the most impartial indictment—even if they are not the *raison d'être* of this society but only its by-product: its sweeping rationality, which propels efficiency and growth, is itself irrational.

The fact that the vast majority of the population accepts, and is made to accept, this society does not render it less irrational and less reprehensible. The distinction between true and false consciousness, real and immediate interest still is meaningful. But this distinction itself must be validated. Men must come to see it and to find their way from false to true consciousness, from their immediate to their real interest. They can do so only if they live in need of changing their way of life, of denying the positive, of refusing. It is precisely this need which the established society manages to repress to the degree to which it is capable of "delivering the goods" on an increasingly large scale, and using the scientific conquest of nature for the scientific conquest of man.

Confronted with the total character of the achievements of advanced industrial society, critical theory is left without the rationale for transcending this society. The vacuum empties the theoretical structure itself, because the categories of a critical social theory were developed during the period in which the need for refusal and subversion was embodied in the action of effective social forces. These categories were essentially negative and oppositional concepts, defining the actual contradictions in nineteenth century European society. The category "society" itself expressed the acute conflict between the social and political sphere—society as antagonistic to the state. Similarly, "individual," "class," "private," "family" denoted spheres and forces not yet integrated with the established conditions—spheres of tension and contradiction. With the growing integration of industrial society, these categories are losing their critical connotation, and tend to become descriptive, deceptive, or operational terms.

An attempt to recapture the critical intent of these categories, and to understand how the intent was canceled by the social reality, appears from the outset to be regression from a theory joined with historical practice to abstract, speculative thought: from the critique of political economy to philosophy. This ideological character of the critique results from the fact that the analysis is forced to proceed from a position "outside" the positive as well as negative, the productive as well as destructive tendencies in society. Modern industrial society is the pervasive identity of these opposites—it is the whole that is in question. At the same time, the position of theory cannot be one of mere speculation. It must be a historical position in the sense that it must be grounded on the capabilities of the given society.

This ambiguous situation involves a still more fundamental ambiguity. *One-Dimensional Man* will vacillate throughout between two contradictory hypotheses: (1) that advanced industrial society is capable of containing qualitative change for the foreseeable future; (2) that forces and tendencies exist which may break this containment and explode the society. I do not think that a clear answer can be given. Both tendencies are there, side by side—and even the one in the other. The first tendency is dominant, and whatever preconditions for a reversal may exist are being used to prevent it. Perhaps an accident may alter the situation, but unless the recognition of what is being done and what is being prevented subverts the consciousness and the behavior of man, not even a catastrophe will bring about the change.

The analysis is focused on advanced industrial society, in which the technical apparatus of production and distribution (with an increasing sector of automation) functions, not as the sum-total of mere instruments which can be isolated from their social and political effects, but rather as a system which determines *a priori* the product of the apparatus as well as the operations of servicing and extending it. In this society, the productive apparatus tends to become totalitarian to the extent to which it determines not only the socially needed occupations, skills, and attitudes, but also individual needs and aspirations. It thus obliterates the opposition between the private and public existence, between individual and social needs. Technology serves to institute new, more effective, and more pleasant forms of social control and social cohesion. The totalitarian tendency of these controls seems to assert itself in still another sense—by spreading to the less developed and even to the preindustrial areas of the world, and by creating similarities in the development of capitalism and communism.

In the face of the totalitarian features of this society, the traditional notion of the "neutrality" of technology can no longer be maintained. Technology as such cannot be isolated from the use to which it is put; the technological society is a system of domination which operates already in the concept and construction of techniques.

The way in which a society organizes the life of its members involves an initial *choice* between historical alternatives which are determined by the inherited level of the material and intellectual culture. The choice itself results from the play of the dominant interests. It *anticipates* specific modes of transforming and utilizing man and nature and rejects other modes. It is one "project" of realization among others.[2] But once the project has become operative in the basic institutions and relations, it tends to become exclusive and to determine the development of the society as a whole. As a technological universe, advanced industrial society is a *political* universe, the latest stage in the realization of a specific historical *project*—namely, the experience, transformation, and organization of nature as the mere stuff of domination.

As the project unfolds, it shapes the entire universe of discourse and action, intellectual and material culture. In the medium of technology, culture, politics, and the economy merge into an omnipresent system which swallow up or repulses all alternatives. The productivity and growth potential of this system stabilize the society and contain technical progress within the framework of domination. Technological rationality has become political rationality.

In the discussion of the familiar tendencies of advanced industrial civilization, I have rarely given specific references. The material is assembled and described in the vast sociological and psychological literature on technology and social change, scientific management, corporative enterprise, changes in the character of industrial labor and of the labor force, etc. There are many unideological analyses of the facts—such as Berle and Means, *The Modern Corporation*

and *Private Property,* the reports of the 76th Congress' Temporary National Economic Committee on the *Concentration of Economic Power,* the publications of the AFL-CIO on *Automation and Major Technological Change,* but also those of *News and Letters* and *Correspondence* in Detroit. I should like to emphasize the vital importance of the work of C. Wright Mills, and of studies which are frequently frowned upon because of simplification, overstatement, or journalistic ease—Vance Packard's *The Hidden Persuaders, The Status Seekers,* and *The Waste Makers,* William H. Whyte's *The Organization Man,* Fred J. Cook's *The Warfare State* belong in this category. To be sure, the lack of theoretical analysis in these works leaves the roots of the described conditions covered and protected, but left to speak for themselves, the conditions speak loudly enough. Perhaps the most telling evidence can be obtained by simply looking at television or listening to the AM radio for one consecutive hour for a couple of days, not shutting off the commercials, and now and then switching the station.

My analysis is focused on tendencies in the most highly developed contemporary societies. There are large areas within and without these societies where the described tendencies do not prevail—I would say: not yet prevail. I am projecting these tendencies and I offer some hypotheses, nothing more.

The New Forms of Control

A comfortable, smooth, reasonable, democratic unfreedom prevails in advanced industrial civilization, a token of technical progress. Indeed, what could be more rational than the suppression of individuality in the mechanization of socially necessary but painful performances; the concentration of individual enterprises in more effective, more productive corporations; the regulation of free competition among unequally equipped economic subjects; the curtailment of prerogatives and national sovereignties which impede the

---

[2] The term "project" emphasizes the element of freedom and responsibility in historical determination: it links autonomy and contingency. In this sense, the term is used in the work of Jean-Paul Sartre.

international organization of resources. That this technological order also involves a political and intellectual coordination may be a regrettable and yet promising development.

The rights and liberties which were such vital factors in the origins and earlier stages of industrial society yield to a higher stage of this society: they are losing their traditional rationale and content. Freedom of thought, speech, and conscience were—just as free enterprise, which they served to promote and protect—essentially *critical* ideas, designed to replace an obsolescent material and intellectual culture by a more productive and rational one. Once institutionalized, these rights and liberties shared the fate of the society of which they had become an integral part. The achievement cancels the premises.

To the degree to which freedom from want, the concrete substance of all freedom, is becoming a real possibility, the liberties which pertain to a state of lower productivity are losing their former content. Independence of thought, autonomy, and the right to political opposition are being deprived of their basic critical function in a society which seems increasingly capable of satisfying the needs of the individuals through the way in which it is organized. Such a society may justly demand acceptance of its principles and institutions, and reduce the opposition to the discussion and promotion of alternative policies *within* the status quo. In this respect, it seems to make little difference whether the increasing satisfaction of needs is accomplished by an authoritarian or a non-authoritarian system. Under the conditions of a rising standard of living, non-conformity with the system itself appears to be socially useless, and the more so when it entails tangible economic and political disadvantages and threatens the smooth operation of the whole. Indeed, at least in so far as the necessities of life are involved, there seems to be no reason why the production and distribution of goods and services should proceed through the competitive concurrence of individual liberties.

Freedom of enterprise was from the beginning not altogether a blessing. As the liberty to work or to starve, it spelled toil, insecurity, and fear for the vast majority of the population. If the individual were no longer compelled to prove himself on the market, as a free economic subject, the disappearance of this kind of freedom would be one of the greatest achievements of civilization. The technological processes of mechanization and standardization might release individual energy into a yet uncharted realm of freedom beyond necessity. The very structure of human existence would be altered; the individual would be liberated from the work world's imposing upon him alien needs and alien possibilities. The individual would be free to exert autonomy over a life that would be his own. If the productive apparatus could be organized and directed toward the satisfaction of the vital needs, its control might well be centralized; such control would not prevent individual autonomy, but render it possible.

This is a goal within the capabilities of advanced industrial civilization, the "end" of technological rationality. In actual fact, however, the contrary trend operates: the apparatus imposes its economic and political requirements for defense and expansion on labor time and free time, on the material and intellectual culture. By virtue of the way it has organized its technological base, contemporary industrial society tends to be totalitarian. For "totalitarian" is not only a terroristic political coordination of society, but also a non-terroristic economic-technical coordination which operates through the manipulation of needs by vested interests. It thus precludes the emergence of an effective opposition against the whole. Not only a specific form of government or party rule makes for totalitarianism, but also a specific system of production and distribution which may well be compatible with a "pluralism" of parties, newspapers, "countervailing powers," etc.

Today political power asserts itself through its power over the machine process and over the technical organization of the apparatus. The government of advanced and advancing industrial societies can maintain and secure itself only when it succeeds in mobilizing, organizing, and exploiting the technical, scientific, and mechanical productivity available to industrial civilization. And this productivity mobilizes society as a whole, above and beyond any particular individual or group interests. The brute fact that the machine's physical (only physical?) power surpasses that of the individual, and of any particular group of individuals, makes the machine the most effective political instrument in any society whose basic organization is that of the machine process. But the political trend may be reversed; essentially the power of the machine is only the stored-up and projected power of man. To the extent to which the work world is conceived of as a machine and mechanized accordingly, it becomes the *potential* basis of a new freedom for man.

Contemporary industrial civilization demonstrates that it has reached the stage at which "the free society" can no longer be adequately defined in the traditional terms of economic, political, and intellectual liberties, not because these liberties have become insignificant, but because they are too significant to be confined with the traditional forms. New modes of realization are needed, corresponding to the new capabilities of society.

Such new modes can be indicated only in negative terms because they would amount to the negation of the prevailing modes. Thus economic freedom would mean freedom *from* the economy—from being controlled by economic forces and relationships; freedom from the daily struggle for existence, from earning a living. Political freedom would mean liberation of the individuals *from* politics over which they have no effective control. Similarly, intellectual freedom would mean the restoration of individual thought now absorbed by mass communication and indoctrination, abolition of "public opinion" together with its makers. The unrealistic

sound of these propositions is indicative, not of their utopian character, but of the strength of the forces which prevent their realization. The most effective and enduring form of warfare against liberation is the implanting of material and intellectual needs that perpetuate obsolete forms of the struggle for existence.

The intensity, the satisfaction and even the character of human needs, beyond the biological level, have always been preconditioned. Whether or not the possibility of doing or leaving, enjoying or destroying, possessing or rejecting something is seized as a *need* depends on whether or not it can be seen as desirable and necessary for the prevailing societal institutions and interests. In this sense, human needs are historical needs and, to the extent to which the society demands the repressive development of the individual, his needs themselves and their claim for satisfaction are subject to overriding critical standards.

We may distinguish both true and false needs. "False" are those which are superimposed upon the individual by particular social interests in his repression: the needs which perpetuate toil, aggressiveness, misery, and injustice. Their satisfaction might be most gratifying to the individual, but this happiness is not a condition which has to be maintained and protected if it serves to arrest the development of the ability (his own and others) to recognize the disease of the whole and grasp the chances of curing the disease. The result then is euphoria in unhappiness. Most of the prevailing needs to relax, to have fun, to behave and consume in accordance with the advertisements, to love and hate what others love and hate, belong to this category of false needs.

Such needs have a societal content and function which are determined by external powers over which the individual has no control; the development and satisfaction of these needs is heteronomous. No matter how much such needs may have become the individual's own, reproduced and fortified by the conditions of his existence; no matter how much he identifies himself with them and finds himself in their satisfaction, they continue to be what they were from the beginning—products of a society whose dominant interest demands repression.

The prevalence of repressive needs is an accomplished fact, accepted in ignorance and defeat, but a fact that must be undone in the interest of the happy individual as well as all those whose misery is the price of his satisfaction. The only needs that have an unqualified claim for satisfaction are the vital ones—nourishment, clothing, lodging at the attainable level of culture. The satisfaction of these needs is the prerequisite for the realization of *all* needs, of the unsublimated as well as the sublimated ones.

For any consciousness and conscience, for any experience which does not accept the prevailing societal interest as the supreme law of thought and behavior, the established universe of needs and satisfactions is a fact to be questioned—questioned in terms of truth and falsehood. These terms are historical throughout, and their objectivity is historical. The judgment of needs and their satisfaction, under the given conditions, involves standards of *priority*—standards which refer to the optimal development of the individual, of all individuals, under the optimal utilization of the material and intellectual resources available to man. The resources are calculable. "Truth" and "falsehood" of needs designate objective conditions to the extent to which the universal satisfaction of vital needs and, beyond it, the progressive alleviation of toil and poverty, are universally valid standards. But as historical standards, they do not only vary according to area and stage of development, they also can be defined only in (greater or lesser) *contradiction* to the prevailing ones. What tribunal can possibly claim the authority of decision?

In the last analysis, the question of what are true and false needs must be answered by the individuals themselves, but only in the last analysis; that is, if and when they are free to give their own answer. As long as they are kept incapable of being autonomous, as long as they are indoctrinated and manipulated (down to their very instincts), their answer to this question cannot be taken as their own. By the same token, however, no tribunal can justly arrogate to itself the right to decide which needs should be developed and satisfied. Any such tribunal is reprehensible, although our revulsion does not do away with the question: how can the people who have been the object of effective and productive domination by themselves create the conditions of freedom?

The more rational, productive, technical, and total the repressive administration of society becomes, the more unimaginable the means and ways by which the administered individuals might break their servitude and seize their own liberation. To be sure, to impose Reason upon an entire society is a paradoxical and scandalous idea—although one might dispute the righteousness of a society which ridicules this idea while making its own population into objects of total administration. All liberation depends on the consciousness of servitude, and the emergence of this consciousness is always hampered by the predominance of needs and satisfactions which, to a great extent, have become the individual's own. The process always replaces one system of preconditioning by another; the optimal goal is the replacement of false needs by true ones, the abandonment of repressive satisfaction.

The distinguishing feature of advanced industrial society is its effective suffocation of those needs which demand liberation—liberation also from that which is tolerable and rewarding and comfortable—while it sustains and absolves the destructive power and repressive function of the affluent society. Here, the social controls exact the overwhelming need for the production and consumption of waste; the need for stupefying work where it is no longer a real necessity; the need for modes of relaxation which soothe and prolong this stupefication; the need for maintaining such deceptive liberties as free competition at administered prices, a free press which censors itself, free choice between brands and gadgets.

Under the rule of a repressive whole, liberty can be made into a powerful instrument of domination. The range of choice open to the individual is not the decisive factor in determining the degree of human freedom, but *what* can be chosen and what *is* chosen by the individual. The criterion for free choice can never be an absolute one, but neither is it entirely relative. Free election of masters does not abolish the masters or the slaves. Free choice among a wide variety of goods and services does not signify freedom if these goods and services sustain social controls over a life of toil and fear—that is, if they sustain alienation. And the spontaneous reproduction of superimposed needs by the individual does not establish autonomy; it only testifies to the efficacy of the controls.

Our insistence on the depth and efficacy of these controls is open to the objection that we overrate greatly the indoctrinating power of the "media," and that by themselves the people would feel and satisfy the needs which are now imposed upon them. The objection misses the point. The preconditioning does not start with the mass production of radio and television and with the centralization of their control. The people enter this stage as preconditioned receptacles of long standing; the decisive difference is in the flattening out of the contrast (or conflict) between the given and the possible, between the satisfied and the unsatisfied needs. Here, the so-called equalization of class distinctions reveals its ideological function. If the worker and his boss enjoy the same television program and visit the same resort places, if the typist is as attractively made up as the daughter of her employer, if the Negro owns a Cadillac, if they all read the same newspaper, then this assimilation indicates not the disappearance of classes, but the

extent to which the needs and satisfactions that serve the preservation of the Establishment are shared by the underlying population.

Indeed, in the most highly developed areas of contemporary society, the transplantation of social into individual needs is so effective that the difference between them seems to be purely theoretical. Can one really distinguish between the mass media as instruments of information and entertainment, and as agents of manipulation and indoctrination? Between the automobile as nuisance and as convenience? Between the horrors and the comforts of functional architecture? Between the work for national defense and the work for corporate gain? Between the private pleasure and the commercial and political utility involved in increasing the birth rate?

We are again confronted with one of the most vexing aspects of advanced industrial civilization: the rational character of its irrationality. Its productivity and efficiency, its capacity to increase and spread comforts, to turn waste into need, and destruction into construction, the extent to which this civilization transforms the object world into an extension of man's mind and body makes the very notion of alienation questionable. The people recognize themselves in their commodities; they find their soul in their automobile, hi-fi set, split-level home, kitchen equipment. The very mechanism which ties the individual to his society has changed, and social control is anchored in the new needs which it has produced.

The prevailing forms of social control are technological in a new sense. To be sure, the technical structure and efficacy of the productive and destructive apparatus has been a major instrumentality for subjecting the population to the established social division of labor throughout the modern period. Moreover, such integration has always been accompanied by more obvious forms of compulsion: loss of livelihood, the administration of justice, the police, the armed forces. It still is. But in the contemporary period, the technological controls appear to be the very embodiment of Reason for the benefit of all social groups and interests—to such an extent that all contradiction seems irrational and all counteraction impossible.

No wonder then that, in the most advanced areas of this civilization, the social controls have been introjected to the point where even individual protest is affected at its roots. The intellectual and emotional refusal "to go along" appears neurotic and impotent. This is the sociopsychological aspect of the political event that marks the contemporary period: the passing of the historical forces which, at the preceding stage of industrial society, seemed to represent the possibility of new forms of existence.

But the term "introjection" perhaps no longer describes the way in which the individual by himself reproduces and perpetuates the external controls exercised by his society. Introjection suggests a variety of relatively spontaneous processes by which a Self (Ego) transposes the "outer" into the "inner." Thus introjection implies the existence of an inner dimension distinguished from and even antagonistic to the external exigencies—an individual consciousness and an individual unconscious *apart from* public opinion and behavior.[3] The idea of "inner-freedom" here has its reality: it designates the private space in which man may become and remain "himself."

Today this private space has been invaded and whittled down by technological reality. Mass production and mass distribution claim the *entire* individual, and industrial psychology has long since ceased to be confined to the factory. The manifold processes of introjection seem to be ossified in almost mechanical reactions. The result is, not adjustment but *mimesis:* an immediate identification of the individual with

his society and, through it, with the society as a whole.

This immediate, automatic identification (which may have been characteristic of primitive forms of association) reappears in high industrial civilization; its new "immediacy," however, is the product of a sophisticated, scientific management and organization. In this process, the "inner" dimension of the mind in which opposition to the status quo can take root is whittled down. The loss of this dimension, in which the power of negative thinking—the critical power of Reason—is at home, is the ideological counterpart to the very material process in which advanced industrial society silences and reconciles the opposition. The impact of progress turns Reason into submission to the facts of life, and to the dynamic capability of producing more and bigger facts of the same sort of life. The efficiency of the system blunts the individuals' recognition that it contains no facts which do not communicate the repressive power of the whole. If the individuals find themselves in the things which shape their life, they do so, not by giving, but by accepting the law of things—not the law of physics but the law of their society.

I have just suggested that the concept of alienation seems to become questionable when the individuals identify themselves with the existence which is imposed upon them and have in it their own development and satisfaction. This identification is not illusion but reality. However, the reality constitutes a more progressive stage of alienation. The latter has become entirely objective; the subject which is alienated is swallowed up by its alienated existence. There is only one dimension, and it is everywhere and in all forms. The achievements of progress defy ideological indictment as well as justification; before their tribunal, the "false consciousness" of their rationality becomes the true consciousness.

This absorption of ideology into reality does not, however, signify the "end of ideology." On

---

[3] The change in the function of the family here plays a decisive role: its "socializing" functions are increasingly taken over by outside groups and media. See my *Eros and Civilization* (Boston: Beacon Press, 1955), p. 96 ff.

the contrary, in a specific sense advanced industrial culture is *more* ideological than its predecessor, inasmuch as today the ideology is in the process of production itself.[4] In a provocative form, this proposition reveals the political aspects of the prevailing technological rationality. The productive apparatus and the goods and services which it produces "sell" or impose the social system as a whole. The means of mass transportation and communication, the commodities of lodging, food, and clothing, the irresistible output of the entertainment and information industry carry with them prescribed attitudes and habits, certain intellectual and emotional reactions which bind the consumers more or less pleasantly to the producers and, through the latter, to the whole. The products indoctrinate and manipulate; they promote a false consciousness which is immune against its falsehood. And as these beneficial products become available to more individuals in more social classes, the indoctrination they carry ceases to be publicity; it becomes a way of life. It is a good way of life—much better than before—and as a good way of life, it militates against qualitative change. Thus emerges a pattern of *one-dimensional thought and behavior* in which ideas, aspirations, and objectives that, by their content, transcend the established universe of discourse and action are either repelled or reduced to terms of this universe. They are redefined by the rationality of the given system and of its quantitative extension.

The trend may be related to a development in scientific method: operationalism in the physical, behaviorism in the social sciences. The common feature is a total empiricism in the treatment of concepts; their meaning is restricted to the representation of particular operations and behavior. The operational point

of view is well illustrated by P. W. Bridgman's analysis of the concept of length:[5]

> We evidently know what we mean by length if we can tell what the length of any and every object is, and for the physicist nothing more is required. To find the length of an object, we have to perform certain physical operations. The concept of length is therefore fixed when the operations by which length is measured are fixed: that is, the concept of length involves as much and nothing more than the set of operations by which length is determined. In general, we mean by any concept nothing more than a set of operations; *the concept is synonymous with the corresponding set of operations.*

Bridgman has seen the wide implications of this mode of thought for the society at large:[6]

> To adopt the operational point of view involves much more than a mere restriction of the sense in which we understand 'concept,' but means a far-reaching change in all our habits of thought, in that we shall no longer permit ourselves to use as tools in our thinking concepts of which we cannot give an adequate account in terms of operations.

Bridgman's prediction has come true. The new mode of thought is today the predominant tendency in philosophy, psychology, sociology, and other fields. Many of the most seriously troublesome concepts are being "eliminated" by showing that no adequate account of them in terms of operations or behavior can be given.

---

[4] Theodor W. Adorno, *Prismen, Kulturkritik und Gesellschaft* (Frankfurt: Suhrkamp, 1955), p. 24 f.

[5] P. W. Bridgman, *The Logic of Modern Physics* (New York: Macmillan, 1928), p. 5. The operational doctrine has since been refined and qualified. Bridgman himself has extended the concept of "operation" to include the "paper-and-pencil" operations of the theorist (in Philipp J. Frank, *The Validation of Scientific Theories* [Boston: Beacon Press, 1954], Chap. II). The main impetus remains the same: it is "desirable" that the paper-and-pencil operations "be capable of eventual contact, although perhaps indirectly, with instrumental operations."
[6] P. W. Bridgman, *The Logic of Modern Physics*, loc. cit., p. 31.

The radical empiricist onslaught (I shall subsequently, in chapters VII and VIII, examine its claim to be empiricist) thus provides the methodological justification for the debunking of the mind by the intellectuals—a positivism which, in its denial of the transcending elements of Reason, forms the academic counterpart of the socially required behavior.

Outside the academic establishment, the "far-reaching change in all our habits of thought" is more serious. It serves to coordinate ideas and goals with those exacted by the prevailing system to enclose them in the system, and to repel those which are irreconcilable with the system. The reign of such a one-dimensional reality does not mean that materialism rules, and that the spiritual, metaphysical, and bohemian occupations are petering out. On the contrary, there is a great deal of "Worship together this week," "Why not try God," Zen, existentialism, and beat ways of life, etc. But such modes of protest and transcendence are no longer contradictory to the status quo and no longer negative. They are rather the ceremonial part of practical behaviorism, its harmless negation, and are quickly digested by the status quo as part of its healthy diet.

One-dimensional thought is systematically promoted by the makers of politics and their purveyors of mass information. Their universe of discourse is populated by self-validating hypotheses which, incessantly and monopolistically repeated, become hypnotic definitions or dictations. For example, "free" are the institutions which operate (and are operated on) in the countries of the Free World; other transcending modes of freedom are by definition either anarchism, communism, or propaganda. "Socialistic" are all encroachments on private enterprises not undertaken by private enterprise itself (or by government contracts), such as universal and comprehensive health insurance, or the protection of nature from all too sweeping commercialization, or the establishment of public services which may hurt private profit. This totalitarian logic of accomplished facts has its Eastern counterpart. There, freedom is the way of life instituted by a communist regime, and all other transcending modes of freedom are either capitalistic, or revisionist, or leftist sectarianism. In both camps, non-operational ideas are non-behavioral and subversive. The movement of thought is stopped at barriers which appear as the limits of Reason itself

Such limitation of thought is certainly not new. Ascending modern rationalism, in its speculative as well as empirical form, shows a striking contrast between extreme critical radicalism in scientific and philosophic method on the one hand, and an uncritical quietism in the attitude toward established and functioning social institutions. Thus Descartes' *ego cogitans* was to leave the "great public bodies" untouched, and Hobbes held that "the present ought always to be preferred, maintained, and accounted best." Kant agreed with Locke in justifying revolution *if and when* it has succeeded in organizing the whole and in preventing subversion.

However, these accommodating concepts of Reason were always contradicted by the evident misery and injustice of the "great public bodies" and the effective, more or less conscious rebellion against them. Societal conditions existed which provoked and permitted real dissociation from the established state of affairs; a private as well as political dimension was present in which dissociation could develop into effective opposition, testing its strength and the validity of its objectives.

With the gradual closing of this dimension by the society, the self-limitation of thought assumes a larger significance. The interrelation between scientific-philosophical and societal processes, between theoretical and practical Reason, asserts itself "behind the back" of the scientists and philosophers. The society bars a whole type of oppositional operations and behavior; consequently, the concepts pertaining to them are rendered illusory or meaningless. Historical transcendence appears as metaphysical transcendence, not acceptable to science and scientific thought. The operational and behavioral point of view, practiced as a "habit of thought" at large, becomes the view of the established universe of discourse and action, needs and aspirations. The "cunning of Reason" works, as it so often did, in the interest of the powers that be. The insistence on operational and behavioral concepts turns against the efforts to free thought and behavior *from* the given reality and *for* the suppressed alternatives. Theoretical and practical Reason, academic and social behaviorism meet on common ground: that of an advanced society which makes scientific and technical progress into an instrument of domination.

"Progress" is not a neutral term; it moves toward specific ends, and these ends are defined by the possibilities of ameliorating the human condition. Advanced industrial society is approaching the stage where continued progress would demand the radical subversion of the prevailing direction and organization of progress. This stage would be reached when material production (including the necessary services) becomes automated to the extent that all vital needs can be satisfied while necessary labor time is reduced to marginal time. From this point on, technical progress would transcend the realm of necessity, where it served as the instrument of domination and exploitation which thereby limited its rationality; technology would become subject to the free play of faculties in the struggle for the pacification of nature and of society.

Such a state is envisioned in Marx's notion of the "abolition of labor." The term "pacification of existence" seems better suited to designate the historical alternative of a world which—through an international conflict which transforms and suspends the contradictions within the established societies—advances on the brink of a global war. "Pacification of existence" means the development of man's struggle with man and with nature, under conditions where the competing needs, desires, and aspirations are no longer organized by vested interests in domination and scarcity—an organization which perpetuates the destructive forms of this struggle.

Today's fight against this historical alternative finds a firm mass basis in the underlying population, and finds its ideology in the rigid orientation of thought and behavior to the given universe of facts. Validated by the accomplishments of science and technology, justified by its growing productivity, the status quo defies all transcendence. Faced with the possibility of pacification on the grounds of its technical and intellectual achievements, the mature industrial society closes itself against this alternative. Operationalism, in theory and practice, becomes the theory and practice of *containment*. Underneath its obvious dynamics, this society is a thoroughly static system of life: self-propelling in its oppressive productivity and in its beneficial coordination. Containment of technical progress goes hand in hand with its growth in the established direction. In spite of the political fetters imposed by the status quo, the more technology appears capable of creating the conditions for pacification, the more are the minds and bodies of man organized against this alternative.

The most advanced areas of industrial society exhibit throughout these two features: a trend toward consummation of technological rationality, and intensive efforts to contain this trend within the established institutions. Here is the internal contradiction of this civilization: the irrational element in its rationality. It is the token of its achievements. The industrial society which makes technology and science its own is organized for the ever-more-effective domination of man and nature, for the ever-more-effective utilization of its resources. It becomes irrational when the success of these efforts opens new dimensions of human realization. Organization for peace is different from organization for war; the institutions which served the struggle for existence cannot serve the pacification of existence. Life as an end is qualitatively different from life as a means.

Such a qualitatively new model of existence can never be envisaged as the mere by-product of economic and political changes, as the more or less spontaneous effect of the new institutions which constitute the necessary prerequisite. Qualitative change also involves a change in the *technical* basis on which this society rests—one which sustains the economic and political institutions through which the "second nature" of man as an aggressive object of administration is stabilized. The techniques of industrialization are political techniques; as such, they prejudge the possibilities of Reason and Freedom.

To be sure, labor must precede the reduction of labor and industrialization must precede the development of human needs and satisfactions. But as all freedom depends on the conquest of alien necessity, the realization of freedom depends on the *techniques* of this conquest. The highest productivity of labor can be used for the perpetuation of labor, and the most efficient industrialization can serve the restriction and manipulation of needs.

When this point is reached, domination—in the guise of affluence and liberty—extends to all spheres of private and public existence, integrates all authentic opposition, absorbs all alternatives. Technological rationality reveals its political character as it becomes the great vehicle of better domination, creating a truly totalitarian universe in which society and nature, mind and body are kept in a state of permanent mobilization for the defense of this universe.

JÜRGEN HABERMAS: THREE NORMATIVE MODELS OF DEMOCRACY

In what follows I refer to the idealized distinction between the "liberal" and the "republican" understanding of politics—terms which mark the fronts in the current debate in the United States initiated by the so-called communitarians. Drawing on the work of Frank Michelman I will begin by describing the two polemically contrasted models of democracy with specific reference to the concept of the citizen, the concept of law, and the nature of processes of political will-formation. In the second part, beginning with a critique of the "ethical overload" of the republican model, I introduce a third, procedural model of democracy for which I propose to reserve the term "deliberative politics."

Jürgen Habermas, *The Inclusion of the Other: Studies in Political Theory*, (eds.) Ciaran Cronin and Pablo De Greiff. Reprinted with permission from MIT Press. This translation © 1998, Massachusetts Institute of Technology.

I

The crucial difference between liberalism and republicanism consists in how the role of the democratic process is understood. According to the "liberal" view, this process accomplishes the task of programming the state in the interest of society, where the state is conceived as an apparatus of public administration, and society is conceived as a system of market-structured interactions of private persons and their labor. Here politics (in the sense of the citizens' political will-formation) has the function of bundling together and bringing to bear private social interests against a state apparatus that specializes in the administrative employment of political power for collective goals.

On the republican view, politics is not exhausted by this mediating function but is constitutive for the socialization process as a whole. Politics is conceived as the reflexive form of substantial ethical life. It constitutes the medium in which the members of quasi-natural solidary communities become aware of their dependence on one another and, acting with full deliberation as citizens, further shape and develop existing relations of reciprocal recognition into an association of free and equal consociates under law. With this, the liberal architectonic of government and society undergoes an important change. In addition to the hierarchical regulatory apparatus of sovereign state authority and the decentralized regulatory mechanism of the market—that is, besides administrative power and self-interest—*solidarity* appears as a third source of social integration.

This horizontal political will-formation aimed at mutual understanding or communicatively achieved consensus is even supposed to enjoy priority, both in a genetic and a normative sense. An autonomous basis in civil society independent of public administration and market-mediated private commerce is assumed as a precondition for the practice of civic self-determination. This basis prevents political communication from being swallowed up by the government apparatus or assimilated to market structures. Thus, on the republican conception, the political public sphere and its base, civil society, acquire a strategic significance. Together they are supposed to secure the integrative power and autonomy of the communicative practice of the citizens.[1] The uncoupling of political communication from the economy has as its counterpart a coupling of administrative power with the communicative power generated by political opinion- and will-formation.

These two competing conceptions of politics have different consequences.

(a) In the first place, their concepts of the citizen differ. According to the liberal view, the citizen's status is determined primarily by the individual rights he or she has vis-à-vis the state and other citizens. As bearers of individual rights citizens enjoy the protection of the government as long as they pursue their private interests within the boundaries drawn by legal statutes—and this includes protection against state interventions that violate the legal prohibition on government interference. Individual rights are negative rights that guarantee a domain of freedom of choice within which legal persons are freed from external compulsion. Political rights have the same structure: they afford citizens the opportunity to assert their private interests in such a way that, by means of elections, the composition of parliamentary bodies, and the formation of a government, these interests are finally aggregated into a political will that can affect the administration. In this way the citizens in their political role can determine whether governmental authority is exercised in the interest of the citizens as members of society.[2]

According to the republican view, the status of citizens is not determined by the model of negative liberties to which these citizens can lay claim as private persons. Rather, political rights—preeminently rights of political participation and communication—are positive liberties. They do not guarantee freedom from external compulsion, but guarantee instead the possibility of participating in a common practice, through which the citizens can first make themselves into what they want to be— politically responsible subjects of a community of free and equal citizens.[3] To this extent, the political process does not serve just to keep government activity under the surveillance of citizens who have already acquired a prior social autonomy through the exercise of their private rights and prepolitical liberties. Nor does it act only as a hinge between state and society, for democratic governmental authority is by no means an original authority. Rather, this authority proceeds from the communicative power generated by the citizens' practice of self-legislation, and it is legitimated by the fact that it protects this practice by institutionalizing public freedom.[4]

The state's *raison d'être* does not lie primarily in the protection of equal individual rights but in the guarantee of an inclusive process of opinion- and will-formation in which free and equal citizens reach an understanding on which goals and norms lie in the equal interest of all. In this way the republican citizen is credited with more than an exclusive concern with his or her private interests.

(b) The polemic against the classical concept of the legal person as bearer of individual rights reveals a controversy about the concept of law itself. Whereas on the liberal conception the point of a legal order is to make it possible to determine which individuals in each case are entitled to which rights, on the republican conception these "subjective" rights owe their existence to an "objective" legal order that both enables and guarantees the integrity of an autonomous life in common based on equality and mutual respect. On the one view, the legal order is conceived in terms of individual rights; on the other, their objective legal content is given priority.

To be sure, this conceptual dichotomy does not touch on the *intersubjective* content of rights that demand reciprocal respect for rights and duties in symmetrical relations of recognition. But the republican concept at least points in the direction of a concept of law that accords equal weight to both the integrity of the individual and the integrity of the community in which persons as both individuals and members can first accord one another reciprocal recognition. It ties the legitimacy of the laws to the democratic procedure by which they are generated and thereby preserves an internal connection between the citizens' practice of self-legislation and the impersonal sway of the law:

> For republicans, rights ultimately are nothing but determinations of prevailing political will, while for liberals, some rights are always grounded in a "higher law" of transpolitical reason or revelation. . . . In a

republican view, a community's objective, common good substantially consists in the success of its political endeavor to define, establish, effectuate, and sustain the set of rights (less tendentiously, laws) best suited to the conditions and *mores* of that community. Whereas in a contrasting liberal view, the higher-law rights provide the transactional structures and the curbs on power required so that pluralistic pursuit of diverse and conflicting interests may proceed as satisfactorily as possible.[5]

The right to vote, interpreted as a positive right, becomes the paradigm of rights as such, not only because it is constitutive for political self-determination, but because it shows how inclusion in a community of equals is connected with the individual right to make autonomous contributions and take personal positions on issues:

> [T]he claim is that we all take an interest in each others' enfranchisement because (i) our choice lies between hanging together and hanging separately; (ii) hanging together depends on reciprocal assurances to all of having one's vital interests heeded by others; and (iii) in the deeply pluralized conditions of contemporary American society, such assurances are not attainable through virtual representation, but only by maintaining at least the semblance of a politics in which everyone is conceded a voice.[6]

This structure, read off from the political rights of participation and communication, is extended to *all* rights via the legislative process constituted by political rights. Even the authorization guaranteed by private law to pursue private, freely chosen goals simultaneously imposes an obligation to respect the limits of strategic action which are agreed to be in the equal interest of all.

(c) The different ways of conceptualizing the role of citizen and the law express a deeper disagreement about the nature of the political process. On the liberal view, politics is essentially a struggle for positions that grant access to administrative power. The political process of opinion- and will-formation in the public sphere and in parliament is shaped by the competition of strategically acting collectives trying to maintain or acquire positions of power. Success is measured by the citizens' approval of persons and programs, as quantified by votes. In their choices at the polls, voters express their preferences. Their votes have the same structure as the choices of participants in a market, in that their decisions license access to positions of power that political parties fight over with a success-oriented attitude similar to that of players in the market. The input of votes and the output of power conform to the same pattern of strategic action.

According to the republican view, the political opinion- and will-formation in the public sphere and in parliament does not obey the structures of market processes but rather the obstinate structures of a public communication oriented to mutual understanding. For politics as the citizens' practice of self-determination, the paradigm is not the market but dialogue. From this perspective there is a structural difference between communicative power, which proceeds from political communication in the form of discursively generated majority decisions, and the administrative power possessed by the governmental apparatus. Even the parties that struggle over access to positions of governmental power must bend themselves to the deliberative style and the stubborn character of political discourse:

> Deliberation . . . refers to a certain attitude toward social cooperation, namely, that of openness to persuasion by reasons referring to the claims of others as well as one's own. The deliberative medium is a good faith exchange of views—including participants' reports of their own understanding of their

respective vital interests— . . . in which a vote, if any vote is taken, represents a pooling of judgments.[7]

Hence the conflict of opinions conducted in the political arena has legitimating force not just in the sense of an authorization to occupy positions of power; on the contrary, the ongoing political discourse also has binding force for the way in which political authority is exercised. Administrative power can only be exercised on the basis of policies and within the limits laid down by laws generated by the democratic process.

II

So much for the comparison between the two models of democracy that currently dominate the discussion between the so-called communitarians and liberals, above all in the US. The republican model has advantages and disadvantages. In my view it has the advantage that it preserves the radical democratic meaning of a society that organizes itself through the communicatively united citizens and does not trace collective goals back to "deals" made between competing private interests. Its disadvantage, as I see it, is that it is too idealistic in that it makes the democratic process dependent on the virtues of citizens devoted to the public weal. For politics is not concerned in the first place with questions of ethical self-understanding. The mistake of the republican view consists in an ethical foreshortening of political discourse.

To be sure, ethical discourses aimed at achieving a collective self-understanding—discourses in which participants attempt to clarify how they understand themselves as members of a particular nation, as members of a community or a state, as inhabitants of a region, etc., which traditions they wish to cultivate, how they should treat each other, minorities, and marginal groups, in what sort of society they want to live—constitute an important part of politics. But under conditions of cultural and social pluralism, behind politically relevant goals there often lie interests and value-orientations that are by no means constitutive of the identity of the political community as a whole, that is, for the totality of an intersubjectively shared form of life. These interests and value-orientations, which conflict with one another within the same polity without any prospect of consensual resolution, need to be counterbalanced in a way that cannot be effected by ethical discourse, even though the results of this nondiscursive counterbalancing are subject to the proviso that they must not violate the basic values of a culture. The balancing of interests takes the form of reaching a compromise between parties who rely on their power and ability to sanction. Negotiations of this sort certainly presuppose a readiness to cooperate, that is, a willingness to abide by the rules and to arrive at results that are acceptable to all parties, though for different reasons. But compromise-formation is not conducted in the form of a rational discourse that neutralizes power and excludes strategic action. However, the fairness of compromises is measured by presuppositions and procedures which for their part are in need of rational, indeed normative, justification from the standpoint of justice. In contrast with ethical questions, questions of justice are not by their very nature tied to a particular collectivity. Politically enacted law, if it is to be legitimate, must be at least in harmony with moral principles that claim a general validity that extends beyond the limits of any concrete legal community.

The concept of deliberative politics acquires empirical relevance only when we take into account the multiplicity of forms of communication in which a common will is produced, that is, not just ethical self-clarification but also the balancing of interests and compromise, the purposive choice of means, moral justification, and legal consistency-testing. In this process the two types of politics which Michelman distin-guishes in an ideal-typical fashion can interweave and complement one another in a rational manner. "Dialogical" and "instrumental" politics can *interpenetrate* in the medium of deliberation if the corresponding forms of communication are sufficiently institutionalized. Everything depends on the conditions of communication and the procedures that lend the institutionalized opinion- and will-formation their legitimating force. The third model of democracy, which I would like to propose, relies precisely on those conditions of communication under which the political process can be presumed to produce rational results because it operates deliberatively at all levels.

Making the proceduralist conception of deliberative politics the cornerstone of the theory of democracy results in differences both from the republican conception of the state as an ethical community and from the liberal conception of the state as the guardian of a market society. In comparing the three models, I take my orientation from that dimension of politics which has been our primary concern, namely, the democratic opinion- and will-formation that issue in popular elections and parliamentary decrees.

According to the liberal view, the democratic process takes place exclusively in the form of compromises between competing interests. Fairness is supposed to be guaranteed by rules of compromise-formation that regulate the general and equal right to vote, the representative composition of parliamentary bodies, their order of business, and so on. Such rules are ultimately justified in terms of liberal basic rights. According to the republican view, by contrast, democratic will-formation is supposed to take the form of an ethical discourse of self-understanding; here deliberation can rely for its content on a culturally established background consensus of the citizens, which is rejuvenated through the ritualistic reenactment of a republican founding act. Discourse theory takes elements from both sides and integrates them into the concept of an ideal procedure for deliberation and decision making. Weaving together negotiations and discourses of self-understanding and of justice, this democratic procedure grounds the presumption that under such conditions reasonable or fair results are obtained. According to this proceduralist view, practical reason withdraws from universal human rights or from the concrete ethical life of a specific community into the rules of discourse and forms of argumentation that derive their normative content from the validity-basis of action oriented to reaching understanding, and ultimately from the structure of linguistic communication.[8]

These descriptions of the structures of democratic process set the stage for different normative conceptualizations of state and society. The sole presupposition is a public administration of the kind that emerged in the early modern period together with the European state system and in functional interconnection with a capitalist economic system. According to the republican view, the citizens' political opinion- and will-formation forms the medium through which society constitutes itself as a political whole. Society is centered in the state; for in the citizens' practice of political self-determination the polity becomes conscious of itself as a totality and acts on itself via the collective will of the citizens. Democracy is synonymous with the political self-organization of society. This leads to a polemical understanding of politics as directed against the state apparatus. In Hannah Arendt's political writings one can see the thrust of republican arguments: in opposition to the civic privatism of a depoliticized population and in opposition to the acquisition of legitimation through entrenched parties, the political public sphere should be revitalized to the point where a regenerated citizenry can, in the forms of a decentralized self-governance, (once again) appropriate the governmental authority that has been usurped by a self-regulating bureaucracy.

According to the liberal view, this separation of the state apparatus from society cannot be eliminated but only bridged by the democratic process. However, the weak normative connotations of a regulated balancing of power and interests stands in need of constitutional channeling. The democratic will-formation of self-interested citizens, construed in minimalist terms, constitutes just one element within a constitution that disciplines governmental authority through normative constraints (such as basic rights, separation of powers, and legal regulation of the administration) and forces it, through competition between political parties, on the one hand, and between government and opposition, on the other, to take adequate account of competing interests and value orientations. This state-centered understanding of politics does not have to rely on the unrealistic assumption of a citizenry capable of acting collectively. Its focus is not so much the input of a rational political will-formation but the output of successful administrative accomplishments. The thrust of liberal arguments is directed against the disruptive potential of an administrative power that interferes with the independent social interactions of private persons. The liberal model hinges not on the democratic self-determination of deliberating citizens but on the legal institutionalization of an economic society that is supposed to guarantee an essentially nonpolitical common good through the satisfaction of the private aspirations of productive citizens.

Discourse theory invests the democratic process with normative connotations stronger than those of the liberal model but weaker than those of the republican model. Once again, it takes elements from both sides and fits them together in a new way. In agreement with republicanism, it gives center stage to the process of political opinion- and will-formation, but without understanding the constitution as something secondary; on the contrary, it conceives the basic principles of the constitutional state as a consistent answer to the question of how the demanding communicative presuppositions of a democratic opinion- and will-formation can be institutionalized. Discourse theory does not make the success of deliberative politics depend on a collectively acting citizenry but on the institutionalization of corresponding procedures. It no longer operates with the concept of a social whole centered in the state and conceived as a goal-oriented subject writ large. But neither does it localize the whole in a system of constitutional norms mechanically regulating the interplay of powers and interests in accordance with the market model. Discourse theory altogether jettisons the assumptions of the philosophy of consciousness, which invite us either to ascribe the citizens' practice of self-determination to one encompassing macrosubject or to apply the anonymous rule of law to competing individuals. The former approach represents the citizenry as a collective actor which reflects the whole and acts for its sake; on the latter, individual actors function as dependent variables in systemic processes that unfold blindly because no consciously executed collective decisions are possible over and above individual acts of choice (except in a purely metaphorical sense).

Discourse theory works instead with the *higher-level intersubjectivity* of communication processes that unfold in the institutionalized deliberations in parliamentary bodies, on the one hand, and in the informal networks of the public sphere, on the other. Both within and outside parliamentary bodies geared to decision making, these subjectless modes of communication form arenas in which a more or less rational opinion- and will-formation concerning issues and problems affecting society as a whole can take place. Informal opinion-formation result in institutionalized election decisions and legislative decrees through which communicatively generated power is transformed into administratively utilizable power. As on the liberal model, the boundary between state and society is respected; but here civil society, which provides the social underpinning of autonomous publics, is as distinct from the economic system

as it is from the public administration. This understanding of democracy leads to the normative demand for a new balance between the three resources of money, administrative power, and solidarity from which modern societies meet their need for integration and regulation. The normative implications are obvious: the integrative force of solidarity, which can no longer be drawn solely from sources of communicative action, should develop through widely expanded autonomous public spheres as well as through legally institutionalized procedures of democratic deliberation and decision making and gain sufficient strength to hold its own against the other two social forces—money and administrative power.

III

This view has implications for how one should understand legitimation and popular sovereignty. On the liberal view, democratic will-formation has the exclusive function of *legitimating* the exercise of political power. The outcomes of elections license the assumption of governmental power, though the government must justify the use of power to the public and parliament. On the republican view, democratic will-formation has the significantly stronger function of *constituting* society as a political community and keeping the memory of this founding act alive with each new election. The government is not only empowered by the electorate's choice between teams of leaders to exercise a largely open mandate, but is also bound in a programmatic fashion to carry out certain policies. More a committee than an organ of the state, it is part of a self-governing political community rather than the head of a separate governmental apparatus. Discourse theory, by contrast, brings a third idea into play: the procedures and communicative presuppositions of democratic opinion- and will-formation function as the most important sluices for the discursive rationalization of the decisions of a government and an administration bound by law and statute. On this view, *rationalization* signifies more than mere legitimation but less than the constitution of political power. The power available to the administration changes its general character once it is bound to a process of democratic opinion- and will-formation that does not merely retrospectively monitor the exercise of political power but also programs it in a certain way. Notwithstanding this discursive rationalization, only the political system itself can "act." It is a subsystem specialized for collectively binding decisions, whereas the communicative structures of the public sphere comprise a far-flung network of sensors that respond to the pressure of society-wide problems and stimulate influential opinions. The public opinion which is worked up via democratic procedures into communicative power cannot itself "rule" but can only channel the use of administrative power in specific directions.

The concept of *popular sovereignty* stems from the republican appropriation and revaluation of the early modern notion of sovereignty originally associated with absolutist regimes. The state, which monopolizes the means of legitimate violence, is viewed as a concentration of power which can overwhelm all other temporal powers. Rousseau transposed this idea, which goes back to Bodin, to the will of the united people, fused it with the classical idea of the self-rule of free and equal citizens, and sublimated it into the modern concept of autonomy. Despite this normative sublimation, the concept of sovereignty remained bound to the notion of an embodiment in the (at first actually physically assembled) people. According to the republican view, the at least potentially assembled people are the bearers of a sovereignty that cannot in principle be delegated: in their capacity as sovereign, the people cannot let themselves be represented by others. Constitutional power is founded on the citizens' practice of self-determination, not on that of their representatives. Against this, liberalism offers the more realistic view that, in the

constitutional state, the authority emanating from the people is exercised only "by means of elections and voting and by specific legislative, executive, and judicial organs."[9]

These two views exhaust the alternatives only on the dubious assumption that state and society must be conceived in terms of a whole and its parts, where the whole is constituted either by a sovereign citizenry or by a constitution. By contrast to the discourse theory of democracy corresponds the image of a *decentered* society, though with the political public sphere it sets apart an arena for the detection, identification, and interpretation of problems affecting society as a whole. If we abandon the conceptual framework of the philosophy of the subject, sovereignty need neither be concentrated in the people in a concretistic manner nor banished into the anonymous agencies established by the constitution. The "self" of the self-organizing legal community disappears in the subjectless forms of communication that regulate the flow of discursive opinion- and will-formation whose fallible results enjoy the presumption of rationality. This is not to repudiate the intuition associated with the idea of popular sovereignty but rather to interpret it in intersubjective terms. Popular sovereignty, even though it has become anonymous, retreats into democratic procedures and the legal implementation of their demanding communicative presuppositions only to be able to make itself felt as communicatively generated power. Strictly speaking, this communicative power springs from the interactions between legally institutionalized will-formation and culturally mobilized publics. The latter for their part find a basis in the associations of a civil society distinct from the state and the economy alike.

The normative self-understanding of deliberative politics does indeed call for a discursive mode of socialization for the *legal community*; but this mode does not extend to the whole of the society in which the constitutionally established political system is *embedded*. Even on its own proceduralist self-understanding, deliberative politics remains a component of a complex society, which as a whole resists the normative approach of legal theory. In this regard, the discourse-theoretic reading of democracy connects with an objectifying sociological approach that regards the political system neither as the peak nor the center, nor even as the structuring model of society, but as just *one* action system among others. Because it provides a kind of surety for the solution of the social problems that threaten integration, politics just indeed be able to communicate, via the medium of law, with all of the other legitimately ordered spheres of action, however these may be structured and steered. But the political system remains dependent on other functional mechanisms, such as the revenue-production of the economic system, in more than just a trivial sense; on the contrary, deliberative politics, whether realized in the formal procedures of institutionalized opinion- and will-formation or only in the informal networks of the political public sphere, stands in an internal relation to the contexts of a rationalized lifeworld that meets it halfway. Deliberatively filtered political communications are especially dependent on the resources of the lifeworld—on a free and open political culture and an enlightened political socialization, and above all on the initiatives of opinion-shaping associations. These resources emerge and regenerate themselves spontaneously for the most part—at any rate, they can only with difficulty be subjected to political control.

NOTES

1. Cf. H. Arendt, *On Revolution* (New York, 1965); *On Violence* (New York, 1970).
2. Cf. F. I. Michelman, "Political Truth and the Rule of Law," *Tel Aviv University Studies in Law* 8 (1988): 283: "The political society envisioned by bumper-sticker republicans is the society of private rights bearers, an association whose first principle is the protection of the lives, liberties, and estates of its individual members. In that society, the state is justified by the protection it gives to those prepolitical interests; the purpose of the constitution is to ensure that the state apparatus, the government, provides such protection for the people at large rather than serves the special interests of the governors or their patrons; the function of citizenship is to operate the constitution and thereby to motivate the governors to act according to that protective purpose; and the value to you of your political franchise—your right to vote and speak, to have your views heard and counted—is the handle it gives you on influencing the system so that it will adequately heed and protect *your* particular, prepolitical rights and other interests."
3. On the distinction between positive and negative freedom see Ch. Taylor, "What is Human Agency?" in *Human Agency and Language: Philosophical Papers 1* (Cambridge, 1985), pp. 15–44.
4. Michelman, "Political Truth and the Rule of Law," p. 284: "In [the] civic constitutional vision, political society is primarily the society not of rights bearers, but of citizens, an association whose first principle is the creation and provision of a public realm within which a people, together, argue and reason about the right terms of social coexistence, terms that they will set together and which they understand as comprising their common good. . . . Hence, the state is justified by its purpose of establishing and ordering the public sphere within which persons can achieve freedom in the sense of self-government by the exercise of reason in public dialogue."
5. Michelman, "Conceptions of Democracy in American Constitutional Argument: Voting Rights," *Florida Law Review* 41 (1989): 446f. (hereafter "Voting Rights").

6. Michelman, "Voting Rights," p. 484.

7. Michelman, "Conceptions of Democracy in American Constitutional Argument: The Case of Pornography Regulation," *Tennessee Law Review* 291 (1989): 293.

8. Cf. J. Habermas, "Popular Sovereignty as Procedure," in *Between Facts and Norms*, trans. W. Rehg (1996), pp. 463–490.

9. Cf. *The Basic Law of the Federal Republic of Germany*, article 20, sec. 2.

Chapter 14

Post-Modernism

Introduction

The term post-modernism or post-modernity has come to mean many different things. Some associate it with the post-industrial society, others with the post-Marxist world, still others view it as a movement in literary criticism, and some view it as a legitimation for new voices in a diverse and multicultural society. It is obviously difficult to give a single, encompassing definition to an intellectual movement that has developed in so many different directions. Two basic themes are explored in the excerpts on the following pages: one deals with the question of the Enlightenment promise, and the other, and related, theme deals with the relationship of theory to knowledge.

In the discussion of Habermas's work, reference was made to his commitment to the Enlightenment project, a view which proposes a democratic and just social order as an evolutionary outcome of modernity. This view is predicated on the assumption that people will be able to come to a rational understanding of the public good, and that this political knowledge can be obtained, under appropriate conditions, without recourse to the distortions of interest and power. In other words, knowledge of the good can be rationally apprehended, or put differently, knowledge and power are separate and distinct spheres of human action.

It is the burden of Michel Foucault's work to demonstrate the opposite: to claim that knowledge and power are inextricably linked. Foucault was born in 1926 in Poitiers, France, where he was educated in Catholic schools and eventually

made his way into the Sorbonne and took his degree in philosophy at the École Normale Supérieure. He subsequently studied psychology and took a diploma in psychopathology, which led to research and publication on mental illness in a book entitled *Mental Illness and Psychology*. Foucault taught at a number of foreign universities but returned to France and in 1964 was appointed to the Chair of Philosophy at the University of Clermont-Ferrand. In 1970 Foucault was designated "Professor of the History of Systems of Thought" in the Collège de France.

In *Discipline and Punish*, which is excerpted on the following pages, as well as in other works, such as *Madness and Civilization, The Birth of the Clinic,* and the first volume of *The History of Sexuality*, Foucault demonstrates how the human sciences have become techniques of power by shaping the views and behaviors of human subjects. Scientific knowledge, in this instance the human sciences, is not a separate sphere of activity engaging the talents and interests of a rarified community of scholars. On the contrary, the knowledge produced in these disciplines has had a profound impact on the lives of ordinary people and has shaped their views of themselves and others around concepts of normality and deviance. The human sciences have taken human subjects and instead of empowering them with knowledge, they have made them the objects of inquiry and subjected them to norms and rules of appropriate behavior that have been legitimated by the idea of science itself. Knowledge, therefore, brings power in its wake as it produces new types of human beings who are deemed better because they are normal.

In formulating the problem in these terms, Foucault reconceptualizes power and embeds it in the socialization processes of everyday life. This is what he means by the "carceral society." The real transactions of power are not in the relationships of citizens to the state, but in the relationships of people to teachers, doctors, therapists, social workers, and psychiatrists. These are not the benign and amelioratory aides of the welfare state but rather moral agents whose disciplinary power is based on their membership in the credentialed knowledge elite.

A related theme of post-modernism is explored by Jean François Lyotard in his book, *The Post-Modern Condition: A Report on Knowledge.* Here Lyotard launches a direct assault on "metanarratives," by which he means the broadly philosophical discourses, like Marxism and other Enlightenment theories, that have distorted our ability to see the truth of our condition by coloring our perceptions with claims of emancipation, progress, and justice. Metanarratives have given meaning and purpose to scientific explorations in the past, but what Lyotard tells us is that metanarratives operate like Kuhnian paradigms and tend to impose meaning onto historical events rather than explore the significance of those events empirically. To abandon these metanarratives is to accept the idea that history may have no purpose, that it is not an evolutionary or progressive march toward an emancipatory *telos*, but rather a contingent set of events, often accidental and with many unanticipated consequences.

One consequence of this claim is that the privileged position of theorists and philosophers is undermined and they are seen as upholding a viewpoint that promises an objective truth but reveals a partial view that suppresses other views as false or unworthy of consideration. Played out on the contemporary political stage, post-modernism has legitimated the expression of voices from many quarters, each asserting its own truths, and each engaged in a struggle for power to legitimate itself politically because there is no longer any higher intellectual authority that can sit in judgment.

In debunking the modernists' commitment to reason, to disinterested knowledge, and to truths that are universal, the writings of Foucault and Lyotard go far in delegitimating intellectual structures that surreptitiously exercise power under the guise of engaging in science. The contrasts with Habermas could not be greater.

MICHEL FOUCAULT: THE CARCERAL

Were I to fix the date of completion of the carceral system, I would choose not 1810 and the penal code, nor even 1844, when the law laying down the principle of cellular internment was passed; I might not even choose 1838, when books on prison reform by Charles Lucas, Moreau-Christophe and Faucher were published. The date I would choose would be 22 January 1840, the date of the official opening of Mettray. Or better still, perhaps, that glorious day, unremarked and unrecorded, when a child in Mettray remarked as he lay dying: "What a pity I left the colony so soon." This marked the death of the first penitentiary saint. Many of the blessed no doubt went to join him, if the former inmates of the penal colonies are to be believed when, in singing the praises of the new punitive policies of the body, they remarked: "We preferred the blows, but the cell suits us better."

Why Mettray? Because it is the disciplinary form at its most extreme, the model in which are concentrated all the coercive technologies of behaviour. In it were to be found "cloister, prison, school, regiment". The small, highly hierarchized groups, into which the inmates were divided, followed simultaneously five models: that of the family (each group was a "family" composed of "brothers" and two "elder brothers"); that of the army (each family, commanded by a head, was divided into two sections, each of which had a second in command; each inmate had a number and was taught basic military

exercises; there was a cleanliness inspection every day, an inspection of clothing every week; a roll-call was taken three times a day); that of the workshop, with supervisors and foremen, who were responsible for the regularity of the work and for the apprenticeship of the younger inmates; that of the school (an hour or an hour and a half of lessons every day; the teaching was given by the instructor and by the deputy-heads); lastly, the judicial model (each day "justice" was meted out in the parlour: "The least act of disobedience is punished and the best way of avoiding serious offences is to punish the most minor offences very severely: at Mettray, a useless word is punishable"; the principal punishment inflicted was confinement to one's cell; for "isolation is the best means of acting on the moral nature of children; it is there above all that the voice of religion, even if it has never spoken to their hearts, recovers all its emotional power"; the entire parapenal institution, which is created in order not to be a prison, culminates in the cell, on the walls of which are written in black letters: "God sees you."

This superimposition of different models makes it possible to indicate, in its specific features, the function of "training". The chiefs and their deputies at Mettray had to be not exactly judges, or teachers, or foremen, or non-commissioned officers, or "parents", but something of all these things in a quite specific mode of intervention. They were in a sense technicians of behaviour; engineers of conduct, orthopaedists of individuality. Their task was to produce bodies that were both docile and capable; they supervised the nine or ten working hours of every day (whether in a workshop or in the fields); they directed the orderly movements of groups of inmates, physical exercises, military exercises, rising in the morning, going to bed at

---

From Michel Foucault, "The Carceral," in *Discipline and Punish: The Birth of the Prison* (New York: Pantheon, 1977). Originally published in French as *Surveiller et Punir: Naissance de la Prison* by Editions Gallimard, Paris. Copyright © 1975 by Editions Gallimard. Reprinted by permission of Georges Bourchardt, Inc., for Editions Gallimard.

night, walks to the accompaniment of bugle and whistle; they taught gymnastics;[1] they checked cleanliness, supervised bathing. Training was accompanied by permanent observation; a body of knowledge was being constantly built up from the everyday behaviour of the inmates; it was organized as an instrument of perpetual assessment: "On entering the colony, the child is subjected to a sort of interrogation as to his origins, the position of his family, the offence for which he was brought before the courts and all the other offences that make up his short and often very sad existence. This information is written down on a board on which everything concerning each inmate is noted in turn, his stay at the colony and the place to which he is sent when he leaves." The modelling of the body produces a knowledge of the individual, the apprenticeship of the techniques induces modes of behaviour and the acquisition of skills is inextricably linked with the establishment of power relations; strong, skilled agricultural workers are produced; in this very work, provided it is technically supervised, submissive subjects are produced and a dependable body of knowledge built up about them. This disciplinary technique exercised upon the body had a double effect: a "soul" to be known and a subjection to be maintained. One result vindicated this work of training: in 1848, at a moment when "the fever of revolution fired the imagination of all, when the schools at Angers, La Flèche, Alfort, even the boarding schools, rose up in rebellion, the inmates of Mettray were calmer than ever" (Ferrus).

Where Mettray was especially exemplary was in the specificity that it recognized in this operation of training. It was related to other forms of supervision, on which it was based: medicine, general education, religious direction. But it cannot be identified absolutely with them. Nor with administration in the strict sense. Heads or deputy-heads of "families", monitors and foremen, had to live in close proximity to the inmates; their clothes were "almost as humble" as those of the inmates themselves; they practically never left their side, observing them day and night; they constituted among them a network of permanent observation. And, in order to train them themselves, a specialized school had been organized in the colony. The essential element of its programme was to subject the future cadres to the same apprenticeships and to the same coercions as the inmates themselves: they were "subjected as pupils to the discipline that, later, as instructors, they would themselves impose." They were taught the art of power relations. It was the first training college in pure discipline: the "penitentiary" was not simply a project that sought its justification in "humanity" or its foundations in a "science", but a technique that was learnt, transmitted and which obeyed general norms. The practice that normalized by compulsion the conduct of the undisciplined or dangerous could, in turn, by technical elaboration and rational reflection, be "normalized". The disciplinary technique became a "discipline" which also had its school.

It so happens that historians of the human sciences date the birth of scientific psychology at this time: during these same years, it seems, Weber was manipulating his little compass for the measurement of sensations. What took place at Mettray (and in other European countries sooner or later) was obviously of a quite different order. It was the emergence or rather the institutional specification, the baptism as it were, of a new type of supervision—both knowledge and power—over individuals who resisted disciplinary normalization. And yet, in the formation and growth of psychology, the appearance of these professionals of discipline, normality and subjection surely marks the beginning of a new stage. It will be said that the quantitative assessment of sensorial responses could at least derive authority from the prestige of the emerging science of physiology and that for this alone it deserves to feature in the history of the sciences. But the supervision of normality was firmly encased in a medicine or a psychiatry that provided it with a sort of "scientificity"; it was supported by a judicial apparatus which, directly or indirectly, gave it legal justification. Thus, in the shelter of these two considerable protectors, and, indeed, acting as a link between them, or a place of exchange, a carefully worked out technique for the supervision of norms has continued to develop right up to the present day. The specific, institutional supports of these methods have proliferated since the founding of the small school at Mettray; their apparatuses have increased in quantity and scope; their auxiliary services have increased, with hospitals, schools, public administrations and private enterprises; their agents have proliferated in number, in power, in technical qualification; the technicians of indiscipline have founded a family. In the normalization of the power of normalization, in the arrangement of a power-knowledge over individuals, Mettray and its school marked a new era.

But why choose this moment as the point of emergence of the formation of an art of punishing that is still more or less our own? Precisely because this choice is somewhat "unjust". Because it situates the "end" of the process in the lower reaches of criminal law. Because Mettray was a prison, but not entirely; a prison in that it contained young delinquents condemned by the courts; and yet something else, too, because it also contained minors who had been charged, but acquitted under article 66 of the code, and boarders held, as in the eighteenth century, as an alternative to paternal correction. Mettray, a punitive model, is at the limit of strict penality. It was the most famous of a whole series of institutions which, well beyond the frontiers of criminal law, constituted what one might call the carceral archipelago.

Yet the general principles, the great codes and subsequent legislation were quite clear on the matter: no imprisonment "outside the law", no detention that had not been decided by a qualified judicial institution, no more of those arbitrary and yet widespread confinements. Yet the very principle of extra-penal incarceration was in fact never abandoned. (A whole study remains to be done of the debates that took place during the Revolution concerning family courts, paternal correction and the right of parents to lock up their children.) And, if the apparatus of the great classical form of confinement was partly (and only partly) dismantled, it was very soon reactivated, rearranged, developed in certain directions. But what is still more important is that it was homogenized, through the mediation of the prison, on the one hand with legal punishments and, on the other, with disciplinary mechanisms. The frontiers between confinement, judicial punishment and institutions of discipline, which were already blurred in the classical age, tended to disappear and to constitute a great carceral continuum that diffused penitentiary techniques into the most innocent disciplines, transmitting disciplinary norms into the very heart of the penal system and placing over the slightest illegality, the smallest irregularity, deviation or anomaly, the threat of delinquency. A subtle, graduated carceral net, with compact institutions, but also separate and diffused methods, assumed responsibility for the arbitrary, widespread, badly integrated confinement of the classical age.

I shall not attempt here to reconstitute the whole network that formed first the immediate surroundings of the prison, then spread farther and farther outwards. However, a few references and dates should give some idea of the breadth and precocity of the phenomenon.

There were agricultural sections in the *maisons centrales* (the first example of which was Gaillon in 1824, followed later by Fontevrault, Les Douaires, Le Boulard); there were colonies for poor, abandoned vagrant children (Petit-Bourg in 1840, Ostwald in 1842); there were almshouses for young female offenders who "recoiled before the idea of entering a life of disorder," for "poor innocent girls whose mothers' immorality has exposed to precocious perversity," or for poor girls found on the doorsteps of hospitals and lodging houses. There were penal colonies envisaged by the law of 1850: minors, acquitted or condemned, were to be sent to these colonies and "brought up in common, under strict discipline, and trained in agricultural work and in the principal industries related to it"; later, they were to be joined by minors sentenced to hard labour for life and "vicious and insubordinate wards of the Public Assistance." And, moving still farther away from penality in the strict sense, the carceral circles widen and the form of the prison slowly diminishes and finally disappears altogether: the institutions for abandoned or indigent children, the orphanages (like Neuhof or Mesnil-Firmin), the establishments for apprentices (like the Bethléem de Reims or the Maison de Nancy); still farther away the factory-convents, such as La Sauvagère, Tarare and Jujurieu (where the girl workers entered about the age of thirteen, lived confined for years and were allowed out only under surveillance, received instead of wages pledged payment, which could be increased by bonuses for zeal and good behaviour, which they could use only on leaving). And then, still farther, there was a whole series of mechanisms that did not adopt the "compact" prison model, but used some of the carceral methods: charitable societies, moral improvement associations, organizations that handed out assistance and also practised surveillance, workers' estates and lodging houses—the most primitive of which still bear the all too visible marks of the penitentiary system.[2] And, lastly, this great carceral network reaches all the disciplinary mechanisms that function throughout society.

We have seen that, in penal justice, the prison transformed the punitive procedure into a penitentiary technique; the carceral archipelago transported this technique from the penal institution to the entire social body. With several important results.

1. This vast mechanism established a slow, continuous, imperceptible gradation that made it possible to pass naturally from disorder to offence and back from a transgression of the law to a slight departure from a rule, an average, a demand, a norm. In the classical period, despite a certain common reference to offence in general,[3] the order of the crime, the order of sin and the order of bad conduct remained separate in so far as they related to separate criteria and authorities (court, penitence, confinement). Incarceration with its mechanisms of surveillance and punishment functioned, on the contrary, according to a principle of relative continuity. The continuity of the institutions themselves, which were linked to one another (public assistance with the orphanage, the reformitory, the penitentiary, the disciplinary battalion, the prison; the school with the charitable society, the workshop, the almshouse, the penitentiary convent; the workers' estate with the hospital and the prison). A continuity of the punitive criteria and mechanisms, which on the basis of a mere deviation gradually strengthened the rules and increased the punishment. A continuous gradation of the established, specialized and competent authorities (in the order of knowledge and in the order of power) which, without resort to arbitrariness, but strictly according to the regulations, by means of observation and assessment hierarchized, differentiated, judged, punished and moved gradually from the correction of irregularities to the punishment of crime. The "carceral" with its many diffuse or compact forms, its institutions of supervision or constraint, of discreet surveillance and insistent coercion, assured the communication of punishments according to quality and quantity; it connected in series or disposed according to subtle divisions the minor and the serious penalties, the mild and the strict forms of treatment, bad marks and light sentences. You will end up in the convict-ship, the slightest indiscipline

seems to say; and the harshest of prisons says to the prisoners condemned to life: I shall note the slightest irregularity in your conduct. The generality of the punitive function that the eighteenth century sought in the "ideological" technique of representations and signs now had as its support the extension, the material framework, complex, dispersed, but coherent, of the various carceral mechanisms. As a result, a certain significant generality moved between the least irregularity and the greatest crime; it was no longer the offence, the attack on the common interest, it was the departure from the norm, the anomaly; it was this that haunted the school, the court, the asylum or the prison. It generalized in the sphere of meaning the function that the carceral generalized in the sphere of tactics. Replacing the adversary of the sovereign, the social enemy was transformed into a deviant, who brought with him the multiple danger of disorder, crime and madness. The carceral network linked, through innumerable relations, the two long, multiple series of the punitive and the abnormal.

2. The carceral, with its far-reaching networks, allows the recruitment of major "delinquents." It organizes what might be called "disciplinary careers" in which, through various exclusions and rejections, a whole process is set in motion. In the classical period, there opened up in the confines or interstices of society the confused, tolerant and dangerous domain of the "outlaw" or at least of that which eluded the direct hold of power: an uncertain space that was for criminality a training ground and a region of refuge; there poverty, unemployment, pursued innocence, cunning, the struggle against the powerful, the refusal of obligations and laws, and organized crime all came together as chance and fortune would dictate; it was the domain of adventure that Gil Blas, Sheppard or Mandrin, each in his own way, inhabited. Through the play of disciplinary differentiations and divisions, the nineteenth century constructed rigorous channels which, within the system, inculcated docility and produced delinquency by the same mechanisms. There was a sort of disciplinary "training," continuous and compelling, that had something of the pedagogical curriculum and something of the professional network. Careers emerged from it, as secure, as predictable, as those of public life: assistance associations, residential apprenticeships, penal colonies, disciplinary battalions, prisons, hospitals, almshouses. These networks were already well mapped out at the beginning of the nineteenth century: "Our benevolent establishments present an admirably coordinated whole by means of which the indigent does not remain a moment without help from the cradle to the grave. Follow the course of the unfortunate man: you will see him born among foundlings; from there he passes to the nursery, then to an orphanage; at the age of six he goes off to primary school and later to adult schools. If he cannot work, he is placed on the list of the charity offices of his district, and if he falls ill he may choose between twelve hospitals . . . Lastly, when the poor Parisian reaches the end of his career, seven almshouses await his age and often their salubrious régime has prolonged his useless days well beyond those of the rich man" (Moreau de Jonnès, quoted in Touquet).

The carceral network does not cast the unassimilable into a confused hell; there is no outside. It takes back with one hand what it seems to exclude with the other. It saves everything, including what it punishes. It is unwilling to waste even what it has decided to disqualify. In this panoptic society of which incarceration is the omnipresent armature, the delinquent is not outside the law; he is, from the very outset, in the law, at the very heart of the law, or at least in the midst of those mechanisms that transfer the individual imperceptibly from discipline to the law, from deviation to offence. Although it is true that prison punishes delinquency, delinquency is for the most part produced in and by an incarceration which, ultimately, prison perpetuates in its turn. The prison is merely the natural consequence, no more than a higher degree, of that hierarchy laid down step by step. The delinquent is an institutional product. It is no use being surprised, therefore, that in a considerable proportion of cases the biography of convicts passes through all these mechanisms and establishments, whose purpose, it is widely believed, is to lead away from prison. That one should find in them what one might call the index of an irrepressibly delinquent "character": the prisoner condemned to hard labor was meticulously produced by a childhood spent in a reformatory, according to the lines of force of the generalized carceral system. Conversely, the lyricism of marginality may find inspiration in the image of the "outlaw", the great social nomad, who prowls on the confines of a docile, frightened order. But it is not on the fringes of society and through successive exiles that criminality is born, but by means of ever more closely placed insertions, under ever more insistent surveillance, by an accumulation of disciplinary coercion. In short, the carceral archipelago assures, in the depths of the social body, the formation of delinquency on the basis of subtle illegalities, the overlapping of the latter by the former and the establishment of a specified criminality.

3. But perhaps the most important effect of the carceral system and of its extension well beyond legal imprisonment is that it succeeds in making the power to punish natural and legitimate, in lowering at least the threshold of tolerance to penality. It tends to efface what may be exorbitant in the exercise of punishment. It does this by playing the two registers in which it is deployed—the legal register of justice and the extra-legal register of discipline—against one another. In effect, the

great continuity of the carceral system throughout the law and its sentences gives a sort of legal sanction to the disciplinary mechanisms, to the decisions and judgements that they enforce. Throughout this network, which comprises so many "regional" institutions, relatively autonomous and independent, is transmitted, with the "prison-form", the model of justice itself. The regulations of the disciplinary establishments may reproduce the law, the punishments imitate the verdicts and penalties, the surveillance repeat the police model; and, above all these multiple establishments, the prison, which in relation to them is a pure form, unadulterated and unmitigated, gives them a sort of official sanction. The carceral, with its long gradation stretching from the convictship or imprisonment with hard labour to diffuse, slight limitations, communicates a type of power that the law validates and that justice uses as its favourite weapon. How could the disciplines and the power that functions in them appear arbitrary, when they merely operate the mechanisms of justice itself, even with a view to mitigating their intensity? When, by generalizing its effects and transmitting it to every level, it makes it possible to avoid its full rigour? Carceral continuity and the fusion of the prison-form make it possible to legalize, or in any case to legitimate disciplinary power, which thus avoids any element of excess or abuse it may entail.

But, conversely, the carceral pyramid gives to the power to inflict legal punishment a context in which it appears to be free of all excess and all violence. In the subtle gradation of the apparatuses of discipline and of the successive "embeddings" that they involve, the prison does not at all represent the unleashing of a different kind of power, but simply an additional degree in the intensity of a mechanism that has continued to operate since the earliest forms of legal punishment. Between the latest institution of "rehabilitation," where one is taken in order to avoid prison, and the prison where one is sent after a definable offence, the difference is (and must be) scarcely perceptible. There is a strict economy that has the effect of rendering as discreet as possible the singular power to punish. There is nothing in it now that recalls the former excess of sovereign power when it revenged its authority on the tortured body of those about to be executed. Prison continues, on those who are entrusted to it, a work begun elsewhere, which the whole of society pursues on each individual through innumerable mechanisms of discipline. By means of a carceral continuum, the authority that sentences infiltrates all those other authorities that supervise, transform, correct, improve. It might even be said that nothing really distinguishes them any more except the singularly "dangerous" character of the delinquents, the gravity of their departures from normal behaviour and the necessary solemnity of the ritual. But, in its function, the power to punish is not essentially different from that of curing or educating. It receives from them, and from their lesser, smaller task, a sanction from below; but one that is no less important for that, since it is the sanction of technique and rationality. The carceral "naturalizes" the legal power to punish, as it "legalizes" the technical power to discipline. In thus homogenizing them, effacing what may be violent in one and arbitrary in the other, attenuating the effects of revolt that they may both arouse, thus depriving excess in either of any purpose, circulating the same calculated, mechanical and discreet methods from one to the other, the carceral makes it possible to carry out that great 'economy' of power whose formula the eighteenth century had sought, when the problem of the accumulation and useful administration of men first emerged.

By operating at every level of the social body and by mingling ceaselessly the art of rectifying and the right to punish, the universality

of the carceral lowers the level from which it becomes natural and acceptable to be punished. The question is often posed as to how, before and after the Revolution, a new foundation was given to the right to punish. And no doubt the answer is to be found in the theory of the contract. But it is perhaps more important to ask the reverse question: how were people made to accept the power to punish, or quite simply, when punished, tolerate being so. The theory of the contract can only answer this question by the fiction of a juridical subject giving to others the power to exercise over him the right that he himself possesses over them. It is highly probable that the great carceral continuum, which provides a communication between the power of discipline and the power of the law, and extends without interruption from the smallest coercions to the longest penal detention, constituted the technical and real, immediately material counterpart of that chimerical granting of the right to punish.

4. With this new economy of power, the carceral system, which is its basic instrument, permitted the emergence of a new form of "law": a mixture of legality and nature, prescription and constitution, the norm. This had a whole series of effects: the internal dislocation of the judicial power or at least of its functioning; an increasing difficulty in judging, as if one were ashamed to pass sentence; a furious desire on the part of the judges to judge, assess, diagnose, recognize the normal and abnormal and claim the honour of curing or rehabilitating. In view of this, it is useless to believe in the good or bad consciences of judges, or even of their unconscious. Their immense "appetite for medicine" which is constantly manifested—from their appeal to psychiatric experts, to their attention to the chatter of criminology—expresses the major fact that the power they exercise has been "denatured"; that it is at a certain level governed by laws; that at another, more fundamental

level it functions as a normative power; it is the economy of power that they exercise, and not that of their scruples or their humanism, that makes them pass "therapeutic" sentences and recommend "rehabilitating" periods of imprisonment. But, conversely, if the judges accept ever more reluctantly to condemn for the sake of condemning, the activity of judging has increased precisely to the extent that the normalizing power has spread. Borne along by the omnipresence of the mechanisms of discipline, basing itself on all the carceral apparatuses, it has become one of the major functions of our society. The judges of normality are present everywhere. We are in the society of the teacher-judge; the doctor-judge, the educator-judge, the "social worker"-judge; it is on them that the universal reign of the normative is based; and each individual, wherever he may find himself, subjects to it his body, his gestures, his behaviour, his aptitudes, his achievements. The carceral network, in its compact or disseminated forms, with its systems of insertion, distribution, surveillance, observation, has been the greatest support, in modern society, of the normalizing power.

5. The carceral texture of society assures both the real capture of the body and its perpetual observation; it is, by its very nature, the apparatus of punishment that conforms most completely to the new economy of power and the instrument for the formation of knowledge that this very economy needs. Its panoptic functioning enables it to play this double role. By virtue of its methods of fixing, dividing, recording, it has been one of the simplest, crudest, also most concrete, but perhaps most indispensable conditions for the development of this immense activity of examination that has objectified human behaviour. If, after the age of "inquisitorial" justice, we have entered the age of "examinatory" justice, if, in an even more general way, the method of examination has been able to spread so widely

throughout society, and to give rise in part to the sciences of man, one of the great instruments for this has been the multiplicity and close overlapping of the various mechanisms of incarceration. I am not saying that the human sciences emerged from the prison. But, if they have been able to be formed and to produce so many profound changes in the episteme, it is because they have been conveyed by a specific and new modality of power: a certain policy of the body, a certain way of rendering the group of men docile and useful. This policy required the involvement of definite relations of knowledge in relations of power; it called for a technique of overlapping subjection and objectification; it brought with it new procedures of individualization. The carceral network constituted one of the armatures of this power-knowledge that has made the human sciences historically possible. Knowable man, (soul, individuality, consciousness, conduct, whatever it is called) is the object-effect of this analytical investment, of this domination-observation.

6. This no doubt explains the extreme solidity of the prison, that slight invention that was nevertheless decried from the outset. If it had been no more than an instrument of rejection or repression in the service of a state apparatus, it would have been easier to alter its more overt forms or to find a more acceptable substitute for it. But, rooted as it was in mechanisms and strategies of power, it could meet any attempt to transform it with a great force of inertia. One fact is characteristic: when it is a question of altering the system of imprisonment, opposition does not come from the judicial institutions alone; resistance is to be found not in the prison as penal sanction, but in the prison with all its determinations, links and extrajudicial results; in the prison as the relay in a general network of disciplines and surveillances; in the prison as it functions in a panoptic régime. This does not mean that it cannot be altered, nor that it is once and for

all indispensable to our kind of society. One may, on the contrary, site the two processes which, in the very continuity of the processes that make the prison function, are capable of exercising considerable restraint on its use and of transforming its internal functioning. And no doubt these processes have already begun to a large degree. The first is that which reduces the utility (or increases its inconveniences) of a delinquency accommodated as a specific illegality, locked up and supervised; thus the growth of great national or international illegalities directly linked to the political and economic apparatuses (financial illegalities, information services, arms and drugs trafficking, property speculation) makes it clear that the somewhat rustic and conspicuous work force of delinquency is proving ineffective; or again, on a smaller scale, as soon as the economic levy on sexual pleasure is carried out more efficiently by the sale of contraceptives, or obliquely through publications, films or shows, the archaic hierarchy of prostitution loses much of its former usefulness. The second process is the growth of the disciplinary networks, the multiplication of their exchanges with the penal apparatus, the ever more important powers that are given them, the ever more massive transference to them of judicial functions; now, as medicine, psychology, education, public assistance, "social work" assume an ever greater share of the powers of supervision and assessment, the penal apparatus will be able, in turn, to become medicalized, psychologized, educationalized; and by the same token that turning-point represented by the prison becomes less useful when, through the gap between its penitentiary discourse and its effect of consolidating delinquency, it articulates the penal power and the disciplinary power. In the midst of all these mechanisms of normalization, which are becoming ever more rigorous in their application, the specificity of the prison and its role as link are losing something of their purpose.

If there is an overall political issue around the prison, it is not therefore whether it is to be corrective or not; whether the judges, the psychiatrists or the sociologists are to exercise more power in it than the administrators or supervisors; it is not even whether we should have prison or something other than prison. At present, the problem lies rather in the steep rise in the use of these mechanisms of normalization and the wide-ranging powers which, through the proliferation of new disciplines, they bring with them.

In 1836, a correspondent wrote to *La Phalange:* "Moralists, philosophers, legislators, flatterers of civilization, this is the plan of your Paris, neatly ordered and arranged, here is the improved plan in which all like things are gathered together. At the centre, and within a first enclosure: hospitals for all diseases, almshouses for all types of poverty, madhouses, prisons, convict-prisons for men, women and children. Around the first enclosure, barracks, courtrooms, police stations, houses for prison warders, scaffolds, houses for the executioner and his assistants. At the four corners, the Chamber of Deputies, the Chamber of Peers, the Institute and the Royal Palace. Outside, there are the various services that supply the central enclosure, commerce, with its swindlers and its bankruptcies; industry and its furious struggles; the press, with its sophisms; the gambling dens; prostitution, the people dying of hunger or wallowing in debauchery, always ready to lend an ear to the voice of the Genius of Revolutions; the heartless rich. . . . Lastly the ruthless war of all against all" (*La Phalange,* 10 August 1836).

I shall stop with this anonymous text. We are now far away from the country of tortures, dotted with wheels, gibbets, gallows, pillories; we are far, too, from that dream of the reformers, less than fifty years before: the city of punishments in which a thousand small theatres would have provided an endless multicoloured representation of justice in which the punishments, meticulously produced on decorative scaffolds, would have constituted the permanent festival of the penal code. The carceral city, with its imaginary "geo-politics," is governed by quite different principles. The extract from *La Phalange* reminds us of some of the more important ones: that at the centre of this city, and as if to hold it in place, there is, not the "centre of power," not a network of forces, but a multiple network of diverse elements—walls, space, institution, rules, discourse; that the model of the carceral city is not, therefore, the body of the king, with the powers that emanate from it, nor the contractual meeting of wills from which a body that was both individual and collective was born, but a strategic distribution of elements of different natures and levels. That the prison is not the daughter of laws, codes or the judicial apparatus; that it is not subordinated to the court and the docile or clumsy instrument of the sentences that it hands out and of the results that it would like to achieve; that it is the court that is external and subordinate to the prison. That in the central position that it occupies, it is not alone, but linked to a whole series of "carceral" mechanisms which seem distinct enough—since they are intended to alleviate pain, to cure, to comfort—but which all tend, like the prison, to exercise a power of normalization. That these mechanisms are applied not to transgressions against a "central" law, but to the apparatus of production—"commerce" and "industry"—to a whole multiplicity of illegalities, in all their diversity of nature and origin, their specific role in profit and the different ways in which they are dealt with by the punitive mechanisms. And that ultimately what presides over all these mechanisms is not the unitary functioning of an apparatus or an institution, but the necessity of combat and the rules of strategy. That, consequently, the notions of institutions of repression, rejection, exclusion, marginalization, are not adequate

to describe, at the very centre of the carceral city, the formation of the insidious leniencies, unavowable petty cruelties, small acts of cunning, calculated methods, techniques, "sciences" that permit the fabrication of the disciplinary individual. In this central and centralized humanity, the effect and instrument of complex power relations, bodies and forces subjected by multiple mechanisms of "incarceration," objects for discourses that are in themselves elements for this strategy, we must hear the distant roar of battle.

At this point I end a book that must serve as a historical background to various studies of the power of normalization and the formation of knowledge in modern society.

NOTES

1. "Anything that helps to tire the body helps to expel bad thoughts; so care is taken that games consist of violent exercise. At night, they fall asleep the moment they touch the pillow" (Ducpétiaux, 1854, 375–6).

2. Cf., for example, the following description of workers' accommodation built at Lille in the mid-nineteenth century: "Cleanliness is the order of the day. It is the heart of the regulations. There are a number of severe provisions against noise, drunkenness, disorders of all kinds. A serious offence brings expulsion. Brought back to regular habits of order and economy, the workers no longer desert the workshops on Mondays. . . The children are better supervised and are no longer a cause of scandal. . . Prizes are given for the upkeep of the dwellings, for good behaviour, for signs of devotion and each year these prizes are competed for by a large number of competitors" (Houzé de l'Aulnay, 13–15).

3. Crime was explicitly defined by certain jurists such as Muyart de Vouglans and Rousseaud de la Combe.

JEAN-FRANÇOIS LYOTARD: THE POST-MODERN CONDITION: A REPORT ON KNOWLEDGE

I define *postmodern* as incredulity toward meta-narratives. This incredulity is undoubtedly a product of progress in the sciences: but that progress in turn presupposes it. To the obsolescence of the metanarrative apparatus of legitimation corresponds, most notably, the crisis of metaphysical philosophy and of the university institution which in the past relied on it. The narrative function is losing its functors, its great hero, its great dangers, its great voyages, its great goal. It is being dispersed in clouds of narrative language elements—narrative, but also denotative, prescriptive, descriptive, and so on. Conveyed within each cloud are pragmatic valencies specific to its kind. Each of us lives at the intersection of many of these. However, we do not necessarily establish stable language combinations, and the properties of the ones we do establish are not necessarily communicable.

Thus the society of the future falls less within the province of a Newtonian anthropology (such as structuralism or systems theory) than a pragmatics of language particles. There are many different languages games—a heterogeneity of elements. They only give rise to institutions in patches—local determinism.

The decision makers, however, attempt to manage these clouds of sociality according to input/output matrices, following a logic which implies that their elements are commensurable and that the whole is determinable. They allocate our lives for the growth of power. In matters of social justice and of scientific truth alike, the legitimation of that power is based on its optimizing the system's performance—efficiency. The application of this criterion to all of our games necessarily entails a certain level of terror, whether soft or hard: be operational (that is, commensurable) or disappear.

The logic of maximum performance is no doubt inconsistent in many ways, particularly with respect to contradiction in the socioeconomic field: it demands both less work (to lower production costs) and more (to lessen the social burden of the idle population). But our incredulity is now such that we no longer expect salvation to rise from these inconsistencies, as did Marx.

Still, the postmodern condition is as much a stranger to disenchantment as it is to the blind positivity of delegitimation. Where, after the metanarratives, can legitimacy reside? The operativity criterion is technological; it has no relevance for judging what is true or just. Is legitimacy to be found in consensus obtained through discussion, as Jürgen Habermas thinks? Such consensus does violence to the heterogeneity of language games. And invention is always born of dissension. Postmodern knowledge is not simply a tool of the authorities; it refines our sensitivity to differences and reinforces our ability to tolerate the incommensurable. Its principle is not the expert's homology, but the inventor's paralogy.

Here is the question: is a legitimation of the social bond, a just society, feasible in terms of a paradox analogous to that of scientific activity? What would such a paradox be?

The text that follows is an occasional one. It is a report on knowledge in the most highly developed societies and was presented to the Conseil des Universités of the government of

Quebec at the request of its president. I would like to thank him for his kindness in allowing its publication.

It remains to be said that the author of the report is a philosopher, not an expert. The latter knows what he knows and what he does not know: the former does not. One concludes, the other questions—two very different language games. I combine them here with the result that neither quite succeeds.

The philosopher at least can console himself with the thought that the formal and pragmatic analysis of certain philosophical and ethico-political discourses of legitimation, which underlies the report, will subsequently see the light of day. The report will have served to introduce that analysis from a somewhat sociologizing slant, one that truncates but at the same time situates it.

Such as it is, I dedicate this report to the Institut Polytechnique de Philosophie of the Université de Paris VIII (Vincennes)—at this very postmodern moment that finds the University nearing what may be its end, while the Institute may just be beginning.

* * *

Transformation in the nature of knowledge, then, could well have repercussions on the existing public powers, forcing them to reconsider their relations (both de jure and de facto) with the large corporations and, more generally, with civil society. The reopening of the world market, a return to vigorous economic competition, the breakdown of the hegemony of American capitalism, the decline of the socialist alternative, a probable opening of the Chinese market—these and many other factors are already, at the end of the 1970s, preparing States for a serious reappraisal of the role they have been accustomed to playing since the 1930s: that of guiding, or even directing investments. In this light, the new technologies can only increase the urgency of such a reexamination, since they make the information used in decision making (and therefore the means of control) even more mobile and subject to piracy.

It is not hard to visualize learning circulating along the same lines as money, instead of for its "educational" value or political (administrative, diplomatic, military) importance; the pertinent distinction would no longer be between knowledge and ignorance, but rather, as is the case with money, between "payment knowledge" and "investment knowledge"—in other words, between units of knowledge exchanged in a daily maintenance framework (the reconstitution of the work force, "survival") versus funds of knowledge dedicated to optimizing the performance of a project.

If this were the case, communicational transparency would be similar to liberalism. Liberalism does not preclude an organization of the flow of money in which some channels are used in decision making while others are only good for the payment of debts. One could similarly imagine flows of knowledge traveling along identical channels of identical nature, some of which would be reserved for the "decision makers," while the others would be used to repay each person's perpetual debt with respect to the social bond.

The Problem: Legitimation

That is the working hypothesis defining the field within which I intend to consider the question of the status of knowledge. This scenario, akin to the one that goes by the name "the computerization of society" (although ours is advanced in an entirely different spirit), makes no claims of being original, or even true. What is required of a working hypothesis is a fine capacity for discrimination. The scenario of the computerization of the most highly developed societies allows us to spotlight (though with the risk of excessive magnification) certain aspects of the transformation of knowledge and its effects on public power and civil institutions—effects it would be difficult to perceive from other points of view. Our hypothesis, therefore, should not be accorded predictive value in relation to reality, but strategic value in relation to the question raised.

Nevertheless, it has strong credibility, and in that sense our choice of this hypothesis is not arbitrary. It has been described extensively by the experts[1] and is already guiding certain decisions by the governmental agencies and private firms most directly concerned, such as those managing the telecommunications industry. To some extent, then, it is already a part of observable reality. Finally, barring economic stagnation or a general recession (resulting, for example, from a continued failure to solve the world's energy problems), there is a good chance that this scenario will come to pass: it is hard to see what other direction contemporary technology could take as an alternative to the computerization of society.

This is as much as to say that the hypothesis is banal. But only to the extent that it fails to challenge the general paradigm of progress in science and technology, to which economic growth and the expansion of sociopolitical power seem to be natural complements. That scientific and technical knowledge is cumulative is never questioned. At most, what is debated is the form that accumulation takes—some picture it as regular, continuous, and unanimous, others as periodic, discontinuous, and conflictual.[2]

But these truisms are fallacious. In the first place, scientific knowledge does not represent the totality of knowledge; it has always existed in addition to, and in competition and conflict with, another kind of knowledge, which I will call narrative in the interests of simplicity (its characteristics will be described later). I do not mean to say that narrative knowledge can prevail over science, but its model is related to ideas of internal equilibrium and conviviality[3] next to which contemporary scientific knowledge cuts a poor figure, especially if it is to undergo an exteriorization with respect to the "knower" and an alienation from its user even greater than has previously been the case. The resulting demoralization of researchers and teachers is far from negligible; it is well known that during the 1960s, in all of the most highly developed societies, it reached such explosive dimensions among those preparing to practice these professions—the students—that there was noticeable decrease in productivity at laboratories and universities unable to protect themselves from its contamination.[4] Expecting this, with hope or fear, to lead to a revolution (as was then often the case) is out of the question: it will not change the order of things in postindustrial society overnight. But this doubt on the part of scientists must be taken into account as a major factor in evaluating the present and future status of scientific knowledge.

It is all the more necessary to take it into consideration since—and this is the second point—the scientists' demoralization has an impact on the central problem of legitimation. I use the word in a broader sense than do contemporary German theorists in their discussions of the question of authority.[5] Take any civil law as an example: it states that a given category of citizens must perform a specific kind of action. Legitimation is the process by which a legislator is authorized to promulgate such a law as a norm. Now take the example of a scientific statement: it is subject to the rule that a statement must fulfill a given set of conditions in order to be accepted as scientific. In this case, legitimation is the process by which a "legislator" dealing with scientific discourse is authorized to prescribe the stated conditions (in general, conditions of internal consistency and experimental verification) determining whether a statement is to be included in that discourse for consideration by the scientific community.

The parallel may appear forced. But as we will see, it is not. The question of the legitimacy of science has been indissociably linked to that of the legitimation of the legislator since the time of Plato. From this point of view, the right to decide what is true is not independent of the right to decide what is just, even if the statements consigned to these two authorities differ in nature. The point is that there is a strict interlinkage between the kind of language called science and the kind called ethics and politics: they both stem from the same perspective, the same "choice" if you will—the choice called the Occident.

When we examine the current status of scientific knowledge—at a time when science seems more completely subordinated to the prevailing powers than ever before and, along with the new technologies, is in danger of becoming a major stake in their conflicts—the question of double legitimation, far from receding into the background, necessarily comes to the fore. For it appears in its most complete form, that of reversion, revealing that knowledge and power are simply two sides of the same question: who decides what knowledge is, and who knows what needs to be decided? In the computer age, the question of knowledge is now more than ever a question of government.

* * *

Delegitimation

In contemporary society and culture—postindustrial society, postmodern culture[6]—the question of the legitimation of knowledge is formulated in different terms. The grand narrative has lost its credibility, regardless of what mode of unification it uses, regardless of whether it is a speculative narrative or a narrative of emancipation.

The decline of narrative can be seen as an effect of the blossoming of techniques and technologies since the Second World War, which has shifted emphasis from the ends of action to its means; it can also be seen as an effect of the redeployment of advanced liberal capitalism after its retreat under the protection of Keynesianism during the period 1930–60, a renewal that has eliminated the communist alternative and valorized the individual enjoyment of goods and services.

Anytime we go searching for causes in this way we are bound to be disappointed. Even if we adopted one or the other of these hypotheses, we would still have to detail the correlation between the tendencies mentioned and the decline of the unifying and legitimating power of the grand narratives of speculation and emancipation.

It is, of course, understandable that both capitalist renewal and prosperity and the disorienting upsurge of technology would have an impact on the status of knowledge. But in order to understand how contemporary science could have been susceptible to those effects long before they took place, we must first locate the seeds of "delegitimation"[7] and nihilism that were inherent in the grand narratives of the nineteenth century.

First of all, the speculative apparatus maintains an ambigious relation to knowledge. It shows that knowledge is only worthy of that name to the extent that it reduplicates itself ("lifts itself up," *hebt sich auf;* is sublated) by citing its own statements in a second-level discourse (autonymy) that functions to legitimate them. This is as much as to say that, in its immediacy, denotative discourse bearing on a certain referent (a living organism, a chemical property, a physical phenomenon, etc.) does not really know what it thinks it knows. Positive science is not a form of knowledge. And speculation feeds on its suppression. The Hegelian speculative narrative thus harbors a certain skepticism toward positive learning, as Hegel himself admits.[8]

A science that has not legitimated itself is not a true science; if the discourse that was meant to legitimate it seems to belong to a prescientific form of knowledge, like a "vulgar" narrative, it is demoted to the lowest rank, that of an ideology or instrument of power. And this always happens if the rules of the science game that discourse denounces as empirical are applied to science itself.

Take for example the speculative statement: "A scientific statement is knowledge if and only if it can take its place in a universal process of engendering." The question is: Is this statement knowledge as it itself defines it? Only if it can take its place in a universal process of engendering. Which it can. All it has to do is to presuppose that such a process exists (the Life of spirit) and that it is itself an expression of that process. This presupposition, in fact, is indispensable to the speculative language game. Without it, the language of legitimation would not be legitimate; it would accompany science in a nosedive into nonsense, at least if we take idealism's word for it.

But this presupposition can also be understood in a totally different sense, one which takes us in the direction of postmodern culture: we could say, in keeping with the perspective we adopted earlier, that this presupposition defines the set of rules one must accept in order to play the speculative game.[9] Such an appraisal assumes first that we accept that the "positive" sciences represent the general mode of knowledge and second, that we understand this language to imply certain formal and axiomatic presuppositions that it must always make explicit. This is exactly what Nietzsche is doing, though with a different terminology, when he shows that "European nihilism" resulted from the truth requirement of science being turned back against itself.[10]

There thus arises an idea of perspective that is not far removed, at least in this respect, from the idea of language games. What we have here is a process of delegitimation fueled by the demand for legitimation itself. The "crisis" of scientific knowledge, signs of which have been accumulating since the end of the nineteenth century, is not born of a chance proliferation of sciences, itself an effect of progress in technology and the expansion of capitalism. It represents, rather, an internal erosion of the legitimacy principle of knowledge. There is erosion at work inside the speculative game, and by loosening the weave of the encyclopedic net in which each science was to find its place, it eventually sets them free.

The classical dividing lines between the various fields of science are thus called into question—disciplines disappear, overlappings occur at the borders between sciences, and from these new territories are born. The speculative hierarchy of learning gives way to an immanent and, as it were, "flat" network of areas of inquiry, the respective frontiers of which are in constant flux. The old "faculties" splinter into institutes and foundations of all kinds, and the universities lose their function of speculative legitimation. Stripped of the responsibility for research (which was stifled by the speculative narrative), they limit themselves to the transmission of what is judged to be established knowledge, and through didactics they guarantee the replication of teachers rather than the production of researchers. This is the state in which Nietzsche finds and condemns them.[11]

The potential for erosion intrinsic to the other legitimation procedure, the emancipation apparatus flowing from the *Aufklärung*, is no less extensive than the one at work within speculative discourse. But it touches a different aspect. Its distinguishing characteristic is that it grounds the legitimation of science and truth in the autonomy of interlocutors involved in ethical, social, and political praxis. As we have seen, there are immediate problems with this form of legitimation: the difference between a denotative statement with cognitive value and a prescriptive statement with practical value is one of relevance, therefore of competence. There is nothing to prove that if a statement describing a real situation is true, it follows that a prescriptive statement based upon it (the effect of which will necessarily be a modification of that reality) will be just.

Take, for example, a closed door. Between "The door is closed" and "Open the door" there is no relation of consequence as defined in propositional logic. The two statements belong to two autonomous sets of rules defining different kinds of relevance, and therefore of competence. Here, the effect of dividing reason into cognitive or theoretical reason on the one hand, and practical reason on the other, is to attack the legitimacy of the discourse of science. Not directly, but indirectly, by revealing that it is a language game with its own rules (of which the a priori conditions of knowledge in Kant provide a first glimpse) and that it has no special calling to supervise the game of praxis (nor the game of aesthetics, for that matter). The game of science is thus put on a par with the others.

If this "delegitimation" is pursued in the slightest and if its scope is widened (as Wittgenstein does in his own way, and thinkers such as Martin Buber and Emmanuel Lévinas in theirs)[12] the road is then open for an important current of postmodernity: science plays its own game; it is incapable of legitimating the other language games. The game of prescription, for example, escapes it. But above all, it is incapable of legitimating itself, as speculation assumed it could.

The social subject itself seems to dissolve in this dissemination of language games. The social bond is linguistic, but is not woven with a single thread. It is a fabric formed by the intersection of at least two (and in reality an indeterminate number) of language games, obeying different rules. Wittgenstein writes: "Our language can be seen as an ancient city: a maze of little streets and squares, of old and new houses, and of houses with additions from various periods; and this surrounded by a multitude of new boroughs with straight regular streets and uniform houses."[13] And to drive home that the principle of unitotality—or synthesis under the authority of a metadiscourse of knowledge—is inapplicable, he subjects the "town" of language to the old sorites paradox by asking: "how many houses or streets does it take before a town begins to be a town?"[14]

New languages are added to the old ones, forming suburbs of the old town: "the symbolism of chemistry and the notation of the infinitesimal calculus."[15] Thirty-five years later we can add to the list: machine languages, the matrices of game theory, new systems of musical notation, systems of notation for nondenotative forms of logic (temporal logics, deontic logics, modal logics), the language of the genetic code, graphs of phonological structures, and so on.

We may form a pessimistic impression of this splintering: nobody speaks all of those languages, they have no universal metalanguage, the project of the system-subject is a failure, the goal of emancipation has nothing to do with science, we are all stuck in the positivism of this or that discipline of learning, the learned scholars have turned into scientists, the diminished tasks of research have become compartmentalized and no one can master them all.[16] Speculative or humanistic philosophy is forced to relinquish its legitimation duties,[17] which explains why philosophy is facing a crisis wherever it persists in arrogating such functions and is reduced to the study of systems of logic or the history of ideas where it has been realistic enough to surrender them.[18]

Turn-of-the-century Vienna was weaned on this pessimism: not just artists such as Musil, Kraus, Hofmannsthal, Loos, Schönberg, and Broch, but also the philosophers Mach and Wittgenstein.[19] They carried awareness of and theoretical and artistic responsibility for delegitimation as far as it could be taken. We can say today that the mourning process has been completed. There is no need to start all over again. Wittgenstein's strength is that he did not opt for the positivism that was being developed by the Vienna Circle,[20] but outlined in his investigation of language games a kind of legitimation not based on performativity. That is what the postmodern world is all about. Most people have lost the nostalgia for the lost narrative. It in no way follows that they are reduced to barbarity. What saves them from it is their knowledge that legitimation can only spring from their own linguistic practice and communicational interaction. Science "smiling into its beard" at every other belief has taught them the harsh austerity of realism.[21]

* * *

Legitimation by Paralogy

Let us say at this point that the facts we have presented concerning the problem of the legitimation of knowledge today are sufficient for our purposes. We no longer have recourse to the grand narratives—we can resort neither to the dialectic of Spirit nor even to the emancipation of humanity as a validation for postmodern scientific discourse. But as we have just seen, the little narrative [*petit récit*] remains the quintessential form of imaginative invention, most particularly in science.[22] In addition, the principle of consensus as a criterion of validation seems to be inadequate. It has two formulations. In the first, consensus is an agreement between men, defined as knowing intellects and free wills, and is obtained through dialogue. This is the form elaborated by Habermas, but his conception is based on the validity of the narrative of emancipation. In the second, consensus is a component of the system, which manipulates it in order to maintain and improve its performance.[23] It is the object of administrative procedures, in Luhmann's sense. In this case, its only validity is as an instrument to be used toward achieving the real goal, which is what legitimates the system—power.

The problem is therefore to determine whether it is possible to have a form of legitimation based solely on paralogy. Paralogy must be distinguished from innovation: the latter is under the command of the system, or at least used by it to improve its efficiency; the former is a move (the importance of which is often not recognized until later) played in the pragmatics of knowledge. The fact that it is in reality frequently, but not necessarily, the case that one is transformed into the other presents no difficulties for the hypothesis.

Returning to the description of scientific pragmatics (section 7), it is now dissension that must be emphasized. Consensus is a horizon that is never reached. Research that takes place under the aegis of a paradigm[24] tends to stabilize; it is like the exploitation of a technological, economic, or artistic "idea." It cannot be discounted. But what is striking is that someone always comes along to disturb the order of "reason." It is necessary to posit the existence of a power that destabilizes the capacity for explanation, manifested in the promulgation of new

norms for understanding or, if one prefers, in a proposal to establish new rules circumscribing a new field of research for the language of science. This, in the context of scientific discussion, is the same process Thom calls morphogenesis. It is not without rules (there are classes of catastrophes), but it is always locally determined. Applied to scientific discussion and placed in a temporal framework, this property implies that "discoveries" are unpredictable. In terms of the idea of transparency, it is a factor that generates blind spots and defers consensus.[25]

This summary makes it easy to see that systems theory and the kind of legitimation it proposes have no scientific basis whatsoever: science itself does not function according to this theory's paradigm of the system, and contemporary science excludes the possibility of using such a paradigm to describe society.

In this context, let us examine two important points in Luhmann's argument. On the one hand, the system can only function by reducing complexity, and on the other, it must induce the adaptation of individual aspirations to its own ends.[26] The reduction in complexity is required to maintain the system's power capability. If all messages could circulate freely among all individuals, the quantity of the information that would have to be taken into account before making the correct choice would delay decisions considerably, thereby lowering performativity. Speed, in effect, is a power component of the system.

The objection will be made that these molecular opinions must indeed be taken into account if the risk of serious disturbances is to be avoided. Luhmann replies—and this is the second point—that it is possible to guide individual aspirations through a process of "quasi-apprenticeship," "free of all disturbance," in order to make them compatible with the system's decisions. The decisions do not have to respect individuals' aspirations: the aspirations have to aspire to the decisions, or at least to their effects. Administrative procedures should make individuals "want" what the system needs in order to perform well.[27] It is easy to see what role telematics technology could play in this.

It cannot be denied that there is persuasive force in the idea that context control and domination are inherently better than their absence. The performativity criterion has its "advantages." It excludes in principle adherence to a metaphysical discourse; it requires the renunciation of fables; it demands clear minds and cold wills; it replaces the definition of essences with the calculation of interactions; it makes the "players" assume responsibility not only for the statements they propose, but also for the rules to which they submit those statements in order to render them acceptable. It brings the pragmatic functions of knowledge clearly to light, to the extent that they seem to relate to the criterion of efficiency: the pragmatics of argumentation, of the production of proof, of the transmission of learning, and of the apprenticeship of the imagination.

It also contributes to elevating all language games to self-knowledge, even those not within the realm of canonical knowledge. It tends to jolt everyday discourse into a kind of metadiscourse: ordinary statements are now displaying a propensity for self-citation, and the various pragmatic posts are tending to make an indirect connection even to current messages concerning them.[28] Finally, it suggests that the problems of internal communication experienced by the scientific community in the course of its work of dismantling and remounting its languages are comparable in nature to the problems experienced by the social collectivity when, deprived of its narrative culture, it must reexamine its own internal communication and in the process question the nature of the legitimacy of the decisions made in its name.

At risk of scandalizing the reader, I would also say that the system can count severity among its advantages. Within the framework of the power criterion, a request (that is, a form of prescription) gains nothing in legitimacy by virtue of being based on the hardship of an unmet need. Rights do not flow from hardship, but from the fact that the alleviation of hardship improves the system's performance. The needs of the most underprivileged should not be used as a system regulator as a matter of principle: since the means of satisfying them is already known, their actual satisfaction will not improve the system's performance, but only increase its expenditures. The only counterindication is that not satisfying them can destabilize the whole. It is against the nature of force to be ruled by weakness. But it is in its nature to induce new requests meant to lead to a redefinition of the norms of "life."[29] In this sense, the system seems to be a vanguard machine dragging humanity after it, dehumanizing it in order to rehumanize it at a different level of normative capacity. The technocrats declare that they cannot trust what society designates as its needs; they "know" that society cannot know its own needs since they are not variables independent of the new technologies.[30] Such is the arrogance of the decision makers—and their blindness.

What their "arrogance" means is that they identify themselves with the social system conceived as a totality in quest of its most performative unity possible. If we look at the pragmatics of science, we learn that such an identification is impossible: in principle, no scientist embodies knowledge or neglects the "needs" of a research project, or the aspirations of a researcher, on the pretext that they do not add to the performance of "science" as a whole. The response a researcher usually makes to a request is: "We'll have to see, tell me your story."[31] In principle, he does not prejudge that a case has already been closed or that the power of "science" will suffer if it is reopened. In fact, the opposite is true.

Of course, it does not always happen like this in reality. Countless scientists have seen their "move" ignored or repressed, sometimes for decades, because it too abruptly destabilized the accepted positions, not only in the university and scientific hierarchy, but also in the problematic.[32] The stronger the "move," the more likely it is to be denied the minimum consensus, precisely because it changes the rules of the game upon which consensus had been based. But when the institution of knowledge functions in this manner, it is acting like an ordinary power center whose behavior is governed by a principle of homeostasis.

Such behavior is terrorist, as is the behavior of the system described by Luhmann. By terror I mean the efficiency gained by eliminating, or threatening to eliminate, a player from the language game one shares with him. He is silenced or consents, not because he has been refuted, but because his ability to participate has been threatened (there are many ways to prevent someone from playing). The decision makers' arrogance, which in principle has no equivalent in the sciences, consists in the exercise of terror. It says: "Adapt your aspirations to our ends—or else."[33]

Even permissiveness toward the various games is made conditional on performativity. The redefinition of the norms of life consists in enhancing the system's competence for power. That this is the case is particularly evident in the introduction of telematics technology: the technocrats see in telematics a promise of liberalization and enrichment in the interactions between interlocutors; but what makes this process attractive for them is that it will result in new tensions in the system, and these will lead to an improvement in its performativity.[34]

To the extent that science is differential, its pragmatics provides the antimodel of a stable system. A statement is deemed worth retaining the moment it marks a difference from what is already known, and after an argument and proof in support of it has been found. Science is a model of an "open system,"[35] in which a statement becomes relevant if it "generates ideas," that is, if it generates other statements and other game rules. Science possesses no general metalanguage in which all other languages can be transcribed and evaluated. This is what prevents its identification with the system and, all things considered, with terror. If the division between decision makers and executors exists in the scientific community (and it does), it is a fact of the socioeconomic system and not of the pragmatics of science itself. It is in fact one of the major obstacles to the imaginative development of knowledge.

The general question of legitimation becomes: What is the relationship between the antimodel of the pragmatics of science and society? Is it applicable to the vast clouds of language material constituting a society? Or is it limited to the game of learning? And if so, what role does it play with respect to the social bond? Is it an impossible ideal of an open community? Is it an essential component for the subset of decision makers, who force on society the performance criterion they reject for themselves? Or, conversely, is it a refusal to cooperate with the authorities, a move in the direction of counterculture, with the attendant risk that all possibility for research will be foreclosed due to lack of funding?[36]

From the beginning of this study, I have emphasized the differences (not only formal, but also pragmatic) between the various language games, especially between denotative, or knowledge, games and prescriptive, or action, games. The pragmatics of science is centered on denotative utterances, which are the foundation upon which it builds institutions of learning (institutes, centers, universities, etc.). But its postmodern development brings a decisive "fact" to the fore: even discussions of denotative statements need to have rules. Rules are not denotative but prescriptive utterances, which we are better off calling metaprescriptive utterances to avoid confusion (they prescribe what the moves of language games must be in order to be admissible). The function of the differential or imaginative or paralogical activity of the current pragmatics of science is to point out these metaprescriptives (science's "presuppositions")[37] and to petition the players to accept different ones. The only legitimation that can make this kind of request admissible is that it will generate ideas, in other words, new statements.

Social pragmatics does not have the "simplicity" of scientific pragmatics. It is a monster formed by the interweaving of various networks of heteromorphous classes of utterances (denotative, prescriptive, performative, technical, evaluative, etc.). There is no reason to think that it would be possible to determine metaprescriptives common to all of these language games or that a revisable consensus like the one in force at a given moment in the scientific community could embrace the totality of metaprescriptions regulating the totality of statements circulating in the social collectivity. As a matter of fact, the contemporary decline of narratives of legitimation—be they traditional or "modern" (the emancipation of humanity, the realization of the Idea)—is tied to the abandonment of this belief. It is its absence for which the ideology of the "system," with its pretensions to totality, tries to compensate and which it expresses in the cynicism of its criterion of performance.

For this reason, it seems neither possible, nor even prudent, to follow Habermas in orienting our treatment of the problem of legitimation in the direction of a search for universal consensus[38] through what he calls *Diskurs*, in other words, a dialogue of argumentation.[39]

This would be to make two assumptions. The first is that it is possible for all speakers to come to agreement on which rules or metaprescriptions are universally valid for language games, when it is clear that language games are heteromorphous, subject to heterogeneous sets of pragmatic rules.

The second assumption is that the goal of dialogue is consensus. But as I have shown in the analysis of the pragmatics of science, consensus is only a particular state of discussion, not its end. Its end, on the contrary, is paralogy. This double observation (the heterogeneity of the rules and the search for dissent) destroys a

belief that still underlies Habermas's research, namely, that humanity as a collective (universal) subject seeks its common emancipation through the regularization of the "moves" permitted in all language games and that the legitimacy of any statement resides in its contributing to that emancipation.[40]

It is easy to see what function this recourse plays in Habermas's argument against Luhmann. *Diskurs* is his ultimate weapon against the theory of the stable system. The cause is good, but the argument is not.[41] Consensus has become an outmoded and suspect value. But justice as a value is neither outmoded nor suspect. We must thus arrive at an idea and practice of justice that is not linked to that of consensus.

A recognition of the heteromorphous nature of language games is a first step in that direction. This obviously implies a renunciation of terror, which assumes that they are isomorphic and tries to make them so. The second step is the principle that any consensus on the rules defining a game and the "moves" playable within it *must* be local, in other words, agreed on by its present players and subject to eventual cancellation. The orientation then favors a multiplicity of finite meta-arguments, by which I mean argumentation that concerns metaprescriptives and is limited in space and time.

This orientation corresponds to the course that the evolution of social interaction is currently taking; the temporary contract is in practice supplanting permanent institutions in the professional, emotional, sexual, cultural, family, and international domains, as well as in political affairs. This evolution is of course ambiguous: the temporary contract is favored by the system due to its greater flexibility, lower cost, and the creative turmoil of its accompanying motivations—all of these factors contribute to increased operativity. In any case, there is no question here of proposing a "pure" alternative to the system: we all now know, as the 1970s come to a close, that an attempt at an alternative of that kind would end up resembling the system it was meant to replace. We should be happy that the tendency toward the temporary contract is ambiguous: it is not totally subordinated to the goal of the system, yet the system tolerates it. This bears witness to the existence of another goal within the system: knowledge of language games as such and the decision to assume responsibility for their rules and effects. Their most significant effect is precisely what validates the adoption of rules—the quest for paralogy.

We are finally in a position to understand how the computerization of society affects this problematic. It could become the "dream" instrument for controlling and regulating the market system, extended to include knowledge itself and governed exclusively by the performativity principle. In that case, it would inevitably involve the use of terror. But it could also aid groups discussing metaprescriptives by supplying them with the information they usually lack for making knowledgeable decisions. The line to follow for computerization to take the second of these two paths is, in principle, quite simple: give the public free access to the memory and data banks.[42] Language games would then be games of perfect information at any given moment. But they would also be non-zero-sum games, and by virtue of that fact discussion would never risk fixating in a position of minimax equilibrium because it had exhausted its stakes. For the stakes would be knowledge (or information, if you will), and the reserve of knowledge—language's reserve of possible utterances—is inexhaustible. This sketches the outline of a politics that would respect both the desire for justice and the desire for the unknown.

NOTES

1. "La Nouvelle Informatique et ses utilisateurs," Annex 3, *L'Informatisation de la société*.

2. B. P. Lécuyer, "Bilan et perspectives de la sociologie des sciences dans les pays occidentaux," *Archives européennes de sociologie* 19 (1978): 257–336 (bibliography). Good information on English and American currents: the hegemony of Merton's school until the beginning of the 1970s and the current dispersion, especially under the influence of Kuhn; not much information on German sociology of science.

3. The term has been given weight by Ivan Illich, *Tools for Conviviality* (New York, Harper & Row, 1973).

4. On this "demoralization," see A. Jaubert and J. M. Lévy-Leblond, eds., *(Auto) critique de la science* (Paris: Seuil, 1973), Pt. 1.

5. Jürgen Habermas, *Legitimationsprobleme im Spätkapitalismus* (Frankfurt: Suhrkamp, 1973) [Eng. trans. Thomas McCarthy, *Legitimation Crisis* (Boston: Beacon Press, 1975)].

6. Certain scientific aspects of postmodernism are inventoried by Ihab Hassan in "Culture, Indeterminacy, and Immanence: Margins of the (Postmodern) Age," *Humanities in Society* 1 (1978): 51–85.

7. Claus Mueller uses the expression "a process of delegitimation" in *The Politics of Communication* (New York: Oxford University Press, 1973), p. 164.

8. "Road of doubt . . . road of despair . . . skepticism," writes Hegel in the preface to the *Phenomenology of Spirit* to describe the effect of the speculative drive on natural knowledge.

9. For fear of encumbering this account, I have postponed until a later study the exposition of this group of rules. [See "Analyzing Speculative Discourse as Language-Game," *The Oxford Literary Review* 4, no. 3 (1981): 59–67.]

10. Nietzsche, "Der europäische Nihilismus" (MS. N VII 3); "der Nihilism, ein normaler Zustand" (MS. W II 1); "Kritik der Nihilism" (MS. W VII 3); "Zum Plane" (MS. W II 1), in *Nietzsches Werke kritische Gesamtausgabe*, vol. 7, pts. 1 and 2

(1887–89) (Berlin: De Gruyter, 1970). These texts have been the object of a commentary by K. Ryjik, *Nietzsche, le manuscrit de Lenzer Heide* (typescript, Département de philosophie, Université de Paris VIII [Vincennes]).

11. "On the future of our educational institutions," in *Complete Works*, vol. 3.

12. Martin Buber, *Ich und Du* (Berlin: Schocken Verlag, 1922) [Eng. trans. Ronald G. Smith, *I and Thou* (New York: Charles Scribner's Sons, 1937)], and *Dialogisches Leben* (Zürich: Müller, 1947); Emmanuel Lévinas, *Totalité et Infinité* (La Haye: Nijhoff, 1961) [Eng. trans. Alphonso Lingis, *Totality and Infinity: An Essay on Exteriority* (Pittsburgh: Duquesne University Press, 1969)], and "Martin Buber und die Erkenntnis theorie" (1958), in *Philosophen des 20. Jahrhunderts* (Stuttgart: Kohlhammer, 1963) [Fr. trans. "Martin Buber et la théorie de la connaissance," in *Noms Propres* (Montpellier: Fata Morgana, 1976)].

13. *Philosophical Investigations*, sec. 18, p. 8.

14. Ibid.

15. Ibid.

16. See for example, "La taylorisation de la recherche," in *(Auto) critique de la science* (note 4), pp. 291–93. And especially D. J. de Solla Price, *Little Science, Big Science* (New York: Columbia University Press, 1963), who emphasizes the split between a small number of highly productive researchers (evaluated in terms of publication) and a large mass of researchers with low productivity. The number of the latter grows as the square of the former, so that the number of high productivity researchers only really increases every twenty years. Price concludes that science considered as a social entity is "undemocratic" (p. 59) and that "the eminent scientist" is a hundred years ahead of "the minimal one" (p. 56).

17. See J. T. Desanti, "Sur le rapport traditionnel des sciences et de la philosophie," in *La*

Philosophie silencieuse, ou critique des philosophies de la science (Paris: Seuil, 1975).

18. The reclassification of academic philosophy as one of the human sciences in this respect has a significance far beyond simply professional concerns. I do not think that philosophy as legitimation is condemned to disappear, but it is possible that it will not be able to carry out this work, or at least advance it, without revising its ties to the university institution. See on this matter the preamble to the *Projet d'un institut polytechnique de philosophie* (typescript, Département de philosophie, Université de Paris VIII [Vincennes], 1979).

19. See Allan Janik and Stephan Toulmin, *Wittgenstein's Vienna* (New York: Simon & Schuster, 1973), and J. Piel, ed., "Vienne début d'un siècle," *Critique*, 339–40 (1975).

20. See Jürgen Habermas, "Dogmatismus, Vernunft unt Entscheidung—Zu Theorie und Praxis in der verwissenschaftlichen Zivilisation" (1963), in *Theorie und Praxis* [*Theory and Practice*, abr. ed. of 4th German ed., trans. John Viertel (Boston: Beacon Press, 1971)].

21. "Science Smiling into its Beard" is the title of chap. 72, vol. 1 of Musil's *The Man Without Qualities*. Cited and discussed by J. Bouveresse, "La Problématique du sujet."

22. It has not been possible within the limits of this study to analyze the form assumed by the return of narrative in discourses of legitimation. Examples are: the study of open systems, local determinism, antimethod—in general, everything that I group under the name *paralogy*.

23. Nora and Minc, for example, attribute Japan's success in the field of computers to an "intensity of social consensus" that they judge to be specific to Japanese society (*L'Informatisation de la Société*, p. 4). They write in their conclusion: "The dynamics of extended social computerization leads

to a fragile society: such a society is constructed with a view to facilitating consensus, but already presupposes its existence, and comes to a standstill if that consensus cannot be realized" (p. 125). Y. Stourdzé, "Les États-Unis," emphasizes the fact that the current tendency to deregulate, destabilize, and weaken administration is encouraged by society's loss of confidence in the State's performance capability.

24. In Kuhn's sense.

25. Pomian ("Catastrophes") shows that this type of functioning bears no relation to Hegelian dialectics.

26. "What the legitimation of decisions accordingly entails is fundamentally an effective learning process, with a minimum of friction, within the social system. This is an aspect of the more general question, 'how do aspirations change, how can the political-administrative subsystem, itself only part of society, nevertheless structure expectations in society through its decisions?' The effectiveness of the activity of what is only a part, for the whole, will in large measure depend on how well it succeeds in integrating new expectations into already existing systems—whether these are persons or social systems—without thereby provoking considerable functional disturbances" (Niklas Luhmann, *Legitimation durch Verfahren*, p. 35).

27. This hypothesis is developed in David Riesman's earlier studies. See Riesman, *The Lonely Crowd* (New Haven: Yale University Press, 1950); W. H. Whyte, *The Organization Man* (New York: Simon & Schuster, 1956); Herbert Marcuse, *One-Dimensional Man* (Boston: Beacon, 1966).

28. Josette Rey-Debove (*Le Métalangage*, pp. 228ff.) notes the proliferation of marks of indirect discourse or autonymic connotation in contemporary daily language. As she reminds us, "indirect discourse cannot be trusted."

29. As Georges Canguilhem says, "man is only truly healthy when he is capable of a number of norms, when he is more than normal" ("Le Normal et la pathologique" [1951], in *La Connaissance de la vie* [Paris: Hachette, 1952], p. 210) [Eng. trans. Carolyn Fawcett *On the Normal and the Pathological* (Boston: D. Reidel, 1978)].

30. E. E. David comments that society can only be aware of the needs it feels in the present state of its technological milieu. It is of the nature of the basic sciences to discover unknown properties which remodel the technical milieu and create unpredictable needs. He cites as examples the use of solid materials as amplifiers and the rapid development of the physics of solids. This "negative regulation" of social interactions and needs by the object of contemporary techniques is critiqued by R. Jaulin, "Le Mythe technologique," *Revue de l'entreprise* 26, special "Ethnotechnology" issue (March 1979): 49–55. This is a review of A. G. Haudricourt, "La Technologie culturelle, essai de méthodologie," in Gille, *Historie des techniques*.

31. Medawar (*Art of the Soluble*, pp. 151–52) compares scientists' written and spoken styles. The former must be "inductive" or they will not be considered; as for the second, Medawar makes a list of expressions often heard in laboratories, including, "My results don't make a story yet." He concludes, "Scientists are building explanatory structures, *telling stories ...*"

32. For a famous example, see Lewis S. Feuer, *Einstein and the Generations of Science* (New York: Basic Books, 1974). As Moscovici emphasizes in his introduction to the French translation [trans. Alexandre, *Einstein et le conflit des générations* (Bruxelles' Complexe, 1979)], "Relativity

was born in a makeshift 'academy' formed by friends, not one of whom was a physicist; all were engineers or amateur philosophers."

33. Orwell's paradox. The bureaucrat speaks: "We are not content with negative obedience, nor even with the most abject submission. When finally you do surrender to us, it must be of your own free will" (*1984* [New York: Harcourt, Brace, 1949], p. 258). In language game terminology the paradox would be expressed as a "Be free," or a "Want what you want," and is analyzed by Watzlawick et al., *Pragmatics of Human Communication*, pp. 203–7. On these paradoxes, see J. M. Salanskis, "Genèses 'actuelles' et genèses 'sérielles' de l'inconsistant et de l'hétérogeme," *Critique* 379 (1978): 1155–73.

34. See Nora and Minc's description of the tensions that mass computerization will inevitably produce in French society (*L'Informatisation de la société*, introduction).

35. Cf. the discussion of open systems in Watzlawick et al., *Pragmatics of Human Communication*, pp. 117–48. The concept of open systems theory is the subject of a study by J. M. Salanskis, *Le Systématique ouvert* (forthcoming).

36. After the separation of Church and State, Paul Feyerabend (*Against Method*) demands in the same "lay" spirit the separation of Science and State. But what about Science and Money?

37. This is at least one way of understanding this term, which comes from Ducrot's problematic, *Dire*.

38. *Legitimationsprobleme* (note 5), passim, especially pp. 21–22: "Language functions in the manner of a transformer . . . changing cognitions into propositions, needs and feelings into normative expectations (commands, values). This transformation produces the far-reaching distinction between the subjectivity of intention, willing, of pleasure and unpleasure on the one hand, and expressions and norms with a *pretension to universality* on the other. Universality signifies the objectivity of knowledge and the legitimacy of prevailing norms; both assure the community [*Gemeinsamkeit*] constitutive of lived social experience." We see that by formulating the problematic in this way, the question of legitimacy is fixated on one type of reply, universality. This on the one hand presupposes that the legitimation of the subject of knowledge is identical to that of the subject of action (in opposition to Kant's critique, which dissociates conceptual universality, appropriate to the former, and ideal universality, or "suprasensible nature," which forms the horizon of the latter, and on the other hand it maintains that consensus (*Gemeinschaft*) is the only possible horizon for the life of humanity.

39. Ibid., p. 20. The subordination of the meta-prescriptives of prescription (i.e, the normalization of laws) to *Diskurs* is explicit, for example, on p. 144: "The normative pretension to validity is itself cognitive in the sense that it always assumes it could be accepted in a rational discussion."

40. Garbis Kortian, *Métacritique* (Paris: Éditions de Minuit, 1979) [Eng. trans. John Raffan, *Metacritique: The Philosophical Argument of Jürgen Habermas* (Cambridge: Cambridge University Press, 1980)], pt. 5, examines this enlightenment aspect of Habermas's thought. See by the same author, "Le Discours philosophique et son objet," *Critique* 384 (1979): 407–19.

41. See J. Poulain, ("Vers une pragmatique nucléaire"), and for a more general discussion of the pragmatics of Searle and Gehlen, see J. Poulain, "Pragmatique de la parole et pragmatique de la vie," *Phi zéro* 7, no. 1 (Université de Montréal, September 1978): 5–50.

42. See Tricot et al., *Informatique et libertés,* government report (La Documentation française, 1975); L. Joinet, "Les 'pièges liberaticides' de l'informatique," *Le Monde diplomatique* 300 (March 1979): these traps *(pièges)* are "the application of the technique of 'social profiles' to the management of the mass of the population; the logic of security produced by the automatization of society." See too the documents and analysis in *Interférences* 1 and 2 (Winter 1974–Spring 1975), the theme of which is the establishment of popular networks of multimedia communication. Topics treated include: amateur radios (especially their role in Quebec during the FLQ affair of October 1970 and that of the "Front commun" in May 1972); community radios in the United States and Canada; the impact of computers on editorial work in the press; pirate radios (before their development in Italy); administrative files, the IBM monopoly, computer sabotage. The municipality of Yverdon (Canton of Vaud), having voted to buy a computer (operational in 1981), enacted a certain number of rules: exclusive authority of the municipal council to decide which data are collected, to whom and under what conditions they are communicated; access for all citizens to all data (on payment); the right of every citizen to see the entries on his file (about 50), to correct them and address a complaint about them to the municipal council and if need be to the Council of State; the right of all citizens to know (on request) which data concerning them is communicated and to whom *(La Semaine media* 18, 1 March 1979, 9).

Further Readings: Moderism and Post-Moderism

CRITICAL THEORY

HABERMAS, JÜRGEN: *Between facts and norms: contributions to a discourse theory of law and democracy,* translated by William Rehg. Cambridge, Mass., MIT Press, c1996.

HABERMAS, JÜRGEN: *Communication and the evolution of society;* translated and introduction by Thomas McCarthy. Boston, Beacon Press, 1979.

HABERMAS, JÜRGEN: *The inclusion of the other: studies in political theory;* edited by Ciaran Cronin and Pablo De Grief. Cambridge, Mass. MIT Press, c1998.

HABERMAS, JÜRGEN: *The theory of communicative action;* translated by Thomas McCarthy. Boston, Beacon Press, c1984.

JAY, MARTIN: *The dialectical imagination; a history of the Frankfurt School and the Institute of Social Research, 1923–1950.* Boston, Little, Brown, 1973.

KELLNER, DOUGLAS: *Herbert Marcuse and the crisis of Marxism.* Berkeley; University of California Press, 1984.

KELLY, MICHAEL, ed.: *Critique and power: recasting the Foucault/Habermas debate.* Cambridge, Mass., MIT Press, c1994.

MARCUSE, HERBERT: *One dimensional man; studies in the ideology of advanced industrial society.* Boston, Beacon Press, c1964.

MARCUSE, HERBERT: *Towards a critical theory of society;* edited by Douglas Kellner. London; New York, Routledge, 2001.

HOY, DAVID COUZENS, and THOMAS MCCARTHY: *Critical theory.* Oxford, UK; Cambridge, Mass., USA: B. Blackwell, 1994.

POSTMODERNISM

BAUMAN, ZYGMUNT: *Intimations of postmodernity.* New, York, Routledge, 1991.

BAUMAN, ZYGMUNT: *Postmodernity and its discontents.* New York, New York University Press, 1997.

BEST, STEVEN, and DOUGLAS KELLNER: *Postmodern theory: critical interrogations.* New York, Guilford Press, 1991.

DICKENS, DAVID R., and ANDREA FONTANA, eds.: *Postmodernism and social inquiry;* foreword by Fred Dallmayr.

FOUCAULT, MICHEL: *Discipline and punish: the birth of the prison;* translated from the French by Alan Sheridan. New York, Pantheon Books, c1977.

FOUCAULT, MICHEL: *The history of sexuality,* vols. 1 and 3; translated from the French by Robert Hurley. New York, Pantheon Books, c1978.

FOUCAULT, MICHEL: *Politics, philosophy, culture: interviews and other writings, 1977–1984;* translated by Alan Sheridan and others; edited with an introduction by Lawrence D. Kritzman. New York: Routledge, 1988.

Giddens, Anthony: *The consequences of modernity.* Stanford, Calif., Stanford University Press, 1990.

HALPERIN, DAVID M.: *Saint Foucault: towards a gay hagiography.* New York, Oxford University Press, c1995.

HARVEY, DAVID: *The condition of postmodernity: an enquiry into the origins of cultural change.* Oxford, England; New York, NY, USA Blackwell, 1989.

KELLNER, DOUGLAS: *Jean Baudrillard: from Marxism to postmodernism and beyond.* Stanford, Stanford University Press, 1989.

LASH, SCOTT: *Sociology of postmodernism.* London, New York, Routledge, 1990.

LYOTARD, JEAN FRANÇOIS: *The postmodern condition: a report on knowledge;* translation from the French by Geoff Bennington and Brian Massumi; foreword by Fredric Jameson. Minneapolis, University of Minnesota Press, 1984.

MILLER, JIM: *The passion of Michel Foucault.* New York, Simon & Schuster, c1993.

NICHOLSON, LINDA, and STEVEN SEIDMAN, eds.: *Social postmodernism: beyond identity politics.* Cambridge; New York, Cambridge University Press, 1995.

POSTER, MARK: *Foucault, Marxism, and history: mode of production versus mode of information.* Cambridge, UK, Polity Press; New York, NY, USA, B. Blackwell, 1984.

ROJEK; CHRIS, and BRYAN S. TURNER, eds.: *The politics of Jean-François Lyotard: justice and political theory.* London, New York, Routledge, 1998.

WOOD, ELLEN MEIKSINS, and JOHN BELLAMY FOSTER, eds.: *In defense of history: Marxism and the postmodern agenda.* New York, Monthly Review Press, c1997.